Oracle Press™

# Oracle Data Guard 11g Handbook

Larry Carpenter    Joe Meeks
Charles Kim       Bill Burke
Sonya Carothers   Joydip Kundu
Michael Smith     Nitin Vengurlekar

D1275405

Mc
Graw
Hill

New York   Chicago   San Francisco
Lisbon   London   Madrid   Mexico City   Milan
New Delhi   San Juan   Seoul   Singapore   Sydney   Toronto

The McGraw·Hill Companies

**Library of Congress Cataloging-in-Publication Data**

Oracle Data guard 11g handbook / Larry Carpenter … [et al.].
        p.      cm.
    ISBN 978-0-07-162111-3 (alk. paper)
    1. Data recovery (Computer science)   2. Data protection.   3. Oracle
(Computer file)   I. Carpenter, Larry.
    QA76.9.D348O73     2009
    005.8'6—dc22                                    2009022071

McGraw-Hill books are available at special quantity discounts to use as premiums and sales promotions, or for use in corporate training programs. To contact a representative, please e-mail us at bulksales@ mcgraw-hill.com.

## Oracle Data Guard 11g Handbook

Copyright © 2009 by The McGraw-Hill Companies, Inc. (Publisher). All rights reserved. Printed in the United States of America. Except as permitted under the Copyright Act of 1976, no part of this publication may be reproduced or distributed in any form or by any means, or stored in a database or retrieval system, without the prior written permission of Publisher, with the exception that the program listings may be entered, stored, and executed in a computer system, but they may not be reproduced for publication.

Oracle is a registered trademark of Oracle Corporation and/or its affiliates. All other trademarks are the property of their respective owners, and McGraw-Hill makes no claim of ownership by the mention of products that contain these marks.

Screen displays of copyrighted Oracle software programs have been reproduced herein with the permission of Oracle Corporation and/or its affiliates.

234567890   DOC DOC   1543210

ISBN    978-0-07-162111-3
MHID       0-07-162111-3

**Sponsoring Editor**
    Lisa McClain

**Editorial Supervisor**
    Janet Walden

**Project Manager**
    Vastavikta Sharma, International
    Typesetting and Composition

**Acquisitions Coordinator**
    Meghan Riley

**Technical Editors**
    Michael Powell
    and Sreekanth Chintala

**Copy Editor**
    Lisa Theobald

**Proofreader**
    Paul Tyler

**Indexer**
    Karin Arrigoni

**Production Supervisor**
    George Anderson

**Composition**
    International Typesetting
    and Composition

**Illustration**
    International Typesetting
    and Composition

**Art Director, Cover**
    Jeff Weeks

**Cover Designer**
    Pattie Lee

Information has been obtained by Publisher from sources believed to be reliable. However, because of the possibility of human or mechanical error by our sources, Publisher, or others, Publisher does not guarantee to the accuracy, adequacy, or completeness of any information included in this work and is not responsible for any errors or omissions or the results obtained from the use of such information.

Oracle Corporation does not make any representations or warranties as to the accuracy, adequacy, or completeness of any information contained in this Work, and is not responsible for any errors or omissions.

This book is dedicated to all Oracle Database administrators in the hope that our words will be their guide to success and restful nights. And to those non–Oracle Database administrators, may you wish you, too, were using Oracle Data Guard!
—*Larry Carpenter*

A quick shout out to the family—Gretchen, and my kids, Emily, Abby, and Ted. We are all hoping a lot of people buy this book so it can help pay the college bills.
—*Joe Meeks*

I dedicate this book to my precious wife, Melissa, and our three boys, Isaiah, Jeremiah, and Noah, for their support during the project and sacrifice of precious family time. Thank you for your unceasing prayers and encouragement.
—*Charles Kim*

I'd like to dedicate this book to my loving wife, Sandra, for the commitment of her time with me; without her support and continued motivation, my contribution to this book would not have been possible.
—*Bill Burke*

To my son, Julian, thanks for your love, encouragement, and laughter.
—*Sonya Carothers*

To my five-year-old daughter, Ria Rajyasri, for making my journey as a father so full of joy and wonder.
—*Joydip Kundu*

I would like to dedicate my portion of this book to my wife, Tina, and two of the best daughters a father could ask for, Jessica and Madison. I know having a "computer geek" for a husband and father can at times be tedious ("but Tina, bandwidth is determined by how quickly a medium can change states") and embarrassing (my T-shirt that has "DAD" spelled out in binary), which makes me love you guys all the more.
—*Mike Smith*

I would like to dedicate this book to my kids, Ishan and Nisha; to my wife, Priya; and most importantly to my parents, whose guidance and support have always been invaluable.
—*Nitin Vengurlekar*

# Contents

Foreword .................................................. xvii

Acknowledgments ........................................... xix

Introduction ............................................... xxi

**1** Data Guard Architecture .................................. 1

Data Guard Overview ..................................... 2

What Is Redo? ......................................... 2

Redo Transport Services ................................... 5

Synchronous Redo Transport ........................... 5

Asynchronous Redo Transport .......................... 7

Redo Transport Compression ........................... 9

Automatic Gap Resolution ............................. 9

Apply Services .......................................... 11

Redo Apply (Physical Standby) ......................... 12

SQL Apply (Logical Standby) ........................... 15

Can't Decide? Then Use Both! ......................... 17

Data Guard Protection Modes ............................. 18

Maximum Performance ................................ 18

Maximum Availability ................................. 18

Maximum Protection .................................. 19

Role Management Services ................................ 19

Switchover .......................................... 20

Failover ............................................. 21

Data Guard Management .................................. 24

Active Standby Databases ................................. 26

Offload Read-Only Queries and Reporting ............... 26

Offload Backups ...................................... 27

Testing .............................................. 27

Data Guard and the Maximum Availability Architecture ....... 29

Conclusion .............................................. 29

**2** Implementing Oracle Data Guard ........................... 31
Plan Before You Implement .............................. 32
Determining Your Requirements ...................... 33
Understanding the Configuration Options ............... 35
Relating the RPO and RTO to the Protection Mode ........ 62
Creating a Physical Standby Database .................... 63
Choosing Your Interface .......................... 63
Before You Start ............................... 64
Using Oracle Enterprise Manager Grid Control ......... 65
The Power User Method ........................... 78
Creating a Logical Standby ........................... 98
Data Guard and Oracle Real Application Clusters ......... 105
Conclusion .................................... 106

**3** Redo Processing .................................. 107
Important Concepts of Oracle Recovery .................. 108
ACID Properties ............................... 108
Oracle Recovery ............................... 109
Life of a Transaction ............................ 111
Nologging Operations ........................... 111
The Components of a Physical Standby ................... 114
Real-time Apply ............................... 117
Scaling and Tuning Data Guard Apply Recovery .......... 118
Parallel Media Recovery ......................... 119
Tools and Views for Monitoring Physical Standby Recovery ... 120
Physical Standby Corruption Detection .................. 124
11g New Data Protection Changes .................... 124
Data Protection and Checking on a Physical Standby ....... 125
Conclusion .................................... 126

**4** Logical Standby .................................. 127
Characterizing the Dataset Available at the Logical Standby ...... 129
Characterizing the Dataset Replicated from the Primary Database ... 129
Protecting Replicated Tables on a Logical Standby ......... 134
Customizing Your Logical Standby Database (or Creating
a Local Dataset at the Logical Standby) ............ 141
Understanding the Operational Aspects of a Logical Standby ... 145
Looking Inside SQL Apply ........................ 145
Tuning SQL Apply ................................ 157
Some Rules of Thumb ........................... 158
Determining Whether SQL Apply Is Lagging ............ 158
Determining Whether SQL Apply Is the Bottleneck ........ 159
Determining Which SQL Apply Component Is the Bottleneck ... 159

Troubleshooting SQL Apply . . . . . . . . . . . . . . . . . . . . . . . . . . . . . . . . . . . . . 164
    Understanding Restarts in SQL Apply . . . . . . . . . . . . . . . . . . . . . . . . 164
    Troubleshooting Stopped SQL Apply . . . . . . . . . . . . . . . . . . . . . . . . 167
Conclusion . . . . . . . . . . . . . . . . . . . . . . . . . . . . . . . . . . . . . . . . . . . . . . . 170

**5**  **Implementing Oracle Data Guard Broker** . . . . . . . . . . . . . . . . . . . . . . . . 171
Overview of the Data Guard Broker . . . . . . . . . . . . . . . . . . . . . . . . . . . . 172
    The Broker Process Model . . . . . . . . . . . . . . . . . . . . . . . . . . . . . . . 173
    The Broker Process Flow . . . . . . . . . . . . . . . . . . . . . . . . . . . . . . . . 174
    The Broker Configuration Files . . . . . . . . . . . . . . . . . . . . . . . . . . . . 176
    The Broker CLI . . . . . . . . . . . . . . . . . . . . . . . . . . . . . . . . . . . . . . 178
Getting Started with the Broker . . . . . . . . . . . . . . . . . . . . . . . . . . . . . . 179
    Configuring the Broker Parameters . . . . . . . . . . . . . . . . . . . . . . . . . 179
    The Broker and Oracle Net Services . . . . . . . . . . . . . . . . . . . . . . . . 183
    RAC and the Broker . . . . . . . . . . . . . . . . . . . . . . . . . . . . . . . . . . . 187
    Connecting to the Broker . . . . . . . . . . . . . . . . . . . . . . . . . . . . . . . 190
Managing Data Guard with the Broker . . . . . . . . . . . . . . . . . . . . . . . . . . 193
    Creating and Enabling a Broker Configuration . . . . . . . . . . . . . . . . . 193
    Changing the Broker Configuration Properties . . . . . . . . . . . . . . . . . 200
    Changing the State of a Database . . . . . . . . . . . . . . . . . . . . . . . . . 211
    Changing the Protection Mode . . . . . . . . . . . . . . . . . . . . . . . . . . . 212
Monitoring Data Guard Using the Broker . . . . . . . . . . . . . . . . . . . . . . . . 214
Removing the Broker . . . . . . . . . . . . . . . . . . . . . . . . . . . . . . . . . . . . . 216
Conclusion . . . . . . . . . . . . . . . . . . . . . . . . . . . . . . . . . . . . . . . . . . . . . . . 217

**6**  **Oracle Enterprise Manager Grid Control Integration** . . . . . . . . . . . . . . . . . 219
Accessing the Data Guard Features . . . . . . . . . . . . . . . . . . . . . . . . . . . . 220
    Configuring Data Guard Broker with OEM Grid Control . . . . . . . . . . . 221
    Verify Configuration and Adding Standby Redo Logs . . . . . . . . . . . . . 224
    Viewing Metrics . . . . . . . . . . . . . . . . . . . . . . . . . . . . . . . . . . . . . 226
    Modifying Metrics . . . . . . . . . . . . . . . . . . . . . . . . . . . . . . . . . . . . 227
    Viewing the Alert Log File . . . . . . . . . . . . . . . . . . . . . . . . . . . . . . 228
    Enabling Flashback Database . . . . . . . . . . . . . . . . . . . . . . . . . . . . 230
    Reviewing Performance . . . . . . . . . . . . . . . . . . . . . . . . . . . . . . . . 231
    Changing Protection Modes . . . . . . . . . . . . . . . . . . . . . . . . . . . . . 234
    Editing Standby Database Properties . . . . . . . . . . . . . . . . . . . . . . . 236
    Performing a Switchover . . . . . . . . . . . . . . . . . . . . . . . . . . . . . . . 238
    Performing a Manual Failover . . . . . . . . . . . . . . . . . . . . . . . . . . . . 240
    Fast-Start Failover . . . . . . . . . . . . . . . . . . . . . . . . . . . . . . . . . . . 243
    Creating a Logical Standby . . . . . . . . . . . . . . . . . . . . . . . . . . . . . . 244
    Managing Active Standby . . . . . . . . . . . . . . . . . . . . . . . . . . . . . . 250
    Managing Snapshot Standby . . . . . . . . . . . . . . . . . . . . . . . . . . . . 250
    Removing a Standby Database from Broker Control . . . . . . . . . . . . . . 250
Keeping an Eye on Availability . . . . . . . . . . . . . . . . . . . . . . . . . . . . . . . 252
Conclusion . . . . . . . . . . . . . . . . . . . . . . . . . . . . . . . . . . . . . . . . . . . . . . . 255

**7** Monitoring Data Guard Implementations .......................... 257
    Monitoring the Data Guard Environment ......................... 258
        Mining the Alert Log File (PS+LS) ......................... 259
        Gathering Statistical Information from Archive Log History (PS+LS) ........ 264
        Detecting Archive Log Gaps (PS+LS) ......................... 266
        Identifying Delays in Redo Transport (PS) ..................... 268
        Monitoring Archive Log Destinations (PS+LS) .................... 269
        Examining Apply Rate and Active Rate (PS) ..................... 271
        Reviewing Transport and Apply Lag (PS+LS) .................... 272
        Determining the Current Time on the Standby Database (PS) ........... 273
        Reporting the Status of Managed Recovery Process (PS) ............. 275
    Data Guard Menu Utility ................................... 276
    Reviewing the Current Data Guard Environment .................... 277
        Checking the Password File (PS+LS) ........................ 278
        Checking for Nologging Activities (PS+LS) .................... 279
        Looking at Archivelog Mode and Destinations (PS+LS) .............. 282
        Checking Standby File Management (PS) ...................... 284
        Revealing Errors in the Data Guard Status View (PS) .............. 284
        Logical Standby Data Guard Menu ......................... 285
    Conclusion ........................................... 297

**8** Switchover and Failover ................................... 299
    Introduction to Role Transition .............................. 300
        Switchover ......................................... 300
        Failover ........................................... 302
        Switchover vs. Failover .................................. 309
    Flashback Technologies and Data Guard ......................... 309
    Performing a Switchover ................................... 311
        Configuration Completeness Check ......................... 311
        Preparatory Checks ................................... 311
        Preprocessing Steps ................................... 314
        Switching over to a Physical Standby ........................ 315
        Switching over to a Logical Standby ........................ 320
        Using the Broker or Grid Control to Switchover ................. 323
        Switchover Health Check ................................ 324
    Performing a Failover ..................................... 324
        Failing over to a Physical Standby .......................... 326
        Failing over to a Logical Standby .......................... 328
        Bringing Back the Old Primary ............................ 329
        Using the Broker or Grid Control to Failover .................. 334
        Automatic Failover .................................... 335
    A Final Word on Multiple Standbys ............................ 348
    Conclusion ........................................... 348

**9**   Active Data Guard . . . . . . . . . . . . . . . . . . . . . . . . . . . . . . 349

    Physical Standby—Open Read-Only . . . . . . . . . . . . . . . . . . . . 350

        Why Read-Only? . . . . . . . . . . . . . . . . . . . . . . . . . . . . . 351

        The Downside of Read-Only or Read-Write Mode . . . . . . . . . . 352

    Snapshot Standby for QA and Test Environments . . . . . . . . . . . . 353

        Read Write Standby in Oracle Database 10*g* . . . . . . . . . . . . . 353

        Snapshot Standbys in Oracle Database 11*g* . . . . . . . . . . . . . 357

    Real Application Testing . . . . . . . . . . . . . . . . . . . . . . . . . . 364

        Database Replay . . . . . . . . . . . . . . . . . . . . . . . . . . . . . 365

        SQL Performance Analyzer . . . . . . . . . . . . . . . . . . . . . . . 370

    Active Data Guard . . . . . . . . . . . . . . . . . . . . . . . . . . . . . . 371

        Configuring Active Data Guard . . . . . . . . . . . . . . . . . . . . 374

    Conclusion . . . . . . . . . . . . . . . . . . . . . . . . . . . . . . . . . . 376

**10**   Automating Site and Client Failover . . . . . . . . . . . . . . . . . . . . 377

    Defining the Problem . . . . . . . . . . . . . . . . . . . . . . . . . . . . 378

        Complete Site Failover . . . . . . . . . . . . . . . . . . . . . . . . . 378

        Partial Site Failover . . . . . . . . . . . . . . . . . . . . . . . . . . . 379

    The Nitty Gritty . . . . . . . . . . . . . . . . . . . . . . . . . . . . . . . 379

        Connection Load Balancing and Connect Time Failover . . . . . . . 380

        Outbound Connect Timeout . . . . . . . . . . . . . . . . . . . . . . 381

        Transparent Application Failover . . . . . . . . . . . . . . . . . . . 382

        Fast Application Notification . . . . . . . . . . . . . . . . . . . . . . 384

        The DB_ROLE_CHANGE System Event . . . . . . . . . . . . . . . . 386

    Implementing Client Failover . . . . . . . . . . . . . . . . . . . . . . . 387

        Complete Site Failover Configuration . . . . . . . . . . . . . . . . . 387

    Conclusion . . . . . . . . . . . . . . . . . . . . . . . . . . . . . . . . . . 394

**11**   Minimizing Planned Downtime Using Data Guard Switchover . . . . . . 395

    Overview of Planned Migration . . . . . . . . . . . . . . . . . . . . . . 396

    Leveraging Data Guard Switchover for Planned Migration . . . . . . . 397

        Case 1–New Data Center . . . . . . . . . . . . . . . . . . . . . . . 397

        Case 2–Move to ASM . . . . . . . . . . . . . . . . . . . . . . . . . 397

    Performing a Database Rolling Upgrade Using Data Guard . . . . . . . 398

        Leveraging Rolling Upgrades Using SQL Apply . . . . . . . . . . . . 399

        Rolling Upgrades Using Transient Logical Standby . . . . . . . . . . 402

    Conclusion . . . . . . . . . . . . . . . . . . . . . . . . . . . . . . . . . . 408

**12**   Backup and Recovery Considerations . . . . . . . . . . . . . . . . . . . 409

    RMAN Basics . . . . . . . . . . . . . . . . . . . . . . . . . . . . . . . . 410

    RMAN Integration with Data Guard . . . . . . . . . . . . . . . . . . . 411

        Block Change Tracking Support . . . . . . . . . . . . . . . . . . . . 411

        Control File Management . . . . . . . . . . . . . . . . . . . . . . . 412

        Resynchronizing the RMAN Catalog . . . . . . . . . . . . . . . . . 412

RMAN Configuration in Data Guard  . . . . . . . . . . . . . . . . . . . . . . . . . . . . . . .  412
   Example Configuration for a Primary Database  . . . . . . . . . . . . . . . . . . . . .  414
   Example Configuration for a Backup Standby Database  . . . . . . . . . . . . . . .  415
   Example Configuration for Other Physical Standby Databases  . . . . . . . . . . .  415
Backup Strategies  . . . . . . . . . . . . . . . . . . . . . . . . . . . . . . . . . . . . . . . . . . .  415
Backup Scenarios  . . . . . . . . . . . . . . . . . . . . . . . . . . . . . . . . . . . . . . . . . . . .  417
   Backup Database Not Backed Up  . . . . . . . . . . . . . . . . . . . . . . . . . . . . . . .  417
   Full Backups on Primary  . . . . . . . . . . . . . . . . . . . . . . . . . . . . . . . . . . . . .  417
   Backup as Copy  . . . . . . . . . . . . . . . . . . . . . . . . . . . . . . . . . . . . . . . . . . .  419
   Image Copy Rolled Forward  . . . . . . . . . . . . . . . . . . . . . . . . . . . . . . . . . .  420
   Standby Database Creation  . . . . . . . . . . . . . . . . . . . . . . . . . . . . . . . . . .  423
   Backups on a Standby Database  . . . . . . . . . . . . . . . . . . . . . . . . . . . . . . .  423
   Archive Backups  . . . . . . . . . . . . . . . . . . . . . . . . . . . . . . . . . . . . . . . . . .  426
General Recovery Strategies  . . . . . . . . . . . . . . . . . . . . . . . . . . . . . . . . . . . .  426
   Media Failure  . . . . . . . . . . . . . . . . . . . . . . . . . . . . . . . . . . . . . . . . . . . .  426
   Block Corruption  . . . . . . . . . . . . . . . . . . . . . . . . . . . . . . . . . . . . . . . . . .  426
   User Errors  . . . . . . . . . . . . . . . . . . . . . . . . . . . . . . . . . . . . . . . . . . . . . .  429
Recovery Scenarios  . . . . . . . . . . . . . . . . . . . . . . . . . . . . . . . . . . . . . . . . . .  430
   Loss of a Datafile on a Primary Database  . . . . . . . . . . . . . . . . . . . . . . . .  430
   Loss of a Datafile on a Standby Database  . . . . . . . . . . . . . . . . . . . . . . . .  431
   Loss of Standby Controlfile  . . . . . . . . . . . . . . . . . . . . . . . . . . . . . . . . . .  432
   Loss of Primary Controlfile  . . . . . . . . . . . . . . . . . . . . . . . . . . . . . . . . . .  432
   Loss of an Online Redo Log File  . . . . . . . . . . . . . . . . . . . . . . . . . . . . . .  432
   Incomplete Recovery of the Primary Database  . . . . . . . . . . . . . . . . . . . . .  436
   Recovering from a Dropped Table  . . . . . . . . . . . . . . . . . . . . . . . . . . . . .  437
   Recover a Missing Datafile from a Backup Taken on the Standby  . . . . . . . .  437
General Best Practices  . . . . . . . . . . . . . . . . . . . . . . . . . . . . . . . . . . . . . . . .  440
Conclusion  . . . . . . . . . . . . . . . . . . . . . . . . . . . . . . . . . . . . . . . . . . . . . . . . .  441

**13  Troubleshooting Data Guard**  . . . . . . . . . . . . . . . . . . . . . . . . . . . . .  443
Diagnostic Information  . . . . . . . . . . . . . . . . . . . . . . . . . . . . . . . . . . . . . . . .  444
   Database Alert Logs  . . . . . . . . . . . . . . . . . . . . . . . . . . . . . . . . . . . . . . . .  444
   Observer Log Files  . . . . . . . . . . . . . . . . . . . . . . . . . . . . . . . . . . . . . . . . .  447
   Data Guard Trace Files  . . . . . . . . . . . . . . . . . . . . . . . . . . . . . . . . . . . . . .  447
   Data Guard Broker Log Files and Tools  . . . . . . . . . . . . . . . . . . . . . . . . . .  448
   Dynamic Performance Views  . . . . . . . . . . . . . . . . . . . . . . . . . . . . . . . . .  449
Data Guard Configuration and Management Errors  . . . . . . . . . . . . . . . . . . . .  450
   Common Management Issues  . . . . . . . . . . . . . . . . . . . . . . . . . . . . . . . . .  450
   Physical Standby Issues  . . . . . . . . . . . . . . . . . . . . . . . . . . . . . . . . . . . . .  456
   Logical Standby Database Failures  . . . . . . . . . . . . . . . . . . . . . . . . . . . . .  459
   Switchover Issues  . . . . . . . . . . . . . . . . . . . . . . . . . . . . . . . . . . . . . . . . . .  461
   Failover Issues  . . . . . . . . . . . . . . . . . . . . . . . . . . . . . . . . . . . . . . . . . . . .  463
   Data Guard Broker Issues  . . . . . . . . . . . . . . . . . . . . . . . . . . . . . . . . . . . .  464
   Errors Converting to a Snapshot Standby  . . . . . . . . . . . . . . . . . . . . . . . . .  468

Helpful Hints and Tips ............................................... 468
    Avoid Refreshing the Standby Control File ........................... 468
    Avoid Using the NOLOGGING Clause ............................. 468
    OMF—Copying Control File ..................................... 469
Conclusion ......................................................... 470

**14** Deployment Architectures ....................................... 471
Manufacturing Company: HA Configuration ............................. 473
Utility Company: Zero Data Loss HA/DR ................................ 476
Retail Brokerage Firm: HA/DR with Zero Data Loss and
    Extended Geographic Separation ...................................... 478
Government Agency: Protection from Multi-site Threats ...................... 480
Pharmaceutical Company: Centralized HA/DR and Data Distribution ............ 483
Web Retailer: HA/DR with Reader-farm Scale Out ......................... 484
Insurance Company: Maximum Availability Architecture ...................... 486
Conclusion ......................................................... 488

**A** Data Guard vs. Array-based Remote Mirroring Solutions ................ 491
The Basics ......................................................... 492
Topology .......................................................... 493
Performance ........................................................ 493
Reliability .......................................................... 494
Final Thoughts ...................................................... 495

Index ............................................................. 497

# Foreword

I've often said that there is one thing a DBA is not allowed to get wrong, and that is recovery. To be more general, it is the DBA's job to ensure that data that cannot ever be lost is never lost. If you cannot provide for continuous, no data loss access to all of your corporate data, you have not done the primary job a DBA should do. Providing a solid disaster recovery contingency is part of the job of the DBA, and Oracle Data Guard is the way to provide for it.

Oracle provides many features and functions to facilitate data backup, recovery, and availability. However, there are so many features that at times the implementation and configuration can be daunting. You'll have questions such as "What is the 'best way' to provide continuous availability given my circumstances?" "How do I decide between all of the configurations possible?" "What is the tradeoff of doing it one way versus the other?" "How does it all actually work under the covers?" This book covers in depth all of these questions, plus others. The authors, Larry Carpenter, Joe Meeks, Charles Kim, Bill Burke, Sonya Carothers, Joydip Kundu, Michael Smith, and Nitin Vengurlekar, are experts in the field. They are the people I go to in order to get answers myself.

The book begins by explaining the Data Guard Architecture, starting with the transaction log (REDO) information—what role it plays, how it is transmitted, and how it is ultimately used. The Data Guard architecture is built up, layer by layer, and presented in a manner that's easy to understand. You'll learn not only how the redo is transmitted, but how the receiving disaster recovery site applies (uses) the redo information. You'll learn the differences between a physical standby database and a logical standby database. You'll be introduced to Data Guard's various configuration modes—either for extreme performance on one hand or for guaranteed zero data loss on the other. You'll also learn about some everyday uses for your standby databases; they are not just for failures anymore.

The book progresses to describe the actual physical installation, setup, and configuration of your standby instances. It starts with a section on "before you even think about setting this up, this is what you need to think about"—an approach I like. Rather than just plowing ahead and making uninformed decisions, you'll learn about what specifically you need to ask. Important terms such as Recovery Point Objective (RPO) (the point in time to which data must be protected, which is a measure of how much "loss" would be acceptable, say from zero to a lot) and Recovery Time Objective (RTO) (the amount of time you can afford to have the data be unavailable, again from zero to a lot) are introduced and discussed. Unless you can assign some values to those metrics, you'll find it difficult, if not impossible, to make decisions about how to configure your disaster recovery solution.

After covering how to install and configure your installation, the book addresses performance considerations, including frequently asked questions. (Believe me, I know. On http://asktom. oracle.com/, I see them asked frequently.) How do you tune Data Guard? How do you measure Data Guard response times? Where am I spending my time in Data Guard? All of these questions and more are covered with sections on tuning the recovery rate (the rate of application of redo at the disaster recovery site), how to perform Data Guard recovery in parallel, troubleshooting redo apply issues, and understanding the operational aspects (how it all works). To me, that is key. If you understand how something works, you are well equipped to "fix" it.

Next in line is a series of chapters on managing your Data Guard environment, either by using automated tools such as Enterprise Manager or by taking a more "do-it-yourself scripting" approach.

What follows are chapters covering something you hope never to have to do: failover. Well, they actually cover switchover, a graceful, reversible process whereby you can turn production into standby and standby into production, as well as failover. These are areas in which you will need to practice; you don't want to find out the day you need to failover that either you don't know how to failover, or, even worse, you cannot failover due to a mistake that was not discovered previously.

The remainder of the book covers other very useful information such as "What else can I use this standby thing for?" "How does this impact my backup and recovery procedures?" "How have other people implemented Data Guard and why did they make the choices they did?" "Why is Data Guard the right way to provide for disaster recovery for my database, and what is wrong with other methods?" And more.

In short, if you need a roadmap describing how to implement disaster recovery, what you need to think about, what are your options, and which ones you should explore, under what circumstances, then this book is for you. It combines the "How does it work?" with "How do I make it work?" in a practical, hands-on way.

—*Thomas Kyte*
asktom.oracle.com

# Acknowledgments

We want to acknowledge our sponsoring editor, Lisa McClain, for her commitment to this book and her patience with all the authors. Thank you for understanding our busy schedules and personal conflicts while pushing us to deliver in a timely manner. This book would be delayed by another year without her involvement and nurturing.

We also want to acknowledge our acquisitions coordinator, Meghan Riley, editorial supervisor, Janet Walden, the meticulous work of copy editor Lisa Theobald, project manager Vastavikta Sharma, proofreader Paul Tyler, and the entire production and marketing team at Oracle Press. We would also like to extend our personal gratitude to our incredible technical editors, Michael Powell and Sreekanth Chintala, for their great review of all the chapters and contributions.

*—Larry, Joe, Charles, Bill, Sonya, Joy, Mike, and Nitin*

First and foremost, I'd like to thank Bernadette, my wife of 35-plus years, for putting up with my insanity and late nights while we were all working on this book. I would not have made it without her. I would also like to thank Rick Anderson and Mark W. Johnson of Oracle for first introducing me to Database Disaster Recovery, first with Oracle Rdb (originally from Digital and an Oracle product since 1994) and then with Oracle Data Guard starting with Oracle8*i*. Their dedication to ensuring that our customers were successful was my guide and support in my endeavors to do the same. Finally, my thanks to my manager, Ashish Ray, and our senior VP, Juan Loaiza, for allowing me to contribute to this book.

*—Larry Carpenter*

Many thanks to the development staff who have made Data Guard the best data protection and data availability solution for enterprise databases. Additional thanks to the members of Oracle's Maximum Availability Architecture team who document and validate best practices for Oracle's high availability solutions. But the biggest thanks of all are reserved for the DBAs and IT managers who recognize the value offered by Data Guard. Their efforts transform Data Guard from a concept represented by lines of code and documentation into real business value for their companies.

*—Joe Meeks*

I want to extend a personal thank you to our lead author, Larry Carpenter, for his enormous sacrifice and commitment to bringing the technical content of this book together. Without Larry's sacrifices, this book would not have been possible.

*—Charles Kim*

First and foremost, I thank the dedicated team of authors involved in our project, and in particular Larry Carpenter, who was always there front and center to support each of us as we worked to complete our contributions to the book. I'd like to thank Charles Kim, who I've worked with for many years and have come to respect for his professionalism and dedication to the Oracle technology arena, for inviting me to participate in this work, and for his patience while we sometimes struggled to meet every deadline. Finally, for the sacrifices my family has made while I worked late and on weekends after arriving home from traveling all week to complete my portions of the book, thank all of you.

*—Bill Burke*

I would like to thank my friend and colleague Charles Kim for the opportunity to work on this project. During the course of writing this book, he has been an invaluable source of knowledge. Thanks for your guidance, recommendations, and time. I would also like to thank Michael Powell and Sreekanth Chintala for their technical reviews. Their expertise and practical knowledge have helped me immensely. My special thanks to Larry Carpenter for his help, patience, and willingness to share his extensive technical expertise.

Lastly, I'd like to thank my family for their understanding, patience, and support while I worked on this book.

*—Sonya Carothers*

Thanks to the members of the LogMiner and the Logical Standby development team for staying the course through fair and foul weather.

*—Joydip Kundu*

I would like to acknowledge all of my teammates on the Maximum Availability Architecture team. Working with such smart, talented people can only be called a privilege. In addition, I would like to thank the High Availability Product Management team and ST developers for all of their help in getting the MAA best practices out to the customer base.

*—Mike Smith*

Thanks to the entire Vengurlekar and Bhide family, the RacPack group, the ASM development group, and the MAA team. Thanks to Larry Carpenter for his tireless efforts in getting this book together and Charles Kim for talking me into writing this book (you owe me a beer). A big thanks to Kirk Mcgowan, Sohan Demel, and Angelo Pruscino for letting me do this book.

*—Nitin Vengurlekar*

# Introduction

Oracle Data Guard provides the best data protection and data availability solution for mission-critical databases that are the life-blood of businesses large and small. As bold as this statement is, Data Guard's rich capabilities did not materialize overnight; Data Guard is a product of more than 15 years of continuous development. We can trace the roots of today's Data Guard as far back as Oracle7 in the early 1990s. Media recovery was used to apply archived redo logs to a remote standby database, but none of the automation that exists today was present in the product. Instead, user-written scripts used FTP to transmit and register archive logs at the standby database. The Oracle7 feature was appropriately referred to as "manual standby." Oracle8i capabilities evolved into the "automatic standby" feature, with automated log shipping (using Oracle Net Services) and apply. User-written scripts were still the order of the day to resynchronize primary and standby databases in case they lost connection with each other. Also in the Oracle8i timeframe, Oracle made available prepackaged scripts for a limited number of platforms that simplified switchover and failover operations. These scripts could be downloaded from the Oracle Technology Network and were called Data Guard, introducing the present-day brand for the first time.

Oracle9i was the first formal release of the Data Guard product that we know today. Replacing the Oracle8i scripts, the new release delivered a comprehensive automated solution for disaster recovery fully integrated with the database kernel—including automated gap resolution and the concept of protection modes, allowing customers to configure Data Guard more easily to meet their recovery point and recovery time objectives. Oracle9i also significantly enhanced redo transport services, adding synchronous and asynchronous redo transport methods as an alternative to traditional log shipping. For the first time, Data Guard could provide zero data loss protection all by itself, without the use of remote-mirroring technologies.

Oracle 9i Release 2 introduced a new type of standby database using SQL Apply, giving users the choice of Redo Apply (physical standby) or SQL Apply (logical standby).

SQL Apply enabled a standby database to be open while the standby apply process was active, making it attractive for offloading read-only queries from the primary database. This new development set the stage for a series of subsequent enhancements to both types of standby databases, physical and logical, to enable their productiveness while in standby role, greatly improving the return on investment (ROI) of standby systems.

As core functionality evolved, so did the tools for managing a Data Guard configuration. A Data Guard configuration can be created, monitored, and managed with Oracle Enterprise Manager (OEM) Grid Control. Mouse-driven switchovers (planned transition of a standby database to a primary role with zero data loss) and failovers (unplanned role transitions where data loss exposure depends upon the Data Guard protection mode used) have made role transition operations less daunting than in earlier Data Guard releases. There is even an option of automating database failover so that no human intervention is required. The current release of Oracle Enterprise Manager Grid Control, release 10.2.0.5, supports all the new Oracle Data Guard 11g features such as Snapshot Standby and Active Data Guard. And as a hint of things to come in future releases, we understand that Oracle is hard at work enhancing capabilities to fail application clients over automatically to a new primary database—something that in the current release requires a more hand-crafted method using the best practices documented later in this book. These features add traditional high availability attributes to a Data Guard configuration, providing an alternative as well as a complement to cluster technologies for protecting against server failure.

It is important to note that Data Guard is not an island unto itself; it is one of many Oracle high availability features that, when each is integrated with the other, provides value that is greater than the sum of the parts. For example, Flashback Database makes it possible to avoid rebuilding a failed primary database after a failover to its standby. Use of a flash recovery area will automate management of archive logs on both primary and standby databases.

Data Guard is integrated with Oracle RAC, with Automatic Storage Management, and with Oracle Recovery Manager. This integration is not by chance. Oracle has methodically inventoried the many sources of planned and unplanned downtime and is following a blueprint to address all possible causes of downtime using capabilities integrated with the Oracle database. Taken together, these capabilities define the Oracle Maximum Availability Architecture. Oracle's work is not yet complete, but an argument can easily be made that the company "is definitely the leader" among the relational database vendors. Sources of unplanned outages have been addressed. Driving planned downtime to zero is the last remaining frontier. Data Guard provides many ways to minimize unplanned downtime in the current release, but you can look forward to increasing Oracle focus on further minimizing planned downtime in upcoming releases.

This book is very timely given the significant enhancements in Data Guard 11g that revolutionize how users can leverage their standby databases for productive purposes while in standby role. A Data Guard physical standby database licensed for the Active Data Guard option can be open for read-only queries and reporting while continuously applying updates received from the primary database. This can improve primary database performance and response time by offloading queries to an active standby database. It can also defer or eliminate new hardware and software purchases by using existing standby databases, previously idle, that are already in place. No other method on the market offers the simplicity, transparency, and high performance of the Active Data Guard standby for maintaining a synchronized replica of a production database that is open read-only.

Data Guard 11g also offers Snapshot standby, a method of fully leveraging a physical standby database for QA testing and other activities that require a database that is independent of the primary and open read-write. When combined with another new Oracle Database 11*g* feature, Real Application Testing, a Data Guard snapshot standby provides an ideal test system for making absolutely sure that no unintended consequences will result from introducing change to your production environment.

This book provides a sound architectural foundation for newcomers to Data Guard as well as important insight for veteran DBAs who have been working with Data Guard since its inception. The authors have been assembled from Oracle Product Management, Development, and Consulting, as well as industry experts with many years of experience using Data Guard. While Data Guard 11*g* is the focus of this book, we will occasionally highlight information from previous releases where helpful.

The authors have worked hard to provide information that expands well beyond what Oracle has documented. You will benefit from a deeper explanation of details and tradeoffs than is provided by the Data Guard documentation. In some cases, the authors have consolidated information under a clear Data Guard context, in contrast to the Oracle documentation that can cross-reference multiple documentation sources and leave it up to you to build your own Data Guard context along the way.

The outline of the book is simple. Regardless of how knowledgeable you believe you are about Data Guard, we strongly recommend that you start with Chapter 1 and don't skip ahead. This will give you a comprehensive view of Data Guard capabilities and a sound conceptual understanding of how it functions. The first chapter sets the stage and provides necessary context for the information that follows.

As you dive into the subsequent chapters, be prepared for in-depth information for configuring and managing a Data Guard configuration. Chapter 2 provides all the information you need to create a Data Guard configuration. Whether you use SQL, the Data Guard Broker, or Enterprise Manager Grid Control, you should read and understand all the information in Chapter 2. Again, this adds to your foundation of knowledge that will be helpful regardless of the management interface you ultimately use.

Later chapters expand additional details for management from the perspective of the Data Guard Broker or Enterprise Manager Grid Control, with in-depth discussion of media recovery, SQL Apply, role transitions, backup and recovery of primary and standby databases, troubleshooting, Active Data Guard, and more.

For command-line DBAs, Chapter 7 is dedicated to monitoring scripts, where we expose both shell and SQL script to help you effectively monitor your Data Guard environment. The monitoring scripts are provided in a menu screen format with prompts for menu options. Because the menu screens are written in Korn shell scripts, the source code is completely exposed. Our complete set of monitoring scripts can be downloaded from the dataguardbook.com web site or from Oracle Press's download site in a single tar format. The best part about Chapter 7 is that we explain not only what the scripts do, but how to deploy them in your environment.

Last but not least, we provide reference architectures that are representative of actual customer configurations encountered by the authors of this book. We don't waste time on the traditional disaster recovery configuration of a single node primary database with remote standby. We focus on more advanced configurations where customers have implemented Data Guard for high availability in addition to disaster recovery, or multi-standby configurations that provide ideal levels of data protection along with various options for using active standby databases for productive purposes while in standby role. Our goals are to expand your thinking with regard to Data Guard's capabilities, increase your confidence to deploy and manage a Data Guard configuration, and provide you with meaningful context so that you can be sure you are using Data Guard in an optimal way for your specific requirements.

# CHAPTER
## 1

# Data Guard Architecture

uman error, hardware failures, software and network failures, and large-scale events such as fires, hurricanes, and earthquakes all jeopardize the availability of databases that are the lifeblood of business applications. The impact to operations when critical databases are unavailable is so obvious that few people need to be convinced of the importance of data protection and availability.

As an Oracle user, you have already done your homework on Oracle Data Guard. You know that Data Guard is purpose-built for protecting Oracle data, offering the highest levels of data protection and availability while still maintaining the best performance for your Oracle database. You know that, as a native capability built into the Oracle kernel, Data Guard's integration with other Oracle High Availability technologies—most notably Oracle Real Application Clusters (RAC), Oracle Recovery Manager (RMAN), and Oracle Flashback Technologies—offers many benefits. You also know that your finance department will be happy that Active Data Guard standby databases will not consume your IT budget on systems, storage, and software that sit idle until a failure occurs. And because there is no such thing as one-size-fits-all, you know that Data Guard offers the flexibility you need to address a wide range of requirements.

On the flip side of things, "comprehensive and flexible" means that you have a number of decisions to make. You might not be sure about the best way to deploy Data Guard for your environment, and while you have read the Oracle documentation, you may find that you still don't completely understand how Data Guard works. You need more insight into the trade-offs inherent in the different configuration options that Data Guard offers and what you need to know to manage a Data Guard configuration. The good news is that you are reading this book. We will provide you with a broader and deeper understanding of Data Guard that will ensure your success.

# Data Guard Overview

Data Guard operates on a simple principle: ship redo, and then apply redo. Redo includes all of the information needed by the Oracle Database to recover a database transaction. A production database, referred to as the *primary database*, transmits redo to one or more independent replicas referred to as *standby databases*. Data Guard standby databases are in a continuous state of recovery, validating and applying redo to maintain synchronization with the primary database. Data Guard will also automatically resynchronize a standby database that becomes temporarily disconnected from its primary database because of a network or standby outage. This simple architecture makes it possible to have one or more synchronized replicas immediately available to resume processing in the event of a planned or unplanned outage of the primary database. A high-level overview of the Data Guard transport and apply architecture is provided in Figure 1-1.

## What Is Redo?

*Redo* is at the center of everything Data Guard does. While Chapter 3 provides more details on redo concepts, a basic knowledge of this feature is fundamental to your understanding of how Data Guard works.

## Data Guard vs. Remote Mirroring: Advantage Data Guard

Data Guard transmits only *redo data*—the information needed to recover a database transaction—to synchronize a standby database with its primary. Data Guard also prevents the primary from propagating corruption by performing Oracle validation before applying changes to a standby database. Before Data Guard became available, companies would use storage or host-based remote mirroring to maintain a synchronized copy of their Oracle database files. Unfortunately, remote mirroring does not have any knowledge of an Oracle transaction; thus it can't distinguish between redo, undo, data block changes, or control file writes. This requires remote mirroring to transmit every write to every file, generating 7 times the network volume and 27 times more network I/O operations than Data Guard.[1] Remote mirroring is also unable to perform Oracle validation, making it impossible to provide the same level of protection as Data Guard. For these reasons and others discussed later in this chapter, Data Guard has become the preferred data availability and protection solution for the Oracle Database.

Primary database transactions generate redo records. Oracle documentation defines a redo record as follows:[2]

A redo record, also called a redo entry, is made up of a group of change vectors, each of which is a description of a change made to a single block in the database. For example, if you change a salary value in an employee table, you generate a redo record containing change vectors that describe changes to the data segment block for the table, the undo segment data block, and the transaction table of the undo segments.

Redo records contain all the information needed to reconstruct changes made to the database. During media recovery, the database will read change vectors in the redo records and apply the changes to the relevant blocks.

Redo records are buffered in a circular fashion in the redo log buffer of the System Global Area (SGA). The log writer process (LGWR) is the database background process responsible for redo log buffer management. At specific times, the LGWR writes redo entries to a sequential file—the online redo log file (ORL)—to free space in the redo log buffer for new entries. The LGWR always writes all redo entries that have been copied into the redo log buffer since the last time it wrote. The LGWR writes the following:

- **A commit record**   Whenever a transaction is committed, the LGWR writes the transaction redo records from the redo log buffer to an ORL and assigns a system change number (SCN) to identify the redo records for each committed transaction. Only when all redo records associated with a given transaction have been written to the ORL is the user process notified that the transaction has been committed.

---

[1] "Oracle Data Guard and Remote Mirroring Solutions," Oracle Technology Network: www.oracle.com/technology/deploy/availability/htdocs/DataGuardRemoteMirroring.html

[2] Oracle Database Administrator's Guide 11g Release 1 (11.1)

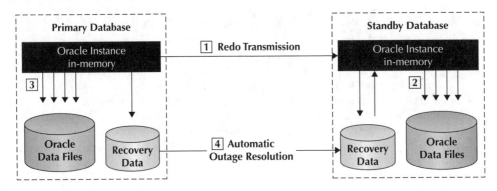

[1] Redo transport services transmit redo data from primary to standby as it is generated.

[2] Apply services validate redo data and update standby database files.

[3] Independent of Data Guard, the database writer process updates primary database files.

[4] Data Guard automatically resynchronizes the standby following network or standby outages using redo data that has been archived at the primary.

**FIGURE 1-1.**   *Overview: Data Guard redo transport and apply*

- **Redo log buffers**   If the redo log buffer becomes a third full or if 3 seconds have passed since the last time the LGWR wrote to the ORL, all redo entries in the log buffer will be written to the ORL. This means that redo records can be written to an ORL before the corresponding transaction has been committed. If necessary, media recovery will roll back these changes using the undo that is also part of the redo entry. The LGWR will also write all redo records to the ORL if the database writer process (DBWn) writes modified buffers to disk and the LGWR had not already completed writing all of the redo records associated with the modified buffers.

It is worth noting that in times of high activity, the LGWR can write to the ORL using "group" commits. For example, assume a user commits a transaction. While the LGWR is writing the commit record to disk, other users may also be issuing COMMIT statements. However, the LGWR cannot write to the redo log file to commit these transactions until it completes the previous write operation. After the first transaction's entries are written to the redo log file, the entire list of redo entries of waiting transactions (not yet committed) can be written to disk in one operation, requiring less I/O than if each transaction entry were handled individually. (The LGWR always does sequential writes—the larger the write, the more efficient it is.) If requests to commit continue at a high rate, every LGWR write from the redo log buffer will contain multiple commit records. This impacts what is referred to as *redo-write size*, one of the factors that influence database performance in a Data Guard synchronous configuration, which is discussed later in this chapter and in Chapter 2.

While the LGWR is going about its business making sure that transactions are recoverable, changes to data blocks in the primary database are deferred until it is more efficient for the DBWn to flush changes in the buffer cache to disk. The LGWR's write of the redo entry containing the transaction's commit record is the single event that determines that the transaction has been committed. Oracle Database is able to issue a success code to the committing transaction, even though the DBWn has not yet flushed data buffers to disk. This enables high performance while guaranteeing that transactions are not lost if the primary database crashes before all data blocks have been written to disk.

Everything discussed in this section is normal processing for any Oracle database, whether or not Data Guard is in use. As transactions commit, they generate redo. This is where a detailed discussion of Data Guard can begin.

# Redo Transport Services

Data Guard Redo Transport Services coordinate the transmission of redo from a primary database to the standby database. At the same time that the primary database LGWR process is writing redo to its ORL, a separate Data Guard process called the *Log Network Server (LNS)* is reading from the redo buffer in SGA and passes redo to Oracle Net Services for transmission to the standby database.

Data Guard's flexible architecture allows a primary database to transmit redo directly to a maximum of nine standby databases. Data Guard is also well integrated with Oracle RAC. An Oracle RAC database has two or more servers (nodes), each running its own Oracle instance and all having shared access to the same Oracle database. Either the primary, or standby, or both can be an Oracle RAC database. Each primary instance that is active generates its own thread of redo and has its own LNS process to transmit redo to the standby database.

Redo records transmitted by the LNS are received at the standby database by another Data Guard process called the *Remote File Server (RFS)*. The RFS receives the redo at the standby database and writes it to a sequential file called a *standby redo log file (SRL)*. In a multi-standby configuration, the primary database has a separate LNS process that manages redo transmissions for each standby database. In a configuration with three standby databases, for example, three LNS processes are active on each primary database instance.

Data Guard supports two redo transport methods using the LNS process: synchronous or asynchronous. A high-level overview of the redo transport architecture is provided in Figure 1-2.

## Synchronous Redo Transport

*Synchronous transport (SYNC)* is also referred to as a "zero data loss" method because the LGWR is not allowed to acknowledge a commit has succeeded until the LNS can confirm that the redo needed to recover the transaction has been written to disk at the standby site. SYNC is described

> **Myth Buster: LGWR Transmits Redo to Standby Databases**
> A common misconception is that the LGWR is the process that transmits data to a standby database. This is *not* the case. The Data Guard LNS process manages all synchronous and asynchronous redo transmissions. Eliminating this perception is the reason why the Data Guard 11*g* documentation simply refers to the redo transport methods as SYNC or ASYNC, rather than LGWR SYNC or LGWR ASYNC as was done in previous releases.

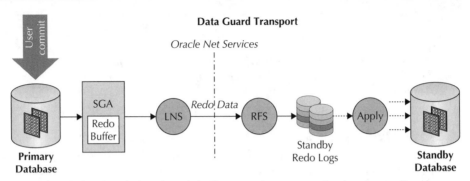

LNS ships redo data directly from the redo buffer—an RFS process receives it at the standby.

**FIGURE 1-2.** *Data Guard redo transport process architecture*

in detail in Figure 1-3. The numbered list that follows outlines each phase of SYNC redo transport and corresponds to the numbers shown in Figure 1-3.

1. The user commits a transaction creating a redo record in SGA. The LGWR reads the redo record from the log buffer, writes it to the online redo log file, and waits for confirmation from the LNS.

2. The LNS reads the same redo record from the log buffer and transmits it to the standby database using Oracle Net Services. The RFS receives the redo at the standby database and writes it to a standby redo log file.

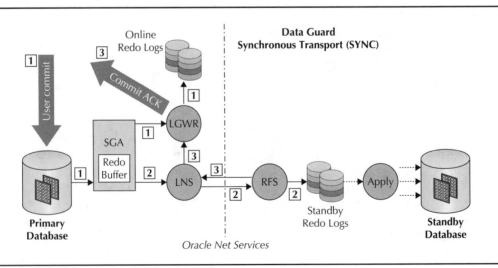

**FIGURE 1-3.** *SYNC redo transport architecture*

3. When the RFS receives a write-complete from the disk, it transmits an acknowledgment back to the LNS process on the primary database, which in turn notifies the LGWR that transmission is complete. The LGWR then sends a commit acknowledgment to the user.

While SYNC guarantees protection for every transaction that the database acknowledges as having been committed, this guarantee can also impact primary database performance. The cause of the performance impact is obvious: the LGWR must wait for confirmation that data is protected at the standby before it can proceed with the next transaction. The degree of impact this has on application response time and database throughput is a function of several factors: the redo-write size, available network bandwidth, round-trip network latency (RTT), and standby I/O performance writing to the SRL. Because network RTT increases with distance, so will the performance impact on your primary database, imposing a practical limit on how far apart you will be able to locate your primary and standby databases. The cumulative impact of these factors can be seen in the wait event "LNS wait on SENDREQ," found in the V$SYSTEM_EVENT dynamic performance view (optimizing redo transport is discussed in Chapter 2).

Having read this, you are probably wondering what happens to the primary database if the network or standby database fails while using SYNC? Will the primary database wait forever for an acknowledgment that will never come? Please hold that thought until the "Data Guard Protection Modes" section and the discussion of the NET_TIMEOUT attribute, later in this chapter.

## Asynchronous Redo Transport

*Asynchronous transport (ASYNC)* is different from SYNC in that it eliminates the requirement that the LGWR wait for acknowledgment from the LNS, creating near zero performance impact on the primary database regardless of the distance between primary and standby locations.

The LGWR will continue to acknowledge commit success even if limited bandwidth prevents the redo of previous transactions from being sent to the standby database immediately (picture a sink filling with water faster than it can drain). If the LNS is unable to keep pace and the log buffer is recycled before the redo can be transmitted to the standby, the LNS automatically transitions to reading and sending from the ORL (Data Guard 11g onward). Once the LNS is caught up, it automatically transitions back to reading/sending directly from the log buffer.

If ASYNC redo transport falls behind to the degree that the LNS is still in the ORL at log switch time, LNS will continue until it completes sending the contents of the original ORL. Once complete, it seamlessly transitions back to reading/sending from the current online log file.

### Data Guard 11g ASYNC Enhancements

ASYNC behavior has varied over previous Data Guard releases. The LNS process in Data Guard 11g ASYNC now reads directly from the redo log buffer, but unlike pre-10.2 releases, there is never a "buffer full" state that can cause transmission to terminate. Instead, the LNS process seamlessly transitions to read and send from the online redo log of the primary database. Data Guard 11g ASYNC is also more efficient in how it utilizes available network bandwidth, increasing the network throughput rate that can be achieved for any given bandwidth. The higher the network latency, the greater the gain in network throughput compared to previous Data Guard releases.

### Optimizing ASYNC Redo Transport

The log buffer hit ratio is tracked in the view X$LOGBUF_READHIST. A low hit ratio indicates that the LNS is frequently reading from the ORL instead of the log buffer. If there are periods when redo transport is coming close, but is not quite keeping pace with your redo generation rate, consider increasing the log buffer size in Data Guard 11*g* to achieve a more favorable hit ratio. This will reduce or eliminate I/O overhead of the LNS reading from the ORL. See Chapter 2 for more details.

When the LNS catches up with the LGWR, it seamlessly transitions back to reading/sending from the redo log buffer.

In the rarer case in which there are two or more log switches before the LNS has completed sending the original ORL, the LNS will still transition back to reading the contents of the current online log file. Any ORLs that were archived between the original ORL and the current ORL are transmitted via Data Guard's *gap resolution process* described in the section "Automatic Gap Resolution" a little later in the chapter. Note that if you find that this "rare case" is a frequent occurrence, it is most likely a sign that you have not provisioned enough bandwidth to transport your redo volume.

The behavior of ASYNC transport enables the primary database to buffer a large amount of redo, called a *transport lag*, without terminating transmission or impacting availability. While the I/O overhead related to the ASYNC LNS reading from the ORL can marginally impact primary database performance, this is insignificant compared to the potential performance impact of SYNC on a high latency network. The relative simplicity of ASYNC is evident when comparing Figures 1-4 and 1-3. The only drawback of ASYNC is the increased potential for data loss. If a failure destroys the primary database before any transport lag is reduced to zero, any committed transactions that are a part of the transport lag will be lost. Provisioning enough network bandwidth to handle peak redo generation rates when using ASYNC will minimize this potential for data loss.

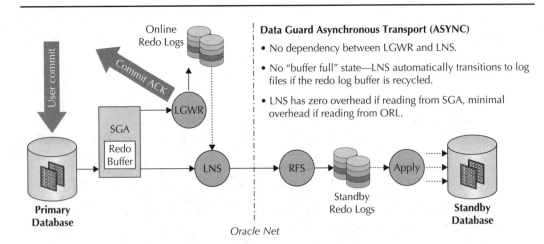

**FIGURE 1-4.** *ASYNC redo transport architecture*

**Enabling ASYNC Redo Transport Compression**

Buried in Oracle MetaLink Note 729551.1 is the information needed to enable redo transport compression for Oracle Database 11g Release 1 and Data Guard ASYNC (Maximum Performance) using the parameter _REDO_TRANSPORT_COMPRESS_ALL. A license for Oracle Advanced Compression is required to enable redo transport compression.

## Redo Transport Compression

An additional consideration when using ASYNC is determining whether it is advantageous to compress redo to reduce your bandwidth requirements. Oracle released a new product for Oracle Enterprise Edition 11g called the *Advanced Compression option*. This new product contains several compression features, one of which is redo transport compression for Data Guard. Initially this feature could only be enabled when Data Guard was transmitting log files needed to resolve an archive log gap. However, in response to customer request, Oracle has published information about an undocumented parameter that enables compression for ASYNC redo transport as well. (See sidebar, "Enabling ASYNC Redo Transport Compression.")

ASYNC redo transport compression will increase CPU utilization; however, in bandwidth-constrained environments it can make the difference between success and failure in accomplishing your recovery point (data loss) objectives. For example, Oracle Japan and Hitachi Ltd. tested the impact of using compression in a bandwidth-constrained environment with a test workload that generated 20 MB/sec of redo. While compression ratios will vary from one workload to the next, the compression ratio achieved in the test was 60 percent. The benefit of using compression was significant, making it possible to sustain a transport lag of less than 10 seconds and achieve recovery point objectives.[3] This compared very favorably to baseline test runs without compression, in which transmission could not keep pace with primary redo generation, resulting in a transport lag that continued to increase linearly over time for the duration of the test. The testing also showed that as long as sufficient CPU resources were available for compression, minimal impact was experienced on database throughput or response time.

## Automatic Gap Resolution

A log file gap occurs whenever a primary database continues to commit transactions while the LNS process has ceased transmitting redo to the standby database. This can occur whenever the network or the standby database is down, depending on how you have chosen to implement your Data Guard configuration (discussed in the section "Data Guard Protection Modes" later in this chapter). While in this state, the primary database LGWR process continues writing to the current ORL, fills it, and then switches to a new ORL while an archive (ARCH) process archives the completed ORL locally. This cycle can repeat itself many times over on a busy system before the connection between the primary and standby is restored, creating a large log file gap.

---

[3] "Batch Processing in Disaster Recovery Configurations: Best Practices for Oracle Data Guard," validation report on Data Guard redo transport compression and proper network configuration by Hitachi Ltd./Oracle Japan GRID Center: www.hitachi.co.jp/Prod/comp/soft1/oracle/pdf/OBtecinfo-08-008.pdf

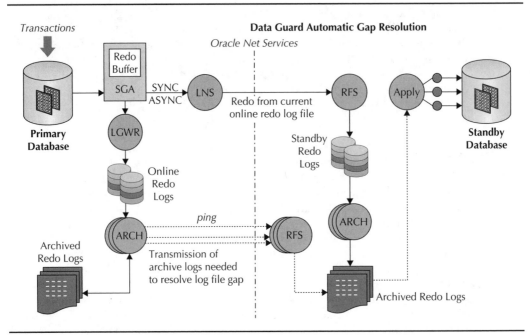

**FIGURE 1-5.** *Automatic gap resolution*

Data Guard uses an ARCH process on the primary database to continuously ping the standby database during the outage to determine its status. When communication with the standby is restored, the ARCH ping process queries the standby control file (via its RFS process) to determine the last complete log file that the standby received from the primary database. Data Guard determines which log files are required to resynchronize the standby database and immediately begins transmitting them using additional ARCH processes. At the very next log switch, the LNS will attempt and succeed in making a connection to the standby database and will begin transmitting current redo while the ARCH processes resolve the gap in the background. The dashed lines in Figure 1-5 portray the transmission and apply of redo needed to resolve the log file gap. Once the standby apply process is able to catch up to current redo records, the apply process automatically transitions out of reading from archived redo logs, and into reading from the current SRL (assuming the user has configured Data Guard *real-time apply*). One last side note: beginning with Data Guard 10g, one ARCH process at the primary database is always dedicated to local archival to ensure that remote archival during gap resolution does not impact the ability of the primary to recycle its ORLs.[4]

The performance of automatic gap resolution is critical. The longer the primary and standby databases remain unsynchronized, the greater the risk of data loss should a failure occur. The primary must be able to transmit data at a much faster pace than its normal redo generation rate if the standby is to have any hope of catching up. The Data Guard architecture enables gaps to be resolved quickly using multiple background ARCH processes, while at the same time the LNS process is conducting normal SYNC or ASYNC transmission of the current log stream.

---

[4] This functionality is available in Oracle9i Data Guard starting at version 9.2.0.5. See MetaLink Note 260040.1.

> **Why Isn't ARCH Redo Transport in the Data Guard 11g Documentation?**
> Three redo transport methods were documented prior to Data Guard 11g: SYNC, ASYNC, and ARCH. *ARCH* refers to traditional archive log shipping, in which Data Guard would wait for an ORL to be archived before the contents of the resulting archive log file where shipped by an ARCH process. Data Guard 11g ASYNC performance enhancements have led Oracle to deprecate ARCH as a documented redo transport method. Though deprecated, the functionally still exists to use ARCH for redo transport and provide backward compatibility for previous customer installations. The ARCH transport infrastructure also continues to be used transparently by Data Guard 11g when automatically resolving archive log gaps between primary and standby databases.

# Apply Services

Data Guard offers two different methods to apply redo to a standby database: Redo Apply (physical standby) and SQL Apply (logical standby). We will describe the differences in a moment, but first let's discuss key objectives that Redo Apply and SQL Apply have in common.

The primary goal of Data Guard is to protect against data loss; thus its first design objective is that the standby database be a synchronized copy of the primary database. Data Guard is designed from the ground up for simple one-way replication of the entire database. Data Guard also has built-in safeguards that prevent any unauthorized modifications from being made at the standby database to data it has replicated from the primary database. These characteristics explain the fundamental difference between Data Guard and Oracle's full-featured replication product, Oracle Streams. Oracle Streams offers various methods for granular, *n*-way replication and transformation of subsets of an Oracle database. By definition, the additional functionality of Oracle Streams means that it has more moving parts with the usual implications for performance and management complexity. Data Guard has been designed for a simpler mission, and this is reflected in the relative simplicity of implementing and managing a Data Guard configuration.

The second objective for Data Guard is to provide a high degree of isolation between primary and standby databases. This prevents problems that occur at the primary database from impacting the standby database and compromising data protection and availability. This also prevents problems that occur at the standby from impacting the availability or performance of the primary database. For example, Data Guard apply processes validate redo before it is applied to the standby database, preventing physical corruptions that can occur at the primary database from being propagated to the standby database. Also, consider for a moment the earlier discussion of redo transport services. Nowhere is there a dependency between redo transport and standby database apply. Primary database availability, performance, and its ability to transmit redo to the standby database are not impacted by how standby apply is configured, or the performance of the apply process, or even whether apply is on or off.

The third objective for Data Guard is to provide data availability and high availability should the primary database fail. Redo Apply and SQL Apply have the same capabilities to transition a synchronized standby database quickly to the primary role. This protects data and restores availability following planned or unplanned outages of the primary database.

### Data Guard Apply and Oracle RAC

Each primary Oracle RAC instance ships its own thread of redo that is merged by the Data Guard apply process at the standby and applied in SCN order to the standby database (see Chapter 8 for a more detailed explanation). If the standby is an Oracle RAC database, only one instance (the apply instance) can merge and apply changes to the standby database. Should the apply instance fail for any reason, the apply process can automatically failover to a surviving instance in the Oracle RAC standby database when using the Data Guard broker, discussed in Chapter 5.

The final objective for Data Guard is to deliver a high return on investment in standby systems, storage, and software, without compromising its core mission of data protection and availability. Both Redo Apply and SQL Apply enable the productive use of standby databases while in a standby role, without impacting data protection or the ability to achieve recovery time objectives (RTO).

Now that you know what Redo Apply and SQL Apply have in common, you need to understand the differences between the two to determine which type of standby database is best suited to your requirements. An overview of the unique characteristics and benefits of Redo Apply and SQL Apply are discussed next. Additional details are provided in Chapters 2, 3, and 4.

## Redo Apply (Physical Standby)

Redo Apply maintains a standby database that is an exact, block-by-block, physical replica of the primary database. As the RFS process on the standby receives primary redo and writes it to an SRL, Redo Apply uses Media Recovery to read redo records from the SRL into memory and apply change vectors directly to the standby database. Media Recovery does parallel media recovery (Figure 1-6) for very high performance. It comprises a Media Recovery Coordinator and multiple parallel apply processes. The Media Recovery Coordinator (MRP0) manages the recovery session, merges redo by SCN from multiple instances (if Oracle RAC primary), and then parses redo into

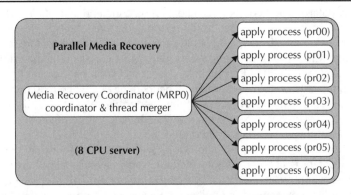

**FIGURE 1-6.**  *Parallel media recovery for Redo Apply (physical standby)*

change mappings partitioned by apply process. The apply processes (pr00, 01, 02...) read data blocks, assemble redo changes from mappings, and then apply redo changes to data blocks. Redo Apply automatically configures a number of apply processes equal to the number of CPUs in the standby system minus one. This architecture, along with significant Media Recovery enhancements in Oracle Database 11g, achieves very high performance. Oracle has benchmarked Data Guard Redo Apply rates up to 47 MB/sec for an online transaction processing (OLTP) workload and 112 MB/sec for a direct path load.[5]

## Oracle Active Data Guard 11*g*

The usefulness of a physical standby database while in the standby role was significantly enhanced by the Active Data Guard Option for Oracle Database 11g Enterprise Edition. In previous Data Guard releases, the database would have to be in the mount state when media recovery was active. Media recovery has always been optimized for the highest possible performance and was never designed to present queries with a read-consistent view while enabled. Querying a physical standby database has required disabling media recovery and opening the standby database in read-only mode. Since standby data can quickly become stale once media recovery is disabled, the usefulness of a physical standby to offload read-only queries and reporting from a primary database was limited.

Active Data Guard 11g solves the read consistency problem without impacting standby apply performance by use of a "query" SCN. The media recovery process on the standby database advances the query SCN after all dependent changes in a transaction have been fully applied (the new query SCN is also propagated to all instances in an Oracle RAC standby). The query SCN is exposed to the user as the CURRENT_SCN column of the V$DATABASE view on the standby database. Read-only users will only see data up to the query SCN, guaranteeing the same read consistency as the primary database. This enables a physical standby database to be open read-only while media recovery is active, making it very useful for offloading read-only workloads from the primary database.

## Corruption Protection

Data Guard Redo Apply provides superior data protection by preventing physical corruptions that can occur at the primary database from being applied to a standby database. Redo transmitted directly from SGA by SYNC or ASYNC is completely isolated from physical I/O corruptions

### Remote Mirroring and Corruption

We frequently hear reports from users of Storage Area Network (SAN) or host-based remote mirroring of cases in which physical corruptions caused by component failure at their primary site were mirrored to remote volumes, making both copies unusable. Since Oracle cannot be mounted on remote volumes while the mirroring session is active, it cannot perform end-to-end validation of changes before they are applied to the standby database. Worse yet, remote mirroring users often do not learn that a problem exists until they need their standby database—and at that point it's too late. Data Guard does not have these limitations.

---

[5] Active Data Guard 11g and media recovery best practices: www.oracle.com/technology/deploy/availability/pdf/maa_wp_11gr1_activedataguard.pdf

caused by component failures at the primary site. The software code-path executed by Redo Apply on a standby database is also fundamentally different from that of a primary—providing the standby database an additional level of isolation from software errors that can impact the primary database. Data Guard uses Oracle processes to validate redo before it is applied to the standby database. Corruption-detection checks occur at the following key interfaces:

- **On the primary database during Redo Transport**   LGWR, LNS, ARCH  On an Oracle Database 11*g* primary database, corruption detection/protection is best enabled using the parameter DB_ULTRA_SAFE.

- **On the standby database during Redo Apply**   RFS, ARCH, MRP, DBWR  On an Oracle Database 11*g* standby database, corruption detection/prevention is best enabled using the parameters DB_BLOCK_CHECKSUM=FULL and DB_LOST_WRITE_PROTECT=TYPICAL.

If Redo Apply detects any corrupt redo at the standby database, Data Guard will automatically fetch new copies of the relevant archive logs from the primary database using the gap resolution process in the hope that the originals are free of corruption.

Physical Standby utilizes the new Oracle Database 11*g* parameter, DB_LOST_WRITE_PROTECT, to provide industry-unique protection against corruptions caused by lost writes. A *lost write* occurs when an I/O subsystem acknowledges the completion of a write, while in fact the write did not occur in persistent storage. On a subsequent block read the I/O subsystem returns the stale version of the data block that is used to update other blocks, spreading corruptions across the database. When the DB_LOST_WRITE_PROTECT initialization parameter is set, the database records buffer cache block reads in the redo log, and this information is used to detect lost writes. Meaningful protection using lost write detection requires the use of a Data Guard physical standby database. You set DB_LOST_WRITE_PROTECT to TYPICAL in both primary and standby databases (setting DB_ULTRA_SAFE at the primary as noted above will automatically set DB_LOST_WRITE_PROTECT=TYPICAL on the primary database). When the standby database applies redo using Redo Apply, it reads the corresponding blocks and compares the SCNs with the SCNs in the redo log. If the comparison shows:

- The block SCN on the primary database is lower than the block SCN on the standby database, then a lost write has occurred on the primary database and an external error (ORA-752) is signaled. The recommended procedure in response to an ORA-752 is to execute a failover to the physical standby and re-create the primary database.

- The block SCN is higher, then a lost write has occurred on the standby database, and an internal error (ORA-600 3020) is signaled. If possible, you can fix the standby using a backup from the primary database of the affected data files. Otherwise, you will have to rebuild the standby completely.

## Redo Apply Benefits
Physical standby databases maintained using Redo Apply are generally the best choice for disaster recovery (DR) based upon their simplicity, transparency, high performance, and superior data protection. In summary, the advantages of a physical standby database include the following:

- Complete application and data transparency—no data type or other restrictions.

- Very high performance, least management complexity, and fewest moving parts.

**Rolling Database Upgrades Using a Physical Standby**

Data Guard 11*g* enables a physical standby database to be used for rolling database upgrades via the KEEP IDENTITY clause and SQL Apply. A physical standby is temporarily converted to a *transient logical standby* and upgraded to the new release. Although the process of upgrading the Oracle Home must be performed on both the primary and standby systems, the execution of the database upgrade script only needs to be performed once on the transient logical standby database. Following a switchover, the original primary database is converted back into a physical standby and is upgraded by applying the redo generated by the execution of the upgrade script previously run on the transient logical standby (see Chapter 11 for details). This eliminates the extra cost and effort of deploying additional storage for a logical standby database solely for the purpose of a rolling database upgrade.

- Oracle end-to-end validation before apply provides the best protection against physical corruptions, including corruptions due to lost writes.

- Able to be utilized for up-to-date read-only queries and reporting while providing DR (Active Data Guard 11*g*).

- Able to offload backups from the primary database while providing DR.

- Able to support QA testing and other activities requiring read-write access, while continuing to provide DR protection for primary data (Data Guard 11*g* Snapshot Standby).

- Able to execute rolling database upgrades beginning with Oracle Database 11*g* (Transient Logical)

# SQL Apply (Logical Standby)

SQL Apply uses the Logical Standby Process (LSP) to coordinate the apply of changes to the standby database. SQL Apply requires more processing than Redo Apply, as can be seen in Figure 1-7 and discussed in detail in Chapter 4. The processes that make up SQL Apply read the SRL and "mine" the redo by converting it to logical change records, and then building SQL transactions and applying SQL to the standby database. Because the process of reconstruction and replaying workload has more moving parts, it requires more memory, CPU, and I/O than Redo Apply.

SQL Apply also does not provide the same level of transparency as Redo Apply. SQL Apply performance can vary from one transaction profile to the next. SQL Apply does not support all data types (such as XML in object relational format, and Oracle supplied types such as Oracle Spatial, Oracle Intermedia, and Oracle Text). Collectively, these attributes result in SQL Apply requiring more extensive performance testing, tuning, and management effort than a physical standby database. (Refer to Oracle MetaLink for an excellent note that provides insight into optimizing SQL Apply performance.[6]) While such characteristics are found to varying degrees in any SQL-based replication solution, whether provided by Oracle or by third parties, SQL Apply

---

[6]MetaLink Note 603361.1: "Developer and DBA Tips for Pro-Actively Optimizing SQL Apply"

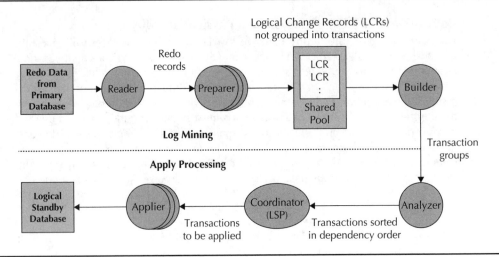

**FIGURE 1-7.** *SQL Apply process architecture*

has an inherent advantage over third-party SQL replication products due to its native integration with the Oracle Database kernel.

## SQL Apply Benefits

The extra processing performed by SQL Apply is also the source of its advantages when compared to Redo Apply. Because SQL Apply applies SQL, a logical standby database is opened read-write while apply is active. While SQL Apply prevents any modifications from being made to the data it is replicating, a logical standby database has the additional flexibility of allowing inserts, updates, and deletes to local tables and schemas that have been added to the standby database independent of the primary. This is very useful, for example, if you want to use the standby to offload a reporting application from the primary database that must make frequent writes to global temporary tables or other local tables that exist only at the standby database. A logical standby database also allows the creation of local indexes and materialized views that don't exist on the primary database. This enables indexes that can be quite expensive to maintain, in terms of their impact on an OLTP system, to be implemented on a logical standby database where they are valuable for optimizing reporting and browsing activities. SQL Apply benefits include the following:

- A native Oracle capability that is simpler and less intrusive on primary database performance and administration than third-party SQL-based replication products. This is accomplished by having a simpler design objective of one-way replication for the entire primary database. (Redo Transport Services efficiently transmit all primary database redo, and SQL Apply always performs all of its processing at the standby database.)

- A standby database that is opened read-write while SQL Apply is active.

- A "guard" setting that prevents applications from modifying data in the standby database that is being maintained by SQL Apply.

**Myth Buster: SQL Apply Is an Immature Feature**

SQL Apply WAS an immature feature when first released in Oracle9*i*, leading early users to believe that SQL Apply could not be used successfully in a production environment. This perception is now a myth as SQL Apply has matured over several major Oracle releases. This statement is substantiated by the growing number of successful production implementations using Data Guard 10*g* Release 2. Data Guard 11*g* SQL Apply is a very attractive solution for the requirements it is designed to address.

■ SQL Apply can be used for rolling database upgrades to new Oracle releases and patchsets, beginning with Oracle Database 10.1.0.4 for logical standby databases, and beginning with Oracle Database 11.1.0.6 for physical standby databases (using the KEEP IDENTITY clause).

We recommend using SQL Apply if you can satisfy its prerequisites and you have the additional requirement for a standby database that is open read-write while it provides DR protection for the primary database.

# Can't Decide? Then Use Both!

We know that making a choice between Redo Apply and SQL Apply can create a dilemma. You want the simplicity and performance of Redo Apply for data protection and availability. Redo Apply when using Active Data Guard 11*g* also offers an excellent solution for offloading read-only queries from your primary databases. However, you may have cases where a reporting application needs read-write access to the standby database, requiring the additional flexibility offered by SQL Apply. Data Guard support for multi-standby configurations having a mix of physical and logical standby databases can provide users with the flexibility to satisfy all requirements in an optimum fashion in a single Data Guard configuration.[7]

**Myth Buster: Standby Apply Performance Can Impact the Primary Database**

A common misperception is that standby apply performance can impact the primary database. This perception is perpetuated by the fact that competing RDBMS products do not deliver the same level of isolation implemented by Data Guard. Standby database apply performance does not have any impact on primary database availability or performance in a Data Guard configuration.

---

[7] "Managing Data Guard Configurations Having Multiple Standby Databases—MAA Best Practices": www.oracle .com/technology/deploy/availability/pdf/maa10gr2multiplestandbybp.pdf

# Data Guard Protection Modes

Many DBAs are interested in the superior data protection of Data Guard SYNC redo transport, but they are often concerned that the primary database may hang indefinitely if it does not receive acknowledgment from its standby database, due to the standby database being unavailable or a network down condition. The last thing that most DBAs want to report to their customers is that while the primary database is completely healthy, it is refusing to process any more transactions until it can guarantee that data is protected by a standby database. Then again, perhaps you have a different set of requirements and you must absolutely guarantee that data is protected even at the expense of primary database availability. Both of these use cases can utilize SYNC transport to provide zero data loss protection, but the two cases require a different response to a network or standby failure. Data Guard protection modes implement rules that govern how the configuration will respond to failures, enabling you to achieve your specific objectives for data protection, availability, and performance. Data Guard can support multiple standby databases in a single Data Guard configuration, and they may all have the same, or different, protection mode setting, depending on your requirements. The different Data Guard protection modes are Maximum Performance, Maximum Availability, and Maximum Protection.

## Maximum Performance

This mode emphasizes primary database performance over data protection. It requires ASYNC redo transport so that the LGWR process never waits for acknowledgment from the standby database. Primary database performance and availability are not impacted by redo transport, by the status of the network connection between primary and standby, or by the availability of the standby database. As discussed earlier in this chapter, ASYNC enhancements in Data Guard 11*g* have made it the default redo transport method for Maximum Performance. Oracle no longer recommends the ARCH transport for Maximum Performance in Data Guard 11*g* given that it provides a lower level of data protection with no performance advantage compared to ASYNC.

## Maximum Availability

This mode emphasizes availability as its first priority and zero data loss protection as a very close second priority. It requires SYNC redo transport, thus primary database performance may be impacted by the amount of time required to receive an acknowledgment from the standby that redo has been written to disk. SYNC transport, however, guarantees 100-percent data protection during normal operation in the event that the primary database fails.

However, events that have no impact on the availability of the primary database can impact its ability to transmit redo to the standby. For example, a network or standby database failure will make it impossible to transmit to the standby database, yet the primary database is still capable of accepting new transactions. A primary database configured for Maximum Availability will wait a maximum of NET_TIMEOUT seconds (a user configurable parameter which is discussed more completely in Chapter 2) before giving up on the standby destination and allowing primary database processing to proceed even though it can no longer communicate with the standby. This prevents a failure in communication between the primary and standby databases from impacting the availability of the primary database.

Data Guard will automatically resynchronize the standby database once the primary is able to re-establish a connection to the standby (utilizing the gap resolution process described earlier in this chapter). Specifically, once NET_TIMEOUT seconds expire, the LGWR process disconnects from the

LNS process, acknowledges the commit, and proceeds without the standby. Processing continues until the current ORL is complete and the LGWR cycles into a new ORL. As the new ORL is opened, the LGWR will terminate the previous LNS process, if necessary, and start a new LNS process that will attempt to make a new connection to the standby database. If it succeeds, the contents of the new ORL will be sent as usual. If the LNS does not succeed within NET_TIMEOUT seconds, the LGWR continues as before, acknowledges the current commit, and proceeds without the standby. This process is repeated at each log switch until LNS succeeds in making a connection to the standby database. (How soon the LGWR retries a failed standby can be tuned using the REOPEN attribute, which is discussed in Chapter 2.)

Meanwhile, the primary database has archived one or more ORLs that have not been completely transmitted to the standby database. A Data Guard ARCH process continuously pings the standby database until it can again make contact and determine which archive logs are incomplete or missing at the standby. With this knowledge in-hand, Data Guard immediately begins transmitting any log files needed to resynchronize the standby database. Once the ping process makes contact with the standby Data Guard will also force a log switch on the primary database. This closes off the current online log file and initiates a new LNS connection to immediately begin shipping current redo, preventing redo transport from falling any further behind while gap resynchronization is in progress. The potential for data loss during this process exists only if another failure impacts the primary database before the automatic resynchronization process is complete.

## Maximum Protection

As its name implies, this mode places utmost priority on data protection. It also requires SYNC redo transport. The primary will not acknowledge a commit to the application unless it receives acknowledgment from at least one standby database in the configuration that the data needed to recover that transaction is safely on disk. It has the same impact on primary database performance as Maximum Availability, except that it does not consider the NET_TIMEOUT parameter. If the primary does not receive acknowledgment from a SYNC standby database, it will stall and eventually abort, preventing any unprotected commits from occurring. This behavior guarantees complete data protection even in the case of multiple failure events (for example, first the network drops, and later the primary site fails). Note that most users who implement Maximum Protection configure a minimum of two SYNC standby databases at different locations, so that failure of an individual standby database does not impact the availability of the primary database.

# Role Management Services

Let's step back for a moment and review what we have covered thus far. Our review of Data Guard transport and apply services has shown the following:

- Data Guard only needs to transmit redo records to synchronize remote standby databases.

- Transmission can be either synchronous (zero data loss) or asynchronous.

- Synchronous transmission can impact primary database throughput and response time because of the time it takes for the primary to receive acknowledgment from the remote standby that data is safely written to disk. We can control how long a primary database will wait for that acknowledgment so that we do not fall into an indefinite hang if the primary loses its link to the standby.

■ Asynchronous transmission will never cause the primary to stall or impact primary database performance or response time in a material way.

■ There are two different types of standby databases: Redo Apply (physical) and SQL Apply (logical). We know their relative strengths, and we know that regardless of the method chosen, standby apply performance will never impact the availability or performance of the primary database. We know that all redo is validated by Oracle before it is applied to the standby database, preventing physical corruptions or lost writes that may occur on the primary database from impacting the standby database. We know that all Data Guard standby databases are active, able to be open for read-only queries and reports in order to offload work from a primary database and get more value from investments in standby systems.

■ The Data Guard protection modes control how the configuration will respond to failures so that availability, performance, and data protection objectives are achieved. We know that the availability of the standby database or the network connection between primary and standby will never impact primary database availability unless explicitly configured to do so to achieve the highest possible level of data protection.

The next area of Data Guard architecture we will discuss is role management services that enable the rapid transition of a standby database to the primary database role. Data Guard documentation uses the term *switchover* to describe a planned role transition, usually for the purpose of minimizing downtime during planned maintenance activities. The term *failover* is used to describe a role transition in response to unplanned events.

# Switchover

Switchover is a planned event in which Data Guard reverses the roles of the primary and a standby database. Switchover is particularly useful for minimizing downtime during planned maintenance. The most obvious case is when migrating to new Oracle Database releases or patchsets using a rolling database upgrade. A Data Guard switchover also minimizes downtime when migrating to new storage (including Exadata storage[8]), migrating volume managers (for example, moving to Oracle Automatic Storage Management), migrating from single instance to Oracle RAC, performing technology refresh, operating system or hardware maintenance, and even relocating data centers. The switchover command executes the following steps:

1. Notifies the primary database that a switchover is about to occur.

2. Disconnects all users from the primary.

3. Generates a special redo record that signals the End Of Redo (EOR).

4. Converts the primary database into a standby database.

5. Once the standby database applies the final EOR record, guaranteeing that no data has been lost, converts the standby to the primary role.

The new primary automatically begins transmitting redo to all other standby databases in the configuration. The transition in a multi-standby configuration is orderly because each standby

---

[8]MAA "Best Practices for Migrating to Oracle Exadata Storage Server": www.oracle.com/technology/products/bi/db/exadata/pdf/migration-to-exadata-whitepaper.pdf

received the identical EOR record transmitted the original primary, they know that the next redo received will be from the database that has just become the new primary database.

The basic principle for using switchover to reduce downtime during planned maintenance is usually the same. The primary database runs unaffected while you implement the required changes on your standby database (e.g. patchset upgrades, full Oracle version upgrades, etc). Once complete, production is switched over to the standby site running at the new release. In the case of a data center move, you simply create a standby database in the new data center and move production to that database using a switchover operation.

Alternatively, before performing maintenance that will impact the availability of the primary site, you can first switch production to the standby site so that applications remain available the entire time that site maintenance is being performed. Once the work is complete Data Guard will resynchronize both databases and enable you to switch production back to the original primary site. Regardless of how much time is required to perform planned maintenance, the only production database downtime is the time required to execute a switchover—a task that can be completed in less than 60 seconds as documented by Oracle best practices[9], and in as fast as 5 seconds as documented in collaborative validation testing performed more recently by Oracle Japan and IBM.[10]

Switchover operations become even more valuable given Oracle's increasing support for different primary/standby systems in the same Data Guard configuration. For example, Oracle Database 11*g* can support a Windows primary and Linux standby, or a 32-bit Oracle primary and a 64-bit Oracle standby, and other select mixed configurations.[11] This makes it very easy to migrate between supported platform combinations with very little risk simply by creating a standby database on the new platform and then switching over. In most cases, you are able to minimize your risk even more by continuing to keep the old database on the previous platform synchronized with the new. If an unanticipated problem occurs and you need to fall back to the previous platform, you can simply execute a second switchover and no data is lost.

## Failover

*Failover* is the term used to describe role transitions due to unplanned events. The process is similar to switchover except that the primary database never has the chance to write an EOR record. From the perspective of the standby database, redo transport has suddenly gone dormant. The standby database faithfully applies the redo from the last committed transaction that it has received and waits for redo transport to resume. At this point, whether or not a failover results in data loss depends upon the Data Guard protection mode in effect at the time of failure. There will never be any data loss in Maximum Protection. There will be zero data loss in Maximum Availability, except when a previous failure (e.g. a network failure) had interrupted redo transport and allowed the primary database to diverge from the standby database. Any committed transactions that have not been transmitted to the standby will be lost if a second failure destroys the primary database. Similarly, configurations using Maximum Performance (ASYNC) will lose any committed transactions that were not transmitted to the standby database before the primary database failed.

---

[9] MAA "Switchover and Failover Best Practices" for Data Guard 10*g*: www.oracle.com/technology/deploy/availability/pdf/MAA_WP_10gR2_SwitchoverFailoverBestPractices.pdf

[10] Oracle Japan GRID Center Performance Validation: Data Guard SQL Apply on IBM Power Systems: http://www.oracle.com/technology/deploy/availability/pdf/gridcenter_sqlapply_validation_powersystem.pdf

[11] MetaLink Note 413484.1

### Myth Buster: You Must Re-create the Original Primary Databases after Failover

Beginning with Oracle 10g Release 1, you can often avoid having to restore a failed primary database from a new backup if Flashback Database was enabled on the primary database before the failover occurred (a minimum flashback retention period of 60 minutes is required). If the failed primary can be repaired and the database brought to a mounted state, it can be flashed back to an SCN that precedes the standby becoming the new primary, and converted to a standby database. When using Redo Apply, this SCN is determined by issuing the following query on the new primary database:

```
SQL> SELECT TO_CHAR(STANDBY_BECAME_PRIMARY_SCN)
FROM V$DATABASE;
```

Once the flashback operation is complete, you convert the failed primary to a physical standby database and Data Guard is able to resynchronize it with the new primary to quickly return the configuration to a protected state. This process is a little more involved for a logical standby, but will accomplish the same end result.

DBAs have the choice of configuring either *manual* or *automatic* failover. Manual failover operations give the administrator complete control of role transitions. Manual failover, however, will lengthen the outage by the amount of time required for the administrator to be notified, to respond to the notification, to evaluate what has happened, make the decision to failover, and manually execute the command. In contrast, Data Guard's Fast-Start Failover[12] feature described in Figure 1-8 automatically detects the failure, evaluates the status of the Data Guard configuration, and, if appropriate, executes the failover to a previously chosen standby database. (Fast-Start Failover is discussed in detail in Chapter 8.) In either case, executing a database failover is very fast once the decision has been made to perform a failover. Oracle has benchmarked Data Guard 11g database failover times ranging from 14 to 25 seconds depending on the configuration.[13]

## Choosing Between Manual or Automatic Failover

Manual or automatic? How do you decide which approach to executing failover is right for you? Your decision is driven by several factors: RTO objectives, the complexity of application failover in your environment, and your personal comfort level using an automated versus a manual process. All things being equal, manual failover will take longer to complete simply because of the human element involved. Even if the status of the primary database is continuously monitored and alerts are automatically sent to administrators when problems occur, the administrator must respond, evaluate the current status, and decide what to do. Not only does this take time, but also the amount of time required can vary widely from one event to the next, making failover time difficult to predict. If your recovery time objective is lax enough that it can be achieved using manual failover, then there is no benefit to be gained from the additional effort required to

---

[12] MAA "Fast-Start Failover Best Practices" for Data Guard 10g: www.oracle.com/technology/deploy/availability/pdf/MAA_WP_10gR2_FastStartFailoverBestPractices.pdf

[13] MAA "Switchover and Failover Best Practices" for Data Guard 10g: www.oracle.com/technology/deploy/availability/pdf/MAA_WP_10gR2_SwitchoverFailoverBestPractices.pdf

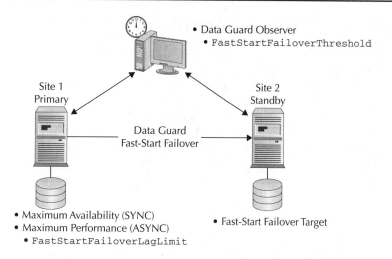

**FIGURE 1-8.**   *Data Guard Fast-Start Failover architecture*

automate failover. However, manual failover can make more aggressive recovery time objectives very difficult, or even impossible to achieve. The more aggressive your recovery time objective, the more there is to be gained from implementing Data Guard Fast-Start Failover.

Application complexity is the second factor to consider in manual versus automatic failover. For example, a U.S. government user of Data Guard since 2003 operates a complex application environment with distributed transactions that execute across multiple databases. A zero data loss failover in Maximum Protection or Maximum Availability mode would be no problem for Fast-Start Failover. The standby database would assume the primary role with no data loss, and there would be no recovery implications for any of the other databases participating in a distributed transaction. An automatic failover in Maximum Performance mode with data loss, however, would be problematic. Manual effort is required because Data Guard is not yet able to coordinate point-in-time recovery across multiple databases participating in a distributed transaction. This user has configured Maximum Performance mode given that primary and standby databases are separated by more than 1000 miles. Even though Data Guard 11*g* supports automatic failover in Maximum Performance mode, it is not practical for this user to implement because of the additional manual effort required to recover multiple databases to the same point in time to preserve global data consistency following a data loss failover.

### How Fast Is Automatic Failover?

Oracle documented Data Guard automatic failover performance for Oracle Database 10*g* Release 10.2.0.2. Failover timings for this early release of Fast-Start Failover were 17 seconds for physical standby databases and 14 seconds for logical standby databases. Users deploying later releases of Data Guard have anecdotally reported that failover times have dropped to less than 10 seconds depending on configuration.

**Myth Buster: Automatic Failover Can Cause Split-Brain**
The last thing you ever want to have are two independent databases, each operating as the same primary database. This can happen if, unknown to you, someone restarts the original primary database after you have performed a failover to its standby database. A common misperception is that automatic failover can increase the chance of this occurring. Not so with Data Guard Fast-Start Failover. A failed primary cannot open without first receiving permission from the Data Guard observer process. The observer will know that a failover has occurred and will refuse to allow the original primary to open. The observer will automatically reinstate the failed primary as a standby for the new primary database, making it impossible to have a "split-brain" condition.

In conversations with DBAs, we also frequently observe a reluctance to "trust" software to execute an automatic failover. This apprehension is natural. Administrators are concerned that the lack of manual control may lead to unnecessary failovers (false failovers) and disrupt operations. They fear that automatic failover may result in more data loss than acceptable, or that it may cause a split-brain condition, in which two primary databases each process transactions independent of the other. They worry that applications may not reconnect to the new primary database, impacting availability even though the database failover was successful. They are concerned that they will be forever rebuilding the original primary database after failovers occur.

While these are legitimate concerns for any automatic solution, Data Guard Fast-Start Failover has been carefully designed to avoid these problems. Data Guard has very specific, user-configurable rules to control an automatic failover for SYNC and ASYNC configurations, preventing false failovers and making it impossible for a split-brain condition to occur. It will never allow an automatic failover if the resulting data loss exceeds the previously configured recovery point threshold. It posts system events that can be used with Oracle Fast Application Notification (FAN), Fast Connection Failover (FCF) and Transparent Application Failover (TAF), or other methods external to Oracle that can reliably direct applications to reconnect to the new primary database (also discussed further in Chapter 10).[14] Data Guard Fast-Start Failover automatically reinstates the failed primary database as a standby for the new primary, assuming it is salvageable, and thus creates no extra work for the DBA compared to manual failover procedures. We expect to see more companies deploy Fast-Start Failover as the increasing cost of downtime drives more aggressive RPOs, and as their internal testing validates Data Guard capabilities, eliminating obstacles to its adoption. See Chapter 8 for more details on Role Transitions.

# Data Guard Management

Data Guard offers three choices for management interface: SQL*Plus, Data Guard broker, and Enterprise Manager. SQL*Plus is the traditional method for managing a Data Guard configuration. SQL*Plus is the most flexible option, but it's also the most tedious to use. Any changes made to a Data Guard configuration require attaching directly to each system and making changes locally for that system.

---

[14]MAA "Client Failover Best Practices for Highly Available Oracle Databases": www.oracle.com/technology/deploy/availability/pdf/MAA_WP_10gR2_ClientFailoverBestPractices.pdf

## Myth Buster: The Data Guard Broker Is a Single Point of Failure

The Data Guard broker is *not* a single point of failure. Broker processes are background processes that exist on each database in a Data Guard configuration and communicate with each other. Broker configuration files are multiplexed and maintained at all times on each database in the configuration. If the system on which you are attached fails, you simply attach to another database in the Data Guard configuration and resume management from there. More details in Chapter 5.

The Data Guard broker is a distributed management framework that automates and centralizes the creation, maintenance, and monitoring of a Data Guard configuration. It has its own command line (DGMGRL) and syntax. It simplifies and automates many administrative tasks for creation, monitoring, and management of a Data Guard configuration. Centralized management is possible by virtue of the broker maintaining a configuration file that includes profiles for all databases in the Data Guard configuration. You can connect to any database in the configuration and the broker will propagate changes to all other databases in the configuration and their server parameter files. The broker also includes commands to start an observer, the process that monitors the status of a Data Guard configuration and executes an automatic failover (Fast-Start Failover) if the primary database should fail.

Oracle Enterprise Manager provides a GUI to the Data Guard broker, replacing the DGMGRL command line and interfacing directly with the broker's monitor processes. The Enterprise Manager Data Guard management overview page is shown in Figure 1-9.

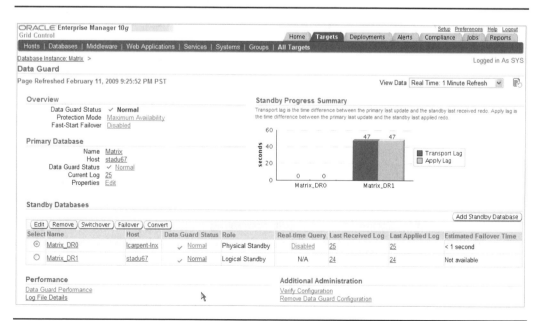

**FIGURE 1-9.**   *The Enterprise Manager Data Guard management page*

Enterprise Manager also provides an easy-to-use creation wizard that provides a simple point-and-click interface to create a Data Guard configuration. Enterprise Manager requires that the Data Guard broker be enabled. If the broker is not enabled, Enterprise Manager cannot be used to manage your Data Guard configuration, and Enterprise Manager's monitoring of Data Guard related metrics is limited to redo rate, transport lag, and apply lag.

# Active Standby Databases

It used to be acceptable for DR solutions to limit their scope to data protection. High availability was considered a separate topic from DR. Then along came Oracle Database 10g and Data Guard Fast-Start Failover, and all of a sudden a DR solution for Oracle Database also possesses high availability attributes. Now, instead of measuring the recovery point objective (RPO) for a DR solution in hours or days, a Data Guard RPO can be measured in seconds or minutes, depending on configuration.

Similarly, DR solutions have traditionally been characterized by standby systems that are unable to be used for any productive purpose while they maintain synchronization with the primary site. This has made DR solutions expensive because they can be used for no other purpose, and has limited their use only to the most critical databases and to companies that could afford their high cost. Sure, some SQL-based replication strategies can be used to work around this limitation, but such approaches do not work transparently with all applications and data types. SQL-based solutions also have difficulty scaling in high workload environments, and they can add considerable management complexity—increasing cost and business risk. With Oracle Database 11g and using Active Data Guard or Data Guard Snapshot Standby, physical standby databases can be used for productive purposes while they also provide DR protection. Asset utilization and performance are enhanced while complexity and the likelihood of disrupting operations when introducing changes to production environments are reduced. This results in higher return on investment with less business risk. Several examples for using your standby databases are described in the sections that follow.

## Offload Read-Only Queries and Reporting

Active Data Guard enables a physical standby database to be open read-only while Redo Apply is active; queries run against the standby database receive results that are up-to-date with the primary database. Read-only queries and reports can be offloaded from the primary to the standby database, reducing I/O and CPU consumption, creating headroom for future growth, and improving quality of service for read-write transactions. The entire time the active standby is servicing queries it is also providing DR. If the primary database should fail, data is protected at the standby and failover is immediate because the standby database is completely up-to-date.

Active Data Guard also makes it very easy to test the readiness of your DR solution. In addition to the usual Data Guard status reporting, you can easily issue the same query against your primary and standby databases and compare results to validate that the standby database is functioning and up-to-date. Active Data Guard is unique in that it offers the simplicity, reliability, and high performance of physical replication, while providing much of the utility of more complex SQL-based replication technologies for read-only queries and reporting.

> **How Fast Are Fast Incremental Backups?**
> Oracle benchmarking has shown that fast incremental backups using RMAN block change tracking are up to 20 times faster than traditional incremental backups. Changed blocks are easily identified without the performance impact of full table scans. Before Active Data Guard, fast incremental backups using RMAN block change tracking could not be performed on a physical standby database.

## Offload Backups

Active Data Guard also includes the ability to use RMAN block change tracking and perform fast, online, incremental backups of your physical standby database. Because backups taken on a physical standby can be used to restore either the primary or standby databases, it is no longer necessary to perform backups on the primary, freeing system resources to process critical transactions. This functionality should be considered even for companies that have previously used storage-based technologies to offload backup overhead from their production databases. For example, it's not uncommon to use storage technologies to take a full copy of a production database and then run backups from this copy. Instead of this practice, the same storage can be repurposed to deploy a local Data Guard physical standby database with Active Data Guard. RMAN fast incremental backups can be performed on the active standby database, providing the same benefit of offloading the primary. But because the standby database is active, it provides additional benefits of better data protection, higher availability, and the ability to offload read-only queries and reports from the primary database.

## Testing

One of the biggest IT challenges is minimizing the risk of introducing changes to systems, databases, and applications in critical production environments. How often have you seen changes implemented over a weekend, when everything looks fine until Monday morning and real users get on the system, performance slows to a crawl, and the CEO wants to know why the problems weren't discovered in test and addressed before they disrupted business operations? Ideally, you could avoid this risk by thoroughly testing any proposed changes on a true replica of your production system and database using actual production workload. Ideally, you would also be able to run multiple tests using the same workload and data. This lets you establish a meaningful baseline against which you can iteratively assess the performance impact of proposed changes, optimizing the strategy chosen without impacting production.

   Data Guard Snapshot Standby in Oracle Database 11*g*, a feature included with the Enterprise Edition license, has been developed to help address this problem. Using a single command, a Data Guard 11*g* physical standby can be converted to a snapshot standby, independent of the primary database, that is open read-write and able to be used for preproduction testing. Behind the scenes, Data Guard uses Flashback Database and sets a guaranteed restore point (GRP)[15] at the

---

[15] Configuring the RMAN Environment: Guaranteed Restore Points: http://download.oracle.com/docs/cd/B28359_01/backup.111/b28270/rcmconfb.htm#BRADV89447

> ### Myth Buster: A Physical Standby Database Can't Receive Primary Redo While Open Read-Write
> A physical standby database does *not* defer shipping of redo from primary to standby when open read-write *if* you use Data Guard 11*g* snapshot standby. Redo for current primary database transactions continues to be received and archived by a snapshot standby database the entire time it is open read-write for testing or other purposes. Primary data is kept safe at the standby, and DR protection is assured at all times.

SCN before the standby was open read-write. Primary database redo continues to be shipped to a snapshot standby, and while not applied, it is archived for later use.

A second command converts the snapshot back into a synchronized physical standby database when testing is complete. Behind the scenes the standby is flashed back to the GRP, discarding changes made while it was open read-write. Redo Apply is started and all primary database redo archived while a snapshot standby is applied until it is caught up with the primary database. While a snapshot standby does not impact recovery point objectives, it can lengthen recovery time at failover due to the time required to apply the backlog of redo archived while it was open read-write.

Oracle Real Application Testing is a new option for the Oracle Database 11*g* Enterprise Edition and is an ideal complement to Data Guard snapshot standby. It enables the capture of an actual production workload, the replay of the captured workload on a test system (your Data Guard snapshot standby), and subsequent performance analysis. You no longer have to invest time and money writing tests that ultimately do an inadequate job of simulating actual workload. You don't have to try to re-create your transaction profile, load, timing, and concurrency. Using Data Guard, the process is simple:

1. Convert a physical standby database to a snapshot standby and begin capturing workload on your primary database.

2. Explicitly set a second guaranteed restore point on your snapshot standby database.

3. Replay the workload captured from the primary database on the snapshot standby to obtain a base line performance sample.

4. Flash the snapshot standby back to your explicit guaranteed restore point set in step 2.

5. Implement whatever changes you want to test on the snapshot standby.

6. Replay the workload captured from the primary database on the snapshot standby and analyze the impact of the change by comparing the results to your baseline run.

7. If you aren't satisfied with the results and want to modify the change, simply flash the snapshot standby back to your explicit guaranteed restore point set in step 2, make your modifications, replay the same workload, and reassess the impact of the change.

8. When testing is complete, convert from snapshot standby back to a physical standby. Data Guard will discard any changes made during testing and resynchronize the standby with redo it had received from primary and archived while the snapshot standby was open read-write.

**Maximum Availability Architecture**
The Oracle Technology network portal for MAA best practices is at http://otn.oracle.com/goto/maa.

Not only are you able to quickly run a series of tests using actual production workload, you are also able to run them on an exact copy of the production database, and on servers and storage sized similarly to production (given that standby systems are usually sized to run production should a failover ever be necessary). You have eliminated considerable time, effort, and expense of deploying a test system by using the DR system already in place. Most importantly, you achieve a better test result and significantly reduce the risk of impacting performance or availability when implementing changes to production systems.

# Data Guard and the Maximum Availability Architecture

Data Guard is only one of the many Oracle Database capabilities that provide high availability and data protection. This chapter has touched on Oracle Real Application Clusters, Oracle Automatic Storage Management, Oracle Recovery Manager, Oracle Flashback Technologies, and Oracle Streams. Other significant features include a growing set of planned maintenance capabilities—online patching, online redefinition, online addition/subtraction of cluster nodes and storage, online configuration of memory and database parameters, and rolling database upgrades. The collective deployment of these capabilities using Oracle documented best practices is referred to as the Oracle *Maximum Availability Architecture (MAA)*. Unlike any third-party DR solution, Data Guard can leverage numerous Oracle technologies to deliver a high availability architecture that provides better data protection, higher availability, better systems utilization, and better performance and scalability, all under a common management environment. This translates into lower cost, less business risk, and greater agility to respond more quickly to changing business requirements.

# Conclusion

The Latin phrase *Prodeo quod victum,* meaning "Go forth and conquer," is an excellent note on which to end this first chapter. We have shared enough information to help you understand the basic architecture of Data Guard and what is possible to achieve. Now you are prepared for Chapter 2 and ready to begin adding to your knowledge of how to implement, manage, and get the most out of your Data Guard configuration.

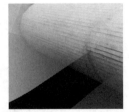

# CHAPTER
2

## Implementing Oracle
Data Guard

ince you have arrived at Chapter 2, you must be ready to start putting your Oracle Data Guard configuration in place. You have read Chapter 1, haven't you? Now that you have a complete understanding of how Data Guard is put together—its terminology, parts, processes, and functionality—you might realize that a little knowledge can be a dangerous thing. Many people make the mistake of getting this far and then jumping straight into Chapter 3 of the *Data Guard Concepts and Administration* manual and creating standby databases. Then they wonder why they have problems later. Without careful thought and planning and a very good understanding of the planned and unplanned outages you are trying to avoid, you run the risk of your "failure avoidance plan" failing—not a good situation.

In this chapter, you'll learn about the various tasks you must perform well before you start executing Recovery Manager (RMAN) and SQL commands in a Data Guard environment. Then you'll learn how to create your standby databases so that they meet every requirement you have been given.

### Data Guard and Oracle Real Application Clusters

The information and procedures discussed in this chapter are structured to set up Data Guard with single non–Oracle Real Application Clusters (RAC) databases. At the end of the chapter, you'll learn about the changes required to make it all work with Oracle RAC databases.

# Plan Before You Implement

We all know that "stuff" happens to our systems, no matter how well designed and implemented they are. This is a fact of life. Murphy's Law tells us "Anything that can go wrong will go wrong."[1] We believe that Murphy was being optimistic when he put the *'If'* at the front of that sentence. It might be more accurately stated as "Anything can go wrong, and it will." It is not the occurrence of *anything* that brings a business to its knees; it is how the problem is handled and how you recover from the situation that is important.

Before you start executing any computer commands or buying any hardware, software, or networks, you need to know which situations you are trying to avoid and how you need to recover from those situations. The two main pieces of information you need to begin this journey are your company's *recovery point objective (RPO)* and *recovery time objective (RTO)*, which tell you what you need to implement. Everything about setting up Data Guard is directly related to the RPO and RTO. (By the way, the much-discussed service level agreement [SLA] is something that you write *after* you know what you can actually achieve, not something you write up front and commit to—at least you should not agree to it without knowing what you can actually achieve given the requirements and the resources committed to the task.)

---

[1] See http://en.wikipedia.org/wiki/Murphy's_law for more about Murphy's Law.

# Determining Your Requirements

OK, so you're not scared off yet. Good. You are our kind of person—one who wants to develop a disaster recovery implementation that will meet your business's needs. To do that, you must first know your RPO and RTO requirements.

## Recovery Point Objective

An RPO is quite simple. It answers the question "How much data are you willing to lose when the dreaded failure occurs?" People in the industry generally talk about data loss in terms of *time*—a few seconds to double-digit hours—but you need to understand what that means in terms of *transactions*. Six seconds of data loss at 3000 transactions per second (tps) means you could potentially lose 18,000 transactions when you have to failover to your disaster recovery site.

Answers to the following questions will affect your RPO:

- Is data loss acceptable if the primary site fails?

- How much data loss is tolerated if a site is lost?

- Is potential data loss between the primary and the standby databases tolerated when a standby host or network connection is temporarily unavailable?

- How far away should the disaster-recovery site be from the primary site?

- What is the current or proposed network bandwidth and latency between sites?

**Data Loss**    If the answer to the first question, "Is data loss acceptable?", is *no*, your task is simple: you must configure your disaster recovery solution not to allow data loss when you have to failover to your disaster recovery site. If the answer is *yes*, you need to know how much data loss is acceptable.

Don't be fooled by the person who tells you that *some* data loss is acceptable. This person might just be trying to save money, having never experienced a data loss situation. If you are trying to save money, admit that up front and implement accordingly, accepting that you will have to figure out how to go on after you have lost some data, even if it means bringing in a small army of retired data entry people to re-enter data from paper documents (which, by the way, could be happening while you are down).

One company, a payments clearinghouse, decided that it could sustain 20 minutes' worth of data loss when production failed and it had to move to the disaster recovery site. The company accepted the cost of paying for 20 minutes of time that it could never bill to its clients. Sounds like a reasonable and controllable situation, doesn't it? But when the same problem happens several times in a row, the amount of lost revenue can mount up considerably. Another site was

### Myth Buster: Zero Data Loss Configurations Have Too Much Impact on Production Throughput

A common fear among Data Guard implementers is that zero data loss configurations have too much impact on production throughput to be used. Don't be put off until you analyze the true impact of losing that data and know what the requirements really are for achieving zero data loss. It may not be as bad as you think.

> **Myth Buster: You Must Configure Data Guard
> to Be Exclusively Zero Data Loss**
> If you need zero data loss, you do not have to configure Data Guard to be exclusively zero
> data loss. You can mix zero data loss standby databases with minimal data loss standby
> databases in the same Data Guard configuration. Each standby database has its own set of
> attributes and parameters.

happy with its 8-hour data loss SLA. But when the primary database went down, the company discovered that the other 14 databases that fed off the primary were all 8 hours out of sync with the new primary database. Nobody had considered the impact of that downstream data loss.

If you are still convinced that data loss is acceptable (or, admittedly, unavoidable), you need to configure accordingly to reduce your exposure. More on that in the next section, "Networks and Data Loss."

What about those times when the network to your standby goes down? Or what if you need to take the standby down for system maintenance? If you have only one standby, you need to know what you are going to do when production fails, since the changes made to the primary database during this period will not be present and will be lost at the standby database when the failover is executed.

**Networks and Data Loss**  Once you have made up your mind on how you need to handle zero or minimal data loss, you need to pay attention to the network that you will use to transport the primary database changes to your standby databases. Although Data Guard does not require a dedicated network, you would be well served to ensure that Data Guard has either a network of its own or at least enough bandwidth on the existing network to be able to transport the redo your database generates to meet your requirements. Remember that you cannot force a tennis ball through a drinking straw without chopping the tennis ball into many small pieces and then reassembling it at the other end. So, you need to determine your primary database redo generation rate at peak and steady states so you can determine the network latency and bandwidth you can sustain and how it will affect your production throughput. In addition, regardless of your zero or minimal data loss choices, you do need to decide what distance is acceptable to meet all of the potential disasters your business may encounter—remember Murphy? Configuring and tuning the network are discussed in the section "Tuning the Network."

## Recovery Time Objective

The RTO is completely different from the RPO. That much is true. Although the RPO is concerned with data loss, the RTO is defined as how fast you can get back up and running. But the RTO is often considered to be more important than the RPO, and that belief is usually misplaced. The following factors can affect your RTO:

- How you have configured your standby

- Not having a standby and having to resort to backups

- Having the database and applications failover at the same time

- Did the middle tier have to failover too?

- Are people stressed and make mistakes?

**Myth Buster: A Low RTO Cannot Be Achieved with Data Guard**

Many people believe that a low RTO cannot be achieved with Data Guard; in fact, many think that it takes minutes if not hours to failover to a Data Guard standby. This is just not true. Like any transition to a different system it is the manual operations that take time. Remove the manual intervention, however, and failing over to your Data Guard standby can be accomplished in seconds. (We'll discuss this in Chapter 8.) Even the manual operation of moving a Data Guard standby database over to the production role itself takes only a couple of minutes. It is usually the client reconnections that take the extra time. We'll show you how to automate client failover in Chapter 10.

We are all concerned about *high availability*, which is what the RTO is all about. But having your system available without all the data could be a bigger problem than you might expect. That is why we're discussing the RTO after we discuss the RPO. You may not like to hear that but you didn't come here to hear things you already know. You came here to learn what the right way to think of things is and how you can plan and implement for those eventualities. Armed with all of this information, you will be able to make better decisions.

So what are your RTO expectations? Everyone wants zero downtime, which is an RTO of zero—who wouldn't?

An RTO of zero isn't impossible, depending on how you look at failures. In general, high availability is viewed as getting users hooked up again as fast as possible, and in a cluster environment, only the users who were on the failed system actually have to be relocated, which is done automatically by the cluster software. The users on the surviving systems in the cluster notice only a slight pause, if anything. Of course, that implies that you are using an Active-Active cluster environment such as Oracle RAC. If you use a Cold Failover Cluster, you will experience a longer failover time than with Data Guard. In addition, Data Guard extends high availability to a distinct copy of the primary database located anywhere from the next computer room to across the globe. The amazing thing is that it's not the distance between the primary database and the standby database that can impact your RTO, it's how fast you can apply the changes to the standby database and how fast you can actually execute the failover when necessary. As mentioned, the distance will affect the RPO, not the RTO.

Armed with your RPO and RTO requirements (and a realistic view of the world), you are now ready to start examining what Data Guard decisions you need to make. After you make those decisions, you'll be ready to start creating Data Guard standby databases.

# Understanding the Configuration Options

Disaster recovery and high availability are a set of configuration and operational decisions, not a black box that you stick onto your system that magically works. Data Guard is no different, although once set up correctly, it almost becomes a black box for the Oracle database. You need to understand four main categories of Data Guard before you can make the correct implementation decisions for your disaster recovery solution:

■ Protection modes
■ Redo transport

- Apply methods
- Role transitions

These four categories are discussed in this order, since you must follow this order when making your decisions.

For the most part, the discussions that follow center around a single Data Guard parameter called LOG_ARCHIVE_DEST_n, where the n is a number from 1 to 9—which means you can have from 1 to 9 standby databases. These parameters define where and how redo is sent to either a local archive log file or a remote standby database, asynchronously (ASYNC) or synchronously (SYNC), as introduced in Chapter 1. These parameters also use the attribute SERVICE, which takes a TNSNAME definition as its argument. All of the nuances of the TNSNAME with regard to Data Guard are discussed later in this chapter as well as in Chapter 10.

## Choosing a Protection Mode

The Data Guard protection modes are, simply put, a set of rules that the primary database must follow when running in a Data Guard configuration. A protection mode is set only on the primary database and defines the way Data Guard will maximize your Data Guard configuration for performance, availability, or protection, so that you achieve the desired RPO when your primary database or site fails. Once you choose your protection mode, you agree to the set of rules that your primary database must obey.

Each of the three protection modes is the degree to which your data is protected, and as such they define two major components of your configuration: how the redo will be transported to the standby and what the primary database will do when a standby or the network fails. Data Guard's automatic failover capability, Fast-Start Failover, adds one more level to the behavior of your primary database at failure time, which we will discuss in Chapter 8.

**NOTE**
*We discuss the rules, requirements, and behaviors for each mode here, but the details of the parameters settings are discussed in later sections of this chapter. The procedure for performing a failover is discussed in Chapter 8.*

**Maximum Performance**    This is the default protection mode that any Oracle database since Oracle9*i* Release 2 actually runs in, with or without a standby database. The rule is this: "Allow as little data loss as possible without impacting the performance of my primary database." As such, this protection mode provides the highest degree of performance for your primary database. It is also the lowest degree of protection you can have, which means that when you have to failover to a standby database you will lose some data. (We will explain why you lose data in Chapter 8.) How much data you lose depends on your redo generation rate and how well your network can handle that amount of redo, which is referred to as *transport lag*. However, a transport lag of zero still means you will lose some data at failover time, because when the primary database is a RAC, the final apply of the remaining redo must find a common point in the redo streams from the primary, which will result in some data loss, potentially 3 to 6 seconds, regardless of the transport mode. Bear in mind, though, that even with a non-RAC primary database, there is no guarantee that zero data loss will be the result in Maximum Performance.

The requirements for this protection mode are 0 (zero) to 9 standby databases using asynchronous transport (ASYNC), with no affirmation of the standby I/O (NOAFFIRM). You might

**Standby Redo Log Files**

While it is true that SRL files are not mandatory in Maximum Performance, you should still create them because they will improve redo transport speed, data recoverability, and apply speed. We'll discuss how to create them later in the chapter.

ask, "How much will ASYNC impact my primary database?" and "How far apart can my primary and standby databases be?" The answers are, as of Oracle Database 11g, "Almost nothing," and "Pretty much across the planet," respectively. There are times when, even though the standby is on this planet, the network latency is such that the redo transport cannot keep up with the redo generation. In such cases, some redo compression might still be in order to help improve the transport lag. This is discussed in the next section.

While it is not mandatory to have standby redo log (SRL) files in Maximum Performance mode, we strongly recommend that you configure them. The SRL files must be the same size as your online redo log (ORL) files, and you also need to have the same number of SRL files as you do ORL files, plus one. If you have a RAC primary, you need "plus one" per RAC instance. These files need to be created on your standby as well as on your primary in preparation for switchover.

When a standby database that is operating in Maximum Performance mode is disconnected from the primary database (either by network, system, or standby database failure), the primary database is not affected—that is, redo generation is not stopped or even paused. If the primary database is an Oracle RAC, the node that lost its connection to the standby database will stop sending redo, but the other nodes in the cluster that can still communicate with the standby database will continue sending redo. The disconnected standby is ignored by the RAC node that lost its connection until its Arch ping process can determine that it is reachable again. At that time, any gaps in the redo will be sent to the standby, but the log writer process (LGWR) will not restart the Log Network Server (LNS) process for the current redo stream until the next normal log switch at the primary database. We expect that this behavior will change in a future release, and a log switch will be executed automatically to reconnect all instances with the recently reconnected standby database.

The Maximum Performance protection mode is useful for applications that can tolerate some data loss in the event of a loss of the primary database.

**Automatic Log Switch**

Many users set up an O/S batch job to force a log switch at the primary database so that logs continue to switch even when the database is idle or they have very small redo log files. This was usually done to ensure a known level of data loss for the standby when you used the ARCH process to send redo. As the true minimum mode is now ASYNC, it is no longer necessary to do this. In fact, your ORLs should be larger today. And if you really want to switch logs on a regular basis, set the `ARCHIVE_LAG_TARGET` parameter, which will force a log switch for you.

**Maximum Availability** This is the first zero data loss protection mode, with some caveats. The rule here is, Do not allow any data loss without impacting the availability of my primary database. This means that when you have to failover to a standby database configured with SYNC transport, and that is synchronized with the primary database, you will not lose any data provided no redo was generated at the primary database that was not received by the standby database. In other words, as long as the primary database or a complete production site failed first, your failover at a synchronized standby database will result in zero data loss. However, if the network went down first or the standby went down and didn't have a chance to resynchronize before the failover, then all redo generated at the primary database will be lost when you failover. A standby database cannot recover something that it never received.

The requirements for this protection mode are one or more standby databases using synchronous (SYNC) redo transport with affirmation of the standby I/O (AFFIRM) and SRL files. A Data Guard configuration that is in Maximum Availability is not considered synchronized until it has at least one standby that meets these requirements.

SYNC transport is different from ASYNC transport. A distinct wait time is required for the LGWR to allow a transaction to commit—the time it takes to send the redo to every SYNC standby database, to write the redo to the SRL file, and to acknowledge that the deed is done. (Of course, if a standby database does not answer, the wait time will be the time it takes for the NET_TIMEOUT value to be exceeded—that is, to become a failed destination. More on that next.) Although you can place a SYNC standby database across the globe, your production throughput is going to suffer from the impact of this wait period. If your network has the bandwidth to meet your redo generation rate and you have tuned it to meet your requirements (more on that later), you should look at the latency (the distance between the primary and standby sites) for a round-trip across the network.

Our experience has shown that Data Guard can perform acceptably in synchronous transport with low production impact at much larger distances than other solutions. Testing has shown about 4 percent impact to database throughput at 10ms latency up to 10 percent impact at 20ms latency. Of course, the lower the latency the lower the impact. Network latencies of 1ms to 20ms translate from 0 miles up to 200 miles (320 km) distance between your primary and your standby. Of course, some network tuning is always necessary to get the best performance, and this will be discussed in the next section. If you need to have a standby (or standbys) outside this distance, you need to test even more diligently to ensure that your production impact is acceptable with SYNC transport (supporting Maximum Availability). If not, you need to consider using Maximum Performance and accepting the data loss that you will incur—or find a site closer to your primary database. If you are ready to accept the performance impact, then read on.

When a standby database that is operating in Maximum Availability is disconnected from the primary database (either by network, system, or standby database failure), the primary database will wait the number of seconds defined in the attribute NET_TIMEOUT (which defaults to 30 seconds). If no response from the LNS process is received within that many seconds, the standby database is marked as failed and the log writer continues committing transactions and ignores the failed standby database. If a failure response is received in less than the number of seconds defined in NET_TIMEOUT, then the LGWR and LNS may attempt to reconnect, provided there is enough time left before abandoning the standby database.

When a SYNC standby database is deemed failed, the primary database forces a log switch to "fix" the zero data loss point and then begins generating redo that is not sent to that standby database. In an Oracle RAC primary, this log switch causes all primary instances to stop sending redo even if they can still see the standby. If this was your last SYNC standby, the protection mode

**Myth Buster: Any Zero Data Loss Data Guard Configuration Will Result in Production Downtime if the Standby Database Is Not Reachable**
It is a common misconception that any zero data loss Data Guard configuration will result in production downtime if the standby database is not reachable. This is simply not true. In Maximum Availability, a failed standby database will create only a small pause on the primary database before continuing to process transactions and generate redo. In addition, starting with Oracle Database 10*g* Release 2, you can increase your protection by going to Maximum Availability without taking a production outage. You can always decrease your protection mode without an outage.

drops to Unprotected; otherwise, the protection mode stays at Maximum Availability. As with Maximum Performance mode, the failed standby is ignored until the Arch ping process can determine that it is reachable again. At reconnect time, any gaps in the redo will be sent to the disconnected standby and a log switch will be forced across all primary nodes to restart the LNS process for the current redo stream on each thread.

Once the gap resolution is complete and each primary instance is sending the current redo stream, the status of standby database is marked as SYNCHRONIZED again. If this was the only standby database (or the last surviving one), the protection level of the primary database also goes back to Maximum Availability. It is a misconception that the protection mode falls to Maximum Performance. When the standby database is disconnected, Data Guard stops shipping redo. When it comes back, it uses the ARCH processes to resolve any gaps and begins sending the redo synchronously (SYNC) again. Monitoring the protection mode and levels is discussed in Chapter 7.

The Maximum Availability protection mode is useful for those applications that cannot tolerate data loss in the event of a loss of the production database, but whose SLA requires no downtime if possible due to standby and/or network failures.

**Maximum Protection**   This is the highest level of zero data loss protection, which has no caveats but does have different rules and behavior. The rule here is, Do not allow any data loss even at the expense of the availability of my primary database. This means that when you have to

**Mixing Standby Databases**
Even in the higher protection modes that require SYNC and AFFIRM standby databases, you can implicitly define other standby databases as Maximum Performance standby destinations using ASYNC, which implies NOAFFIRM. But these standby databases do not figure in meeting the requirements for the zero data loss protection modes and are not considered when Data Guard is evaluating what it is going to do when it runs out of standby databases that meet the requirements for the higher protection modes. Only if you were to increase their settings to SYNC and AFFIRM and allow them to become synchronized would they figure in the higher protection mode rules and evaluation.

failover to a SYNC standby database running in this mode, you will not lose any data. Maximum Protection mode provides the highest degree of protection for your data since no redo can be generated that is not also safe at a minimum of one zero data loss standby database.

The requirements for Maximum Protection mode are the same as those for Maximum Availability mode—one to nine standby databases using synchronous transport (SYNC) with affirmation of the standby I/O (AFFIRM) and SRL files. However, to move to this degree of protection, you must bounce the primary database. If at least one standby database meets these requirements and is reachable at open time, the primary database will open; otherwise, it will not be allowed to open and the database will crash. If it crashes, you will see an error message such as the output in the alert log of the primary database:

```
LGWR: Primary database is in MAXIMUM PROTECTION mode
LGWR: Destination LOG_ARCHIVE_DEST_1 is not serviced by LGWR
LGWR: Minimum of 1 LGWR standby database required
Errors in file /OracleHomes/diag/rdbms/matrix/Matrix/trace/Matrix_lgwr_8095.trc:
ORA-16072: a minimum of one standby database destination is required
Errors in file /OracleHomes/diag/rdbms/matrix/Matrix/trace/Matrix_lgwr_8095.trc:
ORA-16072: a minimum of one standby database destination is required
LGWR (ospid: 8095): terminating the instance due to error 16072
Instance terminated by LGWR, pid = 8095
```

As with Maximum Availability, when a standby database that is operating in Maximum Protection mode is disconnected from the primary database (either by network, system, or standby database failure), the primary database will wait for the number of seconds defined in the attribute NET_TIMEOUT. If no response from the LNS process is received within that many seconds, the standby database is marked as failed and the log writer continues committing transactions, ignoring the failed standby database as long as at least one synchronized standby database meets the requirements of Maximum Protection.

This is where the behavior changes between Maximum Availability and Maximum Protection. If the unreachable standby is the last remaining synchronized standby database, then the primary instance that can no longer send to a qualified standby database is going to be on its way down in a hurry. To avoid crashing (so that no redo can be generated by this thread that is not at a standby database), the LGWR will attempt to reconnect before abandoning the last standby database. Currently, the LGWR will try a reconnect about 20 times, sleeping for 15 seconds between each attempt in the hope that it was just a network brownout. During these attempts (which usually amount to 10 minutes or so), the primary instance is not allowed to generate any redo at all and is, for all intents and purposes, stalled. Since the LGWR process is stalled, it can cause the entire RAC to stall as well for the reconnect attempt period.

If the last standby database does come back before the retries are exhausted, the LGWR will reconnect, send the last bit of redo, and then processing will resume. If the missing standby database does not come back in time, then that primary *instance* will crash and another instance in the Oracle RAC will perform crash recovery, sending all the final bits of redo to its synchronized standby database. At this point, you will not be able to open the failed primary instance until either one standby database with the correct requirements is reachable or you lower the protection mode either to Maximum Availability or Maximum Performance.

You will notice that we use *instance* in this case. Unlike the other two protection modes, there is no concept of asking the other nodes to switch logs and mark a point of zero data loss in the redo stream. This *instance* is going down. If the other instances can still send to a synchronized

## A Note About Parameters

In addition to setting the appropriate transport mode attributes based on the protection mode and creating the SRL files, you should also be using the parameters DB_UNIQUE_NAME and LOG_ARCHIVE_CONFIG as well as the DB_UNIQUE_NAME destination attribute when setting up your Data Guard configuration. By using these parameters, you will avoid all the historical problems that occur when trying to start up a primary database in Maximum Availability with an Oracle RAC primary database.

standby database, they will continue accepting transactions and generating redo. As each instance encounters the same problem, it will also go down until the entire database has crashed. Of course, if you have a single instance primary database, the entire database will go down.

Because of this behavior, you are encouraged to create at least two standby databases that meet the requirements for the Maximum Protection mode. That way, when one of them becomes unreachable, the primary database will continue generating redo without a pause of more than NET_TIMEOUT seconds. As long as the failed standby comes back and is resynchronized before you lose contact with the second standby database, your production continues to run. This flip-flopping between the two databases can go on forever—as long as you never lose the second standby database before the first standby database has come back and been resynchronized.

The Maximum Protection mode is required for applications that cannot tolerate any data loss whatsoever in the event of a loss of the production database. Of course, the SLA must allow for downtime due to standby and/or network failures to avoid the possibility of data loss—that is, a committed transaction at the primary that is not safely at a standby database somewhere.

**Setting the Protection Mode**    As you have seen, each Data Guard protection mode has its own set of rules. Your rule to live by when you make your protection mode decision is *The lower the impact to my primary database the higher the risk to my data.* Or, on a "high" note, *The higher the protection of my data the higher the impact on my primary database.*

After you have made a protection mode decision and accepted the rules, caveats, and behaviors, how do you actually put those rules into play? First, you need to create a standby database or two, set up the redo transport attributes to meet the requirements of your chosen mode, create the SRL files on your primary and standby databases, and then execute one of the following SQL statements on your primary database:

```
ALTER DATABASE SET STANDBY TO MAXIMIZE PERFORMANCE;
ALTER DATABASE SET STANDBY TO MAXIMIZE AVAILABILITY;
ALTER DATABASE SET STANDBY TO MAXIMIZE PROTECTION;
```

This will set up the rules in your primary database and communicate the setting to your standby databases so that they run in the same protection mode when they become the primary database. You never have to issue the first command to go to Maximum Performance since your primary database runs in that mode by default, unless you are lowering the protection mode to Maximum Performance. And remember that you cannot set the protection mode to Maximum Protection unless your primary database is at the MOUNT state, not OPEN.

After you have made this decision, you need to understand the actual process and parameters used for creating and configuring your standby databases.

> **NOTE**
> *If you decide to run in Maximum Protection, you need to consider a few factors when you do have to failover to one of your standby databases. These are discussed in Chapter 8.*

## Defining the Redo Transport Mode

You should now understand the main parts of your standby redo transport mechanism. If you are going to run in Maximum Performance mode, your standby databases will be using ASYNC and NOAFFIRM (which are the defaults in Oracle Database 11g). If you are going to run in either of the two higher protection modes, the databases will use SYNC and AFFIRM. You are also going to create SRL files on the primary and standby databases. Remember that even though it is not mandatory to have SRL files in Maximum Performance mode, best practice is to do so.

So for Maximum Performance mode, the LOG_ARCHIVE_DEST_*n* parameter will look like this (we don't like using defaults because they're not obvious enough):

```
LOG_ARCHIVE_DEST_2='SERVICE=Matrix_DR0 ASYNC NOAFFIRM'
```

And for Maximum Availability or Maximum Protection mode, the parameter will look like this:

```
LOG_ARCHIVE_DEST_2='SERVICE=Matrix_DR0 SYNC AFFIRM'
```

Of course, you will want to set the DB_UNIQUE_NAME and VALID_FOR attributes as well as tune the NET_TIMEOUT and REOPEN attributes, and we will discuss all of the parameters and attributes in more detail in the sections that follow. The topic of configuring multiple standbys with different transport attributes is covered in Chapter 8 when we talk about choosing a standby database for a failover.

Defining your redo transport is only part of the picture. You also need to perform an important tuning exercise—configuring and tuning the network so that Data Guard can make the most of what you have. In addition, there are a few things you can do to optimize your ASYNC transport above and beyond the network tuning.

## Tuning the Network

As mentioned, you need to know how much redo your primary database will be generating at peak times and steady state. This is important, because it is the redo (and only the redo) that Data Guard transports across the network. In addition, you need to know the network bandwidth and latency to the furthest standby database at a minimum. Once you have these figures, you can start to set up the network to allow Data Guard to transport the redo as fast as possible to all standby databases.

Several categories of configuration and tuning information are required:

- Required bandwidth
- Oracle Net Services session data unit (SDU) size
- TCP socket buffer sizes
- Network device queue sizes
- SRL files' I/O tuning

All these will have a major impact on how fast Data Guard can send the redo across your network to the standby database, regardless of how much bandwidth you have. Too little bandwidth is bad, but more than you need is not necessarily enough if you cannot use it efficiently. You should (if you can) perform some commonsense tasks before you even start down this tuning road. If you cannot affect these factors, you need to be aware of them as they will impact how well Data Guard can function:

- Throw out low-speed interfaces and networks.
- Make sure the route your redo is taking goes through high-speed interfaces.
- Make sure you have plenty of bandwidth with room to spare.
- Use routers sparingly.

Let's start looking at what you can tune to get Data Guard to perform as fast as it can, given your networks and systems. Don't worry that we have not yet explained all the details of the Data Guard parameters—we haven't even mentioned that how they are set depends on what interface you use to manage your Data Guard configuration. The examples in this section give you instructions on how to make Data Guard work the best it can and translate easily to the real parameter definitions you will be using to create your standby database. We'll also remind you of this when you start actually doing some real work.

**Network Bandwidth**    Bandwidth isn't *speed*, it is *capacity*, so *high-speed networks* is a misnomer since this usually refers to the larger bandwidth networks. A bit will travel from one end to the other at the same speed, regardless of network size—for example, an OC-3 with 155 Mbits/sec or a T3 with 45 Mbits/sec on a network of the same length or latency. Bandwidth is the number of bits that can be sent at the same time. Hence, the highest bandwidth network is not always the fastest route, which is determined by the latency. An OC-3 (155 Mbits/sec) path that goes from Boston to Newark via Chicago will not necessarily be better for your redo than the T3 (45 Mbits/sec) that goes directly from Boston to Newark. However, the longer but broader path will be chosen by the network more times than you can imagine. Think of Galileo's alleged experiment[2] in which he proved that two cannon balls of different sizes both hit the ground at the same time when they were dropped off of the Leaning Tower of Pisa. (No one is really sure if Galileo actually performed this experiment, and some reports say that it was vindicated by a similar experiment using a vacuum in 1999, but we don't care because we like the legend.)

Using the redo generation rate, you can determine how much bandwidth you will need. Remember that you cannot push a tennis ball through a drinking straw without a lot of effort and time. That is not your goal here. Your goal is to allow tennis balls to fly through the pipe so efficiently that you cannot serve them fast enough.

The easiest method to get your redo generation rate is to use Automatic Workload Repository (AWR) reports taken during steady state times and peak times. If you do not have AWR licensed, you can get a good estimation of your redo generation rate by looking at the alert log and calculating the time between log switches during steady state and peak periods. You can then add up the megabytes of the archive logs for those log switches and divide that number by the total time to get the average megabytes per second. You can make it more granular by doing the math for each log switch. The idea is to get a reasonably accurate number for your redo generation rate.

---

[2] See http://en.wikipedia.org/wiki/Galileo_Galilei for information about Galileo.

### Factors that Affect Throughput

You must consider various characteristics of your network and the underlying Transmission Control Protocol/Internet Protocol (TCP/IP) that will influence the actual throughput that can be achieved. These include the overhead caused by network acknowledgments, network latency, and other factors. Their impact will be unique to your workload and network and will reduce the actual network throughput that you will be able to achieve.

Bear in mind that you must do this for all nodes in an Oracle RAC to get a number for each node and for the total across all nodes. Each node's number indicates what that node will need, but the total number is your starting place for calculating the required bandwidth.

If you obtain enough bandwidth to handle the steady state, then during peak times you will experience performance impact at the primary database in SYNC mode or an increasing transport lag (and subsequent potential data loss) if you are running in ASYNC mode. If you size the network for the peak times, Data Guard may be twiddling its thumbs during steady state, which is actually a better position to be in. In this case more is not less; it's better.

So let's say that you have a three-node RAC, and two of the nodes are used for online transaction processing (OLTP), and the third is used for batch (loads and other processing). You figure out, using one of the methods just described (or one of your own), that the two OLTP nodes generate about 2 MB/sec during steady state and 5 MB/sec during peak times. The batch node generates a steady 12 MB/sec when batch jobs are running. At first glance, this looks like you need a minimum of 16 MB/sec up to 22 MB/sec bandwidth. You will always need more bandwidth than your redo rate—how much is the question. At a minimum, it is always a good idea to start with at least 20 percent more than that number to allow for spikes, network overhead, and miscalculations, but some schools of thought say perhaps 50 percent more. Only your testing will show what you really need.

Your numbers grow at least to around 19 MB/sec to 26 MB/sec, so let's start with those numbers for the following examples. Since networks are measured in megabits, those numbers need to be multiplied by 8, or 152 Mbits/sec to 208 Mbits/sec. At the low end, this is about an OC-3[3] for the wide area network (WAN) to more than an OC-3, but less than a T4 for the peak rate and better than fiber distributed data interface (FDDI) for a local area network (LAN) in both cases. But look closer. Is it possible that these redo rates are not generated at the same time? Perhaps the OLTP systems run between 2 MB/sec and 5 MB/sec during the day but less than 0.1 MB/sec in the night when the batch jobs are running. That could mean that you really need only enough bandwidth for the highest rate, 12 MB/sec plus the 20 percent, or 14.4 MB/sec in this example. Now you are talking 115 Mbits/sec, which is well inside the OC-3 range for the WAN and just more than FDDI for the LAN. This all depends on your system's redo generation characteristics.

Bear in mind that these bandwidth calculations do not take into account the latency or round trip time (RTT) of the network. If you have chosen Maximum Performance mode, you probably don't need to care about the latency with the new Data Guard 11g ASYNC streaming model.

---

[3] See http://en.wikipedia.org/wiki/List_of_device_bandwidths for more about device bandwidths.

### Hidden Impact to ASYNC

The amount of data sent by the LNS (the redo write size) can vary depending on the workload. Knowing the LNS send size enables network and I/O testing to be performed to determine where the LNS is spending its time. The bigger the maximum write and average write size, the better for the LNS to communicate with the network layer. You cannot control this because it depends on your redo generation rate, but you can discover it by using LOG_ ARCHIVE_TRACE.[4]

But that requires that you do all of the tuning described in this section, and that your network has the required bandwidth. There may still be optimization tunings to perform, depending on your situation, such as increasing your primary database log buffers or using redo compression, which is discussed later in this chapter in the section "Optimizing ASYNC Redo Transport."

If, however, you have chosen Maximum Availability or Maximum Protection mode, then that latency is going to have a big effect on your production throughput. Several calculations can be used to determine latency, most of which try to include the latency introduced by the various hardware devices at each end. But since the devices used in the industry all differ, it is difficult to determine how long the network has to be to maintain a 1 millisecond (ms) RTT. A good rule of thumb (in a perfect world) is that a 1 ms RTT is about 33 miles (or 53 km). This means that if you want to keep your production impact down to the 4 percent range, you will need to keep the latency down to 10ms, or 300 miles (in a perfect world, of course). You will have to examine, test, and evaluate your network to see if it actually matches up to these numbers. Remember that latency depends on the size of the packet, so don't just ping with 56 bytes, because the redo you are generating is a lot bigger than that. For example, here is the output from a ping going from Texas to New Hampshire (about 1990 miles) at night, when nothing else is going on (edited a bit to make it fit on the page) using 56 bytes and 64,000 bytes.

**Packet size of 56 bytes of data:**

```
ping -c 2 matrix
PING matrix 56(84) bytes of data.
64 bytes from matrix : icmp_seq=0 ttl=57 time=49.1 ms
64 bytes from matrix : icmp_seq=1 ttl=57 time=49.0 ms

--- matrix ping statistics ---
2 packets transmitted, 2 received, 0% packet loss, time 1000ms
rtt min/avg/max/mdev = 49.047/49.122/49.198/0.234 ms, pipe 2
```

**Packet size of 64,000 bytes of data:**

```
ping -c 2 -s 64000 matrix
PING matrix 64000(64028) bytes of data.
64008 bytes from matrix : icmp_seq=0 ttl=57 time=61.6 ms
64008 bytes from matrix : icmp_seq=1 ttl=57 time=72.0 ms
```

---

[4] For information about setting .LOG_ARCHIVE_TRACE, see the Oracle documentation at http://download .oracle.com/docs/cd/B28359_01/server.111/b28294/trace.htm#i637070.

```
--- matrix ping statistics ---
2 packets transmitted, 2 received, 0% packet loss, time 1000ms
rtt min/avg/max/mdev = 61.691/66.862/72.033/5.171 ms, pipe 2
```

Quite a difference, as you can see. The small packet is getting about 40 miles to the millisecond, but the larger packet is getting around only 27 miles per millisecond. Still not bad and right around our guess of about 33 miles to the millisecond. So given this network, you could potentially go 270 miles and keep it within the 4 percent range, depending on the redo generation rate and the bandwidth, which are not shown here. Of course, you would want to use a more reliable and detailed tool to determine your network latency—something like traceroute. (As before, this output is edited to fit on the page and be a bit more readable.)

```
traceroute matrix
traceroute to matrix, 30 hops max, 38 byte packets
1q6-z2-rtr-1-v222-hsrp   0.381 ms   0.200 ms    0.443 ms
1q7-rtr-13-tg3-2         1.234 ms   0.276 ms    0.233 ms
1q7-rtr-24-g1-9          0.365 ms   1.858 ms    0.299 ms
1q7-rtr-15-g-2-2         0.409 ms   0.357 ms    0.241 ms
1q7-rtr-7-g1-0-0         0.541 ms   0.367 ms    0.463 ms
1-rtr-2-pos5-0-0        49.047 ms  49.086 ms   49.196 ms
1-swi-2-rtr-1-v108      50.313 ms  49.573 ms   50.439 ms
matrix   49.448 ms      49.441 ms  49.196 ms
```

These examples are just that, examples. A lot of things affect your ability to ship redo across the network. As we have shown, these include the overhead caused by network acknowledgments, network latency, and other factors. All of these will be unique to your workload and need to be tested.

**SDU Size**   Oracle Net buffers data into what is called a *session data unit (SDU)*, with a default size of 8192 bytes in Oracle Database 11g. These data units are then sent to the network layer when they are either full, flushed, or read by the client. Generally Data Guard sends redo in much larger chunks than 8192 bytes, so this default is insufficient, as you can end up having to send more pieces (chopping up the data) to Oracle Net Services. Since large amounts of data are usually being transmitted to the standby, increasing the size of the SDU buffer can improve performance and network utilization. You can configure SDU size within an Oracle Net connect descriptor or globally within the sqlnet.ora file. To configure the SDU globally, set the following parameter in the sqlnet.ora file:

```
DEFAULT_SDU_SIZE=32767
```

However, most database administrators and network analysts would rather that this change occur only to a specific connection to reduce the risk of adversely affecting other Oracle Net connections. With Oracle Database 11g, there is no need to set the SDU globally with Data Guard. Instead, on the primary database (which is the client in our case), we set it at the Transparent Networking Substrate (TNS) level in our connection descriptor for our standby database. Remember the short example parameter we used before?

```
LOG_ARCHIVE_DEST_2='SERVICE=Matrix_DR0 SYNC AFFIRM'
```

In this case, the TNS name is `Matrix_DR0`, and in the TNSNAMES.ORA file, we would define the following definition for `Matrix_DR0`:

```
Matrix_DR0.domain=
(DESCRIPTION=
      (ADDRESS=(PROTOCOL=tcp)(HOST=Matrix_DR.domain)(PORT=1521))
     (CONNECT_DATA=
      (SERVICE_NAME=Matrix_DR0.domain))
  )
```

To add in the maximum SDU size of 32,767 bytes (which is the best practice for Data Guard), we would add the `SDU` attribute:

```
Matrix_DR0.domain=
(DESCRIPTION=
     (SDU=32767)
       (ADDRESS=(PROTOCOL=tcp)(HOST=Matrix_DR.domain)(PORT=1521))
     (CONNECT_DATA=
      (SERVICE_NAME= Matrix_DR0.domain))
  )
```

This will cause Data Guard to request 32,767 bytes for the session data unit whenever it makes a connection to the standby called `Matrix_DR0`.

Since we have chosen not to use the SQLNET.ORA method, we will also need to set it in the LISTENER.ORA file at the primary database so that incoming connections from the standby database also get the maximum SDU size. So, in the LISTENER.ORA, we add the `SDU` attribute to the SID list as well:

```
SID_LIST_listener_name=
   (SID_LIST=
     (SID_DESC=
     (SDU=32767)
     (GLOBAL_DBNAME=Matrix.domain)
     (SID_NAME=Matrix)
     (ORACLE_HOME=/scratch/OracleHomes)))
```

Notice here that the `SID` and `GLOBAL_DBNAME` are `Matrix`, not `Matrix_DR0`. This is because we are still working on the primary database system. We are preparing the primary database to make outgoing connections to the standby databases and accept incoming connections from the standby databases using the maximum SDU size of 32,767 bytes.

Now that this is complete, we also need to set up the standby system to use the same SDU size. At this point, since we have not yet started to create a standby database, we may not have installed the software at the standby server. That's all right, though, because we can note down the following steps to take after we install the software later in this chapter.

Our TNS name and destination parameter is going to be different at the standby server. It will use a name that points back to the primary database, so that when this standby becomes the primary database (see Chapter 8), Data Guard will know where to send the redo. We are going to use `Matrix` for this purpose. So our parameter would look like this:

```
LOG_ARCHIVE_DEST_2='SERVICE=Matrix SYNC AFFIRM'
```

Now our TNS name is `Matrix`, so in our TNSNAMES.ORA file we would define the following for `Matrix`:

```
Matrix.domain=
(DESCRIPTION=
      (ADDRESS=(PROTOCOL=tcp)(HOST=Matrix.domain)(PORT=1521))
    (CONNECT_DATA=
     (SERVICE_NAME=Matrix.domain))
)
```

And to add in the maximum SDU size of 32,767, we would add the SDU attribute:

```
Matrix.domain=
(DESCRIPTION=
    (SDU=32767)
      (ADDRESS=(PROTOCOL=tcp)(HOST=Matrix.domain)(PORT=1521))
    (CONNECT_DATA=
     (SERVICE_NAME=Matrix.domain))
)
```

Data Guard will now request 32,767 bytes for the session data unit whenever it makes a connection to the primary database called Matrix.

Don't forget the listener file on the standby. As we are not using the SQLNET.ORA method, we also need to set it in the LISTENER.ORA file at the standby database so that incoming connections from the primary database also get the maximum SDU size. So, in the standby LISTENER.ORA, we add the SDU attribute as well:

```
SID_LIST_listener_name=
  (SID_LIST=
    (SID_DESC=
    (SDU=32767)
    (GLOBAL_DBNAME=Matrix_DR0.domain)
    (SID_NAME=Matrix_DR0)
    (ORACLE_HOME=/scratch/OracleHomes)))
```

We have now prepared the primary database to make outgoing connections to the standby databases and accept incoming connections from the standby databases using the maximum SDU size of 32,767, and vice versa (from standby to primary).

**TCP Tuning**   Setting the Oracle Net SDU is only the first part of tuning a network—the Oracle part. Now we need to go deeper than Oracle Net and prepare our TCP network layer to handle the large amounts of redo we are going to throw at it during Data Guard processing. As mentioned earlier, our redo is usually generated in large amounts, much more than the amounts of data being sent back and forth between client applications.

Of several aspects of the TCP layer, the most important is the amount of memory on the system that a single TCP connection can use. All systems have a built-in limit to this amount of memory at the TCP layer, called the *maximum TCP buffer space*, and this value is regulated by the operating system. For example, using `sysctl -a`, we can find the maximum read and write TCP buffer sizes:

```
net.core.rmem_max = 524288
net.core.wmem_max = 524288
```

This shows the maximum memory that a TCP connection will ever be allowed to use. For some Data Guard configurations, this maximum will be sufficient, but as you will see in this section, it could be necessary to have your system administrator increase this maximum.

Some parameters define the values that a TCP connection will use for its send and receive buffers, also called the socket size. Using `sysctl -a` again, they are as follows:

```
net.ipv4.tcp_rmem = 4096        87380    174760
net.ipv4.tcp_wmem = 4096        16384    131072
```

This shows the minimum, default, and maximum values for writing and reading the network. There will never be a need to change the minimum or default values for the sockets, and even the maximum value for this memory usage can be sufficient when you are tuning your sockets. The tuning discussed here will include settings you can set at the Oracle Net level and do not normally require changing any system or network-level parameter unless your socket size turns out to be larger than the maximum allowable size as defined by the system parameters. If your calculations do show that the amount of socket size you need is larger than the maximums, you can work with your system administrators to determine the best approach. We are not recommending that you go out and blindly change these parameters!

So how does the TCP socket buffer size actually work? An application that makes a connection over the TCP network can ask for a larger socket buffer than the defaults, which will allocate more memory to that connection, essentially increasing the bandwidth available to the connection. TCP will slowly increase the size of the buffer as your database begins to send redo until it reaches the size you set. The buffer can also shrink if there is a lot of network congestion. This is a buffer that determines how much data can be transferred to the network layer before the server stops and waits for acknowledgments of received packets, which can severely limit your network throughput. Since databases generate a lot of redo, the faster it can be put on the network the faster it is sent to the standby and protected. This is even more important when the network latency is high.

But how do you determine what size your socket buffer should be? This is where the *bandwidth-delay product (BDP)*[5] comes into play. Data Guard's utilization of the available bandwidth is essentially bound by the BDP. If the BDP is lower than the *latency × available bandwidth*, Data Guard cannot fill the line, since the acknowledgments don't come back fast enough. Basically, the socket buffers must be large enough to hold a full BDP of TCP data, plus some operating system–specific overhead at a minimum. So what is the math that you have to do? The basic calculation is as follows:

$$BDP = Bandwidth \times Latency$$

Of course, we're going to up that number to account for overhead, network congestion that you didn't think about, and plain errors. In this case, more really is better. TCP networks often need a minimum of 2 times the BDP to recover from errors efficiently. But it is a standard belief that 3 times the BDP is usually required to achieve maximum speed. You need to test your resultant BDP to see which works best for you. We'll go with the proposed maximum speed calculation, 3 times the BDP, for our discussion:

$$BDP = Bandwidth \times Latency \times 3$$

So, taking our example redo generation rate from the start of this section, we'll go with the assumption that we have an OC-3 network between our primary database and our standby database.

---

[5] For more on the bandwidth-delay product (BDP), see http://en.wikipedia.org/wiki/Bandwidth-delay_product.

**Bits vs. Bytes**

In case you're wondering why we used 1,000,000 to multiply the megabits per second to get bits per second, it's because in data communication, one kilobit is 1000 bits, whereas in data storage, one kilobyte is 1024 bytes. So if we were doing storage calculations, then 155 megabytes would be 155 × 1,024,000, or 158,720,000 bytes. Just thought we'd clear that up.

That is 155 Mbits/sec of bandwidth available. We'll also assume to start that we're going to put our standby in a location that is 50 miles (80 km) away (Boston, Massachusetts, to Manchester, New Hampshire) and that we have a tested latency of 8 ms (no one lives in a perfect world). So our calculation looks like this:

$$BDP = 155 \text{ Mbits/sec} \times 8 \text{ ms} \times 3$$

We can plug those numbers into a BDP calculator, like the speedguide.net[6] BDP calculator, and multiply its answer by our overhead of 3:

```
BDP = 155,000 * 3
BDP = 465,000 bytes
```

So our socket buffer size would be 465,000 bytes (or about 0.45MB). But how did we really get that number? Here's the real math:

```
Bandwidth: 155Mbits/sec = 155,000,000 bits/sec (155 * 1,000,000)
Latency: 8ms = .008 sec (8 / 1000)
BDP = 155,000,000 * .008 * 3
BDP = 3,720,000 bits / 8 (8 bits to a byte)
BDP = 465,000 bytes
```

As you can see, these amounts are much larger than the default socket size of 16K.

Now what happens if we move the standby database from Manchester, New Hampshire, and put it in Newark, New Jersey? That is about 226 miles (361 km), so if we assume we have the same OC-3 and that we'll get the same speed as before, our latency is going to go to about 36 ms. So what does that do to our BDP?

```
BDP = 155Mbits/sec * 36ms * 3
BDP = 697,500 * 3
BDP = 2,092,500 bytes
```

So now we need to set our socket size to 2,092,500 bytes, or roughly 2MB. But what about the case in which we have two standby databases—one in Manchester, New Hampshire (using SYNC), and the other in Newark, New Jersey (using ASYNC)? Do we add the two bandwidth delay products together for a combined total of 2,557,500 bytes? No, and that is the beauty of using Oracle Database 11g: you can configure each standby database to have the appropriate socket size for its latency, although you do need to take care during role transitions.

---

[6] You can access the "SG Bandwidth*Delay Product Calculator" at www.speedguide.net/bdp.php.

Which bring us to the job of actually setting these values. For this exercise, we will use a double standby configuration with one in Manchester and the other in Newark. So we have three systems, Matrix.domain, Matrix_DR.domain, and Matrix_DR1.domain, and the three databases, Matrix, Matrix_DR0, and Matrix_DR1. As with the SDU, the socket size must be set at both ends of the network; otherwise our socket size will be reduced to the lowest common denominator. And remember that means we get the default of 16K if we are not careful. Matrix (our primary) will now have two redo destination log_archive_dest_$n$ parameters, as follows:

```
LOG_ARCHIVE_DEST_2='SERVICE=Matrix_DR0 SYNC AFFIRM'
LOG_ARCHIVE_DEST_3='SERVICE=Matrix_DR1 ASYNC NOAFFIRM'
```

This means we have two entries in our TNS names file. To set them up to use the appropriate socket sizes, we add in two more attributes to each entry, just as we did with the SDU. But this time they will be different for each database:

```
Matrix_DR0.domain=
(DESCRIPTION=
    (SDU=32767)
    (SEND_BUF_SIZE=465000)
    (RECV_BUF_SIZE=465000)
      (ADDRESS=(PROTOCOL=tcp)(HOST=Matrix_DR)(PORT=1521))
    (CONNECT_DATA=
     (SERVICE_NAME=Matrix_DR0.domain))
)

Matrix_DR1.domain=
(DESCRIPTION=
    (SDU=32767)
    (SEND_BUF_SIZE=2092500)
    (RECV_BUF_SIZE=2092500)
      (ADDRESS=(PROTOCOL=tcp)(HOST=Matrix_DR1.domain)(PORT=1521))
    (CONNECT_DATA=
     (SERVICE_NAME=Matrix_DR1.domain))
)
```

But we are not done yet. We still have to go to each standby and update the listener, just as you did with the SDU. In the Matrix_DR system's LISTENER.ORA, it looks like this:

```
LISTENER =
  (DESCRIPTION =
    (ADDRESS = (PROTOCOL = TCP)(HOST = Matrix_DR.domain)(PORT = 1521))
  )
```

Add in the socket sizes (called the send and receive buffers) and it looks like this:

```
LISTENER =
  (DESCRIPTION =
    (SEND_BUF_SIZE=465000)
    (RECV_BUF_SIZE=465000)
    (ADDRESS = (PROTOCOL = TCP)(HOST = Matrix_DR.domain)(PORT = 1521))
  )
```

In the LISTENER.ORA on the Matrix_DR1 system, we would use the larger value:

```
LISTENER =
  (DESCRIPTION =
    (SEND_BUF_SIZE=2092500)
    (RECV_BUF_SIZE=2092500)
    (ADDRESS = (PROTOCOL = TCP)(HOST = Matrix_DR1.domain)(PORT = 1521))
  )
```

At this point, we have configured Matrix to make Data Guard connections to Matrix_DR0 using a socket size of 465,000 bytes and to Matrix_DR1 using 2,092,500 bytes.

To complete our configuration, we need to take into account what we will have to do so that our configuration works the same way after a role transition. We will set up Matrix_DR0 as the role transition target first. To configure for a switchover (or failover) to Matrix_DR0, we will have to set up the TNS names and the listener on the Matrix_DR system to make the same connections with the correct socket sizes for Matrix and Matrix_DR1. This means that the TNS names file will need to have the two entries for Matrix and Matrix_DR1 with the correct socket sizes:

```
Matrix.domain=
(DESCRIPTION=
    (SDU=32767)
    (SEND_BUF_SIZE=465000)
    (RECV_BUF_SIZE=465000)
      (ADDRESS=(PROTOCOL=tcp)(HOST=matrix.domain)(PORT=1521))
    (CONNECT_DATA=
     (SERVICE_NAME=Matrix.domain))
 )

Matrix_DR1.domain=
(DESCRIPTION=
    (SDU=32767)
    (SEND_BUF_SIZE=2092500)
    (RECV_BUF_SIZE=2092500)
      (ADDRESS=(PROTOCOL=tcp)(HOST=Matrix_DR1.domain)(PORT=1521))
    (CONNECT_DATA=
     (SERVICE_NAME=Matrix_DR1.domain))
 )
```

Finally, we set up the listener files. We already configured the listener in the Matrix_DR1 system when we did the original setup on Matrix. So a connection from Matrix_DR0 to Matrix_DR1 will use the socket size of 465,000 bytes. So all that is left is to go back to Matrix and add in the socket size to the Matrix listener:

```
LISTENER =
  (DESCRIPTION =
    (SEND_BUF_SIZE=465000)
    (RECV_BUF_SIZE=465000)
    (ADDRESS = (PROTOCOL = TCP)(HOST = Matrix.domain)(PORT = 1521))
  )
```

At this point, Oracle Net Services is configured to perform well based on our tuning calculations regardless of whether or not Matrix or Matrix_DR0 is the primary database. Of course, we would need to set the `log_archive_dest_n` redo transport parameters in the Matrix_DR1 spfile, but we'll discuss that when we actually get to creating our standbys in the next section.

Had enough? Well, we're not quite yet done with this subject. Remember Matrix_DR1 and Murphy? Murphy, and we agree with him, says that there will come a time when we need to failover to Matrix_DR1. So we need to configure for it now, not when it happens, because it will of course occur at 3 A.M. and no one will remember what we did and we would like to keep sleeping.

We need to set the TNS names descriptors on Matrix_DR1 to point back to Matrix and Matrix_DR0, as we did on Matrix and Matrix_DR0. But the difference here is that before we had one TNS descriptor using the smaller size, 465,000 bytes, and one using the larger size of 2,092,500 bytes, because one standby database was always close and the other farther away. Now, from Matrix_DR1, both standby databases are far away. For simplicity sake, we assume that the latency from Matrix_DR1 to Matrix or Matrix_DR0 is the same 36 ms latency. So that means both TNS descriptors need to use the 2,092,500 setting:

```
Matrix.domain=
(DESCRIPTION=
    (SDU=32767)
    (SEND_BUF_SIZE=2092500)
    (RECV_BUF_SIZE=2092500)
      (ADDRESS=(PROTOCOL=tcp)(HOST=matrix.domain)(PORT=1521))
    (CONNECT_DATA=
      (SERVICE_NAME=Matrix.domain))
)

Matrix_DR0.domain=
(DESCRIPTION=
    (SDU=32767)
    (SEND_BUF_SIZE=2092500)
    (RECV_BUF_SIZE=2092500)
      (ADDRESS=(PROTOCOL=tcp)(HOST=Matrix_DR.domain)(PORT=1521))
    (CONNECT_DATA=
      (SERVICE_NAME=Matrix_DR0.domain))
)
```

However, the listeners on Matrix and Matrix_DR0 are both set to 465,000 from our previous setup. If Matrix_DR1 makes a connection to either of them, the socket size is going to be the lower of the two, in this case 465,000, which is not going to be enough to get the performance we need. Of course, after the role transition from Matrix or Matrix_DR0 to Matrix_DR1, we could always put a procedure in place to have someone update the listener files on both systems and change the 465,000 to 2,092,000. A better solution is just to set all three listeners to accept connections up to a socket size of 2,092,000 bytes. That way, when Matrix_DR1 becomes the primary database and starts sending redo to Matrix and Matrix_DR0, it will get the necessary 2,092,000 socket size and life will be good.

But, wait, says our system and network administrators, that means that when Matrix and Matrix_DR0 connect (in either direction), they will get a lot more socket size than they need which will waste memory and affect our system and network overall performance! Not true. Remember that a connection between different socket sizes will always result in a connection of the lower number. So Matrix connecting to Matrix_DR0 asking for 465,000 bytes with a listener willing to provide 2,092,000 bytes, the connection will be made with 465,000. Now we don't have to mess with the listener files on Matrix and Matrix_DR0 after a role transition to Matrix_DR1.

Does all this sound complex? It isn't really. Setting up Oracle Net Services is something you have been doing for years for your applications to connect to your database. Now you just need to do the same things for Data Guard so that databases can connect to each other. The tuning is necessary because of the amount of data being pushed across the line. In the end, we are left with the following definitions on the three systems:

- **Matrix**
  Matrix_DR0 TNS using 465000
  Matrix_DR1 TNS using 2092000
  Listener using 2092000

- **Matrix_DR0**
  Matrix TNS using 465000
  Matrix_DR1 TNS using 2092000
  Listener using 2092000

- **Matrix_DR1**
  Matrix TNS using 2092000
  Matrix_DR0 TNS using 2092000
  Listener using 2092000

Of course, you could simplify all of this and set everything to 2,092,000, your highest value, and be done with it. But the system administrator will most definitely complain at this approach, especially when you are asked to put a standby database in London with a latency of 120 ms (or a socket size of 6 megabytes). That would be a lot of wasted memory for the closer connections.

**Queue Lengths**    The tuning parameters discussed so far have been changes you can make at the Oracle Net Services level that affect Data Guard's ability to use the network efficiently and that hopefully do not require changing any system or network-level parameter unless your socket size turns out to be larger than the maximum allowable size, as defined by the system parameters. Communication drivers also have many tunable parameters used to control their transmit and receive resources, but here we are concerned only with the parameters that control the transmit queue and receive queue limits. These queues should be sized so that losses do not occur due to local buffer overflows. This is especially important for TCP, because losses on local queues cause TCP to fall into congestion control, which limits the TCP sending rates and as such Data Guard's ability to keep your data protected.

These parameters limit the number of buffers or packets that may be queued for transmit or they limit the number of receive buffers that are available for receiving packets. Careful tuning is required to ensure that the sizes of the queues are optimal for your network connection, particularly for high-bandwidth networks. Following are some general guidelines on when to tune these queues:

- Tune the transmit queues when the CPU is faster than the network.
- Tune the transmit queues when the socket buffer sizes are large.

- Tune the receive queues when it is possible to have bursts of traffic.

- Tune both queues when there is high rate of small-sized packets.

In the last section, we did create larger socket sizes, so tuning the transmit queue will probably help. But also noteworthy is that many Data Guard configurations have bursts of redo as well, depending on your workloads. The transmit queue size is configured with the network interface option `txqueuelen`, and the network receive queue size is configured with the kernel parameter `netdev_max_backlog`. For example, to display the transmit queue setting, use `ifconfig`:

```
eth0
      Link encap:Ethernet   HWaddr 00:11:85:7C:5D:A5
      inet addr:10.149.249.107  Bcast:10.149.251.255  Mask:255.255.252.0
      inet6 addr: fe80::211:85ff:fe7c:5da5/64 Scope:Link
      UP BROADCAST RUNNING MULTICAST  MTU:1500  Metric:1
      RX packets:4542160 errors:0 dropped:0 overruns:0 frame:0
      TX packets:1503398 errors:0 dropped:0 overruns:0 carrier:0
      collisions:0 txqueuelen:100
      RX bytes:2635631386 (2.4 GiB)  TX bytes:362113440 (345.3 MiB)
      Interrupt:5
```

Here you can see that `txqueuelen` is set to a length of 100, the default for Linux. This default is probably fine for our Matrix to Matrix_DR0 and maybe even for our Matrix to Matrix_DR1 link. But if you are asked to put that standby database in London and the company springs for a big bandwidth network, then a length of 100 for `txqueuelen` is inadequate. A general belief among network tuning gurus is that for long-distance, high-bandwidth network links, a gigabit network with a latency of 100 ms, for example, you will benefit from a `txqueuelen` setting of at least 10000. If you did have to set the transmit queue length to 10000, for example, you would use `ifconfig`:

```
ifconfig eth0 txqueuelen 10000
```

For the receiver side, there is a similar queue for incoming packets. This queue will build up in size when an interface receives packets faster than the system can process them. If this queue is too small (the default is 300), you will begin to lose packets at the receiver, rather than on the network. The global variable `netdev_max_backlog` describes the maximum number of incoming packets that can be queued up for upper-layer processing. Using `sysctl -a`, you can find the current length of your receive queue:

```
net.core.netdev_max_backlog = 300
```

Since the default transmit queue is 100 and the receive queue on the other end is 300, you need to keep them in sync. If you have increased the transmit queue length, it is considered a good idea to increase the receive queue as well. The general consensus is that your receive queue length is anything from the same as the transmit queue length to two or three times greater. To change the receive queue length, use `sysctl` again:

```
sysctl -w net.core.netdev_max_backlog=20000
```

If you make these queue length changes, remember to make them in both directions, just as you did with the TNS connect descriptors and the listeners. When a pair of databases in your Data

Guard configuration change roles, you will want the same tuning you perform on the primary system to work in the reverse direction.

Before changing anything, of course, you, your system administrators, and your network administrators should consult with your operating system vendor for additional information on setting the queue sizes for various latencies to be sure that you are setting it to a good value. It is possible to decrease performance if the value is set too high when it is not necessary.

### SRL File I/O

The SRL files are where the Remote File Server (RFS) process at your standby database writes the incoming redo so that it is persistent on disk for recovery. We have mentioned that you should configure them on the standby databases for better redo transport performance and data protection. We have also stated that you need to configure them on your primary database as well in preparation for a role transition.

Why do SRL files provide better performance just by having them? Aside from the fact that in Maximum Availability or Maximum Protection mode you must have SRL files, they will improve the performance of redo transport in Maximum Performance mode as well since they are a pool of already created files of the right size, saving the RFS process (and hence making the LNS process at the primary wait) from having to create the archive log file. If no SRL files are at the standby database, then when the primary database starts up and at each log switch, the RFS process on the standby database that is serving an asynchronous standby destination has to create an archive log of the right size. Since Data Guard sends the redo as it is created, and that generation rate is increasing all the time, database administrators have begun to increase the size of their ORL files to reduce the number of log switches and checkpoints at that log switch—so you can imagine how long the LNS would have to wait while the RFS creates a 5GB archive log file at the standby.

It is no longer uncommon to have ORL files of 1GB or larger. At that size, it will take the RFS process quite some time to initialize that archive log. While the RFS is busy doing this, the LNS process at the primary database has to wait, getting further and further behind the LGWR, and your potential data loss grows. Prior to Oracle Database 10g Release 2, the LGWR was also waiting on the LNS. At least that is no longer true. But the impact is still considerable. If there are SRL files at the standby, the RFS process registers the previous file to be archived, selects a new SRL file, and signals the LNS that it is ready to receive the redo.

What about protection? If you are not worried by the performance implications of not using SRL files, at least the protection dangers should make you sit up and pay attention. In Maximum Performance mode with asynchronous transport, you are expecting that your data loss will be minimal. That is supposed to mean that when a primary database failure occurs and you need to failover, the bulk of the redo sent in the current redo stream will be recovered at the standby.

### Myth Buster: Redo Only Gets Sent at Log Switch Time

Data Guard has had the capability to send the redo to the standby database as it is generated, since ASYNC and SYNC transport modes were introduced in version 9.0.1. As of Oracle Database 10g Release 1, even ARCH destinations would use SRL files, considerably improving ARCH transport as well. As mentioned in Chapter 1, the ARCH transport has been deprecated as of Oracle Database 11g anyway, so all you really have left is ASYNC and SYNC.

This is true if you have SRL files when the primary goes down, and the connection to the standby is terminated causing the corresponding RFS process to run down. The redo that was already received is safe in the SRL file and can be recovered at failover time. However, without the SRL file, the redo is lost since that partial archive log file is deleted. So, for example, if you have 500MB ORL files and lose the primary database at megabyte 490, then when you failover, those 490MB of redo that were actually sent to the standby will be lost!

Data Guard no longer tries to save those partial archive log files when a connection from the primary database is lost. Even though the file that remains on disk looked like a real archive log file, it was not registered in the control file. Data Guard would not even know it existed unless you registered it at failover time. However, if you blindly used manual recovery, bypassing the checks and balances of Data Guard, that partial archive log file would be processed. At that point, your standby database is finished. Trying to restart recovery, whether manually or using Data Guard Managed recovery, would result in the dreaded ORA-00326 error:

```
Media Recovery Log  +FLASH/matrix_dr0/.../1_seq_131.419.672830973
MRP0: Background Media Recovery terminated with error 326
Mon Oct 18 23:00:28 2004
Errors in file /scratch/OracleHomes/.../Matrix_DR0_mrp0_540.trc:
ORA-00326: log begins at change 7249201863711,
           need earlier change 7249198180208
ORA-00334: archived log: '+FLASH/matrix_dr0/.../1_seq_131.419.672830973'
Recovery interrupted.
MRP0: Background Media Recovery process shutdown
```

This error was a clear indication that one of those partial archive logs had been applied. Your only choice was to finish with an ACTIVATE STANDBY DATABASE, or, if you were not failing over, re-create the standby database from scratch. Too many people made this mistake, and since SRL files were used all the time by Data Guard, that functionality was removed from 11g and later versions of 10g Releases 1 and 2.

You are going to have SRL files, and as such you need to make sure they work as fast as they can. We've explained that as redo is received by the standby it is written to disk. In Maximum Availability and Maximum Protection modes, the disk write to the SRL file must occur prior to sending an acknowledgment back to the primary that the redo has been received—called AFFIRM processing. Even in Maximum Performance mode with NOAFFIRM, without fast SRL files, the RFS may end up waiting on the asynchronous I/O to empty its buffer, thereby slowing down the LNS. Therefore, it is important that you optimize I/O of the SRL files on the standby. To improve I/O performance on the standby, consider the following best practices:

- Ensure that Oracle is able to utilize ASYNC I/O. Note that, by default, the Oracle database is configured for asynchronous I/O. However, you must also properly configure the operating system, host bus adapter (HBA) driver, and storage array.

- Maximize the I/O write size through all layers of the I/O stack. The layers will include one or more of the following: operating system (including async write size), device drivers, storage network transfer size, and disk array.

- Place SRL files in an ASM diskgroup that has at least the same number of disks as the ASM diskgroup where the primary ORLs reside.

- Do not multiplex SRLs. Since Data Guard will immediately request a new copy of the archive log if an SRL file fails, there is no real need to have more than one copy of each.

### Gap Resolution and Your Network

When Data Guard has to resolve gaps in the redo stream, it will send the redo in 10MB chunks to the standby that is missing the redo. In prior versions, it was send, wait for an ACK, and then send some more. Now with Oracle Database 11g, the ARCH processes use the new streaming architecture, and the amount of redo that will be placed on the network will increase from previous versions. It is important that you take this into account when testing your tuning efforts. Create a large gap and verify that Data Guard does not flood your network with redo beyond your expectations.

■ Typically, RAID controllers configured in RAID 5 perform writes slower than those configured with mirroring. If the process of writing to the SRL becomes the bottleneck, consider changing the RAID configuration.

**The Proof Is in Your Testing**    If you don't believe that all these tuning exercises are worth the payback, then consider the following. The Oracle Maximum Availability Architecture (MAA) team made adjustments only to the TCP socket buffer sizes and the network device queue sizes we have discussed, based on their network bandwidth and latency, and were able to show considerable network improvements in their test lab.

Using a raw network transport without any Data Guard in place, the team ran a transport test three times to see what improvement would be realized from its tuning efforts. The baseline without any tuning was a throughput of 10.8 Mbits/sec for a total of 77.2MB of redo transferred in 60 seconds. That is about 1.28 MB/sec.

After increasing the network socket buffer sizes to 3 × BDP from the default of 16K, the team was able to achieve a throughput of 731.0 Mbits/sec for a total of 5.11GB worth of data being transferred in the same 60 seconds. Right away, that was a jump from 1.28 MB/sec to 87.2 MB/sec—or a 6668 percent improvement over the baseline prior to tuning.

Finally the network queue lengths were increased to 1000 from default of 100 and the same test rerun. The data transferred grew to 6.55GB and the network throughput grew to 937.0 Mbits/sec. That is 111.8 MB/sec for an additional 28 percent improvement.

Overall, the tuning exercises increased the raw network transfer throughput by a whopping 8575 percent! While you may not experience this kind of increase in your Data Guard configuration, you will experience a considerable improvement in redo transport. Only your testing will tell you exactly how much.

**NOTE**
*You should be aware of some caveats to this tuning exercise if you are still using Oracle Database 10g Release 2. This information is contained in the Oracle Maximum Availability paper "Data Guard Redo Transport & Network Configuration."[7] At the time of this writing, the paper had not yet been updated to reflect Oracle Database 11g.*

---

[7] See www.oracle.com/technology/deploy/availability/pdf/MAA_WP_10gR2_DataGuardNetworkBestPractices.pdf.

### Optimizing ASYNC Redo Transport

The tuning discussed so far applies both to synchronous and asynchronous redo transport mechanisms. As you have seen, tuning the network can help you avoid as much of the impact to your primary database as possible. You have also learned about transport attributes, including NET_TIMEOUT and AFFIRM, and how they can affect your transport, especially with synchronous transport. You need to think about two additional factors if you are going to be using Maximum Performance and ASYNC transport: sizing of the primary database log buffers and compressing the redo stream before it goes across the network.

Tuning the log buffers on the primary database can reduce I/O to the ORL files, and redo compression can be performed if a standby destination is starved of bandwidth or you have a requirement not to use more than a certain amount of bandwidth.

As of Oracle Database 11g, in a Data Guard configuration where redo is being shipped in asynchronous mode, the LNS process will attempt to read redo directly from the log buffer. In Oracle Database 10g Release 2, an asynchronous LNS process would read directly from the ORL file. (While this could cause extra I/O on the primary and potentially get in the road of the LGWR, it was better than the Oracle9i and Oracle Database 10g Release 1 method of having a user-sized ASYNC buffer.) In Oracle Database 11g, if the redo to be sent is not found in the log buffer, then the LNS process will go to the ORL to retrieve it. Since reading from memory (log buffer) is much faster than reading from disk (ORL), you want to size the log buffer so that LNS is always able to find the redo that it needs to send within the log buffer. Monitoring the I/O to the ORL files for an increase above normal will tell you whether the ASYNC LNS processes are falling into the ORL file. Increasing the LOG_BUFFER parameter can help keep the LNS process reading from memory. As we mentioned in Chapter 1, the log buffer hit ratio is tracked in the view X$LOGBUF_READHIST. A low hit ratio indicates that the LNS is frequently reading from the ORL instead of the log buffer. The default for log buffers is 512KB, or 128KB × CPU_COUNT, whichever is greater. If transactions are long or numerous, then increasing the size of the log buffer will reduce I/O in general to the online log file. By reducing the I/O to the ORL file, you will be keeping redo longer in memory so that the asynchronous LNS process can read as much as possible from memory, thereby avoiding I/O to the online log files. Of course, in a bandwidth-strapped network, as compared to your redo generation rate, it is still possible that the LNS will not only fall out of memory to the ORL file but all the way down to reading from the archive log file if the ORL is archived before it is done.

Increasing the log buffers improves the read speed of the LNS process—that is, how fast the LNS can get the redo. The rest of LNS's work is to send that redo across the network. We have already shown you how to tune the network send and receive buffers so that the LNS process can use as much of the bandwidth available as possible to obtain the highest level of performance for redo transport. But what about the case in which you just don't have the bandwidth? Or perhaps the bandwidth exists, but you are told that your Data Guard configuration is allowed to consume only a limited amount of that bandwidth? In such cases, you need to reduce the amount of redo you are sending to achieve a high rate of transfer to the standby. In the past, the only way to achieve this was to use some kind of hardware compression unit on the network or enable a secure shell (SSH) tunnel that would compress the redo stream.

As of Oracle Database 11g, Data Guard provides redo compression as part of the Redo Transport Services. Before we go any further, remember that redo transport compression is a feature of the Oracle Advanced Compression option. You must purchase a license for this option before you can use the redo transport compression feature. Several other compression capabilities are included in the Advanced Compression option, all of which you can access with a license. For more information on this option, refer to the *Oracle Database 11g Oracle Database Licensing Information* manual, in the "Advanced Compression" section.[8] In a limited bandwidth environment, Data Guard compression can provide the following benefits:

- Improved data protection by reducing redo transport lag
- Reduced network utilization
- Faster redo gap resolution
- Reduced redo transfer time

Data Guard redo compression can be performed while Data Guard is resolving redo gaps and with asynchronous redo transport on a per-destination basis. As with any compression technique, Data Guard compression will provide you with the best results when you have low-bandwidth networks. With higher bandwidth networks, the benefits of using compression are reduced. Using Data Guard compression will be beneficial in the following situations:

- Data Guard experiences a disconnect from a standby database and needs to resolve the gaps in the redo, but you have a network with bandwidth less than or equal to 100 Mbits/sec.
- There is not enough bandwidth, despite tuning, to meet your primary database redo generation rate when configured with Maximum Performance mode using asynchronous redo transport.

These reasons to use compression apply to configurations for which you either do not have the bandwidth to support you redo generation rate or you are required to restrict Data Guard's access to the network bandwidth artificially by reducing your tuning efforts.

Once you have decided that you could benefit from using Data Guard compression, you need to have sufficient CPU resources available for the compression processing. All compression takes CPU, and somebody has to do all that math. While the compression algorithm is very efficient, Data Guard will consume CPU resources when it is processing the redo, whether for the ARCH process doing gap resolution to a standby database or for the LNS process that is sending the redo to an asynchronous standby database. In addition, CPU consumption will increase in higher network bandwidth environments since potentially a larger percentage of time is spent compressing redo compared to transmitting redo. For example, Oracle's testing of gap resolution showed that with an OC1 network (51.8 Mbits/sec) and a T3 network (44.7 Mbits/sec), 50 percent of one CPU was consumed per ARCH process during the compression operation, while with a 100 Mbits/sec network, an entire CPU was consumed per ARCH process.

A good rule of thumb[9] is that it is not necessarily a wise idea to enable compression when you have a network of more than 100 Mbits/sec. So, if you have decided that you need to use compression, you have a couple of decisions to make.

First, is your redo compressible? It does no good to waste CPU resources when you are going to get only marginal results from the work required to compress the data. The compression ratio is not directly dependent on workload; instead, it depends on the compressibility of the data. For example, if your redo has a lot of unstructured data in it (such as images in binary large object, or BLOB, or Oracle Intermedia ORDImage columns, for example), you will not get a lot of payback

---

[8] See http://download.oracle.com/docs/cd/B28359_01/license.111/b28287/options.htm#sthref43.

[9] http://en.wikipedia.org/wiki/Rule_of_thumb

for your compression, because that data is already pretty well compressed. So you could have a very light workload with lots of this type of data, resulting in very low compression ratios. You also cannot make a general characterization of the compressibility of batch versus OLTP data, because it really is the data itself. A simple test is to take a selection of your archive logs and run them through WinZip to see how much space you save. If it's not more than 30 to 35 percent, you shouldn't bother with compression. Oracle MAA testing showed that with a redo compression ratio of 35 percent or more, redo transmission time was reduced by 15 to 35 percent, depending on the size of the network.[10] The good news is that compression can be applied to any workload. If you make a mistake and enable it without checking, the compression back-off algorithm will detect whether the redo data is insufficiently compressible, and it will respond accordingly and dynamically.

Second, do you want to perform compression for gap resolution only or for gap resolution and asynchronous standby destinations? Data Guard, by default, does not compress the redo. You can configure your standby destination parameters to compress the redo, but it will occur only on those standby destinations where you actually use the compression attribute. By default, if you define compression on a standby destination, compression will be used, but only when Data Guard needs to resolve a gap. However, you can, with the aid of a hidden parameter, tell Data Guard to compress the redo when sending to one or more of your asynchronous standby databases. If you decide that you want Data Guard to compress the redo stream to one or more asynchronous standby databases, set the initialization parameter _REDO_TRANSPORT_COMPRESS_ ALL to TRUE. Changing this hidden parameter requires a restart of the database so use accordingly. Something else to remember is that when you set this parameter, you are saying only that redo will be compressed for gaps and asynchronous (ASYNC) destinations when you include the attribute on a standby database's redo transport LOG_ARCHIVE_DESTINATION_n parameter. If you define compression for a synchronous (SYNC) destination, compression will be used only to resolve gaps. SYNC standby destinations do not use compression at this time.

Once you have determined which of your standby databases require compression, you enable it by adding the compression attribute to the destination parameter:

```
LOG_ARCHIVE_DEST_2='SERVICE=MATRIX_DR0 ASYNC NOAFFIRM COMPRESSION=ENABLE'
```

If you are going to be using the Data Guard Broker, a property is used to set the compression attribute, and we'll discuss that in Chapter 5. Remember that the preceding example will use compression only when resolving gaps to Matrix_DR0, unless you set the hidden parameter _REDO_TRANSPORT_COMPRESS_ALL; then it will use compression for all redo transport to Matrix_DR0. If you decide to go with Maximum Availability and choose Matrix_DR0 for your synchronous standby, Data Guard will use compression only for gaps to Matrix_DR0.

### Choosing an Apply Method

Believe it or not, everything discussed so far in the last two sections has dealt with getting your RPO set at the required level—that is, getting the redo to the standby as fast as possible so it is protected, reducing or eliminating any data loss at failure time. Nowhere have we actually talked about getting that redo into a standby database and how long that will take, which is related directly to your RTO. And the RTO is further influenced by the type of failover configuration you choose to use, which we will deal with in Chapter 8.

---

[10] Note 729551.1 "Redo Transport Compression in a Data Guard Environment"

So what are your options for the apply method? Basically, the apply method is the type of standby database you choose to set up—a *physical* standby database using Redo Apply or a *logical* standby database using SQL Apply. Chapter 1 detailed the differences between these two types of Data Guard standby databases, so we won't go over those topics here. (We asked at the beginning of this chapter if you had read Chapter 1, remember?).

The first important point about the type of standby is that everything we have been discussing so far in this chapter applies to both types of standby databases. How redo is transported to a standby, the tuning you can and should do, the SRL files, the protection modes, compression—everything—is exactly the same regardless of the type of standby database at the other end of the pipe. How that redo gets processed is what is different.

Now that you have been examining the characteristics of your redo generation rates, you need to realize what impact it may have on the type of standby you choose. With redo generation rates in the 1 to 15 MB/sec range, you can tune either type of standby (given sufficient hardware resources) to meet a short RTO, in seconds to single-digit minutes. Note that in a workload dominated by LOB inserts, SQL Apply optimizations have been able to handle up to 60 MB/sec apply rates, beyond which the apply lag, and thus RTO, will grow. Other than the special case for LOB inserts, once your redo rate passes the 15 MB/sec threshold, the RTO for a logical standby database will start to grow some as it will begin to fall behind. A physical standby database has been shown to reach apply rates in the area of 50 to 60 MB/sec for OLTP workloads and more than 100 MB/sec for batch workloads. Of course, to reach the maximum apply rates, you need to have enough hardware and you will have to do some tuning of the standby database, system, and I/O as well as the apply process itself. Those tuning exercises are discussed in Chapters 3 and 4.

In the final parts of this chapter, where you actually get to create something, you will be configuring a physical standby database since you always start with a physical standby database. If you want to add in a logical standby database to your configuration, you start by creating a physical standby database, letting it get caught up with the primary database, and then converting it to a logical standby database, which will also be discussed.

### Considering Role Transitions

One final thing to think about now before we get into creating a standby database. A Data Guard standby database, like any other kind of disaster recovery solution, is never built just to look pretty. It is created for a purpose, and that purpose is to save your business when you experience a failure (remember, it's *when*, not *if*). In addition, Data Guard can be used in a multitude of ways that are non–failure related to save you precious downtime. These are all accomplished by role transitions, *switchover*, and *failover*. Get used to those words, because you are going to use them a lot in the future. We will go much deeper into role transitions in Chapter 8.

# Relating the RPO and RTO to the Protection Mode

Now that you have made your decisions, understand all of your options, and have performed the required setup and tuning tasks for your systems and networks, you are finally ready to start implementing standby databases and putting the operational practices into place.

As you have seen so far in this chapter, disaster recovery and high availability are basically a set of tradeoffs. You must accept that to get the best performance out of your production system, you will potentially lose some data at failure time, and you have to examine and tune your network to meet your RPO. And if you put a standby outside of your local geographical area, you need a network that can handle the amount of change that will occur on your primary database.

Zero data loss isn't free by a long shot. Science-fiction writer Robert A. Heinlein put it best when he wrote TANSTAAFL—There Ain't No Such Thing As A Free Lunch.[11]

# Creating a Physical Standby Database

Finally, you get to start creating a standby database! If you skipped the first part of this chapter, these procedures will still get your standby database up and running, but you will not understand what you are configuring, nor will it perform in the manner you might expect. So make sure you've read everything in this chapter up to this point before you begin.

## Choosing Your Interface

Before you get started, you need to make a decision about the interface are you going to use when you configure, manage, and use your Data Guard setup. You have three choices: Oracle Enterprise Manager Grid Control, the Data Guard Broker, and SQL*Plus, each with its own command line interface (CLI) or graphical user interface (GUI), as shown in Figure 2-1.

You need to choose an interface now because, once you choose to use the Broker (either directly or through Grid Control), you cannot perform Data Guard management using SQL*Plus unless you completely remove the Broker from the picture. This is because the Broker considers itself (rightly so) the keeper of your Data Guard configuration's health, and as such it will put things back the way it believes things should be, regardless of your changes. Not only will this become very confusing for you, but it can, in some cases, prevent functions such as switchover and failover from occurring smoothly, causing you to have to troubleshoot a situation at a time when you really don't want your attention diverted from the cause at hand—that is, getting back up and running in production as quickly as possible.

Choosing one or the other does not mean that you cannot change your mind in the future; it just means that you have to know what you are doing so the change can happen flawlessly. Grid Control uses the Data Guard Broker to set up and manage the configuration, so it is very easy to move from one of those two interfaces as long as you do some basic setup, which is discussed at the end of the next section. If you want to return to using SQL*Plus to perform management, you need to remove the Broker configuration, which also means that you can no longer use Grid Control with your Data Guard configuration other than to monitor some of the performance information. Of course, you can always use SQL*Plus to look at things in your Data Guard databases, even if you are using the Broker—but you cannot change things. More on that in Chapter 7.

Another reason to choose your interface now is because you just don't have to worry about the following things if you choose to go with Grid Control and the Data Guard Broker:

- Parameter definitions
- SRL creation
- Force logging
- Password file, init files
- Starting the apply

These are done for you by Grid Control when you use the Grid Control Data Guard Wizard to create your standby database.

---

[11] See http://en.wikipedia.org/wiki/TANSTAAFL.

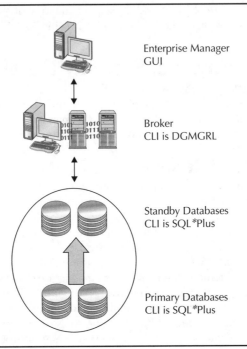

Enterprise Manager
GUI

Broker
CLI is DGMGRL

Standby Databases
CLI is SQL*Plus

Primary Databases
CLI is SQL*Plus

**FIGURE 2-1.** *Data Guard management interfaces*

## Before You Start

In all of the standby creation methods we discuss in the following sections, it is assumed that you have already performed these prerequisites:

- Enabled archiving on your primary database

- Installed Oracle Database 11g on all systems where you will be creating standby databases (you do not need to create a database, just do a software only install)

- Configured and started ASM (although ASM is not mandatory, it is recommended)

- Created any necessary directories on the standby system

- Configured and started the listener on the standby system

- Added your primary and all standby databases connection descriptors to all the TNSNAMES files on each system; even if you did not perform network tuning, you must perform at least this task:

```
MATRIX_DR0 =
  (DESCRIPTION =
    (ADDRESS_LIST =
      (ADDRESS = (PROTOCOL = TCP)(HOST = matrix_dr0.com)(PORT = 1521))
    )
```

```
    (CONNECT_DATA =
      (SERVICE_NAME = Matrix_DR0)
    )
  )

MATRIX =
  (DESCRIPTION =
    (ADDRESS = (PROTOCOL = TCP)(HOST = matrix.com)(PORT = 1521))
    (CONNECT_DATA =
      (SERVER = DEDICATED)
      (SERVICE_NAME = Matrix)
    )
  )
```

You do not have to add any static entries to the LISTENER files yet. We will tell you when that is necessary and why. Just remember this: Setting up a Data Guard standby database is no different from setting up your primary database in the first place. You need a database, which means the following:

- Listener
- TNSNAMES to find the standby and the primary
- Initialization parameters
- Password file (plus service if you are on Windows)
- Control file
- Data, undo, and temporary files
- Redo logs

Pretty much the same things you've been doing for years, right?

# Using Oracle Enterprise Manager Grid Control

It is beyond the scope of this book to describe the entire installation and setup of Grid Control; that part is left up to you. However, you will need the following components if you want to use Grid Control to create and manage Data Guard: an Oracle Management Server (OMS) and its repository database (which can have its own Data Guard standby) installed and operating somewhere in your network. Then you will need the Grid Control Agent installed on every system in your proposed Data Guard configuration—the primary database systems and any standby database systems.

You can use Grid Control 10.2.0.4 to create and manage Oracle Database 11g standby databases, but you will not be able take advantage of any of the Data Guard 11g features, including using the new RMAN method for creating the standby, setting parameters and attributes that are new in 11g, and using Snapshot Standby or Active Data Guard. In addition, since you will be using the Oracle Database 10g creation method, any of the network tuning you did at the TNS name descriptor will be lost unless you chose to put your tuning directly into the sqlnet.ora file for system-wide configuration. If you have only Grid Control 10.2.0.4, we recommend that you skip this section and go to "The Power User Method" later in the chapter to create your standby database. Once done, you can skip to Chapter 5, as instructed, to create the Data Guard

Broker configuration. When that is done, you will be able to connect to your Data Guard configuration through Grid Control 10.2.0.4 and manage it, but still without access to any of the Data Guard 11g features directly. You will have to use the Data Guard Broker CLI DGMGRL to effect those changes.

Using Grid Control 10.2.0.5 will give you access to everything mentioned so far in this book, including the new creation methods. In addition, your network tuning will remain as is, since Grid Control will use the new Broker properties. So once you have installed and configured Grid Control, log in to Grid Control and connect to your production database.

### Step 1: Navigate to Data Guard Setup

Upon launching Grid Control, click the Targets tab and then the Databases tab. Select your primary database. In our case, this is Matrix.

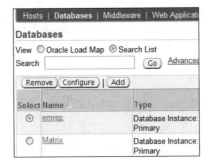

Once on the home page for the primary database, click the Availability tab.

Under this tab, you will find the Data Guard—Add Standby Database link, as shown here:

Click this link to get started. You are prompted to configure the Data Guard Broker since Grid Control requires it. Click the Add Standby Database link to get started:

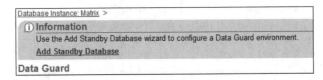

### Step 2: Choose What You Want to Do

The next page shows you a list of operations that the wizard can perform for you:

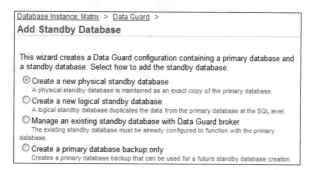

Here you can create a new standby database (either physical or logical), manage an existing standby database (one created outside of Grid Control that does not utilize the Broker), or create an RMAN backup of the primary database that can be used to create multiple standby databases. Let's create a new physical standby database.

### Step 3: Choose Your Creation Method

The next screen asks you what type of backup you are going to use to create the standby: Perform An Online Backup Of The Primary Database or Use An Existing Primary Database Backup. The first option (which you will see only when your primary database is 11g or higher) is where Grid Control will use the FROM ACTIVE DATABASE method to create the standby database. We will explain that feature more in the "The Power User Method" section a bit later. The second option is a staging operation, where Grid Control will perform a hot backup of each data file and place it in a staging area, copy the file to the standby system, and restore it to the standby database. This operation is then repeated for each data file. When your primary database is an Oracle Database 10g database, the staging operation is the only available option.

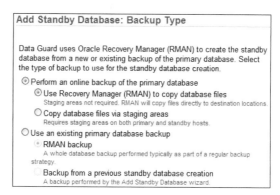

Your other option is to use a previously existing backup, whether created from a previous standby creation or any RMAN backup that already exists. We will choose the new Oracle Database 11g method.

## Step 4: Specify the Backup Files Area

If you chose to use the new 11g method for creating the standby (directly over the network), you will not be asked to specify where you want to place the backup files, because there won't be any. What you will be asked is how many parallel processes you want to use and the primary system logon credentials, as shown next. If you had previously configured your preferred credentials, these fields would be filled in for you.

```
┌─────────────────────────────────────────────────────────────────────────────┐
│ Add Standby Database: Backup Options                                          │
│                    Primary Database  Matrix                                    │
│                       Primary Host   stadu67                                   │
│ ............................................................................. │
│ The primary database files will be copied directly to the standby database Oracle Home. No staging areas are required. │
│   Concurrent File Copy Processes  │4    │                                      │
│                                   The number of concurrent processes (up to 50) used by Recovery Manager (RMAN) to │
│                                   database files. Increased concurrency may speed the process if sufficient network ban │
│                                   is available.                               │
│                                                                               │
│ Primary Host Credentials                                                      │
│ Enter the credentials of the user who owns the primary database Oracle server installation. │
│               * Username  │oracle                                    │        │
│               * Password  │••••••••                                  │        │
│                           ☑ Save as Preferred Credential                      │
└─────────────────────────────────────────────────────────────────────────────┘
```

If you chose to use the 10g method, you will have to choose what you want Grid Control to do with the backup files that will be created to establish your standby database. By default, these files will go into the Oracle home directory under the DBS directory, but you can place it wherever you want. You can also compress the backup (which does not require the Advanced Compression option, as this is the standard compression) to speed up transmission of the backup to the standby site if you do not have the necessary network bandwidth available. If you choose to keep this backup file for a future standby creation, you will need more permanent space on disk, and Grid Control will tell you how much. Since we are using the new Oracle Database 11g method, you will not be asked for a location to place the backup files, since there is no staging area.

One other difference is that the Data Guard Wizard will always create the SRL files on the standby and primary databases. It is important that they always be created, but currently this can create multiplexed SRL files, which is not recommended at this time. We will discuss this in more detail a bit later on in the chapter.

## Step 5: Specify the SID of the Standby

At this point, you need to specify the system ID (SID) or Instance Name that will be used for the standby database. This is what you would set your ORACLE_SID variable to when trying to attach to the standby when you are on the standby server. In addition, you need to specify the standby database system and Oracle home as well as the username and password for the remote host that has the privileges to create the standby database, as shown next. Grid Control will assume that you use the same username and password for both systems and will prefill these fields for you, so you must reenter the data if they are different.

```
A discovered ASM instance will be required on the standby host you choose below. You will be prompted to login to the ASM instance if necessary.
☑ TIP If there is no ASM instance running on the specified standby host, it must be created and discovered in order to proceed with standby database
      creation.

    Standby Database Attributes
                                    ∗ Instance Name    Matrix_DR0
                                                       The instance name (also referred to as the SID) must be unique on the standby host.

    Standby Database Location
    Specify the host and Oracle Home where the standby database will be created. The host should be a discovered Enterprise Manager target and match the
    operating system of the primary database host. The Oracle Home should exist on the specified host and match the version of the primary database.
                                            ∗ Host     lcarpent-lnx
                                    ∗ Oracle Home       /scratch/OracleHomes/OraHome111

    Standby Host Credentials
    Enter the credentials of the user who owns the Oracle Home selected above.
                                        ∗ Username      oracle
                                        ∗ Password      ••••••••
                                                       ☑ Save as Preferred Credential
```

The host for the standby database will default to the same system you are currently on, so you will have to change it. You can either enter the information manually or click the little flashlight icon to get a list of all the hosts that Grid Control has discovered, where you can select the standby host and click Select. The list will contain only hosts that have an Oracle home that exactly match the Oracle version of the primary database. They must match *exactly*.

**Optionally Choose Your Transfer Method and Standby Locations**   If you selected the old staging area method to transfer the data files to the standby system, you will be presented with a File Access page and asked to provide the disk directories where it can put the backup files on the standby system. You can also choose how you want the backup copied over to the standby system—via HTTP or FTP. You won't see this page when you select the 11*g* backup method, as we have.

When you use this backup method, Grid Control also provides the option of specifying a network mount location of the primary host's backups. This option is a viable solution if you decide that you cannot afford to have the database copied over the network at creation time by HTTP or FTP. The second option specifies a directory on the standby system that points to the temporary directory on the primary system that you specified in step 4. For example, suppose you put the backup that Grid Control will create in /u03/backups/Matrix. You then mount that directory with NFS or some sort or network mount on the standby server, perhaps as /u04/primarybackup/Matrix/. You would put that directory specification in the second option to have Grid Control perform the restore directly from that directory. This is the directory where the backup of the primary database is located. In this way, you can avoid doubling the storage for the backup files and let the network mount handle the transfer of the data as it is being restored.

## Step 6: Specify the Location of the Standby Data Files

Since we are using Automatic Storage Management (ASM) on the primary database, Grid Control insists that ASM also be configured on the standby system. If not, you cannot create your standby there using Grid Control. You can, however, create an ASM standby from a non-ASM primary using Grid Control. Since we're using ASM, it will ask for the login credentials for the remote ASM instance.

| Database Location: ASM Instance Login | |
|---|---|
| Standby Host | lcarpent-lnx.us.oracle.com |
| ASM Instance | +ASM_lcarpent-lnx |
| * SYS Password | •••••• |

On the screen shown next, you will be asked where the standby data files and flash recovery area should be placed—in our case, ASM:

**Standby Database File Locations**

Specify the disk groups to use for the database and recovery files.

**Database Area**

Specify the location where datafiles, tempfiles, redo log files, and control files will be created.

| | |
|---|---|
| Total Disk Space Required | **2400 MB** |
| * Database Area | DATA |
| Tablespace Storage Locations | Default ( Customize ) |
| Redo Log and Control File Locations | Default ( Multiplex ) |

If multiplex locations are not specified, these files will be created in both the database and flash r

**Flash Recovery Area**

☑ Use flash recovery area

To enhance data protection and performance, Oracle recommends that a flash recovery area be used.

Specify the location where recovery-related files (archived redo log files, RMAN backups, etc.) will be created.

| | |
|---|---|
| Flash Recovery Area | FLASH |

Archived redo log files received from the primary database will be put in this location.

| | |
|---|---|
| ⓘ Flash Recovery Area Size (MB) | 4801 |

Limit on the total space used by files created in the flash recovery area. The default value is twi

☑ Automatically delete applied archived redo log files when space is needed

**Network Configuration File Location**

Configuration information for the standby database will be added to the network configuration files in the specified directory on

| | |
|---|---|
| * Configuration File Location | /scratch/OracleHomes/OraHome111/network/admin |

If you are not using ASM, you will enter the normal disk path and directory information. If you are storing the data files in more than one place, click Customize and enter the different disk groups, as shown next:

Override storage for all tablespaces or choose different disk groups for each tablespace below.

**Tablespaces**

Set storage for all tablespaces [                    ] ( Go )

| Name △ | Size (MB) | Status | Type | Standby Location |
|---|---|---|---|---|
| EXAMPLE | 101 | ONLINE | PERMANENT | DATA |
| SYSAUX | 644 | ONLINE | PERMANENT | DATA |
| SYSTEM | 701 | ONLINE | PERMANENT | DATA |
| TEMP | 30 | ONLINE | TEMPORARY | DATA |
| UNDOTBS1 | 36 | ONLINE | UNDO | DATA |
| USERS | 79 | ONLINE | PERMANENT | DATA |

You do not have a choice of whether or not to use a flash recovery area. The Data Guard Wizard in Grid Control enforces the best practices, and having a flash recovery area is a must.

At the bottom of the page (see the next illustration) is a place to specify the location of the network configuration files on the standby system. This is not where you would like Grid Control to put the files, but where they are actually located. If you change this to some location and the files are not there, Grid Control will not be able to build your standby. You would only have to change this if your system network admin location was somewhere other than what Grid Control placed in this field.

**Standby Database File Locations**
Specify the disk groups to use for the database and recovery files.

Database Area
Specify the location where datafiles, tempfiles, redo log files, and control files will be created.
Total Disk Space Required  **2400 MB**
＊ Database Area  DATA
Tablespace Storage Locations  **Default**  ( Customize )
Redo Log and Control File  **Default**  ( Multiplex )
Locations
If multiplex locations are not specified, these files will be created in both the database and flash r

Flash Recovery Area
☑ Use flash recovery area
To enhance data protection and performance, Oracle recommends that a flash recovery area be used.
Specify the location where recovery-related files (archived redo log files, RMAN backups, etc.) will be created.
Flash Recovery Area  FLASH
Archived redo log files received from the primary database will be put in this location.
ⓘ Flash Recovery Area Size (MB)  4801
Limit on the total space used by files created in the flash recovery area. The default value is twi
☑ Automatically delete applied archived redo log files when space is needed

## Step 7: Name the Standby Database

You are almost done. Next, as shown in the following image, you configure three items. First you specify the Database Unique Name, which must be different from the name of the primary database. This uniqueness was enforced in prior releases at the Data Guard Broker and Grid Control levels, but not at the SQL*Plus level. As of Oracle Database 11g, this uniqueness between a primary database and its standby databases is enforced at the Data Guard level. Grid Control has never let you specify the same database unique name for the standby in any release since 10g.

**Standby Database Parameters**
ⓘ ＊ Database Unique Name  Matrix_DR0
Used to set the standby database DB_UNIQUE_NAME parameter, which must be unique withir
＊ Target Name  Matrix_DR0
The display name used by Enterprise Manager for the standby database. Oracle recommends
Name.

**Standby Database Monitoring Credentials**
Specify the database user credentials that will be used by Enterprise Manager to monitor the standby database.
○ Use non-SYSDBA monitoring credentials
If non-SYSDBA monitoring credentials are used, Data Guard performance monitoring will not be available for a mounted physical stan
Username
Password
Confirm Password
◉ Use SYSDBA monitoring credentials
The SYSDBA credentials supplied earlier when connecting to the primary database will be used by Enterprise Manager to monitor the

The second parameter is the Target Name, which is the value that Grid Control will use when displaying the standby database in the Data Guard pages.

Grid Control 10.2.0.5 also allows you to specify the username of the monitoring user so that you no longer have to configure this after the standby database is created. You can specify a normal user that does not have SYSDBA credentials (and suffer reduced monitoring capabilities) or use the SYSDBA username you have already supplied.

At the bottom of the page are two other items of interest—you can choose whether to use the Broker or not and how Grid Control should set up the network connections.

Grid Control 10.2.0.5 will create a standby database for you using the Broker and will then remove the Broker configuration when it is done. This means that you must manage your Data Guard configuration using SQL*Plus. You will be able to do only some basic monitoring or your Data Guard setup in Grid Control if you choose not to use the Broker.

The next item you can supply is the connect identifier. In previous versions of Oracle Database, the Data Guard Broker (and Grid Control) would use a specially constructed connect identifier to connect to the standby database. If you provided it with a TNSNAME identifier, it would convert that to the full connect descriptor and store that value in its configuration files. As we mentioned earlier, this would erase all your tuning efforts at the Oracle Net Services and TCP level. So after clicking the plus sign (+), you would expand the connect identifiers and specify the TNSNAME that you already created in the TNSNAMES.ORA file, as shown next.

**▼Data Guard Connect Identifiers**

Data Guard requires a connect identifier for each database in the configuration. The connect identifier will be used for all Data Guard communication, including redo transport for standby databases.

☑ TIP If an existing net service name is specified, ensure that is is resolvable by all databases in the Data Guard configuration.

* Primary Database Connect Identifier ◯ Use Enterprise Manager connect descriptor
Uses the connect descriptor used by Enterprise Manager for the primary database.
◉ Use existing net service name

```
Matrix
```

An existing net service name that can be used by all databases in the Data Guard configuration to connect to the primary database.

* Standby Database Connect Identifier ◯ Use Enterprise Manager connect descriptor
Uses the connect descriptor used by Enterprise Manager for the standby database.
◉ Use existing net service name

```
Matrix_DR0
```

An existing net service name that can be used by all databases in the Data Guard configuration to connect to the standby database.

If you want to let the Broker use the old method of connecting to the standby databases, you can click the appropriate radio buttons. In fact, when you first arrive at this page, the primary database connect string has already been processed and prefilled in the old style. We erased it and added *Matrix*, as you can see.

## Step 8: Ready To Go!

At this point, you have finished answering questions. The following illustration shows all the various parts of your configuration and the answers you made to all the preceding questions.

| Primary Database | | Standby Database | |
|---|---|---|---|
| Target Name | **Matrix** | Target Name | **Matrix_DR0** |
| Database Name | **matrix** | Database Name | **Matrix** |
| Instance Name | **Matrix** | Instance Name | **MatrixD0** |
| Database Version | **11.1.0.6.0** | Oracle Server Version | **11.1.0.6.0** |
| Oracle Home | **/scratch/OracleHomes /OraHome111** | Oracle Home | **/scratch/OracleHomes/OraHome111** |
| Host | **stadu67** | Host | **lcarpent-lnx** |
| Operating System | **Enterprise Linux Enterprise Linux AS release 4 (October Update 7) 2.6.9** | Operating System | **Red Hat Enterprise Linux AS release 4 (Nahant Update 3) 2.6.9** |
| Host Username | **lcarpent** | Host Username | **oracle** |
| Staging Area Location | **/scratch/OracleHomes /OraHome111/dbs** | Backup Type | **New backup** |
| Retain staging area | **No** | Staging Area Location | **/scratch/OracleHomes /OraHome111/dbs** |
| Compress Backup Files | **No** | File Transfer Method | **RMAN duplicate, HTTP/S** |
| | | Database Unique Name | **Matrix_DR0** |
| | | Database Storage | **Automatic Storage Management** |
| | | ASM Instance | **+ASM_lcarpent-lnx** |
| | | Standby Type | **Physical Standby** |
| | | Database Area | **DATA** |
| | | Flash Recovery Area | **FLASH** |
| | | Flash Recovery Area Size (MB) | **4801M** |
| | | Automatically Delete Archived Redo Log Files | **Yes** |

▷ Standby Database Storage

At the bottom of the page you will also see a complete outline of where the wizard will be placing the various files and redirecting any external directory specifications:

▼ Standby Database Storage

| | |
|---|---|
| Database Area | **DATA** |
| Flash Recovery Area | **FLASH** |
| Multiplex Redo Log Files and Control Files | **No** |

Tablespaces

| Name | Size (MB) | Status | Type | Standby Location |
|---|---|---|---|---|
| EXAMPLE | 101 | ONLINE | PERMANENT | DATA |
| SYSAUX | 636 | ONLINE | PERMANENT | DATA |
| SYSTEM | 701 | ONLINE | PERMANENT | DATA |
| TEMP | 30 | ONLINE | TEMPORARY | DATA |
| UNDOTBS1 | 36 | ONLINE | UNDO | DATA |
| USERS | 79 | ONLINE | PERMANENT | DATA |

If all is good, the standby creation job will be created. When it is submitted, you will see the Data Guard home page. On this page, check over everything before you click Finish.

## Step 9: The Job Is Submitted

When you proceed, Grid Control will create the Data Guard Broker configuration and then build and submit a standby creation job; this will actually create the standby. While the job is still running, it will add the standby database to the Data Guard Broker configuration. The sequence is displayed in the illustration. Don't worry about how it is doing the Broker work; this will be discussed in detail in Chapter 5.

⇨ Creating Data Guard configuration
Preparing standby database creation job
Submitting standby database creation job
Adding standby database target

ⓘ The process can be cancelled prior to submission of the standby database creation job.

As it says, the process can be cancelled right up to the point at which it submits the job. After that point, the job can no longer be cancelled, as shown here:

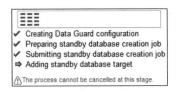

## Step 10: Creation in Progress

Now you can go get a cup of coffee, because it will be awhile before the standby is created. But as soon as the job is submitted and the standby database is added to the configuration, you will be returned to the Data Guard home page. On that page, you will see the standby in progress shown at the bottom of the page, as you see here:

If you click the Creation In Progress link, the Grid Control Jobs page will appear, where you can monitor the progress of the standby creation job. This is also where you will go if an error occurs during the creation process. You will be able to find out what went wrong and where by examining the output log.

Or you can stay here and watch for the creation to be complete. But you won't see anything unless you set the refresh speed at the top of the page, as shown here:

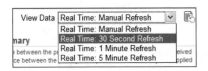

Set that to refresh every 30 seconds, 1 minute, or 5 minutes. Or, if you like manual refreshes better, click the icon with the page and the little green circle arrow on it—that's the manual refresh button.

## Step 11: The Standby Is Ready and Functioning!

Upon successful completion of the job and creation of the standby, a status of Normal will appear, as shown next. If Normal does not appear, click the link to troubleshoot your standby creation.

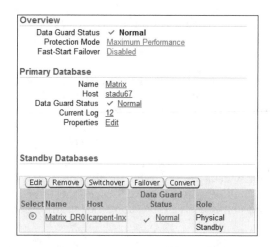

The illustration provides a summary of your configuration including the Protection Mode, Fast-Start Failover status, and the primary database.

From the Data Guard home page, you can edit the various attributes of the primary database (the Edit link above), the standby databases (the Edit button at the bottom), add standby database, perform role transitions, and enable Fast-Start Failover. We will discuss these operations in the chapters in which those features of Data Guard are discussed.

If you decided in the first part of this chapter to use Maximum Availability mode, you can now click the Maximum Performance link on the Data Guard home page. This will begin the Protection Mode Wizard, which will assist you in converting your configuration to the higher mode. The wizard will make all the changes to the redo transport attributes of the primary and the standby database you choose to be the synchronous standby destination.

## Step 12: Correcting Your SRL Files

You need to pay attention to one more thing before you finish up. Remember we said that the SRL files could get multiplexed? By default, with ASM they will have been put into both disk groups, just like the ORL files. If you are not using ASM, they will be multiplexed based on your setting of the DB_CREATE_ONLINE_LOG_DEST_$n$ parameters and will be multiplexed if you have specified more than one location.

On either database, you can query the V$LOGFILE view and obtain a list of the SRL files that have been created:

```
SQL> SELECT GROUP#, MEMBER FROM V$LOGFILE WHERE TYPE='STANDBY';
    GROUP# MEMBER
---------- ----------------------------------------------------------------
         4 +DATA/matrix_dr0/onlinelog/group_4.265.677440617
         4 +FLASH/matrix_dr0/onlinelog/group_4.333.677440625
         5 +DATA/matrix_dr0/onlinelog/group_5.268.677440629
         5 +FLASH/matrix_dr0/onlinelog/group_5.329.677440637
         6 +DATA/matrix_dr0/onlinelog/group_6.300.677440645
         6 +FLASH/matrix_dr0/onlinelog/group_6.292.677440653
         7 +DATA/matrix_dr0/onlinelog/group_7.298.677440663
         7 +FLASH/matrix_dr0/onlinelog/group_7.291.677440669
8 rows selected.
```

If your SRL files do get multiplexed, you should remove the multiplexed copy of each SRL on the standby and primary databases—in our case, the ones in the +DATA disk group.

On the primary database, where the SRL files are not currently being used, you can drop the multiplexed members immediately by executing the following command for each multiplexed member:

```
SQL> ALTER DATABASE DROP STANDBY LOGFILE MEMBER
          '+DATA/matrix/onlinelog/group_4.265.677440617';
Database altered.
```

On the standby database, you first need to stop the MRP and, if possible, redo transport at the same time. If you do not want to stop the transport, you will receive an error for the SRL currently being used by the RFS process and you will have to switch log files at the primary database to free it up before dropping the extra member. You can stop the MRP using SQL*Plus (normally a no-no but OK this one time!), or you can use Grid Control and stop the apply in the correct fashion:

```
SQL> ALTER DATABASE RECOVER MANAGED STANDBY DATABASE CANCEL;
Database altered.
SQL> ALTER DATABASE DROP STANDBY LOGFILE MEMBER
          '+DATA/matrix_dr0/onlinelog/group_4.265.677440617';
Database altered.
SQL> ALTER DATABASE DROP STANDBY LOGFILE MEMBER
          '+DATA/matrix_dr0/onlinelog/group_5.268.677440629';
SQL> ALTER DATABASE DROP LOGFILE MEMBER
          '+DATA/matrix_dr0/onlinelog/group_6.300.677440645';
Database altered.
SQL> ALTER DATABASE DROP STANDBY LOGFILE MEMBER
          '+DATA/matrix_dr0/onlinelog/group_7.298.677440663';
Database altered.
ALTER DATABASE DROP STANDBY LOGFILE MEMBER
          '+DATA/matrix_dr0/onlinelog/group_5.268.677440629'
*
ERROR at line 1:
ORA-00261: log 5 of thread 1 is being archived or modified
```

```
ORA-00312: online log 5 thread 1:
        +DATA/matrix_dr0/onlinelog/group_5.268.677440629'
ORA-00312: online log 5 thread 1:
        +FLASH/matrix_dr0/onlinelog/group_5.329.677440637'
```

The last one we'll try (Group 5) is the one currently in use by redo transport, since we chose not to turn off transport. Go to the primary database and switch logs. This will free up Group 5 so that you can drop its member once it has been archived at the standby. When it has been archived at the standby, you can try the drop again, and this time it will succeed.

```
SQL> ALTER DATABASE DROP STANDBY LOGFILE MEMBER
            '+DATA/matrix_dr0/onlinelog/group_5.268.677440629';
Database altered.
SQL> SELECT GROUP#, MEMBER FROM V$LOGFILE WHERE TYPE='STANDBY';
    GROUP# MEMBER
---------- -------------------------------------------------------------
         4 +FLASH/matrix_dr0/onlinelog/group_4.333.677440625
         5 +FLASH/matrix_dr0/onlinelog/group_5.329.677440637
         6 +FLASH/matrix_dr0/onlinelog/group_6.292.677440653
         7 +FLASH/matrix_dr0/onlinelog/group_7.291.677440669
```

Now that you have dropped the multiplexed members, you can restart the MRP by going back to Grid Control and correcting the error status that is displayed. Simply click the error link and then click Reset.

### Step 13: Finished!

You now have a fully functioning Data Guard standby database. You can go back and create another standby database at a different location, modify this one, or perform role transitions.

You need to take the following into account when creating your standby database with the Grid Control Data Guard Wizard:

- If you have an Oracle RAC primary database, the wizard will not create an Oracle RAC standby database, even if the system is configured for RAC. You will have to create a single instance standby and then use the conversion utility to convert it to RAC.

- If you need to go cross-platform (as defined by the Data Guard Cross Platform Note[12]), you cannot use Grid Control to create the standby database.

If you want to create your standby in one of these situations, you will need to use the procedure outlined in the next section and then import the configuration into Grid Control.

### A Last Note

If this was your chosen method for creating your standby databases, you can skip the rest of this chapter and go directly to Chapter 3. However, if you want to know how things actually function under the covers, the rest of this chapter will give you in-depth details about how standby databases are created by hand.

---

[12] Note 413484.1 "Data Guard Support for Heterogeneous Primary and Standby Systems in Same Data Guard Configuration"

# The Power User Method

So you are here either because you are a die-hard SQL user or you just want to know what goes on behind the scenes when you use Grid Control. Either way, you will benefit from the following discussions and examples.

You have always been able to create a physical standby database in many ways. These methods have traditionally ranged from manually copying the files across the network yourself (whether hot or cold backup), using a mirroring snapshot, or an RMAN backup. With the proliferation of ASM on Oracle databases, RMAN is fast becoming the only way to create a Data Guard standby and is in fact the best method to use.

In this section, you'll learn two methods for using RMAN to create your standby database—the original Oracle Database 10g method and the new 11g FROM ACTIVE DATABASE method. The older method is still a valid way to create a standby database, as there will be situations for which copying the entire database across the network may not be what you want to do, such as in the following examples:

- The size of the database makes you nervous about putting that much traffic on the network.

- Your network is sufficient to handle your redo generation rate but it would take days to move the entire database.

- You need to fully re-create a failed primary database as a standby database after performing a failover and you already have a fairly recent full backup at the primary site.

- You have high-speed tape drives at both sites and can transport the backup to the standby site faster than a network transfer.

Both of the RMAN creation techniques use the DUPLICATE FOR STANDBY command, but, as you will see, the new Oracle Database 11g method eliminates a lot of the work you have to do with the original method. We will start with the new method so you can see just how easy it is to use, followed by the older method. But first we need to discuss the parameters and their attributes that you will need to configure for Data Guard—which Grid Control and the Broker does for you.

## Parameters of Interest to Data Guard

Three types of parameters exist as far as Data Guard is concerned: those that are independent of the role of the database, those that are used only when the database is a primary, and those that are used only when the database is a standby. While numerous parameters can be used with a Data Guard configuration, you really need to configure only a few. And because so much of Data Guard's functionality is being moved into the code, many of these parameters and attributes have been deprecated in the last few releases. It is important to note that just like your TNS names, listeners, and SRL files, these parameters need to be defined on all databases in your configuration in preparation for role transition. So what are these parameters?

### Role-independent Parameters

- **DB_UNIQUE_NAME**   This parameter defines the unique name for a database. Since the DB_NAME parameter must be the same for a physical standby database and different for a logical standby database, this was introduced in 10g to provide a way to identify each database in a Data Guard configuration. You need to set this on all of your databases, but it does require a bounce. If the parameter is not defined, it is defaulted to the `DB_NAME`, which means you do not have to take an outage on production to create a standby. You can set it there later.

```
db_unique_name='Matrix'
```

■  **LOG_ARCHIVE_CONFIG**   This defines the list of valid `DB_UNIQUE_NAME` parameters for your Data Guard configuration. When used with the `DB_UNIQUE_NAME` attribute of the destination parameter (discussed in a moment), it provides a security check for Data Guard that the connection between the two databases is allowed. This parameter is dynamic as long as you do not use the `SEND` and `RECEIVE` attributes. Those are leftovers from the old `REMOTE_ARCHIVE_ENABLE` parameter and are no longer needed, so do not use them.

You need to add only the database unique names of the other databases in your configuration. The current database unique name is always added behind the scenes. But for clarity's sake and to have the exact same parameter defined on all the databases, add all the names explicitly. There is no requirement as to the order of the names in this parameter, but it is absolutely mandatory for RAC databases in a Data Guard configuration. This parameter should be used at all times.

```
log_archive_config='dg_config=(Matrix,Matrix_DR0)'
```

**CONTROL_FILES**   Of course, you all know what this parameter is for, but with a standby database it points to the Standby Control File. This is a special control file that is created for you or that you create yourself depending on the method you use to create your standby database. `control_files='/Oracle/oradata/Matrix/control01.ctl'`

■  **LOG_ARCHIVE_MAX_PROCESSES**   We mention this parameter here because the default setting is still 2, which is not enough. Archive processes on the primary database are responsible for archiving the ORL files as they become full and for resolving gaps in the redo stream to a standby database. And on a standby database, they are responsible for archiving the SRL files and forwarding the archive logs to a cascaded standby database.

On the primary, one archive process is limited to servicing only the ORL files and is not allowed to talk to a standby database at all. This special ARCH process is referred to as the "Dedicated ARCH Process." But the others are all allowed to perform both functions. While an archive process is sending an archive log to a standby database, it is not available to assist in archiving the ORL files. Even though the prime directive of an archive process is "Always archive the online log files first before processing a gap," it is still possible in the worst case to have only that one archive process archiving the online log files. If you do not have enough processes, then in a time of a large gap of a slow network, you could be reduced to one archive process for the ORL files. And we are all painfully aware that if the ORL files all get full at the same time, production stalls until one gets archived. The multi-threaded gap resolution attribute (`MAX_CONNECTIONS`), introduced in Oracle Database 10g, allows Data Guard to use more than one archive process to send a single log file to a standby, which uses even more of the processes. So, at a minimum, set this parameter at 4 with a maximum of 30.

```
log_archive_max_processes='4'
```

### Standby Dedicated ARCH Process

It is important to note that even a physical standby database has a "Dedicated ARCH" process, but that this just means that you have one less ARCH process available on the standby database to archive the SRL files. In a physical standby the dedicated ARCH process is also not allowed to archive the standby redo log files either.

One note on using multiple archive processes: While you need quite a few of them to ensure that you do not have stalls on production, a large number of archive processes can slow down switchovers because they all have to be awakened and asked to exit. You can avoid this by reducing the parameter before starting a switchover. In addition, in Oracle Database 11g with the new streaming capability, you can saturate your network with too many archive processes if you happen to suffer a very large redo gap.

- **DB_CREATE_FILE_DEST** Although this is not a Data Guard–specific parameter, it is worth mentioning here since you will need to define it at the standby database if you are using ASM.

```
db_create_file_dest=+DATA
```

### Primary Role Parameters

- **LOG_ARCHIVE_DEST_n** This is the main parameter for Data Guard redo transport and is usually in action when used on a primary database. Some exceptions to that rule mainly deal with cascaded standby destinations. This parameter can also be used to specify where the archive log files from the ORL files or the SRL files are supposed to go. But as of Oracle Database 10g Release 1 and the introduction of the flash recovery area, the local archiving is defaulted to the flash recovery area and you no longer need to define a local destination. We will discuss local archiving and the LOCATION attribute, but since you should be using the flash recovery area, you will not be setting a local destination.

  This parameter has seventeen attributes, all of which you can configure when setting up redo transport to a standby database. You need to set only seven of them to have a properly functioning Data Guard redo transport to a standby database. We will talk about those seven first and will then show you some examples of how to use them. Then we'll discuss the remaining attributes and describe where you may use them and why. We recommend that you do not use six of them.

The following attributes are required:

- **SERVICE** Specifies the TNSNAMES descriptor you created that points to your standby database. The network tuning you performed earlier will come from here.

- **SYNC** Specifies that you want the redo sent using a synchronous method, meaning that the LGWR process will wait for acknowledgment from the LNS before telling the client that the transaction has committed. This is required on at least one standby destination for Maximum Availability or Maximum Protection mode.

- **ASYNC** This is the default, and if you do not specify a transport type you will get asynchronous redo transport. This is the Maximum Performance redo transport method.

- **NET_TIMEOUT** Specifies the number of seconds that the LGWR process will wait for an LNS process to respond before abandoning the standby as failed. The default is 30 seconds, but 10 to 15 seconds would be a better value depending on the reliability of your network. Do not set it below 10 as you will experience failed reconnects after a standby database comes back, since it take a few seconds to reconnect everything. Reconnection requires the following:

  - Stopping a stale LNS process

  - Starting a new LNS process

  - Making the connection to the standby database

  - Detecting and stopping a stale RFS process

  - Starting a new RFS process

  - Selecting and opening a new SRL

  - Initializing the header of the SR

  - Responding back to the LNS that all is ready to go

  All of this occurs before the LNS process can tell the LGWR that it is ready to go. If this process takes longer than your value for NET_TIMEOUT the LGWR will abandon the standby anew and this whole thing will happen again at every log switch.

- **REOPEN** Controls the wait time before Data Guard will allow the primary database to attempt a reconnection to a failed standby database. Its default is 300 seconds (5 minutes), and this is usually the reason people complain that Data Guard isn't reconnecting after they abort their standby. Generally speaking, in test mode we all do things very fast. So the actions are SHUTDOWN ABORT the standby, watch the alert log of the primary database to see it disconnect from the standby, restart the standby database, and then switch logs on the primary database in hopes of seeing Data Guard reconnect. And all of this happens in less than 300 seconds, so Data Guard does not reconnect at the first log switch or a few more if you try them too fast. This attribute was designed to avoid a potentially stalling reconnect attempt if a log switch occurred immediately after a standby database destination failed. You will want to reduce this attribute to 30 or even 15 seconds so that Data Guard gets reconnected as fast as possible.

- **DB_UNIQUE_NAME** Using this attribute in your LOG_ARCHIVE_DEST_*n* parameter requires that you also set the LOG_ARCHIVE_CONFIG parameter; otherwise, Data Guard will refuse to connect to this destination. The name you would use here for a SERVICE destination (a remote one) is the unique name you specified for the database at the other end of the connection—that is, the standby database.

  You must also enter this unique name into the LOG_ARCHIVE_CONFIG parameter on both databases. When a primary database makes a connection to a standby database, it will send its own unique database name to the standby and ask for the standby's unique name in return. The standby will check in its configuration parameter, LOG_ARCHIVE_CONFIG, to make sure that the primary's unique name is present. If it is not the connection is refused. If it is present, the standby will send its own unique name back to the primary LNS process. If that returned value does not match the value you specified in this attribute, the connection is terminated.

Like the LOG_ARCHIVE_CONFIG parameter, this attribute is mandatory for RAC databases in a Data Guard configuration.

- **VALID_FOR** This is the last of the required attributes. Even if you think that your Data Guard configuration will function just fine without this attribute (and it will), it is a very good idea to use it anyway. The main function of this attribute is to define *when* the LOG_ARCHIVE_DEST_n destination parameter should be used and on what *type* of redo log file it should operate.

Following are the legal values for log files:

- **ONLINE_LOGFILE** Valid only when archiving ORL files
- **STANDBY_LOGFILE** Valid only when archiving SRL files
- **ALL_LOGFILES** Valid regardless of redo log files type

Following are the legal values for roles:

- **PRIMARY_ROLE** Valid only when the database is running in the primary role
- **STANDBY_ROLE** Valid only when the database is running in the standby role
- **ALL_ROLES** Valid regardless of database role

A VALID_FOR will allow the destination parameter to be used if the answer to both of its parameters is TRUE. This attribute enables you to predefine all of your destination parameters on all databases in your Data Guard configuration knowing that they will be used only if the VALID_FOR is TRUE. No more enabling or disabling destinations at role transition time.

So what will your LOG_ARCHIVE_DEST_n parameter look like? Up to nine destinations are available, meaning that you can have up to nine standby databases. In reality, ten destinations are available, but one is reserved for the default local archiving destination, which we will discuss in a moment. We'll use parameter number 2 to start and add a standby database that is in Manchester and will be our Maximum Availability standby database (edited for appearance):

```
log_archive_dest_2='service=Matrix_DR0
                    SYNC REOPEN=15 NET_TIMEOUT=15
                    valid_for=(ONLINE_LOGFILES,PRIMARY_ROLE)
                    db_unique_name=Matrix_DR0'
```

Now let's add in our Newark standby as parameter number 3, which has a network latency greater than we would like for SYNC so it will operate in asynchronous mode:

```
log_archive_dest_3='service=Matrix_DR1
                    ASYNC REOPEN=15
                    valid_for=(ONLINE_LOGFILES,PRIMARY_ROLE)
                    db_unique_name=Matrix_DR1'
```

And of course since we used the proper DB_UNIQUE_NAME attribute, we need to define our LOG_ARCHIVE_CONFIG parameter, too:

```
log_archive_config='dg_config=(Matrix,Matrix_DR0,Matrix_DR1)'
```

The following attributes are optional:

- **AFFIRM**   Default for SYNC destinations. Requires that the LNS process waits for the RFS to perform a direct I/O on the SRL file before returning a success message. Required for SYNC in Maximum Availability or Maximum Protection. You do not need to set this as it will default based on the destination. And even though you can set it for an ASYNC destination in 10g, there is no reason to do so. In fact, it will slow down the LNS process. AFFIRM is ignored for ASYNC destinations in Oracle Database 11g.

- **NOAFFIRM**   Default for ASYNC destinations if not specified. Used in Maximum Performance destinations. Again, there's no need to specify this as it is the default for ASYNC destinations. And if you try to set NOAFFIRM with a SYNC destination, your protection mode will fail to meet the rules and will be marked as being resynchronized. If this is your only SYNC standby and you are in Maximum Availability mode, you will not be able to perform a zero data loss failover and you will lose data. If this is your only SYNC destination, you are running in Maximum Protection mode, and you set NOAFFIRM, your primary database will crash!

- **COMPRESSION**   This attribute turns on compression using the Advanced Compression option for this standby destination. By default, this means that any ARCH process that is sending a gap to this destination will compress the archive as it is sending it. If you set the hidden parameter,[13] then it will also compress as the current redo stream is being sent. For example, assuming we set the hidden parameter, with our previous two destinations let's add the COMPRESSION attribute:

```
log_archive_dest_2='service=Matrix_DR0
                    LGWR SYNC REOPEN=15 NET_TIMEOUT=15
                    COMPRESSION=ENABLE
                    valid_for=(ONLINE_LOGFILES,PRIMARY_ROLE)
                    db_unique_name=Matrix_DR0'

log_archive_dest_3='service=Matrix_DR1
                    LGWR ASYNC REOPEN=15
                    COMPRESSION=ENABLE
                    valid_for=(ONLINE_LOGFILES,PRIMARY_ROLE)
                    db_unique_name=Matrix_DR1'
```

  Matrix_DR0 will be compressed only when an ARCH process is sending a gap (no compression for SYNC, remember?), and Matrix_DR1 will have the redo compressed at all times. This does not mean that the redo remains compressed on disk, as this compression is only during transport. The data is uncompressed at the standby side before it is written to the SRL file.

- **MAX_CONNECTIONS**   This attribute was introduced in 10g Release 2 to allow you to specify the number of archive processes that should be used for the standby destination

---

[13] Note 729551.1 "Redo Transport Compression in a Data Guard Environment"

when sending a gap; it is no longer used in 11*g*. But if you are using 10*g*, you can specify 1 to 5 (with 1 being the default). If you specify more than 1, whenever this standby destination needs to receive a gap, that many archive processes will be assigned to send the archive log. The file will be split up among them, sent in parallel streams across the network, and reassembled on the standby side.

```
log_archive_dest_2='service=Matrix_DR0
                    LGWR SYNC REOPEN=15 NET_TIMEOUT=15
                    MAX_CONNECTIONS=5
                    valid_for=(ONLINE_LOGFILES,PRIMARY_ROLE)
                    db_unique_name=Matrix_DR0'
```

Now when Matrix_DR0 suffers a disconnect from the primary, the gap resolution process on the primary will use multiple streams of redo for each missing archive log file.

**CAUTION**
*Do not use the* `MAX_CONNECTIONS` *attribute if you are running Oracle Database 11*g *as it will impede the redo transport performance.*

- **DELAY**   Rather than delaying the shipment of the redo, which is what a lot of people think it does, this attribute merely instructs the apply processes of the target standby database not to apply the redo without a lag of the number of seconds defined by this attribute. With Flashback Database, this attribute is almost obsolete, especially since we recommend that you always enable Flashback Database on your standby databases and your primary database. If you tend to do a lot of things that Flashback Database cannot handle, then you might want to specify a delay. Flashback Database and Data Guard will be discussed in Chapter 8.

- **ALTERNATE**   Alternate destinations were originally used to keep a database up and running when the local disk where you are archiving the ORL files fills up. Using an alternate destination, you could redirect the archive processes to use an auxiliary disk for the archive logs. This problem has basically disappeared with the flash recovery area, which self-manages its space.

  You could also use this attribute for remote standby destinations if you had multiple network paths to a standby database. Obviously, you would use multiple paths to the standby database with an Oracle RAC, but that is not what `ALTERNATE` was designed to do. It is easier in both the single instance with multiple network interfaces case or the Oracle RAC case to use connect time failover in your TNS descriptor for the standby database.

You are discouraged from using the following attributes:

- **LOCATION**   Prior to Oracle Database 10*g* Release 2, this attribute was required to specify a location where the archive processes could store the archive log files. And this was true on both the primary database (for the ORL files) and the standby database (for the SRL files). With the flash recovery area and local archiving defaults, you no longer need to define a destination with this attribute. Destination number 10 will automatically be set to use the flash recovery area.

  ```
  SQL> SELECT DESTINATION FROM V$ARCHIVE_DEST WHERE DEST_ID=10;
  USE_DB_RECOVERY_FILE_DEST
  ```

```
SQL> ARCHIVE LOG LIST
Database log mode                Archive Mode
Automatic archival               Enabled
Archive destination              USE_DB_RECOVERY_FILE_DEST
Oldest online log sequence       19
Next log sequence to archive     21
Current log sequence             2
```

If you are using a flash recovery area and you want to define a local destination, you should also use the same syntax:

```
log_archive_dest_1='location=USE_DB_RECOVERY_FILE_DEST
                    valid_for=(ONLINE_LOGFILES,PRIMARY_ROLE)
                    db_unique_name=Matrix'
```

If you are still not using the flash recovery area, you would use the old disk path structure:

```
log_archive_dest_1='location=/u03/oradata/Matrix/arch/
                    valid_for=(ONLINE_LOGFILES,PRIMARY_ROLE)
                    db_unique_name=Matrix'
```

Note that in both cases, the DB_UNIQUE_NAME points to the database on which you define this destination, not a remote standby database. In this case, we are on the primary Matrix, so if you are using the DB_UNIQUE_NAME attribute, you need to specify Matrix as the target DB_UNIQUE_NAME.

**NOTE**
*If you are using a flash recovery area, you do not need to set up a local archiving destination using the LOCATION attribute.*

■   **MANDATORY**   This is one of the most dangerous attributes to a standby destination. Basically, it *requires* that the redo from an ORL file *must* be sent to this destination. If the redo cannot be sent, the ORL file that contains the redo cannot be reused until it has been sent to this standby database. If the standby database is not reachable and the primary database cycles through all the available ORL files, production will stall. Of course, a local destination is mandatory so that the file is on disk somewhere, but you do not need to set it at that location either. One of your local archiving destinations will be mandatory by default.

**CAUTION**
*Do not set the MANDATORY attribute.*

■   **MAX_FAILURE**   This attribute is the most misunderstood of all the attributes. People tend to think it indicates how many times the LGWR will attempt to reconnect to a failed standby before giving up and continuing to allow redo to be generated. This is not the case, however. If you set this attribute, it defines how many times at log switch time the LGWR will attempt to reconnect to a failed standby database. If you set MAX_FAILURE to 5, for example, the LGWR will try to connect to a failed standby database five times as it cycles though its ORL files. If it switches five times and still is unsuccessful in reconnecting to the standby database, it will stop trying—forever. You will either have to manually reenable the destination or it will be reenabled when the primary database restarts.

**CAUTION**
*Do not set the* `MAX_FAILURE` *attribute.*

■ **NOREGISTER** This is the last of the attributes for the `LOG_ARCHIVE_DEST_n` parameter that we will discuss. By default, Data Guard will request that any redo it sends to a standby gets registered at that standby database when it is archived to disk. For a physical standby database, that means it will be registered into the standby control file. For a logical standby database, that means SQL Apply will register the file in its metadata. Data Guard does not require this attribute. It is useful for Streams target databases when using downstream capture.

**CAUTION**
*Do not set the* `NOREGISTER` *attribute.*

■ **LOG_ARCHIVE_DEST_STATE_n** This is the companion parameter to `LOG_ARCHIVE_DEST_n` and was necessary for two reasons in the past: to enable predefinition of primary role `LOG_ARCHIVE_DEST_n` parameters on a standby and not have the archive process try to use them until you enabled the destination with this parameter; and to set up an `ALTERNATE` destination as described previously. The first reason is no longer valid (you now have `VALID_FOR` for that reason) and unless you are using `ALTERNATE`, then the second reason is also unnecessary. Since these default to `ENABLE` anyway, you do not need to set them for your destinations.

```
log_archive_dest_state_1=enable
```

### Standby Role Parameters

■ **DB_FILE_NAME_CONVERT** On a standby database, this parameter allows you to logically move the data files from their primary database location to your standby database location. This is necessary if your on-disk structures and layout are different between the two systems. Until the standby database becomes a primary database, this translation occurs only at runtime. Once you either switchover or failover to the standby, these values are hardened into the control file and the data file headers. It functions by doing simple string replacement.

```
db_file_name_convert='/Matrix/','/Matrix_DR0/'
```

This would translate the data filenames from this

```
'/u03/oradata/Matrix/sysaux.dbf'
```

to this:

```
'/u03/oradata/Matrix_DR0/sysaux.dbf'
```

Similarly,

```
db_file_name_convert='+DATA','+RECOVERY'
```

would point the database to the data files in the ASM diskgroup +RECOVERY instead of +DATA. The rest of the path could remain the same. In our example, standby creation using ASM, you will not need to define this parameter.

- **LOG_FILE_NAME_CONVERT**   The log file convert performs the same function as DB_
  FILE_NAME_CONVERT but for the ORL files and any SRL files.

  ```
  log_file_name_convert='/Matrix/','/Matrix_DR0/'
  ```

- **FAL_SERVER**   *FAL* is the *Fetch Archive Log* capability that is much more today than it
  was in Oracle9*i* Release 1 Data Guard. It is only used on a physical standby database
  and is the process whereby a physical standby can go and fetch a missing archive log file
  from one of the databases (primary or standby) in the Data Guard configuration when it
  finds a problem, sometimes referred to as *reactive gap resolution*. But the FAL technology
  has been enhanced over the last three releases to the point at which you almost no
  longer need to define the FAL parameters. With the arrival of *proactive gap resolution*, in
  Oracle9*i* Release 2, almost every type of gap request from a physical or logical standby
  database can be handled by the ping process of the primary database.

  In normal processing on the primary, the archive process, which has been designated as
  the ping process, will poll all the standby databases looking for gaps in the redo and also
  process any outstanding gap requests that were posted by the Apply processes. A
  physical standby database can use the FAL technology when requesting a gap file from
  more than just the primary. If, for example, the primary was not reachable when a
  physical standby encountered a gap in the redo, it could ask one of the other standby
  databases. To do this, you would define the FAL_SERVER parameter as a list to TNS
  names that exist on the standby server that point to the primary and any of the standby
  databases. On our Matrix_DR0 database, for example, we would add the primary
  (Matrix) and our other standby Matrix_DR1:

  ```
  fal_server='Matrix, Matrix_DR1'
  ```

- **FAL_CLIENT**   The FAL client is the TNS name of the gap-requesting database that the
  receiver of the gap request (the FAL_SERVER) needs so that the archive process on the
  FAL server database can connect back to the requestor. On our standby 'Matrix_DR0'
  we would pass the name 'Matrix_DR0' as the client name so that 'Matrix' or
  'Matrix_DR1' would be able to make a connection back to 'Matrix_DR0' and send
  the missing archive log files.

  ```
  fal_client='Matrix_DR0'
  ```

  'Matrix_DR0' must be defined in the FAL server's TNS names file so that Data Guard
  can make a connection to the standby database. Since we will be setting the redo
  transport parameters between all of these databases, we would have to set up the TNS
  names for them as well, so if you use the same TNS name in the FAL parameters, the TNS
  names will already be defined. If you choose to use a different name, you must add the
  name(s) to all of the TNS names files on all systems. As with FAL_SERVER, the FAL_
  CLIENT parameter is only valid for physical standby databases.

- **STANDBY_FILE_MANAGEMENT**   This is the final parameter we discuss in this chapter.
  This simple parameter is used only for physical standby databases. Whenever data
  files are added or dropped from the primary database, the corresponding changes are
  automatically made on the standby database when this parameter is set to AUTO. As
  long as the top level directory exists on the standby or can be found by virtue of the DB_
  FILE_NAME_CONVERT parameter, Data Guard will execute the data definition language
  (DDL) on the standby to create the data file. It will even go as far as creating any missing

subdirectories if it can. By default, this parameter is set to `'MANUAL'`, which means that the apply process on a physical standby database will not create the new data file and you will have to unwind its attempt and create the data file manually.

```
standby_file_management='AUTO'
```

The only time you may need to change this parameter back to `'MANUAL'` is when you need to manipulate the ORL file definitions on the physical standby. SRL files can be added without changing this parameter. If you do need to add or drop online log files on the physical standby database (due to a change on the primary database, for example), you can dynamically set this parameter to `'MANUAL'`, execute the DDL, and then set it back to `'AUTO'` without bouncing the standby database.

### The End of the Parameters and Attributes

After reading all about the parameters and attributes that you can use (or not use in some cases), you should have a good understanding of the function of each of them as well as the ramifications of configuring them incorrectly.

On that note, we hope that you do not already have a headache, because we're going to shock you now. If you choose to use the Data Guard Broker (even if you do not use Grid Control) you do *not* have to set any of these parameters yourself. The Broker will do it for you. We'll talk about that after you create your standby.

## Using RMAN in Oracle Database 11g

Oracle Recovery Manager (RMAN) has included the ability to create a standby database from a backup of the primary database for many releases. While the process was not much different from the documented procedure in the Data Guard Concepts and Administration manual, it also required extra storage for the backup of the primary database. And unless you were willing to go the extra mile and use a more unconventional (but documented) method, you also had to maintain a connection to the primary database during the entire creation process. RMAN in Oracle Database 11g implemented a new process that removes both of these complications while adding the ability to perform transparently most of the setup and file copying that you had to do by hand just to get up and running. This new creation is invoked by an addition to the DUPLICATE FOR STANDBY command, FROM ACTIVE DATABASE.

Just how simple is this new procedure for creating a physical standby database? It actually takes about 75 percent fewer steps. Let's get started.

**Step 1: Prepare the Standby System**  First we are going to make some more assumptions. You have performed the tasks outlined earlier in the "Before You Start" section. You have also configured the network as per your tuning with the TNS names for each database in the correct files as well as the listener connections. Your next step is to set up the standby system. You need to do four things:

1. *Create a static listener entry for the standby.* Even though we have discussed the Broker listener entry, in this case, you just need a standard static entry in the standby listener:

```
SID_LIST_LISTENER =
  (SID_LIST =
    (SID_DESC =
      (GLOBAL_DBNAME = Matrix_DR0)
      (ORACLE_HOME = /scratch/OracleHomes/OraHome111)
```

```
        (SID_NAME = Matrix_DR0)
  ))
```

Make sure you reload the listener after you put this in the listener file:

```
lsnrctl reload
```

2. *Create an init.ora file with only the DB_NAME in it.* All you need for the parameter file at this point is a one-line initialization file with any value for DB_NAME. This file will be replaced by RMAN during the standby creation process.

```
echo 'DB_NAME=WHATEVER' > $ORACLE_HOME/dbs/initMatrix_DR0.ora
DB_NAME=WHATEVER
```

3. *Create a password file with the primary database SYS password.* To create a standby database, RMAN requires that the SYS user perform the various setup and database creation. Oracle Database 11*g* introduced a new level of security in the password file that makes it necessary to have a copy of the primary database's password in order to operate a physical standby database. Merely creating a new password file with the same password will no longer work, as internally it will be different between the two systems and Data Guard will not be able to connect to the standby. To allow RMAN to create the standby database, you can create a password file with the same SYS password used by the primary database, because RMAN will copy the password file from the primary system as part of the procedure.

```
orapwd file=$ORACLE_HOME/dbs/orapwMatrix password=oracle
```

4. *Start up the standby instance.* Since no control file exists yet for the standby database, you cannot mount the standby instance, but you must start it up NOMOUNT so RMAN can attach to the instance:

```
setenv ORACLE_SID Matrix_DR0
sqlplus '/ as sysdba'
SQL> STARTUP NOMOUNT;
```

**Step 2: Prepare the Primary System**   Unlike older methods of standby creation, where you had to take backups of the primary database and make them available to the RMAN duplicate procedure before you could create the standby database, with the new RMAN functionality in Oracle Database 11*g* you need to do very little at the primary database to create your standby database. Because you should be using SRL files, if you create them on the primary database before you create the standby, RMAN will create them for you on the standby database provided

---

**The Password File**

Whenever a change is made to the primary database SYS password, you must copy the primary database password to all physical standby databases. You can no longer create a password manually at the physical standby. Logical standby databases do not have this restriction as they will execute the password DDL.

## Multiplexing SRL Files

Currently, issues with multiplexed SRL files can cause problems in some cases, potentially at failover time. The presence of a second copy of the SRL files is not always a benefit, as the extra I/O might slow down redo transport, and any failure of an SRL would be treated like a gap by Data Guard. We do not recommend multiplexing the SRLs.

it can find the appropriate directory. We are using ASM, and as such we have defined the appropriate ASM file creation parameters so we can use the short version of the SRL creation SQL. Assuming we have three ORL groups of 50MB each, we will create four SRL groups on the primary database:

```
db_create_file_dest='+DATA'
db_create_online_log_dest_1='+FLASH'
db_create_online_log_dest_2='+DATA'

SQL> ALTER DATABASE ADD STANDBY LOGFILE   '+FLASH' SIZE 50M
SQL> ALTER DATABASE ADD STANDBY LOGFILE   '+FLASH' SIZE 50M
SQL> ALTER DATABASE ADD STANDBY LOGFILE   '+FLASH' SIZE 50M
SQL> ALTER DATABASE ADD STANDBY LOGFILE   '+FLASH' SIZE 50M
```

You will notice that we added the +FLASH to the ADD STANDBY LOGFILE command. This was done to prevent the database from multiplexing the SRL files. By not specifying an actual filename for the SRL, the database will automatically put the file into the flash recovery area using an Oracle Managed Files (OMF) name. But if you are using ASM (as we are), the database will automatically multiplex the SRL files just as it does with the ORL files, once in +DATA and once in +FLASH.

Unlike a fatal error on an ORL file on the primary that will crash the instance, if an error were to occur on an SRL file, the redo transport would merely be terminated and when the primary reconnected the new RFS would choose another SRL and the sequence that was en route at the SRL failure point will be sent as a gap. And since having more than one member for an SRL increases the I/O, which could have an impact on redo transport, you may not want the extra overhead.

At this time, we do not recommend using multiplexed SRL files.

**Step 3: Create the Standby**    This is it: time to create the standby database. The following RMAN script will create your standby database into the standby instance you just started. This script can be run from the primary system "pushing" the data to the standby system, or from the standby system "pulling" the data from the primary system. All that's required is that the TNSNAMES be set up correctly and that you start up RMAN.

```
RMAN> CONNECT TARGET sys/oracle@Matrix;
      CONNECT AUXILIARY sys/oracle@Matrix_DR0;
run {
   allocate channel prmy1 type disk;
   allocate channel prmy2 type disk;
```

```
allocate channel prmy3 type disk;
allocate channel prmy4 type disk;
allocate channel prmy5 type disk;
allocate auxiliary channel stby1 type disk;
duplicate target database for standby from active database
  spfile
      parameter_value_convert 'Matrix','Matrix_DR0'
      set 'db_unique_name'='Matrix_DR0'
      set control_files='+DATA/Matrix_DR0/control.ctl'
      set db_create_file_dest='+DATA'
      set db_create_online_log_dest_1='+FLASH'
      set db_create_online_log_dest_2='+DATA'
      set db_recovery_file_dest='+FLASH'
      set DB_RECOVERY_FILE_DEST_SIZE='10G'
  nofilenamecheck;
}
```

This simple RMAN script will now go off and do all the work you used to have to do
manually to create your standby database. And it will be doing a live backup of the PRIMARY
database and a live restore of the standby database without any interim storage.

When this script is complete, you will have a fully functioning physical standby database that
is ready to receive redo. Of course, it will not yet be receiving redo nor applying it.

If you log in to the physical standby database, you can see the results of the creation and
where it has put everything:

```
[Matrix_DR0] sql
SQL*Plus: Release 11.1.0.6.0 - Production on Tue Aug 5 00:33:05 2008
Copyright (c) 1982, 2007, Oracle.  All rights reserved.
Connected to:
Oracle Database 11g Enterprise Edition Release 11.1.0.6.0 - Production
With the Partitioning, OLAP, Data Mining and Real Application Testing options
Unique Name                Current Role     Open Mode   Protection Mode
-------------------------- ---------------- ----------- --------------------
Matrix_DR0                 PHYSICAL STANDBY MOUNTED     MAXIMUM PERFORMANCE

SQL> select name from v$datafile;
 NAME
-----------------------------------------------------------------------------
+DATA/matrix_dr0/datafile/system.261.661890009
+DATA/matrix_dr0/datafile/sysaux.269.661890013
+DATA/matrix_dr0/datafile/undotbs1.266.661890103
+DATA/matrix_dr0/datafile/users.267.661890057
+DATA/matrix_dr0/datafile/example.268.661890027

SQL> select type, member from v$logfile;
TYPE       MEMBER
--------   -------------------------------------------------------------------
ONLINE     +DATA/matrix/onlinelog/group_3.260.661354309
ONLINE     +FLASH/matrix/onlinelog/group_3.296.661354317
ONLINE     +DATA/matrix/onlinelog/group_2.258.661354293
```

```
ONLINE       +FLASH/matrix/onlinelog/group_2.297.661354303
ONLINE       +DATA/matrix/onlinelog/group_1.301.661354277
ONLINE       +FLASH/matrix/onlinelog/group_1.298.661354285
STANDBY      +FLASH/matrix_dr0/onlinelog/group_4.295.661357229
STANDBY      +FLASH/matrix_dr0/onlinelog/group_5.294.661357269
STANDBY      +FLASH/matrix_dr0/onlinelog/group_6.293.661357285
STANDBY      +FLASH/matrix_dr0/onlinelog/group_6.293.908747594

10 rows selected.
```

The ORL files still have the name of the primary database in their path at this time. This will be corrected when you start up the apply process. You will have to move the SPFILE into ASM manually if required. But since we are using ASM, the data files were all put in the correct place without the CONVERT parameters.

Of course, you notice that apart from the two parameters DB_UNIQUE_NAME and LOG_FILE_NAME_CONVERT (needed to correct the SRL filenames), we set no other Data Guard parameters in our script. This procedure is all you need to do if you are going to use the Data Guard Broker to manage this configuration. If the Data Guard Broker is your choice, then you are done. You can go directly to Chapter 5. The beauty of the Data Guard Broker is that when you create the configuration and add the details about the standby database you just created (a name and a connect identifier), the Broker will set up all the parameters and operations for you.

If you choose not to use the Data Guard Broker, you can finish the job right here by adding the necessary parameters to the standby and the primary databases, starting Redo Apply, and configuring the redo transport at the primary.

Manually add in the standby and primary role initialization parameters to the standby:

```
SQL> ALTER SYSTEM SET FAL_SERVER=Matrix;
SQL> ALTER SYSTEM SET FAL_CLIENT=Matrix_DR0;
SQL> ALTER SYSTEM SET LOG_ARCHIVE_CONFIG='DG_CONFIG=(Matrix,Matrix_DR0)';
SQL> ALTER SYSTEM SET STANDBY_FILE_MANAGEMENT=AUTO;
SQL> ALTER SYSTEM SET LOG_ARCHIVE_DEST_2='service=Matrix
       ASYNC DB_UNIQUE_NAME=Matrix
       VALID_FOR=(primary_role,online_logfile)';
```

Then start the Apply process on the standby database:

```
SQL> ALTER DATABASE RECOVER MANAGED STANDBY DATABASE
       USING CURRENT LOGFILE DISCONNECT;
```

Return to the primary database and configure redo transport and switch logs and add the standby role parameters:

```
SQL> ALTER SYSTEM SET LOG_ARCHIVE_CONFIG='DG_CONFIG=(Matrix,Matrix_DR0)';
SQL> ALTER SYSTEM SET LOG_ARCHIVE_DEST_2='service=Matrix_DR0
       ASYNC DB_UNIQUE_NAME=Matrix_DR0
       VALID_FOR=(primary_role,online_logfile)';
SQL> ALTER SYSTEM SWITCH LOGFILE;
SQL> ALTER SYSTEM SET FAL_SERVER=Matrix_DR0;
SQL> ALTER SYSTEM SET FAL_CLIENT=Matrix;
SQL> ALTER SYSTEM SET STANDBY_FILE_MANAGEMENT=AUTO;
```

We titled this section "The Power User Method" because you are going to create a standby database manually. The preceding RMAN script and subsequent parameter settings as well as the starting of the apply and redo transport can all be done in one single RMAN script, which is an expanded script of the preceding one:

```
RMAN> connect target sys/oracle@Matrix;
      connect auxiliary sys/oracle@Matrix_DR0;
run {
    allocate channel prmy1 type disk;
    allocate channel prmy2 type disk;
    allocate channel prmy3 type disk;
    allocate channel prmy4 type disk;
    allocate channel prmy5 type disk;
    allocate auxiliary channel stby1 type disk;
    duplicate target database for standby from active database
      spfile
          parameter_value_convert 'Matrix','Matrix_DR0'
          set 'db_unique_name'='Matrix_DR0'
          set control_files='+DATA/Matrix_DR0/control.ctl'
          set db_create_file_dest='+DATA'
          set db_create_online_log_dest_1='+FLASH'
          set db_create_online_log_dest_2='+DATA'
          set db_recovery_file_dest='+FLASH'
          set DB_RECOVERY_FILE_DEST_SIZE='10G'
              set log_archive_max_processes='5'
              set fal_client='Matrix_DR0'
              set fal_server='Matrix'
              set standby_file_management='AUTO'
              set log_archive_config='dg_config=(Matrix,Matrix_DR0)'
              set log_archive_dest_2='service=Matrix LGWR ASYNC
                  valid_for=(ONLINE_LOGFILES,PRIMARY_ROLE)
                  db_unique_name=Matrix';
          sql channel prmy1 "alter system set

log_archive_config=''dg_config=(Matrix,Matrix_DR0)''";
          sql channel prmy1 "alter system set
                      log_archive_dest_2=''service=Matrix_DR0 LGWR ASYNC
                      valid_for=(ONLINE_LOGFILES,PRIMARY_ROLE)
                      db_unique_name=Matrix_DR0''";
          sql channel prmy1 "alter system set log_archive_max_processes=5";
          sql channel prmy1 "alter system set fal_client=Matrix";
          sql channel prmy1 "alter system set fal_server=Matrix_DR0";
          sql channel prmy1 "alter system set standby_file_management=AUTO";
          sql channel prmy1 "alter system archive log current";

          allocate auxiliary channel stby type disk;
          sql channel stby "alter database recover managed standby database
                      using current logfile disconnect";
      nofilenamecheck;
}
```

Once this script has run, not only will you have a complete physical standby database created and running, but all the parameters will be configured (on both the primary and the standby databases in preparation for switchover), Redo Apply will be started on the standby, and Redo Transport will be started on the primary database.

## Using the RMAN Oracle Database 10g Method

In both Oracle Database 10*g* and 11*g*, the RMAN DUPLICATE FOR STANDBY command restores the data files from backup sets and recovers the database (applying incremental and archived logs backups) to the current system change number (SCN).

As mentioned, this procedure can be useful for setting up a Data Guard standby database or reinstantiating the old primary database as a new standby database after a failover operation. But it is also paramount for recovering a standby database after media failure or a disaster—stuff happens to standby databases, too!

To get started, you need to meet all the prerequisites set out in the "Before You Start" section as with the 11*g* procedure. But a lot more steps and manual work are required to make this work.

1.  Prepare the standby system.

2.  Get the necessary files and create the backups (database and control file).

3.  Copy the required files.

4.  Prepare the standby database.

5.  Restore the backup.

6.  Configure the standby database.

7.  Finalize the primary database.

**Step 1: Prepare the Standby System**   Make sure you have performed the tasks outlined in the "Before You Start" section. You must configure the network as per your tuning with the TNS names for the primary database in the TNSNAMES file. In addition, create the various directories for the dump parameters and, if you are not using ASM, the directories where the data files, control files, online log files, and archive log files will be placed.

**Step 2: Get the Necessary Files and Create the Backups**   You need to gather four main files for transport to the target standby system to be able to create a standby database using this method:

■   The initialization parameters

■   The password file

■   A backup of the database

■   The control file backup (as a standby control file)

In preparation for these files, create a staging directory in which you will place the required files so that they can be transferred to the standby system:

```
mkdir /scratch/oracle/Stage
```

While it is possible to restore the spfile from an RMAN backup, it is easier to obtain a text version of the parameters from the primary database since you need to edit them by hand on the standby system before you can create your physical standby database:

```
SQL> create pfile=/scratch/oracle/Stage/initMatrix_DR0.ora from spfile;
```

As opposed to the Oracle Database 11g method, you cannot just create a password file with the same SYS password as the primary database, because RMAN in the 10g method will not copy the password file from the primary system as part of the procedure. You need to copy the password file from the primary system to your target standby system. Put a copy of the password file from the primary database into your staging directory:

```
cp $ORACLE_HOME/dbs/orapwMatrix /scratch/oracle/Stage/orapwMatrix_DR0
```

Remember that it is no longer possible to use orapwd and create a password file for the standby database with the same SYS password. You must copy the password file from the primary system to each standby system on which you plan on creating a standby database.

Create a compressed backup file of the entire primary database and place it in the staging directory. It is possible to create a full backup into the usual backup directory (the flash recovery area, for example), and then make sure that you place it in the same location on the standby system. However, since our flash recovery area is in ASM, it is easier to place the backup file directly into our staging area:

```
rman target /
RMAN> BACKUP AS COMPRESSED BACKUPSET DEVICE TYPE DISK
      FORMAT '/scratch/oracle/Stage/Database%U' DATABASE PLUS ARCHIVELOG;
```

At this point, you can obtain a copy of the control file for the standby creation. Remember that you cannot simply copy the current control file, because that will not work to instantiate a Data Guard standby database. This copy of the current primary database control file will be in a standby format and must be made after you have created the backup of the primary database. This can be done with SQL*Plus or RMAN, but since we are already working in RMAN, we will use the following command:

```
RMAN> BACKUP FORMAT '/scratch/oracle/Stage/Control%U'
      CURRENT CONTROLFILE FOR STANDBY;
```

**Step 3: Copy the Required Files**   All of the necessary files are now in your staging directory on the primary system.

```
[Matrix] ls -l
total 349912
-rw-r-----  1 matrix g900   10289152 Sep  7 04:25 Control27jpvcq8_1_1
-rw-r-----  1 matrix g900   97857024 Sep  6 22:56 Database23jpupeu_1_1
-rw-r-----  1 matrix g900  247267328 Sep  6 23:01 Database24jpuph9_1_1
-rw-r-----  1 matrix g900    1146880 Sep  6 23:02 Database25jpupqr_1_1
-rw-r-----  1 matrix g900    1366528 Sep  6 23:02 Database26jpuprg_1_1
-rw-r--r--  1 matrix g900       2182 Sep  6 22:47 initMatrix_DR0.ora
-rw-r-----  1 matrix g900       1536 Sep  6 22:47 orapwMatrix_dr0
```

Copy these files to your standby system into the same directory using a network copy or some kind of external transport mechanism—moving the files on tape, for example, or physically moving the disks to the standby system. If you are going to be using tape to make the RMAN backup, the only things you need to copy are the initialization parameter and password files.

**Step 4: Prepare the Standby Database** If your primary and standby sites are exactly the same, you do not need to modify many of the parameters in the init.ora file from the primary database. At a minimum, you need to change the DB_UNIQUE_NAME to the name of the standby, in our case 'Matrix_DR0'.

```
*.DB_UNIQUE_NAME='Matrix_DR0'
```

If your disk structure is different, you also need to add in the filename conversion parameters so that the files go to the correct location on disk. Again, if you are using ASM, this is not necessary for the creation of the standby but will be required for later data file additions to the primary database. If you are not using the same disk structure, they would look something like this.

```
*.DB_FILE_NAME_CONVERT='/matrix/','/matrix_dr0/', '/MATRIX/','/MATRIX_DR0/'
*.DB_LOG_NAME_CONVERT='/matrix/','/matrix_dr0/' , '/MATRIX/','/MATRIX_DR0/'
```

**Step 5: Restore the Backup** Once the parameters are all set and the various directories have been created, start the standby up in NOMOUNT mode, and using RMAN connect to the primary database as the target (in RMAN terminology) and the standby instance as the auxiliary:

```
setenv ORACLE_SID Matrix_DR0
sqlplus '/ as sysdba'
SQL> STARTUP NOMOUNT;
rman target sys/oracle@Matrix auxiliary /
Recovery Manager: Release 10.2.0.3.0 - Production on Sun Jan 25 13:53:57 2009

Copyright (c) 1982, 2005, Oracle.  All rights reserved.
connected to target database: Matrix (DBID=3892409046)
connected to auxiliary database: Matrix (not mounted)

RMAN> DUPLICATE TARGET DATABASE FOR STANDBY NOFILENAMECHECK DORECOVER;
```

If you encounter an error, RMAN-06024, when running this command, you have most likely encountered a bug that was not fixed until release 10.2.0.4. You would see the following output:

```
RMAN-00571: ===========================================================
RMAN-00569: =============== ERROR MESSAGE STACK FOLLOWS ===============
RMAN-00571: ===========================================================
RMAN-03002: failure of Duplicate Db command at 01/25/2009 15:03:55
RMAN-03015: error occurred in stored script Memory Script
RMAN-06026: some targets not found - aborting restore
RMAN-06024: no backup or copy of the control file found to restore
```

The problem is that when RMAN sets the SCN to restore to, it sets it too low and the backup save set with your standby control file in it cannot be used. Above the error, you would see the script RMAN runs to restore the standby control file:

```
contents of Memory Script:
{
    set until scn  2463499;
```

```
restore clone standby controlfile;
sql clone 'alter database mount standby database';
}
```

A `LIST BACKUP;` in RMAN would show you that your standby control file backup piece is at an SCN higher than the number it is trying to use:

```
BS Key   Type LV Size        Device Type Elapsed Time Completion Time
-------  ---- -- ----------  ----------- ------------ ---------------
11       Full    6.86M        DISK        00:00:01     25-JAN-09
         BP Key: 11   Status: AVAILABLE  Compressed: NO  Tag:
TAG20090125T145951
         Piece Name: /scratch/oracle/Stage/Control0dk5mv77_1_1
   Standby Control File Included: Ckp SCN: 2463571      Ckp time: 25-JAN-09
```

The simple fix to this problem is to switch log files at the primary and restart the duplicate. There is no need to disconnect your RMAN session from the primary and the standby instance while the switch is performed.

**Step 6: Configure the Standby Database**    Add the SRL files to the standby database for redo transport:

```
SQL> ALTER DATABASE ADD STANDBY LOGFILE   '+FLASH' SIZE 50M;
SQL> ALTER DATABASE ADD STANDBY LOGFILE   '+FLASH' SIZE 50M;
SQL> ALTER DATABASE ADD STANDBY LOGFILE   '+FLASH' SIZE 50M;
SQL> ALTER DATABASE ADD STANDBY LOGFILE   '+FLASH' SIZE 50M;
```

The Temp file has been added for you by RMAN. You can now finish defining the Data Guard parameters that will be necessary in the standby role as well as the primary role when a switchover (or failover) occurs:

```
SQL> ALTER SYSTEM SET FAL_SERVER=Matrix;
SQL> ALTER SYSTEM SET FAL_CLIENT=Matrix_DR0;
SQL> ALTER SYSTEM SET LOG_ARCHIVE_CONFIG='DG_CONFIG=(Matrix,Matrix_DR0)';
SQL> ALTER SYSTEM SET STANDBY_FILE_MANAGEMENT=AUTO;
SQL> ALTER SYSTEM SET LOG_ARCHIVE_DEST_2='service=Matrix
        ASYNC DB_UNIQUE_NAME=Matrix
        VALID_FOR=(primary_role,online_logfile);
```

And start the Apply process on the standby database:

```
SQL> ALTER DATABASE RECOVER MANAGED STANDBY DATABASE
        USING CURRENT LOGFILE DISCONNECT;
```

This will create and clear the ORL files so that they exist when the standby becomes a primary.

**Step 7: Finalize the Primary Database**    Add the SRL files so that they are in place for a future role transition:

```
SQL> ALTER DATABASE ADD STANDBY LOGFILE   '+FLASH' SIZE 50M;
SQL> ALTER DATABASE ADD STANDBY LOGFILE   '+FLASH' SIZE 50M;
SQL> ALTER DATABASE ADD STANDBY LOGFILE   '+FLASH' SIZE 50M;
SQL> ALTER DATABASE ADD STANDBY LOGFILE   '+FLASH' SIZE 50M;
```

Set the Data Guard parameters on the primary database that will be used to send redo to the standby. Also set those parameters that will be used when the primary becomes a standby database after a role transition:

```
SQL> ALTER SYSTEM SET LOG_ARCHIVE_CONFIG='DG_CONFIG=(Matrix,Matrix_DR0)';
SQL> ALTER SYSTEM SET LOG_ARCHIVE_DEST_2='service=Matrix_DR0
      ASYNC DB_UNIQUE_NAME=Matrix_DR0
      VALID_FOR=(primary_role,online_logfile)';
SQL> ALTER SYSTEM SET FAL_SERVER=Matrix_DR0;
SQL> ALTER SYSTEM SET FAL_CLIENT=Matrix;
SQL> ALTER SYSTEM SET STANDBY_FILE_MANAGEMENT=AUTO;
```

To start sending redo, switch log files on the primary:

```
SQL> ALTER SYSTEM SWITCH LOGFILE;
```

You now have a fully functioning physical standby database. For more details on this procedure, you can refer to the Oracle paper "Using Recovery Manager with Oracle Data Guard in Oracle Database 10g."[14] This procedure is similar to the procedure that Grid Control uses to create standby databases that are in Oracle Database 10g Release 2 or earlier. The FROM ACTIVE DATABASE method is used for databases that are in Oracle Database 11g.

# Creating a Logical Standby

Over the years since logical standby databases were introduced in Oracle9i, the procedure used to create a logical standby has gotten better, easier, and less intrusive on your primary database. In Oracle9i you pretty much had to suffer downtime of the primary to take a cold backup and build the LogMiner dictionary to be sure that SQL Apply would work when you started the logical standby database. At one point, someone (none of us) wrote a procedure using a hot backup to create a logical standby database in Oracle9i, but it was fraught with potential failures and did not always work. We were party, however, to the authoring of a procedure that used a physical standby database in a very special manner to create a logical standby database in Oracle9i, which resulted in minimal downtime of the primary database.[15] Those procedures became obsolete and should never be used once you are using Oracle Database 10g Release 1 and later.

In Oracle Database 10g Release 1, you could take a hot backup of your primary database to create a logical standby database since the concept of a logical standby control file was introduced. That procedure still stands, but only for 10.1 databases and in a special rolling upgrades case in 10.2 and should otherwise never be used with 10g Release 2 and later.

Starting with Oracle Database 10g Release 2, the procedure became even easier, and next we are going to describe the procedure you should always follow. The old methods (with the one exception in 10.2) are obsolete.

## Make Sure You Can Support a Logical Standby

Unlike a physical standby database, a logical standby database is not an exact copy of your primary database. A lookup by ROWID on the logical standby will not return the same data returned by the primary database. In addition, several data types and storage types are supported by a logical standby.

---

[14] See www.oracle.com/technology/deploy/availability/pdf/RMAN_DataGuard_10g_wp.pdf.
[15] Note 278371.1 "Creating a Logical Standby with Minimal Production Downtime"

It is important that you identify any unsupported objects, as it means the affected table will not be maintained on the logical standby database and no error message will be written to the alert log or anywhere else.

You can run two commands on your primary database that will help you identify the parts of your database that will not be maintained by SQL Apply. The first will show you what schemas in the database are ignored by default by SQL:

```
SELECT OWNER FROM DBA_LOGSTDBY_SKIP WHERE STATEMENT_OPT = 'INTERNAL SCHEMA';
```

Any redo for the schemas listed by this command will be skipped. As such, anything that you might put into one of these schemas will also be skipped.

The second command will tell you which tables in the primary database that are also in supported schemas will be skipped automatically by SQL Apply:

```
SQL> SELECT DISTINCT OWNER,TABLE_NAME FROM DBA_LOGSTDBY_UNSUPPORTED
        ORDER BY OWNER,TABLE_NAME;
OWNER                              TABLE_NAME
--------------------------------   --------------------------------
OE                                 CATEGORIES_TAB
OE                                 CUSTOMERS
OE                                 PURCHASEORDER
OE                                 WAREHOUSES
PM                                 ONLINE_MEDIA
PM                                 PRINT_MEDIA
SH                                 DIMENSION_EXCEPTIONS
 8 rows selected.
```

The database used for this query was a normal seed database with the demo schemas loaded. To look further into why a particular table is not supported, you can drill down into the view and look at the unsupported columns of a table:

```
SQL> SELECT COLUMN_NAME,DATA_TYPE FROM DBA_LOGSTDBY_UNSUPPORTED
        WHERE OWNER='OE' AND TABLE_NAME = 'CUSTOMERS';
COLUMN_NAME                        DATA_TYPE
--------------------------------   --------------------------------
CUST_ADDRESS                       OBJECT
PHONE_NUMBERS                      VARRAY
CUST_GEO_LOCATION                  OBJECT
```

Since OBJECT and VARRAY are data types that SQL Apply does not support, all redo for this table (and all the others in the first query) will be skipped immediately. Do not confuse *apply* with *transport*. The redo for these tables is still going to be sent by Data Guard to the logical standby, as all redo is. But SQL Apply will ignore the redo for those skipped tables as it finds it in the redo stream.

One thing to remember is that all of the tables displayed by the first query will exist in the logical standby because it started its life as a physical standby where everything was supported. You cannot rely on a simple test that looks for the existence of any data in those tables on the logical standby, as they will return data, just not any new data. You need to run these queries and look at each object to make sure you can live without it as well as understand what else will be discarded based on SQL Apply not supporting the feature, such as OLTP Compression in the Advanced Compression option.

Rather than repeat all the unsupported objects here, we suggest that you refer to the *Data Concepts and Administration* manual, Appendix C,[16] to determine whether your primary database can sufficiently support a logical standby database. If you are using a version of Oracle prior to 11g, please refer to the manual for that release, as each version has a different set of what is supported and what is not. If you are using Oracle Database 10g Release 2, also refer to the MAA "SQL Apply Best Practices" white paper.[17]

Once you have passed the "supported or not" test, you also need to make sure that those objects that will be maintained by SQL Apply are uniquely identified. If they are not, you risk falling dramatically behind the primary database. The following command will give you a list of all tables that have a uniqueness problem:

```
SQL> SELECT OWNER, TABLE_NAME FROM DBA_LOGSTDBY_NOT_UNIQUE;
OWNER                                TABLE_NAME
------------------------------       ------------------------------
SCOTT                                BONUS
SCOTT                                SALGRADE
SH                                   SALES
SH                                   COSTS
SH                                   SUPPLEMENTARY_DEMOGRAPHICS
```

On a side note, the manual says you should cross-check this list with the unsupported list by adding a NOT IN to the above query, but this no longer seems to be necessary.

```
SQL> SELECT OWNER, TABLE_NAME FROM DBA_LOGSTDBY_NOT_UNIQUE
       WHERE (OWNER, TABLE_NAME) NOT IN
       (SELECT DISTINCT OWNER, TABLE_NAME FROM DBA_LOGSTDBY_UNSUPPORTED);
OWNER                                TABLE_NAME
------------------------------       ------------------------------
SCOTT                                BONUS
SCOTT                                SALGRADE
SH                                   SALES
SH                                   COSTS
SH                                   SUPPLEMENTARY_DEMOGRAPHICS
```

However, just because a table shows up in the view doesn't mean that it really is bad, just that you will get a lot of extra redo being written to the ORLs and hence sent to the standby databases (all of them, physical or logical—remember that redo transport has nothing to do with the Apply services). The view also has a column called, surprisingly enough, BAD_COLUMN, that if equal to Y, means you have a column that cannot be logged to the redo stream for uniqueness use, so then you could end up updating the wrong row at the logical standby database. You must fix these tables by adding some uniqueness or a disabled rely constraint:

```
SQL> SELECT OWNER, TABLE_NAME FROM DBA_LOGSTDBY_NOT_UNIQUE
       WHERE (OWNER, TABLE_NAME) NOT IN
       SELECT DISTINCT OWNER, TABLE_NAME FROM DBA_LOGSTDBY_UNSUPPORTED)
       AND BAD_COLUMN = 'Y';
no rows selected
```

---

[16] See http://download.oracle.com/docs/cd/B28359_01/server.111/b28294/data_support.htm#CHDGFADJ.

[17] See www.oracle.com/technology/deploy/availability/pdf/MAA_WP_10gR2_SQLApplyBestPractices.pdf.

We don't have any entries where the BAD_COLUMN is equal to Y, so we're OK, right? Well, not really. If you have any tables in the "not unique" view, even without the BAD_COLUMN of Y, you still need to fix the uniqueness on those as well; otherwise, you are going to be writing out a large unnecessary amount of redo. For example, take the Sales History SUPPLEMENTARY_DEMOGRAPHICS table:

```
SQL> DESC SH.SUPPLEMENTARY_DEMOGRAPHICS
 Name                                      Null?    Type
 ----------------------------------------- -------- --------------
 CUST_ID                                   NOT NULL NUMBER
 EDUCATION                                          VARCHAR2(21)
 OCCUPATION                                         VARCHAR2(21)
 HOUSEHOLD_SIZE                                     VARCHAR2(21)
 YRS_RESIDENCE                                      NUMBER
 AFFINITY_CARD                                      NUMBER(10)
 BULK_PACK_DISKETTES                                NUMBER(10)
 FLAT_PANEL_MONITOR                                 NUMBER(10)
 HOME_THEATER_PACKAGE                               NUMBER(10)
 BOOKKEEPING_APPLICATION                            NUMBER(10)
 PRINTER_SUPPLIES                                   NUMBER(10)
 Y_BOX_GAMES                                        NUMBER(10)
 OS_DOC_SET_KANJI                                   NUMBER(10)
 COMMENTS                                           VARCHAR2(4000)
```

All of these columns are going to be written out to the redo stream whether they changed or not, just so SQL Apply can find the right row on the logical standby. We quote from the *Oracle Utilities* manual, Chapter 18, under "Supplemental Logging":[18]

> *If the table has neither a primary key nor a non-null unique index key, then all columns except LONG and LOB are supplementally logged; this is equivalent to specifying ALL supplemental logging for that row. Therefore, Oracle recommends that when you use database-level primary key supplemental logging, all or most tables be defined to have primary or unique index keys.*

By the way, this applies to any table that has this uniqueness problem, even those that SQL Apply says are unsupported. You will be generating redo for them as well, shipping it to the standby databases and having it thrown away.

Finally, when you have these uniqueness issues and you resolve them with a disabled RELY constraint, you still need to go to the logical standby and add an index for the tables that are supported by SQL Apply; otherwise, you are going to be doing a lot of full table scans and SQL Apply performance is not going to be very good.

This, too, is documented in the *Data Guard Concepts and Administration* manual in Chapter 4 for the version you are running.

### Start with a Physical Standby
Using one of the methods described in the preceding section of this chapter, create a physical standby database. If you are using the Broker, do not add this new physical standby database to

---

[18] See http://download.oracle.com/docs/cd/B28359_01/server.111/b28319/logminer.htm#i1021068.

your Broker configuration. If you are using an existing physical standby that is Broker controlled, you must disable the target database from the Broker before continuing. Once the new (or existing) physical standby is synchronized with the primary database, shut down the MRP using the CANCEL qualifier:

```
SQL> ALTER DATABASE RECOVERY MANAGED STANDBY DATABASE CANCEL;
```

You must shut down the MRP at this point because the next thing the physical standby will see from a Data Guard point of view is the redo you are going to generate when you build the LogMiner dictionary. If the MRP applied the redo from the dictionary build, you would be past the point at which you wanted the physical standby to become a logical standby.

At this point, if you are also following the instructions outlined in Chapter 4 of the *Data Guard Concepts and Administration* manual, you are told to modify your local archiving parameters on the primary database to point the archiving of the ORL files to one directory and the archiving of the SRL files to another directory if the primary might ever become a logical standby database due to a role transition. Later on in the process, you are told to do the same thing on the logical standby.

The reason behind this splitting of the archive logs (those generated by the logical standby and those coming in from the primary database) is due to the fact that in previous versions (Oracle Database 10g Releases 1 and 2), a logical standby's incoming archive log files (those being sent by the primary database) could not be placed in the flash recovery area. This was because the flash recovery area did not know what they were and considered them "foreign" files, so it did nothing with them.

If you are not using a flash recovery area, then you do need to make the changes as described in Sections 4.2.3.1 and 4.2.4.2 of the Data Guard manual.[19] Since we are using a flash recovery area, we need make no archiving parameter changes here since SQL Apply and the flash recovery area now cooperate fully with each other and the various log files are maintained by the flash recovery area as normal.

The stage is now set for the dictionary build that has always been necessary to create a logical standby database. In the past, the build was created as a standby alone command (Oracle9i), as part of the logical standby control file build (Oracle10g Release 1), and then back as a command (without the need for a logical standby control file) in 10g Release 2. Go to the primary database and execute the BUILD command:

```
SQL> EXECUTE DBMS_LOGSTDBY.BUILD;
```

This package basically performs these functions:

1.  Enables supplemental logging on the primary database. This is the same result as executing the following SQL command yourself:

    ```
    SQL> ALTER DATABASE ADD SUPPLEMENTAL LOG DATA
            (PRIMARY KEY, UNIQUE INDEX) COLUMNS;
    ```

2.  Builds the LogMiner dictionary of the primary database metadata so that the logical standby will know what to do with the redo that is being sent from the primary.

---

[19] See http://download.oracle.com/docs/cd/B28359_01/server.111/b28294/create_ls.htm#i93974.

3. Figures out how far in the redo the MRP will have to process the redo to apply all transactions that occurred before the build.

4. Identifies at what SCN in the redo SQL Apply has to start mining redo to get all the transactions that committed after the MRP finished apply redo to the physical standby database.

The build process has to wait for all existing update transactions to complete to determine the recovery SCN for the MRP. These transactions will be those that the MRP has to complete on the physical standby before it can become a logical standby. Any transactions that start during the build process are the transactions that SQL Apply has to process and apply after the conversion to logical standby is complete.

One thing to be careful about with this process: The supplemental logging will be enabled on the primary database and only on the target physical standby after it becomes a logical standby. That way, if you switchover between the primary and the logical standby, the new primary will generate the required supplemental logging. However, if you have other physical standby databases that are your disaster recovery failover targets and the logical standby is going to be used primarily as a reporting database, then you must go to each one of the other physical standbys and execute the ALTER DATABASE ADD SUPPLEMENTAL LOG DATA (PRIMARY KEY, UNIQUE INDEX) COLUMNS; command to enable supplemental logging on each physical standby database. Other than the control file being updated, nothing will actually happen until the physical standby database becomes the primary, at which point it would start generating redo with the supplemental logging and the logical standby will quite happily follow along. If, however, you forget to do this and you switchover (or failover) to one of your physical standby databases, it would start generating redo without the supplemental logging and your logical standby would be rendered useless. If you forget, you will have to follow the steps in this section to re-create your logical standby database.

Unfortunately, you do have to shut down all auxiliary instances and disable the cluster on the target standby if your physical standby is a Real Application Clusters (RAC). Shut down all but the instance on which the MRP was running—your actual target instance. Once they are all done, then disable the cluster and bounce the standby.

```
SQL> ALTER SYSTEM SET CLUSTER_DATABASE=FALSE SCOPE=SPFILE;
SQL> SHUTDOWN IMMEDIATE;
SQL> STARTUP MOUNT EXCLUSIVE;
```

When you get close to Chapter 8, you will be quite happy to discover that during a switchover, this RAC instance shutdown is no longer necessary for a logical standby. But that's another chapter. Let's continue, shall we?

### Supplemental Logging

If you create a logical standby you *must* manually enable supplemental logging on all physical standby databases other than the one that is to become the logical standby database using the ALTER DATABASE ADD SUPPLEMENTAL LOG DATA (PRIMARY KEY, UNIQUE INDEX) COLUMNS; SQL command.

Let's recap what we've done so far. We have

1. Created a physical standby database
2. Let it get synchronized with the primary
3. Stopped the MRP
4. Built the LogMiner dictionary
5. Made the standby a single instance temporarily if it was a RAC

If you haven't done all this, then check to see what you might have missed. The order is very important.

You are now ready to tell the MRP that it needs to continue applying redo, but only to the recovery point SCN that was placed in the redo stream by the dictionary build. You would use a special format of the MRP command:

```
SQL> ALTER DATABASE RECOVER TO LOGICAL STANDBY MatrixD1;
```

If you make a mistake at this point and enter the normal managed recovery command, the MRP will process all the redo it has been receiving, including the dictionary build. If this happens, you need to start over at the "get synchronized" part and rebuild the dictionary.

On the other hand, if you entered this command but forgot to build the dictionary or the dictionary build was not successful for some reason, this command will hang. You can, of course, cancel it by entering the CANCEL command in another window, figure out what went wrong, and try the build again.

You will notice that the ALTER DATABASE RECOVER TO LOGICAL STANDBY MatrixD1; command is looking for a database name. If you followed our best practices outlined in this chapter when you created the physical standby, it will already be set up to run under a new SID and DB_UNIQUE_NAME—in our case, we used Matrix_DR0 for clarity. Unfortunately, the DB_NAME parameter is still limited to eight characters (as our primary database is with Matrix). Since everything else is done with the instance name (SID) and a physical standby has the same DB_NAME as the primary, this was not a problem. But now you have to change the actual database name of the standby so it can become a logical standby database. You cannot use 'Matrix_DR1' as that will exceed the limit. So we leave everything else as is and use 'MatrixD1' as our new name. Data Guard will change the database name (DB_NAME) and set a new database identifier (DBID) for the logical standby. Since we are using an SPFILE, the DB_NAME parameter will be changed automatically for us. If we were using a PFILE, then we must edit the file manually before restarting the logical standby database to continue the process.

### The Password File
In 11g you do not re-create the password file when converting your physical standby to a logical standby. If you do, it will not work. If you are in 10g, you must continue to re-create the password file after the RECOVER TO LOGICAL command and before restarting the database.

At this point, you can re-enable the cluster database parameter, if you had a RAC, and then restart and open the new logical standby database:

```
SQL> SHUTDOWN;
SQL> STARTUP MOUNT;
SQL> ALTER DATABASE OPEN RESETLOGS;
```

Before you proceed to the next step and actually start SQL Apply, you need to answer one question: Are you building this logical standby on the same system as the primary database or on a system with a physical standby database that has the exact same on-disk structure as the primary? If you are building this logical standby on the same system as the primary database, then you have to tell SQL Apply to skip any ALTER TABLESPACE DDL; otherwise, SQL Apply could find the primary or physical standby database's data files and potentially do some damage when processing any ALTER TABLESPACE DDL. You do this by executing the following package on your logical standby database:

```
SQL> EXECUTE DBMS_LOGSTDBY.SKIP('ALTER TABLESPACE');
```

This will put information into the logical standby metadata that will tell SQL Apply to ignore any of these DDL commands it finds in the redo stream. We will discuss this package and more in Chapter 4.

Everything is ready now. The physical standby has been through its changes and is now ready to serve in its new capacity as your logical standby. All that remains to do is start SQL Apply. Since we followed the correct procedure when we created our physical standby, several SRL files have already been created, so we can start SQL Apply in real-time apply mode using the IMMEDIATE keyword:

```
SQL> ALTER DATABASE START LOGICAL STANDBY APPLY IMMEDIATE;
```

SQL Apply will now start up the various processes as outlined in Chapter 1 and start to mine the redo that was sent during our creation process. New redo from the primary will start coming in as soon as the primary database switches the online log since redo transport was already set up for our physical standby. Do not expect to see new data from your primary database appear in the logical standby tables right away, as SQL Apply must first parse the redo from the primary, find the dictionary, and build the LogMiner dictionary into the logical standby. After that, the rest of the redo can be applied until the logical standby is caught up with the primary. Many more details on logical standby databases and SQL Apply will be discussed in Chapter 4.

# Data Guard and Oracle Real Application Clusters

How does all of the material in this chapter differ when RAC is involved? To be honest, not as much as many people think. Let's review what is involved in setting up and maintaining a Data Guard standby. As we said at the beginning of the creation section, you need a database, which means the following:

- Listener
- TNS names to find the standby and the primary
- Initialization parameters

- Password file (plus service if you are on Windows)
- Control file
- Data, undo, and temporary files
- Redo logs (online and standby)

Considering that you are setting up your primary, Matrix, to have a standby Matrix_DR0 on a remote system following the steps in this chapter, what do you do and what is different?

You configure the listeners at the primary and standby systems. With RAC, you add listeners at the appropriate systems—we're talking about what Data Guard connects to; though you may have other listeners that the clients use and that perform intelligent load balancing, they do not matter to us at this point.

You define TNS names to point from Matrix to Matrix_DR0, and from Matrix_DR0 to Matrix on the two systems. You now have multiple systems, and you add each system address to each of the TNS names, or you use the virtual IP (VIP) so that each TNS name can find all of the target's RAC systems when one node fails. You make sure all nodes in the cluster have the TNS entries. This is no different from the process you underwent when you set up your client TNS names to the RAC.

Initialization parameters, as far as Data Guard's parameters are concerned, have to be the same on each RAC node—that is, *.whatever. Password files are copied to more than one standby system—nothing different there.

The database is backed up once from the primary, and the backup gets restored once in RAC and non-RAC cases (ASM or no ASM), so you do not have more than one "database." You had to adjust the ORL files to accommodate the extra redo threads, and you do the same for the SRL files.

As far as creation is concerned, that's it. Setting up the standby RAC itself is the most complex part. And even that is made easier in Grid Control 10.2.0.5 with standby databases that are in 11.1.0.7. The Convert to Cluster Database Wizard will now convert a physical standby database from single instance to RAC so you don't even have to perform those manual steps.

Switchover and failover, the Broker, and especially client failover have some features that change the way you work when you introduce RAC into the picture, but even those differences are few and will be discussed in the appropriate chapters.

# Conclusion

It has been a long journey, but we hope it has been worth it. We realize that this chapter has offered a lot of material, but it is important for you to understand what you must do to prepare for Data Guard and to understand the workings and parameters before you begin creating standby databases. More than 70 percent of the trouble people have with Data Guard is due to misunderstanding and incorrect configuration in the standby creation process. If you get this part right, the rest will follow along smoothly and you will get to sleep at night.

# CHAPTER
3

## Redo Processing

he backbone of any physical standby database is essentially its ability to recover from crashes and other mishaps. Before we go too deep into Data Guard physical standby and its architecture, you need to understand how redo is generated and how Oracle's recovery methodology is leveraged in physical standby databases.

This chapter discusses redo recovery essentials, and at the end of the chapter, we will piece it all together by describing the life of a transaction. This chapter also covers best practices and tools to improve managed recovery rates as well as briefly review the 11g corruption detection failures.

# Important Concepts of Oracle Recovery

Recovery deals mainly with *redo*, data that recovery can use to reconstruct all changes made to the database. Even "undo" records are protected by redo data. The following describes the important concepts and components of Oracle recovery:

- **Redo change vectors** A change vector describing a single change to a single data block.

- **Redo record** A collection or group of change vectors that describe an atomic change. The term *atomic* means that this group of changed blocks is either all successful or all unsuccessful during recovery.

- **System change number (SCN)** One of the most important pieces of recovery, because it describes a point in time of the database. When a transaction starts, its reference point for database data consistency is relative to the SCN of when it started. The SCN is bumped up every time a transaction is committed. From a recovery standpoint, the SCN defines where recovery will start and when recovery may end. The SCN is used in various layers within Oracle code—for example, data concurrency, redo ordering, database consistency, and database recovery. The SCN is stored in the redo log as well as the controlfile and datafile headers.

- **Checkpoint** A point in time when all items are of a consistent state. The most important concept of checkpoints is that all recovery is bounded by the database checkpoint—that is, roll-forward recovery is bounded by the checkpoint. An Oracle database includes several types of checkpoints, most notably a *thread* checkpoint (local checkpoint), a *database* checkpoint (global checkpoint), and a *datafile* checkpoint.

- **Online redo log (ORL)** Also known simply as redo logs, ORL files contain persistently stored changed redo records. The redo records in the log files are stored in SCN sequential order—that is, the order in which redo was written. When online redo logs are full, they become archived to the archive redo logs.

- **Archived redo log** Archived versions of online redo logs. These files, deemed inactive files, are archived by the archive processes to one or more defined log archive destinations.

## ACID Properties

Oracle's transactions are protected by the *ACID* properties, which state that when a transaction is started, it must follow these basic rules:

- **Atomicity** The entire sequence of actions must be either completed or aborted. The transaction cannot be partially successful. This is also referred to as the *all-or-nothing rule*.

- **Consistency** The transaction moves the system from one consistent state to another.

- **Isolation** A transaction's effects or changes are not visible to other transactions until the transaction is committed.

- **Durability** Changes made by the committed transaction are permanent and must survive system failure.

Notice that the ACID model includes nothing specifically about Oracle; that's because the ACID model is an essential component of database theory and is not Oracle-specific. So why is the ACID model so important for recovery? ACID provides the guarantee of reliability and consistency, and it is an absolute necessity for any database management system.

# Oracle Recovery

Because Oracle's recovery mechanics are driven by the ACID model, its main purpose is to provide data integrity and consistency across failures. The three main failures types are transaction, instance, and media failures. In this section, we focus on instance and media recovery.

## Instance Recovery

Instance recovery occurs when the database instance fails—in other words, the contents of the System Global Area (SGA), or more specifically the buffer cache, are lost. Recovery from instance failure is driven from the ORL files where the changes have been made persistent (the *durability* part of ACID). Crash recovery is simply another case of instance recovery and occurs when a single-node database has crashed and restarts or when all instances of a RAC database fail. The first instance to start up will initiate (crash) recovery. Nevertheless, the mechanics of instance and crash recovery are the same.

The following output from the database alert.log illustrates the recovery progression after the database has been opened from a previous crash:

```
ALTER DATABASE OPEN
Beginning crash recovery of 1 threads
Started redo scan
Completed redo scan
 94354 redo blocks read, 2982 data blocks need recovery
Started redo application at
 Thread 1: logseq 62, block 427
Recovery of Online Redo Log: Thread 1 Group 2 Seq 62 Reading mem 0
  Mem# 0: +DATA/Matrix/redo_02a.log
  Mem# 1: +DATA/Matrix/redo_02b.log
Completed redo application
Completed crash recovery at
 Thread 1: logseq 62, block 94781, scn 678972
 2982 data blocks read, 2982 data blocks written, 94354 redo blocks read
Mon Jul 07 21:44:34 2008
```

Notice that after the database is opened, crash recovery starts by scanning the redo threads of the failed instance (or instances), which is then read and merged by SCN, beginning at the log sequence of the last incremental checkpoint for each thread. This scan generates a list of blocks that require recovery. Recovery then starts at this point, applying recovery redo to these blocks. At the completion of the recovery, a summary of the redo blocks read as well as data blocks read are written to the alert log.

### Thread Merging

*Thread merging* of the redo records is performed to ensure that no update is made to the database out of order, so that all changes are made in the order they were originally made. Thread merging is discussed in detail in Chapter 8.

## Media Recovery

Media recovery occurs when there is a loss of one or more database datafiles or the entire database. Once the necessary database datafiles are restored, the database needs to be recovered either to a specific point in time or up to the point just before the failure. It is important to note that recovery brings the entire database (all online datafiles) to the same consistent point in time, or SCN. Media recovery is driven from the archived redo logs. Since the physical standby architecture is built upon media recovery, it is emphasized here.

The following excerpt from the database alert.log displays media recovery for standby databases:

```
Completed: ALTER DATABASE RECOVER MANAGED STANDBY DATABASE
           THROUGH ALL SWITCHOVER DISCONNECT USING CURRENT LOGFILE
Wed Jul 23 08:43:54 2008
Media Recovery Waiting for thread 1 sequence 35
Wed Jul 23 08:44:01 2008
Redo Shipping Client Connected as PUBLIC
-- Connected User is Valid
RFS[10]: Assigned to RFS process 20724
RFS[10]: Identified database type as 'physical standby'
Primary database is in MAXIMUM PERFORMANCE mode
Primary database is in MAXIMUM PERFORMANCE mode
RFS[10]: Successfully opened standby log 5:
'+FLASH/Matrix_DR0/onlinelog/group_5.257.660730583'
Wed Jul 23 08:44:04 2008
Recovery of Online Redo Log: Thread 1 Group 5 Seq 35 Reading mem 0
  Mem# 0: +FLASH/Matrix_DR0/onlinelog/group_5.257.660730583
Wed Jul 23 08:44:39 2008
Redo Shipping Client Connected as PUBLIC
-- Connected User is Valid
RFS[11]: Assigned to RFS process 20805
RFS[11]: Identified database type as 'physical standby'
Wed Jul 23 19:12:54 2008
Media Recovery Waiting for thread 1 sequence 36
Wed Jul 23 19:12:55 2008
Primary database is in MAXIMUM PERFORMANCE mode
kcrrvslf: active RFS archival for log 5 thread 1 sequence 35
RFS[10]: Successfully opened standby log 4:
'+FLASH/Matrix_DR0/onlinelog/group_5.257.660730583'
Wed Jul 23 19:14:05 2008
Recovery of Online Redo Log: Thread 1 Group 4 Seq 36 Reading mem 0
  Mem# 0: +FLASH/Matrix_DR0/onlinelog/group_4.256.660730567
```

## Life of a Transaction

This section will illustrate a walkthrough of "life of a transaction" as it generates its changes and produces redo, and the log writer process (LGWR) flushes the redo to disk. We will revisit this transaction life cycle later in the chapter in the section "The Components of a Physical Standby."

1.  When a session is about to make changes to data blocks via Data Manipulation Language (DML) operations, such as insert, update, and delete, it must first acquire all the buffer cache locks (exclusive locks).

2.  Once the buffer cache locks are obtained, the redo that describes the changes (change vectors) are generated and stored in the processes' Program Global Area (PGA).

3.  The redo copy latch is obtained, and, while holding the redo copy latch, the redo allocation latch is also obtained. After successfully acquiring the redo allocation latch, space is then allocated in the redo log buffer. Once space is allocated, the redo allocation latch is released. Since this latch has high contention, it must be released as soon as possible.

4.  When the logistics of redo space management have been resolved, the redo generated can be copied from the processes' PGA into the redo log buffer. On completion of the copy, the redo copy latch is released.

5.  The session foreground can now safely tell the LGWR to flush the redo log buffers to disk. Note that the database blocks have not yet been updated with DML changes. At this time, buffer cache buffers are updated.

6.  The LGWR flushes the redo buffers to the ORL and acknowledges the completion to the session. At this point, the transaction is persistent on disk. Notice that no commit has occurred thus far.

7.  At some future time, the database buffers that were previously changed will be written to disk by the database writer process (DBWR) at checkpoint time.

Note that before the DBWR process has flushed the database buffers to disks, the LGWR process must have already written the redo buffers to disk. This explicit sequence is enforced by the *write-ahead logging protocol*, which states that no changes appear in the datafiles that are not already in the redo log. The write-ahead logging protocol provides the ability to guarantee that the transaction can be undone in the event of a transaction failure before it commits, thus preserving transaction atomicity.

As a final point to the life cycle of a transaction, the transaction must be *committed*. The committing of a transaction allocates an SCN and undergoes the same transaction life cycle steps illustrated earlier. The COMMIT is an important element of the transaction because it marks the end of the transaction and thus guarantees that the redo previously generated is propagated to disk. This is also referred to as *log-force at commit*.

## Nologging Operations

The only exception to the write-ahead policy is when direct path writes are employed—for example, direct path load (`sqlload`) or `CREATE TABLE AS SELECT`... insert operations. These transactions do not originate in the buffer cache and thus explicitly use the *write-behind logging protocol*. Nevertheless, redo is generated for direct path write operations and is therefore fully recoverable. Direct path loads occur above the high water mark of the table, so the data is not visible until the redo that moves the high water mark is committed. Thus, the redo describing the load is not written before the blocks.

Most direct path write operations are used in conjunction with the UNRECOVERABLE option. Nologging, or UNRECOVERABLE, operations can be specified for several DML operations, such as the following:

```
CREATE TABLE AS SELECT
CREATE INDEX
ALTER INDEX
ALTER TABLE   ..[MOVE] [SPLIT] PARTITION
SQLLOAD
```

When the UNRECOVERABLE option is specified, no redo is generated for this batch transaction; however, redo is still generated for the database dictionary tables, and a small amount of redo is generated to define an invalidation range (with a starting block address and SCN), reflecting the range of blocks are being changed.

Although the UNRECOVERABLE option is very beneficial when loading large amounts of data efficiently, it has a huge downside when used in Data Guard environments. When media recovery encounters the data blocks within this invalidation range, which occurs when the UNRECOVERABLE operation is used, they are marked as *soft-corrupt*, since they are missing the necessary redo. The physical standby database will then throw the following error:

```
ORA-01578: ORACLE data block corrupted (file # 10, block # 514)
ORA-01110: data file 3: '+data/Matrix_DR0/datafile/users.278.56783987'
ORA-26040: Data block was loaded using the NOLOGGING option
```

This same error would occur on the primary database if you had to perform media recovery. For this reason, it is mandatory that you back up the tablespace datafiles on the primary that were loaded in UNRECOVERABLE mode immediately after the nologging operation is completed. On the standby, if you see this error, you must manually recover from it using one of the methods we will describe in a moment.

You can employ several measures to detect an inadvertent use of nologging operations on your standby database:

- Proactively query for nologging operations on the primary:

```
SQL> SELECT  NAME, UNRECOVERABLE_CHANGE#,
       TO_CHAR(UNRECOVERABLE_TIME,'DD-MON-YYYY HH:MI:SS')
       FROM V$DATAFILE;
```

- Proactively run DBVERIFY to check for nologging operations on the standby:

```
$ dbv file=users.dbf
DBVERIFY - Verification starting : FILE = users.dbf
DBV-00200: Block, dba 35283426, already marked corrupted
DBV-00200: Block, dba 35283427, already marked corrupted
DBV-00200: Block, dba 35283428, already marked corrupted
```

If nologging operations are detected, the following steps can be used to recover the affected datafiles.

**Managed Recovery**

Although the Oracle documentation states that you should use ALTER DATABASE MANAGED STANDBY DATABASE <..> to alter the behavior of managed recovery, you can also use the shortened version: RECOVER MANAGED STANDBY DATABASE <..>. Remember to always use the MANAGED keyword; otherwise, you will be performing manual recovery and bypassing Data Guard.

On the standby database:

1.   Perform a RECOVER MANAGED STANDBY DATABASE CANCEL. This will stop the redo apply.

2.   For the affected nologging files, do this:

     ALTER DATABASE DATAFILE <name> OFFLINE DROP

     This will *offline* the affected datafiles.

3.   Perform a RECOVER MANAGED STANDBY DATABASE DISCONNECT. This will restart the redo apply.

On the primary database:

4.   Using RMAN, back up the affected datafiles and copy them to the standby database and replace the affected files.

5.   Perform a RECOVER MANAGED STANDBY DATABASE CANCEL. This will stop the redo apply.

6.   Online the previously offlined datafiles using this:

     ALTER DATABASE DATAFILE <NAME> ONLINE

7.   Perform a RECOVER MANAGED STANDBY DATABASE DISCONNECT. This will restart the redo apply.

The best method, of course, is to avoid this nologging mess and prevent nologging operations on the primary database in the first place. Following are options that can be used on the primary database for the various levels of enforcement:

■   **Database level**   ALTER DATABASE FORCE LOGGING
    This is the recommended Data Guard setting, as this ensures that all transactions are logged and can be recovered through media recovery or redo apply.

■   **Tablespace level**   ALTER TABLESPACE <NAME> FORCE LOGGING
    As stated, force logging at the database level is the recommended option; however, in special cases it is beneficial to set force logging at the tablespace level—for example, if an application generates large amounts of transient table data where load times are more important than the recovery of these tables, and the transient table data can be easily reloaded after media recovery. In these cases, it may be desirable to group and store all these transient tables into one or more tablespaces that do not have force logging enabled to allow nologging operations. All other tablespaces will have force logging. This option provides finer control over force logging; however, it comes at the expense of higher manageability costs, the need to monitor the use of these nologging tablespaces, and the need to resolve the unrecoverable datafiles at switchover or failover.

- **Table level** [CREATE | ALTER] TABLE <NAME> FORCE LOGGING
  This setting is shown only for the sake of completeness. Setting this at a table level can be cumbersome; therefore, it is recommended to do the force logging at the database level.

# The Components of a Physical Standby

As discussed in Chapter 1, the Data Guard architecture can be categorized into three major components.

- **Data Guard Redo Transport Services** Redo Transport Services are used to transfer the redo that is generated by the primary database to the standby database.
- **Data Guard Apply Services** Apply Services receives and applies the redo sent by Redo Transport Services to the standby database.
- **Data Guard Role Management Services** Role Management Services assist in database role changes in switchover and failover scenarios.

Figure 3-1 illustrates the various components and the data flow in Data Guard physical standby. Keep in mind that these services exist in both physical and logical database configurations. In this chapter, the focus will be on Data Guard physical standby.

It is the combination of transport and apply services that allows the synchronization of a primary and its standby databases. To make this all happen, several Oracle background processes play a key role in the physical standby Data Guard framework.

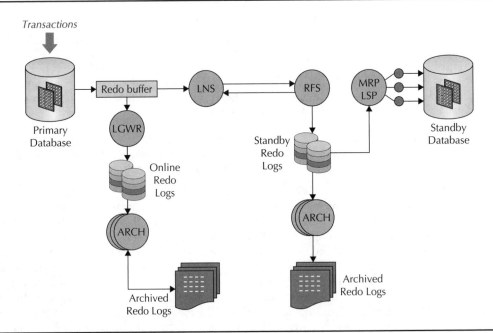

**FIGURE 3-1.** *Data Guard components*

In the primary database, the following processes are important:

- **LGWR**   The log writer process flushes log buffers from the SGA to ORL files.

- **LNS**   The LogWriter Network Service (LNS) reads the redo being flushed from the redo buffers by the LGWR and performs a network send of the redo to the standby site. The main purpose of the LNS process is to alleviate the LGWR process from performing the redo transport role.

- **ARCH**   The archiver processes archives the ORL files to archive log files. Up to 30 ARCH processes can exist, and these ARCH processes are also used to fulfill gap resolution requests. Note that one ARCH process has a special role in that it is dedicated to local redo log archiving only and never communicates with a standby database.

In the standby database, the following processes are important:

- **RFS**   The main objective of the Remote File Server process is to perform a network receive of redo transmitted from the primary site and then writes the network buffer (redo data) to the standby redo log (SRL) files. (SRLs are covered later in this section.)

- **ARCH**   The archive processes on the standby site perform the same functions performed on the primary site, except that on the standby site, an ARCH process generates archived log files from the SRLs.

- **MRP**   The managed recovery process coordinates media recovery management. Recall that a physical standby is in perpetual recovery mode.

- **LSP**   The Logical Standby Process coordinates SQL Apply. This process only runs in a logical standby configuration

- **PR0x**   The recovery server processes read redo from the SRL (when in real-time apply) or the archive log files and apply this redo to the standby database.

Thus far, we have not discussed the standby redo log files (SRLs). The SRLs were introduced to solve two major problems:

- **Data protection**   If SRL files are not used, incoming redo is not kept if the connection to the primary is lost—for example, when the primary database fails, hence when a failover occurs, the data that was being sent at the time of the disconnect is lost. However, if that redo data was written in an SRL, it is persistent and available when the failover occurs.

- **Performance objective**   When the LNS (or an ARCH process after Oracle Database 10gR1) made a connection to the standby, it had to wait while the RFS process created and initialized the archive log on the standby before the LNS/ARCH could start sending redo. This could cause a considerable pause if the log file size was large—such as 500MB or 1GB, which are typical redo log file sizes these days. Since this event occurs at log switch time, the throughput impact on the primary could be high. However, in Oracle Database 10gR2 and 11g, LNS in ASYNC mode will not inhibit the LGWR log switch, but it could potentially impact how far behind the standby could get after a log switch.

As it turns out, Real-TimeApply (RTA) is an inherent side benefit with the advent of configuring the SRL.

SRL files are essentially identical to ORL files, but SLR files are logically distinguished, in that they contain the current redo that is active only on the standby site. Although the primary database will also have SRL files defined, these are inactive on the primary database but will become activated on role management changes (switchover). It is required that the SRL be configured with the same size as the ORL files or the SRLs will not be used. Furthermore, it is recommended to have *N*+1 SRL files per instance defined on the standby site, where *N* is the total number of redo log members per thread on the primary site.

The following `ps` command example shows the important (highlighted) processes on the standby site:

```
racnode1 > ps -ef |grep -i Matrix_DR0
oracle     6507    1  0 21:23 ?        00:00:00 ora_pmon_MATRIX_DR0
oracle     6509    1  0 21:23 ?        00:00:00 ora_vktm_MATRIX_DR0
oracle     6513    1  0 21:23 ?        00:00:00 ora_diag_MATRIX_DR0
oracle     6515    1  0 21:23 ?        00:00:00 ora_dbrm_MATRIX_DR0
oracle     6517    1  0 21:23 ?        00:00:00 ora_psp0_MATRIX_DR0
oracle     6521    1  0 21:23 ?        00:00:11 ora_dia0_MATRIX_DR0
oracle     6523    1  0 21:23 ?        00:00:01 ora_mman_MATRIX_DR0
oracle     6525    1  0 21:23 ?        00:00:01 ora_dbw0_MATRIX_DR0
oracle     6527    1  0 21:23 ?        00:00:01 ora_lgwr_MATRIX_DR0
oracle     6529    1  0 21:23 ?        00:00:02 ora_ckpt_MATRIX_DR0
oracle     6531    1  0 21:23 ?        00:00:00 ora_smon_MATRIX_DR0
oracle     6533    1  0 21:23 ?        00:00:00 ora_reco_MATRIX_DR0
oracle     6535    1  0 21:23 ?        00:00:02 ora_mmon_MATRIX_DR0
oracle     6537    1  0 21:23 ?        00:00:00 ora_mmnl_MATRIX_DR0
oracle     6544    1  0 21:23 ?        00:00:00 ora_arc0_MATRIX_DR0
oracle     6546    1  0 21:23 ?        00:00:01 ora_arc1_MATRIX_DR0
oracle     6548    1  0 21:23 ?        00:00:00 ora_arc2_MATRIX_DR0
oracle     6550    1  0 21:23 ?        00:00:00 ora_arc3_MATRIX_DR0
oracle     8329    1  0 21:31 ?        00:00:00 ora_mrp0_MATRIX_DR0
oracle     8333    1  0 21:31 ?        00:00:01 ora_pr00_MATRIX_DR0
oracle     8335    1  0 21:31 ?        00:00:01 ora_pr01_MATRIX_DR0
```

Now that we have defined the processes that participate in a physical standby Data Guard environment, let's piece together the life cycle of a transaction within the context of a Data Guard environment.

We left off with the LGWR just flushing the redo to disk. This scenario assumes that ASYNC transport is configured along with RTA.

1.  The LNS reads the recently flushed redo from the redo log buffer and sends the redo stream to a standby site using the defined redo transport destination (LOG_ARCHIVE_DEST_n). Since this is ASYNC transport, the LGWR does not wait for any acknowledgment from the LNS on the network send; in fact, it does not communicate with the LNS except to start it up at the database start stage and after a failure of a standby connection.

2.  The RFS on the standby site reads the redo stream from the network socket into network buffers, and then it writes this redo stream to the SRL.

3.  The ARCH process on the standby site archives the SRLs into archive log files when a log switch occurs at the primary database. The generated archive log file is then registered with the standby control file.

**4.** The actual recovery process flow involves three distinct phases, as follows:

- **Log read phase** The managed recovery process (MRP) will asynchronously read ahead the redo from the SRLs or the archived redo logs. The latter case occurs only when recovery falls behind or is not in real-time apply mode. The blocks that require redo apply are parsed out and placed into appropriate in-memory map segments.

- **Redo apply phase** The MRP process ships redo to the recovery slaves using the parallel query (PQ) interprocess communication framework. Parallel media recovery (PMR) causes the required data blocks to be read into the buffer cache, and subsequently redo will be applied to these buffer cache buffers. The "Parallel Media Recovery" section later in this chapter covers the differences between Oracle Database 10g and 11g PMR.

- **Checkpoint phase** This phase involves flushing the recently modified buffers (modified by the parallel recovery slaves) to disk and also the update of datafile headers to record checkpoint completion.

Steps 1 to 4 are continuously repeated until either recovery is stopped or a role transition (switchover or failover) occurs.

## Real-time Apply

When redo is received by an RFS on the standby system, the RFS process writes the redo data to archived redo logs or optionally to the SRL. Since Oracle Database 10g, with RTA, which requires SRL, the Redo Apply will automatically apply redo directly from the SRL. Figure 3-2 illustrates the Redo Apply process flow.

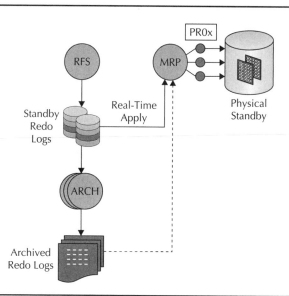

**FIGURE 3-2.** *Redo Apply process flow*

The following command is used to enable the real-time apply feature in physical standby databases. This command is issued on the standby site:

```
SQL> ALTER DATABASE RECOVER MANAGED STANDBY DATABASE
        USING CURRENT LOGFILE DISCONNECT;
```

Keep in mind that if SRLs are not defined when enabling real-time apply, the user will receive an ORA-38500 error message.

To determine whether real-time apply is enabled, query the RECOVERY_MODE column of the V$ARCHIVE_DEST_STATUS view. If the recovery mode indicates MANAGED REAL TIME APPLY, then real-time apply is enabled.

```
SQL> SELECT RECOVERY_MODE FROM V$ARCHIVE_DEST_STATUS
        WHERE DEST_ID=2;
RECOVERY_MODE
----------------------
MANAGED REAL-TIME APPLY
```

Note that if the DELAY attribute is specified in the LOG_ARCHIVE_DEST_n parameter, and real-time apply is enabled, the redo apply lag time is ignored.

In some cases, the redo rate becomes too high and the apply process is unable to keep up with real-time apply. In these scenarios, the MRP (or LSP) automatically performs the redo apply using the archive redo log files. When the redo rate has subsided, the apply will again resume real-time apply using the SRL.

With the advent of real-time apply, Data Guard now provides faster switchover, instant data access, and reporting for read-only (Active Data Guard) physical standby databases. Real-time apply is particularly important for Active Data Guard and logical standby databases as it enables real-time reporting. An additional side benefit of real-time apply is that it allows the apply services to leverage larger redo logs files. As mentioned earlier in the chapter, at redo log boundaries, datafile header updates and checkpoints are performed. Since these are expensive operations, it is recommended that you have larger ORL files (and matching SRL files). Employing larger redo log files with real-time apply allows apply services to recover for longer periods of time, thus minimizing the recovery overhead.

# Scaling and Tuning Data Guard Apply Recovery

Several recommendations can improve the Redo Apply rate as well as redo transmission. The following describes how to scale and tune Redo Apply.

### Top Six Considerations for Tuning the Recovery Rate

The following considerations and best practices can improve the recovery rate. Note that other Data Guard tuning considerations, such as redo shipping, were covered in Chapter 2.

- *During media recovery, at each log boundary (log switch), Oracle does a full checkpoint and updates all the file headers.* It is recommended that you increase the primary database's ORL as well as the standby database's SRL sizes so that a log switch occurs at a minimum of 15-minute intervals.

- *Use the PARALLEL option while in managed recovery.* The next section covers parallel media recovery in more detail.

- *Implement real-time apply*. Although this recommendation does not directly affect recovery rate, it does directly affect (improves) your recovery time objective (RTO).

- *Media recovery hinges on the DBWR's ability to write out modified blocks from the buffer cache to disk as efficiently as possible*. It is very important that the DBWR processes have enough I/O bandwidth to perform this task. To increase DBWR throughput, always use native asynchronous I/O by setting DISK_ASYNCH_IO=TRUE (default). In the rare case that asynchronous I/O is not available, use DBWR_IO_SLAVES to improve the effective data block write rate with synchronous I/O.

- *As with all cases of database recovery, the most important factor is I/O bandwidth*. Oracle media recovery is driven and predominantly dependent on I/O bandwidth, and without sufficient I/O bandwidth, the apply process will be stalled. Thus it is important to ensure that enough I/O bandwidth is available on the standby site. Calibrate_IO is a new utility introduced in 11g. That allows a user to gauge the overall I/O throughput on the server. For more details on Calibrate_IO see MetaLink Note 727062.1.[1]

- *Remember that media recovery is heavily dependent on the Oracle buffer cache*. Thus a large database cache size can significantly improve media recovery performance. While in managed recovery mode, several standby database SGA components can be reduced, and this memory can be moved and reallocated to the DB_CACHE_SIZE. For example, memory associated with the JAVA_POOL, DB_KEEP_CACHE_SIZE, DB_RECYCLE_CACHE_SIZE, and a portion of the SHARED_POOL_SIZE can be reallocated to the DB_CACHE_SIZE. However, upon switchover or failover, the new primary will require a production-ready set of initialization parameters that can support the production workload.

## Parallel Media Recovery

One of the most frequently asked questions when deploying Data Guard is "How can my standby database keep up with the redo rate of the primary database?" This question can become even more interesting when the primary database is a RAC database.

The answer to this question is *parallel media recovery (PMR)*. In both 10g and 11g, the MRP process will perform a scan (asynchronous read) of the redo logs, and parse and build redo change segment maps. This part of the recovery phase is easily handled by the single MRP process. Once this map segment is built, the apply process can begin, and this is where parallelism occurs. Although Oracle Database 10g and 11g both provide parallel scalable recovery, the two versions have different semantics and approaches.

In Oracle Database 10g, parallel query (PQ) slaves were employed to perform the parallel apply. The PQ slaves used messaging to extract redo segments from MRP. The init.ora parameter PARALLEL_EXECUTION_MESSAGE_SIZE or PEMS defines the size of the message that would be exchanged between PQ slaves and MRP. In Oracle Database 10g physical standby systems, it is advised that you set this parameter to 8KB or 16KB, depending on available memory. On 64-bit systems with large amounts of memory (dedicated to shared pool), an 8KB or 16KB PEMS setting is sufficient. On these types of configurations and using the appropriate PEMS setting, upwards to 24MB/sec apply rate can be achieved.

The main issue with 10g managed recovery was the overhead of PQ slave messaging. In Oracle Database 11g, the PQ slave overhead has been assuaged by leveraging Oracle kernel slave

---

[1] See MetaLink Note 727062.1: Configuring and Using Calibrate I/O.

processes (KSV slaves). The KSV slaves can be seen as the PR0x processes. The MRP will relegate the actual (parallel) recovery to the KSV slaves. The PR0x processes will hash to a segment map, read from this map, and apply redo to the standby database. Leveraging KSV slaves removes the need to set the PEMS parameter or even specify the number of slaves needed for recovery. The number of PR0x processes started is dependent on the number of CPUs on the server.

# Tools and Views for Monitoring Physical Standby Recovery

In cases for which media recovery is not keeping up with the apply rate the primary database, the following views and tools need to be reviewed:

- Review key Data Guard views.
- Review Statspack (Oracle Database 11g with Active Data Guard) top wait events.
- Identify I/O bottlenecks in recovery area and data area.
- Monitor CPU usage.

**NOTE**
*Chapter 6 covers the V$ database views in greater detail.*

## Data Guard Views

The following important views can be used to monitor Data Guard physical standby recovery progress. A sample output of each view is also shown.

**V$MANAGED_STANDBY**   This view displays current status information for specific physical standby database background processes. This view can be used to determine activity by process. If your primary database is not a RAC, the column THREAD# in the following query will always contain the number one:

```
SQL> SELECT PROCESS, CLIENT_PROCESS,THREAD#, SEQUENCE#,STATUS
       FROM V$MANAGED_STANDBY;
PROCESS    CLIENT_P    THREAD#   SEQUENCE# STATUS
---------  --------  ----------  ---------- ------------
ARCH       ARCH           1             0 CONNECTED
ARCH       ARCH           1             0 CONNECTED
RFS        N/A            0             0 IDLE
RFS        N/A            0             0 IDLE
RFS        LGWR           1           774 IDLE
RFS        LGWR           2           236 IDLE
RFS        UNKNOWN        0             0 IDLE
MRP0       N/A            1           774 APPLYING_LOG
8 rows selected.
```

**V$DATAGUARD_STATS**   This view displays various information about the redo data. This includes redo data generated by the primary database that is not yet available on the standby database and how much redo has not yet been applied to the standby database. This indirectly shows how much redo data (at the current point in time) could be lost if the primary database crashed.

```
SQL> SELECT * FROM V$DATAGUARD_STATS;
   NAME                              VALUE
-------------------------------   ----------------
apply finish time                 +00 00:00:00.0
apply lag                         +00 00:00:13
estimated startup time            24
standby has been open             N
transport lag                     +00 00:00:05
```

**V$STANDBY_APPLY_SNAPSHOT**   This view provides the current redo apply rate in KB/second:

```
SQL> select to_char(snapshot_time,'dd-mon-rr hh24:mi:ss')
       snapshot_time, thread#, sequence#,  applied_scn,
       apply_rate from V$standby_apply_snapshot;
SNAPSHOT_TIME       THREAD# SEQUENCE#  APPLIED_SCN      APPLY_RATE
-----------------   ------- ---------  ---------------  ----------
15-05-08 15:45:08   1        31527     3273334169433     68234
15-05-08 15:45:08   2        23346     3273334169449     68234
```

**V$RECOVERY_PROGRESS**   This view can be used to monitor efficient recovery operations as well as to estimate the time required to complete the current operation in progress:

```
SQL> select to_char(start_time, 'DD-MON-RR HH24:MI:SS') start_time,
       item, round(sofar/1024,2) "MB/Sec"
       from v$recovery_progress
       where (item='Active Apply Rate' or item='Average Apply Rate');
START_TIME       ITEM                             MB/SEC
-----------      ------------------------------   --------
07-JUL-08 11:49:44 Active Apply Rate                6.15
07-JUL-08 11:49:44 Average Apply Rate               5.90
06-JUL-08 23:13:34 Active Apply Rate                5.76
06-JUL-08 23:13:34 Average Apply Rate               1.73
```

## Physical Data Guard and Statspack

Analyzing performance of the standby database typically meant navigating through many V$ views to collect the required performance data. In addition, due to the read-only nature of Data Guard physical standby, the Statspack utility could not be executed on the standby database. Thus, for database versions of 10g and earlier, any performance analysis of the standby database was generally a manual effort.

In Oracle Database 11g Release 1, users can now leverage Statspack by invoking Statspack from the primary database to collect and store performance data from the standby database. The standby database will need to be opened read-only for the collection, while it is still performing recovery. Note that this requires using the new Active Data Guard option, which requires an additional license.

This section will review the steps to implement the standby Statspack. Note that the new standby Statspack packaging comes with a new set of scripts and packages, most of which start with sb* and reside in $ORACLE_HOME/rdbms/admin.

**Creating the Schema**   The first step in establishing the standby Statspack infrastructure is to run the sbcreate.sql script. This installation script creates the standby Statspack schema on the primary database. This schema is used to house the standby snapshots.

When the sbcreate.sql script is executed, it will prompt for the following items:

- A password for stdbyperf user
- Default tablespace
- Temporary tablespace

Once the script is completed, the standby Statspack schema will be created. In our example, we specified STDBYPERF as the standby user.

**Defining the Standby Database**   Next, you'll need to connect to the primary database as the STDBYPERF user and execute the sbaddins.sql script:

```
SQL> connect stdbyperf/your_password
SQL> @sbaddins
```

When the sbaddins.sql script is invoked, it will prompt for the following:

- The Transparent Networking Substrate (TNS) alias of the standby database instance
- The password of the perfstat user on the standby site

The sbaddins.sql script performs the following tasks:

- Adds the standby instance to the Statspack configuration
- Creates a private database link to the perfstat schema on the standby site
- Creates a separate Procedural Language/Structured Query Language (PL/SQL) package (on the primary database) for each defined standby database

**Creating Statspack Snapshots**   Once the standby database is defined correctly in the STDBYPERF schema, you can begin to take standby Statspack snapshots.

The statspack_<*instance_name*>.snap procedure on the primary database accesses the stats$ views on the standby database via the database link and stores this data in the STDBYPERF on the primary database. In our example, Matrix_DR0 is defined as our standby database (when sddins.sql was executed). For example, while the standby is opened read-only, log in to the primary database as the STDBYPERF user and execute the snap procedure:

```
SQL> connect stdbyperf/your_password
SQL> exec statspack_Matrix_DR0.snap
```

Although most of the standby Statspack report is similar to a standard Statspack report, some very specific standby statistics are collected and presented in the standby report. The following illustrates two new sections of the standby Statspack report of particular interest to the standby database:

- Recovery progress stats
- Managed standby stats

```
Top 5 Timed Events
Event                             Waits   Time(s)   Avg   %Total
--------------------------------  -------- -------  ------ -----
shared server idle wait              32     960     30005   40.0
recovery read                    93,398     767        8   31.9
parallel recovery control message 25,432    536       21   22.3
CPU time                                     28     1.2
latch free                        3,813      25        1    1.0
```
Recovery Progress Stats  DB/Inst: Matrix_DR0/Matrix_DR0 End Snap: 360
-> End Snapshot Time: 07-Jun-08 05:37:42
-> ordered by Item, Recovery Start Time desc

| Recovery Start Time | Item | Sofar | Units | Redo Timestamp |
|---|---|---|---|---|
| 06-Jun-08 06:52:06 | Active Apply Rate | 1,024 | KB/sec | |
| 06-Jun-08 06:52:06 | Active Time | 30,315 | Seconds | |
| 06-Jun-08 06:52:06 | Apply Time per Lo | 709 | Seconds | |
| 06-Jun-08 06:52:06 | Average Apply Rat | 424 | KB/sec | |
| 06-Jun-08 06:52:06 | Checkpoint Time p | 0 | Seconds | |
| 06-Jun-08 06:52:06 | Elapsed Time | 81,943 | Seconds | |
| 06-Jun-08 06:52:06 | Last Applied Redo | 474,368,821 | SCN+Tim | 07-Jun-08 05:37:49 |
| 06-Jun-08 06:52:06 | Log Files | 41 | Files | |
| 06-Jun-08 06:52:06 | Redo Applied | 33,988 | Megabyt | |

```
-----------------------------------------------------------------
```
Managed Standby Stats  DB/Inst: Matrix_DR0/Matrix_DR0  End Snap: 360
-> End Snapshot Time: 07-Jun-08 05:37:42
-> ordered by Process

| Process | pid | Status | Resetlog Id | Thread | Seq | Block Num |
|---|---|---|---|---|---|---|
| Client Proc | Client pid | Blocks | Delay(mins) | | | |
| ARCH | 262 | CLOSING | 655982533 | 1 | 290 | 2013185 |
| ARCH | 262 | | 758 | 0 | | |
| ARCH | 264 | CLOSING | 655982533 | 1 | 289 | 2041857 |
| ARCH | 264 | | 1,671 | 0 | | |
| ARCH | 266 | CLOSING | 655982533 | 1 | 291 | 2023425 |
| ARCH | 266 | | 623 | 0 | | |
| ARCH | 268 | CONNECTED | 0 | 0 | 0 | 0 |
| ARCH | 268 | | 0 | 0 | | |
| MRP0 | 762 | APPLYING_LOG | 655982533 | 1 | 292 | 1879769 |
| N/A | N/A | 2,097,152 | 0 | | | |
| RFS | 17949 | IDLE | 655982533 | 1 | 292 | 1878764 |
| LGWR | 17272 | | 1,006 | 0 | | |
| RFS | 18121 | IDLE | 0 | 0 | 0 | 0 |
| UNKNOWN | 17524 | | 0 | 0 | | |
| RFS | 18280 | IDLE | 0 | 0 | 0 | 0 |
| UNKNOWN | 17517 | | 0 | 0 | | |

```
-----------------------------------------------------------------
```

The following table displays various scripts used to support and manage the standby Statspack:

| Procedure Name | Description | Prompted Info |
|---|---|---|
| sbreport | Generates the standby statistics report. | Database ID, instance number, high and low snapshots ID to create the report |
| sbpurge | Purges a set of snapshots. The script purges all snapshots between the low and high snapshot IDs for the given instance. | Database ID, instance number, low and high snapshots IDs |
| sbdelins | Deletes an instance from the configuration, as well as associated PL/SQL packages. | Instance name |
| sbdrop | Drops the stdbyperf user and tables. The script must be run when connected to SYS (or internal). | |
| sbaddins | Execute this script from the primary database to add a standby instance to the configuration. | TNS alias of the standby database instance, password of the perfstat user on the standby site |

**NOTE**
*We have authored a MetaLink note[2] on using Statspack and an Active Data Guard standby database. As the use of Statspack with Data Guard evolves, we will update this note.*

# Physical Standby Corruption Detection

Earlier in this chapter, we discussed how to detect and avoid user-created corruption problems when nologging operations are allowed on the primary database. But Data Guard can help you detect and recover from many other hardware-created corruption events much faster than many other disaster recovery solutions.

## 11g New Data Protection Changes

This section covers several of the new corruption detection features introduced in Oracle Database 11g. Note that these features are not all specifically for physical standby databases, but for completeness we'll describe the feature and show how standby databases leverage them. The next section will cover the new corruption features for the physical standby.

In Oracle Database 11g, various database components layers and utilities can automatically detect a corrupt block and record it in the V$DATABASE_BLOCK_CORRUPTION view. In pre-11g versions, only RMAN was capable of recording into this view. An Enterprise Manager alert can be triggered whenever a new block (from an unrecoverable event) is recorded in the V$DATABASE_ BLOCK_CORRUPTION view.

---

[2] See MetaLink Note 454848.1: Installing and Using Standby Statspack in 11g R1.

Oracle Database 11*g* also introduced an internal mechanism to provide even better data protection with a thorough block checking mechanism in the database. This block checking can be enabled by setting the DB_ULTRA_SAFE initialization parameter to TRUE. This parameter lets data corruptions be detected in a timely fashion. The DB_ULTRA_SAFE parameter includes the following checks and validations:

- Detects redo corruptions.

- Provides checksum and internal metadata checks.

- Ensures redo is "next change" appropriate to data block.

- Detects lost writes and data block corruptions.

- Validates data block during reads and after updates.

- Detects data block corruption through checksum during reads and through db_block_ checking after DML block operations.

- If ASM redundancy is in use, it then enforces sequential mirror writes on ASM-based datafiles.

The DB_ULTRA_SAFE initialization parameter implicitly enables the setting of other protection-related initialization parameters, including DB_BLOCK_CHECKING, DB_BLOCK_CHECKSUM, and DB_LOST_WRITE_PROTECT.

Note that there may be a performance impact on the application when the DB_ULTRA_SAFE parameter is set on the primary database. The performance impact may vary depending on the number of block changes and available system resources, but generally varies from 1 to 10 percent. This performance impact is higher on the physical standby than on the primary database.

# Data Protection and Checking on a Physical Standby

Physical standby databases inherently provide a strong level of data protection. Out of the box, physical standby's redo apply mechanism implicitly verifies redo headers for correct format and compares the version of data block header with the tail block for accuracy. When DB_BLOCK_ CHECKSUM is set on the physical standby database, it compares the current block checksum with the calculated value. Checksums catch most data block inconsistencies.

In addition, DB_BLOCK_CHECKING validates more internal data block data structures such as Interested Transaction Lists (ITLs), free space, and used space in the block.

So how does this 11*g* new checking capability work with Data Guard physical standby? When DB_LOST_WRITE_PROTECTION is set to TYPICAL on the primary database, the database instance logs buffer cache reads for read-write tablespaces in the redo log; however, when the parameter is set to FULL on the primary database, the instance also logs redo data for read-only and read-write tablespaces.

When DB_LOST_WRITE_PROTECTION is set to TYPICAL or FULL on the physical standby database, the instance performs lost write detection during media recovery.

When the DB_LOST_WRITE_PROTECTION=TYPICAL is set on the primary and standby database instances, the primary database will record buffer cache block reads in the redo log, and this information can be used to detect lost writes in the standby database. This is done by comparing SCN versions of blocks stored on the standby with those in the incoming redo stream. If a block version discrepancy occurs, this implies that a lost write occurred on either the primary or standby database.

Lost writes generally occur when an I/O subsystem acknowledges the completion of a write block I/O, when the write did not get persistently stored on disk. Lost writes occur for various reasons—the most common are faulty host bus adapters (HBAs), firmware bugs, or faulty storage hardware. Lost writes are essentially silent data corruptions in that the corrupted blocks go undetected until the subsequent read, which could be days, weeks, or months later. For this reason, lost writes are extremely difficult to diagnose when they occur. On the subsequent block read, the I/O subsystem returns a block, which is effectively a stale version of the data block.

If the block SCN on the primary database is lower than on the standby database, it detects a lost write on the primary database and throws an internal error (ORA-752). The recommended procedure to repair a lost write on the primary database is to failover to the physical standby and re-create the primary. If the SCN is higher, it detects a lost write on the standby database and throws an internal error (ORA-600 3020). To repair a lost write on a standby database, you must re-create the standby database or affected data files. In both cases, the standby database will write the reason for the failure in the alert log and trace file.

If database corruption is detected on the primary, this can be resolved by failing over to the standby database and restoring data consistency.

It is highly recommended that DB_LOST_WRITE_PROTECT be set to TYPICAL on your primary database and all physical standby databases for the greatest data protection. This setting provides the highest protection with the minimum performance impact. If greater data protection is required and redo apply performance can be slightly sacrificed, set DB_ULTRA_SAFE.

# Conclusion

Oracle Data Guard ensures high availability, data protection, and disaster recovery for enterprise data. However, to appreciate Data Guard fully, you need to understand the essentials of Oracle recovery mechanisms. We hope that this chapter has provided you with a better understanding of the major recovery components and how they fit into the Data Guard framework, as well as more information on the various V$ views used to support and manage a Data Guard environment.

# CHAPTER
## 4

# Logical Standby

ata Guard logical standby was introduced in Oracle Database 9*i* Release 2 as part of the Enterprise Edition. The idea behind a logical standby database is simple: mine the primary database redo and reconstruct the higher level "equivalent" SQL operations that resulted in the database changes, and then apply these equivalent SQL statements to maintain a standby database. The benefits are obvious: the standby database can not only be open for reads, but it can also support additional entities such as indexes and materialized views that can be too expensive to maintain at the primary database. In addition, you can add other tables or even entire schemas to a logical standby database and have complete read-write access to those tables as they are not maintained by SQL Apply. Logical standby databases are a fully integrated feature of Oracle Data Guard and support all role transition operations that are available in the context of a physical standby database.

Here are some of the ways that you can use a logical standby database:

- Offload any application that uses the data replicated from the primary but does not modify it: from running Business Intelligence (BI) analysis on current data as they are replicated, to offloading complete applications. For instance, in the case of a telephone company, this could mean offloading the billing and customer relationship management applications to the logical standby while keeping the call usage tracking application isolated in the primary database.

- Leverage your logical standby database to do a rolling upgrade of Oracle RDBMS software (both between major and minor releases as well as between patch sets). This feature is available for upgrades from a database running the Oracle RDBMS software at versions 10.1.0.3 or later.

- Use a logical standby database as a staging system to propagate changes (either by running local streams capture or by using asynchronous change data capture mechanism) to other databases that may need only a subset of the primary database's data. This is possible only from Oracle Database 11*g* onward.

Three major aspects should be considered when you're dealing with a logical standby database:

- **Dataset available at the logical standby**   This has two parts: First and foremost, you need to characterize what tables are maintained at the logical standby database and how to customize the set of replicated tables. Second, you need to understand how to customize a logical standby database to take advantage of its true power: the ability to offload your applications, allowing the creation of additional schema objects such as materialized views, indexes, and so on.

- **Steady state operational issues**   At steady state, you need to focus on two components: The first is the redo transport service that makes sure that redo generated at the primary database arrives at the standby site promptly and all network disconnections are handled transparently. This was discussed in detail in Chapter 2. The second is the SQL Apply service that mines and applies the redo records to maintain the logical standby database and provides near real-time reports and queries. We will concentrate on the SQL Apply services in this chapter.

- **Role transitions** The SQL Apply service also provides the ability to change roles between a primary and a logical standby database. Role transition can be more complex in logical standby as opposed to steady state operational processes, because application connectivity needs to be considered in addition to the processes involved with database role transitions on the new primary. Role transition, in the context of SQL Apply, should be routinely tested in your disaster recovery (DR) environment. Role transition will not be covered in this chapter, as a more detailed discussion is provided in Chapter 8.

# Characterizing the Dataset Available at the Logical Standby

In this section, we will discuss various issues related to the replicated data: what gets replicated, how replicated data is protected from accidental modification, and how you can write customize solutions where native redo-based replication support is lacking. Then we will discuss various issues related to customizing a logical standby to realize its full potential—including the ability to offload applications from the primary database.

## Characterizing the Dataset Replicated from the Primary Database

A logical standby is first and foremost a standby, so some questions arise naturally:

- What part of the primary database's dataset will be replicated at the logical standby?

- Can we pick and choose the tables that are replicated at the logical standby?

- What prevents users from modifying the replicated data at the logical standby database?

- Is there any way to replicate schema objects that do not have native redo-based replication support?

### Determining What Gets Replicated at the Logical Standby Database

Data Guard logical standby will replicate database schema objects unless they fall under the following three categories:

- The object belongs to the set of internal schemas that SQL Apply does not maintain explicitly.

- The object contains a data type for which native redo-based support is lacking in SQL Apply.

- The object is the target of an explicit skip rule specified by the DBA.

**Determining the Set of Internal Schemas Not Maintained by SQL Apply** You can find the set with the following query:

```
SQL> SELECT OWNER FROM DBA_LOGSTDBY_SKIP
     WHERE STATEMENT_OPT = 'INTERNAL SCHEMA' ORDER BY OWNER;
```

If you issued this query on a database running the 11*g* R1 software, it will return 17 schemas that are automatically skipped by SQL Apply. The two most important ones to point out are SYS and SYSTEM. Why does SQL Apply skip these? Most objects in these schemas (such as the tables OBJ$, COL$, and so on in SYS schema) are maintained through Data Definition Languages (DDLs) or invocations of supplied PL/SQL procedures. SQL Apply replicates DDLs and such invocation of supplied PL/SQL logically, and thus DMLs encountered on system metadata tables are replicated logically by invoking the higher level operations. So remember that if you are planning to use a logical standby database, do not create a user table in one of these internal schemas. They will not be replicated in your logical standby database.

**Determining the Tables Not Being Replicated Because of Unsupported Data Types**   You can find the set of tables with a simple query as well:

```
SQL> SELECT DISTINCT OWNER, TABLE_NAME FROM DBA_LOGSTDBY_UNSUPPORTED;
```

If you want to use an undocumented view that will return the results faster, try the following:

```
SQL> SELECT OWNER, TABLE_NAME FROM LOGSTDBY_UNSUPPORTED_TABLES;
```

We mentioned the presence of explicit skip rules in the list of characteristics as something that will stop replication of a given table. We explore this in more detail in the next section.

## Customizing a Logical Standby Database to Replicate Only a Subset of Tables

Data Guard allows you to specify rules so that you can skip the replication of a table or a set of tables at the logical standby database. Remember, though, that 100 percent of the redo is always transferred to the standby database. The skipping in this case applies to what SQL Apply will actually process at the standby database with that redo.

**Using DBMS_LOGSTDBY.SKIP to Skip Replication of Tables**   Data Guard provides an interface that allows you to use the power of pattern matching to specify set of objects that should not be replicated at the logical standby database. Let's look at the interface in more detail:

```
DBMS_LOGSTDBY.SKIP (
STMT         IN VARCHAR2,
SCHEMA_NAME IN VARCHAR2 DEFAULT NULL,
OBJECT_NAME IN VARCHAR2 DEFAULT NULL,
```

---

### Myth Buster: Standard Log-based Replication Can Give You an Equivalent of a Logical Standby Database

As with all myths, there is an element of truth to this. If all you want is data stored in your tables, you can get an equivalent of a logical standby through third-party replication solutions. But your database is more than the data contained in your tables. What about your jobs? What about your Virtual Private Database (VPD) policies? What about planned and unplanned events and the guarantee of zero data loss? What about transparent migration of your applications that depend on sequences? The truth is, if you want a turnkey one-way replication of your whole database that provides you with high availability and disaster recovery in one package, there is no substitute for Data Guard Logical Standby.

```
PROC_NAME    IN VARCHAR2 DEFAULT NULL,
USE_LIKE     IN BOOLEAN DEFAULT TRUE,
ESC          IN CHAR1 DEFAULT NULL);
```

In essence, you can specify the type of statements (Data Manipulation Language [DML] or DDL), as specified by the `stmt` argument, on which to apply the skip rules. The `schema_name` and `object_name` arguments can take wildcards. The `use_like` indicates whether SQL Apply should use the `LIKE` condition to match the pattern or look for an exact match, and `esc` behaves the same way you would expect the *escape character* to behave when used in a `LIKE` condition.

The most important argument is `proc_name`, which you can specify for DDL statements. It allows you to specify a procedure that will be invoked before the DDL statement can be executed, and it can return a new DDL statement for SQL Apply to execute or ask SQL Apply to stop with an error. Note that you cannot specify a user-supplied procedure in the `proc_name` argument if you are specifying a DML skip rule; attempting to do so will result in an ORA-16104 error.[1]

Suppose, for example, we want to skip replication of the table HR.EMPLOYEE. We can issue the following statement:

```
SQL> EXECUTE DBMS_LOGSTDBY.SKIP(STMT => 'DML', SCHEMA_NAME => 'HR', -
            OBJECT_NAME => 'EMPLOYEE');
```

That is simple enough. Note that since we specified DML explicitly, this will skip only DMLs on HR.EMPLOYEE; DDL statements encountered for this table will still be replicated. If we want to skip those, too, we can issue the following statement:

```
SQL> EXECUTE DBMS_LOGSTDBY.SKIP(STMT => 'SCHEMA_DDL', SCHEMA_NAME => 'HR', -
            OBJECT_NAME => 'EMPLOYEE');
```

What if we want to skip all DML operations on all objects in the HR schema? It is simple:

```
SQL> EXECUTE DBMS_LOGSTDBY.SKIP(STMT => 'DML', SCHEMA_NAME => 'HR', -
            OBJECT_NAME => '%');
```

If we want to be more selective and skip all DML operations on tables with the prefix *EMP*, we can write that too:

```
SQL> EXECUTE DBMS_LOGSTDBY.SKIP(STMT => 'DML', SCHEMA_NAME => 'HR', -
            OBJECT_NAME => 'EMP%');
```

We will look at examples of the procedure invocation in later sections. Now that we know how to specify the patterns that govern what will not be replicated at the logical standby database, we are in a position to answer the question we posed in the first subsection: What objects are not being replicated because of the presence of skip rules?

**Determining Which Tables Are Not Being Replicated Because of Skip Rules**   First, here's the catalog view to query to find out which skip rules are active in your logical standby database:

```
SQL> SELECT OWNER, NAME, USE_LIKE, ESC FROM DBA_LOGSTDBY_SKIP
        WHERE STATEMENT_OPT = 'DML';
```

---

[1] In other words, SQL Apply does not allow you to transform a DML statement into a different DML statement. However, it allows you to do such a transformation on a DDL statement.

Although this will show you the skip rules in effect, the query does not provide the list of tables being skipped. That is a little more complicated. We will do this in two steps: First, we will show you how to determine whether a table will match any of the patterns as identified by the skip rules. Second, we will iterate over all tables that are present at the logical standby and apply the determinant on each of them. We will present it as three procedures to highlight the steps involved.

1. Create a function that takes a schema and a table name and returns TRUE if the table is skipped at the logical standby and FALSE otherwise:

```
CREATE OR REPLACE FUNCTION SYS.IS_TABLE_SKIPPED(
TAB_OWNER IN VARCHAR2, TAB_NAME IN VARCHAR2)
RETURN NUMBER
IS
COUNT_MATCH NUMBER := 0;
BEGIN
  SELECT COUNT(*) INTO COUNT_MATCH FROM DBA_LOGSTDBY_SKIP S
  WHERE STATEMENT_OPT = 'DML' AND ERROR = 'N' AND
  1 = CASE
        WHEN USE_LIKE = 'Y' THEN
          CASE
          WHEN ESC = 'Y' THEN
            CASE
            WHEN TAB_OWNER LIKE S.OWNER ESCAPE ESC AND
                 TAB_NAME  LIKE S.NAME  ESCAPE ESC THEN 1 ELSE 0
            END
          WHEN ESC = 'N' OR ESC IS NULL THEN
              CASE
              WHEN TAB_OWNER LIKE S.OWNER AND
                   TAB_NAME  LIKE S.NAME THEN 1 ELSE 0
              END
          END
      WHEN USE_LIKE = 'N' THEN
        CASE
          WHEN TAB_OWNER = S.OWNER AND TAB_NAME = S.NAME THEN 1 ELSE 0
        END
      ELSE 0
        END;
RETURN COUNT_MATCH;
END IS_TABLE_SKIPPED;
```

2. Now create the necessary types for the table function that will allow us to iterate over all tables in the `DBA_ALL_TABLES` view and determine whether the table is explicitly skipped at the logical standby:

```
SQL> CREATE TYPE STANDBY_TAB AS OBJECT (
TABLE_OWNER  VARCHAR2(32),
TABLE_NAME    VARCHAR2(32));
/
SQL> CREATE TYPE STANDBY_SKIPPED_TAB AS TABLE OF STANDBY_TAB;
```

**3.**   Now create the table function:

```
SQL> CREATE OR REPLACE FUNCTION GET_ALL_SKIPPED_TABS
RETURN  STANDBY_SKIPPED_TAB PIPELINED
IS
  TYPE  REF1 IS REF CURSOR;
  OUT_REC STANDBY_TAB := STANDBY_TAB(NULL, NULL);
  CUR1    REF1;
BEGIN
  OPEN CUR1 FOR 'SELECT OWNER, TABLE_NAME FROM DBA_ALL_TABLES';
  LOOP
    FETCH CUR1 INTO OUT_REC.TABLE_OWNER, OUT_REC.TABLE_NAME;
    EXIT WHEN CUR1%NOTFOUND;
    IF (SYS.IS_TABLE_SKIPPED(OUT_REC.TABLE_OWNER, OUT_REC.TABLE_NAME) <> 0)
    THEN
       PIPE ROW(OUT_REC);
    END IF;
  END LOOP;
  CLOSE CUR1;
  RETURN;
END GET_ALL_SKIPPED_TABS;
/
```

You can now use the table function to get all skipped tables:[2]

```
SQL> SELECT * FROM TABLE(SYS.GET_ALL_SKIPPED_TABS) ;
```

**Adding a Previously Skipped Table to the Set of Replicated Tables**   Now we have a way of knowing what tables are skipped at the logical standby due to explicit skip rules. What if we change our minds midway through? Well, it seems simple. All we need to do is to use DBMS_ LOGSTDBY.UNSKIP and remove the rule from our set of skip rules. And it is almost that simple. However, we cannot simply start replicating changes to the table; we first need to get a current snapshot of the table. Data Guard provides a way to do this via its DBMS_LOGSTDBY.INSTANTIATE_ TABLE procedure. Note that SQL Apply must be stopped before we can invoke this procedure, so for a large table, we need to perform this operation during off-peak hours.

```
SQL> EXECUTE DBMS_LOGSTDBY.INSTANTIATE_TABLE (-
     SCHEMA_NAME => 'SALES', TABLE_NAME => 'CUSTOMERS', -
     DBLINK³ => 'INSTANTIATE_TABLE_LINK');
```

How does this work? The procedure internally uses the Oracle Data Pump network interface to lock the source table momentarily to obtain the current system change number (SCN) at the primary database. It then releases the lock and gets a consistent snapshot of the table from the primary database; it also remembers the SCN associated with the consistent snapshot. Now you

---

[2] The example does not filter out tables that you have created locally at the logical standby database. Ideally, these tables are in schemas that are separate from those being replicated from the primary database, and you can filter them out by adding a predicate to the query.

[3] The DBLINK should point to the primary database.

can see why SQL Apply needs to be stopped before you can issue INSTANTIATE_TABLE. It is essential that SQL Apply has not been applied past the SCN at which the table snapshot was taken, since we need to apply all changes that occurred to the table in question after this SCN.

## Protecting Replicated Tables on a Logical Standby

Now that you know what tables are being replicated at the logical standby database, you're probably asking, "So I have the tables, but what prevents some user from connecting to the standby database and modifying them?" In a physical standby database or in the recently introduced Active Data Guard, the answer is easy. Even if you made a mistake and issued a DML, it will fail since the database is either mounted or open in read-only mode. But a logical standby database is an open, read and write database! Fear not. Data Guard is not just a cool feature name—indeed it does guard and protect your data from accidental modification by a user.

A database GUARD can have three possible values: NONE, STANDBY, and ALL. By default, on a primary database, the GUARD is set to NONE. This means that user applications are free to modify any tables to which they have privileges necessary to perform modifications. When the database-level GUARD is set to STANDBY, user applications cannot modify any tables that are being replicated by SQL Apply, but users are free to create new tables or modify tables (either through DDL or DML) that are not being replicated from the primary database. A GUARD setting of ALL (the default for a logical standby) is the most stringent, as it prevents user modifications to all tables in a database, replicated by SQL Apply or not. The NONE and ALL settings are available to all databases (primary or otherwise), whereas the STANDBY setting is meaningful only on a logical standby database.

You can set the GUARD to STANDBY by issuing the following SQL statement:

```
SQL> ALTER DATABASE GUARD STANDBY;
```

You probably do not want to set the logical standby GUARD on the primary database explicitly. If you were to do so, it would quickly bring production to a halt.

```
SQL> CONNECT SYS/ORACLE AS SYSDBA
CONNECTED.
SQL> ALTER DATABASE GUARD STANDBY;
DATABASE ALTERED.
SQL> CONNECT SCOTT/TIGER
CONNECTED.
SQL> UPDATE EMP SET SAL=9999 WHERE EMPNO=7902;
UPDATE EMP SET SAL=9999 WHERE EMPNO=7902
            *
ERROR AT LINE 1:
ORA-16224: DATABASE GUARD IS ENABLED
```

You would get the same results with ALL on the primary database. Of course ALL is a very quick way to make your production database a read-only database without a shutdown.

---

**Myth Buster: Standard Log-based Replication Can Give You an Equivalent to Logical Standby – Part 2**

Without Oracle's integrated SQL Apply solution, a replication solution cannot provide the built-in protection of the GUARD.

## Replicating Unsupported Tables

Let's look at the list of data types that SQL Apply will not support in the current release of Oracle RDBMS (11*g* Release 1):

- Object types and REFs
- Collections (VARRAYs and nested tables)
- XML stored as object-relational and binary XML
- SecureFile large objects (LOBs)
- Compressed tables

So what do you do if you have such data types in your primary database, and you simply cannot do without them at the logical standby database? The situation is not as bleak as you might think. With some amount of programming, you can still deploy a logical standby database as long as you can ensure the following:

- The rate of modification on these tables is not very high.[4]
- You can control when DDL statements are executed on these tables that change the shape of the table (add/drop/modify columns).

If you can ensure the two prerequisites, Data Guard provides you with the means to overcome the native limitation of SQL Apply: Extended Datatype Support (EDS).[5] It does it by allowing you to fire triggers at the logical standby database as changes are being applied to the maintained tables. Now usually triggers are disabled in the context of SQL Apply processes. Why? Say, for example, that you have a table HR.EMPLOYEES in the primary database, with a trigger defined such that every time a new employee is added in the table, an entry is inserted into IT.EMPLOYEES to start a work order to allocate a new computer for the employee. So in the redo stream, you will see redo records related to the original insert to HR.EMPLOYEES followed by a triggered insert to IT.EMPLOYEES.

You obviously do not want SQL Apply to fire the trigger at the logical standby database when it inserts the row in the HR.EMPLOYEES table, since it is going to encounter the insert to

> **Myth Buster: Standard Log-based Replication Can Give You an Equivalent to Logical Standby – Part 3**
>
> Third-party replication products do not have the ability to disable firing of the triggers. So to deploy them, you will have to disable the triggers yourself. This can be problematic, however, since on a role transition, before applications can connect to the new primary database, you will have to run a PL/SQL procedure to enable all triggers that you had previously disabled. This increases your downtime.

---

[4]We realize that this is vague. However, whether the rate is high or low depends so much on your data and hardware configuration that we are unable to be more specific.

[5]See the MAA paper "Extended Datatype Support: SQL Apply and Streams" at www.oracle.com/technology/deploy/availability/pdf/maa_edtsoverview.pdf.

the IT.EMPLOYEES in the redo log anyway. However, you do want the trigger to be present at the logical standby database, in case you switchover or failover to it.

So what does this have to do with replicating unsupported data types? Well, a traditional DML trigger has what Oracle calls the `fire_once_only` property: the RDBMS fires them only when a regular user process issues a DML operation. These triggers are automatically disabled in the context of SQL Apply processes. However, you can create a trigger and set the `fire_once_only` property to `FALSE`.[6] In this case, Oracle RDBMS will fire the trigger no matter which process is issuing the DML.

Now that you know you can write a trigger that will also fire at the logical standby database in the context of the SQL Apply processes, let's explore how it can be used to maintain an otherwise unsupported table.[7] For each table you want to replicate using triggers that fire at the logical standby, you will need to create three schema objects:

- **A logging table**  This will be used to capture the transformed modification to the base table such that SQL Apply can replicate the logging table.

- **A base table trigger**  This will fire at the primary database to capture the changes in the logging table.

- **A logging table trigger**  This will fire at both the primary and the logical standby databases, but it will need to be written in such a way that it makes modifications only at the logical standby database.

Let's look at the characteristics of each of these.

**Characteristics of a Logging Table**  For efficient space management, you need to design the logging table as a messaging table (so that the logging table size does not grow proportionally with the base table). Thus, you will need to capture the modification type to the logging table. The logging table must contain the following columns:

- A column to store the action to be taken at the logical standby database.

- Columns to represent each column in the base table:

  - The columns in the base table that can be natively supported by SQL Apply can be identically defined in the logging table.

  - For unsupported columns in the base table, one or more columns needs to be created in the logging table using data types that are natively supported by SQL Apply.

    - User-defined types with attributes of scalar types need to be represented as separate columns using the same scalar types.

    - `VARRAY` columns can be represented as BLOBs. You can convert the `VARRAY` into a BLOB using the Oracle-provided operator `SYS_ET_IMAGE_TO_BLOB` in the base-table trigger, and back into a `VARRAY` using `SYS_ET_BLOB_TO_IMAGE` inside the logging table trigger.

---

[6] There is no way to create a trigger with the `fire_once_only` property set to `FALSE`. You must take three steps to set the trigger: You create a trigger as disabled. You change the `fire_once_only` property to `FALSE`. Then you enable the trigger.

[7] Suppose, for example, that you have a table that contains one or more columns of the unsupported data types.

- SDO_GEOMETRY columns can be represented as a character large object (CLOB). Use the TO_WKTGEOMETRY in the base table trigger and FROM_WKTGEOMETRY inside the logging table trigger. Both procedures are defined in the SDO_UTIL package, in the MDSYS schema.

- You need additional columns in the logging table to identify the row of the base table. These are needed to process the UPDATE and DELETE statements correctly. Let's call these columns *identification columns.*

  - For tables with a primary key, the columns making up the primary key should be the identification columns.

  - If your table does not have a primary key, but has a non-null unique index, make these columns your identification columns.

  - If your table does not have either a primary key or non-null unique index, you will need to use all columns in your identification set.[8]

**Characteristics of the Trigger on the Base Table**   The base table trigger can exist at both the primary and the logical standby databases. Since this is a regular DML trigger, it will not fire in the context of a SQL Apply process.

- The trigger should be a regular trigger with the fire_once_only property set to TRUE.

- For any DML on the base table, the trigger should

  - first insert a row in the logging table identifying the operation and logging all values needed to replay the operation inside the logging table trigger at the logical standby database;

  - next delete the row from the logging table to prevent the size of the logging table from increasing.

**Characteristics of the Trigger on the Logging Table**   The logging table trigger must have the following characteristics:

- The fire_once_only property should be set to FALSE.

- The trigger should not perform any changes at the primary database. You can determine whether the trigger needs to perform any action by invoking the dbms_logstdby.is_apply_server function inside the trigger body.

- The trigger needs to perform the corresponding action in the base table as indicated by the DML_TYPE column in the logging table. If you are working on LOB columns (used to replicate VARRAY or SDO_GEOMETRY), you will need the trigger to perform a second UPDATE statement following any insert or UPDATE of the base table.

**Example of Trigger-based Replication in Action**   The following example shows the logging table definition and trigger source for the EMPLOYEE table in the TEST schema, which contains

---

[8] In this case, your base table better be small in size or have a very low update rate, since you are going to incur the cost of a full-table scan for every updated/deleted row.

an object column that is the user-defined type NAME_TYP. The table has a primary key defined on the column ID.

1. Determine the base table definition and the definition of the user-defined type used by the table:

```
SQL> SET LONG 3200⁹
SQL> SELECT DBMS_METADATA.GET_DDL(OBJECT_TYPE => 'TABLE', NAME =>
     'EMPLOYEE', -
     SCHEMA => 'TEST') AS TABLE_DEF FROM DUAL;
TABLE_DEF
--------------------------------------------------------------------
CREATE TABLE "SYS"."EMP"
   (    "ID"     NUMBER,
        "NAME"      "TEST"."NAME_TYP" ,
         CONSTRAINT "TEST_EMP_PK" PRIMARY KEY ("ID")
   USING …¹⁰
   TABLESPACE "TEST_TBS"  ENABLE
    ) …¹¹ TABLESPACE  "TEST_TBS"


SQL>  SELECT DBMS_METADATA.GET_DDL(OBJECT_TYPE => 'TYPE', NAME =>
'NAME_TYP', -
             SCHEMA => 'TEST') AS TYP_DEF FROM DUAL;

TYP_DEF
--------------------------------------------------------------------
CREATE OR REPLACE TYPE "TEST"."NAME_TYP" AS OBJECT (
FIRST_NAME VARCHAR2(32),
LAST_NAME VARCHAR2(32));
```

Since you used DBMS_METADATA.GET_DDL you already know the primary key for the table: in this case, it consists of one column, ID. The logging table must track the old and new values of ID (the old value is to determine the row to be modified). If a table does not have a primary key defined, you will of course need to use a non-null unique index.

Run the following statement on the primary database to create the logging table. SQL Apply will create the table automatically on the standby database. The logging table contains only built-in data types supported by SQL Apply. The attributes (first_name, last_name) from the NAME_TYP user-defined type are represented as separate columns (log_first_name, log_last_name) in the logging table using the same built-in data type as the type attribute.

---

[9] We need to set this, since dbms_metadata.get_ddl returns a CLOB, and by default SQL*Plus shows only the first 80 characters of a CLOB column.

[10] For readability, we do not show the complete output here.

[11] We have truncated the output here as well.

All remaining columns from the base table (in our case dept) are represented in the
logging table (log_dept) using the same data type used in the base table.

```
SQL> CREATE TABLE TEST.LOG_EMPLOYEE (
     ACTION            VARCHAR2(1),
     LOG_ID_OLD        NUMBER,
     LOG_ID_NEW        NUMBER,
     LOG_FIRST_NAME    VARCHAR2(32),
     LOG_LAST_NAME     VARCHAR2(32),
     LOG_DEPT          NUMBER);


SQL> ALTER TABLE ADD CONSTRAINT TEST_LOG_EMP_PK PRIMARY KEY (LOG_ID_OLD);
```

2. Create the base table trigger that will be fired on the primary database for any DML
   against the base table (TEST.EMPLOYEE in our example). The trigger will insert a row in
   the logging table for each row modified on the base table.

```
SQL> CREATE OR REPLACE TRIGGER TEST.EMPLOYEE_PRIMARY_TRIG
 AFTER DELETE OR INSERT OR UPDATE ON EMPLOYEE FOR EACH ROW DISABLE[12]
DECLARE
L_THIS_ROW ROWID  := NULL;
BEGIN

-- INSERT: 'I', LOG_ID_OLD AND LOG_ID_NEW BOTH GET THE SAME VALUE
IF INSERTING THEN
  -- INSERT (ACTION = 'I'):
  INSERT INTO TEST.LOG_EMPLOYEE VALUES ('I' , :NEW.ID, :NEW.ID, :NEW.ID,
  :NEW.NAME.FIRST_NAME, :NEW.NAME.LAST_NAME, :NEW.DEPT)
  RETURNING ROWED INTO L_THIS_ROW;
ELSIF UPDATING THEN
-- UPDATE (ACTION = 'U'): LOG_ID_OLD AND LOG_ID_NEW ARE DIFFERENT
  INSERT INTO TEST.LOG_EMPLOYEE VALUES ('U' , :NEW.ID, :NEW.ID,
  :NEW.NAME.FIRST_NAME, :NEW.NAME.LAST_NAME, :NEW.DEPT)
  RETURNING ROWID INTO L_THIS_ROW;
ELSIF DELETING THEN
  -- DELETE (ACTION = 'D'): AND WE ONLY NEED LOG_ID_OLD VALUE TO BE LOGGED
  INSERT INTO TEST.LOG_EMPLOYEE(ACTION, LOG_ID_OLD) VALUES ('D', :OLD.ID);
END IF;
-- DELETE THE ROW FROM THE LOGGING TABLE.
-- THE STANDBY TRIGGER WILL NOT FIRE ON THE DELETE.
DELETE FROM TEST.LOG_EMPLOYEE WHERE ROWED = L_THIS_ROW;
END;
/
```

---

[12] You need to create this as disabled in order to synchronize the capturing of the changes with the instantiation of
the unsupported tables at the logical standby database.

3. Creating the logging table trigger. You can create it at the primary database and have SQL Apply replicate it automatically. It is fired on the logical standby database for any DML against the logging table (EMPLOYEE_LOG in this example) that occurs on the standby database.

```
CREATE OR REPLACE TRIGGER TEST.EMPLOYEE_STANDBY_TRIG
AFTER INSERT OR UPDATE ON TEST.EMPLOYEE_LOG
FOR EACH ROW BEGIN
-- ONLY RUN ON STANDBY DATABASE
IF DBMS_LOGSTDBY.IS_APPLY_SERVER() THEN
 IF INSERTING THEN
    CASE :NEW.ACTION
    -- IF INSERT ACTION, INSERT THE NEW ROW
WHEN 'I' THEN
INSERT INTO PLAYERS VALUES (:NEW.LOG_ID_NEW,
NAME_TYP( :NEW.LOG_FIRST_NAME, :NEW.LOG_LAST_NAME),
:NEW.LOG_DEPT );
-- IF UPDATE ACTION, THEN UPDATE ROW IN BASE TABLE
WHEN 'U' THEN
  UPDATE TEST.EMPLOYEE E SET
  E.ID  = :NEW.LOG_ID_NEW,
  E.NAME.FIRST_NAME = :NEW.LOG_FIRST_NAME,
  E.NAME.FIRST_NAME = :NEW.LOG_LAST_NAME,
  E.DEPT = :NEW.LOG_DEPT
  WHERE E.ID = :NEW.LOG_ID_OLD;
-- IF DELETE ACTION, THEN DELETE ROW FROM BASE TABLE
WHEN 'D' THEN
    DELETE FROM PLAYERS WHERE ID = :NEW.LOG_ID_OLD;
END CASE;
END IF;
END IF;
END;
/
```

4. Set the `fire_once_only` property of the logging table trigger to FALSE. You need to do this on both the primary and the logical standby databases.

```
SQL> EXECUTE DBMS_DDL.SET_TRIGGER_FIRING_PROPERTY (-
     SCHEMA_NAME => 'TEST', -
     TRIGGER_NAME => 'EMPLOYEE_STANDBY_TRIG', -
     FIRE_ONCE => FALSE);
```

5. Get a snapshot of TEST.EMPLOYEE from the primary database, and enable the logging table trigger while keeping the table locked. You will need to use SQL*Plus sessions in the database:

```
A. (SESSION#1) LOCK THE TABLE, SO THAT NOTHING CAN UPDATE IT. THIS
STATEMENT WILL WAIT FOR TRANSACTIONS THAT ARE IN THE MIDDLE OF UPDATING
THE TABLE TO COMMIT OR ROLLBACK, BEFORE RETURNING.
SQL> LOCK TABLE TEST.EMPLOYEE IN SHARE MODE;
```

```
B. (SESSION#1) WE NEED TO SWITCH THE LOGFILE HERE, TO GET THE SCN TO BUMP UP
SQL> ALTER SYSTEM SWITCH LOGFILE;

C. (SESSION#1) WE CAN NOW QUERY V$DATABASE TO GET THE CURRENT SCN OF THE DATABASE
SQL> SELECT CURRENT_SCN FROM V$DATABASE;
CURRENT_SCN
----------------------------------
52018672

D. (SESSION#2) ENABLE THE LOGGING TABLE TRIGGER
SQL> ALTER TRIGGER TEST.EMPLOYEE_PRIM_TRIG ENABLE;

E. (SESSION#1) ISSUE COMMIT TO RELEASE THE LOCK. SO THE WRITE OUTAGE ON THE TABLE
IS MINIMAL.
SQL> COMMIT; -- RELEASE THE LOCK

F. (SESSION#1) USE THE SCN OBTAINED IN STEP C, TO EXPORT THE CONTENTS OF THE TABLE
USING THE FLASHBACK_SCN CLAUSE OF DATAPUMP EXPORT
SQL> EXPDP TEST/TEST TABLES=EMPLOYEE DIRECTORY=DPUMP_DIR1
DUMPFILE=EMP_SCN.DMP
FLASHBACK_SCN = 52018672
```

6. Import the data for TEST.EMPLOYEE at the logical standby database:

```
SQL> IMPDP TEST/TEST TABLES=EMPLOYEE DIRECTORY=DPUMP_DIR1
DUMPFILE=EMP_SCN.DMP
```

7. Restart SQL Apply

```
SQL> ALTER DATABASE START LOGICAL STANDBY APPLY IMMEDIATE;
```

# Customizing Your Logical Standby Database (or Creating a Local Dataset at the Logical Standby)

Now that you know how to determine what dataset your logical standby database is maintaining, it is time to explore the capabilities that made you want to deploy a logical standby database in the first place: the ability to customize it to offload processing from the primary database.

## Creating Materialized Views on the Logical Standby Database

SQL Apply does not replicate any DDLs related to the materialized views (MVs) or MV logs.[13] However, you are free to create MVs and MV logs on maintained tables at the logical standby database, and these local MVs will be refreshed in a way that you expect: On-commit refresh will be triggered as SQL Apply processes commit a transaction with modifications to a base table;

---

[13] However, since a logical standby is created from a physical standby, the MVs and MV logs that were created at the primary database before you converted your physical standby database into a logical standby will remain in the logical standby database.

on-demand incremental or full refreshes can be scheduled at the logical standby database using DBMS_SCHEDULER or you can issue the refresh directly.

```
SQL> EXECUTE DBMS_RNVIEW.REFRESH (-
   LIST => 'CUSTOMER.TRADE_TRACK_MV', METHOD => 'F');
```

Yes, it is that simple!

## Creating Scheduler Jobs on the Logical Standby Database

You can create a scheduler job on the logical standby in the usual way. However, you need to know a little bit more about DBMS_JOBS and DBMS_SCHEDULER and their interaction with the logical standby database.

Jobs created with the DBMS_JOBS package at the primary are replicated automatically on the logical standby database. This way, the jobs are available on the logical standby when you switchover or failover to it. You can also create local jobs on your logical standby database.

Jobs created with the DBMS_SCHEDULER package at the primary database are not replicated to the logical standby database. However, jobs created with DBMS_SCHEDULER are role-aware. By default, scheduler jobs created on a database inherit the role of the database, so scheduler jobs created at the primary database will have PRIMARY as their database_role and those created at the standby database will have LOGICAL STANDBY as their database_role attribute. A job can become executable only when its database_role matches the attribute in the V$DATABASE view. Suppose, for example, that you have two databases, Matrix and Matrix_DR0, with Matrix being the current primary and Matrix_DR0 being the current logical standby database.

- **Case 1:** You want scheduler job REFRESH_TRADE_TRACK_MV to run on the primary regardless of which one of the databases is the primary database:

```
(A) AT MATRIX:
EXECUTE DBMS_SCHEDULER.CREATE_JOB (JOB_NAME => 'REFRESH_TT_MV_PRIM', -
      JOB_TYPE => 'PLSQL_BLOCK', -
      ENABLED => FALSE, AUTO_DROP => FALSE, START_DATE => SYSDATE, -
      LIST => 'CUSTOMER.TRADE_TRACK_MV',-
      REPEAT_INTERVAL => 'FREQ=HOURLY;INTERVAL=>12' , -
      JOB_ACTION => 'BEGIN DBMS_MVIEW.REFRESH( -
      LIST => 'CUSTOMER.TRADE_TRACK_MV', METHOD => 'F'); END; ');
SQL> EXECUTE DBMS_SCHEDULER.SET_ATTRIBUTE(NAME => 'REFRESH_TT_MV_PRIM', -
      ATTRIBUTE => 'ENABLED', VALUE => 'TRUE');
(B) AT MATRIX_DR0:
SQL> EXECUTE DBMS_SCHEDULER.CREATE_JOB ((JOB_NAME => 'REFRESH_TT_MV_STDBY', -
      JOB_TYPE => 'PLSQL_BLOCK', -
      ENABLED => FALSE, AUTO_DROP => FALSE, START_DATE => SYSDATE, -
      REPEAT_INTERVAL => 'FREQ=HOURLY;INTERVAL=>12', -
      JOB_ACTION => 'BEGIN DBMS_MVIEW.REFRESH( -
      LIST => 'CUSTOMER.TRADE_TRACK_MV', METHOD => 'F'); END; ');
SQL> EXECUTE DBMS_SCHEDULER.SET_ATTRIBUTE(NAME => 'REFRESH_TT_MV_STDBY', -
      ATTRIBUTE => 'DATABASE_ROLE', VALUE => 'PRIMARY');
SQL> EXECUTE DBMS_SCHEDULER.SET_ATTRIBUTE(NAME => 'REFRESH_TT_MV_STDBY', -
      ATTRIBUTE => 'ENABLED', VALUE => 'TRUE');
```

Note that at the logical standby Matrix_DR0, you needed an additional step of changing the `database_role` attribute for the job to `PRIMARY` as it will default to the role of the database, which is currently `LOGICAL STANDBY`.

■ **Case 2:** You want scheduler job `CHECK_SQL_APPLY_PROGRESS` to run on the database that happens to be the logical standby database at any given moment:

```
SQL> CREATE TABLE SYSTEM.SQL_APPLY_PROGRESS_GATHER AS
       SELECT SYSDATE, TIME_COMPUTED, NAME, VALUE FROM V$DATAGUARD_STATS;
SQL > CREATE OR REPLACE PROCEDURE SYSTEM.SQL_APPLY_PROGRESS_GATHER AS
BEGIN
   EXECUTE IMMEDIATE 'INSERT INTO SYSTEM.SQL_APPLY_PROGRESS_GATHER
       SELECT SYSDATE, TIME_COMPUTED, NAME, VALUE FROM V$DATAGUARD_STATS;
   COMMIT;
END;
/
```

At both Matrix and Matrix_DR0:

```
SQL> EXECUTE DBMS_SCHEDULER.CREATE_JOB (JOB_NAME => 'SQL_APPLY_STATS', -
       JOB_TYPE => 'PLSQL_BLOCK', -
       ENABLED => FALSE, AUTO_DROP => FALSE, START_DATE => SYSDATE, -
       REPEAT_INTERVAL => 'FREQ=MINUTELY;INTERVAL=>15', -
       JOB_ACTION => 'BEGIN SYSTEM.SQL_APPLY_PROGRESS_GATHER; END; ');
SQL> EXECUTE DBMS_SCHEDULER.SET_ATTRIBUTE(NAME => 'SQL_APPLY_STATS', -
       ATTRIBUTE => 'DATABASE_ROLE', VALUE => 'STANDBY');
SQL> EXECUTE DBMS_SCHEDULER.SET_ATTRIBUTE(NAME => 'SQL_APPLY_STATS', -
       ATTRIBUTE => 'ENABLED', VALUE => 'TRUE');
```

Note in this example that we could have created the job as `ENABLED` when we created it at Matrix_DR0 and skipped the next two steps, since it would have inherited the correct `database_role` attribute there.

■ **Case 3:** You want scheduler job `UPDATE_BILLING_SUMMARY` to run on only Matrix_DR0 and only when Matrix_DR0 is a logical standby database:

```
AT MATRIX_DR0
SQL> EXECUTE DBMS_SCHEDULER.CREATE_JOB (-
       JOB_NAME => 'UPDATE_BILLING_SUMMARY', JOB_TYPE => 'PLSQL_BLOCK', -
       ENABLED => FALSE, AUTO_DROP => FALSE, START_DATE => SYSDATE, -
       REPEAT_INTERVAL => 'FREQ=HOURLY;INTERVAL=>24', -
       JOB_ACTION => 'BEGIN SYSTEM.UPD_BILLING_SUMMARY; END; ');
```

■ **Case 4:** You want scheduler job `UPDATE_BILLING_SUMMARY` to run only on Matrix_DR0, regardless of the role of the database:

```
AT MATRIX_DR0
SQL> EXECUTE DBMS_SCHEDULER.CREATE_JOB (-
       JOB_NAME => 'UPDATE_BILLING_SUMMARY', JOB_TYPE => 'PLSQL_BLOCK', -
       ENABLED => FALSE, AUTO_DROP => FALSE, START_DATE => SYSDATE, -
       REPEAT_INTERVAL => 'FREQ=HOURLY;INTERVAL=>24', -
       JOB_ACTION => 'BEGIN SYSTEM.UPD_BILLING_SUMMARY; END; ');
```

```
SQL> EXECUTE DBMS_SCHEDULER.CREATE_JOB (-
      JOB_NAME => 'UPDATE_BILLING_SUMMARY', JOB_TYPE => 'PLSQL_BLOCK', -
      ENABLED => FALSE, AUTO_DROP => FALSE, START_DATE => SYSDATE, -
      REPEAT_INTERVAL => 'FREQ=MINUTELY;INTERVAL=>15', -
      JOB_ACTION => 'BEGIN SYSTEM.SQL_APPLY_PROGRESS_GATHER; END; ');
SQL> EXECUTE DBMS_SCHEDULER.SET_ATTRIBUTE(NAME => 'UPDATE_BILLING_
SUMMARY', -
      ATTRIBUTE => 'DATABASE_ROLE', VALUE => 'PRIMARY');
SQL> EXECUTE DBMS_SCHEDULER.SET_ATTRIBUTE(NAME => 'UPDATE_BILLING_
SUMMARY', -
      ATTRIBUTE => 'ENABLED', VALUE => 'TRUE');
```

### Offloading Log-based Replication (Streams Capture) to the Logical Standby

You may be familiar with Oracle Streams capture, which is Oracle's log-based multi-master replication solution. Streams capture and apply have a lot in common with Data Guard logical standby, since both features take advantage of a lot of the common infrastructure inside the Oracle RDBMS. You can use a logical standby database in conjunction with Streams capture.

Suppose you have an online transaction processing (OLTP) database with a physical and logical standby, and you need to replicate a table T to a third database. You can of course set up Streams capture on the primary database. In this case, if you were to failover or switchover to your physical standby, the Streams capture will continue to run[14] on the new primary database. However, since you already have a logical standby database in the mix, you can simply create the Streams capture on the logical standby, as long as the table T is being maintained at the logical standby. This way, you can offload the Streams capture overhead from the primary database. There will be additional latency in capturing changes, however: when you are running at the logical standby, the capture process has to wait for the changes to be shipped from the primary to the logical standby and applied by SQL Apply. In most cases, it is in the order of a few seconds, and in many cases it is a small price to pay to be able to offload applications from the primary database.

You do need to keep one particular item in mind. If you have only two databases, the primary (say, Matrix) and a logical standby (say, Matrix_DR0), you will not be able to move the Streams capture processing from one database to the other as you go through role transitions. For instance, if you created a Streams capture on Matrix_DR0 when it was a logical standby, the Streams capture will remain on Matrix_DR0, even when Matrix_DR0 becomes the primary as a result of a role transition operation such as switchover and failover. For the Streams capture to continue working on the logical standby, you will need to write a role transition trigger like the following:

```
CREATE OR REPLACE TRIGGER STREAMS_AQ_JOB_ROLE_CHANGE1
AFTER DB_ROLE_CHANGE ON DATABASE
DECLARE
CURSOR CAPTURE_AQ_JOBS IS
  SELECT JOB_NAME, DATABASE_ROLE
    FROM DBA_SCHEDULER_JOB_ROLES
    WHERE JOB_NAME LIKE 'AQ_JOB%';
```

---

[14]The physical standby database has the same DBID and global database name as the primary database, so the Streams capture will not even realize that a switchover or failover has happened underneath it. It would look like someone simply bounced the database instances.

```
U AQ_JOBS%ROWTYPE;
MY_DB_ROLE   VARCHAR2(16);
BEGIN
 DBMS_SYSTEM.KSDWRT(DBMS_SYSTEM.ALERT_FILE, 'CHANGING ROLE OF AQ JOBS');
 CURRENT_DB_ROLE := DBMS_LOGSTDBY.DB_ROLE();
 OPEN AQ_JOBS;
 LOOP
   FETCH AQ_JOBS INTO U;
   EXIT WHEN AQ_JOBS%NOTFOUND;

   IF (U.DATABASE_ROLE != MY_DB_ROLE) THEN
     DBMS_SCHEDULER.SET_ATTRIBUTE(U.JOB_NAME,
                                'DATABASE_ROLE',
                                MY_DB_ROLE);

     DBMS_SYSTEM.KSDWRT(DBMS_SYSTEM.ALERT_FILE,
        'AQ JOB ' || U.JOB_NAME || ' CHANGED TO ROLE ' || MY_DB_ROLE);
   END IF;
 END LOOP;
 CLOSE AQ_JOBS;

EXCEPTION
 WHEN OTHERS THEN
 BEGIN
   DBMS_SYSTEM.KSDWRT(DBMS_SYSTEM.ALERT_FILE,
     'FAILED TO CHANGE ROLE OF AQ JOBS');
   RAISE;
 END;
END;
```

# Understanding the Operational Aspects of a Logical Standby

Before delving into the operational aspects of SQL Apply, it helps to get an idea about how it is implemented. So we will take a brief detour inside the internals of SQL Apply.

## Looking Inside SQL Apply

SQL Apply is the layer of code (and also the process group) that maintains the Oracle logical standby database. Three software components are responsible for maintaining a logical standby database: the redo transport service that ships the redo stream of the primary database and performs gap resolution, the mining service that mines the redo and reconstructs the equivalent SQL statements and original transaction grouping, and the apply service that schedules the mined transactions for concurrent application and actually applies them. A fourth service is hidden in plain sight—the core database engine that performs the modification as directed by the apply service. Although this may be obvious to everyone, we mention it to highlight an important fact about a logical standby database: it is an independent database, although it serves as a standby to the primary database, and as a result all aspects of best practices related to database tuning and management that you generally employ in keeping your database running without interruption still apply in the context of a logical standby database.

Stating it differently, you should have a regular backup scheduled for your logical standby database, you should have database flashback enabled at your logical standby, and the first place to go to analyze your performance problem should still be the Automated Workload Repository (AWR) and Active Session History (ASH) reports.

Since this chapter is focused on logical standby, we will look at the mining and apply engines under SQL Apply in more detail. The mining and apply engines form a producer-consumer pair, with the mining engine producing transactions to be consumed by the apply engine. The mining engine transforms the redo records into logical change records (LCRs) and stages them in System Global Area (SGA) memory. You can specify how much SGA memory will be used by SQL Apply to stage the LCR. Two other producer-consumer setups exist in the whole SQL Apply processing: one formed by the transport services (producer) and the mining engine (consumer), and the other formed by the apply engine (producer) and the rest of the RDBMS code (consumer). So if you have a RDBMS tuning issue or a saturated I/O system (we are aggregating the hardware under RDBMS here), the apply engine will become slow. In that case, although you will notice the slowdown in SQL Apply, the underlying problem is the system or I/O load. So keep in mind all three of these producer-consumer pipelines and look at all of them when trying to tune SQL Apply for your logical standby database. Remember that it is, after all, only another database.

## Understanding the Process Architecture of SQL Apply

As we said earlier, SQL Apply consists of two components: the mining engine and the apply engine. When you issue the `alter database start logical standby apply` statement, the first background process to start is the logical standby coordinator process (LSP0). This is the COORDINATOR process for SQL Apply. This in turn spawns two sets of processes: the mining processes (in 11*g* these have the prefix *ora_ms*, implying mining servers) and the apply processes (in 11*g* these have the prefix *ora_as*, implying apply servers).

The mining engine comprises three types of processes:

- **READER**   There is only one reader process. Its job is to read the redo stream (either from the archived logs or from the standby redo log file [SRL]). It does not do any transformation of the redo records except to make a copy in its shared buffer.

- **PREPARER**   There can be multiple preparers. Data Guard uses a step function to determine the right number of preparers with a step of 20. So for the first 20 appliers, only a single preparer will be spawned. A second preparer will be spawned if you were to ask for 21 to 40 appliers, and so on. Each preparer reads a set of redo records and does the initial transformation of the redo records into an LCR. A single redo record can generate multiple LCRs (think of a direct load block).

- **BUILDER**   There is only one builder process. The builder is the process interfacing with the pipeline between the mining and the apply engines. The builder handles three different kinds of tasks:

  - Grouping LCRs into transactions.

  - Merging of multiple LCRs into a single LCR (in case of chained rows for instance).

  - Performing administrative tasks such as paging out memory, advancing the log mining checkpoints, and so on. We will talk about these administrative tasks shortly.

The apply engine comprises three types of processes (we include the COORDINATOR process here as well, since it mostly does apply-specific work):

- **ANALYZER** There is only one such process. Its job is to fetch transactions from the mining engine and compute a safe schedule that can be used to order the commits of the transaction.

- **COORDINATOR** There is only one such process. It coordinates between the appliers, assigning work to the APPLIER processes and coordinating commit ordering.

- **APPLIER** There can be multiple APPLIER processes. These are the true workhorses inside the SQL Apply engine, and they actually replicate the changes.

Where can you find information about the processes? Look at `v$logstdby_process` view. In the next section, we discuss a few aspects of how the mining and apply engines work.

## Understanding the Memory Management Inside SQL Apply

Since the overall SQL Apply engine can be considered a producer-consumer setup with the LCR cache in the middle used as the pipeline, the salient memory-related issue is how the memory gets managed. As we indicated earlier, you can set the size allocated to LCR cache. A good rule of thumb in today's machines with a large amount of shared pools is to set the memory allocated to the LCR cache to 200MB, like so:

```
SQL> EXECUTE DBMS_LOGSTDBY. APPLY_SET ( 'MAX_SGA', 200);
```

Let's look in more detail at the organization of the LCR cache.

As shown in Figure 4-1, the LCR cache is divided into four main components: one that holds the redo records (the size of this is constant), another where the redo records are transformed into LCRs (but not yet grouped into transactions), a third where LCRs are grouped into transactions and are ready for consumption by the apply component, and a fourth section that is made up of unused memory. The reader process reads from the redo logs (archived logs or the SRL) and fills

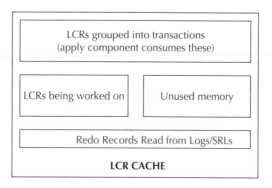

**FIGURE 4-1.** *Inside the LCR cache*

**Setting Various SQL Apply–Related Parameters**
You can change almost all aspects of SQL Apply by using `dbms_logstdby.apply_set()`
without first having to stop SQL Apply. The exception to this rule is the parameter `preserve_commit_order`. If you want to change this parameter, you will first need to stop SQL Apply.

in the region allocated for redo records. The preparers read the redo records and perform the first level of transformation from redo record to LCR. The builder process moves the LCRs into the apply-visible section of the LCR cache by grouping LCRs into transactions and performing second-level transformation such as chained row processing, merging LCRs related to LOB DMLs, and so on.

How is this memory managed? Based on your setting of `MAX_SGA`, the mining engine will start consuming memory from the LCR cache. Depending on the workload you are running at the primary database and the redo generation rate, you may not see the entire memory being used by SQL Apply. But on a very active system with a high redo generation rate, the mining engine will consume all of the LCR cache and fill it with transactions to be applied by the apply engine. Usually the mining component is much faster than the apply component (hence the ratio of 20:1 between the appliers and preparers) and will fill the entire memory allocated to LCR cache before the appliers have a chance to start consuming the prepared transactions. The mining engine then backs off and goes to sleep until the appliers consume and release enough transactions so that the LCR cache is 50 percent empty. At this point, the mining processes will wake up and look for additional redo records to transform into LCRs and group into transactions. If you want to find out how much of the `MAX_SGA` is actually getting used by SQL Apply processes, you can issue the following query:

```
SQL> SELECT USED_MEMORY_SIZE FROM V$LOGMNR_SESSION
        WHERE SESSION_ID = (SELECT VALUE FROM V$LOGSTDBY_STATS
                        WHERE NAME = 'SESSION ID');
USED_MEMORY_SIZE
----------------
167600
```

Why do you need to issue the subquery to restrict the output to a single `session_id`? Refer back to the section, "Offloading Log-based Replication (Streams Capture) to the Logical Standby." The core mining engine[15] used underneath SQL Apply is also used underneath Streams capture, and mining sessions active for a Streams capture will also show up in the shared `v$logmnr_session` view. If you were to run this query every few seconds and chart the output, you would see the memory used by LCR cache increasing up to 95 percent of the `MAX_SGA` setting and then gradually reducing until it reaches 50 percent of the `MAX_SGA` setting before going back up again.

So what happens if you do not allocate enough memory to SQL Apply? You may notice that the mining engine is paging out memory from LCR cache to disk (`system.logmnr_spill$ table`). A moderate amount of paging out is tolerable, but if you have grossly underconfigured the size of

---

[15] The mining engine is also used underneath other Oracle features such as Asynchronous Change Data Capture (CDC) and underneath the redo-based auditing feature in Oracle Audit Vault.

your LCR cache, the performance will deteriorate drastically. Later in this chapter in the section "Tuning SQL Apply" we discuss how to determine whether page out[16] activity is excessive.

## Understanding How SQL Apply Uses Checkpoints

Two kinds of checkpoints are used inside SQL Apply. The apply engine has to remember which transactions it has successfully applied, so that it does not try to apply them again. This is done by inserting a row identifying the XID[17] that was assigned at the primary database into a metadata table (system.logstdby$apply_progress) as part of the transaction that replicates the changes done at the primary database. We can hear you screaming already, "Wait! SQL Apply can run forever. This table will get huge and eat up my whole database!" Yes, it would. But SQL Apply periodically purges the table by creating a new partition and dropping the old one, and it remembers an SCN below which all transactions have been successfully applied. This SCN (shown in v$logstdby_progress.applied_scn) and the rows in system.logstdby$apply_progress form the apply engine's checkpoint information.

The mining engine needs to keep more elaborate checkpoint information. Imagine the following scenario: Some rogue application (one that forgot to log you out of your session even after it has been left idle for a couple of days) started a write transaction *W* and left it open for couple of days. The transaction made a few changes, but it did not commit or roll them back. Now it is two days later, and you stop SQL Apply. Obviously, SQL Apply could not commit the changes done by transaction *W*. It cannot wait indefinitely for *W* to make up its mind. So it stops after applying changes such that the database is at a consistent state. Now when you start SQL Apply again, it really would have to go back to the archived logs where *W* made its changes and read two days' worth of archived logs (most of which is useless work, since *W* may have made only one change two days back). But all these inefficiencies are avoided, since SQL Apply would have checkpointed the changes made by *W* in one of its metadata tables (system.logmnr_age_spill$).

The mining engine has a counterpart to v$logstdby_progress.applied_scn and this is v$logstdby_progress.restart_scn. The mining engine will read only redo logs that contain redo records with SCN greater than or equal to restart_scn. Since the mining engine's checkpoint contains more elaborate information, it has to weigh the costs and benefits related to such checkpoints. The name LOGMNR_AGE_SPILL$ suggests what is going on underneath: the mining engine is spilling data based on its age.

You need to keep two things in mind. First, age is a relative thing. If you have a system that is generating redo at a rate of 100MB/hour, you can say no transaction is old unless it has remained uncommitted for 10 hours. Why is that? The cost of rereading 1GB worth of redo through the mining engine and discarding most of it is quite small. It will probably take no more than a minute to do this. However, if you are working on a system that is generating 10MB/sec, you cannot use 10 hours as your yardstick to determine age, because you may have to read 360GB of redo. So the mining engine computes age based on how much redo has been generated since the candidate redo to determine whether a redo record is old. This adapts nicely with the rate of redo generation: as the redo generation rate waxes and wanes in the primary database, so does the checkpoint intervals. By default, the mining engine sets the redo threshold to be 5 x MAX_SGA. Thus if you

---

[16] In your interactions with Oracle tech support, you may also encounter the term *logminer memory spill*. This is the same as logminer paging out memory from the LCR to the spill tablespace in the database.

[17] *XID* refers to the transaction identifier that is assigned by the Oracle RDBMS to every transaction that modifies the database.

are running with MAX_SGA size of 200MB (which is a reasonable lower bound for SQL Apply), a redo record will become a candidate for checkpointing once 1GB of redo has been generated (and mined by the mining engine) since the time it was mined at the logical standby site.

The second aspect of such a checkpointing scheme is to avoid checkpointing for a large transaction (a transaction that modifies a large number of rows). Why is this? Well, in a sense, any transaction is already checkpointed in the redo stream, except it may be done in a sparse manner. So, ideally, the mining engine should checkpoint only sparse, small transactions and leave large, dense transactions alone.

Getting back to our scenarios in the last paragraph, suppose you are generating 10MB/sec of redo with a direct load of 10 million rows in one transaction *X*. Also assume that each row results in 200 bytes' worth of redo, and this large load is interspersed with some small OLTP-like transactions. Our large load by itself will generate 2GB worth of redo records. According to the default settings, if we were running with 200MB of MAX_SGA, the mining engine will encounter 1GB of redo from the large load as a candidate for checkpointing. However, SQL Apply's checkpointing algorithm detects the fact that transaction *X* is a large transaction, and it is not cost-efficient to checkpoint parts of this transaction, so the mining engine will not checkpoint any data from this transaction. As a result, the restart_scn column in v$logstdby_progress will get stuck at the SCN at which *X* started to modify the database, until SQL Apply has successfully committed all changes made by *X*. If you notice that v$logstdby_progress.restart_scn is not moving for a long time, you have likely encountered one or more large transactions, and the mining engine has suspended its checkpointing until the large transactions have all been successfully committed.

### Understanding Transaction "Chunking" Inside SQL Apply

One important way that SQL Apply differs from most other log-based replication solutions available for Oracle Database is its ability to apply large transactions even before the transaction has been committed at the primary database. SQL Apply uses an internal heuristic to determine whether a transaction is large or not.[18] The mining engine delivers a small transaction as a whole unit, once it encounters the commit record, to the apply engine. Large transactions are divided into chunks,[19] and chunks are delivered to the apply engine as they are filled. It is this ability of chunking transactions and starting to work on them even before the transaction has committed at the primary database that sets SQL Apply apart from other replication solutions.

This chunking of transactions has two beneficial effects. First, since chunks can be applied eagerly (in other words, without having to know whether the transaction will commit or rollback), the memory consumed by a large transaction can be kept to a minimum as long as you allocate enough apply processes to the task. Second, it allows for an adequately sized logical standby to keep its data close to synchronized with the primary database, providing for near–real-time availability of the data at the logical standby database, regardless of transaction size. Chunking of

---

[18] The threshold value is partly determined by the hidden SQL Apply parameter _EAGER_SIZE, which is defaulted to 201. So a transaction that does less than or equal to 200 DML operations is deemed to be a small transaction by SQL Apply.

[19] The hidden SQL Apply parameter _EAGER_SIZE also sets the default number of LCRs making up a transaction chunk. However, not all transaction chunks contain the same number of LCRs. There can be more (for instance, during a partition load operation on a table with LOB columns) or less (for instance, in case of transactions involving product data markup language [PDML] operations). So you should not make any assumption about the number of operations contained within a transaction chunk.

transactions and its associated optimistic scheduling do have a subtle impact on SQL Apply performance, and that is the topic of our next subsection.

## Understanding How DML Transactions Are Scheduled

SQL Apply allows for two modes of transaction application: one where the commit ordering at the primary database is maintained strictly at the logical standby (this is the default setting of transaction scheduling), and the other where the commit ordering is not strictly enforced as long as no row dependency exists between two transactions. You get the second, less strict setting and potentially one with more performance, especially if your workload is OLTP-like with small/medium-sized transactions committing at high rate. You do this with the following statement:

```
SQL> EXECUTE DBMS_LOGSTDBY.APPLY_SET (NAME => 'PRESERVE_COMMIT_ORDER', -
     VALUE => FALSE);
```

Note that no matter which mode you set, SQL Apply will preserve transaction boundaries (changes that committed atomically at the primary database commit atomically at the standby database) and will honor row dependencies (if two transactions modify the same row, they will be committed in the same order at the logical standby as they were at the primary database).

**NOTE**
*Many third-party replication solutions do not offer the integrity of the transaction boundary. The performance numbers that they cite are often collected when they are violating the integrity of the transaction (by applying changes that happened together in the context of multiple transactions).*

For some applications, this may be enough. But if you are running the supply chain of a major retailer, you cannot afford to update the cargo manifest in three different transactions when it was done in a single transaction at the primary. So what does strict ordering mean? Strict ordering (or preserving commit order) means that commits are issued and executed in the same order as in the primary. A valid transaction history ($H_1$) is shown in Table 4-1.

Table 4-2 shows a possible transaction history at the logical standby if the property preserve_commit_order is set to TRUE. Note that although at the primary database, rows $R_3$ and $R_4$ of table $T_2$ were updated after transaction X has committed, SQL Apply is free to apply them before it commits X, since X and Y modify disjoint sets of rows. SQL Apply will, however, delay the commit of transaction Y and issue it after X has been successfully committed, since we have directed it to preserve the commit ordering encountered at the primary database.

Let's now see how this will differ if preserve_commit_order was set to FALSE (see Table 4-3). Note that in this case, SQL Apply can go ahead and commit Y, since transactions X and Y are truly independent.[20] Had they not been independent (or, in other words, there is a row that both X and Y modified), the scheduling of commits would need to be identical regardless of the preserve_commit_order setting. In other words, if true row dependency exists between two transactions, the setting of the preserve_commit_order parameter does not matter; we always have to honor commit ordering that we saw at the primary database.

---

[20] In other words, they do not modify overlapping sets of rows.

| Time (or SCN) | Transaction X | Transaction Y |
|---|---|---|
| 10 | Update Row $R_1$ of Table $T_1$ | Insert Row $R_1$ of Table $T_2$ |
| 20 | | Insert Row $R_2$ of Table $T_2$ |
| 30 | Update Row $R_2$ of Table $T_1$ | |
| 40 | Commit X | |
| 50 | | Insert Row $R_3$ of Table $T_2$ |
| 60 | | Insert Row $R_4$ of Table $T_2$ |
| 70 | | Commit Y |

**TABLE 4-1.** *An Example Transaction History $H_1$ at the Primary Database*

| Time (or SCN) | APPLIER#1 | APPLIER#2 |
|---|---|---|
| 100 | Update Row $R_1$ of Table $T_1$ | Insert Row $R_1$ of Table $T_2$ |
| 110 | | Insert Row $R_2$ of Table $T_2$ |
| 120 | | Insert Row $R_3$ of Table $T_2$ |
| 130 | | Insert Row $R_4$ of Table $T_2$ |
| 140 | Update Row $R_2$ of Table $T_1$ | |
| 150 | Commit X | |
| 160 | | Commit Y |

**TABLE 4-2.** *An Example Transaction History (Associated with $H_1$) at the Logical Standby with* `preserve_commit_order` *Set to TRUE*

| Time (or SCN) | APPLIER#1 (Applying X) | APPLIER#2 (Applying Y) |
|---|---|---|
| 100 | Update Row $R_1$ of Table $T_1$ | Insert Row $R_1$ of Table $T_2$ |
| 110 | | Insert Row $R_2$ of Table $T_2$ |
| 120 | | Insert Row $R_3$ of Table $T_2$ |
| 130 | | Insert Row $R_4$ of Table $T_2$ |
| 140 | Update Row $R_2$ of Table $T_1$ | Commit Y |
| 150 | Commit X | |

**TABLE 4-3.** *An Example Transaction History (Associated with $H_1$) at the Logical Standby with* `preserve_commit_order` *Set to FALSE*

This brings us to the next topic of discussion: How does SQL Apply compute row dependency? It does this by computing several hash values for each LCR, one for each unique constraint on the table of interest, and then uses the hash values to determine whether two LCRs have any collisions. If so, the transaction with the later commit SCN will wait for the first transaction to commit before applying the change that collided with the former. SQL Apply computes the dependency for all complete transactions and for some of the chunks of the large transactions. One reason it does not compute dependencies for all LCRs is the fundamental issue in software engineering (and all other disciplines of engineering): there is always a cost associated with every computation. In this case, the cost is paid in memory consumption. You need memory to stage the dependency computation, and you need memory to stage the dependency graph. So SQL Apply uses a different strategy to handle large transactions. It assumes that if two transactions X and Y are ongoing at the same time, Oracle row-locking strategy must have prevented them from acquiring the same row lock, and hence they must be independent. (This is not strictly true, since Oracle does allow transactions to lock rows with "select for update" and then release them by issuing a rollback to savepoint statement.) So dependency computation is useful only when you are trying to apply a change that occurs after the commit of another transaction. In this case, you need the dependency to tell you whether you need to wait for the other transaction to commit first (as in Case 2) or whether you can go ahead without having to wait for the other transaction to commit (Case 1). So what do you do when you have suspended dependency computation for a given transaction? You wait for that transaction to commit before you can schedule any LCR that occurred after the commit of that transaction. This is essentially an apply barrier, and it is raised any time a large transaction commits.

### Understanding How DDL Statements Are Handled Inside SQL Apply

Now that we have explored how SQL Apply schedules DML transactions, it is time to look at DDL scheduling. Two aspects of DDL transactions are important to keep in mind: DDL statements act as the barrier synchronization point in the context of SQL Apply, and DDL statements are scheduled serially by SQL Apply (with the exception of `Create Table As Select` statements, which may be scheduled concurrently).

---

### Myth Buster: Third-party Replication Products Provide Better Latency, Because the Mining Is Usually Done at the Primary Site

This myth has the potential for being true only for small transactions. Remember that the latency of interest is not just in how quickly the data is captured, but when it is applied. In almost all cases, third-party replication products do not have the eager transaction scheduling feature that's available in SQL Apply. Thus the response time for a large transaction involving millions of rows will be quite high. Assuming that a transaction will take equal time to apply both at the primary and the standby (a good assumption for data loads), if you start a data load that takes 2 hours to complete, most third-party replication solutions will not start applying the transaction until they have seen the commit of the large transaction. So if the load completes at 12 P.M. at the primary, that data will be available at 2 P.M. at your standby—not a good place to be in terms of data loss. SQL Apply will start applying the transaction as soon as it is deemed to be large and will have the data available at the standby much faster.

Let's look at the barrier synchronization aspect of DDL transactions. Although this seems like an obscure academic fact, it turns out that you can use this to your advantage to ameliorate the effects of serial DDL execution. Whenever the mining engine encounters a commit redo for a DDL transaction that it needs to examine and apply to its internal data dictionary (also known as the LogMiner dictionary), it raises a barrier. The barrier condition is not satisfied until all transactions that have committed before the commit of the DDL transaction have been applied successfully.

Until the barrier condition is satisfied, no new transactions that committed after the DDL transaction are handed out to the ANALYZER process. Once the barrier condition is satisfied, the mining engine applies the DDL to the LogMiner dictionary, lifts its barrier, and then hands the DDL transaction to the ANALYZER process to be scheduled. The mining engine barrier shows up in the `v$logstdby_process` view for the `BUILDER` process:

```
SQL> SELECT STATUS_CODE AS SC, STATUS FROM V$LOGSTDBY_PROCESS
        WHERE TYPE = 'BUILDER' ;
SC     STATUS
-----  ------------------------------------------------------------
44604  BARRIER SYNCHRONIZATION ON DDL WITH XID 1.15.256 (WAITING ON 17
       TRANSACTIONS)
```

This tells you that the mining engine is waiting to apply transaction 1.15.256 and that 17 transactions need to be applied for the barrier condition to be satisfied. The apply engine also enters a barrier synchronization point when it receives the DDL transaction. This means although the mining engine's barrier is lifted and the ANALYZER process can start receiving transactions that committed after the DDL, the COORDINATOR process will not assign any transaction until the DDL transaction (except for `Create Table As Select` statements) at hand has been applied successfully. What does this mean? It means that when a DDL transaction is getting applied, all DML transactions that committed before the DDL have been successfully applied and no transaction chunk that committed after the DDL transaction (or handed to the ANALYZER after the DDL transaction, since there can be two transactions that commit at the same SCN) is in process of being applied by an APPLIER process.

From this description, it follows that SQL Apply schedules DDL statements (other than `Create Table As Select` statements) serially. This is done to maintain safety, but it does have an impact. Suppose you performed partition maintenance operations on two tables concurrently at the primary, and each took one hour to complete. At the logical standby site, they will be scheduled serially, and hence will take a total of two hours to complete. Thus it is important to offload large reorganization operations to off-peak hours. SQL Apply also allows you to skip specific DDL operations if you would like to do them out-of-band. We can take advantage of the barrier synchronization that we discussed earlier to perform DDL statements concurrently out-of-band without violating safety. Remember the following points:

■ The DDLs that you are planning to perform concurrently should be safe for concurrent operations. Examples of such operations are index rebuilds on separate tables, segment shrink operations on separate tables, and so on.

■ You have control over such DDLs and know that the DDLs are not issued by some application unbeknownst to you during the normal processing hours. This is unlikely, however, since you would have noticed the slowdown.

So the idea is to stop SQL Apply at the right point, perform the operations concurrently and out-of band at both the primary and the logical standby, and then restart SQL Apply so that it does not try to execute the DDL statements itself.

1.  First make sure that SQL Apply does not execute INDEX REBUILD statements itself. Suppose you have identified two large indexes, TRADE_HISTORY_IDX and PAYMENT_ HISTORY_IDX, both in the CUSTOMER schema, that are candidates for nightly rebuilds. You can direct SQL Apply not to apply ALTER INDEX statements for these two indexes with the following statements:

```
SQL> AlTER DATABASE STOP LOGICAL STANDBY APPLY;
SQL> EXECUTE DTMS_LOGSTDBY.SKIP(STMT => 'ALTER INDEX', -
        SCHEMA_NAME => 'CUSTOMER', OBJECT_NAME => 'TRADE_HISTORY_IDX');
SQL> EXECUTE DTMS_LOGSTDBY.SKIP(STMT => 'ALTER INDEX', -
        SCHEMA_NAME => 'CUSTOMER', OBJECT_NAME => 'PAYMENT_HISTORY_IDX');
```

2.  Next you need to make sure that SQL Apply stops before it encounters such an index rebuild operation. You can design it by always performing a sentinel DDL at the primary database before you rebuild the indexes, and registering a skip handler at the logical standby so that SQL Apply will stop when it sees the sentinel DDL. To keep the discussion simple, assume that the sentinel DDL is a TRUNCATE operation, so that you can issue it over and over again.

    Create the sentinel table first:

```
SQL> CREATE TABLE TEST.STOP_SQL_APPLY(A NUMBER);
```

    At the logical standby, you need to do two things: stop SQL Apply when you see the TRUNCATE operation on the test.stop_sql_apply table, and once the index rebuilds have been done successfully and SQL Apply has been restarted, you need to make sure you do not stop again on encountering the TRUNCATE table. So you need to write two procedures at the logical standby: one needs to be invoked before you start the index rebuild operations at the primary, and the other after the index rebuilds are done at the logical standby:

```
SQL> CREATE TABLE TEST.SQL_APPLY_MESG(CHECK_MSG VARCHAR2, MSG_TIME DATE);
SQL> CREATE OR REPLACE PROCEDURE SYS.STANDBY_START_REBUILD AS
BEGIN
   INSERT INTO TEST.SQL_APPLY_MESG VALUES ('STOP', SYSDATE);
   COMMIT;
END;
/
SQL> CREATE OR REPLACE PROCEDURE SYS.STANDBY_END_REBUILD AS
BEGIN
   DELETE FROM TEST.SQL_APPLY_MESG;
   COMMIT;
END;
/
```

You also create a procedure for the primary database (which is simply to truncate the sentinel table):

```
SQL> CREATE OR REPLACE PROCEDURE SYS.PRIMARY_START_REBUILD AS
BEGIN
  EXECUTE IMMEDIATE 'TRUNCATE TABLE TEST.STOP_SQL_APPLY';
END;
/
```

3. Now you can write the skip handler at the logical standby that will stop only on encountering the TRUNCATE operation on the test.sentinel_table only if there is a row in the test.sql_apply_mesg table:

```
SQL> CREATE OR REPLACE PROCEDURE SYS.STOP_SQL_APPLY_ON_DDL
(OLD_STMT IN VARCHAR2,
STMT_TYP IN VARCHAR2,
SCHEMA IN VARCHAR2,
NAME IN VARCHAR2,
XIDUSN IN NUMBER,
XIDSLT IN NUMBER,
XIDSQN IN NUMBER,
ACTION OUT NUMBER,
NEW_STMT OUT VARCHAR2)
AS
CHECK_MSG NUMBER := 0;
BEGIN
SELECT COUNT(MESSAGE_BODY) INTO CHECK_MSG FROM TEST. SQL_APPLY_MESG;
-- WE ARE SIMPLY CHECKING WHETHER A ROW EXISTS OR NOT IN THE TABLE
IF (CHECK_MSG = 1) THEN
  ACTION := DBMS_LOGSTDBY.SKIP_ACTION_ERROR;
  NEW_STMT := NULL;
ELSE
  ACTION := DBMS_LOGSTDBY.SKIP_ACTION_APPLY;
  NEW_STMT := OLD_STMT;
END IF;
END;
/
```

4. You now need to register the skip handler to a specific DDL operation:

```
SQL> EXECUTE DBMS_LOGSTDBY.SKIP( STMT => 'TRUNCATE TABLE', -
    SCHEMA_NAME => 'TEST', OBJECT_NAME => 'STOP_SQL_APPLY');
```

Now that you have all the building blocks, you can describe the procedure for index rebuilds:

```
STEP 1: AT THE LOGICAL STANDBY:
MAKE SURE THAT SQL APPLY WILL STOP AT THE APPROPRIATE TIME.
SQL> EXECUTE SYS.STANDBY_START_REBUILD;

STEP 2: AT THE PRIMARY DATABASE:
MAKE SURE THAT SQL APPLY STOPS BEFORE IT ENCOUNTERS THE INDEX REBUILD
OPERATIONS
SQL> EXECUTE SYS.PRIMARY_START_REBUILD;
```

At the primary database, you can start your index rebuilds in parallel. You will have to wait for SQL Apply to stop before you can start the rebuild operations. You do not need to take any more actions at the primary related to the index rebuilds. At the logical standby though, once the rebuilds have been finished, you will need to make sure that on restart, SQL Apply does not stop on encountering the TRUNCATE operation on the sentinel table:

```
STEP 3: AT THE LOGICAL STANDBY DATABASE:
SQL> EXECUTE SYS.STANDBY_END_REBUILD;
SQL> ALTER DATABASE START LOGICAL STANDBY APPLY IMMEDIATE;
```

Note that this time, although the skip handler (`sys.stop_sql_apply_on_ddl`) is active and will be invoked for the truncate table DDL, it will apply it and continue on.

# Tuning SQL Apply

If you were to look at the SQL Apply engine as a producer-consumer setup, the tuning at a high level involves choosing the three levers that you have:

- Increase the buffer between the producers (the mining servers) and the consumers (the apply servers). The only way to do this is to increase the MAX_SGA parameter that controls the size of the LCR_CACHE.

- Increase the throughput of the producer or the mining engine if the producer side of the system is the bottleneck.[21] The mining processes can be the bottleneck for several reasons:

  - There are not enough mining processes. In this case, you can increase the number of mining processes.

  - The workload is causing the mining engine to do unproductive work (such as paging out memory or performing checkpoints).

- Increase the throughput of the consumer, or the apply engine, if the consumer side of the system is the bottleneck. This can occur for several reasons:

  - You have not allocated enough apply processes. In this case, you can increase the number of appliers.

  - The workload is causing throughput to reduce. As discussed earlier, DDLs are applied serially at the logical standby. If you have an overabundance of DDLs in your workload, you may see a slowdown.

The performance tuning exercise should proceed in the following manner:

1. Determine whether SQL Apply is lagging more than expected.

2. If so, first determine whether SQL Apply is indeed the bottleneck:

   - Is the redo transport experiencing issues with the network?

   - Has SQL Apply encountered a problematic workload?

   - Look at AWR and ASH reports to rule out other components of the RDBMS.

---

[21] This is rarely the case, since it takes a lot less instructions to transform a redo records into LCRs than to apply an LCR via SQL to the database.

3. At this point, you know that SQL Apply is indeed part of the problem. Which engine is the bottleneck? Is it the mining or the apply engine?

   ■ If it is the apply engine, increase the number of appliers.

   ■ If it is the mining engine, do you need to increase memory size for the `lcr_cache` or the number of mining processes?

4. Repeat the steps.[22]

## Some Rules of Thumb

The default values for several parameters that control SQL Apply are not ideal for production systems. So we suggest the following:

■ Set `MAX_SERVERS` to 8 × number of cores:

```
SQL> EXECUTE DBMS_LOGSTDBY.APPLY_SET[23] ('MAX_SERVERS',  64);
```

■ Set `MAX_SGA` to 200MB:

```
SQL> EXECUTE DBMS_LOGSTDBY.APPLY_SET('MAX_SGA',  200);
```

■ Set `_HASH_TABLE_SIZE` to 10000000[24] (10 million):

```
SQL> EXECUTE DBMS_LOGSTDBY.APPLY_SET('_HASH_TABLE_SIZE', 10000000);
```

■ Defer DDLs to off-peak hours.

■ Set `PRESERVE_COMMIT_ORDER` to FALSE.

Note that for many applications, the default strict ordering imposed by SQL Apply is not necessary, and you can relax this without affecting the correctness of your applications that are offloaded to the logical standby.

```
SQL> EXECUTE DBMS_LOGSTDBY.APPLY_SET('PRESERVE_COMMIT_ORDER', FALSE);
```

## Determining Whether SQL Apply Is Lagging

This is quite simple. A simple select from the `V$DATAGUARD_STATS` view will provide you with the apply statistics:

```
SQL> SELECT NAME, VALUE, UNIT FROM V$DATAGUARD_STATS;
NAME                     VALUE          UNIT
----------------------   -------------  -----------------------------
APPLY FINISH TIME        +00 00:00:03   DAY(2) TO SECOND(1) INTERVAL
APPLY LAG                +00 00:00:05   DAY(2) TO SECOND(0) INTERVAL
TRANSPORT LAG            +00 00:00:00   DAY(2) TO SECOND(0) INTERVAL
```

---

[22] You need to repeat the ASH and AWR analysis. Although the RDBMS tuning was not needed initially, once you allocate more memory and processes to SQL Apply, it may then highlight the need to tune the RDBMS or the I/O subsystem. We have encountered a number of such instances in the field.

[23] Assuming you have a four-CPU box with dual core processors.

[24] `HASH_TABLE_SIZE` determines the size of an internal structure used to track dependencies between different transactions.

The values of interest are *apply lag* and *transport lag*. The apply lag value indicates how current the replicated data at the logical standby is, and the transport lag value indicates how much of the redo data that has already been generated is missing at the logical standby in terms of redo records. So if apply lag is larger than your expected value, you have an issue and you need to drill down. The view also answers the redo transport question of the next step.

**NOTE**
*If the* [apply lag > expected lag at the logical standby] *but* [(apply lag – transport lag) < expected lag at the logical standby], *then it is the redo transport that is keeping SQL Apply behind, and you need to look at your network.*[25]

# Determining Whether SQL Apply Is the Bottleneck

We have already shown you how to eliminate the redo transport as the bottleneck. The next thing to do will be to look at your AWR and ASH report. This will enable you to identify other bottlenecks in the system. For instance, you may be able to identify a query that is doing a full table scan and competing with SQL Apply in terms of CPU and I/O resources, or you may find that an update statement issued from SQL Apply is using a bad plan and not picking up an index that it should have, and so on.

# Determining Which SQL Apply Component Is the Bottleneck

Once you have established that SQL Apply is indeed the bottleneck, you need to find out which part of SQL Apply to focus on. The first query to make such a determination is to look at the producer-consumer pipeline. Is the pipeline full?

```
SQL> SELECT NAME, VALUE FROM V$LOGSTDBY_STATS WHERE NAME LIKE
     'TRANSACTIONS%';
NAME                      VALUE
--------------------      -------
TRANSACTIONS APPLIED      3764
TRANSACTIONS MINED        4985
```

The depth of the pipeline at any given time is *(transactions mined – transactions applied)*. You will have to run this query around 10 or more times at 1-minute intervals. If the size of the pipeline is always around two times the number of appliers or more, the mining engine is doing its job just fine, and it is the apply component that is behind. If, on the other hand, the size of the pipeline is decreasing or staying at a low value, you have to look at the mining engine more closely.

## Tuning the Mining Engine

You can tune the mining engine in two ways: increase the number of preparers[26] or increase the size of the LCR cache.

---

[25] SQL Apply cannot apply something that has not been received at the standby. Refer to Chapter 2.

[26] There can be only one reader process and one builder process.

**Increasing the Number of Preparers**   This needs to be done only rarely, and only if the following conditions are met:

- All PREPARER processes are busy doing work.
- The peak size of the LCR cache is significantly smaller than the maximum allocated for the (via the MAX_SGA setting).
- The number of transactions available in the LCR cache is less than the number of APPLIER processes available.
- Some APPLIER processes are idle.

So let's see how we will ensure that all these conditions are met. Remember that all queries need to be issued multiple times to ensure that the data is consistent and reliable.

1. Make sure all PREPARERS are busy doing work.[27]

```
SQL> SELECT COUNT(1) AS IDLE_PREPARERS FROM V$LOGSTDBY_PROCESS
WHERE TYPE = 'PREPARER' AND STATUS_CODE = 16166[28];
IDLE_PREPARER
-------------
0
```

2. Make sure that the peak size is well below the amount allocated:

```
SQL> SELECT USED_MEMORY_SIZE FROM V$LOGMNR_SESSION
     WHERE SESSION_ID = (SELECT VALUE FROM V$LOGSTDBY_STATS
       WHERE NAME = 'LOGMINER SESSION ID');

USED_MEMORY_SIZE
----------------
32522244
```

3. Verify that the PREPARER does not have enough ready work for the APPLIER processes:

```
SQL> SELECT (AVAILABLE_TXN - PINNED_TXN) AS PIPELINE_DEPTH FROM
V$LOGMNR_SESSION
     WHERE SESSION_ID = (SELECT VALUE FROM V$LOGSTDBY_STATS
                         WHERE NAME = 'LOGMINER SESSION ID');
PIPELINE_DEPTH
--------------
8
SQL> SELECT COUNT(*) AS APPLIER_COUNT
FROM V$LOGSTDBY_PROCESS WHERE TYPE = 'APPLIER';
APPLIER_COUNT
-------------
20
```

---

[27] Note it is difficult to find a PREPARER that is not in an idle state, because in most cases they are way ahead of the APPLIER processes. So you will need to run this query in a tight loop to get a valid result.

[28] ORA-16166: SQL Apply process is idle.

At this point, all three conditions for increasing the number of PREPARERS have been met. Now how do you increase the number of preparers? Before you do that, we need to look at how SQL Apply allocates processes in its disposal. SQL Apply exposes three parameters to control the number of processes: MAX_SERVERS, PREPARE_SERVERS, and APPLY_SERVERS. The following condition holds:

MAX_SERVERS[29] = PREPARE_SERVERS + APPLY_SERVERS + 3

Usually you simply specify MAX_SERVERS and let SQL Apply divide the available processes among the apply component and the mining component. By default, SQL Apply uses a process allocation algorithm that allocates one PREPARE_SERVER for every 20 server processes allocated to SQL Apply as specified by MAX_SERVERS. It also limits the number of PREPARE_SERVERS to 5.

Thus, if you set MAX_SERVERS to any value between 1 and 20, SQL Apply allocates one server process to act as a PREPARER, and allocates the rest of the processes as APPLIERS while satisfying the relationship previously described. Similarly, if you set MAX_SERVERS to a value between 21 and 40, SQL Apply allocates two server processes to act as PREPARERS and the rest as APPLIERS. SQL Apply allows you to override this process allocation formula by setting APPLY_SERVERS and PREPARE_SERVERS directly, provided that the relationship among the three parameters stays true.

So, in our case, we would like to increase the PREPARER processes to the value 3, while keeping the APPLIER processes at the same number of 30. To do this, we will first need to increase the number of MAX_SERVERS from 35 to 36, and then specifically set PREPARE_SERVERS to 3.[30]

```
SQL> EXECUTE DBMS_LOGSTDBY.APPLY_SET('MAX_SERVERS', 36);
SQL> EXECUTE DBMS_LOGSTDBY.APPLY_SET('PREPARE_SERVERS', 3);
```

Note that in 11*g*, you can change most parameters that control SQL Apply without having to stop SQL Apply. The change will take effect sometime in the future, as SQL Apply will detect our request and spawn the extra processes and bring them into the fold under the appropriate component.

**Increasing the Size of the LCR Cache**    You will need to increase the size of the LCR cache in two cases.

In case 1, the following conditions happen:

- Overall throughput is lower than expected.

- Not enough work is available in the LCR cache (number of available transactions is below number of APPLIERs).

- Peak value for v$logmnr_session.used_memory_size is almost equal to the amount allocated to the LCR cache.

In case 2, either of the following two conditions might occur:

- You see mining processes idle most of the time (generally speaking, the mining engine should be active one-sixth of the time).

---

[29] The constant *3* comes from the fact that we will always have one READER, one BUILDER, and one ANALYZER process. The COORDINATOR (or the LSP0) process is not counted within the scope of MAX_SERVERS.

[30] Without an explicit setting, SQL Apply will allocate the extra process to the apply engine.

■ You see the mining engine paging out memory at an unacceptable rate (a normalized rate of more than 5 percent is unacceptable).

We have already shown you how to determine the first three conditions. We want to reiterate that to see the variation in size, you will need to run the query against `v$logmnr_session` every few seconds.

We have also shown how to compute IDLE preparers. You can determine whether the BUILDER process is idle in a similar fashion. This query needs to be run every few seconds as well.

Now we'll show you how to compute the normalized pageout activity. To do this, you will have to obtain at least two snapshots of pageout activity over an interval of 5 to 10 minutes.

```
STEP 1. ISSUE THE FIRST QUERY.
SQL> SELECT NAME, VALUE FROM V$LOGSTDBY_STATS
WHERE NAME LIKE '%PAGE%' OR NAME LIKE '%UPTIME%' OR NAME LIKE '%IDLE%';


NAME                          VALUE
----------------------------  -------------
COORDINATOR UPTIME (SECONDS)  1200856
BYTES PAGED OUT               30000
SECONDS SPENT IN PAGEOUT      78
SYSTEM IDLE TIME IN SECS      3210


STEP 2. ISSUE THE QUERY AGAIN SAY IN 10 MINUTES.
SQL> SELECT NAME, VALUE FROM V$LOGSDTBY_STATS
WHERE NAME LIKE '%PAGE%' OR NAME LIKE '%UPTIME%' OR NAME LIKE '%IDLE%';


NAME                          VALUE
--------------------------    ---------------
COORDINATOR UPTIME(SECONDS)   1201456
BYTES PAGED OUT               1020000
SECONDS SPENT IN PAGEOUT      205
SYSTEM IDLE TIME IN SECS      3210
STEP 3. COMPUTE THE NORMALIZED PAGEOUT ACTIVITY.
FOR EXAMPLE:
CHANGE IN COORDINATOR UPTIME (U)= (1201456 - 1200856) = 600 SECS
AMOUNT OF ADDITIONAL IDLE TIME (I)= (3210 - 3210) = 0
CHANGE IN TIME SPENT IN PAGEOUT (P) = (205 - 78) = 127 SECS
PAGEOUT TIME IN COMPARISON TO UPTIME = P/(U-I) = 127/600 ~ 20%
```

You should write a PL/SQL procedure that takes an interval and provides the normalized pageout number. Ideally, time spent in pageout should be less than 5 percent of the uptime. Now it is usually acceptable for normalized pageout to be higher than the expected threshold infrequently, but if you continue to take snapshots and compute this value, and you find that the normalized pageout keeps violating the acceptable threshold, you will need to increase the LCR cache size. Once you have determined that you will need to change the MAX_SGA, the statement is very simple:

```
SQL> EXECUTE DBMS_LOGSTDBY.APPLY_SET( NAME => 'MAX_SGA', VALUE => 1024);
```

## Tuning the Apply Engine

At this point, you have determined that the apply component is the bottleneck.

**Increasing the Number of APPLIER Processes**   The following conditions must be met:

- The pipeline between the mining and apply component, in other words the LCR cache, has enough ready work available.

- There is no idle APPLIER process or there are unassigned large transactions.

We have already showed you how to determine whether there are no idle APPLIER processes. Now let's look at how you determine whether unassigned large transactions exist.

```
STEP 1 (LOOK AT THE DEPTH OF THE PIPELINE BETWEEN THE MINING ENGINE AND THE
APPLY ENGINE)
SQL> SELECT (AVAILABLE_TXN - PINNED_TXN) AS PIPELINE_DEPTH FROM V$LOGMNR_SESSION
     WHERE SESSION_ID = (SELECT VALUE FROM V$LOGSTDBY_STATS
                         WHERE NAME = 'LOGMINER SESSION ID');
PIPELINE_DEPTH
---------------
256
SQL> SELECT COUNT(*) AS APPLIER_COUNT
FROM V$LOGSTDBY_PROCESS WHERE TYPE = 'APPLIER';
APPLIER_COUNT
-------------
20


STEP 2(A): LOOK FOR IDLE APPLIERS
SQL> SELECT COUNT(1) AS IDLE_APPLIER FROM V$LOGSTDBY_PROCESS
WHERE TYPE = 'APPLIER' AND STATUS_CODE = 16166;
IDLE_APPLIER
------------
3
```

Note that SQL Apply uses a kSafe algorithm for transaction assignment: it holds $k$ appliers aside for applying complete committed transactions. By default, SQL Apply sets $k$[31] to be approximately 1/6 of the number of applier processes. Thus, you may have an issue, even though you find appliers that are idle in your system.

```
STEP 2(B): LOOK FOR UNASSIGNED LARGE TRANSACTIONS
SQL> SELECT VALUE FROM V$LOGSTDBY_STATS
WHERE NAME = 'LARGE TXNS WAITING TO BE ASSIGNED';
VALUE
----------
12
```

---

[31] Note $k$ must at least be 1 or greater, otherwise you may assign all appliers to uncommitted transactions and get into a deadlock.

**Determining Ill-behaved Workloads**    As mentioned, SQL Apply schedules DDL statements serially. You can determine the number of DDL transactions in your workload by querying the v$logstdby_stats view:

```
SQL> SELECT NAME, VALUE FROM V$LOGSTDBY_STATS WHERE NAME = 'DDL TXNS DELIVERED';
NAME                     VALUE
---------------          ---------------------------
DDL TXNS DELIVERED       510
```

Note that this provides the total number of DDL transactions that have been delivered to the apply engine since the last restart. You will need to issue this query over a large interval and subtract the two values to see how many DDL statements were delivered to the apply engine. Note that not all DDL statements delivered to the apply engine will be applied—that is, DDL statements that are associated with skipped internal schemas are not applied by SQL Apply.

# Troubleshooting SQL Apply

Tuning SQL Apply was discussed in a separate section—it is always important to ensure that you are getting the most out of your logical standby. There are, however, other areas in which problems can occur. Since we include a separate troubleshooting chapter in this book, we will concentrate on only a few issues here regarding SQL Apply.

## Understanding Restarts in SQL Apply

Since all good DBAs are in the habit of monitoring their alert logs, if you are managing a logical standby database, you will need to monitor the DBA_LOGSTDBY_EVENTS view with equal intensity.

### Understanding Restarts Due to ORA-4031

You may see the following in the alert log:

```
ORA-4031: UNABLE TO ALLOCATE 2904 BYTES OF SHARED MEMORY ("SHARED
POOL","UNKNOWN OBJECT","LOGMINER LCR C","KRVXRGR")
INCIDENT DETAILS IN:
/U01/APP/ORACLE/DIAG/RDBMS/APPLY/APPLY1/INCIDENT/INCDIR_6246890/APPLY1_MS00_13
611_I6246890.TRC
KRVXERPT: ERRORS DETECTED IN PROCESS 47, ROLE READER.
KRVXMRS: LEAVING BY EXCEPTION: 4031
ERRORS IN FILE
/U01/APP/ORACLE/DIAG/RDBMS/APPLY/APPLY1/TRACE/APPLY1_MS00_13611.TRC:
...
ORA-16234: RESTARTING TO RESET LOGICAL STANDBY
LOGSTDBY STATUS: ORA-16111: LOG MINING AND APPLY SETTING UP
LOGSTDBY STATUS: APPLY LWM 5368712584, HWM 5368712584, SCN 5368712584
LOGMINER: PARAMETERS SUMMARY FOR SESSION# = 1
LOGMINER: NUMBER OF PROCESSES = 3, TRANSACTION CHUNK SIZE = 201
LOGMINER: MEMORY SIZE = 200M, CHECKPOINT INTERVAL = 1000M
```

What is going on? Why did SQL Apply go down with ORA-4031? And why did it not encounter the error once it restarted? The answer has to do with how the mining engine manages memory.

Remember the LCR cache? It keeps LCRs that are associated with modifications made to the database, and different LCRs require different amounts of memory. This is obvious: an insert statement inserting values to a table with 10 columns will most likely require less space than one that inserts values into a table with 300 columns of the same type. To optimize performance, the mining engine recycles memory within its own list and does not free it to the heap. Most of the time, this works well. However, when the working set changes drastically (say, the LCR cache was filled with LCRs for tables with 10 columns and then you encounter a series of direct path loads for tables with 200 columns each), the mining engine may not find enough memory in its list, due to memory fragmentation, although the total amount of memory available in its free list is enough to satisfy the memory requirement. In this case, SQL Apply will first release all the memory from its internal lists to the top-level heap and see if the memory requirement can be met. In very rare circumstances, where the memory fragmentation pattern is such that a refreshing of the internal lists will not do the trick, SQL Apply will perform a controlled restart. This is extremely rare. If you see this in your alert log, you should not be alarmed.

## Understanding Restarts to Break Deadlocks

As mentioned, SQL Apply performs optimistic scheduling and then keeps a lookout for unsafe anomalies and handles these as they arise. This is prevalent throughout the design, and it's one of the primary reasons why SQL Apply can keep up with a high redo rate while honoring transaction boundaries established at the primary database.

Let's look at an unsafe anomaly: the possibility of deadlock while applying large transactions concurrently. We will illustrate the issue in the context of two small transactions, if they were scheduled the same way SQL Apply schedules large transactions. As discussed earlier, SQL Apply schedules concurrent large transactions without computing row dependencies between them, since the very fact that the transactions are running concurrently implies that they must be independent, until one of them commits. Since SQL Apply will go through a commit barrier on such a commit, the scheduling is safe. There is, however, one subtle issue: Oracle RDBMS allows a transaction to release row locks when it executes a rollback to a savepoint, which may cause a false dependency to be introduced and hence cause a deadlock in the context of SQL Apply.

Table 4-4 shows a valid schedule, since by the time transaction Y touches $R_1$ of $T_1$, X had rolled it back, and as a result the row lock on $R_1$ has been released.

Now let's see a possible SQL Apply schedule, if row dependencies were computed for these two transactions (Table 4-5).

| Time | Transaction X | Transaction Y |
|------|---------------|---------------|
| 10 | Savepoint A | |
| 20 | Modify $R_1$ of $T_1$ | Modify $R_2$ to $T_1$ |
| 30 | Rollback to A | |
| 40 | Modify $R_3$ of $T_1$ | Modify $R_1$ of $T_1$ |
| 50 | | Commit |
| 60 | Commit | |

**TABLE 4-4.** *Sample Valid Transaction History ($H_2$) at the Primary Database*

| Time/SCN | Applier#1 (X) | Applier#2 (Y) |
|---|---|---|
| 110 | | Modify $R_2$ of $T_1$ |
| 120 | | Modify $R_1$ of $T_1$ |
| 130 | | Commit |
| 140 | Savepoint A | |
| 150 | Modify $R_1$ of $T_1$ | |
| 160 | Rollback to A | |
| 170 | Modify $R_3$ of $T_1$ | |
| 180 | Commit | |

**TABLE 4-5.** *Transaction Schedule (Associated with $H_2$) at the Logical Standby if* `preserve_commit_order` *Is Set to* `TRUE` *and with Computation of Row Dependencies*

Note that since Y committed before X, the row dependency on $R_1$ resolved in Y's favor and SQL Apply scheduled Y before it allowed X to modify row $R_1$.[32]

Now we'll look at a possible schedule[33] at the logical standby that will result in a deadlock, when row dependencies are not computed (such as in the case of large transactions). See Table 4-6.

| Time/SCN | Applier#1 (X) | Applier#2 (Y) |
|---|---|---|
| 110 | Savepoint A | Modify $R_2$ of $T_1$ |
| 120 | Modify $R_1$ of $T_1$ | |
| 130 | | Modify $R_1$ of $T_1$ (Applier#2 is blocked now, and RDBMS puts the process in the TX-ENQ of Applier#1. It will be unblocked only when X commits.) |
| 140 | Rollback to A | |
| 150 | Modify $R_3$ of $T_1$ | |
| 160 | X cannot make progress now (if `preserve_commit_order` is set). Its commit is after that of Y. So although it sees the commit record, it cannot commit. | |

**TABLE 4-6.** *Transaction Schedule (Associated with $H_2$) Leading to Deadlock at the Logical Standby if* `preserve_commit_order` *Is Set to* `TRUE` *and Without the Computation of Row Dependencies*

---

[32] Although at the primary database, X modified $R_1$ before Y did.

[33] Note that SQL Apply may even get the same scheduling that was used at the primary database. In this case, no deadlock will occur.

The COORDINATOR process performs a deadlock detection based on a timeout value. Once it detects the deadlock, it will ask Applier#1 to rollback. In many cases (if this is the first chunk that Applier#1 is applying), this is enough, since Applier#2 will make progress and we will get back to the schedule shown in Table 4-4. However, if we run into a deadlock midway through a large transaction, SQL Apply will need to perform a controlled restart: but before doing a restart, it will remember that it had run into a deadlock and that on restart it needs to schedule X before Y to get a safe schedule.

Because you now know how this works, you won't be alarmed when you see the following warnings in the alert log:

```
LSP0: ROLLING BACK APPLY SERVER 2
LSP0: APPLY SERVER 2 ROLLED BACK
LSP0: CAN'T RECOVER FROM ROLLBACK OF MULTI-CHUNK TXN, ABORTING..
LOGSTDBY APPLY PROCESS AS05 SERVER ID=5 PID=41 OS ID=17169 STOPPED
LOGSTDBY APPLY PROCESS AS04 SERVER ID=4 PID=40 OS ID=17167 STOPPED
LOGSTDBY APPLY PROCESS AS03 SERVER ID=3 PID=39 OS ID=17164 STOPPED
...
LOGMINER: SESSION#=1, BUILDER MS01 PID=28 OS ID=17141 SID=86 STOPPED
...
LOGSTDBY STATUS: ORA-16222: AUTOMATIC LOGICAL STANDBY RETRY OF LAST ACTION
LOGSTDBY STATUS: ORA-16111: LOG MINING AND APPLY SETTING UP
...
```

## Troubleshooting Stopped SQL Apply

Two important issues can cause SQL Apply to stop. More cases and their solutions appear in Chapter 13.

### Handling ORA-26786 and ORA-26787 with "Skip Failed Transaction"

At times you will find that SQL Apply has stopped with one of the following errors:

- **ORA-26786** This is raised when SQL Apply finds the row to be modified using the primary or unique key information contained within the LCR, but the before-image of the row does not match the image contained within the LCR.

- **ORA-26787** This is raised when SQL Apply cannot find the row to be modified using the primary or unique key information contained within the LCR.

SQL Apply provides two ways to skip a failed transaction:

- Use the SKIP_FAILED_TRANSACTION clause when starting the SQL Apply processes
- Use the dbms_logstdby.skip_transaction procedure.

Our advice is threefold:

- When you skip a failed transaction (in other words, a transaction that caused SQL Apply to stop), you will need to take compensating actions at the logical standby.

- You can use the SKIP_FAILED_TRANSACTION clause if you know that the transaction is a DDL transaction, and you can either ignore the DDL safely at the logical standby or reissue it yourself.

- Be very wary of using SKIP_TRANSACTION or SKIP_FAILED_TRANSACTION when dealing with DML transactions. You will simply be moving the problem to appear sometime in the future.

Before you skip a transaction, SQL Apply writes the following in the alert log (and also in DBA_LOGSTDBY_EVENTS) before it stops:

```
LOGSTDBY STMT: UPDATE "SALES"."CUSTOMER"
SET
"FIRST_NAME" = 'JOHN'
WHERE
"CUSTOMER_ID" = 21340 AND
"FIRST_NAME" = 'JAHN' AND
ROWID = 'AAAAAAAAEAAAAAPAAA'
LOGSTDBY STATUS: ORA-26786: A ROW WITH KEY 21340 EXISTS BUT HAS CONFLICTING
COLUMNS FIRST_NAME IN TABLE SALES.CUSTOMER
LOGSTDBY PID 1006, ORACLE@STACO03 (P004)
LOGSTDBY XID 0X0006.00E.00000417, THREAD 1, RBA 0X02DD.00002221.10
```

This does not give you any information about where the transaction started. You can, however, use the FLASHBACK_TRANSACTION_QUERY[34] view at the primary database to find out the SCN at which the transaction started.

```
SQL> SELECT START_SCN, COMMIT_SCN FROM FLASHBACK_TRANSACTION_QUERY
WHERE XID = HEXTORAW(000600E00000417);
START_SCN          COMMIT_SCN
----------         ----------
56152032           56159340
```

Now that you have the start_scn and commit_scn, you can run the following query at the primary database to mine the archived logs using Oracle's LogMiner utility:

```
SQL> EXECUTE DBMS_LOGMNR.START_LOGMNR (STARTSCN => 56152032, -
     ENDSCN => 56159340, -
     OPTIONS => DBMS_LOGMNR.DICT_FROM_ONLINE_CATALOG[35] + -
DBMS_LOGMNR.CONTINUOUS_MINE);
SQL> SELECT DISTINCT SEG_OWNER, TABLE_NAME FROM V$LOGMNR_CONTENTS
     WHERE XID = HEXTORAW(000600E00000417);
```

This will return all the distinct tables modified by the transaction. If you want to know what the actual changes were, you can then issue the following query:

```
SQL> SELECT SQL_REDO FROM V$LOGMNR_CONTENTS
WHERE XID  = HEXTORAW(000600E00000417);
```

---

[34] Note that the column XID is of type RAW instead of the three-tuple printed in the alert log. You can simply append the three components and apply the HEXTORAW function on that to get the XID needed for the FLASHBACK_ TRANSACTION_QUERY view.

[35] The query tells Oracle LogMiner to find the archived log files between the SCN range (56152032 and 56159340) from the control file (the directive continuous_mine), and use the online data dictionary of the database (the directive dict_from_online_catalog) to interpret the redo records found.

Make sure that you have spooled the output to a text file. Once you are done using LogMiner, simply end the LogMiner session by issuing the following:

```
SQL> EXECUTE DBMS_LOGMNR.END_LOGMNR();
```

## Handling ORA-04042 "Procedure, Function, Package, or Package Body Does Not Exist"

This error is most likely due to SQL Apply encountering a GRANT/REVOKE on a procedure or a function that exists in one of the internally skipped schemas. You can handle this by registering an error handler with SQL Apply to skip errors encountered during the apply of such statements. The following is an example of how to skip these bothersome transactions:

```
STEP 1: DEFINE THE ERROR HANDLER
CREATE OR REPLACE PROCEDURE SYS.HANDLE_ERROR_DDL (
OLD_STMT  IN VARCHAR2,
STMT_TYPE IN VARCHAR2,
SCHEMA IN VARCHAR2,
NAME    IN VARCHAR2,
XIDUSN IN VARCHAR2,
XIDSLT IN VARCHAR2,
XIDSQN IN VARCHAR2,
ERROR IN VARCHAR2,
NEW_STMT OUT VARCHAR2
) AS
INTERNAL_SCHEMA NUMBER := 0;
BEGIN
-- DEFAULT TO WHAT WE ALREADY HAVE
NEW_STMT := OLD_STMT;
-- IGNORE ANY GRANT ERRORS ON INTERNALLY SKIPPED SCHEMAS
IF ((INSTR(UPPER(OLD_STMT),'GRANT')) > 0) OR
((INSTR(UPPER(OLD_STMT),'REVOKE')) > 0)
THEN
  IF SCHEMA IS NULL THEN
    INTERNAL_SCHEMA := 1;
  ELSE
    SELECT COUNT(1) INTO INTERNAL_SCHEMA FROM DBA_LOGSTDBY_SKIP
    WHERE OWNER = SCHEMA AND STATEMENT_OPT = 'INTERNAL SCHEMA';
  END IF;
END IF;
IF INTERNAL_SCHEMA <> THEN
    NEW_STMT := NULL;
    -- RECORD THE FACT THAT WE JUST SKIPPED AN ERROR (CODE NOT SHOWN HERE)
  END IF;
END IF;
END HANDLE_ERROR_DDL;
/


2. REGISTER THE SKIP_ERROR PROCEDURE WITH SQL APPLY
SQL> EXECUTE DBMS_LOGSTDBY.SKIP_ERROR ( -
STATEMENT => 'NON_SCHEMA_DDL', -
```

```
SCHEMA_NAME => NULL, -
OBJECT_NAME => NULL, -
PROC_NAME => 'SYS.HANDLE_ERROR_DDL');
```

# Conclusion

Once again, the chapter has been long, but we hope it has been instructive. The majority of the problems that people encounter in the context of a Data Guard implementation can be attributed to misunderstandings. The fact that you are reading this book before diving into deployment is a sign that you are in the prudent minority. Here's one more piece of advice regarding a logical standby deployment: *The performance of a logical standby depends heavily on your workload at the primary.*

Your first order of business is to create a logical standby off your current primary database and let it run for a while. This way, you will get a chance to try it out on live data, and you can also validate some of the issues we discussed in this chapter.

# CHAPTER
## 5

# Implementing Oracle
# Data Guard Broker

n simple terms, the Data Guard Broker is the management framework for Data Guard. Even if you are a die-hard SQL*Plus user and are used to managing your Data Guard configurations by hand, it is still worth it for you to have a look at the Data Guard Broker. Whether you arrived at this chapter directly from Chapter 2, looking for the Broker to finish the creation job for you, or you are just curious about what the Broker can do for you, the information you will glean from this chapter will help you travel the Data Guard management road. And if you are an Oracle Enterprise Manager Grid Control user, you are using the Broker by default, and it will be good to understand what goes on underneath when you create and manage Data Guard standby configurations. We will discuss the interaction between Grid Control and the Broker in detail in this chapter.

One thing to remember is that the Broker is a part of Data Guard, and if you are using standby databases but not using the Broker you are still using Data Guard. You are just not using the Broker to manage your configuration, and you are using SQL*Plus instead.

This chapter is not intended to replace the Broker manual. It is intended to ensure that you understand how the Broker works, how to set it up to avoid surprises, and what goes on when you create, manage, and monitor Broker configurations.

# Overview of the Data Guard Broker

The Broker is not a feature that is installed separately, nor is it a entity separate from Data Guard. It is part of the normal Oracle Database Enterprise Edition installation and an integral part of Data Guard. Its function is to present a single integrated view of a Data Guard configuration that allows you to connect through any database in a configuration and propagate changes to the configuration or any of the databases in that configuration, primary or standby. Changes that can be made to the Data Guard–related parameters are configuration, transport methods, apply setup and role change services, as well as the overall protection mode. In addition, through this single connection, you can monitor the health of the entire configuration or any of the databases that are part of this configuration.

The Broker is also responsible for implementing and managing the automatic failover capability of Data Guard, called Fast-Start Failover. This will be discussed at length in Chapter 8.

Basically, the Broker is made up of three parts: a set of background processes on each database, a set of configuration files, and a command line interface (CLI) called DGMGRL. It is important that you understand the workings of each of these parts before you delve into the details of creating and managing your Data Guard configurations.

### Myth Buster: The Broker Is Not a Mature and Reliable Interface for Data Guard

Nothing could be further from the truth. The Broker has been evolving since Oracle9i and is not only a reliable interface to Data Guard, but is the very foundation upon which many of the Data Guard features are built, including Fast-Start Failover.

**TIP**
*Once you start using the Broker you must always use the Broker to make any changes to your Data Guard configuration. This means that you must use Grid Control or the Broker CLI DGMGRL to change any Data Guard settings. If you use SQL\*Plus to make configuration changes, the Broker will put things back the way it sees the world or this will lead to inconsistencies between the Broker configuration parameters and the database.*

# The Broker Process Model

As with Data Guard's transport and apply functions, the Broker uses a set of background processes on each database in a Data Guard configuration to monitor and manage the setup. The basic processes are shown in Figure 5-1.

All the Broker processes are started by the Broker when it is enabled and the database is started. You, as the DBA, have no control over what processes are started or how many; that is completely up to the Broker. It will start each of these processes on all the databases in your configuration, the first being the Data Guard Monitor (DMON), explained next. The processes and files in Figure 5-1 are defined as follows:

- **Data Guard Monitor (DMON)** This Broker-controller process is the main Broker process and is responsible for coordinating all Broker actions as well as maintaining the Broker configuration files. This process is enabled or disabled with the `DG_BROKER_START` parameter.

- **Broker Resource Manager (RSM)** The RSM is responsible for handling any SQL commands used by the Broker that need to be executed on one of the databases in the configuration. These SQL commands are made as a result of a change to the configuration made through DGMGRL or are the configuration commands executed by the Broker during database startup.

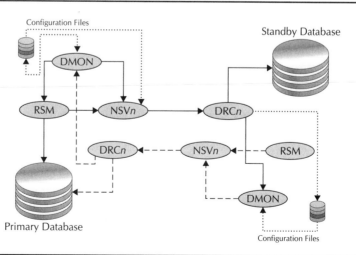

**FIGURE 5-1.** *Data Guard Broker main processes*

- **Data Guard Net Server (NSV*n*)**   From 1 to *n* of these network server processes can exist. They are responsible for making contact with the remote database and sending across any work items to the remote database. Connections to the remote database are made using the same connect identifier that you specified for the database when you created the configuration.

- **DRC*n***   These network receiver processes establish the connection from the source database NSV*n* process. An NSV*n* to DRC*n* connection is similar to the LogWriter Network Service (LNS) to Remote File Server (RFS) connection for Redo Transport. As with Redo Transport, when the Broker needs to send something (data or SQL, for example) between databases, it uses this NSV to DRC connection. These connections are started as needed.

- **Configuration files**   The Broker stores all of the configuration details in these two binary command files. Through the data in these files, the Broker knows what databases make up the configuration, their current intended states, how to connect to each one, and what parameters to set up when each database starts up.

**NOTE**
*Configuration files are flat files stored either on the operating system or inside Automatic Storage Management (ASM). The Broker manages these files, and they are not to be manipulated by you.*

## The Broker Process Flow

In a Broker configuration it is the Data Guard Monitor (DMON) process on the primary database that is the owner of the configuration. Even though you may attach to any database in a configuration using the DGMGRL CLI, all standby databases must get their marching orders from the primary DMON, and all commands to modify the configuration, regardless of which database you are connected to, are done through the primary.

In Figure 5-1, the communication between the primary DMON process and the databases is shown by solid lines. When the DMON needs to communicate with the standby databases, it uses one of the NSV processes to send work to a standby. This is intended to protect the DMON from a network hang if the link goes down in the middle of this send and receive process. An example of this kind of work would be a periodic health check, where the status and state of each standby database is retrieved and stored in the configuration files. Whenever the DMON needs to execute some SQL, it will enlist the aid of the RSM process on the primary database.

The RSM process will execute the SQL directly if it is intended for the primary database; otherwise, if the SQL is targeted for one of the standby databases, the RSM process asks an NSV process to send the SQL to the target standby. This also protects the RSM process from a network hang, the same way the DMON process avoids a hang.

Each NSV process will have a partner DRC process on the target database, which will perform the actual work on behalf of the source database NSV process and return the results or status.

Upon startup of the primary database, the DMON process will attempt to connect to each standby database (using the NSV–DRC connection pair) to establish communication and send the necessary configuration information so that the standby can be configured and start the apply services. If a standby database is not available, you will see the following Transparent

Networking Substrate (TNS) error in the primary database alert log right after an NSV process starts up:

```
NSV1 started with pid=21, OS id=8962
***********************************************************************
Fatal NI connect error 12514, connecting to:
 (DESCRIPTION=(ADDRESS=(PROTOCOL=TCP)(HOST=Matrix_DR.domain.com)(PORT=1521))
 (CONNECT_DATA=(SERVICE_NAME=Matrix_DR0_DGB.domain.com)
 (CID=(PROGRAM=oracle)(HOST=Matrix_DR)(USER=oracle))))
 ...
TNS-12564: TNS:connection refused
    ns secondary err code: 0
    nt main err code: 0
    nt secondary err code: 0
    nt OS err code: 0
```

Because the primary database cannot connect, no information can be sent to the standby. The primary database will continue to startup and the Broker will execute all the setup commands using the local RSM process to execute the SQL statements. You will see other TNS-12564 errors after this in the alert log when the Redo Transport LNS process tries to connect as well as any Fetch Archive Log (FAL) (gap) resolution attempts.

When the primary DMON is successful in connecting to the standby database, it will instruct the local RSM to send the setup commands to the standby database. These commands would define the necessary Data Guard parameters and start the apply services if required. The RSM will send these commands using the NSV–DRC connection pair.

The communication between a standby database and the primary database is shown in Figure 5-1 by the dashed lines. Whenever a standby database starts up, the DMON process will initiate a connection to the primary database to find out what it should be doing. Remember that the primary database controls the configuration. If the primary database is not reachable (the network or primary database is down), this connection will fail, and you will see a TNS error in the standby database's alert log, as follows:

```
Fatal NI connect error 12514, connecting to:
 (DESCRIPTION=(ADDRESS=(PROTOCOL=TCP)(HOST=Matrix.domain)(PORT=1521))
 (CONNECT_DATA=(SERVER=DEDICATED)
 (SERVICE_NAME=Matrix.domain)(CID=(PROGRAM=oracle)
 (HOST=Matrix)(USER=oracle))))
 . . .
TNS-12564: TNS:connection refused
    ns secondary err code: 0
    nt main err code: 0
    nt secondary err code: 0
    nt OS err code: 0
```

You can tell from the TNS information that this is a connection to the primary database called Matrix and not some other kind of network error. The fix here is either to start up the primary or fix the network error condition. This kind of error will cause a delay in the startup of the standby database as the Broker tries to determine what it should be doing. Generally, this error is caused by a delay in making the network connection and the time the Broker waits before trying again. You can tune this by setting the CommunicationTimeout property, which we will explain later

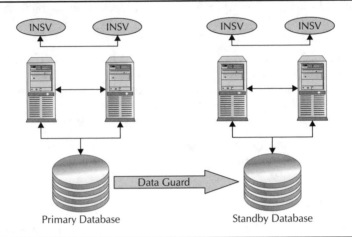

**FIGURE 5-2.**   *Data Guard Broker RAC processes*

in this chapter. Once the Broker has tried to connect to the primary a couple of times, the startup of the standby database will continue after which the Broker will continue to attempt to connect to the primary. When communication is restored, the standby database will get its marching orders and start receiving and applying the redo from the primary database.

In addition to these Broker processes, another set of Broker processes come into play when the primary, the standby, or both are Real Application Clusters (RAC), as shown in Figure 5-2.

These internode servers (INSVs) maintain a connection between the nodes in the cluster to ensure that the Broker on each node knows the state of the cluster. The primary database will always start up an INSV process even if the database is not a RAC.

As other RAC instances start, the Broker will start the INSVs, and they will make queries between all the instances to determine the current state of each node in a Broker-controlled database. In this manner, the Broker is able to maintain information about each instance in the RAC. To make sure that this does not have an adverse impact to performance, this querying is optimized to avoid any unnecessary RAC traffic.

In addition to these Broker processes we have been discussing, you may see one more process on the primary database in a Broker-controlled configuration: the Fast-Start Failover process (FSFP) which is used only when the primary is under the control of Data Guard's automatic failover feature, Fast-Start Failover. The FSFP process will establish a connection to the Fast-Start Failover target database by connecting to a DRC process on that database, much like the NSV to DRC process connection. Fast-Start Failover is discussed at length in Chapter 8.

## The Broker Configuration Files

As shown in Figure 5-1, the Broker maintains configuration files at each database in the configuration to keep track of the Data Guard–wide settings and the intended states for each database in the configuration. Two copies of the configuration files are always stored on each database for redundancy, and their location is controlled by the following two parameters:

- `DG_BROKER_CONFIG_FILE1`
- `DG_BROKER_CONFIG_FILE2`

By default, these are set to the $ORACLE_HOME/dbs directory with a filename of dr1<*DB_UNIQUE_NAME*>.dat and dr2<*DB_UNIQUE_NAME*>.dat, but you should never leave them as the defaults unless you are just playing around. If the database is a RAC, you must store these files on a shared location that is accessible to all RAC instances, because only one copy of these files can exist for the entire RAC and both files must be visible to all instances in the RAC.

**TIP**
*Make sure you change the default location of the Broker configuration files before you start using the Broker. Their placement is controlled by the database parameters* `DG_BROKER_CONFIG_FILE1` *and* `DG_BROKER_CONFIG_FILE2`.

This configuration information is referred to as the *properties* of the configuration and is divided into Configuration-Wide and Individual Database properties. In addition, the Broker uses the configuration files to keep track of the intended state information for each database. The configuration files of all databases are kept in sync by the Broker, but the DMON process of the primary database is the owner of the master copy of the files. Changes made to any database configuration property, regardless of which database you have connected to, are channeled back to the primary database DMON process, which then updates the primary database configuration files.

The configuration file update flow is shown in Figure 5-1 by dotted lines. The primary DMON process updates the local configuration file when the Database Administrator (DBA) makes changes to the properties of the configuration. This information is then sent to all standby databases using the normal NSV–DRC process pair. Once the remote configuration file is updated, the DRC process of the standby notifies the DMON process to refresh its in-memory copy of the configuration file.

If the DBA is connected to the standby and makes changes to the configuration properties, the changes are communicated back to the primary DMON using an NSV–DRC pair. The primary DMON updates the configuration file and the process is repeated to communicate the changes to all standby databases in the configuration.

The fact that the primary DMON is the master of the configuration determines when something will happen on a standby database. For example, if you start up a standby and it cannot connect to the primary database, no Data Guard functionality (starting up the apply process, checking for gaps, and so on) will be performed until the standby database can connect to the primary database (via the same NSV–DRC pair) and determine what it is supposed to do.

**TIP**
*You can watch when the Broker sets up a standby database by shutting down the primary and standby databases, performing a* `tail -f` *of the standby alert log (if you are on UNIX or Linux), and then starting the standby database. You will see the standby attempt to make contact with the primary, fail a couple of times, and then wait. Once you start up the primary, you will see all of the Broker setup commands being executed on the standby database.*

You may ask, "What happens when my primary is gone and I need to failover?" This is why the Broker keeps redundant copies of the configuration files at each database in the configuration, so when you do failover a standby database, it can determine the original settings for the entire configuration as it becomes the "master" of the configuration files by becoming the primary database. Role transitions will be discussed in Chapter 8.

# The Broker CLI

The last part of the puzzle is how to interact with the Broker. You have two choices: Enterprise Manager Grid Control or the Broker CLI DGMGRL. These are actually interchangeable, with the few setup steps mentioned in the next section. You will see that certain configuration options in a Broker setup are available only through DGMGRL and not at all with Grid Control.

If you choose to use Grid Control to manage your Data Guard configurations, you will either need to create a Broker configuration on top of your current standby setup or use the Grid Control Data Guard Wizard to create your standby databases, as Grid Control uses the Broker to manage all Data Guard configurations. Grid Control does have the ability to view certain items of an existing Data Guard configuration without having the Broker configured. You can determine whether a primary database participates in a Data Guard configuration (without the Broker), and you can monitor some of the performance information about the standby setup. But you cannot use Grid Control to manage Data Guard actively or perform any of the functions of Data Guard without the Broker configured. You can use Grid Control 10.2.0.5 to create non-Broker standby databases, but the same restrictions apply. In short, to gain full functionality of Data Guard through Grid Control, you must use the Broker.

The Broker CLI DGMGRL is included in the Oracle Database Enterprise Edition and Client kits and is the only part of Data Guard that can be run on any platform. This does not mean that the Broker itself or any other part of Data Guard is running on a different platform, just the client you use to manage your configuration. Data Guard does allow some mixed platform configurations, but these are few and they have special requirements in certain cases.[1] For example, you can have your primary and standby databases all running on Linux and use a Windows systems to run DGMGRL to manage Data Guard. All that is needed are the appropriate Oracle Net Services definitions.

To access DGMGRL, type **dgmgrl** at the command prompt and the CLI will start up and return a DGMGRL> prompt:

```
[Matrix] dgmgrl
DGMGRL for Linux: Version 11.1.0.6.0 - Production
Copyright (c) 2000, 2005, Oracle. All rights reserved.
Welcome to DGMGRL, type "help" for information.
DGMGRL>
```

This does not connect you to any database—not even our current SID Matrix. To connect to your Data Guard configuration, you either add a slash (/) or the username and password on the command line or you use the CONNECT command after you have started DGMGRL.

---

[1] At the time of this writing, Oracle MetaLink Note 413484.1 provides information about Data Guard mixed platform support.

# Getting Started with the Broker

Now that you have a picture of the various parts of the Broker and know how they interact, you might think that you can jump right into DGMGRL and start configuring your Data Guard setup. You could, but you would run into problems down the line. It is important that you understand the prerequisites of a Broker configuration and how the Broker performs its magic so you get the most out of the Broker. These prerequisites fall into the following four categories:

- Configuring the Broker parameters

- The Broker and the listener

- RAC and the Broker

- Connecting to the Broker

If you are an Enterprise Manager Grid Control user, you may think that you do not have to worry about these prerequisites—but the truth is, you still need to know about and follow these rules. While Grid Control does handle most of this for you, there may come a time when you cannot get to your Grid Control setup and you need to fall back to the CLI. We will discuss what you need to do in each of these categories, after which you will be ready to implement your Broker configuration.

## Configuring the Broker Parameters

First off, if you are not using an spfile on your databases, you must configure it now on all databases in your Data Guard configuration. Since this requires a restart of your production database, you may have to schedule this change before you can start configuring the Broker. The spfile is required since the Broker dynamically sets various Data Guard–related parameters, as discussed in Chapter 2.

As mentioned, the two database parameters that specify where the Broker configuration files are going to be placed when you enable the Broker are DG_BROKER_CONFIG_FILE1 and DG_BROKER_CONFIG_FILE2. Since these parameters do have a default directory ($ORACLE_HOME/dbs/) and filename, you can quite easily forget to change them and the Broker will still appear to work. We say "appear to work" because in a RAC environment, the dbs directory is not always visible cluster-wide, and each instance in the RAC would be updating a different file, causing untold havoc with your Data Guard setup. But RAC considerations aside, it is bad practice to leave these parameters in the Oracle Home and both files in the same place—especially on the primary database, because the Broker is primary-centric (that is, it gets all its orders from the primary). So you must change these parameters before you enable the Broker.

You must set these parameters on the primary (production) database as well as on any standby databases that you have already created using one of the non–Grid Control methods shown in Chapter 2. If you used Grid Control to create the standby database, these parameters would have been set for you, but they may not be stored where you would like, so it is important that you understand them and make the appropriate changes.

The naming conventions used here are for the primary database Matrix. These names would be changed depending on the database where they are being defined—Matrix_DR0 for the first standby, for example.

If you are not using ASM or raw devices, you can place these files anywhere you like. But put them on different disk spindles so a single disk failure does not destroy your entire Broker configuration!

```
SQL> ALTER SYSTEM SET DG_ BROKER_CONFIG_FILE1 = '</directory/file>';
SQL> ALTER SYSTEM SET DG_ BROKER_CONFIG_FILE2 = '</directory/file>';
```

The indicators `directory/file` would be some directory path and filename—as in /U03/Broker/dr1Matrix.dat and /U04/Broker/dr2Matrix.dat, respectively.

If you are configuring for a RAC and you are using a Cluster File System (CFS), these two specifications must point to a directory in the CFS, and each instance in the RAC has the exact same definitions for these parameters, as in `*.DG_ BROKER_CONFIG_FILE1 = ...`. Remember that only one set of configuration files may exist across the entire RAC.

Now, if you are still using raw devices (RAC or not), you need to define a link to a filename that you can use in place of the `/directory/file` since you cannot specify the raw device directly. To do this, create two raw devices of 1MB each and then assign the two filenames to them via the link. Here's an example:

```
ln -s /dev/raw/raw1 dr1Matrix.dat
ln -s /dev/raw/raw2 dr2Matrix.dat
```

Note that in Windows you would use the Oracle-supplied Object Manager, just as you would for data files and control files that would be placed on raw devices.

Of course, today's best practice is to use ASM (although, as we mentioned in Chapter 2, it is not mandatory), and since we used ASM in the original creation of our standby database in Chapter 2, we'll use ASM to store these Broker configuration files. In this case, the values for the `/directory/file` specification for our Broker configuration files would look like this:

```
/+DATA/Matrix/Broker/dr1Matrix.dat
/+FLASH/Matrix/Broker/dr2Matrix.dat
```

In this manner, the two configuration files are spread across the two ASM disk groups, providing that much-needed protection from a single point of failure. You will notice that the filename is the same one we've used so far in this section and not (as you would expect) one of those funny Oracle Managed Files (OMF) names assigned to all the other files in your database. This is because you, as the DBA, have to be able to specify a name for the file before the file is actually created so the Broker can create it. It is kind of like the chicken and the egg question—Which one comes first?

An important thing to remember is that the directories you specify in the parameter (in our case `/Matrix/Broker/`) must already exist at the location you specify before you try to create a Broker configuration. Since we are using ASM, they must exist in the ASM disk groups `DATA` and `FLASH`. If you are following policy and you are placing the files in the directory for the database, then Matrix would already exist, of course. But nothing would stop you from placing the configuration files anywhere in ASM that you choose, provided the directories exist. Using ASMCMD, you would navigate to the database directory under `DATA` and `FLASH` and create a directory called BROKER:

```
[+ASM] asmcmd
ASMCMD> cd DATA
ASMCMD> cd MATRIX
ASMCMD> mkdir BROKER
ASMCMD> cd ../..
ASMCMD> cd FLASH
```

```
ASMCMD> cd MATRIX
ASMCMD> mkdir BROKER
ASMCMD> exit
```

**TIP**

*Remember to pre-create the directories that you are going to use
for the configuration files; otherwise the Broker will not be able to
function and you won't really know why unless you read the Broker
logs and understand what they are saying.*

When you create your configuration later on in this chapter, you will see that the Broker
actually keeps the real configuration data file in another directory when you use ASM. As you can
see from the preceding commands, we created a subdirectory in the database directories called
BROKER, and when we create the configuration, the Broker will put a file in that directory with
the name we specified in the parameter. But if you look closer, you will see that the name is
actually a link to another file in another directory called DATAGUARDCONFIG:

```
[+ASM] asmcmd
ASMCMD> cd DATA/MATRIX/BROKER
ASMCMD> ls
dr1matrix.dat
ASMCMD> ls -l
Type              Redund   Striped   Time                  Sys   Name
                                                           N     dr1matrix.dat =>
+DATA/MATRIX/DATAGUARDCONFIG/Matrix.298.671576301
ASMCMD> cd ../DATAGUARDCONFIG
ASMCMD> ls -l
Type              Redund   Striped   Time                  Sys   Name
DATAGUARDCONFIG   UNPROT   COARSE    NOV 23 20:00:00       Y     Matrix.298.671576301
ASMCMD>
```

The second configuration file in the FLASH disk group will also be linked to the same
directory in the FLASH directory tree.

If you set these parameters but forget to create the directories on the primary database, your
CREATE CONFIGURATION command will return a file not found error from DGMGRL:

```
Error: ORA-16571: Data Guard configuration file creation failure
```

But if you got it right on the primary database but set the parameters on the standby database and
then forgot to create the directories there, nothing will happen when you enable the Broker in the
next step by setting the Broker START parameter to TRUE. Even creating the Broker configuration
(coming up soon) will work fine. But it will never exit the "Enabling Configuration" phase
because it cannot create the configuration files. And unless you look in the Broker alert log of the
standby (which resides in the normal database alert log directory and is called drc<*db_unique_
name*>.log—or drcMatrix_DR0.log in our case) and understand what it is saying, you will not
know why this happened. The following example is an edited piece of the Broker log in which the
BROKER ASM directory did not exist under the standby database top directory:

```
DMON: >> Starting Data Guard Broker bootstrap <<
DMON: Broker Configuration File Locations:
dg_broker_config_file1 = "+DATA/matrix_dr0/broker/dr1matrix_dr0.dat"
```

```
dg_broker_config_file2 = "+FLASH/matrix_dr0/broker/dr2matrix_dr0.dat"
DMON: Attach state object
DMON: Entered rfm_get_chief_lock() for CTL_BOOTSTRAP, reason 2
DMON: chief lock convert for bootstrap
DMON: cannot open configuration file "+DATA/matrix_dr0/broker/dr1matrix_dr0.dat"
ORA-17503: ksfdopn:2 Failed to open file +DATA/matrix_dr0/broker/dr1matrix_dr0.dat
ORA-15173: entry 'dr1matrix_dr0.dat' does not exist in directory 'broker'
DMON: Error opening "+DATA/matrix_dr0/broker/dr1matrix_dr0.dat", error = ORA-16572
DMON: Establishing "+FLASH/matrix_dr0/broker/dr2matrix_dr0.dat" as the more
current file
DMON: cannot open configuration file "+FLASH/matrix_dr0/broker/dr2matrix_dr0.dat"
ORA-17503: ksfdopn:2 Failed to open file
+FLASH/matrix_dr0/broker/dr2matrix_dr0.dat
ORA-15173: entry 'dr2matrix_dr0.dat' does not exist in directory 'broker'
DMON: Error opening "+FLASH/matrix_dr0/broker/dr2matrix_dr0.dat", error = ORA-16572
DMON: Boot configuration,loading from
"+FLASH/matrix_dr0/broker/dr2matrix_dr0.dat"
DMON: cannot open configuration file "+FLASH/matrix_dr0/broker/dr2matrix_dr0.dat"
ORA-17503: ksfdopn:2 Failed to open file
+FLASH/matrix_dr0/broker/dr2matrix_dr0.dat
ORA-15173: entry 'dr2matrix_dr0.dat' does not exist in directory 'broker'
DMON: Configuration does not exist, server ready.
```

As you can see, it is not obvious that the problem is the missing directory BROKER under the database MATRIX_DR0 directory on both the DATA and FLASH disk groups. This sequence of errors will be repeated forever until you disable the configuration, create the missing directory, and then enable the configuration again.

Once you have performed all the necessary directory work and set the parameters in all of your databases, you are ready to start up the Broker. This is done by connecting to each database with SQL*Plus and setting the Broker START parameter to TRUE.

```
SQL> ALTER SYSTEM SET DG_BROKER_START=TRUE SCOPE=BOTH;
```

This does not create any kind of Broker configuration for you, because that is done by executing commands in DGMGRL, which we will discuss in a bit. Nor does it create the configuration files yet. What it does do is start all of those processes we discussed earlier in this chapter.

Do not enable the Broker START parameter before you have made all the necessary modifications to your configuration parameters; otherwise, you will not be allowed to change those parameters.

```
SQL> SHOW PARAMETER DG_BROKER_START
NAME                              TYPE        VALUE
dg_broker_start                   boolean     TRUE
SQL> ALTER SYSTEM SET
  2 DG_BROKER_CONFIG_FILE1='+DATA/Matrix/Broker/dr1Matrix.dat';
ALTER SYSTEM SET DG_BROKER_CONFIG_FILE1='+DATA/Matrix/Broker/dr1Matrix.dat'
  *
```

```
ERROR at line 1:
ORA-02097: parameter cannot be modified because specified value is invalid
ORA-16573: attempt to change or access configuration file for an enabled broker
configuration
```

To resolve this error, you need to set the START parameter to FALSE and then re-execute the configuration parameter changes. Once complete, set the START parameter back to TRUE.

Once you have created your Broker configuration with DGMGRL, do not change the configuration file parameters since the Broker will have created them already and will not be able to find them in the new location. If you need to move the files, you must stop the Broker using the DG_BROKER_START parameter, change the configuration parameters, copy the files from the old location to the new location, and then re-enable the Broker. If you do not do this, you would see the ORA-17503 errors in the DRC log.

You can also remove the Broker configuration completely, delete the old configuration files, change the parameters, re-enable the Broker, and then re-create the configuration—but that is a lot more work. And if you are using ASM, you can imagine how hard it would be to copy that linked file. It is better to get this correct now rather than later.

# The Broker and Oracle Net Services

As with any Oracle interface, the Broker uses Oracle Net Services to make connections to the databases, set up both Redo Transport and archive log gap resolution, and perform role transitions. But the manner in which the Broker uses Oracle Net Services has changed from previous releases and Oracle Database 11*g*. In this section we will discuss what changed (and what has not) and how you should take advantage of these changes.

## Transparent Networking Substrate and Connect Strings

Since its creation in Oracle 9*i* Release 1, the Broker has taken the user-provided TNSNAME and converted it to a connect string that it used for Data Guard Redo Transport and gap resolution connections. This was done so that the Broker could detach itself from the TNSNAME files on the systems and prevent anyone from making a change to those files that would break the Data Guard configuration, an admirable goal. The problem was that this approach also prevented the user from taking advantage of many Oracle Net Services features such as network tuning and specific network paths. It also caused problems when the databases were RAC systems with many instances, something we will discuss in the next section.

In addition, starting with Oracle Database 10*g* Release 2, the Broker discarded the user's service and started using a new service called XPT (for Transport). The XPT service was constructed from the *DB_UNIQUE_NAME* of the database and appending the string *_XPT* to the end of the DB_UNIQUE_NAME, as in *Matrix_XPT*. All databases running in 10.2 or later have this XPT service registered with the listener. Apparently this new service created quite a stir with some users who didn't use the Broker and wanted the service removed from their systems. This could be accomplished by setting the hidden parameter "__DG_BROKER_SERVICE_NAMES" to a blank string and restarting the database:

```
SQL> ALTER SYSTEM SET "__DG_BROKER_SERVICE_NAMES"='' SCOPE=SPFILE;
```

**NOTE**
*Two underscores appear at the front of* `__DG_BROKER_SERVICE_`
`NAMES`, *and you must enclose the parameter name in double
quotation marks. You have to change the SPFILE only. You cannot
change this parameter in memory. To stop the service, you must restart
the database.*

This new service did not bother us nearly as much as the way the Broker converted our
TNSNAMEs to an expanded connect string. For example, if you provide the Broker with Matrix_DR0
as the Transparent Networking Substrate (TNS) connection, when you create your configuration, as in

```
MATRIX_DR0 =
  (DESCRIPTION =
    (ADDRESS_LIST =
      (ADDRESS = (PROTOCOL = TCP)(HOST = matrix_dr0.domain)(PORT = 1521))
    )
    (CONNECT_DATA =
      (SERVER = DEDICATED)
      (SERVICE_NAME = Matrix_DR0.domain)
    )
  )
```

your TNSNAME would be translated and stored as the property `InitialConnectIdentifier` in
the Broker configuration file, as the following connect string:

```
(DESCRIPTION=(ADDRESS_LIST=(ADDRESS=(PROTOCOL=TCP)(HOST=matrix_dr0.domain)
(PORT=1521)))(CONNECT_DATA=(SERVICE_NAME=Matrix_DR0_XPT.domain)
(INSTANCE_NAME=Matrix_DR0)(SERVER=dedicated)))
```

This connection string would be used as the argument to the `SERVICE` attribute of a `LOG_`
`ARCHIVE_DEST_n` parameter for Redo Transport to the target database. When the primary
database starts up (or you create and enable the Broker configuration in the first place), you
would see something like the following in the alert log:

```
ALTER SYSTEM SET log_archive_dest_2= service="(DESCRIPTION=
(ADDRESS_LIST=(ADDRESS=(PROTOCOL=TCP)(HOST=matrix_dr0.domain)(PORT=1521)))
(CONNECT_DATA= SERVICE_NAME=Matrix_DR0_XPT.domain)(INSTANCE_NAME=Matrix_DR0)
(SERVER=dedicated)))" LGWR ASYNC db_unique_name=Matrix_DR0 valid_for=(online_
logfiles,primary_role) reopen=30' SCOPE=BOTH;
```

In this manner, the TNSNAME file would be ignored forever more, and so would any
particular settings that you had configured that the Broker did not handle, such as the send and
receive buffer sizes.

The great news is that as of Oracle Database 11g, this no longer happens. The
`InitialConnectIdentifier` went away and a new property was introduced called the
`DGConnectIdentifier`. This property is loaded when you provide your TNSNAME to specify
how the Broker should connect to a specific database. Now, instead of converting that TNSNAME
to a connect string, the TNSNAME is stored in the configuration file as is, and all connections to
that database are made using your TNSNAME. This means that any special configuration settings
that you have made in your TNSNAME entry are used by the Broker and are no longer discarded.

Of course, all of this is documented in the manual, but as reference material only. Nowhere does it mention just how fantastic an improvement this really is to the Broker. It solves several problems that the old method inadvertently caused, such as requiring a complete re-creation of your configuration if you moved a standby database, making it impossible to force the redo onto a specific network, tune the network, or add any other specific network parameters, to name a few.

For example, when you did all your network tuning, as described in Chapter 2, you most likely increased the session data unit (SDU) and the Transmission Control Protocol (TCP) send and receive buffer sizes to suit your network. If you were using 10*g* and you wanted to use the Broker you would have to use the sqlnet.ora method, which would apply to every Oracle Net Services connection to and from those systems. Now with the `DGConnectIdentifier`, you can place those tuning parameters where they should be, in the TNSNAME and listener files.

```
MATRIX_DR0 =
  (DESCRIPTION =
    (SDU=32767)
    (SEND_BUF_SIZE=2092500)
    (RECV_BUF_SIZE=2092500)
    (ADDRESS_LIST =
      (ADDRESS = (PROTOCOL = TCP)(HOST = matrix_dr0.domain)(PORT = 1521))
    )
    (CONNECT_DATA =
      (SERVER = DEDICATED)
      (SERVICE_NAME = Matrix_DR0.domain)
    )
  )
```

For the new Oracle Database 11*g* user, this new property is an obvious operation, but what about the current Broker user in Oracle 10*g*? What happens when the database is upgraded from 10*g* to 11*g*? The original configuration will continue to work, but the connect string that the Broker put into the `InitialConnectIdentifier` will be migrated to the new configuration as the `DGConnectIdentifier` property. This means that you will still be using the old method where the Broker uses the connect string instead of your TNSNAME. Which brings us back to the subject of that Broker XPT service. This also means that you will still be using the old service as long as you choose not to change the `DGConnectIdentifier`. So do not disable the XPT service, as described earlier, until you fix the connect identifier.

**TIP**
*When you already have a Broker configuration, always change the* `DGConnectIdentifier` *property for all of your databases to a real TNSNAME after you upgrade from 10*g* to 11*g!*

## The Broker and the Listener
Obviously, as with any Oracle Net Services connection, the Broker uses the TNSNAME to resolve the path to the database and then initiates a connection to the listener at the target system using the service name you put into your TNSNAME entry. And since the two main places that these connections are initiated, Redo Transport and connecting to DGMGRL, require that the target database be at least mounted, then as long as you have configured the target database to start the necessary service, all will work well. Or so you might think. But if you tried to do a switchover or

use Fast-Start Failover, all would not work correctly. During these operations, one of the databases shuts down and needs to be restarted. Since the database is down, the service specified by your TNSNAME is not registered so an Oracle Net Services connection cannot be made. When the remote database is down and you try to connect with SQL*Plus or DGMGRL, you would get the dreaded "ORA-12514: TNS:listener does not currently know of service requested in connect descriptor" error message. Of course, there is a way around this, and it is noted as a prerequisite in Chapter 2 of the Data Guard Broker manual and has been there since Oracle Database 10g Release 1. But for some unknown reason, many users miss it, and then, when they try a switchover, it fails.

The configuration prerequisite for the listener is to create a specially named static listener entry for each database in your Broker configuration. This entry makes it possible for the Broker to connect to an idle instance using a remote SYSDBA connection and perform the necessary startup. This static entry has to be made up of the database unique name (as you specified in the DB_UNIQUE_NAME parameter) with the string _DGMGRL appended to it followed by the domain of the database. For example, our primary database, Matrix, would have the following entry in the SID list of the listener.ora file on the primary system:

```
SID_LIST_LISTENER =
  (SID_LIST =
    (SID_DESC =
      (GLOBAL_DBNAME = Matrix_DGMGRL.domain)
      (ORACLE_HOME = /scratch/OracleHomes/OraHome111)
      (SID_NAME = Matrix)
    )
  )
```

You do not need a TNSNAME entry pointing to this static entry since the Broker knows how to construct a connect string from the information you have already provided. The host the database is on and what port the listener is using comes from the connection information you provided when you created the configuration in the first place. It also knows the database unique name and domain from the database properties. In this manner, the Broker is able to construct a valid connect string that will allow a connection to the instance even if it is down.

**TIP**
*Do not forget to define the <db_unique_name>_DGMGRL.domain static entry in the listener.ora file of each database including the primary database, even if you use Grid Control.*

This is the one thing that you need to do even if you use Grid Control, just in case you cannot get access to Grid Control when you need to manage your Data Guard configuration. As we have already mentioned, in a Broker-controlled configuration, if you need to use a CLI, you must use the Data Guard Broker DGMGRL CLI. Sometimes you will need to use DGMGRL to change attributes that are not exposed in Grid Control.

When you use Grid Control to create a new standby database, this static listener entry is added to the standby listener.ora file. But if you have created your standby database manually and imported it into Grid Control, this static entry will not be made to the standby listener. And it is never added to the primary database listener unless you enable Fast-Start Failover. You must ensure that this entry is defined on all databases in your configuration, even if you use Grid Control exclusively.

### Configuring Oracle Net for the Broker

Now that you understand how the Broker uses the various parts of Oracle Net Services, let's recap what we need to do before we create a Broker configuration.

First, as we described in Chapter 2, we need to define TNSNAMEs entries on each system in our configuration that Data Guard will use for Redo Transport and gap resolution, as specified in the LOG_ARCHIVE_DEST_$n$ parameter. So our primary system will have a TNSNAME entry called Matrix_DR0 that points to our standby database, and our standby system will have a TNSNAME entry called Matrix that points to our primary database. We need to do this even if we created a standby without any of the parameters configured, as in the short RMAN example in Chapter 2. The Broker must have these entries so it can complete the configuration.

Second, in addition to the listener on each system and any tuning we have done, we need to create the special static entry for each database in the configuration that follows the <db_unique_name>_DGMGRL.domain format.

Now our network is ready for the Broker to complete the setup when we use DGMGRL to create a configuration.

# RAC and the Broker

The Broker has been RAC aware since Oracle Database 10g Release 1 and will handle all the setup tasks for you, just as it does when the databases involved are single instance. As you will see when you actually create your Broker configuration, the commands are very simple, and by default there is no difference between creating a RAC or non-RAC configuration.

The fact that a Broker configuration is transparent when a cluster is involved goes back to our discussion of the configuration files. Remember that the configuration files must be RAC visible, and only one copy of the configuration files may exist for an entire RAC. In this way, configuration properties are maintained consistently across a cluster, and all instances have the same view of the Broker settings. Unlike the database parameter file, which can use specific settings for some parameters per instance (although that's not necessarily a best practice), the Broker configuration settings cannot vary between instances. That is why it is so important that you get this right the first time! You need to set up the configuration file parameters correctly and set the Broker START parameter to TRUE for each instance in the RAC.

When you create your initial configuration, the Broker writes all the necessary information to the configuration files. If the database is a RAC, the INSV process where you are connected will inform all the other currently running instances of the configuration parameters, and Data Guard setup will be executed as necessary on each node. If an instance is down when you create the configuration, when it comes up again the Broker will start up, read the configuration file, and perform the necessary setup steps. This process applies to the primary and all standby databases in the configuration since the Broker is aware of all instances in a RAC and their current states at all times.

You can optionally configure where the apply processing will occur on a standby database. If the standby is a single-instance database, then the apply will be placed on that system. But if the standby database is a RAC, one of the instances must be chosen as the apply instance. This is because Data Guard Apply services cannot be run on more than one instance at a time, regardless of the type of standby, be it physical or logical. By default, the Broker will randomly choose an available instance in a RAC standby and place the apply processing there.

If you want to specify where the apply will run on a particular standby database, you can modify the PreferredApplyInstance property to point to one of the standby instances.

We will discuss how to change properties a little later in the chapter in the Changing the Broker Configuration Properties section, but it is important for now that you understand why you might want to move the apply instance and what will actually happen when you do. Merely changing the `PreferredApplyInstance` property will not move the apply if it is already running on another standby instance. The change will occur when the current apply instance is restarted. But it you change the `PreferredApplyInstance` property as part of a state change command, the Broker will stop the apply on the current instance and restart it on the desired instance.

Why would you want to make this kind of change? The Broker will handle placement of the apply services automatically and will move them to another surviving instance in the event that the current apply instance fails for some reason. Historically, when clusters were configured, a lot of them used raw devices, and as such the archive logs on the standby database were not visible across the cluster. So users felt it necessary to place the apply on the instance where the redo was arriving so that the archive logs were all available to the apply services. But since the Broker always put the apply services automatically on the same system where the Redo Transport was sending the redo, changing the location of the apply was usually unnecessary. Another reason for making the change might involve a standby RAC in which the systems are not comprised of the same number of CPUs and/or memory and you want to place the apply services on the largest node. Or you might need to take down the current apply instance for maintenance, and you want to move the apply to another instance so that you know your recovery time objective (RTO) remains steady before you take the outage. Whatever the reason for making this change, just remember that when the Broker does fail the apply over to a surviving instance (when the apply instance crashes), it will not put the apply back on your chosen instance when that system comes back up. It will move the apply back to your preferred instance only when you make the property change again.

The second and more important RAC difference is in the way Redo Transport is configured. And this has changed from previous releases and Oracle Database 11g as well. Remember that the Broker enforces database property equality across any RAC in its configuration. This means that when it comes to the Redo Transport Services, the Broker will set the parameters (LOG_ ARCHIVE_DEST_*n*) the same way for each primary RAC instance. You do not have any control over this.

But in Oracle Database 10g (Release 1 or 2), you did not have to worry about how to set up the connect strings to the standby. In fact, you couldn't change them if you wanted to. The Broker stored all the information about each standby instance and constructed the connect string to point all redo traffic from the primary to the first instance in the standby. If that standby instance went down, the Broker would automatically reconfigure the parameters across the primary RAC to point to another standby instance. This use of long connect strings sometimes caused parameter length problems when the size of the cluster grew beyond a certain number of nodes.

As discussed earlier, the Broker no longer constructs the connect string out of your `InitialConnectIdentifier`. It remembers and uses the TNSNAME you provided (unless you are running an upgraded and unchanged configuration), and you are now responsible for ensuring that the Broker can connect to all the instances in the standby RAC. Once you move to the new, fantastic, and tunable method of specifying the `DGConnectIdentifier`, you have to make sure that your TNSNAME for the standby has all the RAC systems configured. And you must make use of the Transparent Application Failover (TAF) connect time failover capability so that the Redo Transport Services move seamlessly from a failed standby node to a surviving standby node.

For example, consider that our standby Matrix_DR0 is a two-node RAC database. The TNSNAME that we use to create the database in our Broker configuration must look like this:

```
MATRIX_DR0 =
   (DESCRIPTION =
     (ADDRESS_LIST =
        (ADDRESS = (PROTOCOL = TCP)(HOST = Matrix1_DR0.domain)(PORT = 1521))
        (ADDRESS = (PROTOCOL = TCP)(HOST = Matrix2_DR0.domain)(PORT = 1521))
     )
     (CONNECT_DATA =
        (SERVICE_NAME = Matrix_DR0.domain)
     )
   )
```

In this way, the Redo Transport Services will use the TNSNAME Matrix_DR0, and if host Matrix1_DR0 is not available, connect time failover will automatically take the transport to the second entry. Of course you could also use the Virtual IP (VIP) for the standby cluster.

One last thing about your TNSNAMEs in a RAC: If you do not have a single cluster-wide tnsnames.ora file, you must make sure that the TNSNAME entry for the standby is the same on all nodes in the primary cluster. Your standby databases must also have a similar entry across the standby cluster pointing back to the primary database RAC hosts for switchover.

The last RAC-specific item is actually something you no longer have to worry about in Oracle Database 11*g*. In 10*g* you needed to modify the RAC Cluster Ready Services (CRS) to make sure that the various standby databases were always started up in the MOUNT state, and then the Broker would take care of opening the database if necessary:

```
srvctl modify database -d <Matrix> -o <$oracle_home> -s mount
srvctl modify database -d <Matrix_DR0> -o <$oracle_home> -s mount
```

**TIP**

*When you set the CRS database options in Oracle Database 10*g*, you do not need to specify the role (-r) option for your standby databases. It was never implemented to do anything and is ignored by the Broker.*

If the database is a primary, the Broker would always bring it to the OPEN state when the instance was started. This would happen even if you used STARTUP MOUNT. (If you simply wanted to mount the primary database, you needed to disable the Broker first.) If the database were a standby, the Broker would bring the instance to the state that you last specified, which was stored in the configuration file. (Database state will be discussed in the next section.)

With Oracle Database 11*g*, setting the START mode option in CRS is no longer necessary or encouraged as far as the Broker in concerned. The Broker will now always honor the startup choice of the DBA, regardless of the database type. If the database is the primary and the DBA uses STARTUP MOUNT, the database will remain in the MOUNT state, whereas in 10*g* the database would be opened anyway.

**TIP**

*The Broker no longer opens the primary database when you use STARTUP MOUNT. In 11*g* it leaves the database at the MOUNT state. You must change your scripts and the CRS startup mode options in 11*g* if you set them to MOUNT in 10*g*.*

At switchover and failover, the Broker will leave the databases in the correct mode for their new role. When a standby becomes the primary, it will be opened for use and the primary that becomes a standby will be put into the correct state for that standby (MOUNT for a physical and OPEN for a logical). This means that if you have the CRS startup mode options set to MOUNT in 11*g*, any subsequent restarts of the new primary database will leave it in the MOUNT state and it will not be open for business! So you will want to remove the MOUNT start mode.

## Connecting to the Broker

Finally, you are now ready to connect to the Broker and start managing Data Guard. However, you still need to understand a couple of things about connecting to the Broker. As with any interface to a database, you have to connect DGMGRL (your client) to a database (your server). And as with other interfaces in the Oracle world, there are multiple ways to do this, such as putting the login information on the command line or using the DGMRGL CONNECT command. For example, you can connect to the current local database (as defined by the ORACLE_SID) on the DGMGRL command line using host authentication:

```
[Matrix] dgmgrl /
DGMGRL for Linux: Version 11.1.0.6.0 - Production
Copyright (c) 2000, 2005, Oracle. All rights reserved.
Welcome to DGMGRL, type "help" for information.
Connected.
DGMGRL>
```

Or you can use the CONNECT command:

```
[Matrix] dgmgrl
DGMGRL for Linux: Version 11.1.0.6.0 - Production
Copyright (c) 2000, 2005, Oracle. All rights reserved.
Welcome to DGMGRL, type "help" for information.
DGMGRL> CONNECT /
Connected.
DGMGRL>
```

You are now connected to the database, but this does not mean that a Broker configuration is associated with the database at this point. For that matter, being connected does not even mean that you have enabled the Broker. If you did not follow the steps to enable the Broker correctly (as described earlier) and you tried a SHOW CONFIGURATION command, you would get the following error message:

```
DGMGRL> SHOW CONFIGURATION;
Error:
ORA-16525: the Data Guard broker is not yet available
ORA-06512: at "SYS.DBMS_DRS", line 157
ORA-06512: at line 1
DGMGRL>
```

But if you performed the correct steps and enabled the Broker correctly, you would get the following result from your SHOW CONFIGURATION command:

```
DGMGRL> SHOW CONFIGURATION;
Error: ORA-16532: Data Guard broker configuration does not exist
```

```
Configuration details cannot be determined by DGMGRL
DGMGRL>
```

While still an error, this is the "correct error," since you haven't actually created a configuration yet. But let's go back to connecting to the Broker for the moment.

You might ask, "Why does this matter? Isn't how to connect to a database pretty clear overall?" Well, yes and no. The problem with this "/ only" method is that the Broker does not have a username and password that it can use when you begin to manage the configuration. While this will not break anything permanently or endanger your Data Guard setup, it does means that certain procedures will not be able to complete correctly and your configuration will remain in a weird state, which you will have to resolve manually.

For example, in a switchover operation, the Broker starts the process on the primary and then, when the standby is ready, completes the switchover on the standby. In parallel, the Broker will shut down the old primary so that it can restart it as a standby and get Redo Transport and apply running again. But without a username and password, the Broker processes (that NSV to DRC connection we talked about in the first part of this chapter) will not be able to log in to the old primary since you cannot log in as SYSDBA to a remote database that is currently shut down without a username and password. So you are left with a functioning new primary but without any standby until you go to the old production system and manually STARTUP MOUNT the old primary using SQL*Plus. When the old primary comes up (as a standby now), the Broker will connect and finish up the configuration.

Worse, if you happen to be running in Maximum Protection mode (which requires at least one SYNC standby), your new primary will not come up and your system will remain down longer than you expect. (We'll revisit this issue in Chapter 8 when we discuss the mechanics of role transition.) How do you avoid this problem? Always specify a username/password that has SYSDBA privileges when you connect to the Broker

```
[Matrix] dgmgrl sys/oracle
DGMGRL for Linux: Version 11.1.0.6.0 - Production
Copyright (c) 2000, 2005, Oracle. All rights reserved.
Welcome to DGMGRL, type "help" for information.
Connected.
DGMGRL>
```

Or

```
[Matrix] dgmgrl
DGMGRL for Linux: Version 11.1.0.6.0 - Production
Copyright (c) 2000, 2005, Oracle. All rights reserved.
Welcome to DGMGRL, type "help" for information.
DGMGRL> CONNECT sys/oracle
Connected.
DGMGRL>
```

As with the "/ method," these two connections will attach to the current database as defined by the ORACLE_SID. Normally, the database to which you connect can be the primary or any of the standby databases. But in this case you have not set up the configuration yet so you need to make sure you connect to the primary database when you create your configuration.

**TIP**
*If you plan on using the Broker, the best practice when creating your standby database is to use as few Data Guard parameters as possible and let the Broker configure everything for you.*

You can also connect to a remote database with DGMGRL by using the normal @TNSNAMES format.

```
[Matrix] dgmgrl sys/oracle@Matrix
DGMGRL for Linux: Version 11.1.0.6.0 - Production
Copyright (c) 2000, 2005, Oracle. All rights reserved.
Welcome to DGMGRL, type "help" for information.
Connected.
DGMGRL>
```

Or

```
[Matrix] dgmgrl
DGMGRL for Linux: Version 11.1.0.6.0 - Production
Copyright (c) 2000, 2005, Oracle. All rights reserved.
Welcome to DGMGRL, type "help" for information.
DGMGRL> CONNECT sys/oracle@Matrix
Connected.
DGMGRL>
```

This means that you can manage any Data Guard configuration from any system in your network without actually being on one of the database systems. You just need to fulfill a few requirements:

- Your Oracle home must be set to an Enterprise Edition or client Oracle home.

- The Oracle home of your local system must be using the same version used by the database homes of the configuration.

- You must have TNSNAME entries on the local system that point to the various databases in your Broker configuration.

- You must have the privileges to connect over the ports defined in the TNSNAME file—that is, if the database systems are behind a firewall, then you must have the port opened so you can connect.

You are now ready to begin your Data Guard Broker configuration. To recap, you have done the following:

- Set up your Broker configuration file parameters

- Created any necessary directories

- Enabled the Broker by setting the START parameter to TRUE on your primary and all standby databases

- Made the appropriate TNSNAME entries on all of the systems involved in the configuration

- Set up the static listener entries on all of the systems

- Sorted out the CRS settings
- Used a username and password to connect to DGMGRL
- Connected to the primary database

After the configuration is set up and enabled, you can connect through any of the databases in the configuration and manage the entire configuration from there. Let's get started!

# Managing Data Guard with the Broker

As discussed earlier, DGMGRL is the CLI to the Broker and the DGMGRL commands can be divided into four main areas:

- **Connection and help**   CONNECT, HELP, and EXIT
- **Creation and editing**   CREATE, ADD, ENABLE, EDIT, and CONVERT
- **Monitoring**   SHOW
- **Role transition**   SWITCHOVER, FAILOVER, and REINSTATE

In this section, we will discuss how to use the commands in the first two areas, which will include the creation, enabling, and editing of a Broker configuration. The monitoring-specific commands for the most part are discussed in the next section and the transition commands will be saved for Chapter 8.

Before we get started, you need to know that if you are a Broker user from the Oracle9i days, you have to forget everything you know about the DGMGRL commands and Enterprise Manager. The Enterprise Manager Data Guard interface changed completely because of the rewrite of Grid Control. The DGMGRL commands changed too—almost 100 percent—because the concepts the Broker employed in Oracle9i changed with the arrival of Oracle Database 10g. A Broker RESOURCE became a DATABASE, an ALTER command became EDIT, and the concept of a SITE disappeared completely. With that understood, let's create a Broker configuration.

## Creating and Enabling a Broker Configuration

DGMGRL cannot create a standby database for you. It cannot copy the database files to the standby server and do all the things necessary to create the standby database. Grid Control has that capability, and if you used it to create your standby database, you do not need to perform this creation exercise, because it has already been done for you. You should read through the process so that you understand what was done for you.

But if you used any other method to create your standby, including "The Power User Method" discussed in Chapter 2, the state in which you left the standby database when you finished your creation will affect how the Broker configures everything. While the commands you are going to use are exactly the same no matter how you created the standby, the Broker will make different decisions when setting the various properties that relate directly to database parameters.

The first step is to create the base configuration by connecting to the primary database and then using the CREATE CONFIGURATION command. Make sure that you connect to the primary database; otherwise, you will see the following ORA-16642 error:

```
[Matrix_DR0] dgmgrl
DGMGRL for Linux: Version 11.1.0.6.0 - Production
Copyright (c) 2000, 2005, Oracle. All rights reserved.
```

```
Welcome to DGMGRL, type "help" for information.
DGMGRL> CONNECT sys/oracle
Connected.
DGMGRL> CREATE CONFIGURATION MATRIX AS
> PRIMARY DATABASE IS MATRIX
> CONNECT IDENTIFIER IS matrix;
Error: ORA-16642: DB_UNIQUE_NAME mismatch
Failed.
DGMGRL>
```

Looking into the DRC log (remember that it is in the same place as the database alert log), you will see the following message (edited to fit here):

```
0 2 0 DMON: Cannot add the primary database with db_unique_name matrix
0 2 0        My db_unique_name is Matrix_DR0.
0 2 671586149 DMON: ADD_DATABASE: (error=ORA-16642)
```

As you can see from the DRC log, the Broker requires that the DB_UNIQUE_NAME of the database to which we are attached matches the primary database name we specified.

One thing that did happen from this mistaken attempt is that the configuration file was created on our standby database, complete with the link to the DATAGUARDCONFIG file, although it is currently empty. So let's try again. We will move to the primary system and set our ORACLE_SID to the primary SID, Matrix:

```
[Matrix] dgmgrl
DGMGRL for Linux: Version 11.1.0.6.0 - Production
Copyright (c) 2000, 2005, Oracle. All rights reserved.
Welcome to DGMGRL, type "help" for information.
DGMGRL> CONNECT sys/oracle
Connected.
DGMGRL> CREATE CONFIGURATION MATRIX AS
> PRIMARY DATABASE IS MATRIX
> CONNECT IDENTIFIER IS matrix;
Configuration "matrix" created with primary database "matrix"
DGMGRL>
```

At this point, we have a configuration created and stored in the primary database configuration files. But nothing is happening yet as we do not have a standby database nor is the configuration enabled. A simple SHOW CONFIGURATION will show us the current state of our configuration:

```
DGMGRL> show configuration
Configuration
  Name:               matrix
  Enabled:            NO
  Protection Mode:    MaxPerformance
  Databases:
    matrix - Primary database
Fast-Start Failover: DISABLED
Current status for "matrix":
DISABLED
```

The next step is to add our standby database that we created in Chapter 2 using one of the Power User methods. This is done with the ADD DATABASE command. The arguments are similar to those of the CREATE CONFIGURATION command and require a database name for the standby (DB_UNIQUE_NAME of the standby), a connect identifier (the TNSNAME for the standby), and, optionally, an indication of whether the standby is a physical or a logical standby database. This is where the way you created the standby starts to make a difference. The Broker can use the database name alone to set up the properties for the standby database, but only if you already configured a transport parameter (LOG_ARCHIVE_DEST_n) in the proper manner. If not, you will see the following error:

```
DGMGRL> ADD DATABASE MATRIX_DR0;
Error: ORA-16796: one or more properties could not be imported from the database
Failed.
```

So what is the proper way to set up the transport parameter? You must have your Redo Transport parameters defined using the DB_UNIQUE_NAME method, meaning that each Redo Transport parameter must contain the DB_UNIQUE_NAME=<*name*> attribute. The Broker will search all of your LOG_ARCHIVE_DEST_n parameters looking for a database unique name that matches the database name you entered for the command. Merely using the same name in the service attribute, SERVICE=name..., is not enough. The Broker will not be able to find the proper connection information and will fail to add the database. In our case, we have not defined any of the Data Guard parameters in our current setup. So we must use the full set of arguments to the ADD DATABASE command to allow the Broker to connect to the standby:

```
DGMGRL> ADD DATABASE MATRIX_DR0
> AS CONNECT IDENTIFIER IS MATRIX_DR0
> MAINTAINED AS PHYSICAL;
Database "matrix_dr0" added

DGMGRL> SHOW CONFIGURATION;
Configuration
  Name:                matrix
  Enabled:             NO
  Protection Mode:     MaxPerformance
  Databases:
    matrix      - Primary database
    matrix_dr0 - Physical standby database
Fast-Start Failover: DISABLED
Current status for "matrix":
DISABLED
DGMGRL>
```

We now have a Broker configuration ready to go. All that is left to start things up is to ENABLE the configuration. But before we do that, let's look at what actually happened behind these simple and fast commands.

The Broker will set the properties of the configuration to default values based on what it finds when you create the configuration. If you have created a standby database but not set any of the Data Guard parameters, the Broker will set every property in the configuration to the default value. (We will discuss these default values in a moment.) But if you have set some of the Data Guard parameters when you created your standby (in other words, you already have a running Data Guard setup), the Broker will "harvest," or gather up, as many of the values as it can and set those properties for which it found no value to the default. To add to the confusion, some of the default values change depending on what protection mode the Broker finds, and some defaults have even changed between 10g and 11g. In addition, some of the parameters in your database are considered by the Broker to be "'Broker controlled," such as LOG_ARCHIVE_MAX_PROCESSES, and the Broker will harvest those parameters accordingly. Confused? Don't be, because it's not as bad as it sounds; you just need to be aware of what is happening behind the scenes.

Let's take the simplest example first: No Data Guard parameters have been manually set when we created our standby database (which is the situation for our examples anyway). After we created the configuration, the Broker set all of the Redo Transport properties to their default values, some coming from the database and some set by the Broker rules. For other properties, the Broker either found an explicit value or it looked up the default value for the parameter. And others were set to the Broker's own default settings, such as ApplyParallel. You can see the various properties by issuing the SHOW DATABASE VERBOSE command:

```
DGMGRL> show database verbose matrix;
Database
  Name:            matrix
  Role:            PRIMARY
  Enabled:         NO
  Intended State:  OFFLINE
  Instance(s):
    Matrix
  Properties:
    DGConnectIdentifier           = 'matrix'
    LogXptMode                    = 'ASYNC'
    DelayMins                     = '0'
    Binding                       = 'OPTIONAL'
    MaxFailure                    = '0'
    MaxConnections                = '1'
    ReopenSecs                    = '300'
    NetTimeout                    = '30'
    RedoCompression               = 'DISABLE'
    LogShipping                   = 'ON'
    PreferredApplyInstance        = ''
    ApplyInstanceTimeout          = '0'
    ApplyParallel                 = 'AUTO'
    StandbyFileManagement         = 'MANUAL'
    ArchiveLagTarget              = '0'
    LogArchiveMaxProcesses        = '4'
    LogArchiveMinSucceedDest      = '1'
    DbFileNameConvert             = ''
    LogFileNameConvert            = ''
    HostName                      = 'matrix.domain'
    SidName                       = 'Matrix'
    StandbyArchiveLocation        = 'USE_DB_RECOVERY_FILE_DEST'
    AlternateLocation             = ''
    LogArchiveTrace               = '0'
    LogArchiveFormat              = '%t_%s_%r.dbf'
```

```
Current status for "matrix":
DISABLED
DGMGRL>
```

This example has been edited to show only those properties that you would be able to change at this moment. The monitoring and Fast-Start Failover properties have been removed. If you look at the standby database Matrix_DR0, you will see the same defaults but for the standby database.

If, on the other hand, you had set up Data Guard to ship and apply redo, then the Broker would pick up the values for the parameters and attributes that you set and use the defaults for those for which no explicit value exists. For example, assume we set up Redo Transport as follows:

```
LOG_ARCHIVE_DEST_2='SERVICE=MATRIX_DR0 SYNC NET_TIMEOUT=15 REOPEN=30
VALID_FOR=(ONLINE_LOGFILES,PRIMARY_ROLE) DB_UNIQUE_NAME=MATRIX_DR0'
```

In this case, the Broker would gather up all of these attributes and set the associated properties to our values and default anything we did not explicitly set.

One parameter to watch out for is the local archiving on the primary and standby databases. The Broker will modify your local archiving parameters if necessary to add the VALID_FOR attribute in preparation for the archival of your standby redo log files. For example, if you have the following local archiving destination defined,

```
LOG_ARCHIVE_DEST_1='LOCATION=/path/'
```

the Broker will change it to the following when you enable the configuration:

```
LOG_ARCHIVE_DEST_1='LOCATION=/path VALID_FOR=(ALL_ROLES,ALL_LOGFILES)'
```

It will make this change on all the databases in the configuration. If you followed best practices and are using a flash recovery area, you should have your local archiving defined using the special attribute for the flash recovery area as follows:

```
LOG_ARCHIVE_DEST_1='LOCATION=USE_DB_RECOVERY_FILE_DEST'
```

And the Broker will change it to the following when you enable the configuration:

```
LOG_ARCHIVE_DEST_1='LOCATION= USE_DB_RECOVERY_FILE_DEST
VALID_FOR=(ALL_ROLES,ALL_LOGFILES)'
```

However, if you explicitly defined a local archiving destination using the VALID_FOR attribute as follows,

```
LOG_ARCHIVE_DEST_1='LOCATION= USE_DB_RECOVERY_FILE_DEST
VALID_FOR=(PRIMARY_ROLE,ONLINE_LOGFILE)'
```

then the Broker cannot change it and will add another destination parameter explicitly defined for the standby redo log files, as follows:

```
LOG_ARCHIVE_DEST_3='LOCATION=$ORACLE_HOME/dbs/arch
VALID_FOR=(STANDBY_ROLE,STANDBY_LOGFILE)'
```

The $ORACLE_HOME in the example represents the actual directory string. This won't mean much on the primary at this time since the standby redo log files are not being used. But it will cause the standby database to start putting archive logs into the directory specified by this new parameter the moment redo starts to come in from the primary. Everything will continue to work, including the apply service and your RMAN backups, but you will see files in places you did not expect. If you have your local archiving defined in this manner, you should change it to specify `VALID_FOR=(ALL_ROLES,ALL_LOGFILES)` before you enable the configuration.

**TIP**
*Always use a flash recovery area and define your local archiving parameters to be* `LOG_ARCHIVE_DEST_1='LOCATION=USE_DB_RECOVERY_FILE_DEST'`.

Other changes have been made, especially to the default values of some of these properties, between the various versions. Because the default in the database Redo Transport view `V$ARCHIVE_DEST` did not hold the correct default for the `NET_TIMEOUT` attribute, the Broker set the `NET_TIMEOUT` to `NONET_TIMEOUT` in 9*i* and early 10.1. The view was corrected and was set correctly by the Broker starting in version 10.2 with the default value being 180 seconds. Starting with 11*g* the attribute was made available to the DGMGRL user as a property and was set to a default of 30 seconds.

The default Redo Transport mode also changed between 10*g* and 11*g*. If you did not specify `ARCH`, `ASYNC`, or `SYNC` in 10.2, the Broker would default the Redo Transport to `ARCH`. But in 11*g* it defaults the transport mode to `ASYNC`, and the Redo Transport mode `ARCH` cannot actually be set through the Broker anymore. As mentioned in Chapter 1, `ARCH` has been deprecated as a transport mode.

Another even more important default action is the way the Broker will configure Redo Transport if the protection mode of the configuration has already been set to a degree higher than the default of Maximum Performance. If the configuration is set to one of the higher modes, Availability or Protection, you should have already set at least one standby database to use the `SYNC` transport mode. In 10*g* the Broker would harvest the attributes for the `SYNC` standby and set its properties correctly. But it would not set the primary database transport property (`LogXptMode`) to `SYNC`, even though you had a parameter in the standby that specified that the redo should be sent to the new standby (the old primary after a switchover, for example) using synchronous (`SYNC`) transport. So unless you set the primary transport mode property to `SYNC` manually, when you switched over to the standby you would find yourself running in a unsynchronized manner (or even down if you were in Maximum Protection) because the Redo Transport being used to send redo to the old primary (now a standby) would be running in `ASYNC` or even `ARCH` mode. This has been corrected in 11*g,* and the primary will be automatically set to `SYNC` whenever the Broker harvests or sets a protection mode higher than Maximum Performance.

But with this correction comes another wrinkle in the default value discussion. What happens when we add a second standby database? For this discussion, we will assume that we have a Broker configuration already running in Maximum Availability with the primary and first standby about 100 km (about 62 miles) apart and using the `SYNC` Redo Transport mode. You want to add a second standby that is 1600 km (1000 miles) away for geographic separation. If you have created the remote standby and configured the Redo Transport parameters to be `ASYNC`, then all will be well and the standby will continue to run in `ASYNC` mode when you enable it. But if you created the remote standby using the short method, expecting the Broker to take care of things for you, then this second standby will default to `SYNC` transport due to the elevated protection mode of the configuration. Since all new databases added to the configuration have to be manually enabled, you will not have a problem and can change the property for this standby to be `ASYNC` before you enable it. But if you blindly enable the new database in this example, your production would suffer a major hit as it is all of a sudden waiting for redo to be shipped over the WAN. Since Redo Transport is dynamic, you can quickly correct this by setting the property down to `ASYNC` for the second standby and then switching logs on the primary database. But it will cause some excitement for a while!

**TIP**
*Always check the database properties for a newly added database before issuing the* `ENABLE DATABASE` *command to ensure that everything is set the way you want it to be.*

This is why we said that it is important to understand what is going on behind the scenes before you enable a database or a new configuration. If you need to change properties, you must do so before you enable the database or configuration. We will discuss editing properties in the next section.

Since the defaults are acceptable for our current setup, we can enable the configuration and let the Broker start everything up:

```
DGMGRL> ENABLE CONFIGURATION;
Enabled.
```

This single command will perform several operations on the primary and all standby databases. It will issue `ALTER SYSTEM` commands on the primary to set the Data Guard parameters that are required for a database that is running as the primary, and start Redo Transport to the standby databases. The Broker will also issue `ALTER SYSTEM` commands on the standby databases to set up the parameters required for a database that is running in the standby mode and will start up the apply services. As it takes a bit of time for all of this to occur, you will most likely see an ORA-16610 if you issue a `SHOW CONFIGURATION` command too quickly after the enable command returns:

```
DGMGRL> SHOW CONFIGURATION;
Configuration
  Name:                matrix
  Enabled:             YES
  Protection Mode:     MaxPerformance
  Databases:
    matrix      - Primary database
    matrix_dr0 - Physical standby database
Fast-Start Failover: DISABLED
Current status for "matrix":
Warning: ORA-16610: command "ENABLE DATABASE matrix_dr0" in progress
```

You can watch the Broker perform its magic by issuing a `tail -f` of the database alert log files. After waiting for a few minutes, a second `SHOW CONFIGURATION` command will return success:

```
DGMGRL> SHOW CONFIGURATION;
Configuration
  Name:                matrix
  Enabled:             YES
```

```
   Protection Mode:        MaxPerformance
   Databases:
     matrix        - Primary database
     matrix_dr0 - Physical standby database
Fast-Start Failover: DISABLED
Current status for "matrix":
SUCCESS
DGMGRL>
```

A simple way to check the current status of Redo Transport and the apply services is to use SQL*Plus. Connect to the standby database with SQL*Plus and examine the V$MANAGED_ STANDBY view:

```
SQL> SELECT CLIENT_PROCESS, PROCESS, THREAD#, SEQUENCE#, STATUS
  2  FROM V$MANAGED_STANDBY;
CLIENT_P PROCESS       THREAD#  SEQUENCE# STATUS
-------- ---------  ---------- ---------- ------------
ARCH     ARCH               1         31 CLOSING
ARCH     ARCH               0          0 CONNECTED
ARCH     ARCH               1         32 CLOSING
ARCH     ARCH               0          0 CONNECTED
N/A      MRP0               1         33 APPLYING_LOG
LGWR     RFS                1         33 IDLE
UNKNOWN  RFS                0          0 IDLE
UNKNOWN  RFS                0          0 IDLE
UNKNOWN  RFS                0          0 IDLE
9 rows selected.
SQL>
```

From this output, you can verify that the redo is being shipped using either SYNC or ASYNC (you cannot tell which one from this view) because there is a LGWR to RFS connection. Remember that the LGWR is not really connected—it is an LNS process that is connected on behalf of the LGWR.

You can also verify that real-time apply is being employed since the MRP is in the APPLYING_LOG state and is processing the sequence that the LGWR–RFS pair is currently sending. Remember that verifying the apply services in this view works only on a physical standby database. If this were a logical standby database, you would use the logical standby views.

At this point, to add more standby databases, you would repeat the setup tasks and execute another ADD DATABASE command.

As you have seen in this section, while you need to understand a lot and configure a lot up front, actually creating a Broker configuration and getting your database protected is very simple, involving basically two commands. Your next task is managing your Data Guard configuration, and we will start by editing the properties, both at the database and configuration levels.

## Changing the Broker Configuration Properties

In the preceding section we introduced the Broker properties for the databases in your configuration, a primary and one standby database at the moment. You can modify three levels of properties—configuration, database, and instance—using the EDIT command. You can also change the STATE of a database in your configuration using the same command. Each of the three levels of properties has its own variation of the EDIT command that will tell the Broker where to look for the property you want to change:

- EDIT CONFIGURATION SET PROPERTY <*name*>=<*value*>

- EDIT DATABASE <*db_name*> SET PROPERTY <*name*>=<*value*>

- EDIT INSTANCE <*in_name*> SET PROPERTY <*name*>=<*value*>
  If the instance name is not unique across the entire Broker configuration, you will need to add ON DATABASE <*db_name*> before SET PROPERTY.

The Broker views its properties from a database role perspective and will act upon a property change only if it considers that the role of the database you are changing meets the role requirements of the property. The Broker properties can be further divided into five main categories:

- **Broker-specific properties**   These affect the way the Broker operates and how Fast-Start Failover is configured.

- **Database parameters**   These are the database parameters that the Broker owns and are considered Data Guard parameters.

- **Attributes of the LOG_ARCHIVE_DEST_*n* parameter**   These are your settings for Redo Transport for each database.

- **SQL syntax**   This property modifies a particular Data Guard SQL command. Currently one property is explicitly defined to modify a SQL command.

- **Logical standby procedure arguments**   These properties are arguments to the logical standby DBMS packages that allow you to modify the way SQL Apply operates.

Some of these properties won't even be visible to you with the SHOW command if the role of the database you are examining does not meet the role of the property. The logical standby properties are a good example in which the Broker will not display the properties if the database is not a logical standby.

## Configuration-level Properties

At the configuration level, all the properties are Broker-specific with all but one related to Fast-Start Failover, which will be discussed in Chapter 8. Each of these properties is global to the entire configuration no matter where the Broker functions are taking place and are not role-specific—that is, they apply no matter which database is the PRIMARY.

Following are the configuration-level properties:

- BystandersFollowRoleChange

- FastStartFailoverAutoReinstate

- FastStartFailoverLagLimit

- FastStartFailoverPmyShutdown

- FastStartFailoverThreshold

- CommunicationTimeout

The first five properties are related to Fast-Start Failover, but the sixth is particularly important at this point. `CommunicationTimeout` is the amount of time that the Broker will wait for a response from a network connection between two databases in the configuration before giving up.

In older versions, this property was not configurable and could sometimes result in communication hangs between Broker databases. The Broker architecture was changed to prevent an important Broker process from getting stuck in a network hang by timing out after a number of seconds. The `CommunicationTimeout` property was added to ensure that there was a default for this eventual occurrence and to allow the DBA to tune the wait. The default is 3 minutes (180 seconds) and can be tuned from 0 seconds up. Setting this property to 0 (zero) will remove any timeout and always cause the Broker communication to wait for an answer. We recommend that you never set this property to zero as you would cause the Broker to wait forever. If you begin to see lots of ORA-16713 errors in the Broker DRC log, you might need to increase this property using the `EDIT CONFIGURATION` command in DGMGRL after connecting to any one of the databases:

```
DGMGRL>  EDIT CONFIGURATION SET PROPERTY CommunicationTimeout=200;
Property "communicationtimeout" updated
DGMGRL>
```

However, for situations in which the Broker takes longer than 180 seconds to get an answer from a remote database, you should examine the network rather than modify this timeout.

### Database-level Properties

Database-level properties comprise all five types of Broker properties and are defined individually for each database in the configuration. This means that each database entry in your configuration has a set of these properties that defines the way the database is to be configured. The way that a particular property is used in your configuration, though, depends on the role characteristics of the property. Some of the properties are defined only for a standby database, others only for a primary, and in some cases for both roles. Although a property may not apply to the current role of a database, most properties can be edited regardless of the database's current role.

**Broker-specific Properties**   Four Broker-specific properties are used:

- `FastStartFailoverTarget`
- `ObserverConnectIdentifier`
- `ApplyInstanceTimeout`
- `PreferredApplyInstance`

The first two are for Fast-Start Failover and will be explained in detail in Chapter 8. The last two are specific to the standby role and are used only when the target database becomes a standby. These two properties are unique because they both have *Instance* in the name, but both are database-level properties. Both define the way the Broker should handle certain parts of the apply regardless of the instance where the apply might be running.

The `ApplyInstanceTimeout` property defines how long the Broker should wait before moving the apply process to another instance in a standby RAC database if it loses contact with the current apply instance. By default, this is set to 0 (zero), which tells the Broker to failover the apply processing immediately. If you experience frequent network brownouts, it might be worthwhile to increase this property:

```
DGMGRL>  EDIT DATABASE Matrix_DR0 SET PROPERTY ApplyInstanceTimeout=20;
Property "applyinstancetimeout" updated
DGMGRL>
```

The `PreferredApplyInstance` property allows you to tell the Broker where you would like the apply to run when you have a multiple-node RAC standby. By default, this property is empty, which tells the Broker it can put the apply processing on any standby instance it chooses. In some cases, it may be necessary to put the apply services on a predefined node. For example, if you have a four-node RAC standby but you want to use three of the four nodes for testing or even for another production database, you might want to try and keep the apply processing on one particular node. You would do so by setting this property to the SID (which is also the instance level property `SidName`) of that instance:

```
DGMGRL>  EDIT DATABASE SET PROPERTY PreferredApplyInstance='Matrix_DR01';
Property "preferredapplyinstance" updated
DGMGRL>
```

You need to remember two things about this property:

- If the apply is already running on some system in the standby RAC, modifying this property will not move the apply services.

- The apply will be moved when the Broker decides it needs to failover the apply services to another instance (of its choosing) when it can no longer contact the current apply node. The Broker will not automatically move the apply services back to your preferred instance when it is reachable again.

Unless you have not yet enabled the target database (and hence the apply services are not yet running), it makes no sense to modify this property. In both cases mentioned, you can use the STATE change part of the EDIT command to move the apply services to a specific instance. We will dive into the states in a bit, but an example of this command follows:

```
DGMGRL> EDIT DATABASE 'Matrix_DR0' SET STATE='APPLY-ON' WITH
APPLY INSTANCE='Matrix_DR01';
Succeeded.
DGMGRL> SHOW DATABASE 'Matrix_DR0' 'PreferredApplyInstance';
PreferredApplyInstance = 'Matrix_DR01'
```

This would set the `PreferredApplyInstance` property for you and move the apply services to the desired instance.

**TIP**
*Unless you have a specific reason for setting the*
`PreferredApplyInstance` *property, leave it blank*
*and let the Broker choose the apply instance.*

**Database Parameter Properties** Several Broker properties equate directly to a database parameter on each of the databases in your configuration. The properties and the parameters they equate to are listed here:

- `ArchiveLagTarget` `ARCHIVE_LAG_TARGET`
- `DbFileNameConvert` `DB_FILE_NAME_CONVERT`
- `LogArchiveMaxProcesses` `LOG_ARCHIVE_MAX_PROCESSES`
- `LogArchiveMinSucceedDest` `LOG_ARCHIVE_MIN_SUCCEED_DEST`
- `LogFileNameConvert` `LOG_FILE_NAME_CONVERT`
- `LogShipping` **(Standby role only)** `LOG_ARCHIVE_DEST_STATE_`*n*
- `StandbyFileManagement` **(Standby role only)** `STANDBY_FILE_MANAGEMENT`

When you modify one of these properties, the corresponding parameter of that database gets set to the appropriate value when necessary. But what does *when necessary* mean? Suppose you were not using the Broker; then any change you make to these parameters using the SQL*Plus `ALTER SYSTEM SET` command would get set immediately if the parameter is dynamic. The Broker, on the other hand, would make the parameter change only if the current role of the target database meets the Broker's requirements, and if the parameter were not dynamic it would automatically add the `SCOPE=SPFILE`, as you would have to do with SQL*Plus. So, for example, changing the `LogArchiveFormat` property to specify a different name for the database archive log files would be executed on the database regardless of the role, but with the `SCOPE=SPFILE` qualifier:

```
DGMGRL> EDIT DATABASE MATRIX SET PROPERTY LogArchive Format='%t%s%r_new.dbf'
```

But in the alert log of Matrix, you would see the following:

```
ALTER SYSTEM SET log_archive_format='%t%s%r_new.dbf'
SCOPE=SPFILE SID='Matrix';
```

And until you restarted the target database (Matrix, in this case), you would see the following error when you perform a `SHOW DATABASE VERBOSE MATRIX`, since the current in-memory value no longer matches the `SPFILE` value:

```
Current status for "matrix":
Warning: ORA-16792: configurable property value is inconsistent with database
setting
```

On the other hand, a property such as `StandbyFileManagement` is considered by the Broker to be a standby-only property. It will change the value of the property in the configuration files but the `ALTER SYSTEM SET STANDBY_FILE_MANAGEMENT=AUTO|MANUAL` command will be issued only when the database is started in the standby role. In SQL*Plus, the parameter would be set immediately but not used until the database became a physical standby.

The same does not apply to the property `LogShipping`, which enables or defers Redo Transport to that standby database. This is one of those *reverse properties—reverse* in the sense that you set it on a database but the resulting SQL command to change the database parameter is executed on whatever database is the primary at the time. Assume, for example, that Matrix is our primary database and Matrix_DR0 is our standby database. Changing the `LogShipping` property of Matrix will not cause any SQL to be issued at this time. Changing the `LogShipping` property on our standby Matrix_DR0 will set the property for Matrix_DR0 in the configuration files, but the SQL will be executed on the Matrix database. Here's an example:

```
DGMGRL> SHOW DATABASE MATRIX LogShipping;
  LogShipping = 'ON'
DGMGRL> EDIT DATABASE MATRIX SET PROPERTY LogShipping='OFF';
Property "logshipping" updated
DGMGRL> SHOW DATABASE MATRIX LogShipping;
  LogShipping = 'OFF'
DGMGRL> SHOW DATABASE MATRIX_DR0 LogShipping;
  LogShipping = 'ON'
DGMGRL> EDIT DATABASE MATRIX_DR0 SET PROPERTY LogShipping='OFF';
Property "logshipping" updated
DGMGRL>
DGMGRL> SHOW DATABASE MATRIX_DR0 LogShipping;
  LogShipping = 'OFF'
```

This would set up Matrix not to receive redo when it becomes a standby database and will stop the transport of redo to Matrix_DR0 immediately. You can verify this by examining the alert log of Matrix. The only entry you will see is the following:

```
ALTER SYSTEM SET log_archive_dest_state_2='RESET' SCOPE=BOTH;
```

The destination parameter number 2 is currently being used by Data Guard to transport redo to our standby and is now deferred until we change the `LogShipping` property back to ON.

**TIP**
*Never use SQL*Plus to modify any of the parameters for which the Broker has a corresponding property when you have enabled the Broker. If you do make these changes, you will see error messages and the Broker will put those parameters back to its view of the world at the next restart of the database. Always use DGMGRL and the EDIT command to make these changes.*

**LOG_ARCHIVE_DEST_*n* Attribute Properties**  All of the LOG_ARCHIVE_DEST_*n* attribute properties are individual attributes that modify the way Data Guard ships the redo to each standby, with each property being one of the attributes that is set in a LOG_ARCHIVE_DEST_*n* database parameter. Not all of the Redo Transport attributes are available through the Broker and you cannot set any attributes that are not visible directly with SQL*Plus, because the Broker will reset the parameter to its view of the world. What you see is what you get. These properties and the attributes they relate to are shown here:

- **Binding**  MANDATORY or OPTIONAL
- **LogXptMode**  ASYNC or SYNC
- **MaxConnections**  MAX_CONNECTIONS
- **MaxFailure**  MAX_FAILURE

- **NetTimeout** NET_TIMEOUT
- **RedoCompression** COMPRESSION
- **ReopenSecs** REOPEN
- **DelayMins** DELAY=n

These properties are handled differently from the other properties, because although you set them on a particular database, they are never actually set on that database regardless of the role. This is similar to the *reverse property* mentioned in the preceding section and is the one part of the Broker logic that has always seemed to confound users.

As with the other database properties, each database in your configuration has a set of these properties. But what they define is the manner in which the LOG_ARCHIVE_DEST_n parameter will be created on the primary database to ship redo to this database. Let's examine this further using our Matrix primary database and our Matrix_DR0 standby database.

If you were setting up the standby configuration manually, you would (if you followed the best practices in Chapter 2), add a LOG_ARCHIVE_DEST_n parameter to Matrix that would include the attribute SERVICE=Matrix_DR0 and any other settings you wanted, which would send the redo to Matrix_DR0. You would also include the VALID_FOR attribute to enable this destination only when Matrix is the primary database. Then you would make similar changes to Matrix_DR0, but with SERVICE=Matrix and the same VALID_FOR, and so on. This parameter would not be used until Matrix_DR0 becomes the primary database. So if you look at this logically, Matrix is currently shipping redo to Matrix_DR0, and Matrix_DR0 will begin to ship redo to Matrix when a role switch occurs.

The Broker attribute properties, on the other hand, are set on the database that is going to receive redo when it is in the standby role. So to make sure that redo is sent from Matrix to Matrix_DR0, you would set the properties on Matrix_DR0 accordingly. And to make sure that the same Redo Transport goes into effect when Matrix_DR0 becomes the primary, you would set these properties on Matrix.

So, for example, if we were to change the transport mode (LogXptMode) so that we ship redo in the SYNC mode to Matrix_DR0, we would update the property on Matrix_DR0 but the result of the change would be an ALTER SYSTEM command on Matrix:

```
DGMGRL> SHOW DATABASE MATRIX_DR0 LogXptMode;
  LogXptMode = 'ASYNC'
DGMGRL> EDIT DATABASE MATRIX_DR0 SET PROPERTY LogXptMode='SYNC';
Property "logxptmode" updated
DGMGRL> SHOW DATABASE MATRIX_DR0 LogXptMode;
  LogXptMode = 'SYNC'
DGMGRL>
```

You would then see the following ALTER SYSTEM command being executed on Matrix from the alert log (note that the Broker sets the AFFIRM property automatically when you move to SYNC):

```
ALTER SYSTEM SET log_archive_dest_2='service="matrix_dr0"','  LGWR SYNC
AFFIRM delay=0 OPTIONAL compression=DISABLE max_failure=0 max_connections=1
reopen=300 db_unique_name="matrix_dr0" net_timeout=30
valid_for=(online_logfile,primary_role)' SCOPE=BOTH;

ALTER SYSTEM SET log_archive_dest_state_2='ENABLE' SCOPE=BOTH;
```

We are now shipping redo from Matrix to Matrix_DR0 synchronously. But if we stopped here, we would have configuration problems when we do a switchover.

Remember that you set these attributes on a database to define how you want Data Guard to ship redo to that database when it becomes a standby. So, in our case, we have not modified Matrix, and since the `LogXptMode` property for Matrix is still set to `ASYNC`, the Broker would set Matrix to receive redo asynchronously when it became a standby database. We need to change the `LogXptMode` property for Matrix as well:

```
DGMGRL> SHOW DATABASE MATRIX LogXptMode;
  LogXptMode = 'ASYNC'
DGMGRL> EDIT DATABASE MATRIX SET PROPERTY LogXptMode='SYNC';
Property "logxptmode" updated
DGMGRL> SHOW DATABASE MATRIX LogXptMode;
  LogXptMode = 'SYNC'
DGMGRL>
```

In this case, nothing would actually happen on Matrix since this is done just to set up Matrix to receive redo synchronously when it relinquishes its role as primary and becomes a standby database.

Be aware of the fact that every time you modify one of these properties on a database that currently is a standby, a log switch will occur on the primary database. If you must modify many of these properties, it might be better to disable the database, make the changes, and then re-enable the database afterward. This means that you will not be protected by the standby during this period.

One final note on these attribute properties. Setting the `DelayMins` property does not delay when Data Guard ships the redo. It instructs the target standby database apply services to delay the apply of the incoming redo for that period of time. This was explained in Chapter 2. But this attribute does affect the way the Broker will configure the apply services of the target standby database. If you leave the `DelayMins` property at its default of 0, or you set it manually to 0, the Broker will configure the apply services on the target standby database to use real-time apply. If you set the `DelayMins` property to any value other than 0, the Broker will always start the apply services without real-time apply and the apply will work only from the archive log files and then only after the delay has passed. This is different from the manual method of configuring your Data Guard setup. Starting up the apply services with SQL*Plus using the real-time apply syntax on a standby database will automatically cause any delay specified for that standby database to be ignored. This is not possible with the Broker.

**TIP**
*If you specify a delay using the `DelayMins` property, then that standby cannot perform real-time apply. In a SQL*Plus–managed Data Guard configuration, starting the apply services using real-time apply will override the delay.*

**SQL Syntax Properties**   Only one property currently falls into this category, although changes to the database and attribute properties do cause SQL to be executed somewhere. This property is

■   **ApplyParallel**   PARALLEL=n

By a *SQL property*, we mean that this property does not modify a parameter on a database, nor does it affect the way the Broker executes. What it does is change the way the Broker starts up the apply services for a physical standby. It affects the way media recovery on the physical standby database uses parallel processes. With this property, you can accomplish one of two things: allow media recovery to use parallel processes (set to AUTO), or disallow it from using any parallel processes (set to NO). You cannot specify a number of parallel processes that you would like media recovery to use. The default is AUTO, and we recommend that you leave the property set at its default.

**Logical Standby Properties**    The last set of database-level properties are solely for logical standby databases. These properties correspond directly to arguments to the SQL Apply procedures introduced and discussed in Chapter 4:

- **LsbyASkipCfgPr**   Set the SKIP TABLES
- **LsbyASkipErrorCfgPr**   Set SKIP ERROR rules
- **LsbyASkipTxnCfgPr**   Perform a SKIP TRANSACTION
- **LsbyDSkipCfgPr**   Unset SKIP TABLES
- **LsbyDSkipErrorCfgPr**   Unset SKIP ERROR rules
- **LsbyDSkipTxnCfgPr**   Unset a SKIP TRANSACTION
- **LsbyMaxEventsRecorded**   Set MAX_EVENTS_RECORDED
- **LsbyPreserveCommitOrder**   Modify the PRESERVE_COMMIT_ORDER
- **LsbyRecordAppliedDdl**   Set RECORD_APPLIED_DDL
- **LsbyRecordSkipDdl**   Set RECORD_SKIPPED_DDL
- **LsbyRecordSkipErrors**   Set RECORD_SKIPPED_ERRORS

These properties are available only on a logical standby and do not show up in the SHOW DATABASE VERBOSE command, and if you try to modify them on a physical standby you will get an error.

```
DGMGRL> EDIT DATABASE Matrix_DR0 SET PROPERTY
LsbyPreserveCommitOrder='FALSE';
Error: ORA-16788: unable to set one or more database
configuration property values
Failed.
DGMGRL>
```

However, if you change the property on a primary database, the modification will succeed because the primary could become a logical standby database if a switchover to a logical standby database occurs:

```
DGMGRL> EDIT DATABASE Matrix SET PROPERTY LsbyPreserveCommitOrder='FALSE';
Property "lsbypreservecommitorder" updated
DGMGRL>
DGMGRL> SHOW DATABASE Matrix LsbyPreserveCommitOrder;
  LsbyPreserveCommitOrder = 'FALSE'
DGMGRL>
```

As with the database and attribute properties, you must ensure that any changes you make to these logical standby properties are also made to the primary database properties if you ever plan on performing a switchover from the primary to a logical standby database. Otherwise, your new logical standby database will not be following the rules you set up for your logical standby in the first place.

## Instance-level Properties

These (the last of the properties) are referred to as *instance-level properties* because they can be set to different values across a RAC database if desired. These are the only properties that can be different between RAC instances in a Broker configuration. Three of the five subtypes of property are included in the instance level properties.

Here are the Broker-specific properties:

- **HostName**
- **SidName**

Here are the database parameters:

- **LogArchiveTrace** LOG_ARCHIVE_TRACE
- **LogArchiveFormat** LOG_ARCHIVE_FORMAT
- **StandbyArchiveLocation** LOG_ARCHIVE_DEST_*n*
- **AlternateLocation** An alternative LOG_ARCHIVE_DEST_*n* location

Here are the logical standby procedure arguments:

- **LsbyMaxSga** MAX_SGA
- **LsbyMaxServers** MAX_SERVERS

These properties are only to be changed using the EDIT INSTANCE command, and if the database is a RAC, any attempt to use the EDIT DATABASE command on these properties will fail. However, if the target database is not a RAC database, they will work with the EDIT DATABASE command. Because this could change in the future, we recommend that you always use the EDIT INSTANCE command when modifying any of the instance-level properties. This makes sense anyway, as you never know when one of your databases might just become a RAC!

So why are these few properties labeled *instance* properties? Didn't we already say that database-related properties are set globally to a database regardless of the number of instances? As with any rule, there are exceptions, and these properties prove that. These properties can be set individually for each instance when they need to be modified, which should not be very often.

The two Broker-specific properties would be used only if you had an already running configuration with a RAC database and needed to move or rename one of the instances in the RAC. You would set these two values on the instance you needed to move to a new system. But doing so requires that you first disable the entire database as far as the Broker is concerned—and it might be easier to use the REMOVE INSTANCE command and let the Broker automatically rediscover the instance when it starts up on the new host in the same RAC configuration.

The database parameters and logical standby properties are pretty self-explanatory. You might need to redirect archive logs to a slightly different directory or change the name of the archive logs on a particular instance, both of which would be very unusual with ASM. In fact, these two properties have been around since Oracle Database 10*g* Release 1, when RAC capabilities were introduced with the Broker when users generally had non-ASM RAC databases. You should never have to change these properties. In fact, the property `StandbyArchiveLocation` will default to your flash recovery area if you are using one, and this is a best practice. But if the property does not default, it might be necessary to use different disk paths for the archive logs on a standby if you archive to a non–cluster wide directory.

On the logical standby side, it is likely that you'd want to modify the amount of memory and apply processes for SQL Apply by instance if your RAC logical standby has unequal size systems. Since the apply services could failover to any node in the standby RAC, you would want the apply to run and to consume resources according to the size of the system. And tracing, being used to diagnose Data Guard issues, is always something you would want to set per instance, as it is either one instance that is causing problems or all instances are having the same problem, and diagnosing the issue on one system will be enough.

This leaves us with the last database parameter property—`AlternateLocation`. If we already have `StandbyArchiveLocation` as a default database-wide location for the incoming primary redo, why is an instance-level property used to redirect that redo somewhere else? The name of the property, `Alternate`, should give away its purpose. This is not to be confused with the Oracle9*i* Broker property `Alternate`, which related only to the attribute of the same name in the `LOG_ARCHIVE_DEST_n` parameter. (The `Alternate` property was deprecated starting with Oracle Database 10*g* Release 1.) The `AlternateLocation` property's purpose is to provide a second location for Data Guard to place the incoming redo if the location specified by `StandbyArchiveLocation` becomes unavailable for some reason.

By default, the `AlternateLocation` property is blank, which means that if redo is arriving at this instance into the standby redo log files and the archive directory becomes unavailable, the standby redo log files will all fill up (since they cannot be archived to disk) and redo will no longer be shipped to this standby.

So the answer was to archive the redo to a different location on the standby. Most likely, this was a local disk directory on the standby. If you were using ASM with the flash recovery area and it failed, you most likely had other problems, but you would still be able to receive redo if this property was set beforehand. Bear in mind, though, that if your standby was a RAC and you chose a directory local to one instance in the RAC for local archiving, the apply services would not be able to read the archive logs if they were on another system in the RAC. In previous releases, this was not an issue since the Broker would always configure the Redo Transport Services to send redo to the same instance in a RAC standby that had the apply services running. In this manner, the apply services could always see the archive logs if they happened to move to the alternate location. Since the Broker in 11*g* allows you to specify a TNSNAME for the Redo Transport `DGConnectionIdentifier` that has all the standby instances in it and allows you to specify where you want the apply services to run, it is completely possible that the redo could be sent to a different instance than the apply services. So if you plan on setting this property, it would be best to set it to a location on the standby database that is visible across all instances of the RAC.

One final note: If this property is invoked due to a failure of the `StandbyArchiveLocation`, the Broker will also configure a new Redo Transport parameter for the standby that explicitly defines this alternate location; don't be surprised if you see `LOG_ARCHIVE_DEST_n` parameters different from what you had before the change.

This brings us to the end of the section on editing the Broker properties. Remember that no matter what your plans for changes in the Broker configuration, any property that corresponds to a database parameter must follow the rules of that parameter.

# Changing the State of a Database

The state of a database is another area of the Broker that has changed considerably since Oracle9*i* Release 2. The command and the qualifier used to change a state is completely different in 9*i*, and although the command used to change a state has been the same since 10*g* Release 1 through 11*g*, the qualifier used to specify the state change evolved yet again in 11*g*. Specific state commands were used for a physical standby database and a logical standby database in 9*i*, such as PHYSICAL-APPLY-READY and LOGICAL-APPLY-READY, which have been changed to APPLY-ON. So if you are using the Broker in one of the older versions, you should read the Broker manual for that release to make sure you are using the correct syntax. The underlying function has pretty much remained the same. When you want to turn the apply services off, you just use the correct state command.

The state model of a database in the Broker can be regarded as a database-level property since the state is set using the EDIT DATABASE command like a property update. The difference from the general data properties is that specific states are used for a primary database and other states are used for a standby database.

The primary database states consist of turning on or off the Redo Transport Services for all standby databases in your configuration. This state can be modified only using the name of the database that is currently acting in the primary role, which in our case is still Matrix, so an attempt to change this state on our standby Matrix_DR0 would fail:

```
DGMGRL> EDIT DATABASE MATRIX_DR0 SET STATE=TRANSPORT-OFF;
Error: ORA-16516: current state is invalid for the attempted operation
Failed.
DGMGRL> EDIT DATABASE MATRIX SET STATE=TRANSPORT-OFF;
Succeeded.
DGMGRL>
```

What you see in the alert log of Matrix as a result of the successful change would be a RESET of every active standby database:

```
ALTER SYSTEM SET log_archive_dest_state_2='RESET' SCOPE=BOTH;
```

Turning the transport back on is the same command using TRANSPORT-ON. Remember that this shuts down Redo Transport to all standby databases. You would use this command only if you needed to isolate the primary database for some reason and enter into a completely unprotected state. If you are looking just to stop Redo Transport to one standby database, you would edit the LogShipping property of that database, as discussed earlier. This would perform the reset only on the Redo Transport for that standby database and leave the other standby databases quite happily receiving the redo.

Two states for a standby database are used to turn the apply services on or off. The default for a physical or a logical standby database is on when the database or configuration is first enabled. The apply state is modified just as the transport state but can be executed only on a standby database.

```
DGMGRL> EDIT DATABASE MATRIX SET STATE=APPLY-OFF;
Error: ORA-16516: current state is invalid for the attempted operation
Failed.
DGMGRL> EDIT DATABASE MATRIX_DR0 SET STATE=APPLY-OFF;
Succeeded.
DGMGRL>
```

This time you would see nothing change in the primary database alert log, but the following (or something like it) would appear in the target standby's alert log:

```
ALTER DATABASE RECOVER MANAGED STANDBY DATABASE CANCEL
Mon Dec 01 23:32:28 2008
MRP0: Background Media Recovery cancelled with status 16037
 ORA-16037: user requested cancel of managed recovery operation
Managed Standby Recovery not using Real Time Apply
Shutting down recovery slaves due to error 16037
Recovery interrupted!
```

Again, like the transport state, you would use APPLY-ON to restart the apply services.

One state disappeared between 9i/10g and 11g, and that was the physical standby READ-ONLY state. The Broker changed the way it interacted with the user's method of starting up a database and now respects a STARTUP MOUNT or a STARTUP, leaving the database in the end state, MOUNTED, OPEN READ ONLY, or OPEN READ WRITE. (Starting with Oracle Database 10g Release 2, performing a STARTUP on a physical standby will automatically open the standby in read-only.)

With the new ability to read a physical standby while the apply is running, the need for a READ-ONLY state was no longer considered necessary. This is called *real-time query*, and it became a part of the Active Data Guard option with the release of Oracle Database 11g. Since the Broker no longer has a read-only state, it is necessary to use DGMGRL and SQL*Plus to put a database into real-time query mode using the Active Data Guard option:

```
DGMGRL> EDIT DATABASE MATRIX_DR0 SET STATE=APPLY-OFF;
Succeeded.
SQL> ALTER DATABASE OPEN READ ONLY;
Database opened;
DGMGRL> EDIT DATABASE MATRIX_DR0 SET STATE=APPLY-ON;
Succeeded.
DGMGRL>
```

We are confident that a future release of the Data Guard Broker will make this process much more streamlined and bulletproof.

## Changing the Protection Mode

A protection mode property is similar to a configuration-level property in that you execute it using the EDIT CONFIGURATION command and it applies to the entire configuration.

As you saw in Chapter 1 when the protection modes were discussed, each mode applies certain rules to the Data Guard configuration: performance, availability, or protection. The Broker provides the same mechanism to enable a certain level of protection, but it also helps protect you from yourself. For example, to change the protection mode of a Data Guard configuration using SQL*Plus (when it is not controlled by the Broker), you would connect to the primary database and execute the appropriate SQL command:

```
ALTER DATABASE SET STANDBY TO MAXIMIZE PERFORMANCE;
ALTER DATABASE SET STANDBY TO MAXIMIZE AVAILABILITY;
ALTER DATABASE SET STANDBY TO MAXIMIZE PROTECTION;
```

Since the second and third modes require certain standby settings, if you had not taken the required steps to configure your standby database correctly, you might find yourself in an unprotected or shutdown state.

Since Oracle Database 10g Release 2, it is possible to set the Maximum Availability mode without any SYNC standby databases, and your configuration would run in an unsynchronized state. Failing over to a standby would result in data loss since Maximum Availability requires at least one SYNC standby database to allow a zero-data-loss failover.

Since Maximum Protection mode can be set only in the MOUNT state, your primary database would not be allowed to open without any SYNC standby destinations. The Broker will not allow a protection mode to be set unless all the prerequisites of the protection mode have been met:

```
DGMGRL> SHOW CONFIGURATION;
Configuration
  Name:              matrix
  Enabled:           YES
  Protection Mode:   MaxPerformance
  Databases:
    matrix    - Primary database
    matrix_dr0 - Physical standby database
Fast-Start Failover: DISABLED
Current status for "matrix":
SUCCESS
DGMGRL> SHOW DATABASE matrix_dr0 LogXptMode;
  LogXptMode = 'ASYNC'
DGMGRL> EDIT CONFIGURATION SET PROTECTION MODE AS MaxAvailability;
Error: ORA-16627: operation disallowed since no standby databases would remain
to support the protection mode

Failed.
DGMGRL> EDIT DATABASE matrix_dr0 SET PROPERTY LogXptMode='SYNC';
Property "logxptmode" updated
DGMGRL> EDIT CONFIGURATION SET PROTECTION MODE AS MaxAvailability;
Succeeded.
DGMGRL> SHOW CONFIGURATION;
Configuration
  Name:              matrix
  Enabled:           YES
  Protection Mode:   MaxAvailability
  Databases:
    matrix    - Primary database
    matrix_dr0 - Physical standby database
Fast-Start Failover: DISABLED
Current status for "matrix":
SUCCESS
DGMGRL>
```

As you can see, the first attempt to change the protection mode to Maximum Availability met with the ORA-16627 error. The simple fix was to set the LogXptMode property for Matrix_DR0 to SYNC and re-execute the command. Your Data Guard configuration is now running in Maximum Availability, or zero-data-loss, mode. Do not forget to update the LogXptMode property for Matrix as well in preparation for a switchover.

# Monitoring Data Guard Using the Broker

We have already introduced the SHOW command in DGMGRL as the way to look at the status of your configuration or a database and to display the various properties of the databases in your configuration. But so far we have discussed only the properties that you can change. Several other properties are "monitor only" and provide much more information than the standard error message returned by the SHOW CONFIGURATION or DATABASE command.

To demonstrate, we will do something behind the scenes to one of our databases and then use the SHOW command to display the current status of the Broker configuration.

```
DGMGRL> SHOW CONFIGURATION;
Configuration
  Name:               matrix
  Enabled:            YES
  Protection Mode:    MaxAvailability
  Databases:
    matrix      - Primary database
    matrix_dr0 - Physical standby database
Fast-Start Failover: DISABLED
Current status for "matrix":
Warning: ORA-16608: one or more databases have warnings
DGMGRL>
```

Unfortunately, the error message does not tell you which database has the problem. So we have to use the SHOW DATABASE command to get more information:

```
DGMGRL> SHOW DATABASE Matrix_DR0;
Database
  Name:             matrix_dr0
  Role:             PHYSICAL STANDBY
  Enabled:          YES
  Intended State:   APPLY-ON
  Instance(s):
    Matrix_DR0
Current status for "matrix_dr0":
SUCCESS
DGMGRL>
```

It's not the standby database. So let's look at the primary database:

```
DGMGRL> SHOW DATABASE Matrix;
Database
  Name:             matrix
  Role:             PRIMARY
  Enabled:          YES
  Intended State:   TRANSPORT-ON
  Instance(s):
    Matrix
Current status for "matrix":
Warning: ORA-16792: configurable property value is inconsistent with database
setting

DGMGRL>
```

This still does not tell us what property or parameter is out of sync between the Broker and the actual database setting, or where it is incorrect. But we can obtain another level of information from the Broker via one of the read-only properties. These properties are displayed when we use the SHOW DATABASE VERBOSE command and can be divided into three main areas: database and transport, logical standby, and general reports. Remember that, as with the updateable database properties, the read-only logical standby properties will appear only if the database is actually a logical standby or is the primary database.

Following are the read-only properties for database and transport:

- **InconsistentLogXptProps**   Inconsistent Redo Transport properties
- **InconsistentProperties**   Inconsistent database properties
- **LogXptStatus**   Redo Transport status

And here are the logical standby properties:

- **LsbyFailedTxnInfo**   Logical standby failed transaction information
- **LsbyParameters**   Logical standby parameters
- **LsbySkipTable**   Logical standby skip table
- **LsbySkipTxnTable**   SQL Apply skip transaction table

And here are the general reports properties:

- **RecvQEntries**   Receive queue entries
- **SendQEntries**   Send queue entries
- **StatusReport**   List of errors or warnings
- **LatestLog**   Tail of the DRC log file
- **TopWaitEvents**   Five top wait events

You can see the same error message in the StatusReport property:

```
DGMGRL> SHOW DATABASE Matrix StatusReport;
STATUS REPORT
        INSTANCE_NAME    SEVERITY ERROR_TEXT
             Matrix      WARNING ORA-16714: the value of property
                         LogArchiveMaxProcesses is inconsistent
                         with the database setting
```

Using the error message we got from our primary database 'Matrix' we can look at the InconsistentProperties property to obtain more information on the errant parameter:

```
DGMGRL> SHOW DATABASE Matrix InconsistentProperties ;
INCONSISTENT PROPERTIES
  INSTANCE_NAME    PROPERTY_NAME    MEMORY_VALUE    SPFILE_VALUE    BROKER_VALUE
  Matrix           LogArchiveMaxProcesses  4             6               4
DGMGRL>
```

This shows that someone has used SQL*Plus to change a parameter that the Broker considers one of its own. This person also tried to be sneaky and put the change only in the SPFILE thinking that at the next restart of the primary database, six ARCH processes would be started and no one would be the wiser. Well, the culprit would be in for a surprise, since the Broker would return the parameter to four processes, because that is its view of the world. The proper way would have been to use the DGMGRL EDIT DATABASE command and change the property from the Broker. We can resolve this inconsistency in three ways: we can use the Broker to reset this parameter, we can change the Broker property to match the SPFILE, or we can return to SQL*Plus and fix the parameter in the SPFILE.

```
DGMGRL> EDIT DATABASE Matrix SET PROPERTY LogArchiveMaxProcesses=6;
Property "logarchivemaxprocesses" updated
DGMGRL> SHOW DATABASE Matrix StatusReport;
STATUS REPORT
        INSTANCE_NAME    SEVERITY ERROR_TEXT
```

Since we have resolved the property with the parameter setting, the status report shows no problems. The rest of the read-only properties work pretty much the same:

```
DGMGRL> SHOW DATABASE Matrix LogXptStatus;
LOG TRANSPORT STATUS
PRIMARY_INSTANCE_NAME STANDBY_DATABASE_NAME                STATUS
            Matrix          matrix_dr0
```

The one read-only property that will always return lots of information is the `LatestLog` property. Examining this property will display the tail end of the Broker DRC log from the system where the target database resides. This will allow you to look at the latest messages that are being added to the log file.

The `TopWaitEvents` property will also display the top five events from the V$SYSTEM_EVENT view of the target database.

# Removing the Broker

In this chapter, we have attempted to show you how the Broker works, and by doing so, we hope that you can see how the Broker has matured and is a powerful yet simple interface to Data Guard. At this point, the question "How do I remove it?" always seems to come up.

Removing Data Guard completely from your production database and throwing away your standby databases is fairly straightforward. You delete the standby databases and remove any Data Guard parameters from the primary database. To be 100-percent safe, you could create a PFILE from your SPFILE, edit it to remove all Data Guard parameters, and restart after re-creating the SPFILE from your edited PFILE. But removing the Broker and leaving your Data Guard configuration intact and managed again by SQL*Plus is something completely different.

As we have shown, the Broker maintains configuration files on each system where there is a database in your Data Guard configuration. The Broker also configures your databases based on their current role, be it primary or standby. This means that if you want to remove the Broker you will have to do some reconfiguring of Data Guard to return to your original setup.

If you want to remove the Broker control temporarily, you can just disable the configuration or a database and enable it again at a later time, and things will run fine underneath as long as you do not need to failover to a standby. You can also remove a database and then add it again in the event that you moved it to a new system, and continue using the Broker to manage Data Guard.

But if you want to remove the configuration completely, you need to use the REMOVE CONFIGURATION command and reset some of the parameters in your databases. You will have to redo the parameters, because the Broker will not set up the primary role parameters on your standby databases (Redo Transport and so on) or the standby role parameters on your primary database (apply services, standby parameters, and so on). This means a switchover or a failover to a standby will work fine, but no parameters will be set up to ship redo from the new primary database back to the old primary, which is now a standby database (or will be if you did a failover and then reinstated the database as a standby), and the apply will not be started for you on the new standby database. And if you have multiple standby databases, the problems just get more complicated.

To remove the Broker from managing your Data Guard configuration and end up with a fully functioning Data Guard setup, you need to follow these steps.

In DGMGRL, do this:

1.  Connect to the primary database.

2.  Execute this command:

    ```
    REMOVE CONFIGURATION PRESERVE DESTINATIONS;
    ```

Using SQL*Plus, do this:

1.  Connect to the primary database as SYSDBA and do the following:

    First, set the DG_BROKER_START parameter to FALSE:

    ```
    ALTER SYSTEM SET DG_BROKER_START=FALSE ;
    ```

    Then define all of the standby role parameters as described in Chapter 2.

2.  Connect to the standby database as SYSDBA and do the following:

    First, set the DG_BROKER_START parameter to FALSE:

    ```
    ALTER SYSTEM SET DG_BROKER_START=FALSE ;
    ```

    Then define all of the primary role parameters as shown in Chapter 2.

3.  Repeat step 2 for all standby databases in your configuration.

4.  On all database systems, delete the two Broker configuration files from disk.

This will leave you with a fully functioning Data Guard setup ready for switchover and failover. Remember that since Grid Control requires the Broker you will no longer be able to manage your Data Guard configuration using Grid Control.

We hope that you will never have to use these steps and that you will find the Broker as useful a tool as we have in our management of Data Guard.

# Conclusion

It's been a long journey but we hope it has been an informative one. By now you have learned not only how to configure and tune your Data Guard environment, you have learned the various ways you can interact with your configuration. Using the Broker as your interface to Data Guard will simplify your job and it is also the foundation for managing Data Guard with Grid Control. As you will discover later on in this book, certain Data Guard functionality is only available through the Data Guard Broker, and the knowledge you have gained in this chapter will serve you well in the future.

# CHAPTER
6

# Oracle Enterprise Manager Grid Control Integration

racle Enterprise Manager (OEM) Grid Control plays an integral part in an Oracle ecosystem. Advocates of management tools promote OEM Grid Control as a centralized monitoring and maintenance console for the enterprise. With additional plug-ins, OEM Grid Control is intended to become *the* enterprise console and may even replace the network operations console, such as HP OpenView and IBM Tivoli.

You may be surprised to hear that OEM Grid Control can be leveraged to exploit the majority of Data Guard features. Whether you are interested in being alerted for a specific performance metrics or for changing the protection mode, OEM Grid Control can be a powerful ally for the DBA. OEM Grid Control provides an easy to use and friendly user interface for new and seasoned DBAs for performing many of the tasks associated with maintaining a Data Guard environment. With OEM Grid Control, the DBA can perform even what is perceived to be complex tasks, such as switchovers, failovers to a remote site, or reinstating a failed primary database.

This chapter focuses on OEM Grid Control functionality relative to Data Guard. We will take advantage of all the major innovative features offered by OEM Grid Control to manage your Data Guard environment. In Chapter 2, you learned how to set up a physical standby database using OEM Grid Control. This chapter will continue where that chapter left off and maneuver around various screens within OEM Grid Control to help you effectively manage a disaster recovery and/or reporting database.

We start by looking at verifying your existing configuration and then dive into reviewing performance metrics, modifying metrics, and viewing database alert log details. The rest of chapter will focus on the following:

- Enabling flashback logging
- Reviewing performance
- Changing protection modes
- Editing the standby database properties
- Performing a switchover
- Performing a manual failover
- Enabling Fast-Start Failover
- Creating a logical standby
- Managing an active standby
- Managing a snapshot standby

# Accessing the Data Guard Features

The Data Guard home page is a portal entry point for managing and viewing the Data Guard protection mode, enabling and/or disabling Fast Connection Failover, viewing the summary of apply/transport lag, editing standby database properties, viewing Data Guard status, and viewing current redo log activity. You can also observe the primary and standby databases received and applied log sequence numbers. More important, the home page provides the estimated failover time to serve as a quick dashboard indicating your compliance to your corporate recovery point objective/recovery time objective (RPO/RTO).

**NOTE**
*Do not be confused by the terms* Database Control *and* OEM Grid
Control. *Database Control is database-specific and runs locally on the
database server. Each database houses a scaled-down version of the
SYSMAN repository. Database Control is also version-specific to the
database, since it resides locally on the database server whereas OEM
Grid Control encompasses all the supported database versions. With
Database Control, you must log in to each of the database server's EM
login portals. Database Control cannot be used with a physical standby.*

Here's how to access all the Data Guard features:

1.  Click the Targets tab on the Grid Control entry page.

2.  From the Targets page, click Databases to open the Databases page.

3.  From the Databases page, you will see a comprehensive list of all the discovered databases. Select your primary database from this list to be routed to the database home page.

4.  Click the Availability tab, and then click the Setup and Manage link in the Data Guard section to access all the Data Guard services. If you have already configured the Data Guard Broker for this primary database you will be directed to the Data Guard Overview page. We will make reference to this page throughout this chapter as the *Data Guard home page.* You may want to bookmark this page from your browser of choice for quick access in the future. If there is no Data Guard Broker Configuration you will be asked if you want to configure the Broker.

**NOTE**
*This chapter does not spend time on installation and configuration
of the OEM Grid Control. Installing OEM Grid Control is beyond the
scope of this book.*

## Configuring Data Guard Broker with OEM Grid Control

If you are not taking advantage of the GUI of OEM Grid Control with your current Data Guard configuration, you have neither unleashed the effectiveness nor realized how easy Data Guard configuration can be. With each release of OEM Grid Control, Oracle packs in more and more Data Guard support and functionality. As you saw in Chapter 2, you can create your standby database using the OEM Data Guard Wizard. But you can start managing your existing Data Guard environment simply by enabling the Data Guard Broker. Here's how to take advantage of OEM Grid Control in your fully functional Data Guard environment:

1.  Navigate to the Add Standby Database screen, shown in the following illustration, by clicking the *Add Standby Database* link that OEM Grid Control displays when there is no Broker configuration.

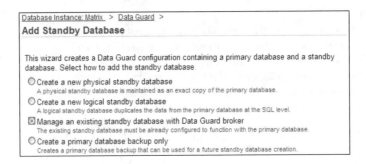

2. On the Add Standby Database screen, select the *Manage An Existing Standby Database With Data Guard Broker* radio button. Note that prior to enabling the Data Guard Broker with OEM Grid Control, the primary database must be started using the SPFILE.

3. Click the Next button to open the Add Standby Database: *Select Existing Standby Database* screen, where you can choose an existing standby database. You can select the standby database that currently provides disaster recovery or reporting services for your primary database, as shown here.

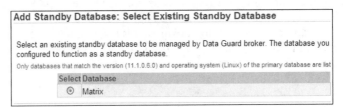

4. Select your standby database and click the Next button.

5. If login credentials have not yet been established, you are prompted to provide SYSDBA login credentials to connect to the physical standby database. Once you have provided SYSDBA login credentials, you can optionally modify the archive location at the standby host, as shown here.

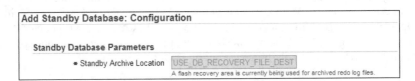

6. If you are not using the flash recovery area, you can optionally modify the local archiving parameter. But if the primary database uses the flash recovery area, the standby archive location will contain USE_DB_RECOVERY_FILE_DEST and will be grayed out to use the same settings.

7.  At the bottom of the page you will now be able to modify how the Broker connects to the primary and standby databases by changing the Enterprise Manager Connect Identifier fields for both databases back to the TNSNAMEs you originally used, as shown here.

---

**▼Data Guard Connect Identifiers**

Data Guard requires a connect identifier for each database in the configuration. The connect identifier will be used for all Data Guard communicatio standby databases.

☑ TIP If an existing net service name is specified, ensure that is is resolvable by all databases in the Data Guard configuration.

\* Primary Database Connect Identifier   ◯ Use Enterprise Manager connect descriptor
Uses the connect descriptor used by Enterprise Manager for the primary database.

◉ Use existing net service name

Matrix

An existing net service name that can be used by all databases in the Data Guard configuration to connect to the primary

\* Standby Database Connect Identifier   ◯ Use Enterprise Manager connect descriptor
Uses the connect descriptor used by Enterprise Manager for the standby database.

◉ Use existing net service name

Matrix_DR0

An existing net service name that can be used by all databases in the Data Guard configuration to connect to the standby

---

8.  Click the Next button and review the proposed changes:

---

**Add Standby Database: Review**

( Cancel )  ( Back )  Step

Standby database **Matrix_DR0** will be added to the Data Guard configuration.

| **Primary Database** | | **Standby Database** | |
|---|---|---|---|
| Target Name | **Matrix** | Target Name | **Matrix_DR0** |
| Host | **stadu67** | Host | **lcarpent-lnx** |
| | | Instance Name | **Matrix_DR0** |
| | | Oracle Home | **/scratch/OracleHomes/OraHome111** |
| | | Standby Type | **Physical Standby** |
| | | Standby Archive Location | **USE_DB_RECOVERY_FILE_DEST** |

---

9.  If you are satisfied with the configuration, click the Finish button, and OEM Grid Control will start enabling the Data Guard Broker, as shown in the following illustration. At this point, you will not be able to cancel this operation after it starts.

---

**⊛ Processing: Add Standby Database**

**The standby database will be added to the Data Guard configuration.**

After the process is complete, you will be returned to the Data Guard overview page.

⇨ Creating Data Guard configuration
Updating standby database target

---

You will be redirected to the Data Guard home page once the physical standby is configured for Broker control.

# Verifying Configuration and Adding Standby Redo Logs

We're assuming that you have already created your standby database as you read Chapter 2 or have an existing standby environment that was just imported into Grid Control in the preceding section. If you haven't created an environment, create a standby database now, as instructed in Chapter 2, and configure the Data Guard environment to be managed by OEM Grid Control. When you have a standby database managed by Grid Control, you can perform a health check of your Data Guard environment.

To perform a health check of your Data Guard environment, click the Verify Configuration link in the Additional Information section of the Data Guard home page. You can click the Verify Configuration link at any time for both the primary and standby databases. Clicking this link will initiate the verification steps displayed in Figure 6-1. Notice that the verification operation validates database settings such as the protection mode, redo log configuration, standby redo log files, redo log switches, and Data Guard status, and it performs a basic health check.

You can cancel the verification process at any time, but you should let the process complete and review the Results page to assess your current environment. Figure 6-2 shows the top portion

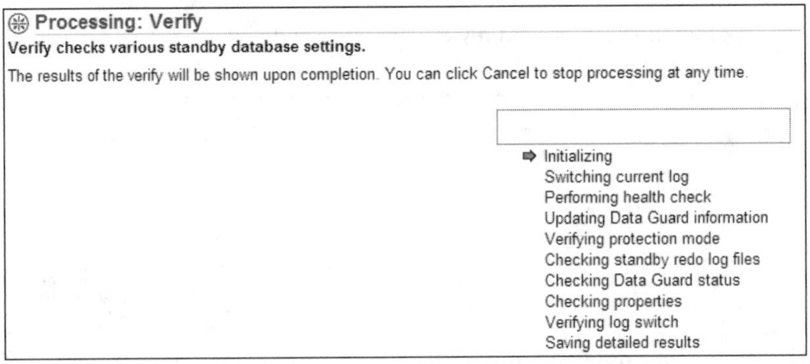

**FIGURE 6-1.** *Processing Data Guard verification*

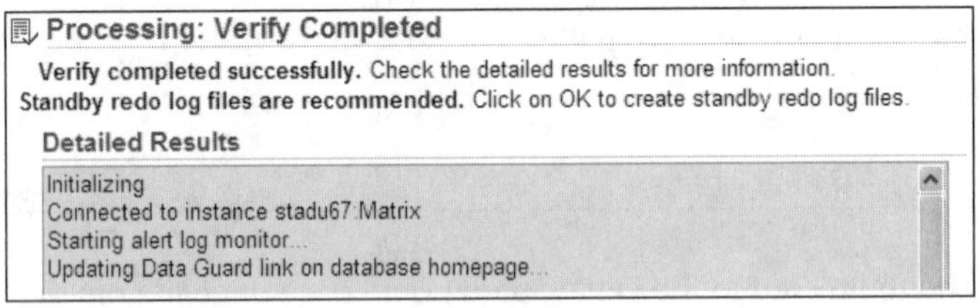

**FIGURE 6-2.** *Data Guard has completed verification.*

of the Results output, indicating that the verification process completed successfully and that standby redo logs are recommended at the primary database.

Following is the detailed output of the verification results:

```
Initializing
Connected to instance Matrix
Starting alert log monitor...
Updating Data Guard link on database homepage...
Data Protection Settings:
  Protection mode : Maximum Performance
  Redo Transport Mode settings:
    Matrix: ASYNC
    Matrix_DR0: ASYNC
  Checking standby redo log files.....Done
    (Standby redo log files needed : 4)
Checking Data Guard status
  Matrix : ORA-16789: standby redo logs not configured
  Matrix_DR0 : Normal
Checking Inconsistent Properties
Checking agent status
  Matrix ... OK
  Matrix_DR0 ... OK
Switching log file 14.Done
  Checking applied log on Matrix_DR0...OK
Processing completed.
```

Standby redo logs are essential for receiving incoming redo instead of archive logs. In addition to checking for availability of standby redo logs, the verification process also checks agent status. At the bottom portion of the results page, shown in Figure 6-3, you are informed that the standby redo logs are missing and need to be created at the standby database server. If you are executing the verification process on the physical standby database and have already created standby redo logs on the standby database, the verification process will switch redo logs on the primary database and confirm that the log was applied on the physical standby.

---

**Standby Redo Log Files**

Standby redo log files are recommended for all transport modes. They are required for certain features such as real-time apply and elevated protection modes.

☑ Create standby redo log files for the following database(s)

☑ Use Oracle-managed files (OMF) for standby redo log files
  Files will be created using OMF for all databases configured to use OMF. Deselect this option to override the default file locations. Overridden file locations for databases configured to use Automatic Storage Management (ASM) must be ASM disk groups.

| Database | Host | Size (MB) | Log File Location |
| --- | --- | --- | --- |
| Matrix | stadu67 | 50.0 | Oracle-managed file |
| Matrix | stadu67 | 50.0 | Oracle-managed file |
| Matrix | stadu67 | 50.0 | Oracle-managed file |
| Matrix | stadu67 | 50.0 | Oracle-managed file |

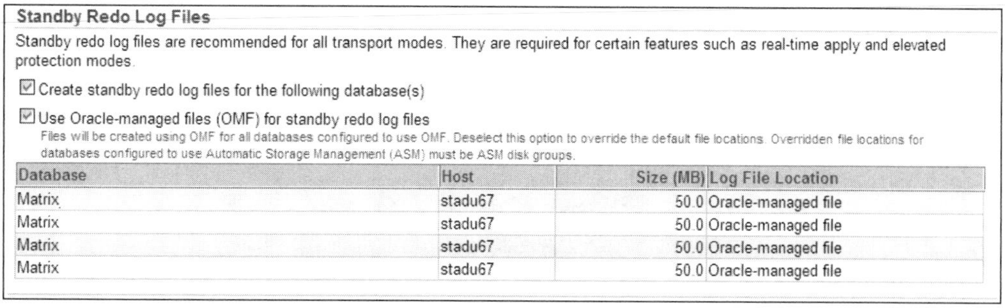

**FIGURE 6-3.**   *Standby redo log file recommendations*

Clicking the OK button will create the standby redo logs as Oracle Managed Files and return you to the Data Guard home page. You will also be prompted to create standby redo logs in other screens within OEM Grid Control, such as while enabling Fast-Start Failover or changing protection modes.

# Viewing Metrics

OEM Grid Control uses the term *metrics* to refer to the assessment of the health of your system. Metrics are units of measurement with associated *thresholds*. When a threshold for a metric is reached, an alert is generated. Targets in OEM Grid Control come with a predefined set of metrics, and alerts are generated when a threshold is reached. A threshold is cleared when a monitored service changes such as database up/down conditions and when a specific condition occurs, such as an ORA-message in the alert log file.

From the Related Links section of the Data Guard home page, you can click the All Metrics link to view all the OEM Grid Control metrics (including Data Guard metrics). From the All Metrics screen, you can expand the metrics summary specific to Data Guard, such as Fast-Start Failover, Fast-Start Failover Observer, performance, and status. The metrics that you will see depend on the current role of the database through which you have connected. For example, Figure 6-4 displays a small subset of the Metrics screen for our physical standby, Matrix_DR0.

Here we see the Data Guard metrics for the apply and transport lags, the apply rate, and failover estimate. However, if we connect to our primary database, Matrix, and look at All Metrics, we'll see a slightly different set of Data Guard metrics, as shown in Figure 6-5.

Notice that the Failover Occurred and Observer Status threshold values are the same as those shown for the standby database, but here you also see the Data Guard Status and the primary database Redo Generation Rate metrics.

You can click any of the metrics that have thresholds set. For instance, click the Data Guard Status metrics, and you can observe that both the primary and physical standby databases are online and operational, as shown in Figure 6-6.

| Metrics | Thresholds |
|---|---|
| ▼ Matrix_DR0 | |
| ▷ Archive Area | Some |
| ▷ Data Failure | All |
| ▼ Data Guard Failover | Not Applicable |
| Failover Occurred | Not Applicable |
| ▼ Data Guard Fast-Start Failover Observer | All |
| Observer Status | Set |
| ▼ Data Guard Performance | None |
| Apply Lag (seconds) | Not Set |
| Estimated Failover Time (seconds) | Not Set |
| Redo Apply Rate (KB/second) | Not Set |
| Transport Lag (seconds) | Not Set |

**FIGURE 6-4.** *Data Guard standby database metrics*

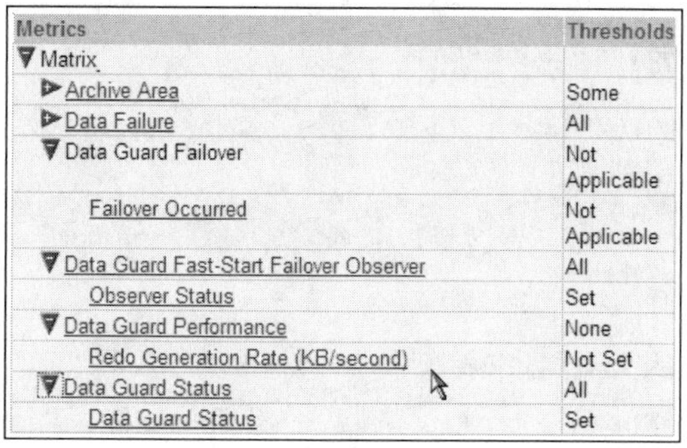

| Metrics | Thresholds |
|---|---|
| ▼ Matrix | |
| ▶ Archive Area | Some |
| ▶ Data Failure | All |
| ▼ Data Guard Failover | Not Applicable |
| Failover Occurred | Not Applicable |
| ▼ Data Guard Fast-Start Failover Observer | All |
| Observer Status | Set |
| ▼ Data Guard Performance | None |
| Redo Generation Rate (KB/second) | Not Set |
| ▼ Data Guard Status | All |
| Data Guard Status | Set |

**FIGURE 6-5.** *Data Guard primary database metrics*

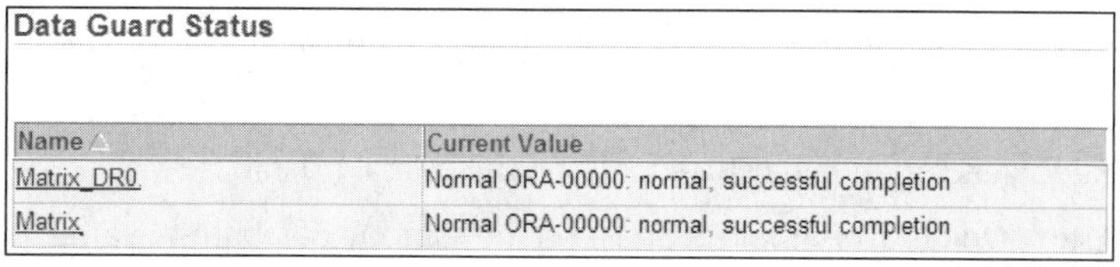

**Data Guard Status**

| Name △ | Current Value |
|---|---|
| Matrix_DR0 | Normal ORA-00000: normal, successful completion |
| Matrix | Normal ORA-00000: normal, successful completion |

**FIGURE 6-6.** *All Metrics: Data Guard Status*

# Modifying Metrics

If you haven't done so already, you need to set up the notification methods to receive e-mails or pages from OEM Grid Control for alerts and metric threshold notifications. To access the Notification Methods page, click the *Setup* link located at the upper-right corner of the page above the tabs. You will see a page with two panes. In the left pane, click the Notification Methods link to open the Notification Methods page, where you can specify the SMTP server, username, password, and sender's e-mail address. You can also stipulate that repeat alert notifications be sent for the same metric or availability alert.

Metrics can be modified by clicking the Metrics and Policy Settings link in the middle column of the Related Links section on the Database home page. However, you have to use the link from the Database home page where the database's current role matches that of the metric. For example, one particular metric of interest in a Data Guard environment is the apply lag metric, which is measured in seconds; you will be able to set this metric only from the Standby Database home page. In the Metrics and Policy Settings page of our standby Matrix_DR0, the apply lag metric is not visible by default since the apply lag is not configured by default. To change the apply lag, simply select the All Metrics option from the View drop-down list. The screen will refresh, and all the modifiable metrics will be displayed, as shown in Figure 6-7.

Set the appropriate values in the Warning Threshold and Critical Threshold columns. Optionally, you can also change the collection schedule. You can continue to make changes to other metrics and then click OK to commit the changes. You will see a confirmation page indicating the successful update.

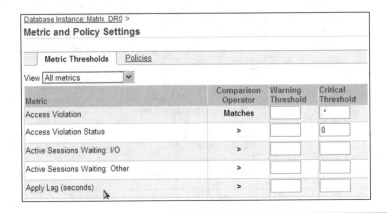

**FIGURE 6-7.** *Metrics and Policy Settings for all metrics*

Other critical metrics that you may want to modify relative to your Data Guard configuration include the following:

- Redo generation rate (KB/second) on the primary database
- Estimated failover time (seconds) on the standby database
- Redo apply rate (KB/second) on the standby database
- Transport lag (seconds) on the standby database
- Archive area used (%) on both the primary and standby databases
- Archive hung alert log error on both the primary and standby databases
- Archive hung alert log error status on both the primary and standby databases

# Viewing the Alert Log File

You can view the database alert log file for both the primary and standby databases through Grid Control. You can gain access to the database alert log file in several ways, but the most sensible route is clicking the Edit link in the Properties field to open the Edit Primary Database Properties page. Or you can click the Status link in either the primary or the standby database. Within the Edit Primary/Standby Database Properties page in the Diagnostics section, you can click the link associated with your database, as shown in Figure 6-8.

| Diagnostics | | |
| --- | --- | --- |
| Role | View Alert Log | Open Telnet Session |
| Primary | Matrix | stadu67 |
| Physical Standby | Matrix_DR0 | lcarpent-lnx |
| General | Standby Role Properties | Common Properties |

**FIGURE 6-8.** *Edit the primary database properties*

**Search Criteria**

| | |
|---|---|
| Begin Date | [____] 📅 Time [▾] : [▾] ◉ AM ○ PM |
| | (example: Feb 10, 2009) |
| End Date | [____] 📅 Time [▾] : [▾] ◉ AM ○ PM |
| | (example: Feb 10, 2009) |

[ Go ]

**FIGURE 6-9.** *Alert log search range*

In this example, we will examine the alert log entries for the Matrix database. The alert log search screen will extract the last 100K characters of the database alert log file. You can define a custom search by entering begin and end dates and time criteria at the top of the page in the Search Criteria area, as shown in Figure 6-9.

You are strongly encouraged to hit the Refresh button since the alert log file is constantly updated. Reviewing the database alert log provides your initial entry point to diagnosing Data Guard–related problems. By viewing the alert log file entries using a web browser, you no longer need physical OS access to the database servers to examine the alert log files. Figure 6-10 shows the bottom of the page, where you can peruse redo log alert entries.

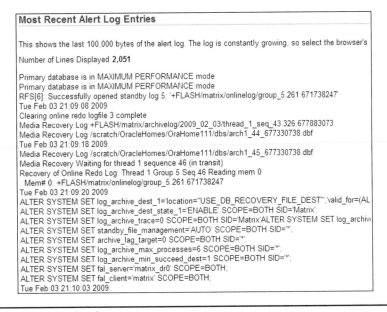

**Most Recent Alert Log Entries**

This shows the last 100,000 bytes of the alert log. The log is constantly growing, so select the browser's

Number of Lines Displayed **2,051**

Primary database is in MAXIMUM PERFORMANCE mode
Primary database is in MAXIMUM PERFORMANCE mode
RFS[6]: Successfully opened standby log 5: '+FLASH/matrix/onlinelog/group_5.261.671738247'
Tue Feb 03 21:09:08 2009
Clearing online redo logfile 3 complete
Media Recovery Log +FLASH/matrix/archivelog/2009_02_03/thread_1_seq_43.326.677883073
Media Recovery Log /scratch/OracleHomes/OraHome111/dbs/arch1_44_677330738.dbf
Tue Feb 03 21:09:18 2009
Media Recovery Log /scratch/OracleHomes/OraHome111/dbs/arch1_45_677330738.dbf
Media Recovery Waiting for thread 1 sequence 46 (in transit)
Recovery of Online Redo Log: Thread 1 Group 5 Seq 46 Reading mem 0
  Mem# 0: +FLASH/matrix/onlinelog/group_5.261.671738247
Tue Feb 03 21:09:20 2009
ALTER SYSTEM SET log_archive_dest_1='location="USE_DB_RECOVERY_FILE_DEST"',valid_for=(AL
ALTER SYSTEM SET log_archive_dest_state_1='ENABLE' SCOPE=BOTH SID='Matrix';
ALTER SYSTEM SET log_archive_trace=0 SCOPE=BOTH SID='Matrix'ALTER SYSTEM SET log_archiv
ALTER SYSTEM SET standby_file_management='AUTO' SCOPE=BOTH SID='*';
ALTER SYSTEM SET archive_lag_target=0 SCOPE=BOTH SID='*';
ALTER SYSTEM SET log_archive_max_processes=6 SCOPE=BOTH SID='*';
ALTER SYSTEM SET log_archive_min_succeed_dest=1 SCOPE=BOTH SID='*';
ALTER SYSTEM SET fal_server='matrix_dr0' SCOPE=BOTH;
ALTER SYSTEM SET fal_client='matrix' SCOPE=BOTH;
Tue Feb 03 21:10:03 2009

**FIGURE 6-10.** *Review alert log entries*

# Enabling Flashback Database

The Flashback Database feature introduced in Oracle Database 10*g* Release 1 provided expedient recovery from logical database corruptions and user errors. With Flashback Database logging, you can flashback a database to the point in time prior to the user error or when the logical corruption occurred. More importantly, the Flashback Database logging capabilities eliminate the need to perform a restore and point-in-time recovery. Oracle flashback logging will enable you to bypass datafile restores.

Another great benefit of Flashback Database logging is that you do not have to delay application of redo data on the standby database server. This allows for the standby database to be closely synchronized with the primary database.

Most important, enabling Flashback Database logging may eliminate the need to rebuild the primary database after a failover. After a failover to the standby database server, the primary database can be flashed back to a point-in-time prior to the failover event (unless media recovery is required) and converted to a standby database to be synchronized with the new primary database server.

If you did not set up the flash recovery area with Database Configuration Assistant (DBCA) while creating your primary database, you can set it up now with OEM Grid Control. Flashback Database logging is required to support Fast-Start Failover, covered in its own section a bit later in the chapter. To setup the flash recovery area, you must navigate to the Recover Setting page on the Availability tab of the Database home page. The Flash Recovery settings are located in the bottom half of the screen and will look similar to that shown in Figure 6-11.

Click the Apply button after you have finished your settings. If you want to make changes only to the SPFILE, click the check box at the bottom of Figure 6-11 that specifies that the changes should be applied only to the SPFILE. On the right side of the Recover Setting page is a pie chart depicting the current usage statistics for the flash recovery area, as shown in Figure 6-12.

**Flash Recovery**

This database is using a flash recovery area. The chart shows space used by each file type that is not reclaimable by Oracle. Performing backups to tertiary storage is one way to make space reclaimable. Usable Flash Recovery Area includes free and reclaimable space.

Flash Recovery Area Location `+FLASH`

Flash Recovery Area Size `8` `GB`
Flash Recovery Area Size must be set when the location is set.

Non-reclaimable Flash Recovery Area (GB) **1.38**
Reclaimable Flash Recovery Area (GB) **2.87**
Free Flash Recovery Area (GB) **3.75**

☑ Enable Flashback Database*
Flashback database can be used for fast database point-in-time recovery, as it returns the database to a prior point-in-time without restoring files. Flashback is the preferred point-in-time recovery method in the recovery wizard when appropriate. The flash recovery area must be set to enable flashback database.

Flashback Retention Time `1` `Hours`
Current size of the flashback logs(MB) **42.094**
Lowest SCN in the flashback data **9466151**
Flashback Time **Feb 10, 2009 4:53:07 AM**

☐ Apply initialization parameter changes to SPFILE only. If not checked, parameter changes will be made to both

**FIGURE 6-11.** *Enable flash recovery*

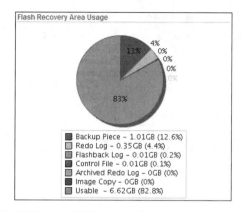

**FIGURE 6-12.** *Flash recovery area usage*

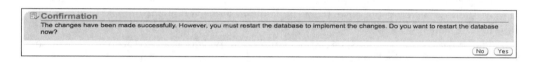

**FIGURE 6-13.** *Confirmation to restart database*

If this chart shows that your flash recovery area is already reaching capacity, you need to allocate more space before enabling Flashback Database, as the flashback logs will increase considerably depending on your retention period. To enable Flashback Database on your primary, you must restart the database, as depicted in Figure 6-13.

Click the Yes button to bounce the database. You will be asked for SYSDBA credentials to shut down and restart the database. If the standby database does not have a flash recovery area enabled, you can repeat these steps on the standby database; however, if the standby database is only mounted and not open read-only, a restart will not be necessary.

## Reviewing Performance

Reviewing Data Guard performance starts at the Data Guard home page in the Standby Progress Summary chart. The Standby Progress Summary chart reveals the transport and apply lag in seconds, minutes, or even hours depending on the amount of delay. The transport lag is measured as the delta from the primary database last update and the standby last received redo, while apply lag is measured as a delta between the primary last update and last applied redo on the standby site. A transport lag impacts your ability to satisfy your RPO. If you have to failover your database at this moment, redo data that did not arrive at the standby database server will be lost. Figure 6-14 shows a transport lag of approximately 0 and an apply lag of more than 3 minutes. This transport lag means that all redo generated by the primary database is available at the standby database so in a Maximum Availability configuration you would be able to satisfy an RPO of zero data loss.

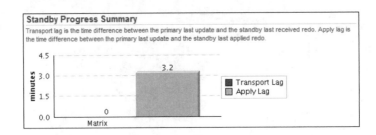

**FIGURE 6-14.** *Standby Progress Summary chart*

The apply lag indicates how far behind your standby database server is compared to the primary when it comes to applying redo data. The apply lag is the indicator of your RTO—how long it takes for you to failover to your standby database server. It also tells you whether your apply process can keep up with the redo generation rate from the primary database server. If the delta between the redo generation rate and apply rate became significant, you may be better off performing an incremental backup from the primary and restoring the incremental backup on the standby database server. In our case, the RTO would be impacted by the time it takes to apply those last 3.2 minutes of redo.

Additional performance statistics can be captured in the Performance Overview link in the Performance section of the Data Guard home page. The Performance Overview page displays performance-related information in graphical line chart format. The graphical charts in each of the quadrants represent current redo generation rate, transport lag, apply lag, and apply rate. You can simulate a workload by clicking the Start button under Test Application, which is a built-in application that will generate a workload on the primary database. You can use this page to switch log files at the primary database.

You can set the collection interval, which causes the charts to be refreshed, by choosing an option from the View Data drop-down list. Figure 6-15 displays the top of a pretty elaborate Performance Overview page that reports redo generation rate, lag times, and apply rate.

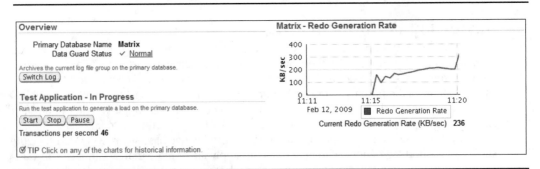

**FIGURE 6-15.** *Primary Performance Overview page*

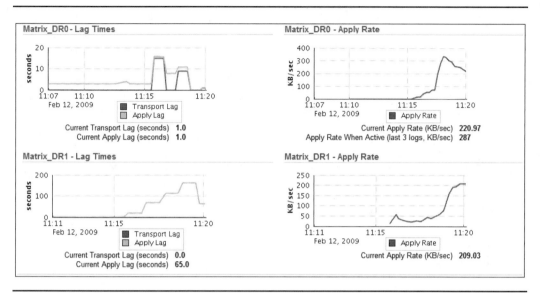

**FIGURE 6-16.** *Standby Performance Overview page*

The redo generation rate chart reveals the redo generation rate measured in kilobytes per second (KB/sec) on the primary. Figure 6-16 displays the performance information from the bottom of the page. These metrics are for the standby databases.

The transport lag time denotes the potential amount of data loss. In Figure 6-16, you can see that our logical standby, Matrix_DR1, does not have a transport lag but our physical standby database, Matrix_DR0, did have a transport lag that has been resolved. The apply rate obviously provides information about data applied on the standby database environment. Clicking each of the charts will route you to another page that reports historical information for the past 24 hours. Again, you can choose an option from the View Data drop-down list to view the data for the past 24 hours, 7 days, 31 days, or a customized date interval.

The redo generation rate is available only through OEM Grid Control. The transport lag and apply lag values are also available from the V$DATAGUARD_STATS view on a standby database.

You can also derive performance information by reviewing the log file details from the Data Guard home page. In the Performance section at the bottom of the Data Guard home page, click the Log File Details link to view the following:

- Status of redo that was generated on the primary database but not received on the standby database server

- Redo that was received but not applied on the standby database server

In our example, Figure 6-17 shows that two archive logs were received on the standby database server but not applied. It also shows six archive logs that have not yet been received by our logical standby due to some error. The error in this case is that the logical standby was only mounted, not open and applying redo.

The log files details page also provides information about redo log transport and apply information for diagnostic purposes. Under normal circumstances, you should not see entries on this page. An example of a good situation is shown in Figure 6-18.

| | | | | | | | |
|---|---|---|---|---|---|---|---|
| Matrix_DR1 | | | | | | | |

Redo Transport Services  **On**
Redo Transport Status  **Normal**

Redo Apply Services  **On**
Status  **ORA-16810: multiple errors or warnings detected for the database**
Apply Delay (minutes)  **0**

| Log | Status | ResetLogs ID # | First Change # (SCN) | Last Change # (SCN) | Size (KB) | Time Generated | Time Completed |
|---|---|---|---|---|---|---|---|
| 26 | Partially Applied | 678489738 | 9590011 | 9590231 | 164 | Feb 11, 2009 9:25:36 PM | Feb 11, 2009 9:29:42 PM |
| 28 | Not Applied | 678489738 | 9590409 | 9590412 | 3 | Feb 11, 2009 9:32:50 PM | Feb 11, 2009 9:32:57 PM |
| 29 | Not Applied | 678489738 | 9590412 | 9590580 | 102 | Feb 11, 2009 9:32:57 PM | Feb 12, 2009 3:43:47 PM |
| 26 | Not Received | 678489738 | 9590011 | 9590231 | 163 | Feb 11, 2009 9:25:36 PM | Feb 11, 2009 9:29:42 PM |
| 27 | Not Received | 678489738 | 9590231 | 9590409 | 169 | Feb 11, 2009 9:29:42 PM | Feb 11, 2009 9:32:50 PM |
| 28 | Not Received | 678489738 | 9590409 | 9590412 | 2 | Feb 11, 2009 9:32:50 PM | Feb 11, 2009 9:32:57 PM |
| 29 | Not Received | 678489738 | 9590412 | 9590580 | 101 | Feb 11, 2009 9:32:57 PM | Feb 12, 2009 3:43:47 PM |
| 30 | Not Received | 678489738 | 9590580 | 9593164 | 6511 | Feb 12, 2009 3:43:47 PM | Feb 12, 2009 4:12:03 PM |
| 31 | Not Received | 678489738 | 9593164 | 9593337 | 71 | Feb 12, 2009 4:12:03 PM | Feb 12, 2009 4:17:03 PM |

**FIGURE 6-17.** *Bad log file details*

Primary Current Log  **35**

| | | | | | | | |
|---|---|---|---|---|---|---|---|
| Matrix_DR0 | | | | | | | |

Redo Transport Services  **On**
Redo Transport Status  **Normal**

Redo Apply Services  **On**
Status  **Normal**
Apply Delay (minutes)  **0**

| Log Status | ResetLogs ID # | First Change # (SCN) | Last Change # (SCN) | Size (KB) | Time Generated | Time Completed |
|---|---|---|---|---|---|---|
| All logs have been received and applied. | | | | | | |

Matrix_DR1

Redo Transport Services  **On**
Redo Transport Status  **Normal**

Redo Apply Services  **On**
Status  **Normal**
Apply Delay (minutes)  **0**

| Log Status | ResetLogs ID # | First Change # (SCN) | Last Change # (SCN) | Size (KB) | Time Generated | Time Completed |
|---|---|---|---|---|---|---|
| 34 Committed Transactions Applied | 678489738 | 9609171 | 9650663 | 50029 | Feb 12, 2009 8:16:18 PM | Feb 12, 2009 8:20:25 PM |

**FIGURE 6-18.** *Good log file details*

As you can see, the physical standby, Matrix_DR0, has received everything and is up to date applying the redo. The logical standby, Matrix_DR1, has received all primary redo and is currently catching up in sequence 34, whereas the primary is currently sending redo from sequence 35 (shown at the top of the page). This page may become particularly helpful if for some reason the redo transport services go offline and you need to view which archive logs have not made it to the standby database server.

# Changing Protection Modes

With just a few clicks in OEM Grid Control, you can easily change the protection mode of the Data Guard configuration. By default, the initial configuration is set up in Maximum Performance mode. You can easily toggle among Maximum Protection, Maximum Availability, and Maximum Performance modes. For detailed information about each of the protection modes, refer to Chapters 1 and 2.

**Change Protection Mode: Select Mode**

Data Guard provides multiple protection modes. Higher protection modes reduce data loss but may affect performance of the primary database. When changing to maximum protection or maximum availability, a SYSDBA connection is required to the primary database and all standby databases to determine if standby redo log files are needed.

○ Maximum Protection
  Provides the highest level of data protection. No data will be lost. Possible primary database downtime if connectivity to the standby database is lost. Requires the SYNC redo transport mode to be set on at least one standby database.

◉ Maximum Availability
  Provides very high data protection. No primary database downtime if connectivity to the standby database is lost but data may diverge. Requires the SYNC redo transport mode to be set on at least one standby database.

○ Maximum Performance
  No performance impact on the primary database. Provides high data protection with the ASYNC redo transport mode. Can also be used with the ARCH redo transport mode.

**FIGURE 6-19.**  *Change Protection Mode: Select Mode page*

From the Data Guard home page, click the URL next to the Protection Mode in the Overview section of the page. The protection mode of the Data Guard configuration will be displayed. Click the Protection Mode link to open the Change Protection Mode: Select Mode page, as shown in Figure 6-19.

You can select from the available protection modes. In this example, let's raise the protection mode from Maximum Performance to Maximum Availability. Click the Maximum Availability option and click Continue. If you are prompted for SYSDBA credentials, enter the username and password with SYSDBA privileges and click Login. As shown in Figure 6-20, choose which database will have its protection mode changed. Since we are changing from Maximum Performance to Maximum Availability, we are notified that the redo transport will be changed to SYNC as part of the process. You must be careful when choosing protection modes. If your transport mode is changed to SYNC, transactions must wait for redo generated from the primary database to be written on the standby redo logs before you will be allowed to continue. If you are comfortable with the proposed changes, you can simply click Continue to proceed.

If you did not have the standby redo log files defined on all the required databases, you would also be required to choose where they would be created. Since these were already defined, choose the SYNC standby database and click Continue. In the Edit Protection Mode Processing page, confirm the selection. Click Yes and observe the progress screen shown in Figure 6-21. Before clicking the final Yes, make sure you want to do this, because once the process starts, it cannot be cancelled.

Once changes are processed, you will be redirected to the Data Guard home page where the new protection mode will be reflected.

**Change Protection Mode: Standby Databases and Standby Redo Log Files**

**Standby Databases**

One or more of the following standby databases can be selected to support the protection mode. The redo transport SYNC (if not currently set to SYNC).

Select All | Select None

| Select | Name | Role | Redo Transport Mode |
|--------|------|------|---------------------|
| ☑ | Matrix_DR0 | Physical Standby | ASYNC |

**FIGURE 6-20.**  *Change Protection Mode: choose the transport mode*

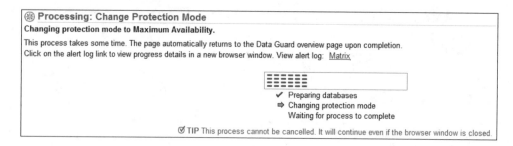

**FIGURE 6-21.** *Processing: Change Protection Mode screen*

# Editing Standby Database Properties

From time to time, you will need to turn on or off Redo Apply on a standby database. You can turn on or off the apply services by navigating to the Edit Standby Database Properties screen. To disable archived redo data from being applied, click the Apply Off radio button and click Apply. The screen will refresh and you will receive a success banner at the top of the page. Similarly, you can re-enable Redo Apply services by clicking the Apply On radio button and clicking Apply. If you want to activate Real-Time Query,[1] you can also check the Enable Real-time Query box and click Apply. Remember that unless you are running Oracle Database 11*g*, redo data will not be applied while the database is open in read-only mode. Figure 6-22 shows the General tab's Standby Database properties that can be modified.

In this example, the Data Guard environment was modified to be open for read-only purposes to service ad hoc read-only reports for the customers.

In the Standby Role Properties tab in Figure 6-23, you can set attributes such as the transport mode (but you will not be allowed to impact the protection mode), the net timeout (in seconds), the apply delay (in minutes), or the standby archive location. In addition, you can expand the

---

**Edit Standby Database Properties: Matrix_DR0**

| General | Standby Role Properties | Common Properties |

ⓘ Status ✓ Normal
Role Physical Standby

**Redo Apply Services**

Redo apply services automatically apply redo data to standby databases to maintain transactional

⦿ Apply On
Redo apply is on. Redo data is being applied.
ⓘ Real-time query allows a physical standby database to be used for real-time reporting, with
☑ Enable Real-time Query
The database is open read-only and redo apply is on.
○ Apply Off
Redo apply is off. No redo data will be applied.

**FIGURE 6-22.** *Edit Standby Database Properties General tab*

---

[1] To activate Real-Time Query, you must be licensed for the Active Data Guard Option.

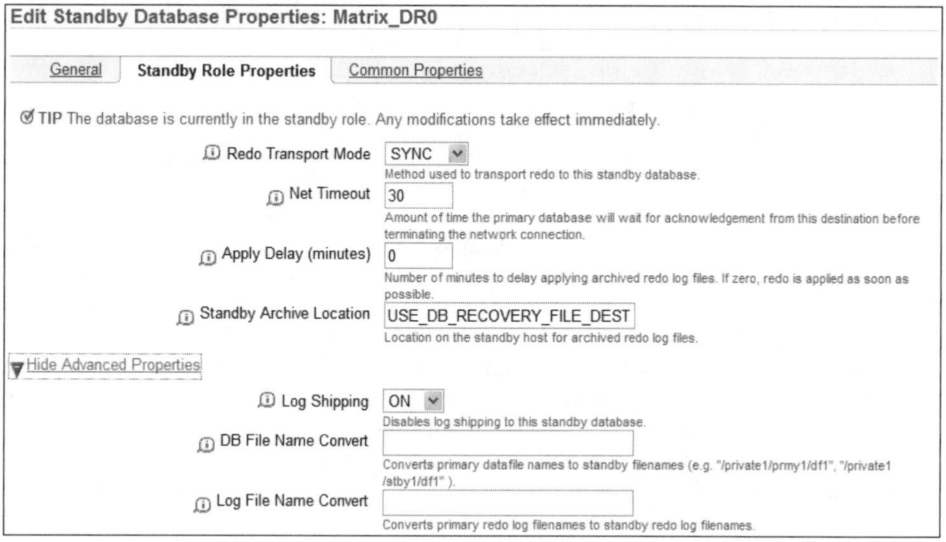

Edit Standby Database Properties: Matrix_DR0

General   **Standby Role Properties**   Common Properties

✅ TIP The database is currently in the standby role. Any modifications take effect immediately.

ⓘ Redo Transport Mode   SYNC ▾
Method used to transport redo to this standby database.

ⓘ Net Timeout   30
Amount of time the primary database will wait for acknowledgement from this destination before
terminating the network connection.

ⓘ Apply Delay (minutes)   0
Number of minutes to delay applying archived redo log files. If zero, redo is applied as soon as
possible.

ⓘ Standby Archive Location   USE_DB_RECOVERY_FILE_DEST
Location on the standby host for archived redo log files.

▼ Hide Advanced Properties

ⓘ Log Shipping   ON ▾
Disables log shipping to this standby database.

ⓘ DB File Name Convert
Converts primary datafile names to standby filenames (e.g. "/private1/prmy1/df1", "/private1
/stby1/df1" ).

ⓘ Log File Name Convert
Converts primary redo log filenames to standby redo log filenames.

**FIGURE 6-23.**   *Edit Standby Database Standby Role Properties tab*

Advanced Properties link to set properties such as enabling/disabling log shipping and changing
the filename conversion parameters. Bear in mind that changing these last two does require a
restart of the standby database.

You can delay application of redo data on the standby database to provide additional
protection from user error or corruption on the primary database. This can protect you against
incidents such as an accidental table drop on the primary database. You can prevent the table
drop from hitting the disaster recovery site. Instead of setting the apply delay time, you should
consider enabling Flashback Database with sufficient amount of space in the flash recovery area.

In the Common Properties tab shown in Figure 6-24, you can specify the connect identifier
for the standby database (how the primary should connect to this standby database), the number

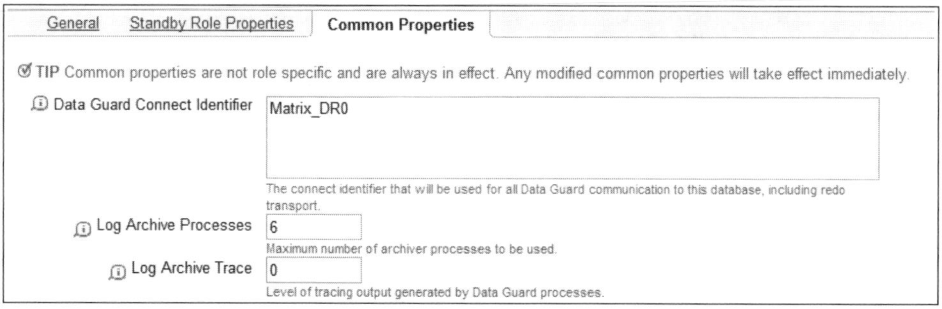

General   Standby Role Properties   **Common Properties**

✅ TIP Common properties are not role specific and are always in effect. Any modified common properties will take effect immediately.

ⓘ Data Guard Connect Identifier   Matrix_DR0

The connect identifier that will be used for all Data Guard communication to this database, including redo
transport.

ⓘ Log Archive Processes   6
Maximum number of archiver processes to be used.

ⓘ Log Archive Trace   0
Level of tracing output generated by Data Guard processes.

**FIGURE 6-24.**   *Edit Standby Database Common Properties tab*

of archive processes to be used for the `LogArchiveMaxProcesses` Broker property, and the level of tracing to be set for the `LogArchiveTrace` property. These properties are not role-specific and will take effect immediately after you click Apply.

# Performing a Switchover

Simply stated, a *switchover* is the process in which the primary database and a standby database perform a role reversal without resetting the online redo logs of the primary database. A switchover is typically done within a planned maintenance time window. In a switchover scenario, the primary database becomes the standby database, and the standby database becomes the new primary database. During the switchover process, the primary database role is changed and the database is shut down and restarted. When this process is complete at the primary, it is finished at the standby you chose and the standby is opened without a restart.[2] In a switchover, no data loss occurs. With OEM Grid Control, performing a switchover has never been easier. Switchovers are initiated only on the primary database, and database connections can be configured to switch over automatically.[3] The switchover process can be initiated by selecting the standby database that you want to become the primary database and clicking Switchover on the Data Guard home page, as shown next.

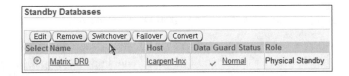

Behind the scenes, the switchover operation ensures that the primary and standby databases are error free, and then it asks you to confirm the switchover. You may have to provide the OS credentials for the physical database server; then do the following:

1. Click Continue. You should see the Confirmation Switchover page as shown in the next illustration.

---

**Confirmation: Switchover to Matrix_DR0**

**Are you sure you want to switchover to Matrix_DR0.?**

A switchover will cause the primary and standby databases to switch roles. The switchover operation cannot be cancelled.

Any active sessions connected to the primary database will be closed automatically during the switchover operation.
Browse Primary Database Sessions

---

[2] In 10*g*, the standby would be restarted if it had been opened read-only since it was last started.
[3] See Chapter 10 for client failover details.

2. At the bottom of the page, you can also decide whether you want the Grid Control Monitoring Settings and Jobs transferred to the new primary database, as shown in the next illustration.

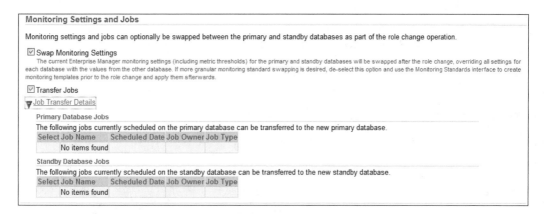

3. If the standby database has archive logs that still need to be applied, you will see a warning message indicating that the unapplied log files will be applied before starting the switchover. You can also see the active sessions by clicking the Browse Primary Database Sessions link. Once you are ready to process, click Yes to finalize the initiation process.

**CAUTION**
*You cannot stop the switchover process once it starts.*

4. Immediately after you click Yes, you will see the Processing: Switchover screen, where the processing operation will perform the steps to switch roles between the primary and standby databases and the Data Guard Broker will restart the original primary database and complete tasks to switch the database roles, as shown in the illustration.

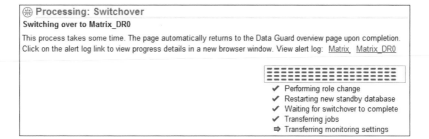

5. While waiting for the switchover process, click the View Alert Log link to review the progress details in another browser window. After the switchover process is complete,

you are routed to the Data Guard home page that shows the new primary database, as depicted in the next illustration.

As you can see, Matrix_DR0 is now the primary database and Matrix is the new physical standby. Switchover role transitions are risk-free and require an insignificant amount of outage to the production database server.

## Performing a Manual Failover

You should consider failing over to your standby database when you experience a complete outage on your primary database. As discussed in Chapters 1 and 2, depending on your protection mode, you may or may not lose data. You should perform a failover only if the primary database is completely down and a switchover is not possible. Even though reinstating a failed primary database using Flashback Database is a relatively simple operation, you should still exercise caution and generally failover only in an emergency. Data loss and failover is discussed in detail in Chapter 8.

Similar to switchover, a database failover can be achieved by navigating through several screens:

1. From the Data Guard home page, you'll see that the current primary database, Matrix_DR0 (remember, we just performed a switchover so Matrix_DR0 was our primary database), is no longer available, as shown here in the illustration.

2. To failover, select the standby database at the bottom of the Data Guard home page; this will be your new primary database. In our example, we will failover to our original primary database, Matrix, as also shown in this illustration.

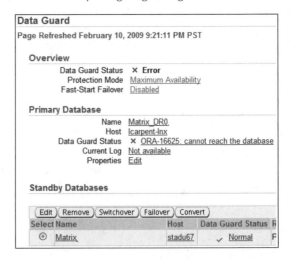

3. Click Failover to open the Confirmation page, where you are asked to confirm the failover, as shown in the following illustration.

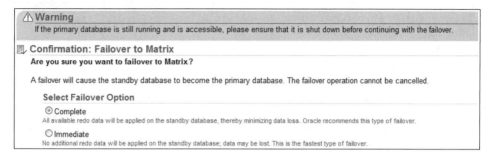

You are warned on this page to make sure the primary is really down, because a failover here with it still running would leave you with two open primary databases. Here you are also asked to select from the type of failover option, Complete or Immediate.

**CAUTION**
*Be aware that even though the text says that Immediate is the fastest type of failover, it is also the failover with the biggest data loss and should be used only if you have a gap in the redo that you cannot resolve.*

At the bottom of the page, as shown in the next illustration, you are asked if you want to move the Grid Control monitoring and job setup to the new primary database. These will be transferred by default, but you can customize them at this point.

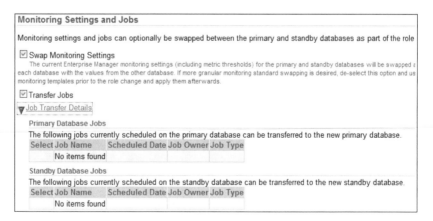

4. In a complete failover scenario, all available redo data is applied on the standby database. Oracle recommends performing a complete failover, and it happens to be the default failover option. When the complete failover scenario is not an option, you have a gap you cannot resolve, and you can perform an immediate failover instead. In an immediate failover situation, no additional redo data is applied on the standby database, resulting in data loss once you initiate the failover. If you had a zero transport lag and

zero apply lag, all your data was applied; however, if you had an apply lag for some reason, data that was not applied would result in data loss when the failover operation is initiated. If you have a transport lag or apply lag, data loss is imminent when the failover operation is initiated. Select the appropriate failover option and click Yes.

**CAUTION**
*You cannot stop the failover process once it starts.*

5. A database failover will be initiated and you will not be able to cancel the database failover. You will be routed to the Processing screen, where you will see the status of the failover process, as shown in the following illustration. Similar to the switchover progress screen, you can click the View Alert Log link to drill down to the alert log file and review the details in another browser window. However, remember that this is a failover and the alert log of the original primary (Matrix_DR0 in our case) may not be available.

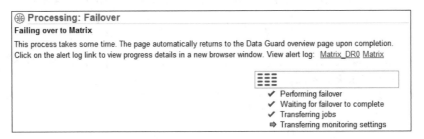

6. When the failover processing gets to the stage where it is transferring the jobs, the failover is complete. You can manually navigate back to the Data Guard home page using your bookmark or you can just wait, and once the processing is complete, you will be returned to the Data Guard home page.

7. If you were running in Maximum Protection or Maximum Availability mode before the failover, you will notice that you have been downgraded to Maximum Performance mode after the failover. To get your new production database back to its original protection level, you must mount the old primary database and reinstate it as the standby database if possible. Exercise caution and make sure that you do not open the old primary database; otherwise, you will have two primary databases up and running. In the Data Guard home page, you will see the Data Guard Status link stating that the Database Must Be Reinstated, as shown in the next illustration.

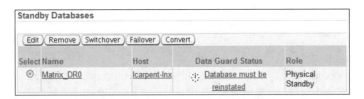

8. Click the Data Guard Status link to open the Edit Standby Database Properties page. If you had Flashback Database enabled and have all the required flashback logs, you can reinstate the old primary database. If you have mounted the old primary database, you will have to follow these steps only once. However, if the old primary database is not

mounted, you will have to execute this procedure twice, because the first time around, Grid Control will mount only the failed primary database.

**TIP**
*Enabling Flashback Database on both the primary and standby databases is strongly recommended. Flashback Database allows for the former primary database to be reinstated after a failover operation without being restored with sufficient flashback log availability.*

9.   In the Edit Standby Database Properties page, click the Reinstate button near to the Status Role, as shown in the illustration.

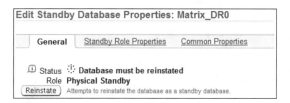

10.   On the Confirmation page, click Yes to initiate the reinstating of the failed primary database and continue to the Processing page, as shown in the illustration.

11.   Once the processing activities complete, the Data Guard home page appears. You may notice an ORA-16778 redo transport error for the Data Guard Status. This error will eventually clear, but if you want to clear it manually, you can click the ORA-16778 error link to open the Edit Properties page.

12.   The errors on the Related Status section are expected errors. Click Reset to reset the log services. When you reinstate a failed primary database, it will be brought back into your configuration as the type of standby that matches the standby type you failed over to in the first place. If OEM Grid Control is not able to reinstate the failed primary, you will have to clean up the failed database manually and create a new standby by clicking Add Standby.

# Fast-Start Failover

Fast-Start Failover allows the Data Guard Broker to failover automatically to a standby database when a failure occurs at the primary database. No manual intervention is required, and Fast-Start Failover effectively increases database availability since it decreases the amount of time for manual failover operations. Like most other Data Guard functionalities, Fast-Start Failover can also be configured and maintained within OEM Grid Control. We will discuss the Fast-Start Failover architecture and how you enable it in Chapter 8.

# Creating a Logical Standby

You learned in Chapter 2 how to create a logical standby database manually, and you learned pretty much everything else about a logical standby in Chapter 4. In this section, we will demonstrate how easy it is to create a logical standby database with OEM Grid Control.

1. To initiate the process to create a logical standby database, click Add Standby Database on the Data Guard home page. (As we mentioned before, for a new database that does not have any standby databases, the Data Guard home page will have just one option to add a standby database.) You will see the Add Standby Database screen, shown in preceding examples in this chapter and in Chapter 2.

2. On the Add Standby Database screen, select Create A New Logical Standby Database, as shown in the following illustration, and then click Continue.

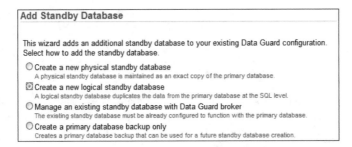

3. The Add Standby Database: Backup Type page is the same page you arrived at when you created your physical standby database, but it now has a lot more information. At the bottom of the screen, look at the SQL Apply Unsupported Tables section. Make sure that your database does not have any unsupported data types.[4] In the next illustration, you can see the tables that contain unsupported data or storage types.

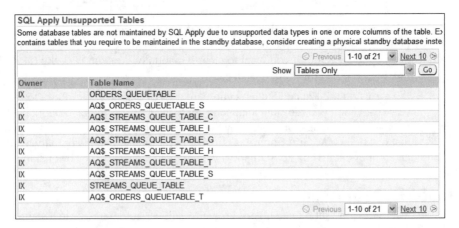

---

[4] For a comprehensive list of all the unsupported data types, refer to the Data Concepts and Administration Manual, Appendix C, to determine whether your primary database can sufficiently support a logical standby database: http://download.oracle.com/docs/cd/B28359_01/server.111/b28294/data_support.htm#CHDGFADJ

4. Instead of viewing only the tables, you may want to view the columns and data types that Oracle detected as not being supported. To view the unsupported columns and data types, click the Show drop-down list and choose Table Columns and Data Types. Then click Go, as shown in the illustration.

| SQL Apply Unsupported Tables | | | |
| --- | --- | --- | --- |
| Some database tables are not maintained by SQL Apply due to unsupported data types in one or more columns of the table. Ex contains tables that you require to be maintained in the standby database, consider creating a physical standby database instea | | | |
| | | Previous 1-10 of 173 ▼ Next 10 ⊗ | |
| | | Show Table Columns and Data Types ▼ (Go) | |
| Owner | Table Name | Column Name | Data Type |
| IX | ORDERS_QUEUETABLE | Q_NAME | VARCHAR2 |
| IX | ORDERS_QUEUETABLE | MSGID | RAW |
| IX | ORDERS_QUEUETABLE | CORRID | VARCHAR2 |
| IX | ORDERS_QUEUETABLE | PRIORITY | NUMBER |
| IX | ORDERS_QUEUETABLE | STATE | NUMBER |
| IX | ORDERS_QUEUETABLE | DELAY | TIMESTAMP(6) |
| IX | ORDERS_QUEUETABLE | EXPIRATION | NUMBER |
| IX | ORDERS_QUEUETABLE | TIME_MANAGER_INFO | TIMESTAMP(6) |
| IX | ORDERS_QUEUETABLE | LOCAL_ORDER_NO | NUMBER |
| IX | ORDERS_QUEUETABLE | CHAIN_NO | NUMBER |
| | | Previous 1-10 of 173 ▼ Next 10 ⊗ | |

5. After you perform a thorough analysis of the unsupported tables and columns, choose to continue to create a logical standby database, click the Backup Type radio button, and click Next to be directed to the Add Standby Database: Backup Options page.

The rest of the steps are identical to those for creating a physical standby database, which is thoroughly covered in Chapter 2. Instead of repeating the same figures here, we simply ask that you review Chapter 2. The only other difference between this procedure and the former is that, after the logical standby is created, the role will be listed as Logical Standby in the Standby Databases section, as shown in Figure 6-25.

## Skipping Table Entries in Logical Standby Database

In the logical standby database world, you can skip certain, or all, types of SQL operations against a specific table or schema from being applied by SQL Apply. You can also specify additional processing on the logical standby database by using stored procedures.

In earlier releases of Oracle Database, you pretty much had to stop SQL Apply before making any changes to these skip rules. In Oracle Database 11g, most changes no longer require that you stop SQL Apply. Grid Control will take care of stopping the apply if necessary so you don't have to worry about it.

| Standby Databases | | | |
| --- | --- | --- | --- |
| (Edit) (Remove) (Switchover) (Failover) (Convert) | | | |
| Select Name | Host | Data Guard Status | Role |
| ⊙ Matrix_DR0 | lcarpent-lnx | ✓ Normal | Physical Standby |
| ○ Matrix_DR1 | stadu67 | ✓ Normal | Logical Standby |

**FIGURE 6-25.** *Standby Databases logical standby role*

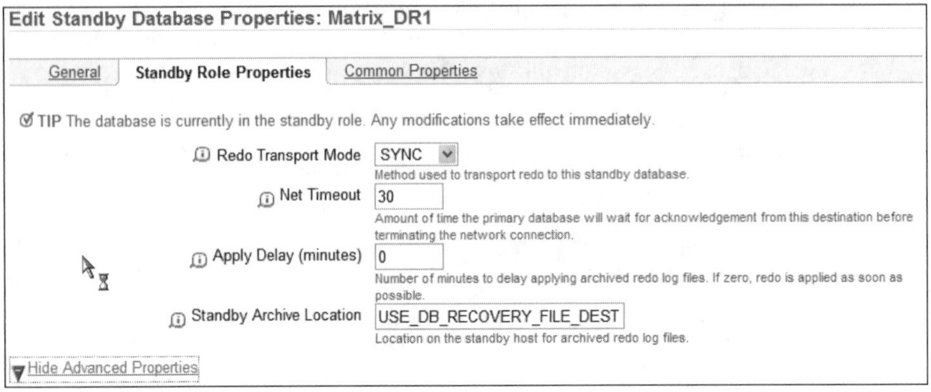

**Edit Standby Database Properties: Matrix_DR1**

General    **Standby Role Properties**    Common Properties

☑ TIP The database is currently in the standby role. Any modifications take effect immediately.

Redo Transport Mode   `SYNC ▾`
Method used to transport redo to this standby database.

Net Timeout   `30`
Amount of time the primary database will wait for acknowledgement from this destination before terminating the network connection.

Apply Delay (minutes)   `0`
Number of minutes to delay applying archived redo log files. If zero, redo is applied as soon as possible.

Standby Archive Location   `USE_DB_RECOVERY_FILE_DEST`
Location on the standby host for archived redo log files.

▼ Hide Advanced Properties

**FIGURE 6-26.** *Edit Standby Database Properties for the logical standby*

To configure skip operations, you have to set up the appropriate SQL Apply properties in the Standby Role Properties page. To get to the Standby Role Properties page, select your logical standby database and click the Edit button shown in Figure 6-25 to be routed to the Edit Standby Database Properties screen. Click the Standby Role Properties tab to see the properties shown in Figure 6-26.

Click Show Advanced Properties to expand the SQL Apply Properties, as shown in Figure 6-27.

You can specify the amount of system resources that SQL Apply can consume in the SQL Apply Properties portion of the screen. By adjusting the MAX SGA in number of megabytes (MB), you can allocate the amount of megabytes for SQL Apply to cache in the system global area (SGA). If you specify a value of 0, SQL Apply will allocate one quarter of the value of the

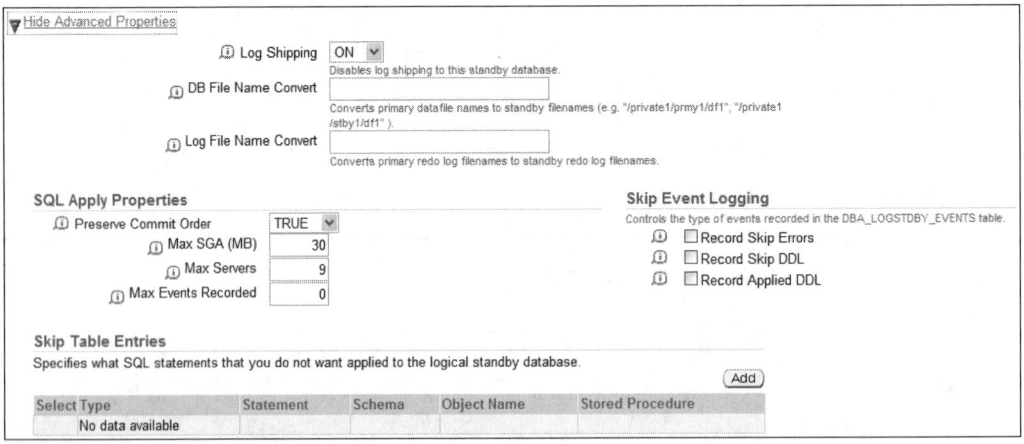

▼ Hide Advanced Properties

Log Shipping   `ON ▾`
Disables log shipping to this standby database.

DB File Name Convert   `_____`
Converts primary datafile names to standby filenames (e.g. "/private1/prmy1/df1", "/private1/stby1/df1").

Log File Name Convert   `_____`
Converts primary redo log filenames to standby redo log filenames.

**SQL Apply Properties**

Preserve Commit Order   `TRUE ▾`
Max SGA (MB)   `30`
Max Servers   `9`
Max Events Recorded   `0`

**Skip Event Logging**
Controls the type of events recorded in the DBA_LOGSTDBY_EVENTS table.
☐ Record Skip Errors
☐ Record Skip DDL
☐ Record Applied DDL

**Skip Table Entries**
Specifies what SQL statements that you do not want applied to the logical standby database.

[Add]

| Select Type | Statement | Schema | Object Name | Stored Procedure |
|---|---|---|---|---|
| No data available | | | | |

**FIGURE 6-27.** *SQL Apply Properties for the logical standby*

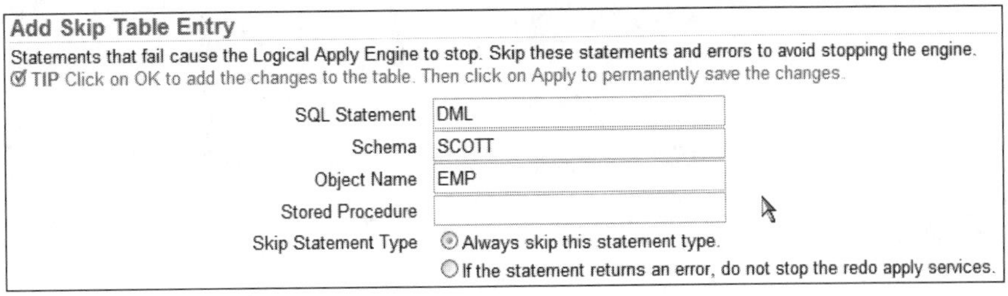

**Add Skip Table Entry**

Statements that fail cause the Logical Apply Engine to stop. Skip these statements and errors to avoid stopping the engine.

☑ TIP Click on OK to add the changes to the table. Then click on Apply to permanently save the changes.

| | |
|---|---|
| SQL Statement | DML |
| Schema | SCOTT |
| Object Name | EMP |
| Stored Procedure | |
| Skip Statement Type | ◉ Always skip this statement type. |
| | ○ If the statement returns an error, do not stop the redo apply services. |

**FIGURE 6-28.**   *Add Skip Table Entry for the logical standby*

SHARED_POOL_SIZE initialization parameter. You can also specify the number of parallel servers specifically reserved for SQL Apply. In the Max Events Recorded field, you can set the number of events that will be stored in the DBA_LOGSTDBY_EVENTS table. At the bottom of the page, you can add tables for SQL Apply to ignore, or skip, by clicking Add and entering more tables.

**TIP**
*The SQL Apply Properties portion of the page is visible only on the logical standby database. If you view the Standby Role Properties page on the primary database server, the SQL Apply Properties portion of the page will not be available.*

After you click the Add button, you'll see the Add Skip Table Entry page, as shown in Figure 6-28.
In this particular example, SQL Apply will be instructed to skip all DML operations on the SCOTT.EMP table. Click OK to go back to the Standby Role Properties page. Click Add once more. This time, change the SQL Statement field to SCHEMA_DDL for the SCOTT.EMP table.
To add more tables to skip, click Add and enter more tables. You can see from Figure 6-29 that the EMP table is set up to have all DML and DDL skipped.
Lastly, once you've identified and entered all the tables you want SQL Apply services to skip, click Apply to save your changes. You'll see an Information bar telling you that the changes have been applied, as shown in Figure 6-30.

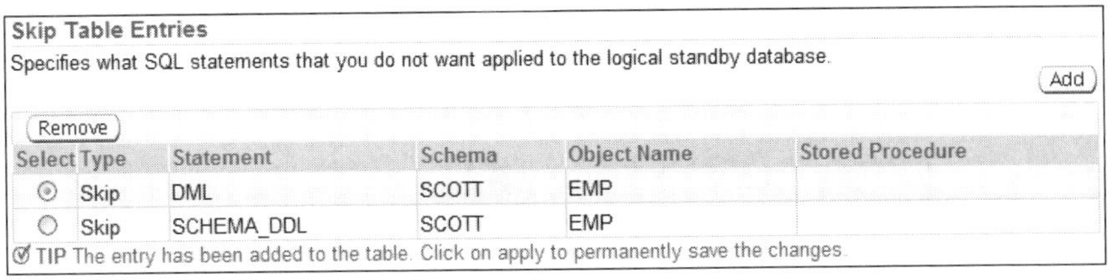

**Skip Table Entries**

Specifies what SQL statements that you do not want applied to the logical standby database.

( Add )

( Remove )

| Select | Type | Statement | Schema | Object Name | Stored Procedure |
|---|---|---|---|---|---|
| ◉ | Skip | DML | SCOTT | EMP | |
| ○ | Skip | SCHEMA_DDL | SCOTT | EMP | |

☑ TIP The entry has been added to the table. Click on apply to permanently save the changes.

**FIGURE 6-29.**   *Skip Tables Entries after tables are added to the logical standby*

**FIGURE 6-30.** *Your changes were successful.*

Later, if you want SQL Apply to start applying DML and DDL changes to the EMP table, you can return to this screen and click Remove, as shown in Figure 6-31.

Once you have removed all the skip rules for the table you want SQL Apply to maintain, click the Apply button at the lower-right corner of the page. You'll see a TIP at the bottom of the page telling you that the entry has been removed from the table, as shown in Figure 6-32.

This will process your request and remove the skip rules for EMP from the logical standby database. But you are not done yet. The moment someone makes a change to the EMP table on a row that either does not exist in the logical standby or has different data, the SQL Apply processes will stop immediately and you will see an error on the Data Guard home page, as shown in the lower-right corner in Figure 6-33.

Click the error message link to see more information about the problem in the Edit Properties page, as shown in Figure 6-34.

You are offered a "Skip" button, but unless you are certain that you understand what happened and you are 100-percent sure that you can skip this error, do not push the Skip button. In general, you should not skip DML transactions for it can corrupt data on the logical standby database. In this case, what you really need to do is reinstantiate the EMP table using the DBMS_LOGSTDBY.INSTANTIATE_TABLE procedure. This procedure requires a Database link that points to the primary database with a user that has the privileges to read and lock the table in the primary database, as well as the SELECT_CATALOG_ROLE on the primary database. In this example, we use the SYSTEM account for our database link.

```
SQL> CREATE DATABASE LINK MATRIX CONNECT TO SYSTEM
     IDENTIFIED BY oracle USING 'MATRIX';
Database link created.
SQL> EXECUTE DBMS_LOGSTDBY.INSTANTIATE_TABLE(SCHEMA_NAME => 'SCOTT',
     TABLE_NAME => 'EMP', DBLINK => 'MATRIX');
PL/SQL procedure successfully completed.
SQL> ALTER DATABASE START LOGICAL STANDBY APPLY IMMEDIATE;
Database altered.
SQL>
```

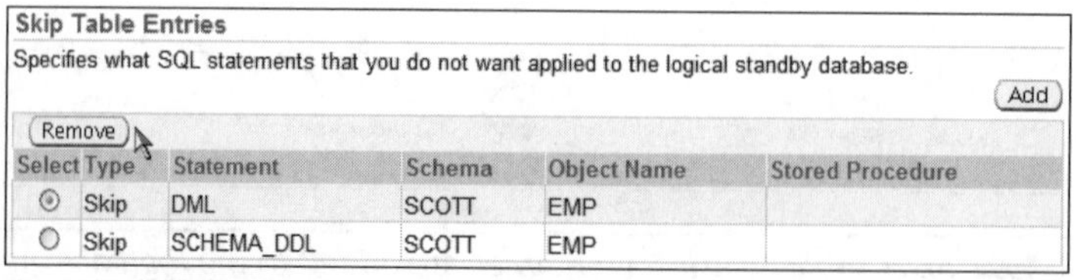

**Skip Table Entries**

Specifies what SQL statements that you do not want applied to the logical standby database.

(Add)

(Remove)

| Select | Type | Statement | Schema | Object Name | Stored Procedure |
|--------|------|-----------|--------|-------------|------------------|
| ⊙ | Skip | DML | SCOTT | EMP | |
| ○ | Skip | SCHEMA_DDL | SCOTT | EMP | |

**FIGURE 6-31.** *Removing a skipped table*

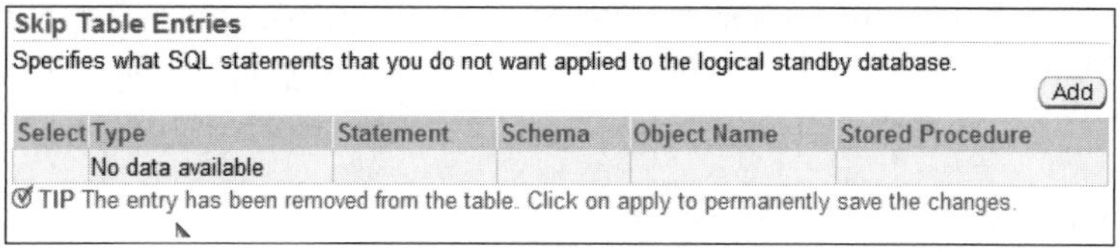

**Skip Table Entries**

Specifies what SQL statements that you do not want applied to the logical standby database.

(Add)

| Select | Type | Statement | Schema | Object Name | Stored Procedure |
|---|---|---|---|---|---|
| | No data available | | | | |

💬 TIP The entry has been removed from the table. Click on apply to permanently save the changes.

**FIGURE 6-32.**    *Skip rules removed for EMP*

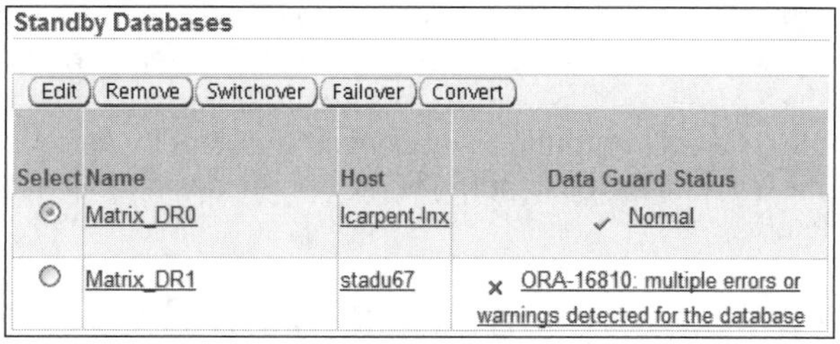

**Standby Databases**

(Edit) (Remove) (Switchover) (Failover) (Convert)

| Select | Name | Host | Data Guard Status |
|---|---|---|---|
| ⦿ | Matrix_DR0 | lcarpent-lnx | ✓ Normal |
| ○ | Matrix_DR1 | stadu67 | ✗ ORA-16810: multiple errors or warnings detected for the database |

**FIGURE 6-33.**    *SQL Apply error*

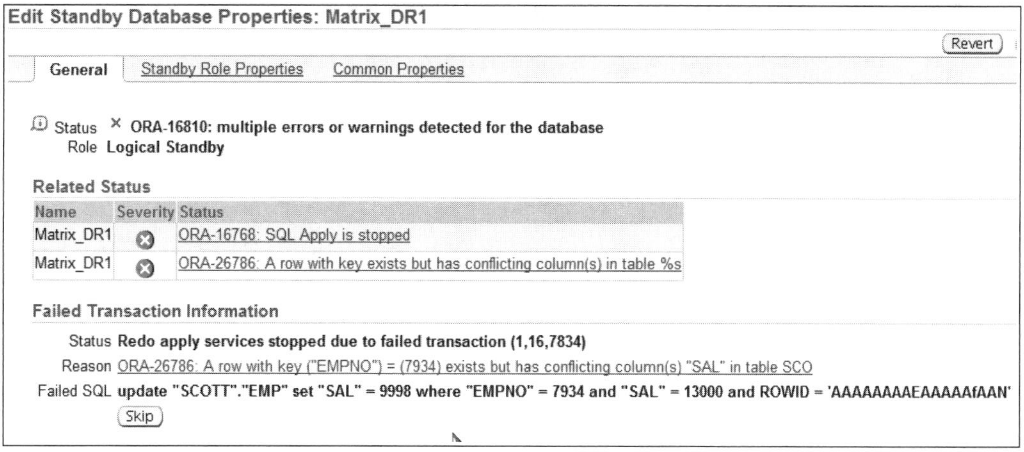

**Edit Standby Database Properties: Matrix_DR1**

(Revert)

**General**    Standby Role Properties    Common Properties

🗔 Status  ✗ ORA-16810: multiple errors or warnings detected for the database
Role  **Logical Standby**

**Related Status**

| Name | Severity | Status |
|---|---|---|
| Matrix_DR1 | ✗ | ORA-16768: SQL Apply is stopped |
| Matrix_DR1 | ✗ | ORA-26786: A row with key exists but has conflicting column(s) in table %s |

**Failed Transaction Information**

Status **Redo apply services stopped due to failed transaction (1,16,7834)**

Reason ORA-26786: A row with key ("EMPNO") = (7934) exists but has conflicting column(s) "SAL" in table SCO

Failed SQL **update "SCOTT"."EMP" set "SAL" = 9998 where "EMPNO" = 7934 and "SAL" = 13000 and ROWID = 'AAAAAAAAEAAAAAfAAN'**

(Skip)

**FIGURE 6-34.**    *SQL Apply error information*

Then you need to restart SQL Apply manually after the procedure is complete, as Grid Control will still show the error state. After SQL Apply has restarted and applied the errant DML to our EMP table, the Data Guard home page will once again show that everything is normal, and you can relax.

## Managing Active Standby

In Chapter 9, you'll learn how to enable an active standby database using SQLPlus and the Data Guard Broker CLI. OEM Grid Control 10*g* Release 5 starts to support the active standby functionality that is available beginning in Oracle Database 11*g*. You can enable active standby with a couple of clicks.

## Managing Snapshot Standby

You will also learn how to create a snapshot standby database in Chapter 9. OEM Grid Control 10*g* Release 5 also supports the snapshot standby feature offered in Oracle Database 11*g* with a simple click of the Convert button on the Data Guard home page and with a Yes click on the confirmation page. The convert button will convert the standby database, depending on the role at the current time, to a snapshot standby if it is a physical standby and to a physical standby if it is a snapshot standby.

## Removing a Standby Database from Broker Control

You can easily remove a standby database or Data Guard Broker configuration from OEM Grid Control. Removing a standby from OEM Grid Control does not remove the database from the file system or ASM, just from the Broker's control. Removing a standby database profile in Grid Control merely removes that database from the Data Guard Broker configuration file. By default, during the Data Guard Broker decoupling phase, the standby destination is removed from the primary database so that logs are no longer shipped to the standby database. You can specify whether or not you want the Broker to leave the redo transport parameters in place after it is no longer controlling the standby database by selecting the Preserve The Destination… check box shown in Figure 6-35.

You can remove a standby database from the Data Guard Broker by selecting the standby database you want to remove and clicking Remove from the Data Guard home page. OEM Grid

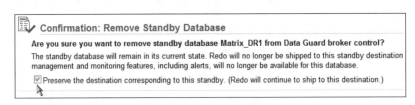

**FIGURE 6-35.**  *Confirming a standby database removal*

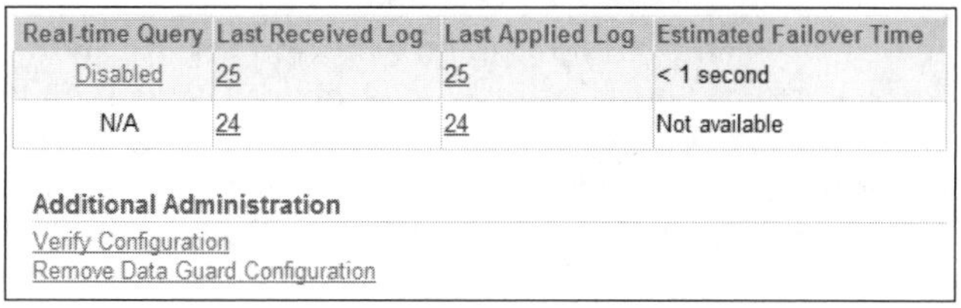

| Real-time Query | Last Received Log | Last Applied Log | Estimated Failover Time |
|---|---|---|---|
| Disabled | 25 | 25 | < 1 second |
| N/A | 24 | 24 | Not available |

**Additional Administration**
Verify Configuration
Remove Data Guard Configuration

**FIGURE 6-36.** *Remove Data Guard Configuration link*

Control forwards you to a confirmation page to make sure that you really want to remove the standby database, as shown in Figure 6-35.

Then click Yes to remove the standby database from Data Guard Broker control. Once the standby database is profile is removed, you are returned to the Data Guard home page.

To remove an entire Broker configuration, navigate to the Data Guard home page and scroll down to the bottom of the screen. In the Additional Administration section, look for the Remove Data Guard Configuration link, as shown in Figure 6-36.

Click the link, and you will be routed to a confirmation page, shown in Figure 6-37, which explains that the database will still stay intact. You also have an option to click the check box to preserve all standby destinations so that redo data will continue to ship to the standby site.

Then click Yes to remove the Data Guard Configuration. When complete, you are returned to the Data Guard home page.

**NOTE**
*You can always add the Data Guard Broker configuration back by clicking Add Standby Database from the Data Guard home page. You can re-add the standby database by selecting the Manage An Existing Standby Database With Data Guard Broker option.*

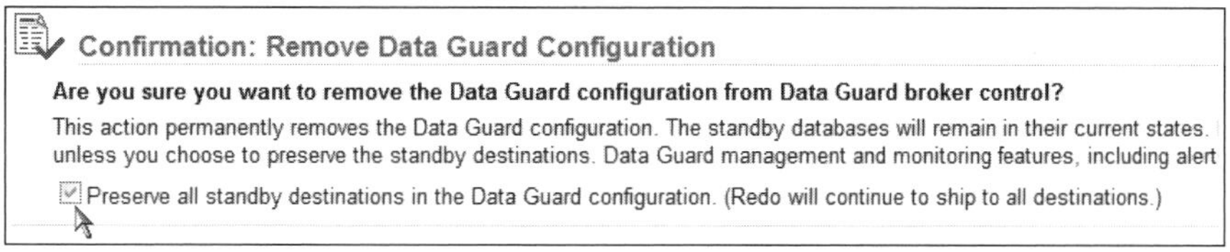

 **Confirmation: Remove Data Guard Configuration**

**Are you sure you want to remove the Data Guard configuration from Data Guard broker control?**

This action permanently removes the Data Guard configuration. The standby databases will remain in their current states, unless you choose to preserve the standby destinations. Data Guard management and monitoring features, including alert

☑ Preserve all standby destinations in the Data Guard configuration. (Redo will continue to ship to all destinations.)

**FIGURE 6-37.** *Confirming that you want to preserve all standby destinations*

# Keeping an Eye on Availability

Now that you have examined what you can do with Grid Control and your Data Guard setup, it's time to get to know one final new feature of Grid Control 10.2.0.5. All the actions and screens shown throughout this chapter, as well as the other chapters in which Grid Control is discussed, are available in prior versions of Grid Control 10g. Starting with Grid Control 10.2.0.5, you can navigate to a new, consolidated High Availability Console under the Availability tab on any of your databases, as shown in the next illustration.

The console offers one place to monitor most things concerning high availability (HA) and disaster recovery (DR). When we first access the console, it will pertain to the database to which we want to connect, displaying the basic layout, as shown the next illustration, which is for our primary database.

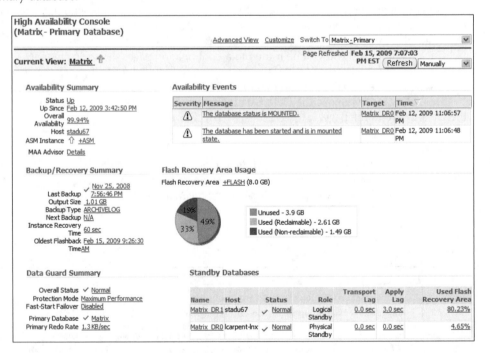

The console shows an Availability Summary, Availability Events, a Backup/Recovery Summary, current Flash Recovery Area statistics if one is configured, and a Data Guard Summary if this database is part of a Data Guard configuration. If it is not, you will see the Add Standby Database link in the Data Guard Summary area. By default, the console screen has a manual refresh that you can configure with the pull-down menu in the upper-right corner.

Click the Advanced View link at the top of the screen, and the console will be expanded with some new charts and other information, as shown in the next illustration.

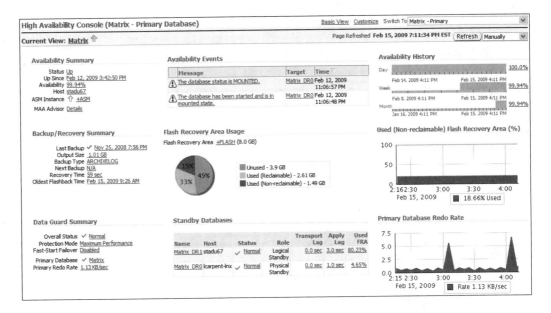

At the right side are three charts that have been added to the console: Availability History, a history of the Used Flash Recovery Area space, and, since this is a primary database, a historical chart of the Redo Generation Rate.

The Redo Generation Rate chart changes to the Standby Apply Lag history if the database you are showing is a physical or a logical standby database. At the upper-right, you can use the pull-down menu to select any one of the databases that are part of the Data Guard configuration. The next illustration shows the console for our physical standby database, Matrix_DR0.

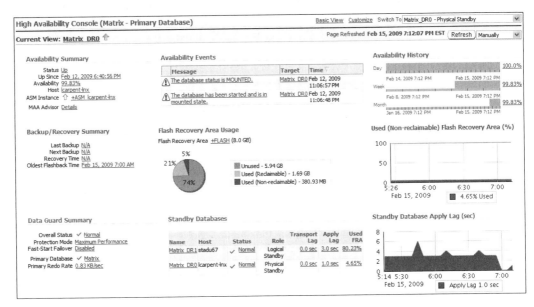

The only difference here is the chart showing the apply lag historical statistics for the last few hours. You can also view advanced information for a logical standby, as shown in the next illustration.

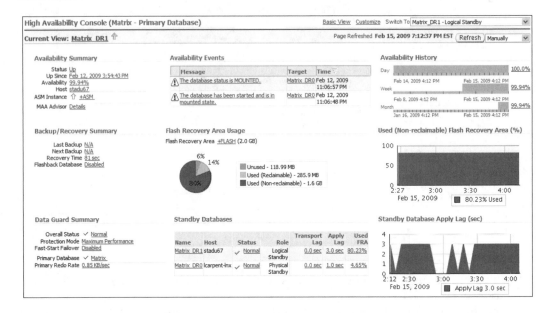

Compare these two screens, and you'll see two major differences between the statistics for the physical standby and the logical standby, the apply lag, and the flash recovery area space usage. It is pretty normal for the apply lag to be greater on a logical standby than a physical standby, as SQL Apply does have more work to do. But you can tune both apply services to keep this number as close to 0 as possible. A big spike in the apply lag for either type of standby database would signify either that you had a burst of redo generation that exceeded your standby's ability to apply at the same speed (compare the spikes to the history of the redo generation rate in the primary console) or something needs your attention on the standby database and should perhaps be tuned.

The other interesting information shown in these two screens is the flash recovery area usage. The logical standby database is 80 percent full with unreclaimable space while the physical standby is only 4.5 percent used. This is due (in our case) to the fact that we have the RMAN Archive Log Deletion Policy set on the physical standby to delete the archive logs when space is needed in the flash recovery area as soon as they have been applied to all standbys, which includes itself. The logical standby database is a read-write database and as such generates its own archive logs as well as those that are coming from the primary database. As mentioned in Chapter 2, you can place the incoming archive log files from the primary and the archive log files generated by the logical standby into the flash recovery area. Data Guard can be configured to automatically delete incoming archive log files that are no longer needed for the recovery or for Flashback Database if enabled. So we would expect the space usage to be greater for a logical standby than for a physical standby. However, the reason that the difference is so high is due to the fact the RMAN deletion policy does not work on the logical standby, as it does on a physical standby, and the generated archive log files are not marked as reclaimable. This is because, unlike a physical standby which can be restored and recovered from the archive logs of the primary database, the log files would be necessary to recover the database if you had to restore your logical standby. So you will want to keep an eye on the flash recovery area for your logical standbys and implement a backup strategy for the logical standby and its archive logs.

A last word on the High Availability Console: You can customize the console by clicking the Customize link at the top of the page and choosing what you would like displayed, as shown in this illustration.

# Conclusion

OEM Grid Control allows a DBA to maintain and monitor what may seem like a complex Data Guard environment with ease from a single GUI. OEM Grid Control can be the jewel of the company, and, at the same time, the single hindrance for DBAs when things do not work as expected. DBAs can effectively set up and manage a Data Guard environment without typing any commands in SQL*Plus.

It would be foolish not to take advantage of the robust feature enabled in OEM Grid Control. At the same time, we strongly advocate that you should also learn the command-line syntax of both the Broker DGMGRL CLI and SQL*Plus and the in-depth architecture so that you can effectively troubleshoot Data Guard behind the scenes. As you manage the Data Guard environment with OEM Grid Control, you will quickly discover that heaps of the under-the-cover SQL commands are exposed in the alert log file.

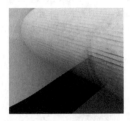

# CHAPTER
## 7

# Monitoring Data Guard
# Implementations

roactive database monitoring is vital to the task of keeping a production database up and running. Monitoring a database for potential outage conditions is the best way to maintain the highest uptime of your production environment. Monitoring solutions such as HP OpenView, IBM Tivoli, and Oracle Grid Control classify database alerts in two or three severity categories: critical, warning, and minor. Basically, a critical condition would indicate that a database outage has occurred or is about to happen. A warning condition would indicate that the database or the application component of the database would become an outage if the condition were not handled by a DBA. A minor condition is an informative message to the DBA. Typically a production database will be monitored for at least the following:

- Tablespace free space
- Database alert log for ORA errors
- Archive log destination for free space thresholds
- Database/listener availability
- Blocking locks

When it comes to Data Guard, DBAs must monitor for conditions that may potentially risk satisfying the company's recovery point objective (RPO) and recovery time objective (RTO) requirements. Proactive monitoring of Data Guard implementations can save DBAs hours or even days of headaches in keeping the physical standby database in sync with the primary database. Monitoring a Data Guard environment involves monitoring both the primary and all associated standby databases. In addition to monitoring the databases for pertinent errors or conditions, the DBA must check the existing configuration for compliance to industry standard practices; this can also alleviate potential issues.

This chapter focuses on providing extensive monitoring solutions delivered in shell script format that can be readily implemented in a Data Guard environment. In addition to the monitoring scripts, a comprehensive checklist is also supplied to assist in diagnosing common configuration issues. You can leverage this checklist to review your Data Guard configuration to ensure that setup complies with the industry standard best practices.

# Monitoring the Data Guard Environment

When it comes to monitoring a Data Guard environment, DBAs must closely monitor selective components of the database topology, such as the file system or Automatic Storage Management (ASM) diskgroup for archive log destination or the alert log file for ORA error messages. The goal of monitoring a Data Guard environment is to detect and proactively eradicate server, network, database, application, Storage Area Network (SAN), file system, operating system, and application problems before they become full-scale outages. None of us wants these errors to jeopardize our ability to failover to our disaster recovery site.

Your company may be deploying physical standby and/or logical standby databases. Depending on the type of standby database being implemented, your monitoring objectives will vary. Even though physical and logical standby databases share common elements to be monitored, such as the alert log file, archive log destination, and archive log history, monitoring a logical standby database is significantly different from doing so on a physical standby database.

**PS and LS**

We have labeled the paragraph headings with *PS* (physical standby) and/or *LS* (logical standby) to let you know the standby database type for which the section applies. A section may be specific to a physical standby database or to a logical standby database, or to both.

In this chapter, we will share our expertise in how to monitor both the logical and physical standby databases effectively.

# Mining the Alert Log File (PS+LS)

Let's start with monitoring the alert log file. Whether you are deploying a logical standby database or a physical standby database, Data Guard monitoring begins by scrutinizing the alert log file, which is your first line of defense against identifying and resolving Data Guard issues. An alert log monitoring script should focus on mining for Data Guard–related ORA error messages, since most of the errors associated with Data Guard are visible in the database alert log. As of Oracle Database 10*g* Release 2, many of the usual Data Guard messages have been removed from the alert log. This will not affect our code examples in this book but if you have your own scripts that look for errors that are no longer there, you can set LOG_ARCHIVE_TRACE=1 on the primary and the standby databases and most of them will be reinstated.

For specific details of Data Guard error(s), you may need to examine the trace files to find the root cause. In this chapter, we provide an alert log monitoring script called alert_log_monitor.ksh.

**NOTE**
*You can review major components of the code in this section or download the entire source code from this book's web site, www .dataguardbook.com, or from Oracle Press's download web site: www .oraclepressbooks.com.*

The alert log monitoring script is designed to read the oratab file in either the /var/opt/oracle directory in the Sun Solaris operating system or in the /etc directory in all other flavors of UNIX. The script checks to see if the auto-startup flag in /etc/oratab is set to Y. If the flag is set to Y, the alert log monitoring script will perform a diff command on the alert log and compare it to the previous diff command output file. If additional ORA errors are encountered, the script will send an alert to the DBA.

When an ORA error is encountered, DBAs will be notified of the issue so that they can examine the root cause of the ORA error. The alert log monitoring shell script has an $IGNORELIST variable that can be used to strip out certain ORA messages before deciphering the alert condition and generating an alert. You can strategically input one or more ORA error codes in the $IGNORELIST concatenated with pipes.

At times, you'll probably not want to be notified of the errors generated by the application queries. Or you may experience sporadic ORA-00600 messages in the alert log file. For example, you may have already logged a technical assistance request (iTAR) with Oracle Support and have identified a corrective action plan, but you do not want to receive alerts for ORA-00600 error messages until the issue is resolved with Oracle Support.

The alert log monitor script will suppress the ORA error number messages specified in the
`$IGNORELIST` variable. All the scripts offered in this chapter source (or execute) a file called
.ORACLE_BASE in the Oracle user's $HOME directory. The .ORACLE_BASE file defines basic
UNIX environment variables such as `ORACLE_BASE`, `PATH`, and `SH`:

```
export BASE_DIR=/apps/oracle
export ORACLE_BASE=/apps/oracle
export PATH=/usr/local/bin:/usr/bin:/usr/sbin:$PATH
export SH=$ORACLE_BASE/general/sh
```

After you source the .ORACLE_BASE file, you can set additional parameters relevant for the
alert log monitoring script such as the oratab file location. Here is the content of the alert_log_
monitor.ksh script for your perusal:

```
#!/usr/bin/ksh

# --------------------------------------------------------------------
# INITIAL SETUP
# --------------------------------------------------------------------
. $HOME/.ORACLE_BASE
[ -f /etc/oratab ] && export ORATAB=/etc/oratab || export
ORATAB=/var/opt/oracle/oratab
echo "oratab is: $ORATAB"

cat $ORATAB|grep -v \^# |grep :Y |cut -d: -f1 |sort |sed 's/ //g' |while read DB
do

export ORACLE_SID=$DB
export ORAENV_ASK=NO
. oraenv
export DECIMAL_VERSION=$(sqlplus -V |sed -e 's/[a-z]//g' -e 's/[A-Z]//g' -e 's/
//g' |sed 's/[*:=-]//g' |grep -v ^$)
export NUMERIC_VERSION=$(echo $DECIMAL_VERSION |sed -e 's/\.//g')
echo "The database version is: $DECIMAL_VERSION - $NUMERIC_VERSION"
echo "Checking Alert Log for: $DB"

export TMPDIR=/tmp
IGNORELIST="03113|19809|19804|01013|07445"
RUNDATE=`date "+%d/%m/%y at %H:%M:%S"`
LOGFILE=${SH}/${DB}_chkalerts.log
DIFFFILE=${TMPDIR}/${DB}_chkalert.diff
ALERT2FILE=${TMPDIR}/${DB}_chkalert2
export  IGNORELIST RUNDATE LOGFILE DIFFFILE ALERT2FILE

[ -f $DIFFFILE ] && rm $DIFFFILE
echo "Execution starts on ${HOSTNAME} on $RUNDATE"

(
```

```
# -----------------------------------------------------------------------
# SETUP Oracle Environment and alias for every database in the $ORATAB file
# -----------------------------------------------------------------------
# -----------------------------------------------------------------------
# ALERTLOG_10g=${BDUMPDIR}/alert_${DB}.log
# ALERTLOG_11g=$ORACLE_BASE/diag/rdbms/$(echo $ORACLE_SID|tr A-Z a-
z)/$ORACLE_SID/trace/alert_$ORACLE_SID.log
# -----------------------------------------------------------------------
if [ "$NUMERIC_VERSION" -lt 11 ]; then
  BDUMPDIR=${ORACLE_BASE}/admin/${DB}/bdump
  [ ! -d $BDUMPDIR ] && echo "BDUMP Dir: $BDUMP does not exist!!!!"
  echo "bdump: $BDUMPDIR"

  ALERTLOG=${BDUMPDIR}/alert_${DB}.log
else
  ALERTLOG=$ORACLE_BASE/diag/rdbms/$(echo $ORACLE_SID|tr A-Z a-
z)/$ORACLE_SID/trace/alert_$ORACLE_SID.log
fi

[ ! -f $ALERTLOG ] && echo "ALert Log File $ALERTLOG does not exist!!!!"
echo "Alert Log is:  $ALERTLOG"

if [ ! -r ${ALERTLOG} ] ; then
  echo "$RUNDATE Could not read alert log ${ALERTLOG} for SID ${DB}"
  break
fi

touch ${SH}/chkalert1_${DB}
cp ${SH}/chkalert1_${DB} ${ALERT2FILE}

grep -n ORA- ${ALERTLOG} | egrep -v "${IGNORELIST}" > ${SH}/chkalert1_${DB}
set `wc -l ${SH}/chkalert1_${DB}`
COUNT1=$1
set `wc -l ${ALERT2FILE}`
COUNT2=$1

if [ $COUNT1 -lt $COUNT2 ] ; then
    > ${ALERT2FILE}
    COUNT2=0
fi

if [ $COUNT1 -gt $COUNT2 ] ; then
   diff ${SH}/chkalert1_${DB} ${ALERT2FILE}|grep "<" > ${DIFFFILE}

  FN=`echo $0 | sed s/\.*[/]//`
  export HOSTNAME=$(hostname)
  echo "Sending Alert - Diff file is: $DIFFFILE"
  echo "$SH/alert_notification.ksh $FN `hostname` $DB "" "Alert log errors for
```

```
${DB}" ${DIFFFILE}"
  $SH/alert_notification.ksh $FN `hostname` $DB "" "Alert log errors for ${DB}"
${DIFFFILE}

fi

) >> ${LOGFILE} 2>&1

done
```

The alert log monitoring script checks the Oracle database version by means of the `sqlplus` –V syntax. We chose this method because you cannot query the database for the version as the database may not be online. As of Oracle Database 11*g*, the database version becomes pertinent for alert log monitoring since the alert log file is located in the trace directory of the DIAG_DEST location.

**TIP**
*DBAs can create symbolic links from the $ORACLE_BASE/ admin/$ORACLE_SID for the bdump directory that points to the trace directory of the new Oracle Database 11g diagnostic repository. Here's a simple example of creating a symbolic link from the older location $ORACLE_BASE/admin/$ORACLE_SID directory to the trace directory:*

```
$ pwd
/apps/oracle/admin/RACQA
ln -s /apps/oracle/diag/rdbms/racqa/RACQA1/trace bdump
```

When the alert log monitor script detects new ORA error code(s) in the alert log, the alert_notification.ksh script is invoked. This script reads another script that is a control file called alert_notification.ctl, and based on the name of the invoking script, the recipients of the alert condition are determined. You can specify any number of recipients in this file based on the script name. Here's an example of an alert_notification.ctl control file:

| SCRIPT_NAME | KEYWORD | SEVERITY | NOTIFICATION_LIST |
|---|---|---|---|
| oraping.ksh | DB | CRITICAL | authors@dataguardbook.com |
| ping_server.ksh | OSE | CRITICAL | authors@dataguardbook.com |
| dgmon.ksh | OSE | WARNING | authors@dataguardbook.com |
| dgmon_arch.ksh | OSE | WARNING | authors@dataguardbook.com |
| archmon.ksh | OSE | MINOR | authors@dataguardbook.com te@dataguardbook.com |
| dg_archivelog_monitor.ksh | DB | MINOR | authors@dataguardbook.com te@dataguardbook.com |
| tbsp_free.ksh_PG | DB | MINOR | authors@dataguardbook.com |
| tbspmon.ksh | DB | MINOR | authors@dataguardbook.com te@dataguardbook.com |
| tbspmon.ksh_PG | DB | MINOR | authors@dataguardbook.com te@dataguardbook.com |

| | | | |
|---|---|---|---|
| `diskfree.ksh` | OSE | MINOR | authors@dataguardbook.com |
| | | | te@dataguardbook.com |
| `[ … ]` | | | |
| `*:` | OTH | MINOR | authors@dataguardbook.com |
| | | | te@dataguardbook.com |
| `#*:` | OTH | MINOR | test@dataguardbook.com |

If a script that matches the invoking script is not found, the alert notification is sent out to a catch-all recipient. The catch-all recipient is configured as the last line of the control script alert_notification.ctl file that is not commented out. The alert notification control file also labels the severity of the alert with the possible severity categories: MINOR, WARNING, and CRITICAL. Obviously, additional categories can be defined, but WARNING and CRITICAL severities happen to be the same categories that are recognized by leading industry management consoles such as HP OpenView and IBM Tivoli.

For larger companies that depend on network operation centers (NOCs) or surveillance teams, the alert notification shell script also has API hooks to HP OpenView and IBM Tivoli. You can send alert notifications directly to the monitoring consoles with the severity levels specified. The alert_notification.ksh script escalates severities if DBAs do not clear the alert within a specified number of alert intervals. By default, the alert notification script will raise up to five alerts. The goal of the alert notification script is not to flood your e-mail inbox with database alerts but to send you proactive information so that you can deal with potential outages. In this example, if the specific alert is not corrected or cleared by the fourth alert, the alert will be escalated to the next higher severity. For certain situations, the script has been modified to change the recipient list as well.

The alert log monitoring script detects the differences in the ORA error messages since the last time it was executed and writes the alert to a file in the /tmp directory. The alert log monitoring script invokes the alert notification script and passes all the necessary parameters to send the alert with all the information required. Here's a sample alert generated by the alert log monitoring script:

```
< 201:      returning error ORA-16191
< 204:ORA-16191: Primary log shipping client not logged on standby
< 216:      returning error ORA-16191
< 219:ORA-16191: Primary log shipping client not logged on standby
< 223:ORA-16055: FAL request rejected
[…]
< 520:ORA-01034: ORACLE not available
< 524:ORA-16055: FAL request rejected
< 551:      returning error ORA-16191
< 554:ORA-16191: Primary log shipping client not logged on standby
< 566:      returning error ORA-16191
< 569:ORA-16191: Primary log shipping client not logged on standby
[…]
< 641:      returning error ORA-16191
< 644:ORA-16191: Primary log shipping client not logged on standby
< 897:ORA-03135: connection lost contact
< 1160:ORA-16055: FAL request rejected
< 1242:ORA-12541: TNS:no listener
< 4459:ORA-12537: TNS:connection closed
< 4491:ORA-01034: ORACLE not available
< 4500:ORA-03135: connection lost contact
```

**Logical Standby Alert Log File Entries**

In the logical standby database alert log file, you will see entries that start with the words "LOGSTDBY status:" followed by the Oracle error message. You may choose to search selectively for the words "LOGSTDBY status:" to scan directly for logical standby–related error messages. Here are several examples of the logical standby errors in the alert log file:

```
LOGSTDBY status: ORA-16081: insufficient number of processes for APPLY
Wed Feb 11 23:27:13 2009
Errors in file /apps/oracle/admin/MATRIXRT/bdump/matrixrt_lsp0_3966.trc:
ORA-16081: insufficient number of processes for APPLY
LOGSTDBY status: ORA-16222: automatic Logical Standby retry of last
action
LOGSTDBY status: ORA-16111: log mining and apply setting up
```

You can perceive from the alert notification that the alert is probably due to the primary database not identifying the archive log on the standby site. The issue in this e-mail output seems to be that either the database was shut down or the listener was not available. Once you receive the alert from e-mail, pager, or cell phone, you can examine the alert log to view additional information relative to the issue(s) causing the alert. By viewing the alert log, you can see detailed messages that are not captured by the alert log monitor script, such as the Remote File Server (RFS) messages:

```
RFS[17]: Possible network disconnect with primary database
Thu Aug 28 06:44:40 2008
Aborting archivelog file creation:
+FRA/matrix-DR0/archivelog/2008_08_28/thread_1_seq_11067.3622.663921821
If this a network disconnect, then this archivelog will be fetched again
by GAP resolution mechanism.
Thu Aug 28 06:44:40 2008
```

# Gathering Statistical Information from Archive Log History (PS+LS)

In general, archive logs should switch about every 30 minutes, but no less than every 15 minutes. You should examine the V$LOG_HISTORY view to review the frequency of archive log switches. If the archive log switches occur at an astronomical rate, you may need to consider increasing the size of the online redo logs. Keep in mind that if you increase the size of the online redo logs, the size of the standby redo logs needs to be increased as well. You must also remember that Oracle recommends $N + 1$ standby redo logs on the standby database. The following formula can be used to compute the number of standby redo logs for a RAC environment:

```
Total Number of Standby Redo Logs = ( No. of ORL per RAC instance +1 )
                                     * No. of  Instances
```

```
For example, for a 3-node RAC that has 3 ORLs per instance:
Total Number of Standby Redo Logs: (3+1)*3 =12 Standby Redo Logs.
```

You can review the alert log historical information, such as number of archive logs generated, in these increments:

- Past one hour
- Past one day

You should also capture related information such as the number of archive logs generated per day and the size of online redo logs. Based on how many archive logs are generated on an hourly basis, database architects can design a proper wide area network (WAN) infrastructure and determine bandwidth requirements to satisfy RTO and RPO requirements. Archive log generation during peak database usage will dictate the bandwidth needed for the WAN. The following query can be used on the primary database to identify peak archive times for a specified day:

```
SELECT TO_CHAR(TRUNC(FIRST_TIME),'Mon DD') "DG Date",
TO_CHAR(SUM(DECODE(TO_CHAR(FIRST_TIME,'HH24'),'00',1,0)),'9999')     "12AM",
TO_CHAR(SUM(DECODE(TO_CHAR(FIRST_TIME,'HH24'),'01',1,0)),'9999')     "01AM",
TO_CHAR(SUM(DECODE(TO_CHAR(FIRST_TIME,'HH24'),'02',1,0)),'9999')     "02AM",
TO_CHAR(SUM(DECODE(TO_CHAR(FIRST_TIME,'HH24'),'03',1,0)),'9999')     "03AM",
TO_CHAR(SUM(DECODE(TO_CHAR(FIRST_TIME,'HH24'),'04',1,0)),'9999')     "04AM",
TO_CHAR(SUM(DECODE(TO_CHAR(FIRST_TIME,'HH24'),'05',1,0)),'9999')     "05AM",
TO_CHAR(SUM(DECODE(TO_CHAR(FIRST_TIME,'HH24'),'06',1,0)),'9999')     "06AM",
TO_CHAR(SUM(DECODE(TO_CHAR(FIRST_TIME,'HH24'),'07',1,0)),'9999')     "07AM",
TO_CHAR(SUM(DECODE(TO_CHAR(FIRST_TIME,'HH24'),'08',1,0)),'9999')     "08AM",
TO_CHAR(SUM(DECODE(TO_CHAR(FIRST_TIME,'HH24'),'09',1,0)),'9999')     "09AM",
TO_CHAR(SUM(DECODE(TO_CHAR(FIRST_TIME,'HH24'),'10',1,0)),'9999')     "10AM",
TO_CHAR(SUM(DECODE(TO_CHAR(FIRST_TIME,'HH24'),'11',1,0)),'9999')     "11AM",
TO_CHAR(SUM(DECODE(TO_CHAR(FIRST_TIME,'HH24'),'12',1,0)),'9999')     "12PM",
TO_CHAR(SUM(DECODE(TO_CHAR(FIRST_TIME,'HH24'),'13',1,0)),'9999')     "1PM",
TO_CHAR(SUM(DECODE(TO_CHAR(FIRST_TIME,'HH24'),'14',1,0)),'9999')     "2PM",
TO_CHAR(SUM(DECODE(TO_CHAR(FIRST_TIME,'HH24'),'15',1,0)),'9999')     "3PM",
TO_CHAR(SUM(DECODE(TO_CHAR(FIRST_TIME,'HH24'),'16',1,0)),'9999')     "4PM",
TO_CHAR(SUM(DECODE(TO_CHAR(FIRST_TIME,'HH24'),'17',1,0)),'9999')     "5PM",
TO_CHAR(SUM(DECODE(TO_CHAR(FIRST_TIME,'HH24'),'18',1,0)),'9999')     "6PM",
TO_CHAR(SUM(DECODE(TO_CHAR(FIRST_TIME,'HH24'),'19',1,0)),'9999')     "7PM",
TO_CHAR(SUM(DECODE(TO_CHAR(FIRST_TIME,'HH24'),'20',1,0)),'9999')     "8PM",
TO_CHAR(SUM(DECODE(TO_CHAR(FIRST_TIME,'HH24'),'21',1,0)),'9999')     "9PM",
TO_CHAR(SUM(DECODE(TO_CHAR(FIRST_TIME,'HH24'),'22',1,0)),'9999')     "10PM",
TO_CHAR(SUM(DECODE(TO_CHAR(FIRST_TIME,'HH24'),'23',1,0)),'9999')     "11PM"
FROM V$LOG_HISTORY
GROUP BY TRUNC(FIRST_TIME)
ORDER BY TRUNC(FIRST_TIME) DESC
/
```

The output of this query will span beyond the width of your UNIX terminal. You may want to maximize your UNIX terminal to view the output in a friendly format. For display purposes, we will execute the SQL statement and truncate the output after 11 A.M. to display the number of archive logs generated from 12 A.M. to 12 P.M.:

| DG Date | 12AM | 01AM | 02AM | 03AM | 04AM | 05AM | 06AM | 07AM | 08AM | 09AM | 10AM | 11AM | |
|---|---|---|---|---|---|---|---|---|---|---|---|---|---|
| Jul 17 | 0 | 0 | 0 | 0 | 10 | 25 | 39 | 0 | 0 | 0 | 0 | 0 | ... |
| Jul 16 | 0 | 0 | 0 | 0 | 6 | 0 | 55 | 6 | 0 | 1 | 0 | 0 | ... |
| Jul 15 | 0 | 0 | 0 | 0 | 7 | 0 | 43 | 5 | 20 | 8 | 11 | 0 | ... |
| Jul 14 | 0 | 0 | 0 | 0 | 7 | 7 | 39 | 25 | 30 | 52 | 0 | 0 | ... |
| Jul 13 | 0 | 0 | 0 | 0 | 6 | 1 | 0 | 0 | 0 | 0 | 0 | 0 | ... |
| Jul 12 | 0 | 0 | 0 | 6 | 0 | 0 | 0 | 0 | 0 | 0 | 0 | 0 | ... |
| Jul 11 | 0 | 0 | 0 | 0 | 6 | 0 | 45 | 20 | 0 | 2 | 1 | 0 | ... |
| Jul 10 | 2 | 0 | 0 | 0 | 7 | 0 | 0 | 32 | 1 | 16 | 24 | 0 | ... |
| **Jul 09** | 0 | 0 | 0 | 30 | 33 | 32 | 32 | 31 | 1 | 25 | 13 | 1 | ... |
| Jul 08 | 0 | 0 | 0 | 6 | 0 | 32 | 29 | 7 | 2 | 3 | 0 | 0 | ... |
| Jul 07 | 0 | 0 | 0 | 6 | 0 | 0 | 42 | 0 | 0 | 0 | 0 | 0 | ... |
| Jul 06 | 0 | 0 | 0 | 7 | 1 | 0 | 1 | 0 | 1 | 0 | 6 | 0 | ... |
| Jul 05 | 0 | 0 | 0 | 12 | 0 | 0 | 0 | 0 | 4 | 6 | 0 | 0 | ... |
| Jul 04 | 0 | 0 | 0 | 12 | 0 | 0 | 0 | 32 | 13 | 7 | 0 | 0 | ... |
| Jul 03 | 0 | 0 | 0 | 14 | 3 | 31 | 33 | 0 | 0 | 8 | 0 | 0 | ... |
| Jul 02 | 1 | 0 | 0 | 12 | 0 | 0 | 46 | 0 | 0 | 24 | 0 | 0 | ... |
| Jul 01 | 0 | 0 | 0 | 13 | 1 | 0 | 0 | 0 | 0 | 6 | 39 | 8 | ... |
| Jun 30 | 0 | 0 | 0 | 12 | 0 | 0 | 57 | 12 | 12 | 18 | 7 | 0 | ... |

When you run the script, the output will display every hour of the day and the number of archive logs generated per hour. Let's review some interesting statistics from this output. On July 9, 30-plus archive logs were generated from 3 A.M. to 7 A.M. Additionally, you will notice that on June 30 and July 16, 55-plus archive logs were generated at 6 A.M. You can use these numbers to determine your bandwidth requirements to satisfy your RPO and RTO.

**NOTE**
*The ARCHIVE_LAG_TARGET parameter forces a log switch after a specified threshold set in seconds. This initialization parameter will influence this report since it influences redo log switches even during low or no activity on the database. By default, ARCHIVE_LAG_TARGET is set to 0, indicating that the primary database does not participate in a time-based redo switch. The recommended setting for this parameter is 1800, which is equivalent to 30 minutes, indicating that the primary must switch online redo log files every 30 minutes at a minimum. Be aware that a low value can cause performance degradations.*

# Detecting Archive Log Gaps (PS+LS)

For one reason or another, you may encounter gaps in archive log sequences on the standby database. Gap sequences typically occur as a result of a network outage. Archive gaps occur when an archive log is generated on the primary database but not received at the standby site. The primary database pings the standby database every minute to detect archive log gaps. Archive log gaps should be monitored to make sure that a gap does not exceed a large number of archive logs or for an extended period of time. Most archive log gaps are resolved by the ping ARCH process or by the Fetch Archive Log (FAL) process; typically, DBA intervention is not required. In the event of an extended outage or multiple gap sequences, manual intervention may be required to copy or restore the archive logs from the primary database to the standby database.

Archive log gaps can be monitored by examining the low and high sequence numbers in the V$ARCHIVE_GAP view, as shown here:

```
SELECT THREAD#, LOW_SEQUENCE#, HIGH_SEQUENCE#
FROM V$ARCHIVE_GAP;
```

By reviewing the THREAD# column, you can detect missing sequences at the Real Application Clusters (RAC) instance level.

If you find that Data Guard cannot resolve a gap automatically, it is probably because a required archive log file no longer resides on disk at the primary. The following script, dg_gap_detect.ksh, not only monitors the archive log gap on the standby database, but the gaps are correlated to the archive log names on the primary database that need to be copied or restored to the standby site:

```
# File Name: dg_gap_detect.ksh
export DR_DB=DEV_STDBY
export GAPFILE=${DR_DB}_gap.log

[ -f $GAPFILE ] && rm $GAPFILE

echo "Gaps in DR DB: $DR_DB"
echo "set head off ver off pages 0 feed off lines 122
SELECT * FROM V\$ARCHIVE_GAP;" |sqlplus -s "sys/${SYSPASSWD}@${DR_DB} as sysdba" >
$GAPFILE

# Print the contents of the GAPFILE
cat $GAPFILE

cat $GAPFILE |while read THREAD LOW HIGH
do
echo "Reporting Archivelogs that need to be manually shipped"
echo "set head off ver off pages 0 feed off lines 222
select name
from v\$archived_log
where thread#=${THREAD}
and dest_id=1
and sequence# between ${LOW} and ${HIGH};" |sqlplus -s / as sysdba
done
```

The following example shows that a gap exists on THREAD #1, and archive log sequences 87 and 88 need to be copied or restored from the primary to the standby database server:

```
$ ./dg_gap_detect.ksh
Gaps in DR DB: DEV_STDBY
        1           87          88
Reporting Archivelogs that need to be manually shipped
/u04/oradata/DEV/recovery_area/arch_1_87_656445787.log
/u04/oradata/DEV/recovery_area/arch_1_88_656445787.log
```

Now you can manually `scp` or `sftp` the archive logs to the physical standby database server if they exist on the primary server (or restore them from a backup) and register the archive logs. For detailed steps on how to troubleshoot archive log gaps, refer to Chapter 13.

## Identifying Delays in Redo Transport (PS)

Delays in redo transport can be monitored by comparing the highest sequence numbers of both primary and physical standby databases. If the maximum sequence number deviates by a specified number of archive logs, you can send an alert indicating that the standby Data Guard is falling behind. To view the highest sequence numbers, you can query the V$ARCHIVED_LOG view:

```
SELECT MAX(SEQUENCE#), THREAD#
FROM V$ARCHIVED_LOG GROUP BY THREAD#;
```

We have provided a script called dg_archivelog_monitor.ksh to detect delays in redo transport (even for a RAC environment) and alert DBAs in conditions where redo transport exceeds a specified threshold. The dg_archivelog_monitor.ksh script accepts three parameters (in the order specified):

1. The primary database name

2. The Transparent Network Substrate (TNS) alias to the physical standby database

3. The archive log threshold specified in numeric format

Here's an example of usage for this script:

```
dg_archivelog_monitor.ksh MATRIX MATRIX_DR0 25
```

This particular example specifies that you want to be alerted if the number of archive logs on the standby site falls behind by 25 or more archive logs. Here's a sample e-mail produced from the dg_alertlog_monitor.ksh script:

```
Subject: :OTH:MINOR:rac05:MATRIX:MATRIX_DR0:Primary: and DG:
Archive Logs are not in sync on 012109:1500 - Alert#: 2

Primary MATRIX and Data Guard MATRIX_DR0 ArchiveLogs are not in sync

There is a gap in Archive Log Sequence of:  27 for Thread#1 and 10 for
Thread#2
thread1                        37918
thread1                        37945
thread2                        30689
thread2                        30699
# ------------------------------------------------#
# -  Here's a look at the status on the DR Site:
# ------------------------------------------------#

NAME
CREATOR     T#    S# APPL FIRST_CHANGE# NEXT_CHANGE#
--------------------------------------------------------------------
------ ------- --- ------- ---- ------------- ------------
```

```
+FRA/matrix_dr0/archivelog/2009_01_20/thread_1_seq_37881.5092.676
652477 ARCH 1   37881 YES      3.273329E+12 3.273329E+12
+FRA/matrix_dr0/archivelog/2009_01_20/thread_1_seq_37882.4980.676
652965 ARCH 1   37882 YES      3.273329E+12 3.273329E+12
+FRA/matrix_dr0/archivelog/2009_01_20/thread_1_seq_37883.4558.676
653449 ARCH 1   37883 YES      3.273329E+12 3.273329E+12
[ ... ]
```

In this particular example, an alert notification was sent since the deviance of 27 archive logs for the sequence numbers exceeded the specified threshold of 25 archive logs. Notice that for Thread #1, the current sequence number is 37945, while the current sequence number on the physical standby is 37918. The dg_archivelog_monitor.ksh script monitors each thread of the RAC environment on the physical standby database to compare the maximum sequence number (of each thread) of the primary thread with the corresponding standby thread.

When you detect a redo transport delay, execute the following query on the primary database to identify archive logs that have not made it to the standby destination:

```
SELECT L.THREAD#, L.SEQUENCE#
FROM
  (SELECT THREAD#, SEQUENCE#
   FROM V$ARCHIVED_LOG
   WHERE DEST_ID=1) L
WHERE L.SEQUENCE# NOT IN
                     (SELECT SEQUENCE#
                      FROM V$ARCHIVED_LOG
                      WHERE DEST_ID=2
                      AND THREAD# = L.THREAD#);
```

# Monitoring Archive Log Destinations (PS+LS)

If the archive log destination happens to be in an ASM diskgroup, DBAs have to monitor the ASM diskgroup for available space. You can compute the percentage of free information by dividing the value of the FREE_MB column with the value in the TOTAL_MB column of the V$ASM_DISKGROUP view. The shell script, dgmon_arch.ksh, computes the percentage of free space and sends a notification to the DBAs based on a given threshold. This script accepts three parameters: the alert notification threshold, the database name, and the diskgroup to which the archive logs are written. If the ASM diskgroup used space threshold exceeds the notification threshold, or if an ORA-00257 error is encountered, the DBAs will be notified according to the escalation procedures.

```
#!/bin/ksh
# Filename: dgmon_arch.ksh
export PAGE_THRESHOLD=$1
export DB=$2
export ARCH_DG=$3

#
# [...] Deleted Portion to reduce page count
#
```

```
function exam_dg_threshold
{
export PAGE_THRESHOLD=$1

sqlplus -s $CONNECT_STRING 2>&1 <<__ENDSQL
  whenever sqlerror exit sql.sqlcode;

  set pages 60
  set lines 90
  set verif off
  set trims on

  col pct_free for 999.9 hea '%_FREE'
  define ORA_SID='$DB'
  define PAGE_THRESHOLD=$PAGE_THRESHOLD
  define LOG_DIR='$LOGDIR'

  spool $LOGFILE

  select name DG_NAME, total_mb/1024 GB, round(free_mb/total_mb,2)*100 pct_free
  from v\$asm_diskgroup
  where round(free_mb/total_mb,2)*100 < &PAGE_THRESHOLD
  and name=upper('$ARCH_DG');
  spool off

  set pages 14
  set lines 80
  set verif on
__ENDSQL

grep "DG_NAME" $LOGFILE
export RC1=$?

grep ORA-00257 $LOGFILE
export RC2=$?

if [[ "$RC1" -eq 0 || "$RC2" -eq 0 ]]; then
  (( EMAIL_COUNTER = ${COUNTER} + 1 ))

    # ------------------------------------------------------------
    # Set ALERT_COUNTER to be passed into alert_notification.ksh
    # ------------------------------------------------------------
    export ALERT_COUNTER=$EMAIL_COUNTER

  print "Sending dgmon Archive Destination alert ... $ALERT_COUNTER for $DB"

   $SH/alert_notification.ksh ${FN} `hostname` $DB "" "ARCH: Alert#: $EMAIL_COUNTER
for Archive Destination Disk Group Free < $PAGE_THRESHOLD percent!" $LOGFILE

  # Increment the counter by one and append it to the LOGFILE filename
  (( COUNTER = ${COUNTER} + 1 ))
```

```
   echo $COUNTER
   mv ${LOGFILE} ${LOGFILE}.${COUNTER}

fi
}


#+++++++++++++++++++++++++++++++++++++++++++++++++++++++++
#  MAIN LOGIC
#+++++++++++++++++++++++++++++++++++++++++++++++++++++++++

   #---------------------------------------------
   # Count the number of error files (LOGFILE)
   # in the /tmp directory
   #---------------------------------------------
   if [ -f ${LOGFILE}.* ]; then
     export COUNTER=$(ls ${LOGFILE}.* |wc -l)
   else
      COUNTER=0
   fi

#show_debug_parameters;

#---------------------------------------------------------
#  If # of error files on disk is greater than
#  $MAX_NUMBER_ALERTS, then skip to the next database
#---------------------------------------------------------
if [ "${COUNTER}" -ge "$MAX_NUMBER_ALERTS" ]; then
  echo "Exceeded Max number of Alerts:  $MAX_NUMBER_ALERTS"
else
  exam_dg_threshold $PAGE_THRESHOLD;
fi
```

This shell script addresses monitoring of the archive destination if the archive destination happens to be written to an ASM diskgroup. Feel free to download its counterpart, called archmon.ksh, to monitor the archive log destination if your archive logs are written to the file system from Oracle Press's script repository or the Data Guard book web site.

# Examining Apply Rate and Active Rate (PS)

The recovery performance can easily be monitored in real time by querying the V$RECOVERY_PROGRESS view as shown here:

```
SELECT TO_CHAR(START_TIME, 'DD-MON-RR HH24:MI:SS') start_time,
       ITEM,  SOFAR
FROM V$RECOVERY_PROGRESS
WHERE ITEM IN ('Active Apply Rate',
               'Average Apply Rate',
               'Redo Applied')
/
```

The output of this query can be used to determine how fast the standby database is able to keep up with the primary database. One thing to consider while diagnosing the performance numbers is that the average apply rate includes the think time for waiting for the redo to arrive. The active apply rate is the calculation of redo applied over time based on a moving average during the last 3 minutes. Here's a sample output of V$RECOVERY_PROGRESS:

```
START_TIME                ITEM                               SOFAR
----------------------    ------------------------------     ----------
30-JUN-08 23:20:14        Active Apply Rate                  26953
30-JUN-08 23:20:14        Average Apply Rate                 742
30-JUN-08 23:20:14        Redo Applied                       843227
```

The Redo Applied value is measured in megabytes while the Active Apply Rate and Average Apply Rate are calculated in KB/sec. For this example, if you divide the output of 26953/1024 to determine the MB/sec, you derive an active apply rate of 26.12 MB/sec.

## Reviewing Transport and Apply Lag (PS+LS)

The V$DATAGUARD_STATS view provides information on how far behind the redo transport and redo apply processes are. Here's an example of how to determine the delay in redo transport and apply processes on the physical standby:

```
COL NAME FOR A13
COL VALUE FOR A20
COL UNIT FOR A30
SET LINES 122
SELECT NAME, VALUE, UNIT, TIME_COMPUTED
FROM V$DATAGUARD_STATS
WHERE NAME IN ('transport lag', 'apply lag');

NAME            VALUE           UNIT                            TIME_COMPUTED
-------------   -------------   ----------------------------    --------------------
apply lag       +00 00:33:41    day(2) to second(0) interval    11-JUL-2008 11:20:13
transport lag   +00 00:01:18    day(2) to second(0) interval    11-JUL-2008 11:20:13
```

The transport lag value of 00:01:18 indicates that shipment of redo from the primary to the physical standby is behind by 1 minute, 18 seconds. In the event of a catastrophe on the primary, you stand to lose 1 minute, 18 seconds' worth of data if you lose the primary site or have to wait 1 minute, 18 seconds if you want to perform a switchover. Notice the apply lag value of 33:41 indicating that the apply lag is more than 33 minutes behind. The apply lag value reflects the 30-minute DELAY attribute in the ARCHIVE_LOG_DEST_*n* parameter.

### Do You Know Where Your Standby Database Is?
Monitoring where your standby database is in relation to the redo generated on your primary database is paramount to knowing whether you are meeting your RPO at any given moment.

# Determining the Current Time on the Standby Database (PS)

Another method for measuring how far behind your physical standby database is from your primary database is to convert the current SCN to timestamp with the SCN_TO_TIMESTAMP function. The current timestamp of the physical standby can be compared to the timestamp of the primary database to find the lag. You cannot convert the CURRENT_SCN to a timestamp on the physical standby. Attempting to convert the CURRENT_SCN on the physical standby will produce an ORA-00904 error:

```
SELECT SCN_TO_TIMESTAMP(CURRENT_SCN) FROM V$DATABASE;
       *
ERROR at line 1:
ORA-00904: "SCN_TO_TIMESTAMP": invalid identifier
```

The CURRENT_SCN column of the V$DATABASE view of a physical standby database must be converted to a timestamp value on the primary database. Once the timestamp values of CURRENT_SCN of both the primary and physical standby databases are available, the delay information of the physical standby relative to the primary database can be computed accurately. Note that the CURRENT_SCN column of an Active Data Guard standby database is actually the query SCN, the most current SCN that queries can access.

The shell script dg_time_lag.ksh connects to the physical standby database, selects the CURRENT_SCN value from V$DATABASE, and stores the output in a log file. The content of the dg_time_lag.ksh script is shown here:

```
export CONF=$PWD/dg.conf
[ ! -f "$CONF" ] && { echo "Configuration file: $CONF is missing."; echo
"Exiting."; exit 1; }
. $CONF

export SYSPASSWD=$(cat .syspasswd)
export DR_LOG=db_db.log
export LOG=db.log

[ -f $DR_LOG ] && rm $DR_LOG
[ -f $LOG ] && rm $LOG

echo "Printing Standby Current SCN and Primary Current SCN"
echo "set echo off ver off feed off head off pages 0;
select current_scn from v\$database;" |
    sqlplus -s "sys/${SYSPASSWD}@${STANDBY_HOST}:${STANDBY_PORT}/${STANDBY_DB} as
sysdba" |
    tee $DR_LOG

echo "set echo off ver off feed off head off pages 0;
select current_scn from v\$database;" |
    sqlplus -s "sys/${SYSPASSWD}@${PRIMARY_HOST}:${PRIMARY_PORT}/${PRIMARY_DB} as
sysdba" |
    tee $LOG

echo ""
```

```
export DR_SCN=$(cat $DR_LOG |sed -e 's/ //g')
export SCN=$(cat $LOG |sed -e 's/ //g')

# Convert SCN to timestamp on the Primary DB
echo "Printing Standby Current SCN To Timestamp and Primary Current SCN To
Timestamp"
echo "set echo off ver off feed off head off pages 0;
select scn_to_timestamp(current_scn) from v\$database;" |
    sqlplus -s "sys/${SYSPASSWD}@${PRIMARY_HOST}:${PRIMARY_PORT}/${PRIMARY_DB} as
sysdba"

echo "set echo off ver off feed off head off pages 0;
select scn_to_timestamp(${DR_SCN}) from dual;" |
    sqlplus -s "sys/${SYSPASSWD}@${PRIMARY_HOST}:${PRIMARY_PORT}/${PRIMARY_DB} as
sysdba"

echo "set echo off ver off feed off
      col Primary for a32
      col DR for a32
      col wks for 999
      col days for 9999
select scn_to_timestamp(${SCN}) Primary
      ,scn_to_timestamp(${DR_SCN}) DR
      ,trunc(to_number(substr((scn_to_timestamp(${SCN})-
scn_to_timestamp(${DR_SCN}))),1,instr(scn_to_timestamp(${SCN})-
scn_to_timestamp(${DR_SCN}),' ')))/7) Wks
      ,trunc(to_number(substr((scn_to_timestamp(${SCN})-
scn_to_timestamp(${DR_SCN}))),1,instr(scn_to_timestamp(${SCN})-
scn_to_timestamp(${DR_SCN}),' '))))   Days
        ,substr((scn_to_timestamp(${SCN})-
scn_to_timestamp(${DR_SCN})),instr((scn_to_timestamp(${SCN})-
scn_to_timestamp(${DR_SCN})),' ')+1,2)                Hrs
        ,substr((scn_to_timestamp(${SCN})-
scn_to_timestamp(${DR_SCN})),instr((scn_to_timestamp(${SCN})-
scn_to_timestamp(${DR_SCN})),' ')+4,2)                Mins
        ,substr((scn_to_timestamp(${SCN})-
scn_to_timestamp(${DR_SCN})),instr((scn_to_timestamp(${SCN})-
scn_to_timestamp(${DR_SCN})),' ')+7,2)                Secs
from dual;" |
    sqlplus -s "sys/${SYSPASSWD}@${PRIMARY_HOST}:${PRIMARY_PORT}/${PRIMARY_DB} as
sysdba"
```

Let's execute the dg_time_lag.ksh script on a Data Guard environment where the archive log gap has gone unresolved for an extended period of time. Executing dg_time_lag.ksh results in the following output:

```
    822999
    1000327


Printing Standby Current SCN To Timestamp and Primary Current SCN To Timestamp
  Standby Current SCN: 822999   Time Stamp: 15-JUL-08 08.28.34.000000000 PM
  Primary Current SCN: 1000327  Time Stamp: 08-JUL-08 12.47.49.000000000 AM
```

```
[SC: Suggested Output]PRIMARY                                DR
WKS  DAYS HR MI SE
-------------------------------- -------------------------------- ---- ---- -- -- --
15-JUL-08 08.28.34.000000000 PM 08-JUL-08 12.47.49.000000000 AM    1   7 19 40 45
```

The output confirms that the physical standby is significantly behind the primary database. In terms of SCN comparisons, the output indicates that the physical database is behind by about 1 week, 7 days, 19 hours, 41 minutes.

## Reporting the Status of Managed Recovery Process (PS)

The V$MANAGED_STANDBY view reports the progress of the standby database in managed recovery mode. This view provides information regarding current activities for Redo Apply and Redo Transport Services. A separate set of views can be used to monitor SQL Apply. Processes that you repeatedly notice in the V$MANAGED_STANDBY view relative to the managed recovery process (MRP) include Media Recovery Process (MRP0), archiver process (ARCH), log writer (LGWR), Remote File Server (RFS), and LogWriter Network Service (LNS). You can execute the following SQL query to view the progress of each of the processes:

```
SET LINES 132
SET PAGESIZE 9999
COL CLIENT_PID FORMAT A12
  1  SELECT PID, PROCESS, STATUS, CLIENT_PROCESS,
  2         CLIENT_PID, THREAD#, SEQUENCE# SEQ#,
  3         BLOCK#, BLOCKS
  4* FROM V$MANAGED_STANDBY
SQL> /
```

Here's a sample output of the V$MANAGED_STANDBY view where the MPR0 (the detached managed recovery process) is applying archive logs:

| PID | PROCESS | STATUS | CLIENT_P | CLIENT PID | THREAD# | SEQ# | BLOCK# | BLOCKS |
|-----|---------|--------|----------|------------|---------|------|--------|--------|
| 5489 | ARCH | CONNECTED | ARCH | 5489 | 0 | 0 | 0 | 0 |
| 5491 | ARCH | CONNECTED | ARCH | 5491 | 0 | 0 | 0 | 0 |
| 5493 | ARCH | CONNECTED | ARCH | 5493 | 0 | 0 | 0 | 0 |
| 5495 | ARCH | CONNECTED | ARCH | 5495 | 0 | 0 | 0 | 0 |
| 5660 | RFS | IDLE | UNKNOWN | 20691 | 0 | 0 | 0 | 0 |
| 23054 | MRP0 | APPLYING_LOG | N/A | N/A | 1 | 89 | 18423 | 24430 |
| 23064 | RFS | IDLE | UNKNOWN | 20687 | 0 | 0 | 0 | 0 |
| 23336 | RFS | IDLE | UNKNOWN | 20693 | 0 | 0 | 0 | 0 |

In this case, Redo Apply is in the process of applying the archive logs from a recent gap. The RFS process receives redo data from the primary database and writes it to the standby redo logs. The output of the query reveals that the Redo Apply process is currently applying archive log sequence 89 for thread 1. The last block that Redo Apply applied was block number 18423. A total of 24,430 512-byte blocks need to be applied. Lastly, the other processes, ARCH and RFS, are idle, and you can see that no current connection exists with the primary for the current redo stream.

# Data Guard Menu Utility

The Data Guard monitoring scripts, DG Menu, are an interactive toolkit designed to help DBAs and architects assess the Data Guard configuration quickly and seamlessly. The purpose of DG Menu is to provide detailed reports so that the Data Guard implementation can be bulletproof. You can leverage the DG Menu to check your existing configuration for requirement compliance or to troubleshoot a configuration with issues.

**TIP**
*You can download the Data Guard monitoring scripts (DG Menu) from Oracle Press's web site or from this book's web site at www.dataguardbook.com. The scripts are provided in a single archived file in a UNIX TAR format. You can download the dg.tar file and extract it using the* `tar -xvf dg.tar` *command. As long as you have access to a korn or bourne shell and SQL\*Plus, you can execute DG Menu. All the monitoring scripts are easily accessible from the initial menu screen.*

The DG Menu utility uses a configuration file called *dg.conf* that defines the topology of the Data Guard environment. This configuration file can be modified to suit your needs. Here's a sample dg.conf file:

```
PRIMARY_HOST=rac3a
PRIMARY_DB=DEV
PRIMARY_PORT=1523
STANDBY_HOST=rac4a
STANDBY_DB=DEVDR
STANDBY_PORT=1523
#
FLASH_DG=/u04/oradata/$ORACLE_SID/recovery_area
DATA_DG=/u02/oradata
DATA_DG2=/u03/oradata
PRIMARY_DOMAIN=dbaexpert.com
PRIMARY_VIP=rac3a-vip
DR_VIP=rac4a-vip
# Valid entries for FS=FS for file system or ASM for automated storage management
FS=FS
FS=FS [SC: suggest to spell FILE_SYSTEM for clarity]
```

In the dg.conf file, you define the primary database server (`PRIMARY_HOST`), the primary database (`PRIMARY_DB`), and the database listener port (`PRIMARY_PORT`). Furthermore, you define the standby database server (`STANDBY_HOST`), the standby database (`STANDBY_DB`), and the standby database listener port (`STANDBY_PORT`).

Optionally, you can define the SYS password in the .syspasswd file. If the .syspasswd file does not exist, you will be prompted to enter the SYS password. Since this is a client application, you should provide the SYS password even to diagnose the primary database configuration. For security considerations, the .syspasswd file is an optional file that is provided at your discretion. It is a simple matter of convenience to include an entry for the .syspasswd file.

To run DG Menu, only an Oracle client with SQL*Plus is required. Even the instant client with SQL*Plus is adequate to launch DG Menu. DG Menu does not use a TNSNAMES.ORA file.

**NOTE**
*If you want to execute DG Menu from the Microsoft Windows environment, you can download and install CYGWIN (www.cygwin .org) or UNIX Services for Windows from Microsoft's web site.*

# Reviewing the Current Data Guard Environment

The DG Menu toolkit includes shell scripts that execute SQL or that run behind the scenes to diagnose a Data Guard configuration. Each of the shell scripts executes SQL*Plus to gather pertinent information from the database. More than half the scripts have been converted to PL/SQL for friendly output purposes. The shell scripts leverage the SYS account to log in to the primary and standby databases. The optional password file, .syspasswd, can be updated to automate the login to the primary and standby databases.

**NOTE**
*The supplied DG Menu does not issue any Data Definition Language (DDL) on the database. Only* SELECT *statements are issued against relevant* V$ *and* DBA_ *views to extract Data Guard–related information.*

The SYSDBA role is required simply because the SQL*Plus connection must be established to the physical standby database, which is in mounted mode. The DG Menu checks the following components and more:

- The existence of a password file is checked in both the primary and standby databases.
- SYSDBA role is granted to the SYS system account.
- Forced logging is enforced on the primary database.
- Unrecoverable activities on the primary database are closely scrutinized.
- The primary database runs in archive log mode.
- The existence of standby redo logs is checked on both the primary and standby databases.
- The existence of TNSNAMES.ORA file entries is checked for both the primary and standby databases.
- Standby file management is set to AUTO.

You can invoke the DG Menu by typing **./dg** in the directory where you have extracted the dg.tar archive. Each of the menu items executes a submenu command via SQL*Plus or another shell script. Here's an example of the DG Menu UI:

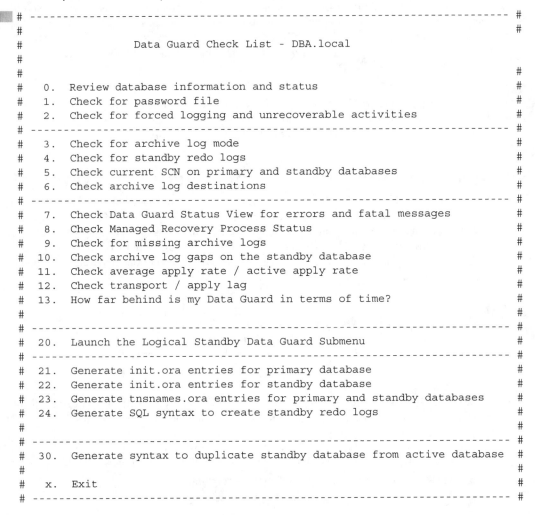

```
# --------------------------------------------------------------------- #
#                                                                       #
#                  Data Guard Check List - DBA.local                    #
#                                                                       #
#                                                                       #
#                                                                       #
#  0.  Review database information and status                           #
#  1.  Check for password file                                          #
#  2.  Check for forced logging and unrecoverable activities           #
# --------------------------------------------------------------------- #
#  3.  Check for archive log mode                                       #
#  4.  Check for standby redo logs                                      #
#  5.  Check current SCN on primary and standby databases              #
#  6.  Check archive log destinations                                   #
# --------------------------------------------------------------------- #
#  7.  Check Data Guard Status View for errors and fatal messages      #
#  8.  Check Managed Recovery Process Status                            #
#  9.  Check for missing archive logs                                   #
# 10.  Check archive log gaps on the standby database                   #
# 11.  Check average apply rate / active apply rate                     #
# 12.  Check transport / apply lag                                      #
# 13.  How far behind is my Data Guard in terms of time?               #
#                                                                       #
# --------------------------------------------------------------------- #
# 20.  Launch the Logical Standby Data Guard Submenu                    #
# --------------------------------------------------------------------- #
# 21.  Generate init.ora entries for primary database                   #
# 22.  Generate init.ora entries for standby database                   #
# 23.  Generate tnsnames.ora entries for primary and standby databases #
# 24.  Generate SQL syntax to create standby redo logs                 #
#                                                                       #
# --------------------------------------------------------------------- #
# 30.  Generate syntax to duplicate standby database from active database #
#                                                                       #
#  x.  Exit                                                             #
# --------------------------------------------------------------------- #
```

**NOTE**
*In the remainder of this chapter, we will discuss individual checklist menu items of the DG Menu starting with checking the password file. Notice that option 20 will invoke a logical standby DG submenu. The logical standby DG submenu can save you hours of troubleshooting-related efforts.*

## Checking the Password File (PS+LS)

If DG Menu is launched from the database server, it checks for the existence of the password file in the $ORACLE_HOME/dbs directory. If DG Menu is launched from the client, it will not check for the password file. DG Menu compares the local hostname to the PRIMARY_HOST and the

STANDBY_HOST defined in the dg.conf file. If the local hostname matches either the PRIMARY_HOST or the STANDBY_HOST, the orapw$ORACLE_SID file will be expected in the $ORACLE_HOME/dbs directory as specified here:

```
ls -l ${ORACLE_HOME}/dbs/orapw${ORACLE_SID}
rc=$?
if [ "$rc" -ne 0 ]; then
  echo "Password file for your database:  $ORACLE_SID does not exist!"
  echo "Please create a password file using the orapwd utility"
[…]
```

Not only does Data Guard require a password file, but it also expects SYS to be granted the SYSDBA role. The V$PWFILE_USERS data dictionary view provides detailed information on database accounts that have been granted the SYSDBA and/or SYSOPER roles:

```
SELECT * FROM V$PWFILE_USERS;
```

# Checking for Nologging Activities (PS+LS)

As discussed in Chapter 3, the impact of allowing nologging operations on your primary database can be immense when you have to failover to your standby database. Although forced logging should be mandated at the database level, your performance requirements may dictate that you use forced logging at the tablespace level instead. If the database forced logging is enabled, all nologging activities will be logged. Users who issue NOLOGGING transactions may think that they have completed successful NOLOGGING transactions, but behind the scenes, Oracle logs the transaction. Forced logging at the database level trumps all other levels of NOLOGGING settings or transactions.

We strongly recommend that you set up forced logging at the database level. If you do not do so, you can set the forced logging option at the tablespace level by using the FORCE LOGGING clause. By default, all tablespaces are created with the logging option enabled but with forced logging disabled. All newly created tablespaces should always be created with the forced logging feature if database logging is not forced. NOLOGGING activities are speculated to increase performance throughput, so users often prefer to trade the benefits of performance for risk of corruption on the standby database.

DBAs should be cognitive of tablespaces that allow NOLOGGING activities. Just as important, DBAs should check for NOLOGGING activities at the datafile level. The script shown here checks for tablespaces in NOLOGGING mode and datafiles with NOLOGGING activity such as SQL*Loader or index rebuilds with the NOLOGGING option enabled:

```
set serveroutput on size 1000000
set feed off ver off pages 0 lines 2000 trims on
DECLARE
cursor c1 is
select file#, name, unrecoverable_change#,
       to_char(unrecoverable_time, 'DD-MON-RR HH24:MI:SS') unrecoverable_time
from v$datafile
where unrecoverable_time is not null;

cursor c2 is
```

```
select tablespace_name, logging ,status
from dba_tablespaces
where logging='NOLOGGING'
and contents <> 'TEMPORARY';

BEGIN
dbms_output.put_line('Checking for datafiles with unrecoverable activities');
FOR r1 in c1 loop
  dbms_output.put_line('FOUND ... File Name: '|| r1.name||' - '||'Unrecoverable
Time: '|| r1.unrecoverable_time);
END LOOP;

dbms_output.put_line('Checking for tablespace(s) that are not being logged');
FOR r2 in c2 LOOP
  dbms_output.put_line('FOUND ... Tablespace Name: '|| r2.tablespace_name||' -
'||'Logging: '|| r2.logging);
END LOOP;

END;
/
```

Here's a sample output with several datafiles with NOLOGGING activities:

```
Checking for forced logging at the database level
# ---------------------------------------------------------------------- #
#          Executing dg_check_unrecoverable.sql on DB:  DEV
# ---------------------------------------------------------------------- #
Checking for datafiles with unrecoverable activities
FOUND ... File Name: /u04/oradata/Matrix_DR0/docs_i_01.dbf - Unrecoverable Time:
04-JUL-08 14:25:45
FOUND ... File Name: /u02/oradata/Matrix_DR0/kb_d_01.dbf - Unrecoverable Time:
04-JUL-08 14:27:39
FOUND ... File Name: /u04/oradata/Matrix_DR0/sox_i_01.dbf - Unrecoverable Time:
04-JUL-08 14:27:39
Checking for tablespace(s) that are not being logged
FOUND ... Tablespace Name: USERS - Logging: NOLOGGING
```

When checking for unrecoverable activities that can invalidate your standby database, you need to note the date of the unrecoverable activity. If the date of the unrecoverable activity occurred after the database restore of your standby database, you must recopy the datafile(s) in question or perform an incremental backup on the primary database based on the SCN and apply the incremental backup on the physical standby database. For detailed instructions on how to perform an SCN-based incremental backup to apply on the standby database, refer to Chapter 13.

If you do not specify forced logging at the database level, you should carefully consider the risk implications. If for some reason you choose to disable forced logging at the database level, we strongly recommend forced logging at the tablespace level for all the tablespaces that are not designated for the NOLOGGING activities, or you risk data corruption on the standby database. For example, your company may drop and/or re-create materialized views on the OLTP database on a nightly basis. In addition to the materialized view reinstantiation, you also need to re-create all the indexes associated with the materialized view. At the same time, you discovered that by adding the NOLOGGING option for creating the materialized views and indexes, you can save three to four hours of processing time. In such situations, you may consider specifying one or two tablespaces for the NOLOGGING activities and set forced logging for the remaining tablespaces in the database. To set the tablespace at FORCE LOGGING mode, you can use the FORCE LOGGING clause shown here:

```
1* CREATE TABLESPACE DATA_FORCE
2  DATAFILE '+DATA' SIZE 1M LOGGING FORCE LOGGING;

Tablespace created.
```

For demonstration purposes, we will create a tablespace with the NOLOGGING option for the tablespace designated for unrecoverable activities:

```
1*  CREATE TABLESPACE DATA_NOLOG
2   DATAFILE '+DG_DBA_DD501' SIZE 1M NOLOGGING;

Tablespace created.
```

You can see from the following SQL output that the FORCE_LOGGING column of the DBA_TABLESPACES view indicates that forced logging is enabled for the DATA_FORCE tablespace we just created. On the other hand, you can also see that the DATA_NOLOG tablespace is set to NOLOGGING, which means that data in this tablespace will not be available after you open the database in the standby database.

```
SQL> SELECT TABLESPACE_NAME, LOGGING, FORCE_LOGGING
       FROM DBA_TABLESPACES;
TABLESPACE_NAME                      LOGGING    FOR
------------------------------------ ---------- ---
SYSTEM                               LOGGING    NO
UNDOTBS1                             LOGGING    NO
SYSAUX                               LOGGING    NO
TEMP                                 NOLOGGING  NO
USERS                                LOGGING    NO
TOOLS                                LOGGING    NO
EGG_WHITE_D                          LOGGING    NO
DATA_FORCE                           LOGGING    YES
DATA_NOLOG                           NOLOGGING  NO
```

In addition to monitoring for NOLOGGING at the database and tablespace levels, you should also monitor for NOLOGGING settings at the object level—objects that need to be monitored are tables and indexes. Tables should always be kept in logging mode. Indexes should also be kept in logging mode even though they can be rebuilt on the standby database after the database is opened. You can issue the following query to determine all the tables that are currently in NOLOGGING mode:

```
  1  SELECT OWNER||'.'||TABLE_NAME, LOGGING FROM DBA_TABLES
  2  WHERE LOGGING ='NO'
  3  AND OWNER NOT IN ('SYS', 'SYSTEM', 'EXFSYS',
                       'WMSYS', 'MDSYS', 'OLAPSYS', 'DBSNMP')
  4* ORDER BY OWNER, TABLE_NAME
SQL> /
```

```
TABLE_NAME                                                             LOG
---------------------------------------------------------------       ---
RODBA.EDBA_NOROWS                                                      NO
```

To disable `NOLOGGING` at the table level, you can issue this command:

```
ALTER TABLE RODBA.EDBA_NOROWS LOGGING;
```

As mentioned earlier, you should also scrutinize the indexes for `NOLOGGING` settings. You can use the following query to determine what indexes are configured for nologging activities:

```
SQL> SELECT OWNER||'.'||INDEX_NAME INDEX_NAME, LOGGING
  2  FROM DBA_INDEXES
  3  WHERE LOGGING ='NO'
  4  AND OWNER NOT IN ('SYS', 'SYSTEM', 'EXFSYS',
  5                          'WMSYS', 'MDSYS', 'OLAPSYS', 'DBSNMP')
  6  /
INDEX_NAME                                                             LOG
---------------------------------------------------------------       ---
TSMSYS.SRSIDX                                                          NO
```

Although indexes can be rebuilt, and you may be tempted to disable logging at the index level, you do not want to be in a situation where you are rebuilding the standby database after a switchover/failover condition. Indexes on large tables can take several to many hours to rebuild.

Although we mentioned how you can check for `NOLOGGING` activities at the tablespace, datafile, and even object levels, the best recommendation that we can make to you is to enable forced logging at the database level. Enforcing database-level logging keeps everything simple.

# Looking at Archivelog Mode and Destinations (PS+LS)

A required prerequisite to implement a physical or logical Data Guard standby is that the database must be running in archive log mode. The DG Menu checks for archive log mode and archive log destinations for errors. During the probe of archive log destinations, relevant information such as archive log destination, archive log status, and error messages are revealed. Starting with Oracle Database 11*g*, Oracle provides the redo compression feature for Data Guard. If your company happens to use the new technology, you can confirm that compression of archive logs is enabled during transmission when Data Guard is resolving a gap. The following script checks the two views, V$ARCHIVE_DEST_STATUS and V$ARCHIVE_DEST, and provides pertinent information related to archive destinations:

```
SET SERVEROUTPUT ON SIZE 1000000
SET LINES 132
COL ERROR FORMAT A32
COL DESTINATION FORMAT A35
SET VER OFF HEAD OFF FEED OFF PAGES 0

DECLARE
pad10 CHAR(10) := ' ';
CURSOR c1 is
select s.db_unique_name,
       s.database_mode,
```

```
        s.dest_id id, s.status stats,
        s.recovery_mode,
        s.protection_mode, s.standby_logfile_count,
        s.standby_logfile_active,
        s.archived_thread#, s.archived_seq#,
        s.applied_thread#, s.applied_seq#,
        d.status, d.destination, d.archiver,
        d.transmit_mode, d.affirm, d.async_blocks,
        d.net_timeout, d.delay_mins, d.reopen_secs,
        d.register, d.binding, d.compression, d.error err
from v$archive_dest_status s, v$archive_dest d
where d.dest_id=s.dest_id
and s.db_unique_name <> 'NONE'
and d.destination is not null;

BEGIN
dbms_output.put_line('-----------------------------------------------------');
FOR r1 IN c1 LOOP
  dbms_output.put_line('Dest ID: '||r1.id||pad10||'Status: '||r1.stats);
  dbms_output.put_line('DB Name: '||r1.db_unique_name||pad10||'DB Mode:
'||r1.database_mode);
  dbms_output.put_line('Recovery Mode: '||r1.recovery_mode);
  dbms_output.put_line('Protection Mode: '||r1.protection_mode);
  dbms_output.put_line('SRL Count: '||r1.standby_logfile_count||pad10||'SRL
Active: '||r1.standby_logfile_active);
  dbms_output.put_line('Archived Thread#: '||r1.archived_
thread#||pad10||'Archived
Seq#: '||r1.archived_seq#);
  dbms_output.put_line('Applied Thread#: '||r1.applied_
thread#||pad10||'Applied
Seq#: '||r1.applied_seq#);

  dbms_output.put_line('Destination: '||r1.destination);
  dbms_output.put_line('Archiver: '||r1.archiver);
  dbms_output.put_line('Transmit Mode: '||r1.transmit_mode);
  dbms_output.put_line('Affirm: '||r1.affirm);
  dbms_output.put_line('Asynchronous Blocks: '||r1.async_blocks);
  dbms_output.put_line('Net Timeout: '||r1.net_timeout);
  dbms_output.put_line('Delay (Mins): '||r1.delay_mins);
  dbms_output.put_line('Reopen (Secs): '||r1.reopen_secs);
  dbms_output.put_line('Register: '||r1.register);
  dbms_output.put_line('Binding: '||r1.binding);
  dbms_output.put_line('Compression: '||r1.compression);
  dbms_output.put_line('Error: '||r1.err);
dbms_output.put_line('-----------------------------------------------------');
END LOOP;
END;
/
```

The script is intentionally written in PL/SQL to provide easier readability. In addition to the COMPRESSION column, you should pay particular attention to the ERROR column from the V$ARCHIVE_DEST view.

## Checking Standby File Management (PS)

Standby file management should be enabled as part of Data Guard best practices. Standby file management enables automatic file creation or deletion on the physical standby when files are added or dropped on the primary database. The files are created based on the value set in the DB_FILE_NAME_CONVERT initialization parameter. Use the following query to verify that the physical standby has standby file management enabled:

```
COL NAME FOR A33
COL VALUE FOR A10
SELECT NAME, VALUE
FROM V$PARAMETER
WHERE NAME='standby_file_management';
```

A value set to AUTO indicates that standby file management is enabled, as shown here:

```
NAME                                 VALUE
--------------------------------- ----------
standby_file_management              AUTO
```

If this parameter is not set, or it accidentally becomes unset, and a datafile is added to the primary database, it is possible that you will encounter an "ORA-1274: cannot add datafile '%s' – file could not be created" error. The datafile will not be generated on the standby file system, but an entry will be added to your standby control file that refers to this datafile as an *UNNAMEDxxx* file. To remedy this, you will have to add the missing datafile manually.[1] Here's an example:

```
SQL> ALTER SYSTEM SET STANDBY_FILE_MANAGEMENT=MANUAL;
SQL> ALTER DATABASE CREATE DATAFILE
  2  '.../dbs/UNNAMED00007'
  3  AS
  4  '.../realfilename/';
```

## Revealing Errors in the Data Guard Status View (PS)

The V$DATAGUARD_STATUS view identifies events that write error messages to the alert log file and/or generate trace files associated with the error. This view reveals information about all the severities including informational messages, but only for the last 256 Data Guard–related messages written to the alert log file. The MESSAGE column may provide more information than you need. DBAs can restrict the output of messages to the important ones by qualifying the CALLOUT column with a value of YES. A YES value indicates that a DBA intervention may be required.

---

[1] See MetaLink Note 388659.1: ORA-1274 Encountered on Physical Standby After Adding Datafile to Primary, and MetaLink Note 304488.1: Using standby_file_management with Raw Devices.

Here's a code example of querying the V$DATAGUARD_STATUS view and restricting the output that requires a DBA response:

```
SET LINES 132
COL MESSAGE FOR A80
COL TIMESTAMP FOR A20

SELECT ERROR_CODE, SEVERITY, MESSAGE,
       TO_CHAR(TIMESTAMP, 'DD-MON-RR HH24:MI:SS') TIMESTAMP
FROM V$DATAGUARD_STATUS
WHERE CALLOUT='YES'
AND TIMESTAMP > SYSDATE-1;
```

Valid values for the SEVERITY column are Informational, Warning, Error, Fatal, and Control. You also want to restrict the output depending on how far back you would like to see by qualifying the TIMESTAMP column.

## Logical Standby Data Guard Menu

The remainder of the chapter is dedicated to logical standby monitoring. We hope to provide you a comprehensive toolkit to monitor a logical standby configuration. We are releasing a full screen's worth of logical standby monitoring scripts. From the tar extract, you can easily determine what is related to the logical standby monitoring versus the physical standby monitoring scripts. All the scripts that start with *dg_* prefix are associated with the physical standby database. Note that quite a few of the scripts that were intended for the physical standby are applicable to the logical standby database as well. All the shell scripts and SQL scripts that pertain to the logical standby monitoring start with the *logical_* prefix.

From the main DG menu screen, menu option 20 invokes the logical standby DG submenu. By invoking task option 20, you will invoke the dg_logical_menu.ksh shell script. You can optionally invoke this shell script independently to access the logical standby menu options directly. The logical standby screen provides specific options to monitor and assist you in troubleshooting the logical standby database.

For demonstration purposes, we will directly execute the logical standby DG submenu. Here's the UI of the logical standby DG submenu:

```
./dg_logical_menu.ksh
# --------------------------------------------------------------------- #
#                                                                       #
#    Logical Standby Data Guard Check List - DBA.local                  #
#                                                                       #
#    1.  Check Logical Progress - View Overall Progress Of SQL Apply    #
#    2.  Check Logical Events - History on Logical Standby Apply Activity #
#    3.  Check Logical Events - Detailed View                           #
#    4.  Check Logical Stats - Logical Standby Stats                    #
#    5.  Check Logical Parameters - Logical Standby Parameters          #
#    6.  Look At What The Logical Standby Processes Are Doing           #
#        Coordinator, Reader, Builder, Preparer, Analyzer, Applier ...  #
#    7.  Look At The Status Codes For The Logical Standby Processes     #
#    8.  Look At Events The Applier Process Is Stuck On                 #
# --------------------------------------------------------------------- #
```

```
#  10.   Check the LCR - Look At Bytes Paged Out                          #
#  11.   Generate Syntax To Skip Transactions                            #
#        Based On MAX(EVENT_TIME) FROM DBA_LOGSTDBY_EVENTS               #
#        DO NOT SKIP DML STATEMENTS                                      #
#  12.   Diagnostic Script Per Metalink Note ID: 241512.1               #
#        Look for output in logical_diag_[ORACLE_SID_MONDD_HHMM.out] format #
# ----------------------------------------------------------------------- #
#  20.   Review What Is NOT Supported In Your Logical Standby Database    #
#                                                                         #
# ----------------------------------------------------------------------- #
#  30.   Start Logical Standby Database                                   #
#  40.   Stop Logical Standby Database - PLEASE BE CAREFUL !!!!!          #
#        THIS WILL STOP THE LOGICAL STANDBY APPLY PROCESS                 #
# ----------------------------------------------------------------------- #
#                                                                         #
#   x.   Exit                                                             #
# ----------------------------------------------------------------------- #
#    Enter Task Number:
```

Each of the menu options can be invoked by typing the corresponding numeric value and pressing ENTER. At the end of execution of each script, you will be presented with a message to press any key to continue. Simply pressing any key will re-invoke the DG submenu.

## Checking the Progress

Our first menu option in the logical standby DG submenu exposes all the relative information about how far the logical standby database has progressed. Here's sample output from the first menu option:

```
1
# ----------------------------------------------------------------------- #
#          Executing logical_progress.sql on DB:   MATRIXRT               #
# ----------------------------------------------------------------------- #
Session altered.

APPLIED_SCN LATEST_SCN MINING_SCN RESTART_SCN
----------- ---------- ---------- -----------
 6590562696 6590562726 6590562700  6590562699


APPLIED_TIME       RESTART_TIME       LATEST_TIME
----------------- ----------------- -----------------
06-apr-09 01:00:48 06-apr-09 01:00:49 06-apr-09 01:00:52


Your Apply Lag
--------------------------------------------------------------
+000000000 00:00:04.000000000


Your Standby Redo Lag
--------------------------------------------------------------
+000000000 00:00:01.000000000
```

You can see from the output that the SQL Apply is only 4 seconds behind the newest SCN recorded in the standby redo logs. The output shown here provides information regarding SCN and time in seconds. The most important aspect of monitoring the logical standby is to compare the APPLIED_TIME relative to the LATEST_TIME. In addition, we compare the LATEST_TIME with the system time to review how fast the standby redo logs are being updated.

**NOTE**
*We recommend that both the primary and the standby database servers' time is synchronized with that of the NTP server.*

As a final output, we save you from calculating the delta between the LATEST_TIME and the APPLIED_TIME with the NUMTODSINTERVAL function. You can see from the following queries how the output is being determined:

```
ALTER SESSION SET NLS_DATE_FORMAT='dd-mon-rr hh24:mi:ss';
SELECT APPLIED_SCN, LATEST_SCN, MINING_SCN, RESTART_SCN FROM V$LOGSTDBY_PROGRESS;

SELECT APPLIED_TIME, RESTART_TIME, LATEST_TIME
FROM V$LOGSTDBY_PROGRESS
/

SELECT NUMTODSINTERVAL(LATEST_TIME - APPLIED_TIME,'day')  "Your Apply Lag"
FROM V$LOGSTDBY_PROGRESS;

SELECT NUMTODSINTERVAL(SYSDATE - LATEST_TIME,'day')  "Your Standby Redo Lag"
FROM V$LOGSTDBY_PROGRESS;
```

The view V$LOGSTDBY_PROGRESS provides the single insight into how well the logical standby is keeping up with the primary database. As someone who has to support a logical standby database in a reporting environment, you may have a stringent requirement that the reporting database server (logical standby database) be at least in sync with the primary database by a margin of 15 minutes or so. In some cases, the expectation can be that the reporting database must be in sync with the primary database in almost real time. Even though we can implement the logical standby with the Maximum Protection or Maximum Availability option, SQL Apply still must be able to keep up with the latest SCN written to the standby redo logs. You should monitor your reporting database server on a regular basis to see if your reporting requirements are satisfied. During peak hours, you should monitor the reporting database server to see if SQL Apply can keep in sync. Following is a simple shell script called *logical_check_every_5min.ksh* that wakes up every 5 minutes and appends entries to two log files: logical_progress.log and logical_metalink.log. You can review two log files and determine whether you are able to satisfy your corporate reporting needs. If you cannot accommodate the SQL Apply rate that you are expecting, you may need to set and tune relevant initialization parameters and logical standby attributes. Review Chapter 4 for additional details on logical standby performance tuning.

You should kick off the logical_check_every_5min.ksh script in the background with the nohup option as shown here:

```
nohup logical_check_every_5min.ksh > /tmp/ logical_check_every_5min.log 2>&1 &
```

Here's the complete shell script for you to review:

```
cat logical_check_every_5min.ksh
echo "CURRENT_TIME           APPLIED      APPLIED_TIME      RESTART
RESTART_TIME      LATEST         LATEST_TIME" >>logical_progress.log
echo "                                SCN                               SCN
SCN                         ">>logical_progress.log
echo "------------------ ---------- ------------------ ----------
------------------ ---------- ------------------" >>logical_progress.log

while true
do

echo "
col applied_time for a18
col restart_time for a18
col latest_time for a18
col current_time for a18
set echo off ver off head off feed off lines 255 pages 0 trims on
SELECT to_char(sysdate, 'dd-mon-rr hh24:mi:ss') current_time, APPLIED_SCN, to_
char(APPLIED_TIME, 'dd-mon-rr hh24:mi:ss') APPLIED_TIME,
        RESTART_SCN, to_char(RESTART_TIME, 'dd-mon-rr hh24:mi:ss') RESTART_TIME,
        LATEST_SCN, to_char(LATEST_TIME, 'dd-mon-rr hh24:mi:ss') LATEST_TIME
FROM V\$LOGSTDBY_PROGRESS;
" |sqlplus -s / as sysdba > logical_progress_temp.log
cat logical_progress_temp.log >> logical_progress.log

sleep 300;
done
```

Shown next is a sample output of the logical_progress.log file. The shell script will append an entry into this file every 5 minutes. You can compare the LATEST_TIME and the APPLIED_TIME columns to determine whether SQL Apply is keeping up. Likewise, you can compare the CURRENT_TIME and LATEST_TIME columns to see if any latencies are of concern.

```
CURRENT_TIME            APPLIED         APPLIED_TIME         RESTART         RESTART_TIME
LATEST          LATEST_TIME
                        SCN                                  SCN
SCN
------------------ ---------- ------------------ ---------- ------------------
---------- ------------------
05-apr-09 08:32:31  6590373143 05-apr-09 08:32:18  6590373144 05-apr-09 08:32:18
6590373160 05-apr-09 08:32:27
05-apr-09 08:37:31  6590373844 05-apr-09 08:37:25  6590373845 05-apr-09 08:37:25
6590373852 05-apr-09 08:37:31
05-apr-09 08:42:31  6590374530 05-apr-09 08:42:13  6590374531 05-apr-09 08:42:13
6590374558 05-apr-09 08:42:31
05-apr-09 08:47:32  6590375156 05-apr-09 08:47:07  6590375157 05-apr-09 08:47:07
6590375205 05-apr-09 08:47:31
```

```
05-apr-09 08:52:32  6590375931 05-apr-09 08:52:13  6590375932 05-apr-09 08:52:13
6590375956 05-apr-09 08:52:31
05-apr-09 08:57:32  6590376581 05-apr-09 08:57:23  6590376582 05-apr-09 08:57:23
6590376594 05-apr-09 08:57:29
...
```

## Checking for Events

You can obtain the history on logical standby apply activity by querying the DBA_LOGSTDBY_EVENTS view. This view can provide relevant information to determine the root cause of failures that occur when applying redo data to the logical standby database. Here's a simple query against the DBA_LOGSTDBY_EVENTS view ordered by the event time and the order it was committed on the primary database:

```
cat logical_events.sql
ALTER SESSION SET NLS_DATE_FORMAT  = 'DD-MON-YY HH24:MI:SS';

SET LONG 999999
SET LINES 255
COLUMN STATUS FORMAT A60
SELECT EVENT_TIME, STATUS, EVENT
FROM DBA_LOGSTDBY_EVENTS
ORDER BY EVENT_TIMESTAMP, COMMIT_SCN;
```

Execution of this script yields the following results:

```
EVENT_TIME          STATUS
EVENT
----------------- -----------------------------------------------------------------
------------------------------------------------------------------
17-MAR-09 22:15:37 ORA-16226: DDL skipped due to lack of support
alter database backup controlfile to '/apps/oracle/admin/MATRIX/bkups/control01_

MATRIX1_17Mar09_1818.ctl.bkup'

18-MAR-09 01:00:44 ORA-16226: DDL skipped due to lack of support
alter database backup controlfile to trace
18-MAR-09 01:00:44 ORA-16226: DDL skipped due to lack of support
alter database backup controlfile to '/apps/oracle/admin/MATRIX/bkups/control01_
MATRIX_18Mar09_0100.ctl.bkup'

18-MAR-09 08:22:00 ORA-16226: DDL skipped due to lack of support
-- Create database link

create public database link DBATOOLS

connect to rodba_web identified by **********using 'DBATOOLS'
```

```
18-MAR-09 08:45:47 ORA-02019: connection description for remote database not
found CREATE OR REPLACE VIEW V_WEB_DOCS
 (DOC_ID, DOC_TIMESTAMP, DESCRIPTION, CREATED, FILE_NAME,
CONTENT, DOC_TYPE)
AS
SELECT /*+ first_rows */ DOC_ID, DOC_TIMESTAMP, DESCRIPTION, CREATED, FILE_NAME,
CONTENT, DOC_TYPE
FROM DOCUMENTS
```

By default, only the last 100 records are stored in the DBA_LOGSTDBY_EVENTS view. You can change the amount of history that is preserved with the DBMS_LOGSTDBY.APPLY_SET package procedure.

In the preceding output, you can determine that the root cause of the failures on the logical standby database was the CREATE DATABASE LINK command. Since the CREATE DATABSE LINK command is skipped in the logical standby database, all subsequent CREATE VIEW commands failed. You can also see that the command ALTER DATABASE BACKUP CONTROL is also skipped on the logical standby database. For a complete list of unsupported commands, review Chapter 4.

On the logical standby DG submenu, the option to check the detailed view of the events displays all the columns of the DBA_LOGSTDBY_EVENTS view. In particular, the columns in which we are interested are XIDUSN (Transaction ID undo segment number), XIDSLT (Transaction ID slot number), XIDSQN (Transaction ID sequence number), and STATUS_CODE (Oracle error code associated with the STATUS message).

### Checking Stats

Valuable SQL Apply information such as LogMiner statistics, current state, and status information on the logical standby database can be obtained by querying the V$LOGSTDBY_STATS view. The V$LOGSTDBY_STATS view also exposes the custom logical standby options set by the DBMS_LOGSTDBY.APPLY_SET procedure including the default values. In addition, you can compare the values for transactions applied and transactions ready to determine whether transactions are being applied as fast as they are being read.

Executing the option to check the stats from the logical standby DG Submenu yields the following results:

```
#   Enter Task Number:
4
# --------------------------------------------------------------------- #
#         Executing logical_stats.sql on DB:  MATRIXRT
# --------------------------------------------------------------------- #


NAME                              VALUE
--------------------------------- ---------------------------------------
number of preparers               4
number of appliers                20
maximum SGA for LCR cache         1500
parallel servers in use           27
maximum events recorded           100
preserve commit order             FALSE
```

```
transaction consistency            NONE
record skip errors                 Y
record skip DDL                    Y
record applied DDL                 N
record unsupported operations      N
coordinator state                  IDLE
transactions ready                 8711
transactions applied               8711
coordinator uptime                 200488
realtime logmining                 Y
apply delay                        0
Log Miner session ID               1
txns delivered to client           95226
DML txns delivered                 22860
DDL txns delivered                 323
CTAS txns delivered                77
Recursive txns delivered           72043
Rolled back txns seen              23019
LCRs delivered to client           357570
bytes of redo processed            552773192
bytes paged out                    0
...

...
33 rows selected.
```

In this environment, you can see that attributes for maximum SGA, preparers, appliers, and commit order have been customized to suit the high amount of transactions on the reporting database.

## Checking the Logical Standby Parameters

The DBA_LOGSTDBY_PARAMETERS view provides a list of parameters used by SQL Apply on the logical standby database. Querying on the NAME and VALUE columns, you can ascertain miscellaneous options and settings on the logical standby. Menu option 5 provides a complete output of the DBA_LOGSTDBY_PARAMETERS view:

```
#   Enter Task Number:
5
# -------------------------------------------------------------------- #
#       Executing logical_parameters.sql on DB:  MATRIXRT
# -------------------------------------------------------------------- #


NAME                               VALUE
--------------------------------   --------------------------------
APPLY_SCN                          6557897644
APPLY_SERVERS                      20
FIRST_SCN                          6557896604
GUARD_STANDBY                      READY
LMNR_SID                           1
LOG_AUTO_DELETE                    FALSE
```

```
MAX_SERVERS                     27
MAX_SGA                         1500
PREP_DICT_RECEIVED
PRESERVE_COMMIT_ORDER           FALSE
PRIMARY                         1135258887
_SYNCPOINT_INTERVAL             4294967295

12 rows selected.
```

## Checking the Logical Standby Processes

You can query the DBA_LOGSTDBY_PROCESS view to analyze the current state of each of the SQL Apply processes. During the log mining process, the READER process reads redo records from the standby redo logs or archive logs, the PREPARER process converts the block records into logical change records (LCR), and the BUILDER process groups the LCRs into transactions and manages the LCR cache in the shared pool of the system global area (SGA). As you can see in the following output, you can have multiple PREPARER processes. Also, you will notice that an ORA-16116 error message appears in the STATUS column indicating that there is no work for the processes:

```
#    Enter Task Number:
6
# ------------------------------------------------------------------- #
#         Executing logical_process.sql on DB:   MATRIXRT
# ------------------------------------------------------------------- #
TYPE          SID SERIAL#   LID SPID      HIGH_SCN STATUS
------------- ----- ------- ----- ------- ---------- --------------------------
COORDINATOR   248        1    -1 31451  6590542563 ORA-16116: no work available
READER        245        1     0 31454  6590542573 ORA-16116: no work available
BUILDER       246        1     1 31456  6590542573 ORA-16116: no work available
PREPARER      244        1     2 31458  6590542401 ORA-16116: no work available
PREPARER      241        1     3 31460  6590542542 ORA-16116: no work available
PREPARER      243        1     4 31462  6590542500 ORA-16116: no work available
PREPARER      242        1     5 31464  6590542506 ORA-16116: no work available
ANALYZER      237        1     6 31466  6590542542 ORA-16116: no work available
APPLIER       238        1     7 31468  6590542509 ORA-16116: no work available
APPLIER       236        1     8 31470  6590540298 ORA-16116: no work available
APPLIER       235        1     9 31472  6590512759 ORA-16116: no work available
...
...
```

During the apply phase, the ANALYZER process identifies dependencies; the COORDINATOR process, also known as the LSP process, assigns and coordinates transactions to different APPLIER processes; and the APPLIER process applies transactions to the logical standby database. Again, you will notice multiple numbers of APPLIERS in the preceding output. Here's the simple query to view the logical standby processes:

```
COLUMN LID FORMAT 9999
COLUMN SERIAL# FORMAT 9999
COLUMN SID FORMAT 9999
COL STATUS FOr a55
```

```
SET LINES 255
COL TYPE FOR a12
COL SPID FOR a7
SELECT TYPE, SID, SERIAL#, LOGSTDBY_ID AS LID, SPID, HIGH_SCN, STATUS
FROM V$LOGSTDBY_PROCESS
/
```

The STATUS column informs you what the process is doing or waiting on or whether work is available for it.

## Checking Status Codes of Logical Standby Processes

Again, we will query from the V$LOGSTDBY_PROCESS view to determine the status codes of each of the SQL Apply processes. In this menu option, we provide a high-level summary report categorized by type and status code:

```
prompt 16113 -> Apply change to a particular object
prompt 16116 -> No work available
prompt 16117 -> Processing
prompt 16123 -> Transaction Waiting for Commit Approval
prompt 16124 -> Transaction Waiting on Another Transaction before proceeding

SELECT TYPE, STATUS_CODE,COUNT(1) NO_OF_TXNS
FROM V$LOGSTDBY_PROCESS
GROUP BY TYPE,STATUS_CODE
/
```

Executing menu option 7 from the logical standby DG submenu produces these results:

```
#    Enter Task Number:
7
# --------------------------------------------------------------------- #
#          Executing logical_trx.sql on DB:  MATRIXRT
# --------------------------------------------------------------------- #
16113 -> Apply change to a particular object
16116 -> No work available
16117 -> Processing
16123 -> Transaction Waiting for Commit Approval
16124 -> Transaction Waiting on Another Transaction before proceeding


TYPE                          STATUS_CODE NO_OF_TXNS
----------------------------- ----------- ----------
APPLIER                             16116         20
COORDINATOR                         16116          1
READER                              16116          1
PREPARER                            16116          4
ANALYZER                            16116          1
BUILDER                             16116          1

6 rows selected.
```

In our output, we provide some common status codes that you will likely encounter that can help you quickly assess your situation.

### Checking on Stuck Appliers

Correlating V$SESSION and V$LOGSTDBY_PROCESS, you can identify the events or resources that the session is waiting on. The following query displays a high-level summary of the number of appliers that may be waiting on a specified event:

```
COL EVENT FORMAT A50 TRUNC
SELECT LS.STATUS_CODE, S.EVENT, COUNT(1) No_Of_Appliers
  FROM V$LOGSTDBY_PROCESS LS
      ,V$STREAMS_APPLY_SERVER SAS
      ,V$SESSION S
  WHERE LS.TYPE = 'APPLIER'
--    AND LS.STATUS_CODE IN ( 16124, 16123 )
   AND LS.LOGSTDBY_ID = SAS.SERVER_ID
   AND S.SID = SAS.SID
 GROUP BY LS.STATUS_CODE, S.EVENT;
```

You may want to also add additional filters for the STATUS_CODE column. Filtering on transactions that are waiting for commit approvals with a STATUS_CODE of 16123, you may encounter a similar kind of output, as shown here:

```
STATUS_CODE EVENT                              NO_OF_APPLIERS
----------- ---------------------------------- --------------
      16123 enq: TX - allocate ITL entry       4
      16123 rdbms ipc message                  4
```

Once you identify wait events to be the delaying factor for SQL Apply, you will want to identify the SQL statements that are causing the issue(s) and take corrective tuning measures.

### Checking the LCR for Paging

The LCR Cache is an area of the shared pool where the PREPARER process stages logical change records (LCRs) as it converts redo change blocks to LCRs. If the LCR Cache is not sized adequately, LCR paging can occur. LCR paging is an operation in which the SQL Apply process writes to a SPILL table in the SYSAUX tablespace from memory to disk. LCR paging is a very expensive operation and should be avoided. To determine whether you are experiencing LCR paging, you can execute the following query:

```
SELECT VALUE BYTES
FROM V$LOGSTDBY_STATS
WHERE NAME = 'bytes paged out'
/
```

If a non-zero value is returned from this query, you should execute this query on a periodic basis and determine what transactions are causing LCR paging. Remember that the 'bytes paged out' value is a cumulative value since the SQL Apply process started. If you see this value increasing, you may want to resize the MAX_SGA logical standby parameter.

## Generating Syntax to Skip DDL Transactions

Rarely, conditions will warrant that you skip transactions on the logical standby database. When you face such events, DDL statements such as CREATE TABLE AS SELECT (CTAS) or other DDL statements will typically be a symptom of unsupported DDLs such as CREATE DATABASE LINK. In general, you should never have to skip a Data Manipulation Language (DML) statement. Skipping DML statements can cause logical corruptions on the logical standby database. The following menu option can be helpful when you have to skip a transaction that is causing SQL Apply to halt:

```
#   Enter Task Number:
11
# ----------------------------------------------------------------------- #
#          Executing logical_skip_transactions.sql on DB:  MATRIXRT
# ----------------------------------------------------------------------- #


XIDUSN XIDSLT XIDSQN
------ ------ ------
     2     40 611166
    10     36 958286


To Skip, Execute:
-------------------------------------------------------------------------
EXECUTE DBMS_LOGSTDBY.SKIP_TRANSACTION(2,40,611166);
EXECUTE DBMS_LOGSTDBY.SKIP_TRANSACTION(10,36,958286);
```

The SKIP_TRANSACTION procedure accepts three parameters in the following order for the transaction that is being skipped:

1. Transaction ID undo segment number (XIDUSN)

2. Transaction ID slot number (XIDSLT)

3. Transaction ID sequence number (XIDSQN)

In our example, the following SQL statement is used to generate the syntax to skip transactions on the logical standby:

```
SET NUMWIDTH 6
SET LINES 155

SELECT XIDUSN, XIDSLT, XIDSQN
FROM DBA_LOGSTDBY_EVENTS
WHERE EVENT_TIME = (SELECT MAX(EVENT_TIME) FROM DBA_LOGSTDBY_EVENTS);

SELECT 'EXECUTE DBMS_LOGSTDBY.SKIP_TRANSACTION('||xidusn||','||xidslt||','
||xidsqn||');' "To Skip, Execute:"
FROM DBA_LOGSTDBY_EVENTS
WHERE EVENT_TIME = (SELECT MAX(EVENT_TIME) FROM DBA_LOGSTDBY_EVENTS);
```

We query the latest event from the `DBA_LOGSTDBY_EVENTS` to determine candidate transactions that can be skipped. You should review the `EVENT` column to examine the statement that caused the failure.

### Executing Diagnostics

Another menu option worth noting is the diagnostic script per MetaLink Note 241512.1. This script will generate a rather comprehensive report for troubleshooting purposes. The script generates a log file with the following naming convention in the current directory: *logical_diag_[ORACLE_SID_MONDD_HHMM].out*. Here's a sample name of the output file: *logical_diag_MATRIXRT_Apr06_1058.out*. Because the date, hour, and minute of the day is appended to the output file, the diagnostic script should generate a new file every time you execute the menu option.

### Executing SQL Apply Lag Scheduled Monitoring

We provide another shell script called logical_lag_alert.ksh. We will not include the source code for this shell script in this chapter, but it will be bundled with the tar extract. The logical_lag_alert .ksh shell script is designed to be invoked from the cron job scheduler or as a daemon and will send an alert to the recipients in the event that the SQL Apply lag exceeds the user-defined threshold or if the standby redo log lag exceeds the user-defined threshold specified in minutes. If you are launching the logical_lag_alert.ksh shell script as a daemon, make sure that it is part of the server startup scripts. Alternatively, you can schedule this shell script to run every 5 minutes from cron. You can create a cron job entry that resembles this:

```
0,5,10,15,20,25,30,35,40,45,50,55 * * * * /apps/oracle/general/sh/logical_lag_
alert.ksh MATRIX 10 10 > /tmp/logical_lag_alert.MATRIX.log 2>&1
```

This cron job entry will execute every 5 minutes 24 hours a day, 7 days a week. The logical_lag_alert.ksh script accepts three parameters:

- Database name
- SQL Apply lag threshold in minutes
- Standby redo log lag threshold in minutes

The database name must exist as an entry in the ORATAB file in /etc/oratab or /var/opt/oracle/oratab depending on the operating system. If you do not provide any parameters, the script will spit out an error indicating that several parameters are required before it even starts the main logic. Once all the required parameters are accepted, the shell script will source the Oracle-supplied oraenv file to create or update the `ORACLE_HOME` and `PATH` environment variables.

# Conclusion

Monitoring a Data Guard environment for proper configuration and performance can potentially mitigate risks when it comes to opening the standby database in a disaster recovery situation. First, you must discover settings in the primary database that can possibly corrupt the standby database, such as nologging activities. Second, you must examine various log files such as Oracle alert logs and trace files in a timely manner to capture any errors generated from the inception of the redo buffer on the primary database to the Redo Apply process on the standby database.

Furthermore, you must monitor the performance of the Data Guard environment so that you do not jeopardize the RPO or RTO of the disaster recovery requirements. By checking to see whether your Data Guard configuration follows the industry best practices, you can be assured that you can easily meet your RPO and RTO requirements.

The complete DG Menu, including the logical standby DG submenu, is available for download from either the Oracle Press web site at www.oraclepress.com or from the Data Guard Handbook web site at www.dataguardbook.com. Obviously, we cannot cover every facet of the Data Guard monitoring components but hope to address the common metrics. As new techniques are discovered, we will update our scripts and post revisions on the web site. You are strongly encouraged to check for updates and download the scripts instead of copying the scripts manually.

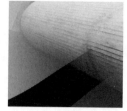

# CHAPTER
## 8

# Switchover and Failover

f you have been reading all the preceding chapters, you should now be fully versed in the Data Guard architecture; standby database creation, management, and monitoring; what the different standby database types offer (and what they do not); and what interfaces you can use to manage Data Guard. But up to now, you have learned only how to set up your database to be protected in the event of some sort of production failure. You haven't yet learned how to use your standby database for the purpose for which it was created: to take over as the production database. This is where *role transition* comes into play.

# Introduction to Role Transition

Role transition is divided into two basic functions: *switchover* and *failover*. Many DBAs use different terms to describe these two functions, such as switchover and switchback or failover and failback, for example. Some even combine or confuse the two functions, believing that they are doing a failover when in fact they are doing a switchover. Let's first clarify the purpose of each function before we dive into the details. The procedures and commands used for each of the three interfaces (SQL*Plus, Data Guard Broker, and Grid Control) are discussed in the appropriate sections.

After both role transition types have been discussed, we will contrast and compare the two methods and the pros and cons of each.

## Switchover

A switchover is the act of changing the primary database to a standby role and changing one of your standby databases to the primary role. This role transition is a planned event in all cases and is safe from data loss because the primary database must complete all redo generation on the production data before allowing the switchover to commence. The *switchback* does not exist as a separate procedure. You would *switchover* to a standby database, and, when you wanted to move production back to the original site, you would perform another *switchover*, but in the reverse direction.

A switchover is usually performed when things are quiet, when no problems are occurring, and you have some reason to move production from the normal site to one of your disaster recovery sites. You might perform a switchover to test your disaster recovery (DR) solution to ensure that everything works as planned when production moves to a different site, that the database starts the correct services, that the middle tier clients can connect, that clients can connect to the middle tier, and so on. Other reasons besides testing can prompt you to perform a switchover in this planned manner. Changes to your hardware configuration (maintenance, new systems), storage changes (newer, faster disks or moving from one storage vendor to another), software changes (OS upgrades, and implementing Real Application Clusters [RAC] or Automatic Storage Management [ASM], upgrading Cluster Ready Services [CRS] or ASM) are some of the reasons you might employ a switchover to reduce the impact on production availability in addition to testing. These scenarios will be discussed in more detail in Chapter 12.

When a switchover is complete, the new primary database will begin sending the new redo to all standby databases, including the original primary database, since it is now a standby database. Remember that when you use the Broker or Grid Control, all the parameters are configured for you automatically after the switchover so that the new primary will send the redo to all standby databases. If you are using SQL*Plus as your management interface, you would have had to preconfigure all of the parameters on your databases before the switchover, which, if you really did read "The Power User Method" in Chapter 2, you will have already done.

## The Switchover Process

Depending on your circumstances (whether you're using RAC or switching over to a logical standby database, for example), you might need to do some preparatory work prior to starting the actual switchover on your primary database, which will be discussed later on in this chapter.

A switchover always starts on the primary database and is completed on the selected standby database regardless of the interface you are using—SQL*Plus, the Broker, or Grid Control. The actual switchover is started by the SQL command ALTER DATABASE COMMIT TO SWITCHOVER TO STANDBY;, which is executed for you if you are using the Broker or Grid Control. When the switchover SQL command is executed at the primary database, redo generation is terminated, all Data Manipulation Language (DML)–related cursors are invalidated and users are either prevented from executing transactions (a logical standby switchover) or terminated (a physical standby switchover), and the current log is archived for each thread. A special switchover marker called the *EOR* (End Of Redo) is then placed in the header of the next sequence for each thread, and the online redo log files are archived a second time, sending the final sequences to the standby databases. If you are performing a physical standby switchover, the primary is closed and the final log switch is done without allowing the primary database to advance the sequence numbers for each thread.

After the EOR redo is sent to the standby databases, the original primary database is finalized as a standby and its control file backed up to the trace file and converted to the correct type of standby control file. The control file backup is recorded in the alert with a line similar to the following:

```
Backup controlfile written to trace file
/scratch/OracleHomes/diag/rdbms/matrix/Matrix/trace/Matrix_ora_32137.trc
```

In the case of a physical standby switchover, the managed recovery process (MRP) is automatically started on the original primary to apply the final archive logs that contain the EOR so that the original primary has processed all redo ever generated. After the EOR has been applied, the database is dismounted and must be restarted as a standby database in at least the MOUNT state.

For a logical standby, this bit of redo does not need to be applied on the original primary by SQL Apply since the database is still open in read-write and the redo has been processed as normal. In this case, the GUARD is enabled, preventing users from modifying the data that is going to be maintained by SQL Apply.

It is extremely important that the EOR redo is received by the standby databases, because a switchover cannot complete without applying the EOR redo. Once the standby databases have received and applied the EOR redo, the switchover is completed at the standby of your choice by the execution of the ALTER DATABASE COMMIT TO SWITCHOVER TO PRIMARY; SQL command. This, too, is automatic if you are using Grid Control or the Broker.

A physical standby switchover will wait for the MRP to exit after processing the EOR redo and then convert the standby control file into a normal production control file. A switchover does require that all readers who were attached using Active Data Guard be disconnected first so the switchover will wait for the sessions to be terminated. All that is left is to open the new primary database for general production use with the ALTER DATABASE OPEN; SQL command.

A logical standby switchover also has to wait for the EOR redo from the primary to be applied and SQL Apply to shut down before the switchover command can complete. Once the EOR has been processed, the GUARD is turned off and production processing can begin. Any users who

**Opening a Physical Standby After Switchover**
Prior to Oracle Database 10g you had to shut down and restart a physical standby database after it became a primary database. In 10g you could go directly to OPEN as long as it had never been opened read-only since it was last started. As of 11g you always go directly to the OPEN state.

were attached to the logical standby database will not have been disconnected during the switchover procedure.

At this point, you have moved production to one of your standby databases. Of course, you have moved only the database role. Middle tiers and clients will have to be moved or redirected depending on your requirements. Physically moving the middle tier and redirecting clients to the new location of the middle tier is an optional step since the production site is not necessarily down. Since a switchover is a planned event, your original middle tier and clients are still capable of running on the original systems and may only need their database connections to be redirected to the new primary database. In either case, you would need to move the required services to the new primary database and clients would connect automatically if you have the connection paths correctly configured. Client failover is discussed in Chapter 11.

# Failover

A failover is an unplanned event that occurs when something bad has happened and you need to move your production database to your DR site. This is a time when people are usually running around trying to figure out what has happened and what needs to be done to get the database back up and running. Phones are ringing from clients asking when the system will be back up. Upper management is roaming the hallways looking for the guilty parties. But you are reading this book, and when that time comes you will be the one calmly sitting at your desk (or even at home in bed), safe in your knowledge that you have prepared for this eventuality and all will be fine. You have a complete failover procedure in place and you have tested it many times using switchovers (if not then you will have after you finish this book). You know that the standby database is OK because it is a database that you can monitor, manage, and even open to check on data—something that you cannot do with a mirroring solution, for example. There is nothing more frightening to a DBA than a dark standby site and you don't know whether it is going to work until you need it. And if that thought doesn't frighten you, remember that bonuses and even careers have been lost due to failover setups that failed when they were needed most.

This is why it is so important that you not only have a complete and tested DR solution, especially for your Oracle database, but that you trust your DR solution so that you are ready to move at a moment's notice when needed. It makes no sense at all to spend the time, effort, and money setting up a DR solution only to avoid using it when you experience a production failure. This does not mean that you always have to failover. Your setup may be so complex that it is easier to solve a problem in the short term instead of resorting to a failover. Or you might be in a position to lose more data than you'd like if you perform a failover. But you do need to be ready to failover when it is necessary.

## The Failover Process

Unlike a switchover, which begins on the primary, no primary is involved in the failover, so there is no possibility of doing a switchover. If the primary is still available, why would you be doing a failover in the first place? As with a switchover, Data Guard must finish up all possible redo before the role transition can be completed. Once you have decided to perform a failover and you've chosen the standby database that will become the primary database (and understood the data loss, if any), you will begin the failover process by telling Data Guard to apply all remaining redo that can be safely applied.

In the case of a physical standby, the finish-up-all-the-redo command will actually cause Data Guard to emulate a switchover in the sense that the EOR marker will be added to the current standby redo log file header and archived just as if that marker came from the primary database. Once this final redo has been applied, the MRP will exit and you can finish the failover using the same switchover command you would normally use to convert a physical standby to a primary database. The idea behind this was to put the physical standby into the same state it would be in if you were performing a switchover, so that the same steps can occur. The control file is converted to a normal production control file, and you finish by opening the database normally for read-write.

A logical standby failover is somewhat different, since the standby database is already open for read-write. Like the switchover, the failover command also instructs SQL Apply to perform the EOR processing and apply all the remaining redo possible, converts the control file to a production control file (essentially activating the standby database), and removes the GUARD so that all data can be updated as usual.

Once the failover is complete, the new primary will be running in Maximum Performance mode even if it were previously running in Maximum Availability or Maximum Protection mode. To return to the proper level, you will have to reinstate the primary or add another standby database and then manually execute the steps (either in SQL*Plus, DGMGRL, or Grid Control) necessary to raise the protection mode back to the desired level. This does mean that if you were running in Maximum Protection mode you will have to suffer yet another outage to bounce the new primary database, as Maximum Protection mode requires the database to be in the mount state before the protection mode can be raised to that level.

## Failover and Data Loss

In both physical and logical standby database failover, there is always the potential for data loss, even if you have configured your Data Guard setup for Maximum Availability. The only absolute zero data loss mode is Maximum Protection, where the primary database would be aborted if no standby database were available to receive the redo for each and every transaction. Maximum Availability can guarantee zero data loss only if the primary and standby were synchronized at the time of the production failure. If the network were to go down for a period of time and you were forced to execute a failover before the two databases could be resynchronized, you would lose any data that was generated at the primary during the network outage period. This is sometimes referred to as a "double failure" for which Maximum Availability cannot provide zero data loss.

Generally, however, data loss is encountered in situations in which you are running in the default Maximum Performance mode (or unsynchronized). The topic of data loss was introduced in Chapters 1 and 2 where the protection modes were discussed. To help you fully understand why data loss occurs, we will expand on the details of a failover and what causes data loss in addition to the network down situation already mentioned.

### Partial Archive Logs

If you use ARCH or ASYNC without standby redo log (SRL) files, Data Guard writes the incoming redo directly to an archive log file at the standby database. If you were operating in this manner in versions of Data Guard prior to 10.2.0.3, then a disconnect from the primary Data Guard would leave a nonregistered partial archive log file on the standby server. This was an attempt to help you avoid some of the data loss if you had to failover. Since this file would ruin your standby database if you manually applied it without doing a failover, Data Guard no longer leaves partial archive log files on disk. Use SRL files to avoid data loss.

During normal operation, Data Guard's apply services, regardless of standby database type, will process and apply the redo as it comes in from the primary database. But redo can only be applied if there is a commit record for the transaction and that transaction is not dependent on another transaction. Obviously, if you were using ARCH mode (deprecated in Oracle Database 11g) to transport the redo, at failover time you would lose whatever redo was not shipped to the standby database. This means the current online redo log files at the primary and potentially the previous one that was archived but not yet sent to the standby.

When ASYNC is used to transport the redo, Data Guard will send the redo as fast as it can to the standby databases, where it will be written to the SRL. But since you are using Maximum Performance mode, there is no guarantee that all of the redo received by the standby database can be applied when you failover. This is due to the thread merging that must occur at the standby to ensure that all transactions are applied to the standby database in the correct order so Data Guard does not compromise the integrity of the data when the primary database is a RAC. There are implications to single node primary systems as well, which we will discuss at the end of this section. Assuming that you are not using real-time apply, you can see the archive logs at the standby database that have been archived by the standby in Figure 8-1.

The apply process has to figure out in what order it should apply the redo that is contained in the six archive log files. Applying them in sequence number order makes no sense because sequence numbers are not contiguous across the cluster.

As your primary database generates redo, normal cluster-wide locking occurs at the row and block level to prevent one transaction from overwriting the updates made by another transaction. But when the standby receives the same redo generated by those transactions, no locking per se is going on, at least not in the same manner, since only one user (the apply process) is actually processing and applying the transactions. To prevent any corruption, the threads of redo are merged together in SCN order, as shown in Figure 8-2, and applied on the standby databases. In this manner, the redo cannot be written to disk in the incorrect order.

A transaction that updates a block, for example, cannot be processed before another transaction that updated the same block but on a different thread and at a previous time. This is usually referred to as a *dependant transaction*. As the apply process reads the redo, it must go back and forth between the archive logs, looking for the appropriate SCN. The thread merging logically makes the redo streams look like a single stream of redo, as shown in Figure 8-3.

This thread merging is the reason you will see the apply processes waiting for something when it would appear that there is sufficient redo to process. And this is also why data will be lost at failover time.

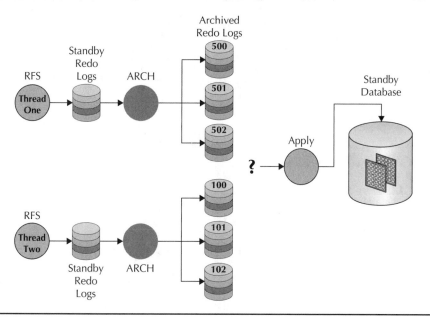

**FIGURE 8-1.** *Redo ready to be applied*

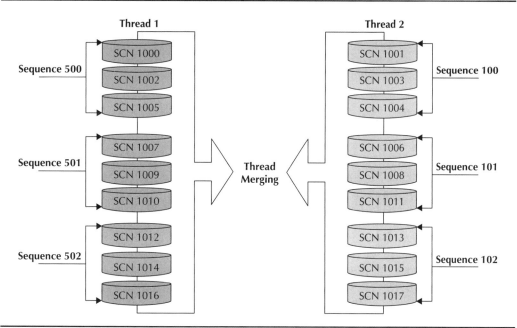

**FIGURE 8-2.** *Transactions by SCN in the redo stream*

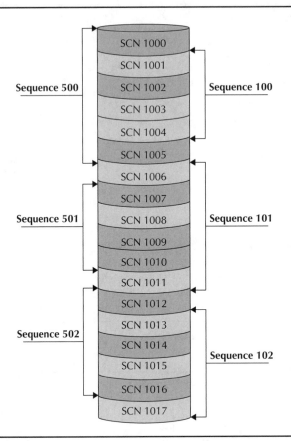

**FIGURE 8-3.** *Merged redo*

When you initiate a failover, the first thing you do is instruct Data Guard to finish applying all the redo that it has received. If you were running real-time apply (with SRL files), then pretty much all the redo that can be applied has been applied. Some redo may still be applied by using the heartbeat redo that each thread sends when it is idle. But Data Guard must look at all of the threads of redo and figure out where the last consistent heartbeat is in the redo stream and then discard all transactions that might be in the redo after that point, as shown in Figure 8-4.

In our example, Thread 2 stopped sending redo at SCN 1008, but Thread 1 continued to send its redo. At failover in Maximum Performance mode, all of the redo after SCN 1009 would be discarded since there is no way for Data Guard to be sure that no transactions in Thread 2's stream that were not received by the standby which should be applied first. Since heartbeat redo is sent every 6 seconds or so, the general rule of thumb is that you might lose around 6 seconds of redo during a failover when all was running perfectly before the failure. But this is just a best guess. There is no way to determine exactly how much redo was lost, and whatever number you do come up with is based on redo volume over a period of time, not user transactions.

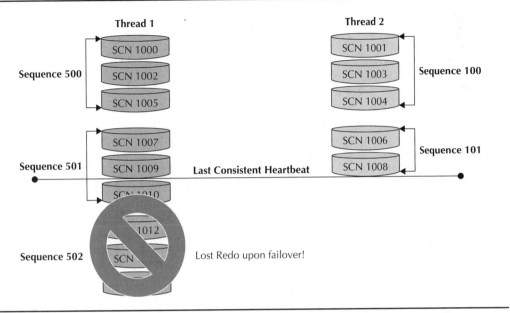

**FIGURE 8-4.** *Lost redo*

In Maximum Availability or Maximum Protection mode, the apply process would know that it was impossible for Thread 2 to have generated any redo after the end of its redo stream and therefore is able to apply the redo past that last consistent heartbeat in the redo stream—that is, all of the transactions past SCN 1009.

This thread merging and failover can have a bigger impact on data loss if some sort of disconnect occurred between the standby and just one of the primary nodes before the failure that required a failover.

So what does that mean? You have multiple RAC nodes on your primary database, and in the event that one of your primary nodes crashes, another node in the cluster will perform crash recovery on the failed instance's redo and ship the final archive log to the standby databases. In that crash recovery log is enough information to tell Data Guard that the instance is in fact down and is no longer generating any redo, and the apply services can safely apply all the redo in that final log when required. In this manner, once that crash recovery archive log is sent to the standbys and processed, that thread is ignored during the failover and the thread merging is done between the surviving threads.

## Closed Threads and Data Guard

As of 10.2, any thread that was shut down is considered to be disabled by Data Guard as long as compatibility was set to 10.2.0.2. If compatibility was not set to 10.2.0.2 or you are using a previous release, those closed threads will have a major impact on data loss (it could increase by one or more complete archive logs of redo). In that case you should manually disable any threads that will be down for a period of time to prevent major data loss.

If one of your primary threads is still generating redo but cannot communicate with the standby (its network link to the standby is down) and the other threads are still sending redo, a failover will have to find a consistent heartbeat redo point at the point at which the thread stopped sending its redo. Since no actual crash occurred when the network connection was lost, none of the surviving threads will perform crash recovery and send that final log notifying Data Guard that the thread is truly down. At failover the thread merging will look at the last log of the disconnected thread and use the last heartbeat in it to define the consistent point, throwing away all the redo that the surviving nodes had been sending all along. The redo that is discarded from Thread 1 in Figure 8-4 would be much larger.

But wait, you say, what about Data Guard's gap resolution? Wouldn't that get the missing logs from the thread that lost its connection prior to the need to do a failover (when you lose the entire cluster/site and so on)? No, it won't. The proactive gap resolution depends on the ping ARCH process on the primary to ask the standbys if they are missing archive logs. But proactive gap handling ping does so only for its own thread, and the primary nodes will not resolve gaps for another thread unless directly asked to do so by a Fetch Archive Log (FAL) request from the standby. The apply process at the standby is responsible for making those FAL requests—but it will make a reactive FAL request only in three cases:

- A log file should be present but is not.
- The apply process is processing a log file but encounters corruption in it.
- An actual hole exists in the sequence of archive logs. (Sequences 100, 101, and 103 are present, but not 102.)

In the case of a lost connection but not a lost instance, none of these three cases exists and the apply services will sit there quite happily sleeping until the next log from that thread arrives and they can continue thread merging. If you encounter this situation, you must either repair the communication problem or shut down that thread and manually resolve the missing log files so you do not risk a large amount of data loss if you had to failover before Data Guard could resolve the gaps itself.

As you can see, a failover in Maximum Performance mode will usually result in some data loss, from at least 6 seconds or so to an unknown amount if the preceding situation occurs. And remember that if some kind of disconnect occurs between the standby and one node in a RAC primary, unless crash recovery exists for that node, Data Guard is going to be functioning using Maximum Performance rules at failover time, even if you were originally in Maximum Availability. If you are wondering what would happen in the lost connection case if you were in Maximum Protection mode, here's the simple answer: If the standby was your last SYNCHRONOUS transport standby and the network connection was lost on only one node, that instance would crash, causing crash recovery to be performed by another instance, and bringing the configuration back in sync.

A final note about data loss: If your setup does not include a RAC primary database and only one thread is to be processed at failover time, there is still no guarantee that you will experience a zero data loss failover in Maximum Performance. It is possible but not a sure thing. You must use at least Maximum Availability and not suffer that dreaded double failure before you have to failover to ensure zero data loss. Only Maximum Protection can positively guarantee zero data loss in all situations in which at least one synchronous standby database survives a failure.

## Switchover vs. Failover

Now that you understand how switchover and failover work, you need to understand when and where you would use each method. Starting with Oracle Database 10g and the use of Flashback Database (discussed in detail in the next section), a failover does not have the same implications toward rebuilding your original primary as a standby that it had in Oracle9i. However, unless you are running in a zero data loss protection mode, a failover is going to lose some data, which is usually the driving force behind your trying to perform switchovers, with failover reserved for those times when it is truly necessary.

Since a switchover has to "drain the redo pipe" (all redo generation has to cease on the primary data), the chance of data loss is impossible. And if you encounter some problem that prevents you from completing the switchover on a standby database, you can always go back to your original primary and be back in business with very little effort. With a failover, you always have to go through the reinstatement procedure (which requires that Flashback Database be enabled before you failed over), which involves more steps and time—something you probably don't want to be involved in if you don't have to be.

In any of your planned outages, you should be using a switchover, and if you have the luxury of even a small amount of notice before an unplanned outage, try a switchover. If it fails to complete on the primary database before the production site becomes unavailable, you can always failover to the standby database. Since it does not normally take much time to send that last EOR redo, chances are the switchover will succeed.

# Flashback Technologies and Data Guard

We kept the topic of flashback in this chapter because it plays an important role in failover. You need to use flashback to undo any error that occurred on the primary database. Flashback is also extremely important when you're getting back to a protected setup as soon as possible after a failure of the primary database or the entire production site. In this section, we will briefly discuss various ways you can use Flashback Database with Data Guard. You can, in fact, employ Flashback Database even if you are not in the process of doing a failover.

Flashback in an Oracle context covers a lot of ground, and most of it is transparent to Data Guard. All but one of the flashback technologies restores data back to a point in time, generating redo in the process. For example, a *flashback query* puts a row back the way it was at some prior point and generates redo that is then processed by your standby databases, and the same "flashback" is performed there. *Flashback drop* puts an entire table back by removing it from the recycle bin, which generates the necessary metadata redo. The same process applies to the other flashback technologies, except for *Flashback Database,* which uses its own flashback logs and some of the redo to put the entire database back to a previous point in time or SCN. This process does not generate any redo, and when used on the primary database, it also requires that OPEN RESETLOGS be executed to open the database again in a read-write mode.

Flashback Database can be enabled on the primary database, on one or more standby databases, or on any combination of the two. To enable it, you need to be in the MOUNT state, have the flash recovery area configured, set the flashback retention period (DB_FLASHBACK_RETENTION_TARGET), and execute the `ALTER DATABASE FLASHBACK ON;` command.[1] In the Data Guard context, Flashback Database is used in the following circumstances:

- On any standby, to recover data in lieu of a `DELAY` on the apply processing. Flashback Database must be enabled and the retention period set to a period sufficient to recover the data based on your requirements. The flash recovery area will need to be sized to handle the amount of flashback logs generated for the retention period.

- On a physical standby, to open a physical standby database in snapshot mode (read-write for testing). In this case, Flashback Database does not have to be expressly enabled since Data Guard uses a guaranteed restore point (GRP) before opening the physical standby in read-write mode. The retention period is also not required as the flashback logs will be maintained as long as necessary. This also means that you will need to size your flash recovery area accordingly, as there is no concept of a rolling flashback log window. If the flash recovery area runs out of space, not only will the snapshot standby come to a halt, but the incoming redo from the primary database will also be stopped.

- On both the primary and *all* standby databases, if you want to be able to flash the primary database back in time. In this case, Flashback Database must be expressly enabled on all of your databases in the Data Guard setup before the flashback at the primary database occurs. The retention period on the standby databases must also be equal to or greater than the primary database retention period. If you perform a Flashback Database operation on your primary database, you must first stop the apply processes on all standby databases. Once the `OPEN RESETLOGS` command has been executed on the primary database after the flashback, you must flash back each standby database to a point in time prior to the primary flashback. When the redo starts to be transmitted again (with the sequence numbers reset to 1), the standby will recognize the change and recover the standby up to the point of the flashback and then start processing the new redo stream.

- On the primary database, to be able to recover the database after a failover. Flashback Database must be enabled before you failover to a standby in this case, but the retention period needs to be set only to 60 minutes if you do not plan on using Flashback Database, as in the preceding case. Data Guard needs only a little bit of flashback log to move the failed primary back in time so that it can be converted to a standby database and resynchronized with the new primary database. This will be discussed in the next section in detail.

As you can see, you should enable Flashback Database in a Data Guard configuration for many reasons. But do not dismiss the last one too quickly. In today's world, databases are growing at a tremendous rate. As we have said before, it is no longer a matter of *if you will failover* but *when you failover*, and that could mean that you will have to take a long protection outage if you did not have Flashback Database enabled on your original primary, even if your production outage is very short. Having to back up and restore several terabytes of data and then ship them to the original primary site just to get a standby up and running again can take a long time. As we said in Chapter 2, Murphy's Law says you will have a failure of the new production

---

[1] See http://download.oracle.com/docs/cd/B28359_01/backup.111/b28270/rcmconfb.htm#BRADV83993 to read about DB_FLASHBACK_RETENTION_TARGET and ALTER DATABASE FLASHBACK ON;.

site before that backup can be completed and resynchronized. Flashback Database enabled on the primary database makes that process take only a few minutes.

# Performing a Switchover

Performing a switchover is not rocket science, at least as far as the Oracle Database and Data Guard are concerned. We realize that many other parts of your environment may need to be included in the switchover process before the database goes down. And they will need to be restarted again afterward, making connections to the new primary database. But other than the client failover we discuss in Chapter 11, it is beyond the scope of this book to go into the details of client and middle tier switchovers—there are just too many possible combinations.

As we mentioned in the beginning of this chapter, you need to take some preparatory steps before starting the switchover. Then, depending on your configuration (RAC or single instance) and target standby (physical or logical), some extra steps may also be necessary.

After we have discussed the preparatory steps, we will go through the actual switchover steps, first for a physical standby database and then for a logical standby database using only SQL*Plus (the Power User Method). After that, we will examine the steps for the Broker and Grid Control. It is important that you understand the SQL*Plus method even if you are using the Broker or Grid Control, because the preparatory work is required in all methods. And some of the tricks and checks are worth doing regardless of your interface to Data Guard.

## Configuration Completeness Check

As we mentioned, unless you are using the Broker or Grid Control, you must make sure that all of the necessary Data Guard parameters have been defined on the primary and the standby database, as outlined in Chapter 2.

Regardless of interface, you must also make sure that the SRL files have been created on the current primary so that it can properly receive the redo when it becomes a standby database. Finally, if you are switching over to a physical standby database, you need to make sure that it has a temporary data file defined. If you followed Chapter 2 and used Recovery Manager (RMAN), this will have been done for you in 11*g*. Prior versions of Oracle required that you manually create the temp file on the physical standby.

**NOTE**
*If you are using the Data Guard Broker, you must make sure that all the prerequisites from Chapter 5 have been met before beginning a role transition.*

If you have not already enabled Flashback Database, now would be a good time to do so. If it is enabled before you begin the switchover, you can use it to return to your original configuration easily if you encounter some kind of failure during the switchover. Since this requires a bounce of the primary, this should be done at some point prior to a switchover when your system can withstand a quick restart of the primary database.

## Preparatory Checks

Our preparatory work for a switchover begins before the pre-switchover work required for your application starts. Since this is a planned event, your first step is to verify that you can in fact perform a switchover. This is done by checking to make sure that the target standby (and preferably your other standby databases as well) is completely synchronized with the current primary database. A switchover cannot complete until it has received and applied all redo up to and including the EOR redo that you are going to generate when you actually start the switchover.

## Verifying That the Standby Has Received All Redo

If you are running in a zero data loss mode (Maximum Availability or Maximum Protection), you can ensure that the target of your switchover is synchronized by examining the V$ARCHIVE_DEST_STATUS view on the primary database:

```
SQL> SELECT DB_UNIQUE_NAME, PROTECTION_MODE, SYNCHRONIZATION_STATUS,
  2> SYNCHRONIZED FROM V$ARCHIVE_DEST_STATUS
DB_UNIQUE_NAME  PROTECTION_MODE      SYNCHRONIZATION_STATUS SYN
--------------- -------------------- ---------------------- ---
NONE            MAXIMUM PERFORMANCE  CHECK CONFIGURATION    NO
matrix_dr0      MAXIMUM AVAILABILITY OK                     YES
NONE            MAXIMUM PERFORMANCE  CHECK CONFIGURATION    NO
NONE            MAXIMUM PERFORMANCE  CHECK CONFIGURATION    NO
NONE            MAXIMUM PERFORMANCE  CHECK CONFIGURATION    NO
NONE            MAXIMUM PERFORMANCE  CHECK CONFIGURATION    NO
NONE            MAXIMUM PERFORMANCE  CHECK CONFIGURATION    NO
NONE            MAXIMUM PERFORMANCE  CHECK CONFIGURATION    NO
NONE            MAXIMUM PERFORMANCE  CHECK CONFIGURATION    NO
NONE            MAXIMUM PERFORMANCE  CHECK CONFIGURATION    NO
10 rows selected.
```

As you can see in this above, our target standby (and our only standby) MATRIX_DR0 is synchronized with the primary database. This is sufficient to verify that the standby has received all the redo. But if SYNCHRONIZED does not say YES or you are running in Maximum Performance mode, you need to do a bit more work to verify the redo status. Go to your target standby database and execute the following SQL command:

```
SQL> SELECT CLIENT_PROCESS,PROCESS,SEQUENCE#,STATUS FROM V$MANAGED_STANDBY;
CLIENT_P PROCESS    SEQUENCE#  STATUS
-------- ---------- ---------- ------------
ARCH     ARCH             326 CLOSING
ARCH     ARCH               0 CONNECTED
ARCH     ARCH             327 CLOSING
ARCH     ARCH               0 CONNECTED
N/A      MRP0             328 APPLYING_LOG
LGWR     RFS              328 IDLE
ARCH     RFS                0 IDLE
N/A      RFS                0 IDLE
8 rows selected.
SQL>
```

The output from this command will show you the current sequence that the primary is sending, as evidenced by the CLIENT_PROCESS equal to LGWR, which is sequence 328 in our case. If you are using SYNC or ASYNC, you will get the same result. If, however, you are using ARCH (remember that ARCH has been deprecated but still exists in 11g and previous versions), you should at least see an ARCH to RFS connection with the last archived sequence from the primary, which should be no more than 1 less than the primary, as shown in the following command executed on the primary:

```
SQL> SELECT THREAD#,SEQUENCE#,STATUS FROM V$LOG;
    THREAD#   SEQUENCE# STATUS
---------- ---------- ----------------
         1        328 CURRENT
         1        326 INACTIVE
         1        327 INACTIVE
SQL>
```

If the standby is not receiving the current redo, you cannot switchover. Note that if your primary is a RAC, you should see multiple LGWR to RFS connections, one for each primary thread. You must validate that each primary thread is caught up.

## Checking That the Apply Is Caught Up

Once you have determined that the redo stream is current, you need to make sure that the redo has all been applied to the standby database.

**Redo Apply**    In the case of a physical standby you will see the MRP0 line in the V$MANAGED_ STANDBY query like so:

```
CLIENT_P PROCESS    SEQUENCE#  STATUS
-------- ---------- ---------- ------------
N/A      MRP0                  328 APPLYING_LOG
LGWR     RFS                   328 IDLE
```

If you are switching over to a physical standby and you do not see the MRP0 line, then the apply is not running. To switchover, you must start the apply service and wait for it to catch up with the current redo stream before starting.

If you see the MRP0 line but it has a status of WAIT_FOR_GAP, you cannot switchover until the gap has been resolved.

Remember that a status of WAIT_FOR_LOG means that either you are not running real-time apply or you have specified a DELAY. In the case of a DELAY, you must stop the apply process and restart it using the NODELAY qualifier; otherwise, your switchover will not be able to complete.

**SQL Apply**    If you are performing a switchover to a logical standby, there will be no indication in the V$MANAGED_STANDBY view about the SQL Apply process, just the redo transport. To verify that the logical standby is caught up with the primary, use the V$LOGSTDBY_PROGRESS view. Here's an example:

```
SQL> SELECT APPLIED_SCN, LATEST_SCN, MINING_SCN FROM V$LOGSTDBY_PROGRESS;
APPLIED_SCN   LATEST_SCN MINING_SCN
----------- ----------- ----------
 7178240496   7178240507 7178240507
```

If the redo transport check from V$MANAGED_STANDBY is up to date and the MINING_SCN and LATEST_SCN from the above command are in sync, then the logical standby is caught up and ready to go. If, on the other hand, transport looks correct but the MINING_SCN is behind the LATEST_SCN, you may have a gap. You can check for this by using this SQL command:

```
SQL> SELECT STATUS FROM V$LOGSTDBY_PROCESS WHERE TYPE = 'READER';
STATUS
-----------------------------------------------------------------------
ORA:01291 Waiting for logfile
```

In this case, you have a gap that must be resolved before beginning the switchover, as with a physical standby.

### Canceling Jobs and Backups

Finally, you must cancel any running jobs on the primary database (and disable any new ones from starting) such as RMAN backups, application cleanup jobs, Oracle Text Sync jobs, and so on. In addition, stop any RMAN backups that are currently running on the target standby database as this can interfere with the switchover. For example, to find out if RMAN is running, try the following command:

```
SQL> SELECT PROCESS, OPERATION, R.STATUS, MBYTES_PROCESSED PCT, S.STATUS
      FROM V$RMAN_STATUS R, V$SESSION S WHERE R.SID=S.SID
PROCESS            OPERATION                 STATUS            PCT STATUS
-----------------  ------------------------  ---------------   --- -------
19507              RMAN                      RUNNING             0 ACTIVE
19507              BACKUP BACKUPSET          RUNNING             0 ACTIVE
```

Once you have performed all of the checks in this section and resolved any problems, you are ready to continue. But if you cannot resolve them, you must abandon the switchover.

## Preprocessing Steps

If your standby database passed the mandatory checks discussed so far, you are ready to begin the switchover. Your first step is to start monitoring the alert logs of the primary and the target standby databases. If possible, do a tail -f of each database's alert log. If you are using Windows, you'll find third-party free tools that let you do this if you want. Here's an example on the primary database system:

```
[Matrix] cd $ORACLE_BASE/diag/rdbms
[Matrix] tail -f  ./matrix/Matrix/trace/alert_Matrix.log
Mon Jan 19 13:20:37 2009
Thread 1 cannot allocate new log, sequence 334
Private strand flush not complete
   Current log# 3 seq# 333 mem# 0:
         +DATA/matrix/onlinelog/group_3.297.671727289
   Current log# 3 seq# 333 mem# 1:
         +FLASH/matrix/onlinelog/group_3.256.671727297
LGWR: Standby redo logfile selected to archive thread 1 sequence 334
LGWR: Standby redo logfile selected for thread 1 sequence 334 for
         destination LOG_ARCHIVE_DEST_2
Thread 1 advanced to log sequence 334
   Current log# 1 seq# 334 mem# 0:
         +DATA/matrix/onlinelog/group_1.300.671727255
```

```
Current log# 1 seq# 334 mem# 1:
        +FLASH/matrix/onlinelog/group_1.266.671727263
```

And here's the corresponding target standby alert log:

```
[Matrix] cd $ORACLE_BASE/diag/rdbms
[Matrix] tail -f ./matrix_dr0/Matrix_DR0/trace/alert_Matrix_DR0.log
Mon Jan 19 16:19:49 2009
Primary database is in MAXIMUM AVAILABILITY mode
Standby controlfile consistent with primary
kcrrvslf: active RFS archival for log 6 thread 1 sequence 333
RFS[8]: Successfully opened standby log 5:
        '+DATA/matrix_dr0/onlinelog/group_5.258.671757777'
Mon Jan 19 16:19:51 2009
Media Recovery Waiting for thread 1 sequence 334 (in transit)
Recovery of Online Redo Log: Thread 1 Group 5 Seq 334 Reading mem 0
  Mem# 0: +DATA/matrix_dr0/onlinelog/group_5.258.671757777
  Mem# 1: +FLASH/matrix_dr0/onlinelog/group_5.421.671757783
```

These two alert logs will tell you what is happening during the switchover process, and you should be monitoring them regardless of which interface you are using to manage Data Guard—SQL*Plus, the Broker, or Grid Control.

If you are paranoid (and who isn't?), you can also turn on Data Guard tracing to the maximum so that all tracing information will be written out to the alert log and trace files for diagnostic purposes:

```
SQL> ALTER SYSTEM SET LOG_ARCHIVE_TRACE=8192;
```

But if you set up tracing, remember to turn it off after you are done or you will be generating a lot of information during production:

```
SQL> ALTER SYSTEM SET LOG_ARCHIVE_TRACE=0;
```

In addition, you can define a Flashback Database guaranteed restore point (GRP) on both the primary database and the target standby database that can be used to reverse the switchover. However, if you have not previously enabled Flashback Database on the primary, you would have to bounce the primary to create the GRP (or enable Flashback Database and create the GRP), which may not be something you want to do at this point. If you create the GRP, make sure that you drop it from both databases after the switchover is complete; otherwise, you will be generating permanent Flashback Database logs forever, which will eventually fill up your flash recovery area.

Finally, switch logs at the primary to flush out any current redo and execute the switchover command.

# Switching over to a Physical Standby

Before you can execute the switchover SQL, you must bring the two databases down to one instance each—the primary instance where you are executing the switchover and the standby instance where the MRP0 (Redo Apply) is running. Obviously, if you do not have RAC on either end, you don't need to worry about this step.

Over the years, much discussion has focused on how to shut down the auxiliary instances, IMMEDIATE or ABORT? Or, to put it another way, "slow but sure" versus "fast but risky." Like everything else in a Data Guard configuration (or any other type of DR solution for that matter), this is one of the trade-off decisions you have to make. If you are sure of your setup and want to execute this part of the process as fast as possible, then perform a SHUTDOWN ABORT on the auxiliary instance, but *do not use* ABORT on the instance from where you will execute the switchover. And be aware of the fact that crash recovery is going to be taking place and ultimately you have to wait until all the aborted instances have been recovered and the final redo log sent to the standby database before you can continue.

If you think we are against using ABORT to shut down the auxiliary instances, this is not necessarily the case. We are careful when it comes to our data, and since a switchover is a planned event, what's a few extra minutes? As we have said, if speed is paramount, then ABORT is probably necessary, but use with care. If client connections are the issue, then shut down the listeners before you begin the shutdown and do not restart them until the switchover is complete. In any event, bring the instances down to 1 on each side and do the auxiliary instance shutdown in parallel between the primary and standby databases

After you are down to one instance, do a final check by examining the column SWITCHOVER_STATUS in V$DATABASE as follows:

```
SQL> SELECT SWITCHOVER_STATUS FROM V$DATABASE;
SWITCHOVER_STATUS
--------------------
SESSIONS ACTIVE
```

Since you are going to use the session shutdown capability of Data Guard, you could ignore the fact that some sessions are active on your remaining primary instance. But to find out what is running, look at V$SESSION:

```
SQL> SELECT PROGRAM, TYPE FROM V$SESSION WHERE TYPE='USER';
PROGRAM                                              TYPE
--------------------------------------------------- ----------
emagent@stadu67 (TNS V1-V3)                          USER
emagent@stadu67 (TNS V1-V3)                          USER
OMS                                                  USER
OMS                                                  USER
oracle@stadu67 (J000)                                USER
sqlplus@stadu67 (TNS V1-V3)                          USER
sqlplus@stadu67 (TNS V1-V3)                          USER
```

In our case, it was the Enterprise Manager Database Console. We don't really need to worry about those sessions, but to clear them out, we shut down the DB Console. Once that was done, another look gives us the signal to move ahead:

```
SQL> SELECT SWITCHOVER_STATUS FROM V$DATABASE;
SWITCHOVER_STATUS
--------------------
TO STANDBY
SQL>
```

This is it! Although it may seem like a long road to get here (and all of those checks were worth it), we can now execute the switchover command:

```
SQL> ALTER DATABASE COMMIT TO SWITCHOVER TO PHYSICAL STANDBY
     WITH SESSION SHUTDOWN;
Database altered.
```

You can see what transpired on the primary by examining the tail of the alert log:

```
Mon Jan 19 18:12:23 2009
ALTER DATABASE COMMIT TO SWITCHOVER TO PHYSICAL STANDBY
      WITH SESSION SHUTDOWN
Mon Jan 19 18:12:27 2009
LGWR: Standby redo logfile selected to archive thread 1 sequence 336
LGWR: Standby redo logfile selected for thread 1 sequence 336 for destination
LOG_ARCHIVE_DEST_2
Thread 1 advanced to log sequence 336
...
Active process 17986 user 'lcarpent' program 'oracle@stadu67 (FBDA)'
Active process 17986 user 'lcarpent' program 'oracle@stadu67 (FBDA)'
CLOSE: waiting for server sessions to complete.
CLOSE: all sessions shutdown successfully.
...
Mon Jan 19 18:12:47 2009
Thread 1 closed at log sequence 337
Successful close of redo thread 1
ARCH: Noswitch archival of thread 1, sequence 337
ARCH: End-Of-Redo Branch archival of thread 1 sequence 337
...
Mon Jan 19 18:12:53 2009
Backup controlfile written to trace file
/scratch/OracleHomes/diag/rdbms/matrix/Matrix/trace/Matrix_ora_32137.trc
Archivelog for thread 1 sequence 337 required for standby recovery
...
Mon Jan 19 18:12:56 2009
MRP0 started with pid=21, OS id=1728
MRP0: Background Managed Standby Recovery process started (Matrix)
Fast Parallel Media Recovery NOT enabled
Managed Standby Recovery not using Real Time Apply
 parallel recovery started with 2 processes
Media Recovery Log
 +FLASH/matrix/archivelog/2009_01_19/thread_1_seq_337.351.676577573
Identified End-Of-Redo for thread 1 sequence 337
Resetting standby activation ID 2212007183 (0x83d88d0f)
Media Recovery End-Of-Redo indicator encountered
Media Recovery Applied until change 7591537
MRP0: Media Recovery Complete: End-Of-REDO (Matrix)
MRP0: Background Media Recovery process shutdown (Matrix)
Switchover: Complete - Database shutdown required (Matrix)
Completed: ALTER DATABASE COMMIT TO SWITCHOVER TO PHYSICAL STANDBY
            WITH SESSION SHUTDOWN
```

From this edited output, you can see the steps covered earlier in the chapter:

1.   Switched log files immediately to sequence 336.

2.   Killed off any remaining users.

3.   Closed the database.

4. Put the EOR in sequence 337 (as shown later by the MRP).

5. Switched logs again without allowing an advance in sequence numbers.

6. Wrote out the command to re-create the control file to the trace files.

7. Started the MRP, which processed the EOR in sequence 337 and shut down.

At this point, the primary database has been dismounted, and when it is restarted it will be a physical standby database. To complete the switchover, you must wait for the EOR to be processed at the target physical standby. Examine the tail of the standby alert log and you will see where the MRP processes the EOR and exits:

```
Mon Jan 19 21:11:39 2009
Media Recovery Waiting for thread 1 sequence 336 (in transit)
RFS[8]: Successfully opened standby log 5:
    +DATA/matrix_dr0/onlinelog/group_5.258.671757777'
Recovery of Online Redo Log: Thread 1 Group 5 Seq 336 Reading mem 0
Mon Jan 19 21:11:51 2009
Media Recovery Waiting for thread 1 sequence 337
Mon Jan 19 21:11:58 2009
Redo Shipping Client Connected as PUBLIC
-- Connected User is Valid
RFS[10]: Assigned to RFS process 19665
RFS[10]: Identified database type as 'physical standby'
RFS[10]: Archived Log:
    +FLASH/matrix_dr0/archivelog/2009_01_19/thread_1_seq_337.350.676588325'
Mon Jan 19 21:12:07 2009
Media Recovery Log
    +FLASH/matrix_dr0/archivelog/2009_01_19/thread_1_seq_337.350.676588325
Identified End-Of-Redo for thread 1 sequence 337
Resetting standby activation ID 2212007183 (0x83d88d0f)
Media Recovery End-Of-Redo indicator encountered
Resetting standby activation ID 2212007183 (0x83d88d0f)
MRP0: Media Recovery Complete: End-Of-REDO (Matrix_DR0)
MRP0: Background Media Recovery process shutdown (Matrix_DR0)
```

Once the MRP has shut down after processing the EOR, the SWITCHOVER_STATUS from V$DATABASE will show TO PRIMARY as long as no users are accessing the database. If it says SESSIONS ACTIVE, then use the WITH SESSIONS SHUTDOWN qualifier on the switchover command.

Complete the switchover with the ALTER DATABASE COMMIT TO PRIMARY command:

```
SQL> ALTER DATABASE COMMIT TO SWITCHOVER TO PRIMARY
     WITH SESSION SHUTDOWN;
Database altered.
```

This command finishes up the processing of the switchover by clearing various memory structures as needed and converting the standby control file to a normal database control file. When complete, the standby can be opened as the primary:

```
Mon Jan 19 21:45:17 2009
ALTER DATABASE COMMIT TO SWITCHOVER TO PRIMARY WITH SESSION SHUTDOWN
```

**Stopping the MRP**

The MRP process must complete applying the EOR redo and then exit. In Oracle10g, if you used the THROUGH ALL SWITCHOVER startup qualifier to the MANAGED RECOVERY command, you had to stop the MRP manually before the switchover command could complete on the standby; otherwise it would fail. In Oracle Database 11g, the switchover command will stop the MRP once there is no more redo to apply. The THROUGH ALL SWITCHOVER qualifier has been deprecated since Oracle Database 10g Release 2.

```
ALTER DATABASE SWITCHOVER TO PRIMARY (Matrix_DR0)
Backup controlfile written to trace file <trace>/Matrix_DR0_ora_20944.trc
SwitchOver after complete recovery through change 7591537
...
Online log +DATA/matrix_dr0/onlinelog/group_1.259.671758349: Thread 1 Group 1 was
previously cleared
Online log +DATA/matrix_dr0/onlinelog/group_2.272.671758359: Thread 1 Group 2 was
previously cleared
Online log +DATA/matrix_dr0/onlinelog/group_3.274.671758367: Thread 1 Group 3 was
previously cleared
Standby became primary SCN: 7591535
Converting standby mount to primary mount.
Switchover: Complete - Database mounted as primary (Matrix_DR0)
Completed: ALTER DATABASE COMMIT TO SWITCHOVER TO PRIMARY
          WITH SESSION SHUTDOWN
```

If you used the THROUGH ALL SWITCHOVER startup qualifier for the MRP, the switchover command will stall for a maximum of 15 minutes for the MRP to stop. You will see the line Media Recovery Continuing in the alert log:

```
Mon Jan 19 21:12:07 2009
Media Recovery Log
 +FLASH/matrix_dr0/archivelog/2009_01_19/thread_1_seq_337.350.676588325
Identified End-Of-Redo for thread 1 sequence 337
Resetting standby activation ID 2212007183 (0x83d88d0f)
Media Recovery End-Of-Redo indicator encountered
Media Recovery Continuing
Resetting standby activation ID 2212007183 (0x83d88d0f)
Media Recovery Waiting for thread 1 sequence 338
```

This means that the MRP has been told to ignore the switchover (you used the THROUGH ALL SWITCHOVER clause to start managed recovery). If you encounter this situation, the switchover will cancel the MRP automatically once it has applied the EOR:

```
Mon Jan 19 21:12:27 2009
alter database commit to switchover to primary with session shutdown
ALTER DATABASE SWITCHOVER TO PRIMARY (Matrix_DR0)
Maximum wait for role transition is 15 minutes.
Mon Jan 19 21:12:57 2009
```

```
Switchover: Media recovery is still active
Role Change: Canceling MRP - no more redo to apply
Mon Jan 19 21:12:58 2009
MRP0: Background Media Recovery cancelled with status 16037
ORA-16037: user requested cancel of managed recovery operation
Managed Standby Recovery not using Real Time Apply
Shutting down recovery slaves due to error 16037
Recovery interrupted!
```

The THROUGH ALL SWITCHOVER qualifier has been deprecated since Oracle Database 10g Release 2.

Finish the switchover by opening the new primary database with ALTER DATABASE OPEN, at which point users can start to reconnect. Restart the old primary as a standby and start Redo Apply (the MRP). Of course, the restart of the old primary can be done in parallel with the switchover processing on the standby.

On the new primary, use this command:

```
SQL> ALTER DATABASE OPEN;
```

And on the original primary, now a standby database, use this command:

```
SQL> SHUTDOWN IMMEDIATE
SQL> STARTUP MOUNT
SQL> ALTER DATABASE RECOVER MANAGED STANDBY DATABASE
  2> USING CURRENT LOGFILE DISCONNECT;
```

Then you can start up the auxiliary RAC instances on the primary and standby databases if you are using RAC. Your client switchover will occur based on your service relocation strategy, which is discussed in Chapter 10.

## Switching over to a Logical Standby

The switchover process for a logical standby is somewhat simpler because of improvements in Oracle Database 11g and the fact that a logical standby is already open read-write. But it also has a second set of steps that guarantee the safety of your data if a failure occurs after the switchover but before the new logical standby database can process new transactions.

Remember, though, that when you switchover to a logical standby, any physical standby databases will no longer receive redo from this new primary as they are not physical copies of the new primary but rather of the old primary. Other logical standby databases can be manually reintegrated.

As of Oracle Database 11g, you no longer need to shut down any database instance (primary or logical standby) when you perform a switchover between your primary and a logical standby database. In Oracle Database 10g Release 2, you do need to shut down all auxiliary instances just like a physical standby switchover as long as your COMPATIBILITY is set to 10.2.0.2 or higher. If COMPATIBILITY is not set to 10.2.0.2 or you are using a prior version of Oracle, then not only do you need to shut down the auxiliary instances, but you must disable their threads on both the primary database and the target logical standby database. Once the switchover is complete, you can re-enable the threads and restart the instances.

**NOTE**
*As of Oracle Database 11g, you no longer need to shut down any database instance (primary or logical standby) when you perform a switchover between your primary and a logical standby database.*

As with a physical standby, you can check the `SWITCHOVER_STATUS` column of V$DATABASE to make sure that the primary is in a state to consider a switchover:

```
SQL> SELECT SWITCHOVER_STATUS FROM V$DATABASE;
SWITCHOVER_STATUS
-----------------
TO STANDBY
```

But before you can commence the switchover, you must first prepare the two databases for the operation. Unlike a physical standby, which is an exact copy of the primary, a logical standby could be different, and once the roles have reversed, the new logical standby database needs to know what the new primary looks like so SQL Apply can process the redo stream. To start the preparation, you execute the following statement on the current primary database:

```
ALTER DATABASE PREPARE TO SWITCHOVER TO LOGICAL STANDBY
```

This tells the primary that a role transition could happen and that it needs to allow redo to be shipped to it from a logical standby database.

Normally, a primary database receives redo from another database only if the primary database is the target of a streams downstream capture setup and a streams client process is responsible for receiving and processing the redo. When the primary is ready, it will show `PREPARING SWITCHOVER` in the `SWITCHOVER_STATUS` column of the V$DATABASE view. You then go to the logical standby database that will become the new primary database and tell it to send the preparation information to the primary in its redo stream:

```
ALTER DATABASE PREPARE TO SWITCHOVER TO PRIMARY;
```

The logical standby will then commence a dictionary build and put it into the redo stream of the logical standby, which will be sent to the primary. You do not need to tell the logical standby where to send the redo because it knows where the primary is and only one primary database can be in a Data Guard configuration. While the prepare is running, you will see `PREPARING DICTIONARY` in the `SWITCHOVER_STATUS` column of V$DATABASE view.

The reason for this extra step is to ensure that the new logical standby database knows how to apply the redo from the new primary the moment new primary transactions start to generate redo. If you skip this preparatory step, you will be generating redo from business transactions that will be sent to your logical standby. The new dictionary would then be behind that redo, and if you had a failure of the new primary before the dictionary was sent to the new logical standby, a failover would results in data loss.

Once the dictionary is built and sent, it will show `PREPARING SWITCHOVER` and you can continue. You can check this by looking at the switchover status again. Now it will say `TO LOGICAL STANDBY` instead of `TO STANDBY` as it has received and processed the new dictionary and knows who is going to be the boss:

```
SQL> SELECT SWITCHOVER_STATUS FROM V$DATABASE;
SWITCHOVER_STATUS
-----------------
TO LOGICAL STANDBY
```

At this point, you are not 100-percent committed to the switchover, as the prepare phase can be canceled using the CANCEL command. Cancel switchover on the primary database first:

```
SQL> ALTER DATABASE PREPARE TO SWITCHOVER CANCEL;
```

And then cancel the switchover on the logical standby database:

```
SQL> ALTER DATABASE PREPARE TO SWITCHOVER CANCEL;
```

This will unwind everything that the prepare has done and put the primary back into its normal TO STANDBY state.

If you are committed to your logical standby switchover, the process is pretty much the same as that for a physical standby from this point on. Tell the primary database that it is going to become a logical standby database:

```
ALTER DATABASE COMMIT TO SWITCHOVER TO LOGICAL STANDBY;
```

This will cause the longest outage to your updating users as the switchover waits for all current read-write transactions to commit and prevents any new read-write transaction from starting. If a lot of activity with long-running read-write transactions is occurring on your primary when you issue this command, you could see a significant stall to the users and the time it takes to complete the switchover. Unlike the physical standby switchover, users are not terminated. As mentioned earlier, since this is a planned event, plan accordingly and perform the switchover in a quiet time. When the read-write transactions have all committed, the switchover completes and Data Guard enables the GUARD on the primary to prevent any more updates to the data, as this is now a logical standby database.

**NOTE**
*When you switchover, the SQL Apply GUARD is enabled to its highest level, ALL, which prevents anyone other than a SYSDBA user from updating anything in the logical standby, not just the tables that SQL Apply is maintaining from the primary. If you need to write to the logical standby and previously lowered the guard to STANDBY, you will have to set the guard manually to STANDBY on the new logical standby.*

Querying the switchover status on the logical standby will tell you when it is ready to assume the primary role:

```
SQL> SELECT SWITCHOVER_STATUS FROM V$DATABASE;
SWITCHOVER_STATUS
-----------------
TO PRIMARY
```

Finish the switchover just as you did for the physical standby switchover by executing the COMMIT command on the logical standby:

```
SQL> ALTER DATABASE COMMIT TO SWITCHOVER TO PRIMARY;
Database altered.
```

**NOTE**
*Notice that we did not use the* WITH SESSION SHUTDOWN *on either of the two switchover commands in this case. This is because there is no need to knock users off to do the switchover with a logical standby.*

Since there was no need to shut down any RAC instances, everything on both sides is up and running, and the only thing left to do is to start up SQL Apply on the new logical standby:

```
SQL> ALTER DATABASE START LOGICAL STANDBY APPLY IMMEDIATE;
```

Any user-added objects to the original logical standby (now the primary) would of course not exist in the new logical standby, and their redo would be skipped until you created and instantiated them again in your new logical standby.

That is it! As with physical standby switchover, your client switchover will occur based on your service relocation strategy.

## Using the Broker or Grid Control to Switchover

We went through the Power User Method first in this chapter so that you understand Data Guard's under-the-cover processing, since none of it is exposed to the user when you use DGMGRL or Enterprise Manager to perform the switchover.

Even though you are not using SQL*Plus to perform the switchover, you still need to perform the steps of checking the configuration completeness, setting up the Broker prerequisites, and performing the preparatory steps before you can begin a switchover. You do not necessarily have to do the preprocessing steps, but it cannot hurt. In fact, you can also tail the Broker log as well as the alert log for even more information. The Broker log is in the same directory as the database alert log and begins with *DRC*.

Once you have completed the mandatory checks, you connect to DGMGRL through the target standby database or the primary and perform the switchover:

```
[Matrix] dgmgrl
DGMGRL for Linux: Version 11.1.0.6.0 - Production
Copyright (c) 2000, 2005, Oracle. All rights reserved.
Welcome to DGMGRL, type "help" for information.
DGMGRL> CONNECT sys@MATRIX_DR0
Password:
Connected.
DGMGRL> SWITCHOVER TO MATRIX_DR0;
```

That's about as simple as it can get! No RAC auxiliary instance shutdown and restart for physical standby switchover, no CRS reconfiguration, no restart of the old primary (if performing a physical standby switchover), no manual startup of the apply process—nothing, just a single command.

The Broker does all of the processing for you regardless of the type of standby you are switching to. And Grid Control is just a button click away, as you can see in Figure 8-5.

You select the target standby by clicking the radio button of that standby and clicking Switchover. This will open a confirmation page, where you can choose YES or NO to have Grid Control set up and submit a job to begin the switchover processing. Then it will return to the Data Guard home page. Here, if you have the page refresh set to automatic, you can watch as the switchover processes and the standby database becomes the primary and the primary a standby.

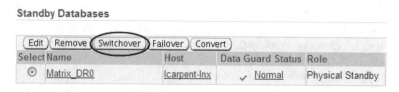

**Standby Databases**

| Select | Name | Host | Data Guard Status | Role |
|--------|------|------|-------------------|------|
| ⊙ | Matrix_DR0 | lcarpent-lnx | ✓ Normal | Physical Standby |

( Edit )( Remove )( Switchover )( Failover )( Convert )

**FIGURE 8-5.**   *Using Grid Control to switchover*

## Switchover Health Check

As you can see, performing a switchover is not a difficult process, even if you use SQL*Plus. The actual commands are very simple and need to be done in order. The bulk of the work is accomplished prior to your even getting close to executing the switchover and are steps that you should be checking all the time:

- Make sure your configuration has been set up correctly and has not been altered.
- Meet all of the Data Guard prerequisites.
- Enable Flashback Database.
- Verify that redo is being sent to the standbys and is being applied.
- Ensure that the standby will not encounter problems during switchover/failover due to nologging DML on the primary if you have not enabled FORCE LOGGING.

A Data Guard configuration that is not set up correctly, not receiving the primary redo, or not applying it is pretty useless when it comes to failover, which is the subject of the next section. As long as you follow the guidelines and rules for configuring your Data Guard implementation and you take the time to understand and perform the switchover steps in the correct manner, you will be able to execute switchovers whenever you need to, whether for testing or other planned outages.

# Performing a Failover

This is it! This is what you have been preparing for ever since you started to read this book: how to get your database back into production as quickly as possible after that dreaded failure. Everything else we have been talking about so far in this book described how to set up your Data Guard configuration correctly to meet the RTO and RPO requirements your business needs, how things work under the covers, and how to use (to some extent) your Data Guard environment. In this section, you can finally test your mettle—you want to be the one sitting calmly at your desk when it seems like the world is ending. You want to prove Evans wrong![2]

When you find that you must perform failover, it is an unplanned event, and there is no way to resolve most of the things that you need to check in the preparatory steps before a switchover. If you have a gap in the redo, that is where the failover will occur; there's no going back and getting the missing redo now, because the primary site is gone. Even though we sometimes talk about trying to resolve a gap after the failure to get as much redo as possible to the standby before

---

[2] Evans's Law says that if you can keep your head when all about you are losing theirs, then you just don't understand the problem.

you failover, in reality, you will not be able to get that data, because it's gone. If you can get it, great; you were extremely lucky this time.

Even though some of the configuration completeness checks can be resolved now (temp files, for example), there is no way to move to zero data loss after the failure at the primary, and you are going to lose data. You made that decision when you configured Data Guard. So plan according to your business requirements and configure for zero data loss before the failure happens!

What do you do before you failover? Stop any jobs (RMAN backups, and so on) and tail the alert log file; that's pretty much it as far as the database is concerned. Your next big task is to figure out which database to failover to if you have more than one standby database. If you only have one, it's a moot point: choose that one. If you have multiple standby databases, you need to examine each one and figure out which one has received the most redo, and then choose that standby database as your failover target.

If you were running in Maximum Protection mode, one standby is guaranteed to be synchronized with the primary database at the time of failure. But if you followed the suggestions in this book and ran with two SYNC standby databases, you need to determine which one has the most redo if both of them are synchronized (look at SYNCHRONIZED in V$ARCHIVE_DEST_STATUS) at the time of failover.

The same thing applies to running in Maximum Availability mode. If a standby were synchronized with the primary database at failure time, it should be your failover target. But if you had two SYNC standby databases that were synchronized at the time of failure (as with Maximum Protection), you also need to figure out which one has the most redo.

And with Maximum Performance, there is no column to examine to determine whether one standby was synchronized or not, as there is no concept of that in Maximum Performance.

Consider the standby databases that you have defined and that meet the protection mode you have defined as your first failover targets. If you have a SYNC standby and an ASYNC standby and are running in Maximum Availability mode, you would choose the SYNC standby first. In addition, choose a physical standby database over a logical standby database if you have both. The logical standby database will easily follow along as a standby to the new primary (you may have to reintegrate it first using Flashback Database) if you failover to a physical standby database, whereas a physical standby database will never cooperate with the new primary if it was a logical standby in a former life.

If you end up with more than one potential failover target, you should examine each one to determine which has the most redo. You can examine (as the Data Guard manual shows) the V$DATAGUARD_STATS view:

```
SQL> SELECT NAME, VALUE, TIME_COMPUTED
      FROM V$DATAGUARD_STATS WHERE NAME LIKE '%lag%';
NAME                  VALUE              TIME_COMPUTED
--------------------  -----------------  -----------------------
apply lag             +00 00:00:00       20-JAN-2009 22:54:18
transport lag         +00 00:00:00       20-JAN-2009 22:54:18
SQL>
```

This will show you where this standby database "thinks" it is in relation to the primary, but it does not show you exactly the last SCN that was received. You can find this information by looking at the standby redo log files using V$STANDBY_LOG:

```
SQL> SELECT THREAD#,SEQUENCE#,LAST_CHANGE#,LAST_TIME FROM V$STANDBY_LOG;
    THREAD#   SEQUENCE# LAST_CHANGE# LAST_TIME
```

```
--------- ---------- ------------ ---------
       1          0            0
       1          5      7671155 21-JAN-09
       0          0            0
       0          0            0
```

**NOTE**
*In versions of Oracle prior to 11g, the* LAST_CHANGE# *and* LAST_
TIME *columns of* V$STANDBY_LOG *are only filled in when the RFS
processes run down after they discover the disconnect from the
primary. You may have to wait until they do run down to get a valid
value from this view at failover time if you are not using Oracle
Database 11g.*

Once you have selected your target, you are ready to failover. The procedure used depends
on the type of standby you have chosen.

## Failing over to a Physical Standby

A failover to a physical standby is executed only on the target standby and uses some of the same
commands used for a switchover. As with a switchover, you must shut down all but the instance
of a RAC standby where the MRP is running. SHUTDOWN IMMEDIATE or ABORT has less importance
other than speed in this case, since no redo is being generated by the standby and hence no real
crash recovery needs to take place.

When those instances are shut down, you must first tell the apply process that the primary is
gone and this standby database is going to become the new primary. You do this by instructing it
to apply all the redo it can using an additional qualifier to the RECOVER MANAGED STANDBY
DATABASE command, FINISH. To do this, you first cancel the MRP and then restart it with the
extra qualifier:

```
SQL> ALTER DATABASE RECOVER MANAGED STANDBY DATABASE CANCEL;
Database altered.
SQL> ALTER DATABASE RECOVER MANAGED STANDBY DATABASE FINISH;
Database altered.
```

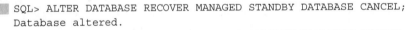

**TIP**
*If you have a gap in the redo and it is not possible for the MRP to
apply all the redo it has received, the* FINISH *command will fail and
you must revert to the old* ALTER DATABASE ACTIVATE PHYSICAL
STANDBY DATABASE; *to failover your standby database, which will
incur data loss from the last redo successfully applied onward. This
command can also be used explicitly to prevent redo from being
applied at failover time.*

This tells the MRP not to wait any longer for more redo and to apply all the redo it can and finish
up by emulating the switchover command at the primary and placing the Terminal EOR (TEOR) in
the header of the last redo log from the primary. You can see this in the alert log output:

```
ALTER DATABASE RECOVER MANAGED STANDBY DATABASE FINISH
Attempt to do a Terminal Recovery (Matrix_DR0)
```

```
Media Recovery Start: Managed Standby Recovery (Matrix_DR0)
Fast Parallel Media Recovery enabled
Managed Standby Recovery not using Real Time Apply
Terminal Recovery timestamp is '01/20/2009 23:56:20'
Terminal Recovery: applying standby redo logs.
Terminal Recovery: thread 1 seq# 377 redo required
Terminal Recovery:
Recovery of Online Redo Log: Thread 1 Group 6 Seq 377 Reading mem 0
  Mem# 0: +DATA/matrix_dr0/onlinelog/group_6.265.671757787
  Mem# 1: +FLASH/matrix_dr0/onlinelog/group_6.420.671757793
Identified End-Of-Redo for thread 1 sequence 377
Incomplete recovery applied all redo ever generated.
Recovery completed through change 7658944 time 01/20/2009 20:55:47
Media Recovery Complete (Matrix_DR0)
Terminal Recovery: successful completion
Resetting standby activation ID 2216964717 (0x8424326d)
Completed: ALTER DATABASE RECOVER MANAGED STANDBY DATABASE FINISH
```

An interesting note regarding the FINISH command is that in prior releases, the existence of RFS processes would cause the failover to fail since the MRP considered the presence of an RFS process evidence that the primary was still functioning. And in that case, why are you failing over? In Oracle Database 10g Release 2, Data Guard added a FORCE qualifier that allows the DBA to force the shutdown of those errant RFS processes. In 11g, FORCE was made the default and the FORCE qualifier deprecated.

Once the FINISH command has completed, the protection mode of the primary database is lowered to Maximum Performance, regardless of its original protection mode. This is done so that the new primary database can open without a standby if you had only one standby database, and it is now the failed primary database. With Maximum Protection mode, it is extremely important that the protection mode is lowered to Maximum Performance in this case, since the absence of a viable standby will prevent the primary database from opening. In addition, the protection level is set to UNPROTECTED at this point in the procedure because Data Guard does not even know if you have a standby database configured to protect it when you open for business:

```
Protection Mode        Protection Level
-------------------- --------------------
MAXIMUM PERFORMANCE  UNPROTECTED
```

The standby database is now in the same place that it was in the switchover when the MRP applied the EOR—in limbo. Now you can issue the switchover command and open the new primary database:

```
SQL> ALTER DATABASE COMMIT TO SWITCHOVER TO PRIMARY WITH SESSION SHUTDOWN;
Database altered.
SQL> ALTER DATABASE OPEN;
Database altered.
SQL>
```

The open will pause while Data Guard tries to establish a connection with the standby databases you have configured, which in our case is the failed primary database. Once it tries a couple of times, the open will finish and the protection level of the database will be set to

**Speeding Up the Open**

When running in Maximum Availability, you can defer the destination used for the original primary database that you defined for switchover until you reinstate the old primary as a standby database. In this manner, Data Guard will not try to attach to the standby before allowing the database to open. If you were running in Maximum Protection mode and no other standby was configured with SYNC transport, you must lower the protection mode to Maximum Performance before performing the failover.

MAXIMUM PERFORMANCE until you manually raise it back to AVAILABILITY or PROTECTION as required:

```
Protection Mode       Protection Level
--------------------  --------------------
MAXIMUM PERFORMANCE   MAXIMUM PERFORMANCE
```

If users were connected to the physical standby using the Active Data Guard option, they will be terminated as with a switchover. You now have a new primary database, and as with switchover, the client failover will occur based on your service relocation strategy.

## Failing over to a Logical Standby

As with physical standby failover, if you have a gap in the redo, you are going to failover to your logical standby with major data loss unless you can somehow find all that missing redo. But this is not all bad news. As with a logical standby switchover, you do not need to shut down any extra RAC instances, nor do you have to terminate any users who might be attached to the logical standby. Once you have decided to failover to your logical standby, you execute one command:

```
SQL> ALTER DATABASE ACTIVATE LOGICAL STANDBY DATABASE FINISH APPLY;
Database altered.
SQL>
```

**CAUTION**
*If you do not specify the FINISH APPLY qualifier to the logical standby activate command, all redo that has not been applied will be discarded. Omitting the FINISH APPLY qualifier should be used only to prevent all the redo from being applied at failover time, after a FLASHBACK DATABASE for example.*

When this command completes, SQL Apply will have applied all the available redo using the same rules applied to the physical standby (remember thread merging and data loss?), converted the control file to a primary control file, and removed the GUARD so that all users can update all data in the database as usual. The same advice on protection modes with physical standby failover mentioned in the last section also applies here, as does client failover.

As with a switchover to a logical standby, you must remember that any physical standby databases will no longer receive redo from this new primary because they are not physical copies of the new primary but rather of the old primary. Other logical standby databases can be manually reintegrated.

# Bringing Back the Old Primary

So what do you do about the original primary database after a failover? Regardless of which type of standby you failed over to, if that was your only standby database you are going to be running unprotected until you can set up a new standby database and get it synchronized.

If you did not follow our suggestion and enable Flashback Database before you had to failover, your only choice is to delete the original primary database (even if it is in perfect condition) and re-create it following the procedures outlined in Chapter 2.

If, on the other hand, you did enable Flashback Database before the primary failure and the original primary database is still intact when the primary site comes back, you can easily bring back the original primary as a standby with a few simple steps. This procedure is usually referred to as *reinstatement*.

**CAUTION**
*Be careful not to let the old primary database come back up as an open read-write primary database after you have failed over to a standby. This could cause your applications to connect to this stale database and begin generating transactions at the same time other client applications are connected to the real primary. We refer to this as a "split brain" situation that is difficult to recover from, at least for those transactions that were run on the old primary by mistake. Never let a failed primary database go beyond the mount phase if you have already failed over to a standby.*

## Reinstating the Primary After a Physical Standby Failover

To begin the process, we need to figure out the point at which our standby database became the primary database. Since redo is applied by SCN, we need the failover SCN from the new primary. When a physical standby becomes the primary, the failover SCN is written to the control file and visible through the column STANDBY_BECAME_PRIMARY_SCN:

```
SQL> SELECT TO_CHAR(STANDBY_BECAME_PRIMARY_SCN) FAILOVER_SCN
     FROM V$DATABASE;
FAILOVER_SCN
----------------------------------------
7658942
```

Armed with this SCN number, we can go back to the original primary database, mount it, flash it back to that SCN, and convert it in place to a physical standby database. Add a restart, and we have a physical standby database again!

```
SQL> STARTUP MOUNT
ORACLE instance started.
Database mounted.
SQL> FLASHBACK DATABASE TO SCN 7658942;
Flashback complete.
SQL> ALTER DATABASE CONVERT TO PHYSICAL STANDBY;
```

```
Database altered.
SQL> SHUTDOWN IMMEDIATE
ORA-01507: database not mounted
ORACLE instance shut down.
SQL> STARTUP MOUNT
ORACLE instance started.
Database mounted.
```

The new primary's Arch ping process will find the standby and immediately begin to resolve any gaps in the redo at the next log switch, and will start sending the current redo stream. Now we can restart the MRP to get the apply going again so we can get caught up as fast as possible:

```
SQL> ALTER DATABASE RECOVER MANAGED STANDBY DATABASE
     USING CURRENT LOGFILE DISCONNECT;
Database altered.
SQL>
```

We now have a running physical standby that is at SCN 7658942, and the MRP will start to look for redo from that point on. In the normal sequence of events, the MRP will need the redo that is contained in sequence number 377, because that is where we were on the original primary when the failure happened. Remember that, unlike a switchover, which forces a log switch followed by the EOR in the header of the next log, the FINISH command puts the EOR into the header of the current log file. This brings us back to the subject of THROUGH ALL SWITCHOVER. If we had specified this deprecated qualifier when we started the MRP, then this EOR would be ignored and the apply would continue. Since we did not use it this time, the MRP stopped. But this also told us that it knows there is more redo beyond the EOR archive log:

```
Media Recovery Log
+FLASH/matrix/archivelog/2009_01_20/thread_1_seq_377.370.676680217
Identified End-Of-Redo for thread 1 sequence 377
Resetting standby activation ID 2216964717 (0x8424326d)
Media Recovery End-Of-Redo indicator encountered
Media Recovery Applied until change 7658944
MRP0: Media Recovery Complete: End-Of-REDO (Matrix)
Media Recovery archivelogs detected beyond End-Of-REDO
MRP0: Background Media Recovery process shutdown (Matrix)
```

All we have to do is restart the MRP once again, and it will continue on until is sees another EOR in the incoming redo at some point in the future. Another interesting point is that a failover in 11g will also reset the sequence numbers for the threads to one much like an open reset logs. In Oracle9i, this would have destroyed our standby database, but not anymore. Since 10g, Data Guard is capable of processing a reset like this and applying only what it needs from the old log stream and then switching over to the new log stream that begins at 1 again:

```
Tue Jan 20 22:45:22 2009
ALTER DATABASE RECOVER MANAGED STANDBY DATABASE
USING CURRENT LOGFILE DISCONNECT
Attempt to start background Managed Standby Recovery process (Matrix)
Tue Jan 20 22:45:22 2009
MRP0 started with pid=30, OS id=21131
MRP0: Background Managed Standby Recovery process started (Matrix)
```

```
Fast Parallel Media Recovery enabled
Managed Standby Recovery starting Real Time Apply
…
 parallel recovery started with 2 processes
Waiting for all non-current ORLs to be archived...
Media Recovery Log
+FLASH/matrix/archivelog/2009_01_20/thread_1_seq_1.372.676680255
Media Recovery Log
+FLASH/matrix/archivelog/2009_01_20/thread_1_seq_2.517.676680255
Completed: ALTER DATABASE RECOVER MANAGED STANDBY DATABASE
          USING CURRENT LOGFILE DISCONNECT
```

Data Guard gap resolution will take place and all the missing redo, since the failover will be sent to the standby and applied, bringing us back to synchronization again, and we will once more be protected. When you have some planned downtime, you can execute a switchover and return production processing to the original site, and return the DR site to its usual function, protecting your data.

## Reinstating After a Logical Standby Failover

If you failed over to a logical standby, then you have to reinstate your old primary database as a logical standby. The old primary cannot be a physical standby, since it is not an exact copy of the new primary. During the reinstatement process it will become a physical standby database for a brief moment before becoming a logical standby.

As with a physical standby reinstatement, you must figure out the SCN at which the logical standby became the new primary database. However, unlike the physical standby process, in this process you cannot use the STANDBY_BECAME_PRIMARY_SCN. The SCNs of a logical standby have no direct bearing on the SCNs that the original primary was generating and sending to the logical standby, where SQL Apply converted them into SQL and data and executed them as transactions, generating other SCNs in the logical standby. You must poke around in the logical standby metadata and determine where you need to flash the old primary back to so you can realign it with the new primary using Flashback Database. But you also need to know how far SQL Apply got in the original primary redo stream during the failover, so you can limit how far the old primary recovers, so that it can then become a logical standby. Make sense? OK… the flashback part should be easy to understand—you have to rewind the failed primary just as with the physical reinstatement to some point in the past before the failover. That is referred to as the *flashback SCN*. But since a recovery of the failed primary would try to apply all the redo it could find, it would recover past the point where SQL Apply finished up at the failover. This would put the reinstated primary in the future at the point where the logical standby became the primary, and you'd have to start all over again. This SCN is referred to as the *recovery SCN*. Still doesn't make sense? Well, don't worry, the command you need is well documented. Just run the following SQL on your new primary database:

```
SQL> SELECT merge_change# AS FLASHBACK_SCN, processed_change#
     AS RECOVERY_SCN
     FROM DBA_LOGSTDBY_HISTORY
     WHERE stream_sequence# = (SELECT MAX(stream_sequence#)-1
     FROM DBA_LOGSTDBY_HISTORY);
 FLASHBACK_SCN RECOVERY_SCN
------------- ------------
     7658942      7659569
```

> **NOTE**
> *If you are using Oracle Database 10g, these columns are not present and you have to use a time-based method to reinstate the old primary database rather than this SCN-based method.*

Take the `FLASHBACK_SCN` number and go to the old primary, start it up in the `MOUNT` state, and flash it back to this number. Then, just as with physical standby reinstatement, convert it to a physical standby database:

```
SQL> STARTUP MOUNT
ORACLE instance started.
Database mounted.
SQL> FLASHBACK DATABASE TO SCN 7658942;
Flashback complete.
SQL> ALTER DATABASE CONVERT TO PHYSICAL STANDBY;
Database altered.
SQL> SHUTDOWN IMMEDIATE
ORA-01507: database not mounted
ORACLE instance shut down.
SQL> STARTUP MOUNT
ORACLE instance started.
Database mounted.
```

This is not a physical standby database in the normal sense; it is a physical standby database all by itself, since it has no primary. The new primary has a different `DBID` and `DB_NAME`, and this physical standby will neither receive nor apply the redo from the primary, which would not help anyway since we are still missing the redo from the flashback time to the failover time. So we have to figure out what archive logs we need from the logical standby metadata and hand-feed them to MRP. Back to the new primary—and, using the two SCNs you obtained, execute this command:

```
SQL> SELECT file_name FROM DBA_LOGSTDBY_LOG
     WHERE first_change# <= recovery_scn
     AND next_change#  > flashback_scn;
NAME
------------------------------------------------------------------
+FLASH/matrix/archivelog/2009_01_20/thread_1_seq_376.370.676680217
+FLASH/matrix/archivelog/2009_01_20/thread_1_seq_377.372.676680255
```

This will give you a short list of archive logs that you need to carry back to the old primary and make them available to the MRP when you start it up to continue this reinstatement process. To make them available to the MRP, once they are there, you need to register them as if you were manually resolving a gap, which, in fact, you are:

```
SQL> ALTER DATABASE REGISTER LOGFILE '<from your list>';
```

If all the archive logs returned by the query are not available to be registered at the old primary, then your work is done here and you must rebuild a logical standby following the procedures outlined in Chapter 2. But if all goes well and you have the logs, and the registration was successful, then you can perform the next part: telling the physical standby database just how far you want it to recover and no further. This requires that you use another qualifier to the managed recovery command to start the MRP, using the UNTIL CHANGE syntax:

```
SQL> RECOVER MANAGED STANDBY DATABASE UNTIL CHANGE 7659569;
Database altered.
```

This qualifier instructs the MRP to recover the redo data up to, but not including, the specified SCN which aligns the physical standby with the failover point of the new primary. When done, the MRP exits, and this is where it ends its short life as a physical standby. Activate and open the database:

```
SQL> ALTER DATABASE ACTIVATE STANDBY DATABASE;
Database altered.
SQL> ALTER DATABASE OPEN;
Database altered.
```

Your failed primary database is now ready to assume its role as the new logical standby database. But before it can do this, it needs to know what the new primary looks like so it can process the redo—that is, it needs the LogMiner dictionary. But, unlike the procedure in Chapter 2 where you did the build on the primary and used the MRP to recover up to the build and then let SQL Apply take over, you are already past that point. So you need to tell your new logical standby to ask the primary database for a new copy of the dictionary and all the redo in between. To do this, you use an additional qualifier on the Logical Standby Process (LSP) command called NEW PRIMARY, which instructs SQL Apply to get the dictionary over a database link that you provide:

```
SQL> CREATE PUBLIC DATABASE LINK reinstatelogical
     CONNECT TO system IDENTIFIED BY password
     USING 'service_name_of_new_primary_database';
SQL> ALTER DATABASE START LOGICAL STANDBY
     APPLY NEW PRIMARY reinstatelogical;
Database altered.
```

SQL Apply will connect to the new primary using the database link and retrieve the LogMiner dictionary. Once the dictionary has been built, SQL Apply will apply all the redo sent from the new primary and get itself synchronized.

**NOTE**
*One thing to remember is that SQL Apply will apply redo only for objects that existed in the old primary database before the failover. As with switchover, any user-added objects to the original logical standby (now the primary) would of course not exist and their redo would be skipped until you created and instantiated them again in your new logical standby.*

You now are protected again by your logical standby. This may seem like a cumbersome process, but the steps are few and really not too difficult or time consuming. And executing these steps is always going to be a lot easier and much faster than using a new backup to create a new logical standby database.

## Using the Broker or Grid Control to Failover

So, after all that, are we going to tell you just how easy it is to failover using the Broker or Grid Control? Of course we are! The only difference is the command (or button) used and the fact that you can connect only to the standby since the primary is not there anymore.

```
[Matrix] dgmgrl
DGMGRL for Linux: Version 11.1.0.6.0 - Production
Copyright (c) 2000, 2005, Oracle. All rights reserved.
Welcome to DGMGRL, type "help" for information.
DGMGRL> CONNECT sys@MATRIX_DR0
Password:
Connected.
DGMGRL> FAILOVER TO MATRIX_DR0;
```

As with switchover, the Broker does all of the processing for you. But what about all those reinstatement steps we just went through? That is a lot easier, too. Once you have verified that the old primary is still viable, mount it and execute a single Broker command:

```
DGMGRL> REINSTATE DATABASE MATRIX;
```

If the Broker discovers it is not possible to reinstate the failed primary, it will tell you so, and you must re-create the standby database. Failover with Grid Control is just a button click away, as you can see in Figure 8-6.

Select the target standby of your choice by clicking the radio button of that standby and then clicking Failover. This will take you to a confirmation page where you can say YES or NO to have Grid Control set up and submit a job to begin the failover processing, after which it will return to the Data Guard home page. Set the page refresh to automatic and watch as the failover processes and the standby database becomes the primary and the original primary disabled.

Now, since the original primary has failed, once the failover is complete, the old primary will appear in the Standby Databases grid and Grid Control will mark it as Needs Reinstatement in the Data Guard Status column. (If the Broker tells Grid Control that the old failed primary cannot be reinstated, it will be flagged as Disabled.)

This status is a live link to a confirmation page. Once you click YES, the process will start. However, if the old primary is not mounted, Grid Control will just start and mount the database and the status will remain as Needs Reinstatement. You will have to click the link a second time to start the actual reinstatement process. If it is mounted already, one click is enough. As you can see, the process of failover and reinstatement is much simpler when the Broker is involved. But if you are a Power User, the steps in the preceding sections are for you.

**FIGURE 8-6.** *Using Grid Control to failover*

> **Myth Buster: No One Will Ever Allow Data Guard to Failover Automatically!**
> This is something we have heard a lot. A lot of people now get to sleep at night because the phone doesn't ring when a failure occurs—Data Guard has already moved production processing to the disaster recovery site. Try it, you might like it!

# Automatic Failover

Now that you have gotten this far into this book, it is time to take a walk on the wild side. If you thought that we had a reason for sprinkling information about the Broker and Grid Control throughout this book, especially this chapter, you are right. We wanted you to see how the Broker can simplify the management of Data Guard. But we had an ulterior motive as well.

Over the years, database administrators have been confronted with the requirement of automating as much as possible of their disaster recovery plans so that anyone on duty can engineer a move to the disaster recovery site at the drop of a hat. Everyone is afraid that if only one person knows how to recover the database, that person won't be around when the failure happens. However, despite many people's best efforts and no matter how scripted you make the process, you still need people to get involved before the transition can take place. Once people get involved, decisions have to be made, doubt is thrown into the mix, investigations occur, phone calls happen, and usually errors are made. These are not things you want to happen when your databases are down and your business is on hold. That is why Data Guard implemented Fast-Start Failover. And Fast-Start Failover requires the Broker.

Fast-Start Failover (FSFO) removes the people from the equation. That is not as harsh as it sounds. It means that when there is a problem, there is no room for error, and people make mistakes, especially when they are stressed. It also means that you do not end up relying on a script or document that was written by someone who may no longer work for the company.

## Fast-Start Failover Architecture

The architecture employed by FSFO is a third-member quorum that ensures that the failover occurs only when everything meets the rules you have defined, and the failed primary is never allowed to open after a failover to avoid any chance of the split brain scenario we discussed earlier in this chapter. That is one of the biggest dangers when someone tries to automate a Data Guard failover without FSFO. There is nothing they can do or write a script for that will prevent someone from mistakenly opening the failed primary after their scripts have performed an automatic failover, or firing off a false failover because their scripts cannot get to the primary, yet the users are still working. In both cases, two databases are open for business, acting as the primary database and advertising all the services. This is not a situation you want to be in, because someone's transactions are going to get discarded when your sort it all out.

The third member is called the *Observer*, and its job is to maintain a connection with the primary and the target standby, monitoring the health of the configuration and performing the failover when required. The Observer is also responsible for performing the automatic reinstatement of the failed primary database when it comes back online, if possible. The other two members are the primary database and the standby database, of course, running in a normal configuration setup as we have discussed in this book.

When everything is running according to plan, redo is being shipped from the primary, the standby is applying it, no gaps exist, and communication between all three parties is normal. The Observer is pinging the primary database on a very frequent basis to keep an eye on things, and at the first sign of trouble goes into a countdown state (which you configure). During the countdown state, the Observer continually attempts to reestablish communication with the primary database. If the connection to the primary returns (either the original instance is reachable again or one of the other RAC instances can be reached) before the timer expires, then the Observer will check to make sure things are OK, and when everything is synchronized again, it goes back to its normal watch mode. When the primary is a RAC, the Observer is connected only to one primary instance at a time, and your Broker connect identifier must include all primary RAC instances so that the Observer can try to connect to any one of them after a disconnect; otherwise, you could failover when the primary was still running fine.

If the countdown timer expires before the Observer can reconnect, it then checks with the standby to see if a failover can be executed. At this point, the standby database must respond that it is synchronized as much as required at that time (we will discuss what *as much as required* means later on). If the standby is ready and capable of failover, the Observer initiates the process and the standby database becomes the primary, just as it did in our manual failover.

In certain types of failures, when the Observer is able to reconnect with the failed primary database, it will automatically reinstate the failed primary as a standby if possible, unless you have explicitly told it not to reinstate the failed database automatically. In user-configured failover events, an automatic reinstate is not performed.

As you can see, the Observer is the piece that makes FSFO work. The rest is really just standard Data Guard managed by the Broker. Before we get into configuring FSFO, you need to spend some time thinking about where you are going to put the Observer; otherwise, things may not happen like you expect or want.

## Observer Placement

Only one Observer can exist per Data Guard FSFO configuration, and if that Observer is not running or is not reachable, then your automatic failover ceases to be automatic. Worse, if the Observer is not reachable from the primary, in certain circumstances it can cause a hang of your production database! For example, if you decide to put the Observer on the production system somewhere, a crash of that node will take out the Observer and no failover would occur. You could put it on the middle tier systems and avoid that problem, but then a complete site failure would have the same effect. What about moving the Observer to the standby site and putting it on the same system as the standby? In this case, when the network between the primary database and the standby site goes down, your primary database will hang, waiting for the go-ahead from

---

### Primary Database Shutdown

In 11g, the stalled primary will abort once the countdown period has expired, as it is assumed that a failover occurred. This can be avoided using a FSFO configuration property. In Oracle Database 10g, where FSFO was introduced, the primary database would remain open for readers even when its FSFO rules told it to stop generating redo. The 11g method of shutting down the primary after the threshold expired was implemented in 10.2.0.4 so a primary database that is stalled because of FSFO will always shut down.

the Observer. In the meantime, the Observer has gone into its countdown phase and will failover the standby if the network does not come back in time. All the while your users who are trying to update the primary database are stalled and unable to generate any redo. And the readers are still capable of reading the data until the primary goes down, which is also configurable in Oracle Database 11*g*.

You can see why it is important to put the Observer where it has a better chance of remaining in contact with both the primary and the standby when they themselves remain up and running. That way, a true crash of the primary database, system, or site will cause a failover to occur (if the configuration was synchronized at the time of failure), and a crash of the standby instance, system, or site will not cause a hang of the primary database; it will just temporarily disable FSFO until things get back to normal.

But wait! Does that mean you have to find a place to put the Observer, a system there that matches the systems used by the databases, install Oracle Enterprise Edition (complete with license), and fire up an instance so you can start the Observer? Not at all. The Observer, unlike the databases in your configuration, does not have to be on the same platform or operating system on which the databases reside, and it does not need Oracle EE and an instance (which means no extra license). The Observer can be installed on any system and requires only the Oracle Client Kit for the version of the database you are using (or higher). The only requirement is for TNSNAMES to be set up to allow the Observer to attach to your standby database.

The Observer system is one point of failure for FSFO, however. If the system crashes or becomes unavailable, FSFO is disabled until the Observer comes back. A failure of the primary during this period would require that you enact those manual failover steps as of old. This is where Grid Control really helps, because it can allow you to specify two systems and Oracle homes where the Observer can run. Then, when the main Observer system becomes unreachable and Grid Control cannot restart the Observer there, it will start up the Observer on the other system in your list, getting FSFO re-enabled as quickly as possible. As with any installation of Grid Control, this does require that you install the agent on the Observer systems. We have placed a sample script on www.dataguardbook .com to restart the observer automatically in the event you are not using Grid Control.

## Conditions That Precipitate FSFO

We touched on the subject of events that can cause a FSFO to occur in the previous section "Observer Placement". But failover can occur in a lot more ways, and you can configure events that the Broker can watch for and handle with an immediate failover.

The usual way that a failover will be triggered is when the Observer and the target standby lose their connections with the primary database, but the Observer and the standby database are still communicating. This can be a database crash, a system crash, the loss of the network, or an entire primary site outage—as in a complete power failure of the locality where the primary is running. The threshold will be honored and the failover will not commence until the timer has expired. Since this is an unexpected event and there is no information as to the health of the primary database, the Observer will attempt to reinstate the failed database automatically as a standby when it is restarted.

You can also force a FSFO by performing a `SHUTDOWN ABORT` on the primary database. Of course, if the primary is a RAC, a `SHUTDOWN ABORT` will only cause a failover if the instance being aborted is the last surviving instance and your `FastStartFailoverThreshold` is exceeded. As with the normal lost connection event, the Observer will reinstate the failed primary when it comes back up.

In addition, you can configure FSFO conditions that the Broker will watch for, and, if it sees one of them happening, FSFO will initiate an immediate abort of the primary and a failover as long as the requirements for the failover have been met. These are set in the Broker using the `ENABLE` command. You can configure five specific conditions:

- **"Datafile Offline"** A primary data file is offline due to a write error.

- **"Corrupted Controlfile"** The primary control file is corrupted.

- **"Corrupted Dictionary"** A critical dictionary object in the primary database is corrupted.

- **"Inaccessible Logfile"** The LGWR is unable to write to any member of an online redo log group due to an I/O error.

- **"Stuck Archiver"** A primary ARCH process is unable to archive an online redo log because the archive log destination is full or unavailable.

The Broker is very specific about the condition tag: you must enter them as above or the command will throw an error. The good news is that if the particular condition is already set, no error is returned. You can also instruct the Broker to fire off a failover if a specific ORA error is generated by the primary database. These conditions would be set as follows:

```
ENABLE FAST_START FAILOVER CONDITION "Corrupted Controlfile";
ENABLE FAST_START FAILOVER CONDITION 27102;
```

Three of the conditions are enabled by default in a FSFO configuration, as shown in the follow excerpt from a `SHOW FAST_START FAILOVER` command:

```
Configurable Failover Conditions
    Health Conditions:
      Corrupted Controlfile          YES
      Corrupted Dictionary           YES
      Inaccessible Logfile           NO
      Stuck Archiver                 NO
      Datafile Offline               YES
    Oracle Error Conditions:
      (none)
```

Finally, you can code an application or script to initiate a failover if your monitoring tools discover something that you know to be a problem, such as the clients not being able to connect to the primary database, and failing over would allow them to connect to the DR site and continue processing. Using the `DBMS_DG.INITIATE_FS_FAILOVER` package, your application can request that a failover be initiated immediately:

```
DECLARE STATUS INTEGER;
STATUS := DBMS_DG.INITIATE_FS_FAILOVER (''Failover Requested'')
```

If `STATUS` is retuned as 0, then a failover will commence. Otherwise, one of six possible errors will be returned and the failover will not happen. These are documented in the *PL/SQL Packages and Types Reference* manual.

These user-defined conditions will cause the Broker to shut down the primary database immediately and perform a failover without waiting for the threshold timer to expire. So you will want to use these conditions carefully.

## Enabling Fast-Start Failover

Now that you have decided where you are going to place the Observer and prepared the system for it, and you understand when a failover will occur, you can start setting up FSFO. You must meet several prerequisites before setting up FSFO, most of which we have been discussing throughout this book:

- Use the Broker with all of its prerequisites.

- Enable Flashback Database on both the primary and the standby.

- Set up the configuration correctly for the protection mode.

  - Standby redo log files on both sides

  - Redo transport setup the same in both directions

- Install the Observer system and configure TNSNAMES.

If you have been following the setup and suggestions in this book, you will have already configured your Data Guard implementation to meet all of the prerequisites, with the exception of the Observer system.

To get started, the Broker needs to know which standby will become your FSFO target. In addition, that database in your configuration needs to know that it is the primary that will become the target after a failover. If you have only one standby database, then the Broker knows which one to use (only one choice of course) and will set the properties accordingly. But if you have more than one standby database, you must explicitly tell the Broker which one to use. The next two commands will make that change and can be run in either case:

```
DGMGRL> EDIT DATABASE MATRIX
        SET PROPERTY FastStartFailoverTarget = 'MATRIX_DR0';
Property "faststartfailovertarget" updated
DGMGRL> EDIT DATABASE MATRIX_DR0
        SET PROPERTY FastStartFailoverTarget = 'MATRIX';
Property "faststartfailovertarget" updated
DGMGRL>
```

Now that the Broker knows which two parties are involved in the setup, it also needs to know how long the Observer should wait (its countdown timer) before starting the failover, just in case the primary is not really down. This is referred to as the *Fast-Start Failover threshold* and is a configuration level property, as discussed in Chapter 5.

In general, if you are not using RAC, you can set any value down to 6 seconds (the default is 30) depending on your network's latency and reliability. But if your primary database is a RAC, you need to take into account the cluster reconfiguration and miscount time. When the Observer

### FSFO and Protection Modes

In Oracle Database 10g, where FSFO was introduced, you had to be running in Maximum Availability mode to enable FSFO. In 11g, both Maximum Availability and Maximum Performance modes are supported. You cannot enable FSFO using Maximum Protection mode.

loses its connection to the primary RAC instance to which it was attached, it will try to get reattached to a surviving instance. But that instance may be busy recovering the failed instance and will not answer right away. If its counter expires before a surviving instance can reply, the Observer will start a failover and the primary will hang and eventually abort. A good rule of thumb for setting the threshold counter is the time it takes your RAC primary to evict a node plus 20 seconds. For more information and current thinking on setting your threshold, refer to the MAA Fast-Start Failover paper.[3]

```
DGMGRL> EDIT CONFIGURATION SET PROPERTY FastStartFailoverThreshold = 45;
Property "faststartfailoverthreshold" updated
DGMGRL>
```

Earlier we talked about the standby database responding to the 'Are you ready to failover?' query from the Observer, and we said that the standby database would failover if the standby was synchronized *as much as required* at the time. This required state is determined purely from the standpoint of data loss.

If you are running in Maximum Availability mode, the required maximum amount of data loss is zero. In a zero data loss protection mode, no data loss can be incurred by FSFO, so the standby would reply that it was not able to failover if it was not 100-percent synchronized with the primary at the time the Observer lost its connection to the primary database. If a data loss would occur, the failover is aborted and nothing happens until the primary database comes back and processing continues, or until you choose to manually failover and accept the data loss.

If, on the other hand, you are running in Maximum Performance mode, data loss will occur at any failover. The question is, how much? As we have said many times in this book, you will lose data when you failover in Maximum Performance mode. So FSFO needs to know how much data loss is acceptable. To that end, you must take into account one other property in Maximum Performance mode, `FastStartFailoverLagLimit`. This is pretty much the only place where you can actually control how much data you will lose if you failover. If the amount of data you will lose is greater than the lag limit you set, FSFO will not failover and you must use the manual procedure:

```
DGMGRL> EDIT CONFIGURATION SET PROPERTY FastStartFailoverLagLimit = 60;
Property "faststartfailoverlaglimit" updated
DGMGRL>
```

Here, since we set the lag to 60 seconds, when the Observer asks the question, Are you ready?, the standby will look at the lag limit and determine whether more than 60 seconds' worth of redo would be lost if a failover occurred at the moment. If less than 60 seconds' worth of data will be lost, the failover proceeds. If more redo would be lost than the lag limit, the failover will not occur and nothing happens until the primary database either comes back and processing continues or you choose to failover manually, suffering the larger data loss.

If you are running in Maximum Availability mode, the property will be set but ignored during the failover. You can set three other FSFO properties—two configuration-level properties and one database-level property.

---

[3] See www.oracle.com/technology/deploy/availability/pdf/MAA_WP_10gR2_FastStartFailoverBestPractices.pdf.

The `FastStartFailoverPmyShutdown` property allows you to tell the Broker whether or not it should shut the primary down if the database is in the hung state and a failover could have happened. If this property is set to `TRUE` (the default), whenever the primary hangs due to a lost connection to the Observer and the standby at the same time, the Broker will abort the database after the `FastStartFailoverThreshold` has expired. When set to `FALSE` (which was the way it worked in early releases of 10g), the Broker will not abort the old primary when it is hung, allowing readers who are already attached to continue to read the data. New users and writers will be hung as all redo generation is stalled. Remember, this property will be ignored when FSFO executes a failover because of a user-defined event, as discussed in the previous section.

Whenever FSFO has executed a failover due to a crash or similar event, it will attempt to reinstate the failed primary automatically when it is reachable again. When the failed primary is restarted after the failure, it will mount but not be allowed to open until it can make contact with the Observer. Once that connection is made, the primary will be reinstated and converted into the appropriate standby using the method discussed earlier. You can instruct the Broker not to reinstate the failed primary automatically by setting the property `FastStartFailoverAutoReinstate` to `FALSE`. However, just like the primary shutdown property, this property is ignored if the reason for the failover was due to a user-defined event or a data file offline error. The Broker will never try an automatic reinstatement in these cases, and you must remedy the problem and perform a manual reinstate using the DGMGRL `REINSTATE DATABASE` command.

Finally, if you would like the Observer to use its own connection identifier other than the `DGConnectIdentifier` you entered for the databases when you created the Broker configuration (you might have a different network route you want the Observer to use for example), you can set the `ObserverConnectIdentifier` for each of the two databases in the FSFO configuration.

Even though we have not started the Observer, we can go ahead and enable FSFO at this point and it will become active when the Observer is started. But if you have not set up everything correctly, you will get the following:

```
DGMGRL> ENABLE FAST_START FAILOVER;
Error: ORA-16651: requirements not met for enabling fast-start failover
```

A quick `oerr ORA 16651` will give you a nice list of what you need to check. Fix the problem and try again:

```
DGMGRL> ENABLE FAST_START FAILOVER;
Enabled.
DGMGRL> SHOW FAST_START FAILOVER;
Fast-Start Failover: ENABLED
   Threshold:          45 seconds
   Target:             matrix_dr0
   Observer:           (none)
   Lag Limit:          60 seconds (not in use)
   Shutdown Primary:   TRUE
   Auto-reinstate:     TRUE
Configurable Failover Conditions
```

```
      Health Conditions:
        Corrupted Controlfile              YES
        Corrupted Dictionary               YES
        Inaccessible Logfile                NO
        Stuck Archiver                      NO
        Datafile Offline                   YES
      Oracle Error Conditions:
        (none)
DGMGRL>
```

Now you can see exactly what you have configured. The only thing left to do is to start the Observer on its system. When the Observer starts, it will open a file called FSFO.dat in the current directory by default, where it will store its configuration information about the FSFO setup it is controlling. Since it is possible to have more than one Observer on the same system controlling multiple FSFO configurations, it is a good idea to qualify where this file should go and what name it should use. This is so the multiple Observers do not get into a fight about who owns FSFO.dat and there is no chance that an Observer might get the wrong configuration file. This is done by placing the FILE qualifier onto the START command:

```
[Matrix] dgmgrl sys/oracle@matrix_dr0
DGMGRL for Linux: Version 11.1.0.6.0 - Production
Copyright (c) 2000, 2005, Oracle. All rights reserved.
Welcome to DGMGRL, type "help" for information.
Connected.
DGMGRL> START OBSERVER FILE=<Your Path>/Matrix.dat;
Observer started
```

The Observer will stay in this window until you stop it from another DGMGRL session with STOP OBSERVER, and it will output what it is doing directly into the window. We'll leave it like that so we can cut and paste the output for examples here, but you should redirect the DGMGRL output to a log file for future reference by using the -logfile qualifier when you log in to DGMGRL on the Observer system:

```
dgmgrl -logfile <Your Path>/Matrix.log sys/oracle@matrix_dr0
```

When you start the Observer from Grid Control, it will place the data file for each Observer in the Oracle Home dbs directory with a filename of afo#####.dat, where the ##### is a unique number and the log files in the rdbms/log directory with a name of dgmgrl#####.log. And remember that Grid Control will automatically attempt to restart the Observer if it fails and will restart on another system if the first system itself fails.

A SHOW CONFIGURATION VERBOSE command will show the Observer running, and you are ready for automatic failover:

```
DGMGRL> SHOW CONFIGURATION VERBOSE;
Configuration
  Name:                 matrix
  Enabled:              YES
  Protection Mode:      MaxAvailability
  Databases:
    matrix     - Primary database
    matrix_dr0 - Physical standby database
               - Fast-Start Failover target
```

```
Fast-Start Failover: ENABLED
  Threshold:          45 seconds
  Target:             matrix_dr0
  Observer:           stadu67
  Lag Limit:          60 seconds (not in use)
  Shutdown Primary:   TRUE
  Auto-reinstate:     TRUE
Current status for "matrix":
SUCCESS
```

The simplest way to test FSFO is to perform a SHUTDOWN ABORT on the primary database. When the primary goes down, the Observer will detect the crash and start its countdown. After the countdown expires, it will initiate the failover. In the Observer window, you can see what the Observer is doing:

```
DGMGRL> START OBSERVER;
Observer started
16:58:50.43  Friday, January 23, 2009
Initiating Fast-Start Failover to database "matrix_dr0"...
Performing failover NOW, please wait...
Failover succeeded, new primary is "matrix_dr0"
17:01:32.76  Friday, January 23, 2009
```

Production is now running on our standby database, Matrix_DR0, and all is well, with the exception of our failed primary database:

```
DGMGRL> SHOW CONFIGURATION VERBOSE;
Configuration
  Name:               matrix
  Enabled:            YES
  Protection Mode:    MaxAvailability
  Databases:
    matrix_dr0 - Primary database
    matrix     - Physical standby database (disabled)
               - Fast-Start Failover target
Fast-Start Failover: ENABLED
  Threshold:          45 seconds
  Target:             matrix
  Observer:           stadu67
  Lag Limit:          60 seconds (not in use)
  Shutdown Primary:   TRUE
  Auto-reinstate:     TRUE
Current status for "matrix":
Warning: ORA-16608: one or more databases have warnings
```

The ORA-16608 is issued because Matrix is down. All we have to do to get our original primary database back into the fold and protecting our new primary is to start it up:

```
SQL> STARTUP
ORACLE instance started.
```

```
Total System Global Area  535662592 bytes
Fixed Size                  1301112 bytes
Variable Size             394265992 bytes
Database Buffers          134217728 bytes
Redo Buffers                5877760 bytes
Database mounted.
ORA-16649: possible failover to another database prevents this database being opened
```

As you can see, the Broker prevented the old primary from coming all the way up because it was told a failover had occurred. In the Observer window, you will see where the Observer starts the reinstatement process:

```
17:07:40.89  Friday, January 23, 2009
Initiating reinstatement for database "matrix"...
Reinstating database "matrix", please wait...
Operation requires shutdown of instance "Matrix" on database "matrix"
Shutting down instance "Matrix"...
ORA-01109: database not open
Database dismounted.
ORACLE instance shut down.
Operation requires startup of instance "Matrix" on database "matrix"
Starting instance "Matrix"...
ORACLE instance started.
Database mounted.
Continuing to reinstate database "matrix" ...
Reinstatement of database "matrix" succeeded
17:09:16.32  Friday, January 23, 2009
```

We did not have to do any of the reinstatement steps we went through earlier in this chapter. They were all done for us, and we are now back up on both sides, fully protected and ready for the next failure:

```
DGMGRL> SHOW CONFIGURATION VERBOSE;
Configuration
  Name:              matrix
  Enabled:           YES
  Protection Mode:   MaxAvailability
  Databases:
    matrix_dr0 - Primary database
    matrix     - Physical standby database
               - Fast-Start Failover target
Fast-Start Failover: ENABLED
  Threshold:         45 seconds
  Target:            matrix
  Observer:          stadu67
  Lag Limit:         60 seconds (not in use)
  Shutdown Primary:  TRUE
  Auto-reinstate:    TRUE
Current status for "matrix":
SUCCESS
```

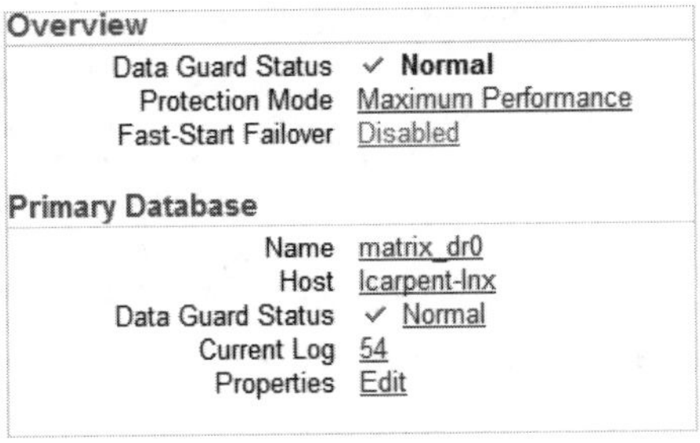

Overview

| | |
|---|---|
| Data Guard Status | ✓ **Normal** |
| Protection Mode | Maximum Performance |
| Fast-Start Failover | Disabled |

**Primary Database**

| | |
|---|---|
| Name | matrix_dr0 |
| Host | lcarpent-lnx |
| Data Guard Status | ✓ Normal |
| Current Log | 54 |
| Properties | Edit |

**FIGURE 8-7.** *Using Grid Control to configure FSFO*

Life is good. So is sleep! But wait, don't go to sleep just yet. Wouldn't you like to see how easy it is to enable FSFO with Grid Control? It will do all of the work we just put you through, including setting up all the prerequisites. We've reset the configuration to its original state, including disabling Flashback Database. On the Data Guard home page, you start the Fast-Start Failover Wizard by clicking the Disabled link next to the FSFO name, as shown in Figure 8-7.

This will take you to the first page, where you will configure the Observer and make any changes to the FSFO settings, as shown in Figures 8-8 and 8-9.

If you had more than one standby database, the wizard would have asked you to make a selection for the FSFO target database. Since you have only the one, it is chosen by default. At the bottom of the page, you will see the Threshold or countdown timer that the Observer will use when a disconnect occurs between it and the primary database. And since you are in Maximum Performance mode, you will also see the Lag Limit or your acceptable data loss limit.

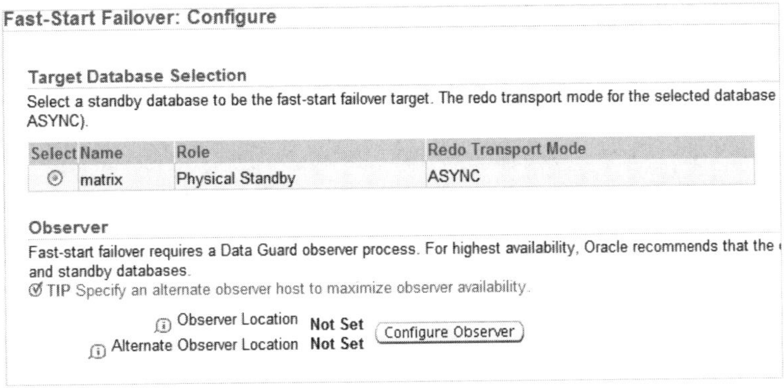

Fast-Start Failover: Configure

**Target Database Selection**

Select a standby database to be the fast-start failover target. The redo transport mode for the selected database ASYNC).

| Select Name | Role | Redo Transport Mode |
|---|---|---|
| ⊙ matrix | Physical Standby | ASYNC |

**Observer**

Fast-start failover requires a Data Guard observer process. For highest availability, Oracle recommends that the and standby databases.
☑ TIP Specify an alternate observer host to maximize observer availability.

ⓘ Observer Location **Not Set** ( Configure Observer )
ⓘ Alternate Observer Location **Not Set**

**FIGURE 8-8.** *Configure the Observer hosts*

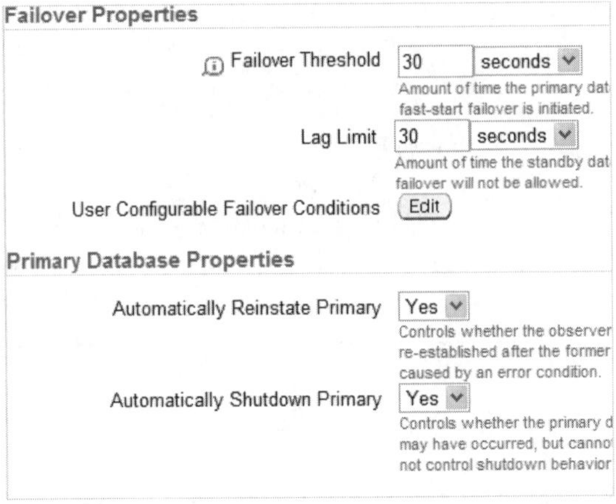

**Failover Properties**

| | | |
|---|---|---|
| ⓘ Failover Threshold | 30 | seconds ⌄ |

Amount of time the primary dat
fast-start failover is initiated.

| | | |
|---|---|---|
| Lag Limit | 30 | seconds ⌄ |

Amount of time the standby dat
failover will not be allowed.

User Configurable Failover Conditions    ( Edit )

**Primary Database Properties**

Automatically Reinstate Primary    [ Yes ⌄ ]

Controls whether the observer
re-established after the former
caused by an error condition.

Automatically Shutdown Primary    [ Yes ⌄ ]

Controls whether the primary d
may have occurred, but canno
not control shutdown behavior

**FIGURE 8-9.** *Configure the FSFO parameters*

At the bottom of this page (shown in Figure 8-9), you can set the two Database Level properties that control automatic reinstatement and automatic primary shutdown.

Clicking Configure Observer (Figure 8-8) will open a page (Figure 8-10) where you can enter two host names that Grid Control is aware of. Remember that the Observer host has to have the Oracle Database Client Kit for the version you are running and the Enterprise Manager Agent installed at a minimum.

You can either directly enter the host names here or use the Search function (the little flashlight) to search for the appropriate hosts. Once you return to the configuration page and click Continue, you will be taken to the Flashback Database configuration page. If Flashback Database was already enabled on both the primary and the FSFO target databases, this page would be skipped. Since you turned Flashback Database off, you have to enable it here.

Figure 8-11 shows the page where you can change the flash recovery area size and the Flashback Database retention time. For purposes of reinstatement, after a failover the default of

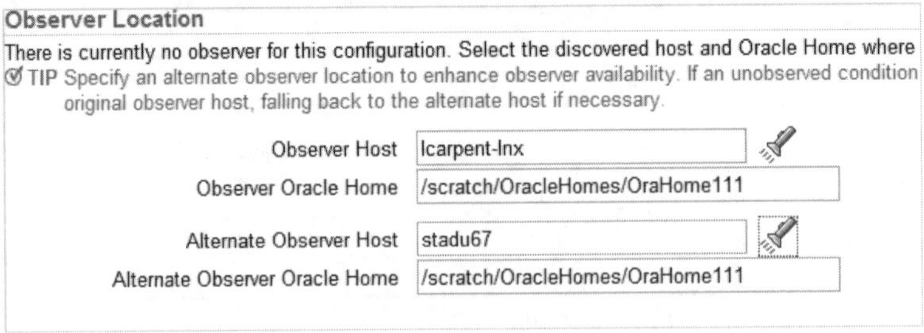

**Observer Location**

There is currently no observer for this configuration. Select the discovered host and Oracle Home where
✔ TIP Specify an alternate observer location to enhance observer availability. If an unobserved condition
     original observer host, falling back to the alternate host if necessary.

| | |
|---|---|
| Observer Host | lcarpent-lnx |
| Observer Oracle Home | /scratch/OracleHomes/OraHome111 |
| Alternate Observer Host | stadu67 |
| Alternate Observer Oracle Home | /scratch/OracleHomes/OraHome111 |

**FIGURE 8-10.** *Enter the Observer hosts*

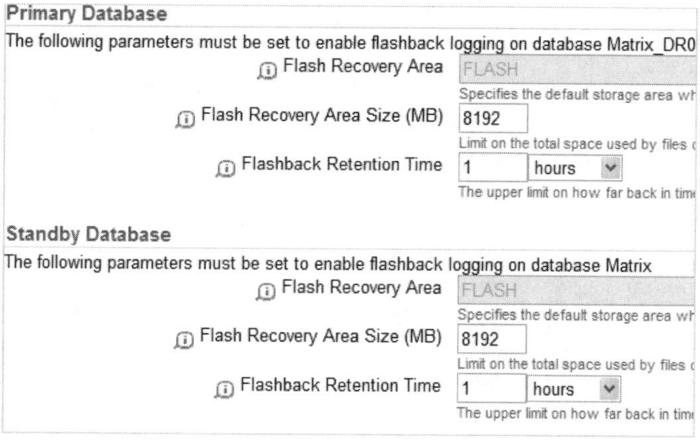

**Primary Database**

The following parameters must be set to enable flashback logging on database Matrix_DR0

Flash Recovery Area        FLASH

Specifies the default storage area wh

Flash Recovery Area Size (MB)    8192

Limit on the total space used by files

Flashback Retention Time    1      hours

The upper limit on how far back in time

**Standby Database**

The following parameters must be set to enable flashback logging on database Matrix

Flash Recovery Area        FLASH

Specifies the default storage area wh

Flash Recovery Area Size (MB)    8192

Limit on the total space used by files

Flashback Retention Time    1      hours

The upper limit on how far back in time

**FIGURE 8-11.** *Configure Flashback Database*

60 minutes is sufficient. You can lengthen this if you plan on using Flashback Database for more than just failed primary reinstatement.

Next you are asked to confirm the FSFO operation, which is very important here, since enabling Flashback Database on our primary will require a restart. If you answer Yes, the process starts. When everything is complete, you are returned to the Data Guard home page, where you can see that FSFO is enabled, which database is the target, and where the Observer is currently running. Figure 8-12 shows the current status.

And that is it! It's much simpler than all those commands in SQL*Plus and DGMGRL that we had to enter. Plus you get the extra benefit of having Grid Control manage your Observer, restarting the Observer if it fails and failing it over to another system if the Observer system fails. This is something you would have to script yourself if you do not use Grid Control to set up FSFO.

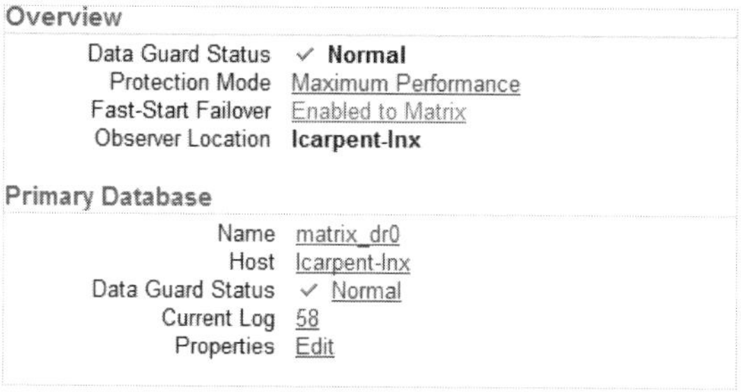

**Overview**

Data Guard Status    ✓ **Normal**
Protection Mode      Maximum Performance
Fast-Start Failover  Enabled to Matrix
Observer Location    **lcarpent-lnx**

**Primary Database**

Name                 matrix_dr0
Host                 lcarpent-lnx
Data Guard Status    ✓ Normal
Current Log          58
Properties           Edit

**FIGURE 8-12.** *Fast-Start Failover enabled*

# A Final Word on Multiple Standbys

We have discussed the topic of the THROUGH ALL SWITCHOVER when using the managed recovery command because it can change the way things operate. To recap, it has been deprecated and was removed (mostly) from the documentation since 10g Release 2. Using it when you start the Redo Apply process will instruct the MRP to process and keep right on working through any EOR it finds in the redo. If you do not use it, the MRP will stop whenever it finds an EOR in the redo. The qualifier was primarily designed for use with other standby databases so that when you performed a switchover or a failover to your target physical standby database those other physical standby databases would keep right on applying.

The problem was, when it was used on the target of a physical standby switchover in 10g, the COMMIT TO SWITCHOVER TO PRIMARY command would hang and ultimately fail, confusing everybody and causing panic. You had to remember to cancel it manually before you started the switchover on the physical standby so the command would work correctly. That problem has been corrected in 11g, where the switchover command, as we have shown, will stop the MRP if required and finish the switchover.

Confusion has also arisen from the fact that the Broker continues to use the qualifier throughout 10g Release 2 and 11g. But the Broker is smart enough always to cancel the MRP and restart it without THROUGH ALL SWITCHOVER before beginning any switchover processing on the target standby, so it never has the hanging problem.

So, where does that leave us, and should we use THROUGH ALL SWITCHOVER or not? If you are using the Broker this is a moot point, because it's all done for you. If you are using SQL*Plus, since the functionality is still there, it is fine to use THROUGH ALL SWITCHOVER, especially if you have multiple physical standby databases. In 11g, you can use THROUGH ALL SWITCHOVER even on your target physical standby, since the switchover command will do the right thing. In 10g, you should not use THROUGH ALL SWITCHOVER on the physical standby you usually switchover to unless you change your procedures always to cancel the MRP and restart it without the qualifier before starting any switchover.

So where does that leave us? The reinstatement of a failed primary database. Again, this is necessary only if you are not using the Broker, as it will just do the right thing for you. When you converted your failed primary back into a physical standby after the failover, it had to process through all the redo it was missing since the standby was failed over, including the archive log with the EOR (TEOR actually) in it. If you do not start the MRP with THROUGH ALL SWITCHOVER, it will stop immediately as that log is always the first one it receives. Again, if you are using 11g, just go ahead and start the MRP with the qualifier and the MRP won't stop. If you are using 10g, this is a judgment call. If you use THROUGH ALL SWITCHOVER you will have to remember to cancel and restart without the qualifier before you start the next switchover process.

# Conclusion

As we said in the beginning of this chapter, you have been learning how to configure Data Guard to suit your requirements throughout this book. But knowing how to failover is what this chapter was really all about. And that is truly the *prime directive* of Data Guard: Protect my data and make it available when production fails. This really is your failover strategy.

Be aware that if you do not trust your failover strategy, it will fail you when you need it most, because you will not have the confidence to use it. You must trust your Data Guard failover strategy 100 percent and have no qualms about using it, even if you do not use Fast-Start Failover.

# CHAPTER
## 9

# Active Data Guard

I n Chapter 2 we discussed the configuration and implementation of physical standby databases. The physical standby database itself is not new to Oracle. In fact, Oracle Database 7.3 was the first version that officially supported standby databases. In Oracle Database 7.3, however, all redo log application had to be performed manually. In Oracle Database 8*i*, the concept of shipping and apply of redo logs was introduced. At the same time, the standby database could be opened in a read-only mode once the application of the logs was stopped. In Oracle Database 9*i*, both the Data Guard Broker and the concept of protection modes to prevent data variances between the primary and standby were introduced. In Oracle Database 9*i* Release 2, logical standby databases were introduced. With Oracle Database 10*g*, we saw the addition of real-time apply for redo data on physical and logical standby databases, and the list goes on and on. Many of the other new features in Oracle Database 10*g* supporting Data Guard's physical standby architecture have paved the way for the implementation of Active Data Guard in Oracle Database 11*g*.

This chapter focuses on four variations to the typical physical Data Guard configuration:

- Physical standby—open read-only

- Snapshot standby—QA and test

- Real Application Testing (RAT)

- Active Data Guard

This chapter will also discuss how you can leverage each of these configurations in the real world to maximize investment in standby and disaster recovery (DR) technologies. In addition, we will include the scripts *necessary* to extend each of the environments beyond the basic physical Data Guard setup. The implementation and configuration scripts are all based on using Data Guard Broker. For more information on the Broker, refer to Chapter 5. Oracle Enterprise Manager Grid Control can also be used for the configuration of read-only, read-write, and snapshot standby databases using a physical standby. Grid Control and its use were discussed in Chapter 6 so you can contrast the differences between using the GUI over the command line interface (CLI) versus Data Guard Broker. Two other key areas, script-based monitoring and troubleshooting, are covered in Chapters 7 and 13, respectively.

# Physical Standby—Open Read-Only

The read-only physical standby database is the simplest extension to the basic physical standby database. In this configuration, applications generally considered to be reporting applications could move the query load they would otherwise put on the primary database to the physical standby database. Moving these read-only operations to the standby database offers a number of advantages that make effective use of the hardware environment in the physical standby that would otherwise remain functionally idle.

Beyond those applications that are exclusively read-only are applications in which a section or module might be read-only. Those modules could be well suited for read-only access to a physical standby database.

While the physical standby is open in read-only mode, the following operations are permitted against it:

- Select statements
- Complex queries
- Calling of stored procedures
- Use of database links
- Use of stored procedures to call remote stored procedures via database links
- Use of `SET ROLE`
- Use of `ALTER SESSION` and `ALTER SYSTEM`

While the physical standby is open in read-only mode, the following operations are disallowed against it:

- Any Data Manipulation Language (DML) except for select statements
- Any Data Definition Language (DDL)
- Access of local sequences
- DMLs on local temporary tables

The primary difference between traditional read-only physical standby databases and Active Data Guard is this: Active Data Guard permits both read-only services and disaster recovery while the standby database is open for operation. This provides for an immediate failover or switchover, without your having to shut down the standby and put it back in managed recovery mode so it can catch up with the recent redo generated by the primary. Most important, you have a real-time reporting database that provides the utmost return on investment while offloading all read-only reporting requirements from the production database.

# Why Read-Only?

We will cover the typical scenarios for which a read-only physical standby would make sense. First and foremost, read-only databases are associated with reporting applications, and as you might suspect, the read-only physical standby is also a prime player in supporting reporting applications. For those who have been involved in performance tuning for any length of time, you know the impact that poorly tuned queries can have on an operational transactional database. These queries are often the direct result of reports built too rapidly to meet business needs without time to tune them adequately, or, even worse, they are the result of ad hoc queries being performed by power users against the production database. The ability to offload and redirect these reporting and ad hoc queries to the read-only physical standby database releases the resources on the primary database that would otherwise be consumed.

Reporting is not the only reason you might open a physical standby in read-only mode. Another application of the read-only physical standby database is in the *document retrieval area*. Medical facilities, police departments, and other businesses that place high demands on the rapid retrieval of large volumes of documents of varying types, while at the same time creating large volumes of new documents, can leverage both the flexibility and scalability that read-only physical standby databases offer.

Even though we're discussing opening a physical standby database in read-only mode, you might have valid reasons for opening the physical standby temporarily in read-write mode, and then returning it to either read-only, or simply a physical standby in managed recovery mode. A physical standby database can be temporarily opened in read-write mode for development, quality assurance (QA) testing, or to resolve break-fix issues, and then reverted to its true physical standby state. This is accomplished through the use of Flashback Database to return the database to a previous point in time. When the database is flashed back, Data Guard automatically synchronizes the standby database with the primary database without the need to re-create the physical standby from a backup copy of the primary database.

## The Downside of Read-Only or Read-Write Mode

In Oracle Database 10g, when the physical standby is opened in read-only or read-write mode, the time it takes to recover from a failure of the primary database and subsequent failover to the standby is lengthened. Once the physical standby has been opened in read-only or read-write mode, it does not apply redo received from the primary database, and hence the primary and standby become inconsistent with one another. In addition, once the physical standby has been opened for either mode, the database must be shut down and restarted following a failover. Because the application of redo is paused while the physical standby is open, the accumulated redo and archive logs must be applied before the physical standby can assume its role as the primary database after a failover. To make matters worse, in Oracle Database 10g, redo is not shipped to a standby that has been opened in a read-write mode. The shutdown and restart, and application of archived redo logs extends the length of time for the failover or switchover to occur in an open physical standby read-only or read-write configuration.

If the physical standby database has not been opened in either read-only or read-write mode since it was last started, no restart of the database is required prior to the failover or switchover occurring in Oracle 10g.

In addition to the lengthened failover and switchover times, queries that are executed against a read-only physical standby are running against stale data immediately. In some applications this is acceptable, but just as often, a current and consistent image of the data is a much preferred view against which queries can be executed.

As will become evident in this chapter, Oracle Database 11g Data Guard has enabled Active Data Guard to accomplish this goal: Provide a read-only physical standby database that can concurrently serve as disaster recovery without a restart being required.

The following steps are required to enable a physical standby database in read-only mode:

- If the physical standby is currently shut down, use this:

  ```
  SQL> STARTUP;
  ```

- If the physical standby is currently in managed recovery mode applying redo, use this:

  1. Cancel the Redo Apply:

     ```
     SQL> ALTER DATABASE RECOVER MANAGED STANDBY DATABASE CANCEL;
     ```

  2. Open the database for read-only access:

     ```
     SQL> ALTER DATABASE OPEN;
     ```

- To return the database from read-only to applying redo, restart the standby database in the MOUNT mode and use this command:

  ```
  SQL> ALTER DATABASE RECOVER MANAGED STANDBY DATABASE
    2> DISCONNECT FROM SESSION;
  ```

- If you want to enable real-time apply of redo, use this:

```
SQL> ALTER DATABASE RECOVER MANAGED STANDBY DATABASE
  2> USING CURRENT LOGFILE DISCONNECT;
```

In review, there is no real difference between the implementation of a physical standby that has been opened read-only in Oracle Database 10*g* or Oracle Database 11*g* in a basic read-only configuration. The most important concept to remember is that no redo will be applied to the physical standby while the instance is open in read-only mode, and all accumulated redo stored in the archive logs on the standby server will have to be applied to the standby database before it can assume the role of the primary instance during a failover or switchover event.

# Snapshot Standby for QA and Test Environments

What differentiates a snapshot standby from the physical standby in read-only mode? The answer is simple: the physical standby becomes fully updatable. Oracle introduced a twist in Oracle Database 10*g* Data Guard that provided similar functionality, albeit with many more steps and hence more complexity, when opening a physical standby in read-write mode. For comparative purposes, we'll discuss both the physical standby database open in read-write mode and the true snapshot standby that is new to Oracle Database 11*g*.

Redo is not shipped from the primary database to the physical standby database while it is being used in read-write mode in Oracle Database 10*g* and, if this is your only standby database, the primary database is unprotected. For this reason, if you plan on opening a physical standby database as a read-write clone of the primary database for testing or other operations, it is highly recommended that a second physical standby database be in place to maintain protection for the primary database.

In Oracle Database 11*g*, though, redo continues to ship from the primary to the snapshot standby, but no redo is applied and your recovery time objective (RTO) will be longer if you have to failover during the snapshot period.

## Read-Write Standby in Oracle Database 10*g*

To create a physical standby and open it as a read-write clone of the primary database, you'll need to perform the following steps:

1.  Prepare the physical standby to enable a guaranteed restore point. Because Flashback Database requires that the flashback logs reside in the flash recovery area (FRA) we need to set up a flash recovery are if we do not have one:

```
SQL> ALTER SYSTEM SET DB_RECOVERY_FILE_DEST_SIZE=20G;
SQL> ALTER SYSTEM SET DB_RECOVERY_FILE_DEST='+FLASH';
```

**NOTE**
*Although we have set up our flash recovery area in Automatic Storage Management (ASM), you can also set up your flashback recovery area in a normal disk directory. In that case, you would use something like this:* `DB_RECOVERY_FILE_DEST= '/arch/oradata'`

2. Create a guaranteed restore point and cancel redo apply:

```
SQL> ALTER DATABASE RECOVER MANAGED STANDBY DATABASE CANCEL;
SQL> CREATE RESTORE POINT before_open_standby GUARANTEE FLASHBACK
DATABASE;
```

Creating an easy-to-remember name such as `before_open_standby` automatically associates it with an SCN or timestamp. When you later need to flash back the database to restore it to a previous point in time as part of synchronizing it with the primary database and restarting the redo apply, having a simple name to reference during the flashback process makes it much easier.

3. Prepare the primary database to be split from the physical standby by archiving the current log file. It's necessary for the SCN of the restore point to be archived on the physical standby database. To accomplish this, you must switch logs on the primary database:

```
SQL> ALTER SYSTEM ARCHIVE LOG CURRENT;
```

If you're using standby redo logs, this step must be accomplished to guarantee that the standby database can be flashed back successfully to the restore point.

4. On the primary database, defer all log archive destinations that are pointing to the physical standby database that will be opened, and switch logs once more to stop redo transport. If it is a single instance, only one instance will have to be modified; if it is a Real Application Clusters (RAC) cluster, all instances of the cluster will need to defer the archival of their redo to the physical standby. On the primary database, and on all nodes of a RAC cluster, do this:

```
SQL> ALTER SYSTEM SET LOG_ARCHIVE_DEST_STATE_2=DEFER;
SQL> ALTER SYSTEM SWITCH LOGFILE;
```

5. Now it is time to activate the physical standby database. On the physical standby database, perform the following steps:

```
SQL> ALTER DATABASE ACTIVATE STANDBY DATABASE;
```

6. Skip the next statement if the physical standby has not been opened read-only since it was last started:

```
SQL>STARTUP MOUNT FORCE;
```

7. The last step is to change the protection mode and open the database for read-write access:

```
SQL> ALTER DATABASE SET STANDBY DATABASE TO MAXIMIZE PERFORMANCE;
SQL> ALTER DATABASE OPEN;
```

The physical standby database is now fully available for update operations. Once again, note that if this is your only disaster protection source for providing failover protection, while the physical standby is open in read-write mode, no redo is being shipped and it is falling behind the primary database. All of the redo that was not shipped would be lost if you had to failover to this standby before you could synchronize with the primary again. The missing redo in the form of archive logs must be sent and applied to the physical standby before a switchover can be performed in addition to the following steps to bring the physical standby back from its read-write mode to a physical standby in managed recovery mode.

While the physical standby database is open in read-write mode, it can be used for testing, benchmarking, reporting, or any other activity completely separate from the primary database.

In the steps that follow, we will revert the database back to its original form as a physical standby database in managed recovery mode. Remember that once this reversion has occurred, any changes that have occurred while the physical standby database was open in read-write mode will be lost.

To revert the physical standby database back to its original state, it must first be returned to the point before the standby was activated. We will leverage the guaranteed restore point we set earlier along with Flashback Database. To complete this next phase we must perform the following steps:

```
SQL> STARTUP MOUNT FORCE;
SQL> FLASHBACK DATABASE TO RESTORE POINT before_open_standby;
SQL> ALTER DATABASE CONVERT TO PHYSICAL STANDBY;
SQL> STARTUP MOUNT FORCE;
```

1.  At this point, your standby database is back to its former role of physical standby but at the point where it became a snapshot standby. Your next steps will depend largely on how far the standby is behind the primary database in terms of redo.

2.  If you have activated the physical standby for a short period of time, the physical standby has not fallen too far behind the primary database. In this case, you can allow the physical standby database to use archive gap resolution to fetch any missing archived redo logs and allow Redo Apply to apply the logs. To complete this process, perform the following step:

    ```
    SQL> ALTER DATABASE RECOVER MANAGED STANDBY DATABASE
            USING CURRENT LOGFILE DISCONNECT;
    ```

However, if the activated physical standby has fallen sufficiently behind the primary database, simply allowing gap resolution to occur is not a viable alternative. It would result in too many archive logs being requested for gap resolution. It could also be that all of the necessary archive logs are not available on disk anymore at the primary database. In this scenario, it becomes necessary to take an incremental backup of the primary database and apply that to the physical standby database using RMAN to resynchronize the standby database with the primary.

**NOTE**
*This procedure can also be used if the apply process was unable to resolve an archive log gap due to corruption of the archive log or a large gap in the redo between the primary and the standby. If this is the case, make sure that Redo Apply has been stopped first by executing the* ALTER DATABASE RECOVER MANAGED STANDBY *DATABASE CANCEL; command.*

To complete this procedure, use the following steps:

1.  Identify the current SCN on the physical standby database before starting the incremental backup, as the backup must be created from this SCN forward. On the physical standby database, execute the following command:

    ```
    SQL>SELECT CURRENT_SCN FROM V$DATABASE;
    ```

2.  Record the SCN returned for the next step.

3.  The incremental backup must be taken to disk on the primary database. Using the SCN from the query, connect to the primary database and create an incremental RMAN backup as follows:

    ```
    RMAN> BACKUP INCREMENTAL FROM SCN <SCN from above query>
          DATABASE FORMAT '/tmp/ForStandby_%U' tag 'FORSTDBYSYNCH';
    ```

    Note that independent incremental RMAN backups are not considered valid backups. Even though default destinations are defined for RMAN backups, backup sets produced by this command are written to the /dbs location by default notwithstanding the existence of a flash recovery area or another destination having been defined as we have with the FORMAT qualifier. The incremental backup will *not* be catalogued on the primary database, and you must manually catalog it on the physical standby after it is moved to a disk location there.

4.  When the incremental backup completes, manually transfer all the backup sets to the physical standby database. Pay particular attention to the fact that more than one backup set may be associated with the incremental backup and all pieces of the incremental backup must be moved to the physical standby database before you catalog them. As an example, to scp the backup sets from the primary database named Matrix to the physical standby database named Matrix_DR0, you would execute the following command:

    ```
    $scp /$ORACLE_HOME/dbs/FORSTDBYSYNCH_* MATRIX_DR0:/tmp
    ```

5.  After moving the incremental backup pieces to the physical standby database, the backup pieces must be cataloged in RMAN. Then you can recover the standby database with the cataloged incremental backup pieces. Here's how to perform these steps from the physical standby database:

    ```
    $rman target /
    RMAN> CATALOG START WITH '/tmp/FORSTDBYSYNCH';
    RMAN> RECOVER DATABASE NOREDO;
    ```

6.  Before the physical standby database can by returned to its original state, a few more steps remain. You must create a standby control file backup on the primary database and restore it on the physical standby database. Connect to the Primary database and execute these commands

    ```
    RMAN> BACKUP CURRENT CONTROLFILE FOR STANDBY
          FORMAT '/tmp/FORSTDBYCTRL.bak';
    $scp /tmp/FORSTDBYCTRL.bak MATRIX_DR0:/tmp
    ```

7.  Back on the physical standby database, do this:

    ```
    RMAN> SHUTDOWN;
    RMAN> STARTUP MOUNT;
    ```

8.  If the primary and standby datafile directories are not identical, you need to complete this intermediate step and on the physical standby database, connect to RMAN and catalog the standby datafiles, and switch the database to use the just-cataloged datafiles:

    ```
    RMAN> CATALOG START WITH '+DATA/MATRIX_DR0/DATAFILE/';
    RMAN> SWITCH DATABASE TO COPY;
    ```

9.  The same situation exists with the redo log directories that existed with the datafile directories. Again, this is an intermediate step, and if the directories are the same, it can be skipped. Otherwise, use asmcmd if it is an ASM-managed database, or use an OS utility to remove all online and standby redo logs from the standby directories.

In addition, make sure that the `LOG_FILE_NAME_CONVERT` parameter has been set to convert the directory paths from Matrix to Matrix_DR0. As an example, you would include the following in your parameter file:

```
LOG_FILE_NAME_CONVERT='/MATRIX/','MATRIX_DR0/'.
```

10. You also need to clear all of the redo log groups on the standby:

```
SQL> ALTER DATABASE CLEAR LOGFILE GROUP1;
SQL> ALTER DATABASE CLEAR LOGFILE GROUP2;
...
```

11. When you have successfully cleared all standby redo log groups, re-enable Flashback Database on the physical standby database:

```
SQL> ALTER DATABASE FLASHBACK OFF;
SQL> ALTER DATABASE FLASHBACK ON;
```

12. Finally, still on the physical standby, restart the managed recovery process:

```
SQL> ALTER DATABASE RECOVER MANAGED STANDBY DATABASE
       USING CURRENT LOGFILE DISCONNECT;
```

So why, you might ask, have we taken you through this painful and lengthy process to return a physical standby to its original state in managed recovery? As was alluded to earlier, in Oracle Database 10g Data Guard, the process of opening a physical standby database in read-write mode and returning to managed recovery mode required more steps and was a more complex process than what is required in Oracle Database 11g Data Guard. And since no redo is shipped from the primary database to a physical standby that has been opened read-write in 10g, you need to know how to get it synchronized again with the primary in the best possible way.

In Oracle Database 11g Data Guard, Oracle introduced a new feature that eliminates this painful procedure. The new feature is known as *snapshot standby*. Lest we digress, we'll discuss what many of you will find to be a favorite feature and one that will greatly increase the flexibility of your database infrastructure.

# Snapshot Standbys in Oracle Database 11g

In the larger scheme of things, how does the Oracle Database 11g snapshot standby database differ from the Oracle Database 10g "open read-write standby" we discussed for QA and test? Operationally, there are no differences, as both are read-write and are fully updatable while they are open.

What you will find, though, is that the process of moving the database to fully updatable and back again takes fewer steps, is simpler, and, most important, has a significantly lower degree of risk to the physical standby database and to the protection of your primary database than the previous version. Setting up the snapshot standby can be accomplished in a number of ways, including the Data Guard Broker CLI, Enterprise Manager 10.2.0.5 , or through SQL*Plus. The Data Guard Broker provides a convenient interface to convert your physical standby to a snapshot standby and back again, so we'll discuss how to implement the snapshot standby using the Data Guard Broker first.

The following examples of enabling snapshot standbys assume you have either built a test environment that includes the sample database or the environment in which you are working includes the sample database. If this is not the case, create appropriate test tables prior to beginning this exercise.

Some basic configuration needs to be completed up front and will stay in place in your Data Guard environment going forward. First, make sure the Data Guard Broker is configured and enabled correctly, as discussed in Chapter 5. Four key items are required in configuring the Data Guard Broker, depending on your environment:

- Set the DG_BROKER_START initialization parameter.
- Create the Data Guard Broker service for the listener.
- Create the Broker configuration.
- Enable the Broker configuration.

Just as with the Oracle Database 10*g* snapshot standby, we need to enable Flashback Database on the physical standby database if it is not already enabled. To determine whether Flashback Database is enabled on the physical standby database, query V$DATABASE as follows:

```
[oracle@matrix_dr0 app]$ sqlplus / as sysdba
SQL*Plus: Release 11.1.0.6.0 - Production on Wed Oct 29 09:58:29 2008
Copyright (c) 1982, 2007, Oracle.  All rights reserved
Connected to:
Oracle Database 11g Enterprise Edition Release 11.1.0.6.0 - Production
With the Partitioning, OLAP, Data Mining and Real Application Testing options
SQL> SELECT FLASHBACK_ON FROM V$DATABASE;
FLASHBACK_ON
------------------
NO
```

You do not need to enable Flashback Database explicitly to use a snapshot standby database as long as the physical standby is not open in read-only mode. Snapshot standby uses a guaranteed restore point (GRP) that can be set even if Flashback Database is not enabled as long as you are in the MOUNT state. But, if Flashback Database is not enabled (FLASHBACK_ON = NO), and you want to enable it, you can use a combination of the Data Guard Broker command line and SQL*Plus.

1. Stop the application of redo by disabling the managed recovery process (MRP) as follows:

   ```
   [oracle@matrix_dr0 ~]$dgmgrl
   DGMGRL> CONNECT sys/oracle
   Connected.
   DGMGRL> EDIT DATABASE 'MATRIX_DR0'SET STATE='APPLY-OFF';
   Succeeded.
   DGMGRL> EXIT
   [oracle@matrix_dr0 ~]
   ```

2. Next, enable Flashback Database on the physical standby database through SQL*Plus while the database is in a MOUNT state. If your physical standby is open read-only at this time, you need to shut it down and bring it back to the MOUNT state as follows:

   ```
   [oracle@matrix_dr0 ~]$sqlplus / as sysdba
   SQL> SHUTDOWN IMMEDIATE
   Database closed.
   Database dismounted.
   ORACLE instance shut down.
   ```

```
SQL>STARTUP MOUNT
ORACLE instance started.
Total System Global Area    422670336 bytes
Fixed Size                    1300352 bytes
Variable Size               276826240 bytes
Database Buffers            138412032 bytes
Redo Buffers                  6131712 bytes
Database mounted.
```

3.  Once back in the MOUNT state, enable Flashback Database:

```
SQL> ALTER DATABASE FLASHBACK ON;
Database altered.
```

4.  Now that Flashback Database is enabled, you can again enable the application of redo
    to the physical standby database in preparation for converting it to fully updatable. Since
    you are using the Broker, use DGMGRL:

```
[oracle@matrix_dr0 ~]$dgmgrl
DGMGRL> CONNECT sys/oracle
Connected.
DGMGRL> EDIT DATABASE 'MATRIX_DR0'SET STATE='APPLY-ON';
Succeeded.
```

5.  You are now ready to do the actual conversion to a snapshot standby. All you have to do
    is enter the following command to DGMGRL using the physical standby database name:

```
DGMGRL> CONVERT DATABASE 'MATRIX_DR0' TO SNAPSHOT STANDBY;
Converting database "MATRIX_DR0" to a Snapshot Standby database, please
wait.
Database "MATRIX_DR0" converted successfully
```

6.  After the conversion completes, like all other work you do as a DBA, you need to
    verify the proper completion of the conversion. This is accomplished with the SHOW
    CONFIGURATION command as follows:

```
DGMGRL> SHOW CONFIGURATION
Configuration
  Name:              DGConfig1
  Enabled:           YES
  Protection Mode:   MaxPerformance
  Databases:
    MATRIX        - Primary database
    MATRIX_DR0    - Snapshot standby database
Fast-Start Failover: DISABLED
Current status for "DGConfig1":
SUCCESS
DGMGRL>
```

7.  You need to do some more verification—in this case to assure yourself that redo is
    actually being sent to the standby from the primary database. You can accomplish this by
    querying V$MANAGED_STANDBY on the snapshot standby database and noting the value
    in the BLOCK# column:

```
SQL> SELECT STATUS, SEQUENCE#, BLOCK#
     FROM V$MANAGED_STANDBY
```

```
       WHERE CLIENT_PROCESS='LGWR';
STATUS          SEQUENCE#  BLOCK#
---------- ---------- -------
IDLE                83    2183
SQL>
```

8. On the primary database, connect via SQL*Plus and insert a row into the hr.regions table as follows:

```
SQL> INSERT INTO HR.REGIONS
  2  VALUES (1, 'TEXAS');
1 row created.
SQL> COMMIT;
Commit complete.
SQL>
```

9. Recheck V$MANAGED_STANDBY as you did earlier on the snapshot standby to verify that redo from the primary database is being applied. You should see that the BLOCK# has changed in the query results:

```
SQL> SELECT STATUS, SEQUENCE#, BLOCK#
  2  FROM V$MANAGED_STANDBY
  3  WHERE CLIENT_PROCESS='LGWR';
STATUS          SEQUENCE#  BLOCK#
---------- ---------- -------
IDLE                83    2786
SQL>
```

10. This shows you that the redo is still coming in from the primary database and you are still protected. One thing to note from this simple example is that the insert to the primary database will not appear in the snapshot standby until it is converted back into a physical standby and the redo has been applied. You can go to the snapshot standby database and insert a row into the same table as you just did on the primary, hr.regions, as follows:

```
SQL> INSERT INTO HR.REGIONS
  2  VALUES (10, 'TEXAS');
1 row created.
SQL> COMMIT;
Commit complete.
SQL>
```

In this case, you have the record in the snapshot standby with different values for the first column. This second update will be removed from the snapshot standby when you convert it back into a physical standby database.

You can now proceed with testing, benchmarking, break-fix work, QA, and so on, on the physical standby, as it has been converted to a fully updatable snapshot standby. All statements executed on the primary database that would have been applied to the physical standby during normal physical standby mode operations will continually be shipped but not applied.

Now, assuming you have completed the work you intended, you want to return the snapshot standby database to its original mode as a physical standby database. We mentioned earlier that returning an Oracle Database 11g snapshot standby database to a physical standby was a much simpler process. Just how much simpler is it? Let's return the snapshot standby you just converted to a physical standby now.

1. Connect to the Data Guard Broker to begin the process:

```
[oracle@matrix_dr0 app]$ dgmgrl
DGMGRL for Linux: Version 11.1.0.6.0 - Production
Copyright (c) 2000, 2005, Oracle. All rights reserved.
Welcome to DGMGRL, type "help" for information.
DGMGRL> CONNECT sys/oracle
Connected.
DGMGRL> CONVERT DATABASE 'MATRIX_DR0' TO PHYSICAL STANDBY;
Converting database "MATRIX_DR0" to a Physical Standby database, please
wait.
Operation requires shutdown of instance "MATRIX_DR0" on database
"MATRIX_DR0"
Shutting down instance "MATRIX_DR0"…
Database closed.
Database dismounted.
ORACLE instance shut down.
Operation requires startup of instance "MATRIX_DR0" on database
"MATRIX_DR0"
Starting instance "MATRIX_DR0"…
ORACLE instance started.
Database mounted.
Continuing to convert database "MATRIX_DR0"…
Operation requires shutdown of instance "MATRIX_DR0" on database
"MATRIX_DR0"
Shutting down instance "MATRIX_DR0"…
ORA-01109: database not open
Database dismounted.
ORACLE instance shut down.
Operation requires startup of instance "MATRIX_DR0" on database
"MATRIX_DR0"
Starting instance "MATRIX_DR0"…
ORACLE instance started.
Database mounted.
Database "MATRIX_DR0" converted successfully
DGMGRL>
```

2. Believe it or not, that is almost all there is to returning the snapshot standby to a physical standby. You again want to perform some verification and validation to assure that everything is as it should be, and the last step is to return the physical standby to managed recovery mode, which you'll do right after a quick SHOW CONFIGURATION:

```
DGMGRL> SHOW CONFIGURATION
Configuration
  Name:                DGConfig1
  Enabled:             YES
  Protection Mode:     MaxPerformance
  Databases:
    MATRIX        - Primary database
    MATRIX_DR0    - Physical standby database
Fast-Start Failover: DISABLED
Current status for "DGConfig1":
SUCCESS
DGMGRL>
```

You are done. The Broker will have restarted the Redo Apply process and the physical standby database will be working on catching up with the primary. If the primary database has not yet reconnected to the standby after the conversion, you can connect as SYSDBA to your primary database and switch log files, although this is not necessary if you are running in Maximum Availabilty:

```
SQL> ALTER SYSTEM SWITCH LOGFILE;
System altered.
SQL>
```

This will reconnect the LogWriter Network Service (LNS) process to its RFS process on the standby. Now you want to have a look at what happened to your data in the Regions table, so back on the physical standby database, use DGMGRL and stop the managed recovery process:

```
DGMGRL> EDIT DATABASE 'MATRIX_DR0'SET STATE='APPLY-OFF';
Succeeded.
```

Using SQL*Plus, open the physical standby in read-only mode:

```
SQL> ALTER DATABASE OPEN READ ONLY;
Database altered.
SQL>
```

You can query any table you changed while the database was a snapshot standby, and the changes made on the snapshot standby will be gone, such as your change to the hr.regions table (10, 'TEXAS'). However, changes made on the primary database, such as the row you entered for hr.regions with the values (1, 'TEXAS') will still be there:

```
SQL> SELECT * FROM HR.REGIONS;
  REGION_ID REGION_NAME
---------- ------------------------
         1 TEXAS
SQL>
```

You are almost finished! Simply shut down the physical standby database and restart it in MOUNT mode. This will take the physical standby out of read-only mode and prepare it for receiving redo from the primary database:

```
SQL> SHUTDOWN
Database closed.
Database dismounted.
ORACLE instance shut down.
SQL> STARTUP MOUNT
ORACLE instance started.
Total System Global Area   422670336 bytes
Fixed Size                   1300352 bytes
Variable Size              343935104 bytes
Database Buffers            71303168 bytes
Redo Buffers                 6131712 bytes
Database mounted.
SQL>
```

Finally, put the physical standby back into managed recovery mode and you're really done!

```
[oracle@matrix_dr0 ~]$dgmgrl
DGMGRL>connect sys/oracle
Connected.
DGMGRL> EDIT DATABASE 'MATRIX_DR0'SET STATE='APPLY-ON';
Succeeded.
DGMGRL>EXIT
[oracle@matrix_dr0 ~]
```

You have two, just two, real steps that you must complete to go from the physical standby database to a fully updatable snapshot standby database and return again to your physical standby database:

1. Convert the physical standby database to a snapshot standby database.

2. Convert the snapshot standby database to a physical standby database.

When we look back at the requirements to accomplish the same fully updatable or open read-write standby database in Oracle Database 10g, the number of steps (15 in total), the level of complexity, and the opportunity for error is significantly higher. This one feature enables testing and QA against real-world environments in an extremely effective manner.

To complete the story, of course you can do this operation with SQL*Plus if you are not using the Broker; it involves a few more steps to issue the commands that the Broker issues for you:

1. Shut down any auxiliary RAC instances of the standby.

2. Put the database in the MOUNT state.

3. Execute ALTER DATABASE CONVERT TO SNAPSHOT STANDBY;.

To go back to a physical standby, do the same thing:

1. Shut down any auxiliary RAC instances of the standby.

2. Put the database in the MOUNT state.

3. Execute ALTER DATABASE CONVERT TO PHYSICAL STANDBY;.

4. Restart the standby database.

Restart Redo Apply. This involves not many more steps, but since the Broker does it all for you, why not take advantage of it? Performing this conversion is also possible in Grid Control 10.2.0.5, which added a new Convert button, as shown in Figure 9-1.

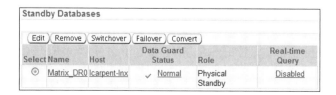

**FIGURE 9-1.** *Grid Control snapshot convert*

Select a physical standby database and click the Convert button, and you will be asked to confirm; then the conversion will take place and the Role column will change to snapshot standby when the Data Guard home page returns.

One final note about snapshot standby databases: They are part of your normal Oracle Enterprise license that you already have with your Data Guard configuration and hence do not cost extra to use.

# Real Application Testing

This chapter has continued to build on the basic physical standby database in both Oracle Database 10g and Oracle Database 11g. From this point forward, however, the database features we'll discuss are all new to Oracle Database 11g. This section introduces two new features:

- **Database Replay** Enables the capture of actual production workloads and the constant, dependable, and steadfast execution of a workload in a mirror environment, which, for our purposes, is an Oracle Database 11g snapshot standby.

- **SQL Performance Analyzer** Provides a granular view of the impact of changes in an environment to a SQL statement's execution plan by running the statements sequentially before and after the changes have been made. In addition to simply executing the statements pre- and post-changes, it provides an assessment based on the workload in both states and generates recommendations to tune the statements with supporting execution plan details.

Snapshot standby databases can be created and opened from a physical standby for read-write testing in one step. And the snapshot standby can be returned to a physical standby in a single step. This is an obvious enabler of proper testing at all levels of the system development life cycle (SDLC), in addition to providing a nearly immediate platform for break-fix testing of production anomalies. As we continue to build on the flexibility of Oracle Database 11g, Real Application Testing (RAT), coupled with a snapshot standby, takes this to a completely new level.

We'll start by discussing Database Replay in detail and cover why you might want to capture a production workload and then execute it in a snapshot standby. Remember that we are capturing the operational workload from the running production environment, and our goal is to determine how it responds to changes in environment. The question, then, is what environmental changes would give us adequate concern to validate the performance of our production workload? Here are some examples:

- Database upgrades, patches, parameter changes

- Configuration changes, such as single instance to RAC, ASM, and so on

- Physical changes, such as storage, network, interconnect, bonding/teaming

- Operating system changes, such as hardware migrations, patches, upgrades, and parameter changes

These are examples of triggers that would cause a prudent IT staff to perform regression testing before implementing changes into an operational production environment. In addition to these changes for Database Replay, some general candidates are triggers for SQL Performance Analyzer:

- Schema changes, including the addition, removal, or change of an index, partition, or materialized view

- Changes in how optimizer statistics are gathered, the direct application of other SQL performance tuning actions such as creating SQL profiles, histograms, and so on

One of the primary goals in RAT is to perform our testing in an environment that mirrors production when we replay our captured workload to assure we are minimizing risk for our actual migration of the changes. Our first step then is to convert the physical standby database to a snapshot standby before we capture our workload using the procedures from the preceding section.

# Database Replay

Once the physical standby has been converted to a snapshot standby, we can begin the steps to complete the process of capturing the production workload with Database Replay.

**NOTE**
*Before you start the Database Replay process, Oracle (and your authors) recommend taking a backup of your primary Oracle Database as a best practice.*

Four main components make up Database Replay:

- **Workload capture**   Workload capture uses binary files on the file system called *capture files*. Once workload capture is enabled, all client or external changes received by the Oracle Database are tracked and written to the capture files on the file system. The location of the capture files, start, and stop times of capture are all controlled by the user.

- **Workload processing**   This process is typically executed on the snapshot standby or test server. Before the captured workload can be replayed in the test environment, it must be converted to replay files and the metadata needed for replaying the workload in the test environment. There is no limit to the number of times the converted files can be replayed on test systems. The converted files can also be copied to another test system if necessary and run there if it supports Database Replay.

- **Workload replay**   To state the obvious, because we are replaying a captured workload that includes DML and queries, the test database must have data that is identical to the source database on which the workload capture was performed if results are to be reliable. Since we're assuming a snapshot standby is being used, we're ready now for the replay component of the Database Replay workflow. The workload replay uses a replay client program that processes the replay files and submits calls to the database with the exact same timing and concurrency as in the workload capture system. A calibration tool is provided to assist you in determining how many replay clients you will need to emulate the workload from the original capture system. It's possible that you will need more than one client system, but the calibration tool will help you determine this.

- **Analysis and reporting**   The purpose of regression testing is to determine the fitness of changes for migration into a production environment, which means analysis of the tests, and reports of that analysis must be produced. Fortunately, Database Replay natively provides extensive reports from simple error listings encountered during the test run to differences in rows returned by DML statements. In addition, you can access AWR reports for detailed comparative analysis between the capture and replay systems.

What about testing? Everybody performs testing—at least they should! But it requires time, effort, and extra storage to populate the test environments frequently. And since workloads usually do not mimic production, they rarely catch production problems. Even simple tests like checking a new index can be very time consuming. The following table contains some of the things you can test with Database Replay and a snapshot standby.

| Production Setup | Test on Snapshot Standby |
|---|---|
| Non-ASM storage | ASM storage |
| No flash recovery area | Uses flash recovery area |
| Flashback Database not enabled | Flashback Database enabled |
| Lower O/S version | Higher O/S version |
| Old hardware (disks/system) | New hardware (disks/system) |
| Simple indexes | Complex/more indexes |
| Parameters | Changed parameters |
| No partitioning | New partitioning |
| No compression | Compression enabled |

Let's look at a simple example of capturing a workload on the primary database and replaying it several times on our snapshot standby.

Database Replay is much easier to use in Database Control, so if you do not have Database Control configured, it would be prudent to configure it now. To do so, execute the following on the primary database to create the Database Control metadata or start it if already configured:

```
[Matrix] emca -config dbcontrol db -repos recreate
[Matrix] emctl start dbconsole
```

To get ready for Database Replay, create a directory in which the capture information will be placed and gather up your testing material, scripts, and other data. You need to convert your physical standby to a snapshot standby before you start your workload generation to maintain the same starting point as the capture on the primary database:

```
DGMGRL> convert database MATRIX_DR0 to snapshot standby;
Converting database "MATRIX_DR0" to a Snapshot Standby database, please
wait...
Database "MATRIX_DR0" converted successfully
```

Remember that this requires extra flash recovery area space as flashback logs are not recycled when a GRP is in effect, which is what converting to a snapshot creates for you.

Next, configure Database Control on the snapshot standby. You won't be able to use the metadata for Database Control from the primary because these are now two separate databases. This step can be done in parallel with the capture on the primary database.

```
[Matrix_DR0] emca -config dbcontrol db -repos recreate
```

While that is running, you can start your capture. The general steps to capture a workload are listed here. Use Database Control on the primary and do the following:

1. Log in to Database Control on your primary database.

2. Click the Software and Support link at the top.

3. Under Real Application Testing, select Database Replay.

4. On the Capture Workload task line, click the Go to Task icon.

5. Read and acknowledge the prerequisites and click Next.

6. On the next page, choose whether to restart the primary or not and create the directory object for your Replay Directory. You should test the file system by clicking the button provided to make sure you got it right. Note that each workload capture that you perform requires its own directory. When the test is successful, click OK.

7. Once the directory object is created, click Next.

8. Set a schedule for your capture (Start and Stop) and submit your capture job. We choose not to set a schedule so that we can run a specific workload and then stop the capture ourselves.

9. Database Replay will now capture your current workload. In our case, we ran a set of programs to simulate a workload:

```
[Matrix] wcr_demo_workload.csh
...
[7]   + Done wcr_demo -d 40 -c salmon -t 0.00001 -u 2000
[6]   + Done wcr_demo -d 30 -c orange -t 0.00001 -u 2000
[5]   + Done wcr_demo -c yellow -d 10 -t 0.00001 -u 2000
[4]   + Done wcr_demo -u 3000 -t 0.01 -c black
[3]   + Done wcr_demo -u 3000 -t 0.01 -c blue
[2]   + Done wcr_demo -u 3000 -t 0.01 -c green
[1]   + Done wcr_demo -u 3000 -t 0.01 -c red
```

10. If you did not set a scheduled time to end the capture, then when the programs complete, return to Database Control and stop the capture, as in our case.

11. When Database Replay asks if you want to export the AWR data, click Yes.

At this point, you are done with your primary database. In the capture directory are all the files needed to rerun the workload. But they must first be processed by Database Replay before they can be used to replay the workload. You can do this preprocessing on the primary system or you can copy the captured workload files to the standby and process them there, which is what we did. Once the files are on the standby system, log in to Database Control on your standby database (which should be created by now) and navigate to the Database Replay page.

1. Select the Preprocess Captured Workload task.

2. Create the capture directory object to point to the copied capture files. You cannot use the directory object you created during the capture process since it will not exist on the snapshot standby. Remember that redo (with that DDL in it) is being shipped to the standby but not applied.

3. Click PreProcess Workload.

4. Configure the job settings as required and verify the replay version. Once complete, click Next.

5. Set the schedule (Run Immediate is the default), click Next, and click Submit the Job.

When the preprocess job is complete, you are ready to start replaying your workload. You will first want to run the replay once without any changes to obtain a baseline set of metrics. After that, make many runs of the replay with your changes and compare the results of the various runs. We will run the baseline first and then add several indexes to the snapshot standby to change the workload execution statistics and do it all again.

Before you start, create a guaranteed restore point in the snapshot standby and restart the standby. This will give you a rewind point that you can return to so that each replay runs on exactly the same database contents and structure. Restarting the database sets the System Global Area (SGA) back to a clean starting point as well:

```
SQL> create restore point beforereplay
       guarantee flashback database;
SQL> shutdown immediate
SQL> startup
```

**NOTE**
*If you are not running in Maximum Availability mode, you need to return to the primary and switch logs at this point to make sure that the primary starts sending redo again to keep you protected.*

Now, in Database Control, navigate to the Database Replay page, select the Replay Workload task, and click the Go to Task icon. Then do the following:

1. Create a directory object to point to the capture files.

2. Click Set Up Replay.

3. Ensure the prerequisites have been met.

4. On the Restore Database Requirement, we are using a snapshot standby and Flashback Database so we do not need to restore the database.

5. Resolve any references to external systems and click Continue. Determine how many clients you need. Database Replay provides a multithreaded replay client program called *wrc* that will handle the clients for you. When run with the mode=calibrate option, wrc

will tell you the minimum number of clients to run so that it can start the appropriate number of user threads.

```
[Matrix_DR0] wrc mode=calibrate REPLAYDIR=/scratch/oracle/Replay/Capture
Workload Replay Client: Release 11.1.0.6.0 - Production
Copyright (c) 1982, 2007, Oracle.  All rights reserved.
Report for Workload in: /scratch/oracle/Replay/Capture
-----------------------
Recommendation:
Consider using at least 1 clients divided among 1 CPU(s).
Workload Characteristics:
- max concurrency: 7 sessions
- total number of sessions: 11

On the next screen, choose your replay options and then start up the
clients using the Database Replay program wrc:[Matrix_DR0] wrc
REPLAYDIR=/path USERID=xxx PASSWORD=xxx
```

6. When replay sees the clients, it will list them in the table at the bottom. When they are all accounted for, you can continue by clicking Next.

7. Click Submit on the next page to start the replay and wait until the replay is completed.

8. Once the replay is complete, using the links on the next page you will create and save the Workload Report and the AWR report for your baseline run.

That was your baseline run. Now the fun starts. You are going to rewind the snapshot standby and do it all over again after making some changes that you want to test:

1. Flashback the snapshot standby to the restore point:

```
SQL> shutdown immediate
SQL> startup mount
SQL> flashback database to restore point beforereplay;
SQL> alter database open resetlogs;
SQL> shutdown immediate
SQL> startup
```

2. The second restart is not technically necessary, but we want to ensure that we start with the database in the same state as the baseline run.

3. Now make your changes to the database. We'll set up some new indexes:

```
SQL> create index wcr_grid_xcoor_ycoor on wcr_grid(xcoor, ycoor);
SQL> create index wcr_grid_pixid_xcoor_ycoor
     on wcr_grid(pixid,xcoor, ycoor);
SQL> create index wcr_grid_pixid_xcoor on wcr_grid(pixid, xcoor);
SQL> create index wcr_grid_pixid_ycoor on wcr_grid(pixid, ycoor);
SQL> create index wcr_grid_pixid_xcoor_color
     on wcr_grid(pixid, xcoor, color);
SQL> create index wcr_grid_pixid_ycoor_color
     on wcr_grid(pixid, ycoor, color);
SQL> create index wcr_grid_pixid_color on wcr_grid(pixid, color);
SQL> create index wcr_grid_xcoor_color on wcr_grid(xcoor, color);
SQL> create index wcr_grid_ycoor_color on wcr_grid(ycoor, color);
```

4. Rerun the entire replay using the same steps used for the baseline run.

5. Save the reports, and run the AWR Differences report between the new run and the baseline run.

6. Compare the results of each of your secondary runs to the baseline.

You can continue in the preceding loop as long as you have the disk for your flashback logs. When you are satisfied with the results of your testing, convert your snapshot standby back into a physical standby and let it resynchronize with the primary by applying all the redo that has accumulated at the standby during your testing runs.

1. Drop the replay restore point:

   ```
   SQL> drop restore point beforereplay;
   ```

2. Convert the snapshot to a physical standby database:

   ```
   DGMGRL> convert database MATRIX_DR0 to physical standby;
   ```

   Redo Apply automatically begins applying the redo that came in while it was in snapshot standby mode and the primary continues to send the current redo.

For more details on this example of using RAT Database Replay, refer to the Oracle OpenWorld 2008 Presentation entitled "Beat-up Your Oracle Data Guard Standby with Oracle Real Application Testing—It's Payback Time!"[1]

# SQL Performance Analyzer

With Database Replay, we've explored the basic steps to approach full-blown regression testing on your physical standby database using a snapshot standby. Being able to predict the results of environmental changes on the application SQL before it is introduced into production means less work for DBAs in tracking down problem SQL and an environment that can reliably tune the SQL before migrating it back into production. The combination of Database Replay and SQL Performance Analyzer, and the ability of the Oracle Database to capture SQL and save it into SQL tuning sets, make this not only feasible, but also pretty straightforward.

A goal in RAT is to identify those SQL statements with degraded performance resulting from the environmental and/or database changes that have been introduced. SQL Performance Analyzer can both predict and prevent SQL execution performance problems as a result of these changes.

SQL Performance Analyzer is tightly integrated with SQL tuning sets, SQL Tuning Advisor, and SQL Plan Management functionality. When Database Replay is running in its Client Replay mode, SQL Performance Analyzer is capturing detailed statistics and plan information for every DML statement and query executed against the test environment sequentially before and after the changes occur. From these statistics and plan information, SQL Performance Analyzer generates a report that outlines where performance in the workload has improved as a result of the changes, in addition to which SQL statements have degraded in performance as a result of the changes. This completely automated process of analyzing the performance of the SQL statements and comparing the before and after execution plans takes what was an extremely time-consuming and manual process to a level of refinement: you can simply review the generated reports to identify the degraded SQL.

---

[1] See www.oracle.com/technology/deploy/availability/pdf/oracle-openworld-2008/298770.pdf

Once the degraded SQL has been identified, it can be isolated and captured into a SQL tuning set for additional focused performance tuning.

Use of the SQL Performance Analyzer encompasses five main steps:

1. Capture the SQL workload you want to analyze with SQL Performance Analyzer. This would normally be done on the production database, using AWR to extract the SQL from the cursor cache into a SQL tuning set. The SQL tuning set is then transferred to the test system where SQL Performance Analyzer can analyze the extracted SQL.

2. Using SQL Performance Analyzer, measure your workload's performance prior to any changes being made by executing the SQL Performance Analyzer against the SQL tuning set.

3. Apply the planned changes to the test environment.

4. Repeat step 2, this time with the changes in place.

5. Compare the performance of the SQL tuning sets, identifying those that have improved, degraded, or stayed the same.

The SQL statements of particular interest to us comes out of step 5—those which have degraded in performance since we measured them in step 2. As mentioned earlier, SQL Tuning Advisor is tightly integrated with SQL Performance Analyzer. At this point you can leverage SQL Tuning Advisor to correct the degraded SQL statements while they are in the test environment and create new plans for them. These plans are then seeded in to SQL Plan Management baselines and exported back into production.

**NOTE**
*For more information on Real Application Testing, read the Oracle white paper "Oracle Database 11g: Real Application Testing Overview."*[2]

# Active Data Guard

So far, we've covered the physical standby database variations related to opening the physical standby in read-only, read-write, or as a snapshot standby. Although each of these variants, once opened, offers significant differences, they all have one thing in common: there is an accepted impact to the recovery time objective (RTO) and potentially to the recovery point objective (RPO). In the case of the read-only physical standby, the application of redo is paused, which means all accumulated redo must be applied to the physical standby when it is returned to managed recovery mode. In the case of Oracle Database 10g, when the physical standby has been opened read-write, the number of steps to return the physical standby to managed recovery mode is actually fairly lengthy, and in some cases involves creating an RMAN incremental backup if the amount of time since the physical standby was opened read-write has been lengthy, or archive logs needed to resynchronize the physical standby are missing. As shown earlier in this chapter, returning to a physical standby from a snapshot standby is simply a matter of a single command:

```
DGMGRL> CONVERT DATABASE 'MATRIX_DR0' TO PHYSICAL STANDBY;
```

[2] See www.oracle.com/technology/products/manageability/database/pdf/wp07/owp_real_application_testing_11g .pdf

In the example we showed earlier, we performed some verification and validation, but following the execution of this command, the snapshot standby was returned to its original state as a physical standby. One thing you should have noted, though, is that during the conversion process, the instance was stopped and restarted. In other words, a delay impacts RTO and RPO. This leads us to our fourth and final configuration in this chapter, Active Data Guard.

First, Oracle Database 11g Active Data Guard enables read-only access to the physical standby while applying redo to the physical standby in real time. Active Data Guard continues to apply redo from the production primary database while allowing you to open a physical standby in read-only mode for reporting any combination of simple or complex queries, sorts, and/or web-based access. Because redo is being applied to the read-only physical standby, all queries execute in real time and return result sets that are current and in sync with the production primary database. Because of this synchronization with the production primary database, any operation requiring read-only, real-time access to production data can be executed against the Active Data Guard database. Opening an Oracle Database 11g physical standby using the Active Data Guard option enables this read-only, real-time access with absolutely no impact on RTO or RPO, as the Active Data Guard physical standby remains in managed recovery mode the entire time it is open for read-only access.

One of the uses for physical standby databases for many years has been to shift the load of RMAN backups from the production server to the physical standby. What has not been possible until Oracle Database 11g Active Data Guard is the ability to use block change tracking as well. With the use of block change tracking to record only those blocks that have been modified, it is now possible to perform fast incremental backups from the physical standby with Active Data Guard enabled. This can increase the performance of backups on the physical standby by a factor of as much as 20 times over using a physical standby without Active Data Guard.

The primary focus of Active Data Guard is to support read-only environments, so let's look at the various architectures for Active Data Guard.

In its simplest form, a single instance primary and a single instance physical standby are required to enable the Active Data Guard option for a read-only environment. In this architecture, updates are made on the primary and redo is applied to the Active Data Guard standby in real time, giving a guaranteed read-consistent view of the data at all times, while being open and available for read-only operations, as shown in Figure 9-2.

Active Data Guard standby also supports Oracle RAC on the primary and/or standby databases, which leads us to our next architecture: Oracle Database 11g RAC on the primary

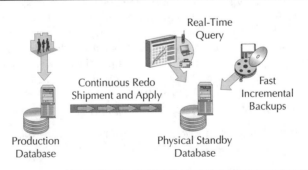

**FIGURE 9-2.** *Basic Active Data Guard configuration*

database and a single-instance physical Data Guard active standby database. This configuration is virtually identical to the basic RAC to single-instance physical standby architectures used in many disaster recovery plans.

We start to see the real opportunity of the Active Data Guard architecture in its flexibility and scalability. This brings us to what is likely to be a new concept within the context of Data Guard, Active Data Guard reader farms. Active Data Guard reader farms are multiple instances all operating as Active Data Guard physical standby databases. Active Data Guard supports multiple physical standby databases (up to nine), so our example of a single-instance primary database and a single-instance physical standby database can easily be modified to a single-instance primary database and multiple single-instance physical standby databases. Prior to Oracle Database 11*g* and Active Data Guard, this was a recommended approach when the conventional path for opening a physical standby read-only was taken and the application of redo had to be paused, leaving you with an extended failover time. Using Active Data Guard reader farms, the same architecture of a single-instance primary database, and multiple physical standby active data guard databases, you literally have the best of all worlds, as shown in Figure 9-3.

The third architecture is an extension of the Active Data Guard reader farms, as shown in Figure 9-4. If the physical standby is on RAC, then leveraging the full power of the RAC for read-only operations and scalability is as simple as adding instances as needed.

**TIP**
*Active Data Guard is a separately licensed option for Oracle Enterprise Edition. An Active Data Guard license is required to use either the Real-Time Query or the RMAN block-change tracking on a standby database.*

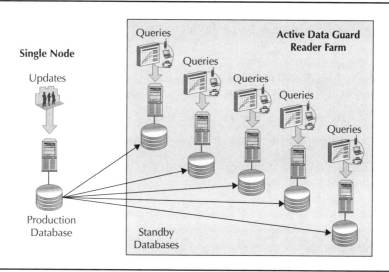

**FIGURE 9-3.** *Reader farm multiple databases*

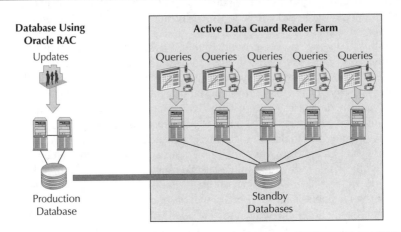

**FIGURE 9-4.** *Active Data Guard RAC reader farm*

## Configuring Active Data Guard

For the purposes of our discussion, you'll need a Data Guard physical standby database that meets prerequisites prior to enabling Active Data Guard. For assistance with configuring a Data Guard physical standby database, refer to Chapter 2.

**TIP**
*The compatible parameter must be set to at least 11.0.0 in either the initialization parameter file or the spfile on both the primary and physical standby databases. The physical standby database must apply some redo after the compatible parameter was set to 11.0.0 or higher.*

The actual process of enabling Active Data Guard is simple: Open the physical standby database in read-only mode and start Redo Apply. The Data Guard physical standby should be in one of two states prior to enabling Active Data Guard:

- The standby database is mounted and Redo Apply is running.
- The standby database has been shut down cleanly and Redo Apply was stopped.

In the first scenario, proceed as follows using SQL*Plus or Data Guard Broker if you prefer. Using SQL*Plus alone, do this:

1. Stop Redo Apply:

   ```
   SQL> RECOVER MANAGED STANDBY DATABASE CANCEL;
   ```

2. Open the database read-only:

   ```
   SQL> ALTER DATABASE OPEN READ ONLY;
   ```

3. Restart Redo Apply:

   ```
   SQL> RECOVER MANAGED STANDBY DATABASE DISCONNECT USING CURRENT LOGFILE;
   ```

Using Data Guard Broker, do this:

1. Stop Redo Apply:

   ```
   DGMGRL> EDIT DATABASE 'MATRIX_DR0' SET STATE='APPLY=OFF'
   ```

2. Using SQL*Plus, open the database read-only:

   ```
   SQL> ALTER DATABASE OPEN READ ONLY;
   ```

3. Restart Redo Apply:

   ```
   DGMGRL> EDIT DATABASE 'MATRIX_DR0; SET STATE='APPLY-ON'
   ```

In the second scenario, where the physical standby and Redo Apply are already shut down, proceed as follows.

Using SQL*Plus alone, do this:

1. Start the physical standby in read-only mode.

   ```
   SQL> STARTUP
   ```

2. Start Redo Apply.

   ```
   SQL> RECOVER MANAGED STANDBY DATABASE DISCONNECT USING CURRENT LOGFILE;
   ```

Using Data Guard Broker, do this:

1. Connect to the database using DGMGRL and start it in read-only mode:

   ```
   DGMGRL> STARTUP
   ```

2. Unless the default for Redo Apply has been changed, issuing this startup command also starts Redo Apply. If the default behavior has been changed, start Redo Apply like so:

   ```
   DGMGRL> EDIT DATABASE 'MATRIX_DR0' SET STATE='APPLY-ON'
   ```

If you are interested in how easy it can be to open a physical standby in Active Data Guard mode, you should try Grid Control 10.2.0.5. After clicking the Disabled link under the Real-Time Query heading on the Data Guard home page (Figure 9-1), check the Enable Real-Time Query checkbox on the next page and select Apply On (Figure 9-5). Grid Control does the rest for you!

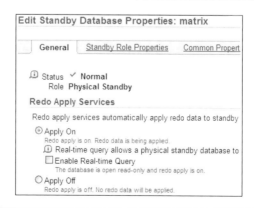

**FIGURE 9-5.** *Enabling Active Data Guard Real-Time Query with Grid Control*

# Conclusion

Oracle Database 11g Active Data Guard introduced a new paradigm in the read-only options when using Data Guard physical standby databases. The ability to open the physical standby read-only and still apply redo assures that RTO and RPO objectives can be met, because the standby is 100-percent available for failover or switchover as necessary. Beyond the read-only availability to applications, the application of Active Data Guard to RMAN fast incremental backups by enabling block change tracking on the Active Data Guard standby is another significant performance enhancer, expediting backup times by a factor of as much as 20 times, based on Oracle's testing.

For more information on Active Data Guard, refer to the MAA white paper "Oracle Active Data Guard: Oracle Data Guard 11g Release 1: Oracle Best Practices for High Availability" (includes best practices for Redo Apply).[3]

---

[3] See www.oracle.com/technology/deploy/availability/pdf/maa_wp_11gr1_activedataguard.pdf

# CHAPTER
## 10

## Automating Site and
## Client Failover

hapter 8 discussed database failover using both a physical and logical standby. You learned that database failover can be achieved simply by entering a couple of commands and can take mere seconds to complete. You might believe that your understanding of database failover is so complete that you would be willing to give yourself a mental checkmark, thinking that in the event of a disaster, you can failover quickly and save the day. Well, we are here to say, Not so fast! You're really only halfway to a complete understanding of database failover. What good is database failover if your application can't connect to it?

In this chapter, we will dig deep into the details of failover configurations. You'll learn how to configure your client applications and databases so your connections seamlessly and transparently reconnect to the new primary database in the event of failure.

The process of configuring client failover can be divided into three broad categories:

- **Service relocation**   The database service used by the primary application to connect to the database should be active only on the primary database. If a failover or switchover occurs, this service should be automatically migrated to the new primary database.

- **Client notification**   Once the failover has completed and the service is available on the new primary database, the application should be notified that a failover has occurred and that connections should be migrated to the new primary database.

- **Efficient reconnection**   The new and previous sessions should quickly be able to locate the new primary database and not get stalled waiting for timeouts on unavailable hosts or networks.

After reading this chapter, you should truly be able to save the day in the event of a failover and give yourself that mental checkmark.

# Defining the Problem

Client failovers typically fall into one of two categories: complete site failover or partial site failover. Let's begin by examining these two categories at a high level. Once you understand the differences, we will begin digging deep into the details that enable clients to failover automatically and seamlessly.

## Complete Site Failover

Users that experience a complete site failover category typically have a disaster recovery data center that, in addition to hosting the standby database, also has a complete set of redundant middle tiers or application servers. Put simply, every application component on the primary site is duplicated exactly at the standby site. In addition to redundant application components, each site typically has a network load balancer or traffic manager that sends incoming requests to the application servers on that site. The traffic manager is usually active only within the primary site. Client connections originate from outside the two data centers and attempt to connect to the application using a single address that resolves to the active traffic manager.

When a complete site failover is performed, the standby database is transitioned to a primary database and the application servers/middle tiers are started. Once the application components have been started, the address of the traffic manager from the failed site is enabled and started on the new site. If a single address floats between the traffic managers in the event of a failover, or a virtual IP address, then client connections can immediately resume. If each traffic manager has its own IP address, then the administrator must update the domain name system (DNS) so that the hostname used for client connections correctly maps to the IP address of the new active traffic manager.

## Partial Site Failover

Partial site failover differs from a complete site failover in that the application servers to which clients are connected remain active while a Data Guard failover transitions the standby database to a primary database. Say, for example, that with clients connected through the application servers, a failure event occurs and takes down all the hosts that make up the primary database cluster. The DBA quickly performs a Data Guard failover to either a local or remote standby so that the application can resume processing. In this scenario, connections from the failed primary cluster must be cleaned up and new connections to the new primary cluster established once it is available for processing.

Partial site failover can also be useful in configurations that are set up for a complete site failover. When performing a failover to a secondary site in a complete site configuration, it can take some time to start up the new application servers. To avoid this lengthy startup time, you may find it beneficial to direct the primary site's application servers to the secondary site. This can be feasible if the outage that triggered the failover involves only the database and the network latency between the sites is such that the application servers on the primary site can access the new primary on the secondary site.

## The Nitty Gritty

You know that the client failover consists of three main components: service relocation, client notification, and client reconnection. You can certainly take these three concepts and go directly to the "Implementing Client Failover" section later in this chapter and get straight to work. However, if you like to feed your inner geek, if you like to lift the hood and see the inner workings, this section is for you. Here we provide the details on how various Oracle technologies and features that have been developed over the years work and how putting the individual technologies together can create a comprehensive client failover solution. While it is not necessary that you have a deep and complete understanding of each feature to understand how to implement the client failover solution, knowing this information does help you understand why certain things work the way they do. In addition, when it comes to troubleshooting an issue, the extra knowledge is a good thing to have in your back pocket.

This section also covers the process flow for each piece, and for that we need an example Oracle Net alias as shown here:

```
SALES =
    (DESCRIPTION =
        (ADDRESS_LIST =
            (ADDRESS = (PROTOCOL = TCP)(HOST = MATRIX1)(PORT = 1521))
            (ADDRESS = (PROTOCOL = TCP)(HOST = MATRIX2)(PORT = 1521))
            (ADDRESS = (PROTOCOL = TCP)(HOST = MATRIX_DR01)(PORT = 1521))
            (ADDRESS = (PROTOCOL = TCP)(HOST = MATRIX_DR02)(PORT = 1521))
            (LOAD_BALANCE = yes)
        )
```

```
(CONNECT_DATA=
   (SERVICE_NAME=SALES)
 )
)
```

**TIP**
*In this example, Oracle Net aliases can also be coded into Java
Database Connectivity (JDBC) thin applications as a URL and achieve
the same functionality as Oracle Call Interface (OCI) clients.*

Using this example's connect descriptor, the following sections will illustrate how new and
existing connections will be properly routed only to the primary database.

# Connection Load Balancing and Connect Time Failover

As the size of database clusters grow, it becomes more and more important for connections to be
evenly distributed across nodes and instances as they are being created. This is true when a large
number of connections are created in a short period of time or for connections that are created in
a trickle. Oracle's basic mechanisms for evenly distributing connections are called *client-side* and
*server-side load balancing.* The following sections focus mainly on client-side load balancing and
connect-time failover, as they have the most impact on a client failover solution. The functionality
described here works with both OCI and Oracle JDBC clients.

### Client-side Load Balancing/Connect-time Failover

The `ADDRESS_LIST` in our example Oracle Net alias (or URL if you are using JDBC thin client) has
four address entries, each of which represents an Oracle listener running on a specific host and port.
When a connection is started, the process chooses an initial address from the `ADDRESS_LIST` to
attempt the connection. If `LOAD_BALANCE = YES` is included within the `ADDRESS_LIST`, the
address to which the connect is made is chosen at random. This is called *client-side load balancing.*
If the connection to the initial address does not succeed, Oracle Net will go back to the `ADDRESS_`
`LIST` and randomly choose a new address. This continues until the connection attempt succeeds.

**NOTE**
*Client-side load balancing is implicitly enabled if a* `DESCRIPTION_`
`LIST` *is included in the Oracle Net alias.*

If `LOAD_BALANCE` is set to `NO`, or is not included in the Oracle Net alias, then connection
attempts will always grab the first address from `ADDRESS_LIST`. If the connection to the initial
address does not succeed, Oracle Net will go back to the `ADDRESS_LIST` and choose the next
address. With client-side load balancing turned off, the addresses are attempted sequentially.

In addition to providing load balancing across different addresses (or nodes) with an
`ADDRESS_LIST`, you can also load balance connections across `DESCRIPTIONS` within a
`DESCRIPTION_LIST`. Consider the following example:

```
SALES =
   (DESCRIPTION =
      (ADDRESS_LIST =
       (LOAD_BALANCE= YES
```

```
            (ADDRESS = (PROTOCOL = TCP)(HOST = MATRIX1)(PORT = 1521))
            (ADDRESS = (PROTOCOL = TCP)(HOST = MATRIX2)(PORT = 1521)))
      (ADDRESS_LIST =
       (LOAD_BALANCE= YES
            (ADDRESS = (PROTOCOL = TCP)(HOST = MATRIX_DR01)(PORT = 1521))
            (ADDRESS = (PROTOCOL = TCP)(HOST = MATRIX_DR02)(PORT = 1521)))
      (CONNECT_DATA=
       (SERVICE_NAME=SALES)
      )
    )
```

In this example, when a connection attempt is made, a random address from the first ADDRESS_
LIST is obtained for the connection attempt. If that connection attempt fails, another address
from the top ADDRESS_LIST is randomly selected. If all addresses from the first ADDRESS_LIST
fail, you move to the second  ADDRESS_LIST and begin pulling addresses from that list in a
random order.

You must consider a few implications when building your Oracle Net alias to handle site
failover and choosing between load balancing against addresses in an ADDRESS_LIST or against
ADDRESS_LIST within a description. In our example, SALES Oracle Net alias, imagine that
MATRIX1 and MATRIX2 are the two nodes in our primary cluster and MATRIX_DR01 and
MATRIX_DR02 are the two nodes within our standby cluster. If the entire primary site cluster is
completely unavailable, then any new connection attempt using the alias with two addresses in
the ADDRESS_LIST will try the two primary hosts first before trying the two standby hosts, which
could take a considerable amount of time. (We will discuss how to mitigate this in the next
section, "Outbound Connect Timeout.")

If you use the Oracle Net alias with a single ADDRESS_LIST, then you at least have a fair
chance a choosing a standby host within the first two attempts.

One more important item to consider is centered on database services. In our CONNECT_
DESCRIPTOR we are connecting to a service called sales. If this service is available on the
primary database as well as a mounted standby database, and the connection attempt happens to
pull a standby host from the ADDRESS_LIST, then the connection attempt will fail with the
"ORA-01033: ORACLE initialization or shutdown in progress" error. If the standby database
happens to be opened read-only, then, worse yet, the connection to the standby will succeed.
We resolve this issue by assuring that the database service the application uses to connect to the
database is available only on the primary database and not the standby database. That way, if a
connection connects to a standby host connection, it will find the service unavailable and go
back to the ADDRESS_LIST and attempt a different host until it finds the service on a primary
host. The process of ensuring that the service is active only on the primary database occurs using
a trigger that is fired at instance startup. The trigger checks the database role, and if the role is
PRIMARY, then the service is started. Otherwise, the service is not started. Later in the chapter,
we will provide an example trigger that you can use to automate the relocation of the database
service during a Data Guard switchover or failover.

# Outbound Connect Timeout

As mentioned, it is quite possible that new connection attempts (or those being failed over) might
attempt to connect to a host that is unavailable. If the host is completely down or the network to
the host is unavailable, the connection attempt will wait for Transmission Control Protocol (TCP)
to timeout. If the client host has a TCP timeout of 10 minutes, it could take up to 30 minutes

before the connection attempt chooses a new primary host. This behavior can be mitigated by the use of the outbound connect timeout.

For OCI clients, outbound connect timeout is set in the sqlnet.ora using the following parameter:

`SQLNET.OUTBOUND_CONNECT_TIMEOUT`

This parameter is set to the number of seconds that you want Oracle Net to wait for a host to respond in a connection attempt. If no response is seen in that amount of time, Oracle Net will go back to the `ADDRESS_LIST` and attempt to find a new host. Setting the parameter to a value of 3 seconds, a recommended value, would allow a connection attempt to traverse an `ADDRESS_LIST` quickly until it finds a new primary host. As the parameter is set in the sqlnet.ora, any connection attempt using an Oracle Net alias that uses that sqlnet.ora will inherit the outbound connect timeout.

For Oracle JDBC clients, similar behavior can be achieved by setting a data source property called `SQLnetDef.TCP_CONNTIMEOUT_STR`. While technically this data source property can be set in milliseconds, we still recommend 3 seconds as a reasonable setting.

# Transparent Application Failover

So far, we have discussed client-side load balancing and connect-time failover, and hopefully you have a good understanding of how new connections can failover to different addresses within an Oracle Net alias. But how do sessions that are already connected to the database get failed over? That is what Transparent Application Failover (TAF) is specifically designed for. With TAF, when an existing session detects an error that would result in a disconnect, Oracle Net will automatically begin attempting to reconnect that session to another instance. This reconnection attempt can be configured to go specifically to a particular instance by using a designated Oracle Net alias, or you can simply use the connect time failover discussed earlier to find an available instance. In addition to failing over the session, TAF can also be configured to failover any running select statements that the session was performing. While TAF cannot failover inserts, updates, or deletes, an application can be configured to use OCI callbacks to capture those statements and replay them once the new session has been created.

In this section, we will discuss how to configure the different TAF options and how TAF plays a role in a client failover solution. If you want more information on how to write callbacks to failover various session state information or transaction statements, consult the Oracle documentation.

**NOTE**
*Transparent Application Failover is supported for all OCI and JDBC thick clients. Currently JDBC thin clients are not supported for use with TAF.*

## Configuring TAF

The first step in configuring TAF is to have a properly defined Oracle Net alias. When a TAF failover begins, we use client-side load balancing and connect-time failover to go back to the `ADDRESS_LIST` and grab a host to perform the reconnect. This means that we should start with an Oracle Net alias that has at least two or more addresses in an `ADDRESS_LIST`. But as with every rule, there is an exception. It is possible to have an Oracle Net alias that contains a single address in the `ADDRESS_LIST` and use the `BACKUP` attribute to point to another Oracle Net alias to use for TAF failover purposes. While using the `BACKUP` attribute does have it advantages, it does not handle all cases, so we won't discuss its usage further.

Once we have a properly formed Oracle Net alias, we need to decide how we want to configure our TAF attributes. TAF attributes include those described in the following sections.

**TYPE**   The TYPE attribute describes the type of failover. Possible values are

- **SESSION**   This specifies that when a failover occurs, TAF should create the session and perform no other action.

- **SELECT**   This specifies that when performing a failover, in addition to creating the session, TAF should also restart any select statements that were running at the time of the failover. When the select states are executed, Oracle Net will return only rows not previously returned to the user prior to failover.

- **NONE**   Do not perform a TAF failover.

**METHOD**   The METHOD attribute determines when the session is created. Possible values are

- **BASIC**   This establishes the session at the time of the failover.

- **PRECONNECT**   When the initial connection to the database is made, this creates the failover session using the Oracle Net alias designed by the BACKUP attribute.

**RETRIES**   The RETRIES attribute specifies the number of times Oracle Net will go back to the ADDRESS_LIST and attempt to connect to the surviving instance.

**DELAY**   The DELAY attribute specifies the number of seconds to wait between each retry.

The values to which you set the various TAF attributes are dictated by your application and business needs. For instance, having TAF precreate the failover session using the PRECONNECT attribute can speed up failover, since it does not have to create the session at failover time, but was mainly designed for active/passive cluster configurations. In addition, the DELAY and RETRIES attributes should be set so that TAF continues to retry long enough for a Data Guard failover or switchover to complete in your environment.

Setting the various TAF attributes can be at the client level within the Oracle Net alias the client uses to connect to the database, or at the server level, where they are associated with the database service used to connect. A client configuration within an Oracle Net alias would look something like the following:

```
SALES =
(DESCRIPTION =
   (ADDRESS_LIST =
    (LOAD_BALANCE= YES
       (ADDRESS = (PROTOCOL = TCP)(HOST = MATRIX1)(PORT = 1521))
       (ADDRESS = (PROTOCOL = TCP)(HOST = MATRIX2)(PORT = 1521))
       (ADDRESS = (PROTOCOL = TCP)(HOST = MATRIX_DR01)(PORT = 1521))
       (ADDRESS = (PROTOCOL = TCP)(HOST = MATRIX_DR02)(PORT = 1521)))
   (CONNECT_DATA=
    (SERVICE_NAME=SALES)
    (FAILOVER_MODE=(TYPE=SELECT)(METHOD=BASIC)(RETRIES=20)(DELAY=15)
   )
 )
```

This configuration instructs TAF to create the session at failover time and to re-execute any selects that were running when the failover occurred. In addition, if the first attempt at creating the session fails, TAF should wait 15 seconds before trying again for a total of 20 attempts.

When configuring TAF settings within an Oracle Net alias, any connection made using that alias inherits the TAF attributes. If you have multiple, or even thousands, of clients on individual hosts, you would need to configure TAF for each individual client. An option to this cumbersome approach is to use what is called *server-side TAF*. With server-side TAF, the TAF attributes are associated with the service on the database. Any client that connects to the database using the service that has the TAF attributes defined will automatically inherit them. In our example Oracle Net alias in the beginning of this section, the client will be connecting to the database using the service SALES. This is a database service that is created and started by including it in the SERVICE_NAMES init.ora parameter, by using SRVCTL in a Real Application Clusters (RAC), or by using the DBMS_SERVICE PL/SQL package. Regardless of which method was used to create or start the service, you use the DBMS_SERVICE PL/SQL to configure the TAF attributes. For example, on the database, execute the following:

```
exec DBMS_SERVICE.MODIFY_SERVICE(
       service_name => 'SALES',
       failover_method => 'BASIC',
       failover_type => 'SELECT',
       failover_retries => 20,
       failover_delay => 15);
```

No matter how you configure TAF, either at the client level or on the server side, you can verify your sessions current TAF setting by querying the V$SESSION view. For each session, V$SESSION will display the failover type, failover method, and if that session has ever been failed over in the past. Here's a simple SQL example to verify your current TAF settings:

```
SQL> SELECT SERVICE, FAILOVER_TYPE, FAILOVER_METHOD,
       FAILED_OVER FROM V$SESSION;
```

## Fast Application Notification

You have learned how new connections can perform failover between addresses in an ADDRESS_LIST and how existing connections can automatically perform failover between instances. But there's still more to learn. Imagine that you are using our example Oracle Net alias after configuring the server-side TAF for the sales service and have created numerous connections across a two-instance RAC cluster. Because this is a Data Guard book, you have dutifully created a two-node standby cluster, which is humming along quite nicely. All of a sudden, disaster strikes and both hosts in your primary cluster go down hard. Within minutes, you failover and transition your standby database to a primary. But for some reason, your existing application connections are just sitting there. Why isn't TAF kicking in and failing over the sessions to your new primary? Well, no one told your application connections that the primary hosts are gone and that you performed a failover.

The application connections have to wait for TCP to tell them that the primary hosts are no longer responding and that they should give up. With some operating systems running with default values, a TCP timeout could take up to 2 hours! The solution is Oracle *Fast Application Notification (FAN)*.

FAN can solve difficult TCP timeout issues by quickly notifying applications whenever a resource or component becomes unavailable. In addition to telling applications when resources have become unavailable, FAN also notifies the application when it should reconnect as new resources come online.

FAN comes in two basic flavors, with each geared specifically toward a distinct client base. FAN *Oracle Notification Service (ONS)* is designed for both JDBC thick and thin clients, while *FAN OCI* is used for all OCI-based clients. Each type of FAN implementation uses a different mechanism to notify clients, covered in the following sections along with client requirements.

## FAN ONS

FAN ONS is for both Oracle JDBC thick and thin drivers. FAN ONS delivers messages to the client application by using ONS daemons that are running on the database or cluster hosts. When you perform an Oracle Clusterware installation, you will see that the ONS daemons are automatically created and started for you. With the ONS daemons in place, you need to configure your JDBC application to subscribe to the available daemons upon application startup. Whenever a resource within the cluster changes state, Oracle Clusterware will publish a message to the ONS daemons, which is then consumed by the JDBC application. Depending on the type and contents of the message, the JDBC application will respond appropriately.

In order for JDBC clients to subscribe to ONS daemons and receive FAN events, they must first be configured for Fast Connection Failover (FCF). To configure for FCF, all JDBC applications must meet the following requirements:

- The JDBC application must do the following:

  - Use the Oracle JDBC driver.

  - Have the implicit connection cache enabled.

  - Connect to the database using services.

- ONS daemons must be running on the database hosts.

- The Java Virtual Machine (JVM) in which your JDBC instance is running must have `oracle.ons.oraclehome` set to point to your `ORACLE_HOME`.

## FAN OCI

FAN OCI is designed for, as you can probably guess, OCI clients. FAN OCI is different from FAN ONS in that it does not use ONS daemons to subscribe to and consume messages; instead, it has the database deliver messages directly to the OCI client. When an OCI client that is configured for FAN OCI connects to the database, an entry is placed in the `reg$` view that describes the application and how it can be contacted. As the state of resources (such as services, instances, or databases) changes, a FAN OCI message is placed into the database alert queue. Once the message is queued, a database process will wake up and send the message to all OCI clients that are registered in the `reg$` view. The OCI application then takes the correct actions depending on the FAN message.

For FAN OCI clients to receive the FAN message, they must meet the following requirements:

- The `OCI_EVENTS` must be enabled at the environment creation time on the client, as shown here:

  ```
  ( OCIEnvCreate(...) )
  ```

- The OCI application must be linked with the client or operating system thread library.

- The database service used by the application to connect to the database must have the AQ_HA_NOTIFICATIONS set to TRUE. Here's an example:

```
exec DBMS_SERVICE.MODIFY_SERVICE(
     service_name => 'SALES',
     failover_method => 'BASIC',
     failover_type => 'SELECT',
     failover_retries => 20,
     failover_delay => 15,
     aq_ha_notifications => true);
```

Note that in order to generate FAN OCI messages during a Data Guard failover, the failover must have been performed using the Data Guard Broker. The Data Guard Broker failover could have been executed by either the Enterprise Manager GUI or the DGMGRL command-line utility and can be a manual failover or a Fast-Start Failover. It is also important to note that due to FAN OCI's reliance on the SYS-owned reg$ table, logical standby databases do not support FAN OCI messaging.

## The DB_ROLE_CHANGE System Event

The process of performing a Data Guard failover is easy and straightforward. However, as you know, there is a lot more to performing a site failover than just reconfiguring the database. Oftentimes, a litany of application-related components must be either started or reconfigured so that they can correctly connect to the new primary database. Automation is the key to making this process as fast as possible and avoiding any mistakes. For that, we have the DB_ROLE_CHANGE system event.

The DB_ROLE_CHANGE system event is fired each time the role of the database is changed. For example, when either a physical or logical standby database is converted to a primary, the

### What if My Client Doesn't Meet the Requirements for FAN?

Not all applications are able to receive FAN events. For example, some application servers might use the Oracle JDBC driver but do not use the Oracle implicit connection cache. Or a third-party OCI application might not have been compiled with OCI_EVENTS mode enabled. How do applications that cannot support FAN achieve timely failovers? The answer is a combination of TCP timeouts and application retry logic.

On the host where the application is executed, you must configure the operating system TCP parameters for efficient timeouts. The OS TCP timeouts should be set to the amount of time it takes for the database layer to failover and the application services to be started. As different operating systems have different default values and different TCP implementations, it is best to consult your operating system manuals for how to configure TCP timeout properly.

In addition to configuring OS TCP timeouts, you must also configure for application retries. For example, when a session from the connection pool receives any exception that results in a disconnect (such as an ORA-3113 error), the application should automatically attempt to reconnect that session. The reconnection attempts should be configured so that they will continue for the length of time that it takes to failover the database layer and bring the application services online.

DB_ROLE_CHANGE system event is fired. The system event also fires whenever a primary is converted to either a physical or logical standby.

We can use this system event to write a trigger that can perform any number of functions at failover time. The next example creates a trigger that fires at failover and uses the DBMS_ SCHEDULER to call an external script:

```
CREATE OR REPLACE TRIGGER failover_actions AFTER DB_ROLE_CHANGE ON DATABASE
  BEGIN
    dbms_scheduler.create_job(
    job_name=>'publish_events',
    job_type=>'executable',
    job_action=>'/u01/oracle/failover_actions.sh',
    enabled=>TRUE
    );
  END;
```

This script can contain any actions that you want performed at failover, such as starting application middle tiers, starting message queues, and so on.

# Implementing Client Failover

This is where the rubber meets the road. Whether you came directly here from the beginning of the chapter or you took the leisurely stroll through the "Nitty Gritty" section, it is now time to get your hands dirty. In this section, we will address configuration details for a complete site failover as well as a partial failover. Each section will cover how to configure client-side components as well as database components.

## Complete Site Failover Configuration

Application deployments that need to configure for a complete site failover have completely redundant application components between the primary and standby data centers. Typically within each site is a network load balancer or traffic manager, which accepts incoming client requests. This traffic manager then distributes the requests to various application servers on that site. When a site failover occurs, the standby on the secondary site is transitioned to a primary database and the secondary site application servers are started.

Once all the application components have been made available, one of the following two events typically occurs:

- The virtual IP address that the client used to connect to the traffic manager is removed from the primary site traffic manager (if it is still available) and started on the secondary site traffic manager.

- The secondary site traffic manager is started with an IP address that is different from the primary site traffic manager and the DNS entries for the hostname used in the connection by the clients are remapped to this new IP address.

### Configuring Clients

The configuration for clients in respect to Oracle Net aliases or a JDBC thin URL is generally unnecessary in a complete site failover case, as they usually reference a single hostname that is mapped to a virtual IP address. Clients could also be configured so that the administrator changes the DNS name mapping to the new IP address after the failover completes.

If the DNS name mapping is changed, then the client may have to flush the DNS name cache on the local machine. For example, the following procedure could occur with the DNS name change:

1. Update the master DNS server to associate the second traffic manager IP address with the hostname that the client used to connect to the database.

2. Slave DNS servers are notified via the DNS NOTIFY announcement.

3. Clear any caching DNS servers using a command similar to the following:

   ```
   rndc flush
   ```

4. Clear any local DNS caching on the client host. In Linux, you can execute the nscd command, and in the Windows environment, you can execute the ipconfig command with the /flushdns option:

   ```
   Linux: /etc/init.d/nscd restart
   Microsoft Windows: ipconfig /flushdns
   ```

### Configuring the Database

Normally we recommend that the database service that the client uses to connect to the database be started and available only on the database that has the primary role. This is to prevent client connections from attempting to connect to the standby database. For the complete site failover scenario, this is not a concern, as the traffic managers are responsible for funneling connections to the correct application servers on the correct site.

One database configuration that can aid in the complete site failover is the creation of a trigger around the DB_ROLE_CHANGE system event. This trigger can be used to automate tasks that need to be performed once the database failover has completed. For example, the database trigger can call an external script that in turns starts the application servers or perhaps message queues. In some cases, the script can be used to configure traffic managers or DNS servers. For an example of this trigger, see the earlier section, "The DB_ROLE_CHANGE System Event."

### Partial Site Failover

With partial site failover, the database is failed over but the original application server connections are maintained. Solving the partial site failover scenario is difficult because you must assure that application connections do not connect to the wrong resources, do not get stuck waiting on long timeouts, and when they do reconnect, they do not get stuck waiting on resources or hosts that are no longer available. To meet these objectives, we will have to deploy the technologies and features discussed in the "Nitty Gritty" section earlier in this chapter.

Due to our experiences working with users, we will explain how to achieve seamless partial site failover in a phased approach. Experience has shown that users situations are typically one of three types:

- While the database can failover in less than 30 seconds, the decision to perform a database failover takes hours. Once the database has failed over, the application servers are restarted and the only the application servers are connected to the new primary without any configuration changes.

- Database failover is automated and can occur in less than 30 seconds and so should the application. However, the client application does not support FAN events.

- Database failover is automated and occurs in less than 30 seconds. The application supports FAN and failover should be automatic and efficient.

As you can guess, the configuration for the third type is far more complex than for the first. We will attack this section in a tiered approach, starting with, as you might guess, the first type. Each section is dependent on the steps undertaken in the preceding section.

## First: The Basics

The basic configuration will allow applications to be restarted after a failover has occurred and will have the application connections correctly find the new primary. The application connections should quickly bypass any old primary hosts, which may be unavailable or may have lost network connectivity.

### Client-side Configuration

1. The client configuration should include a connect descriptor that includes all potential primary hosts in an ADDRESS_LIST and should have connect time failover enabled. In addition, this connect descriptor should be connecting to the database using a database service in the CONNECT_DATA portion instead of a SID entry. Here's an example:

```
SALES =
  (DESCRIPTION =
     (ADDRESS_LIST =
         (ADDRESS = (PROTOCOL = TCP)(HOST = MATRIX1)(PORT = 1521))
         (ADDRESS = (PROTOCOL = TCP)(HOST = MATRIX2)(PORT = 1521))
         (ADDRESS = (PROTOCOL = TCP)(HOST = MATRIX_DR01)(PORT = 1521))
         (ADDRESS = (PROTOCOL = TCP)(HOST = MATRIX_DR02)(PORT = 1521))
        (LOAD_BALANCE = yes)
      )
     (CONNECT_DATA=
       (SERVICE_NAME=SALES)
      )
   )
```

2. When the application connections are being made, if they should happen to attempt to connect to an old primary host that is unavailable, the connection attempt to that host should last no longer than 3 seconds. This allows for connection attempts to get through the ADDRESS_LIST quickly until a new primary host is found. For an OCI client, set the following in the sqlnet.ora file:

```
SQLNET.OUTBOUND_CONNECT_TIMEOUT=3
```

For JDBC thick and thin clients, configure the following property on the DataSource (what a JDBC application uses to define the connection to the database):

```
SQLnetDef.TCP_CONNTIMEOUT_STR=3000
```

### Database Configuration

1. On the primary database, create the database service that the application will use to connect to the database. The service can be created using the DBMS_SERVICE PL/SQL package or via the srvctl Clusterware utility:

```
exec DBMS_SERVICE.CREATE_SERVICE (
      service_name => 'sales',
      network_name => 'sales');
```

Note that you should not include the service name in the SERVICE_NAMES parameter. Instead, you should allow the trigger described in the next step to manage the starting and stopping of the service.

2. For reasons listed in the "Nitty Gritty" section, you want only the service running on the primary database. To automate the starting and stopping of the service, deploy an on database startup trigger:

```
CREATE OR REPLACE TRIGGER manage_service
    after startup on database
DECLARE
role VARCHAR(30);
BEGIN
SELECT DATABASE_ROLE INTO role FROM V$DATABASE;
IF role = 'PRIMARY' THEN
   DBMS_SERVICE.START_SERVICE('SALES');
END IF;
   END;
```

Note that if you are using a logical standby, you should also create the same trigger around the DB_ROLE_CHANGE system event. A logical standby applies changes while it is open. At failover time, the logical is converted to a primary without the need to restart the instance, which means the after startup on database trigger will not fire. Since the DB_ROLE_CHANGE trigger will fire at failover time for a logical, you can use it to start the service at failover time and depend on the after startup on database trigger to start it upon subsequent restarts.

## Second: Stepping It Up a Notch

The next step up in a client failover configuration is to have the database and client connections failover automatically. New and existing connections should be correctly routed to the new primary database. This configuration also accounts for applications that cannot make use of FAN messaging. As mentioned earlier, the steps for this configuration build upon the preceding example.

### Client-side Configuration

1. Since the client application needs to failover its connection automatically and the application doesn't meet the requirements for FAN messaging, you must configure the client operating system TCP timeouts. The TCP timeouts should be set to the amount of time it takes for the database layer to failover and the application services to be started. As different operating systems have different default values and different TCP implementations, it is best to consult your operating system manuals for how to configure

TCP timeout properly. Failing to configure these timeouts will result in your applications hanging for the timeout period before they will failover.

2.  Once the existing application connections receive an exception, the application should be coded to automatically retry. For OCI applications (and JDBC thick applications), you can use TAF to automate this retry. For applications that cannot make use of TAF (JDBC thin applications), retry logic should be built into the application. For example, when a session from the connection pool receives any exception that results in a disconnect (such as an ORA-3113 error), the application should automatically attempt to reconnect that session. The reconnection attempts should be configured so that they will continue for the length of time that it takes to failover the database layer and bring the application services online.

**Database Configuration**   To automate the reconnection of existing sessions for OCI applications, server-side TAF should be configured on the database for the service that the application uses to connect to the database. Here's an example:

```
exec DBMS_SERVICE.MODIFY_SERVICE(
    service_name => 'SALES',
    failover_method => 'BASIC',
    failover_type => 'SELECT',
    failover_retries => 180,
    failover_delay => 1);
```

## Third: Ultimate Client Failover

In this client failover configuration, the database and the application connections are failed over automatically. When the failover has completed, the application should be notified via FAN messages that the old primary is unavailable and the application should connect to the new primary database.

### Client-side Configuration

For OCI applications, the following requirements must be met in order to receive FAN OCI messages:

1.  Enable the `OCI_EVENTS` at the environment creation time on the client as follows:

    ```
    ( OCIEnvCreate(...) )
    ```

2.  OCI application must be linked with the client thread or operating system library.

JDBC applications should be configured for Fast Connection Failover. In addition, JDBC applications should meet the FCF requirements that were discussed in the "Nitty Gritty" section:

1.  The client application must use an implicit JDBC connection cache on its data source by setting the `DataSource` property `FastConnectionFailoverEnabled` to `True`. Here's an example:

    ```
    OracleDataSource ods = new OracleDataSource()
    ...
    ```

```
ods.setUser("hr");
ods.setPassword("hr");
ods.setConnectionCachingEnabled(True);
ods.setFastConnectionFailoverEnabled(True);
ods.setConnectionCacheName("MyCache");
ods.setConnectionCacheProperties(cp);
```

2. Configure the JDBC application to subscribe to remote ONS daemons that exist on the primary and standby hosts. If the primary and standby have Oracle Clusterware installed, these ONS daemons should already exist. If the primary and standby hosts are not part of a cluster, the ONS daemons on each host need to be created. To create and start the ONS daemons, use an ONS configuration file to configure ONS. This file should exist in the $ORACLE_HOME/opmn/conf directory after installation of the Oracle software stack. It should be configured similar to the following:

```
localport=6100
remoteport=4200
loglevel=3
nodes=halinux03:6200,halinux04:6200
```

In this example, the `nodes` parameter points to the primary and standby hosts followed by the remote port for the ONS daemon running on that port. Once the configuration file has been created, you can start the ONS daemon on the middle tier or client nodes by issuing the following command:

```
$onsctl start
```

3. After the ONS daemons have been created and started, configure the JDBC application to remotely subscribe to those daemons:

```
ods.setONSConfiguration("halinux03:6200,halinux04:6200");
```

**Database Configuration**   The good news for those of you with OCI applications is that you are pretty much done at this point. When the OCI application connects to the database, all necessary information to construct the FAN message as well as how to contact the client is placed into the reg$ table. When a Data Guard failover is performed using the Data Guard Broker, the FAN OCI event is automatically created and sent to the application.

For those of you with JDBC applications, you have some work to finish. Currently, FAN ONS is designed to work within a cluster. The Oracle Clusterware processes are primarily designed to publish FAN events. In other words, one cluster cannot send FAN events for other clusters and their resources. However, when we perform a failover to a secondary cluster due to complete loss of the primary cluster, that is exactly what we need to do. To resolve this dilemma, we must configure an external ONS publisher and call that publisher when a failover occurs. With the help of a configuration file, this publisher will create events that tell the application that the old primary database is down and where the new primary database resides. Configuring for this external ONS publisher is the final step for those with JDBC applications.

To configure the ONS publisher, do the following:

1. In the $ORACLE_HOME/dbs directory on each node that has the potential to be a primary, create a file named cfo{$ORACLE_SID}.ora. The configuration file will be used

by the ONS publisher to construct the ONS events prior to sending it to the application. To show how to configure the contents of this file, assume the following values for the Data Guard configuration:

| Database | Host | Instance Name | DB_UNIQUE_NAME |
|----------|------|---------------|----------------|
| Primary | hasun01 | Matrix1 | Matrix |
| Primary | hasun02 | Matrix2 | Matrix |
| Standby | hasun42 | Matrix_DR0 | Matrix_DR0 |

The following example show the FAN ONS configuration file configured using the values shown in the table:

```
Matrix peer=Matrix_DR0
Matrix_DR0 peer=Matrix
Matrix service=SALES location=hasun01,Matrix1:hasun02,Matrix2
Matrix_DR0 service=SALES location=hasun42,Matrix_DR0
```

2. When calling an external program from the database, you need to pass the program the appropriate environment variables such as ORACLE_HOME, ORACLE_SID, and so on. It is often easier to do this by building a wrapper script around the external program that you are calling and set the variables in the wrapper script. When calling the ONS publisher, you would use a wrapper script similar to the following:

```
#!/bin/ksh
export TZ=PST8PDT
export ORACLE_SID=sales
export ORACLE_HOME=/u01/app/oracle/product/10.2.0
export LD_LIBRARY_PATH=/u01/app/oracle/product/10.2.0/lib
export PATH=/u01/app/oracle/product/10.2.0/bin:$PATH
/u01/app/oracle/product/10.2.0/bin/cfo r
```

In this wrapper script's last line, the ONS publisher is called with the r option, which indicates that it should be executed and the events published. Note that when configuring the publisher on a RAC, the ORA_CRS_HOME variable must be set so that the publisher will use the ONS daemons in the Oracle CRS home instead of the ONS daemons in the Oracle database home.

3. Now you are ready to configure the database to call the ONS publisher whenever a failover has occurred. Use the DB_ROLE_CHANGE system event to fire this trigger. On the primary database, create the role-change trigger that will generate the redo that will update the standby. In the following example, a trigger called ons_publish is provided to send events when a database role changes:

```
CREATE OR REPLACE TRIGGER ons_publish
AFTER DB_ROLE_CHANGE ON
    DATABASE
BEGIN
        dbms_scheduler.create_job(
        job_name=>'publish_events',
```

```
        job_type=>'executable',
        job_action=>'/u01/oracle/product/10.2.0/db_1/bin/cfo.sh',
        enabled=>TRUE
        );
END;
```

Once the trigger DDL has been recovered on the standby, your clients are fully prepared for automatic and seamless reconnection in the event of a failover.

# Conclusion

As you have seen, failing over your database with Oracle Data Guard can be done easily and quickly. It's also important to devote considerable effort to assuring that your application connections, both new and existing, can also failover easily and quickly. Configuring for proper application failover can greatly reduce your overall downtime and help you meet even the most stringent service level agreements. Hopefully, this chapter has helped you understand the various Oracle technologies associated with application failover as well as how to configure them to craft a complete solution.

# CHAPTER
## 11

# Minimizing Planned Downtime Using Data Guard Switchover

his chapter discusses how Data Guard can be leveraged in cases of planned migrations. The first part of this chapter covers use case examples of migration to a new system configuration using Data Guard switchover. The second part covers database rolling upgrades. The preceding chapters of this book have already covered the mechanics of Data Guard configuration and switchover, so we draw on those parts of the book to help explain the concepts presented here.

# Overview of Planned Migration

As explained in earlier chapters, you can leverage Data Guard to provide high availability for planned as well as unplanned outages. However, Data Guard can also be used in planned migration strategies such as the following:

- **Data Center migration** Create a standby at the new data center and then switchover.

- **Migrating to Automatic Storage Management (ASM) and/or Real Application Clusters (RAC)** Create an ASM standby from a non-ASM primary and then switchover. A similar scenario can be leveraged for migration to RAC.

- **Refreshing technology stack** Create a standby database on new servers and/or storage and then switchover.

- **Implementing database changes in a rolling fashion—for example, Automatic Segment Space Management (ASSM), `initrans`, and `blocksize`** Build a logical standby database, implement the required database changes, and then switchover.

- **Upgrading database release** Use a transient logical standby database for rolling database upgrades. This is the focus of the second section of this chapter.

- **Migrating to a different OS/platform** Use a physical standby for platform migrations. Currently this is supported only with the following: Windows to Linux, 32-bit to 64-bit, Hewlett Packard Unix (HP-UX) to a reduced instruction set computer (RISC). (See MetaLink Note 413484.1 for more details.)

**NOTE**
*The standby and primary servers of a Data Guard environment do not have to match from a configuration perspective—for example, the size of the servers, number of CPUs, or number of RAC nodes. However, the OS, platform, and database software version need to be same. As we discussed earlier in this book, there are some exceptions to this rule. Although the configuration between the primary and standby systems can differ, it is important to keep in mind that the standby should have enough overall capacity to handle the production workload in the case of a switchover or failover.*

# Leveraging Data Guard Switchover for Planned Migration

Leveraging Data Guard in planned migration scenarios lets you not only switchover to the new configuration with very little downtime, but also lets you streamline failback in case of an emergency. This section addresses a couple of planned migration scenarios, such as data center moves, technology stack changes, or migration to ASM/RAC. Let's take a deeper look at two real-world use cases for a planned migration that leverages Data Guard.

## Case 1–New Data Center

In the first case, customer ABC wants to move to a new data center as well as to a new product stack. The source system is a two-node RAC configuration using third-party Clusterware. The target system is a four-node stack, with Oracle Clusterware, ASM, and RAC. In addition, this customer wants to enable some key new features such as flashback logging. This customer also has a downtime limitation of 6 hours.

Using AWR reports, `iostats`, and `vmstat` reports from the current production configuration, the customer designs the target environment to meet the needs of the expected production workload and SLA, including storage, memory, and CPU. After the new data center is built, the Data Guard standby is put in place using Maximum Performance (LGWR ASYNC). This customer also wants to capitalize on the standby resources by running Active Data Guard on the standby site to offload batch reporting. (Active Data Guard was discussed in Chapter 9.)

Once the standby is built, it is initially relegated to disaster recovery (DR) duties. On designated weekends, a switchover to the standby site is performed, so that maintenance can be performed on the primary (such as upgrading the hardware, enabling flashback database, or patching the O/S and Clusterware), and so that the standby database can take on weekend batch work. This has the side benefit of validating the capability and configuration of the standby Data Guard environment. After the weekend maintenance is completed, a switchback to the original primary site is performed. As more confidence is gained in the standby site configuration, the workload and duration of standby site usage increases—that is, it goes from weekend duties to weeklong activities. After several months of switchover and switchback as well as testing heavier workloads on the standby, the customer decides to migrate the production environment permanently to the standby (the new primary), and the old primary is relegated to standby duties. Once the predefined burn-in time for the new primary production site is met, the standby database site (old primary) is rebuilt to resemble the new production site.

By configuring and using a Data Guard standby database in this migration scenario, this customer saved millions of dollars in outage prevention and also leveraged the Data Guard resources to offload work from the primary database.

## Case 2–Move to ASM

In this use case, customer XYZ has a 5-TB database across seven Veritas file systems and wants to migrate to ASM. This needs to be performed with minimum downtime. A fallback plan must also be in place in case of emergency. In addition, due to budgetary constraints, the customer does not have extra server hardware for configuring a remote Data Guard environment, so the migration to ASM will be done in place—that is, Data Guard will be configured on the same server as the production database, with the Data Guard physical standby residing in ASM. In this case, the physical standby is configured as Maximum Availability.

An RMAN duplicate using the FROM ACTIVE DATABASE feature is used to instantiate the physical standby database. Also, the Real Application Testing (RAT) tool is used to capture/replay the database transaction load. Once the physical standby has caught up with the production database, a restore point is created and the ASM-based physical standby is restarted as a snapshot standby. RAT Capture is used to capture a workload and RAT Database Replay is then used to replay the transaction workload on the ASM based standby database (snapshot standby). AWR reports are captured to analyze the performance of the ASM-based configuration.

The read-write database is subsequently converted back to the physical standby role with SQL*Plus or the Broker, which uses the Flashback Database feature and the guaranteed restore point (GRP). Once it is verified that the ASM-based database can sustain the production workload, a brief, planned outage is scheduled to perform a Data Guard switchover to the ASM-based configuration. This switchover takes only a couple of minutes to complete.

The Veritas file system–based database is kept online as a standby database, but is eventually torn down once the customer is confident that the ASM-based configuration is performing as expected.

# Performing a Database Rolling Upgrade Using Data Guard

One of the key use cases of planned migration is deployment of Data Guard for rolling upgrades. Performing rolling upgrades using standby databases allows you to upgrade the database infrastructure with very little downtime.

Performing an upgrade, say from Oracle Database 10.2 to 11.1, in a non–Data Guard environment would require hours of downtime. Performing a rolling upgrade using Data Guard provides a mechanism to upgrade the database infrastructure without incurring large outages on the production servers.

The database upgrade includes two stages: updating the binary files and updating the database objects. The binary files upgrade is picked up with the new installation of the Oracle Database software. For the upgrade of database objects, once the physical standby has caught up to the new primary, it will be automatically upgraded (by virtue of Redo Apply).

By using the standby database, application downtime primarily due to PL/SQL recompilation is eliminated. In addition, the following intensive efforts are offloaded to the standby site:

■ Validation of the new software release

■ The database upgrade process

■ Any unexpected upgrade problems

■ Any preliminary performance troubleshooting

A rolling upgrade can be performed using SQL Apply or the transient logical standby method. The general, high-level steps are similar for both methods, and the differences are primarily in the state of the standby database after the completion of the upgrade. With the SQL Apply method, the upgrade concludes with one site continuing to be a logical standby database, while in the transient logical standby method, one site will revert back to being a physical standby after the upgrade. However, in both cases, the upgrade incurs very little downtime. The overall downtime is generally the time it takes to perform a switchover.

In the next section, we will examine the steps for deploying both methods. In our sample cases, we will perform a rolling upgrade from Oracle Database 11.1.0.6 to 11.1.0.7.

# Leveraging Rolling Upgrades Using SQL Apply

The steps outlined in this section assume that a logical standby already exists and is currently being used to provide a reporting database solution for the primary database. In addition, we also assume that unsupported database data types (for the logical standby database) are already processed and handled accordingly. (Chapter 4 discusses how to handle unsupported logical standby data types.)

The following high-level steps describe a rolling upgrade using a logical standby database:

1. Prep the environment in order to establish a logical standby configuration. Ensure that flashback logging is enabled on the primary and standby. If it is not enabled, it will require a small outage (database shutdown and startup mount) to enable it:

   ```
   SHUTDOWN IMMEDIATE   <- Note, for Oracle RAC environments this needs to
   be  performed on all instances
   STARTUP MOUNT
   ALTER DATABASE FLASHBACK ON
   ALTER DATABASE OPEN
   ```

2. Data Guard Broker configurations are not supported in this rolling upgrade methodology. If the Broker is being used, the Broker must be disabled on both the primary and standby databases:

   ```
   ALTER SYSTEM SET DG_BROKER_START=FALSE SCOPE=BOTH;
   ```

   The Data Guard Broker can be re-enabled after the completion of the rolling upgrade.

3. The Data Guard protection mode must be set to either Maximum Availability or Maximum Performance:

   ```
   SELECT PROTECTION_MODE FROM V$DATABASE;
   ```

4. To ensure that the primary database can proceed while the logical standby database is being upgraded, the LOG_ARCHIVE_DEST_$n$ init.ora parameter pointing to the logical standby database destination must be set to OPTIONAL if it was set to MANDATORY.

5. The COMPATIBLE init.ora parameter must match the software release prior to the upgrade—for example, if upgrading from 11.1.0.6 to 11.1.0.7, set the COMPATIBLE parameter to 11.1.0.6. Note that once the COMPATIBLE parameter is updated to the target database release, you cannot downgrade to an earlier release. For this reason, it is recommended that you thoroughly test (burn-in) on the current version before advancing the COMPATIBLE value. Once you are satisfied with the upgraded version, the COMPATIBLE value can be increased.

6. You can optionally create an archived redo log repository with the same database release (the target release) and COMPATIBLE setting as the primary database so that redo is still received while applying the patch or upgrading the database. Creating a repository ensures that you can meet the recovery point objective (RPO) if the primary site fails during the upgrade of the logical. Oracle MetaLink Note 434164.1[1] covers this topic.

---

[1] See MetaLink Note 434164.1: "Data Guard Archived Redo Log Repository Example"

7. Install an upgraded ORACLE_HOME, which is separate from the current ORACLE_HOME. For RAC configurations, this needs to be performed on each node of the cluster. This install can be done using the Oracle home cloning utility and then patching this ORACLE_HOME location accordingly. The cloning process is described as below. First, establish the new ORACLE_HOME:

```
cp -pr /u01/app/oracle/product/11.1.0.6 /u01/app/oracle/
product/11.1.0.7
```

Use the Oracle-provided cloning utility to update the Oracle Software Inventory with the new ORACLE_HOME location:

```
/u01/app/oracle/product/11.1.0.7/clone/bin/clone.pl
ORACLE_HOME=/u01/app/oracle/product/11.1.0.7 ORACLE_HOME_NAME=11gR1d07 '-
O"CLUSTER_NODES={node1,node2}"' '-O"LOCAL_NODE=node1"'
```

8. As root user, run /u01/app/oracle/product/11.1.0.7/root.sh.

9. Now upgrade the new ORACLE_HOME to 11.1.0.7 using Oracle Universal Installer to apply the patchset.

10. As part of the pre-upgrade process, stop redo transport to the standby:

```
ALTER SYSTEM SET LOG_ARCHIVE_DEST_STATE_2=DEFER SCOPE=MEMORY
```

11. Perform pre-upgrade steps on the logical standby:

It is also recommended that you create a GRP on the logical standby. This GRP will be used in case issues with the upgrade process are encountered and fallback recovery is needed.

```
CREATE RESTORE POINT SQLAPPLY_PRE_UPGRADE GUARANTEE FLASHBACK DATABASE;
```

12. Upgrade the ORACLE_HOME software on the logical standby system. Note that if the standby database is configured in a RAC environment, then the Oracle Clusterware has to be at the highest version—in this example, 11.1.0.7. Ensure that the Oracle Clusterware is at the highest and same release across all nodes of the cluster before starting the database rolling upgrade. If the Oracle Clusterware needs to be upgraded, it can be upgraded in a rolling upgrade fashion as well. During the Clusterware rolling upgrade, the ASM and standby instance on the node being upgraded will need to be down.

Once the Clusterware is upgraded to 11.1.0.7, you can optionally (though highly recommended) upgrade ASM to 11.1.0.7 as well. ASM is also rolling upgradeable in Oracle Database 11g—that is, rolling upgrade can be used to upgrade from 11.1.0.6 to 11.1.0.7.

13. The upgrade will be performed on the logical standby database; thus you will need to stop SQL Apply:

```
ALTER DATABASE STOP LOGICAL STANDBY APPLY;
```

14. Shut down the logical standby database.

15. Set the ORACLE_HOME environment variable to the new software location, and start up the logical standby using this new upgraded ORACLE_HOME.

16. Execute the Database Upgrade Assistant (DBUA) utility from the new ORACLE_HOME. It is highly recommended that you use the DBUA utility for all upgrade scenarios, such as from 10gR2 to 11g upgrades, because it prevents errors and handles several post-upgrade

tasks such as Clusterware OCR updates as well as `oratab` changes. For an Oracle patchset apply, such as 11.1.0.7, use the Oracle Universal Installer.

**17.** Update the OCR with the new ORACLE_HOME location for this logical standby database srvctl modify database -d MATRIX-0 `/u01/app/oracle/product/11.1.0.7`.

**18.** If an archived redo log repository was used (in step 6), you can use the `RMAN CATALOG` command to catalog the archived redo log repository destination to avoid resending those logs:

```
RMAN> CATALOG START WITH '+FRA/Matrix_DR1/ARCHIVELOG/';
```

**19.** Restart the logical standby database:

```
STARTUP MOUNT;
ALTER DATABASE START LOGICAL STANDBY APPLY IMMEDIATE;
```

**20.** You can now restart the transport services for redo to the logical standby from the primary database:

```
ALTER SYSTEM SET LOG_ARCHIVE_DEST_STATE_2=ENABLE SCOPE=MEMORY
```

At this point, the primary is running the lower version of the software and the logical standby is running the upgrade software version. To finish up the rolling upgrade process, you should upgrade/patch the primary database. A switchover will be performed to change the primary database role to the logical standby role, and will go through the same upgrade process.

**21.** On the current primary, before proceeding with the switchover, query the V$DATABASE view for the SWITCHOVER_STATUS. If the status indicates TO STANDBY, then it is safe to proceed. Otherwise, switchover with SESSION DISCONNECT:

```
SELECT SWITCHOVER_STATUS FROM V$DATABASE;
ALTER DATABASE COMMIT TO SWITCHOVER TO LOGICAL STANDBY;
```

**22.** Similarly, on the logical standby, before proceeding with the switchover, query the V$DATABASE view for the SWITCHOVER_STATUS. If the status indicates TO PRIMARY, then it is safe to proceed. Otherwise switchover with SESSION DISCONNECT:

```
ALTER DATABASE COMMIT TO SWITCHOVER TO PRIMARY;
```

**23.** The former logical standby database is now the primary database and also running the latest upgraded code. However, the new standby (former primary) cannot receive or apply redo because it is running at a lower database version than the new primary database; therefore, you must disable redo transmission on the new primary:

```
ALTER SYSTEM SET LOG_ARCHIVE_DEST_STATE_2=DEFER SCOPE=MEMORY;
```

**24.** Repeat the upgrade process starting from step 7 for this new logical standby.

**25.** Once you are satisfied with the new Oracle version, it is recommended that you set the COMPATIBLE settings to the rolling upgraded versions. You can plan this change for a later time since changing COMPATIBLE requires an outage.

**26.** Optionally, for customers who want to return back to the original configuration (the primary-logical configuration prior to starting the rolling upgrade), a switchover can be performed.

**27.** Drop the restore point created in step 9. If you forget to do this, your flash recovery area will be consumed with flashback logs.

```
DROP RESTORE POINT SQLAPPLY_PRE_UPGRADE
```

**28.** Enable Data Guard Broker if it was previously in place. This needs to performed on the primary and standby databases:

```
ALTER SYSTEM SET DG_BROKER_START=TRUE SCOPE=BOTH;
```

# Rolling Upgrades Using Transient Logical Standby

In this method, a rolling upgrade is performed using a physical standby database that is temporarily converted to a logical standby. The logical standby database is upgraded, and when the switchover has occurred, the logical standby is reverted back to being the physical standby.

The rolling database upgrade process using the transient logical standby is illustrated in Figure 11-1.

This method is applicable in Oracle Database 10gR2 and 11gR1 standby database environments. The notable difference between the Oracle Database 10gR2 and 11gR1 is that new syntax is included to facilitate this conversion and many fewer steps are required to accomplish this in 11g.

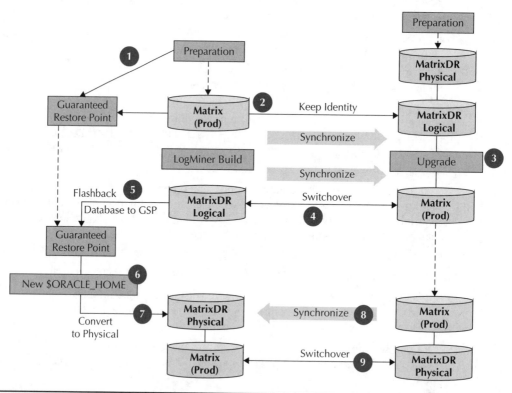

**FIGURE 11-1.** *Rolling database upgrade with transient logical standby*

Some differences also exist between the Oracle Database 11*g* and 10*g*R2 process flow with regard to RAC configurations: see Oracle MetaLink Note 300479.1[2] for more details.

Performing a rolling upgrade using a transient logical standby is similar to the standard SQL Apply rolling upgrade process, described earlier, with the following differences:

- A GRP is created on the primary database for the purpose of flashing it back to become a physical standby after the switchover.

- The conversion of a physical standby to a logical standby uses the new KEEP IDENTITY clause to retain the same DB_NAME and DBID as that of its primary database.

- The ALTER DATABASE CONVERT TO PHYSICAL STANDBY statement is used to convert the original primary from a logical standby to a physical standby.

  - The original primary is actually upgraded by means of Redo Apply after it is converted from a logical standby to a physical standby.

The high-level steps for this process are shown next:

1. Prep the environment to establish a logical standby configuration. First, review for any unsupported datatypes on the primary database. Unsupported datatypes will be skipped on the logical standby. Chapter 4 covers the handling of unsupported data types with logical standby databases.

2. Ensure that enough SRLs are created on the standby site.

3. Data Guard Broker configurations are not supported in this rolling upgrade methodology, and thus the Broker must be disabled on both the primary and standby databases:

   ```
   ALTER SYSTEM SET DG_BROKER_START=FALSE SCOPE=BOTH;
   ```

   The Broker can be re-enabled after the completion of the rolling upgrade.

4. The Data Guard protection mode must be set to either Maximum Availability or Maximum Performance. Verify the protection mode using the following query:

   ```
   SELECT PROTECTION_MODE FROM V$DATABASE
   ```

5. To ensure that the primary database can proceed while the logical standby database is being upgraded, set the LOG_ARCHIVE_DEST_*n* init.ora parameter pointing to the logical standby database destination to OPTIONAL.

6. Set the COMPATIBLE init.ora parameter to match the software release prior to the upgrade. For example, if upgrading from 11.1.0.6 to 11.1.0.7, then set the COMPATIBLE parameter to 11.1.0.6. Note that once you have updated the COMPATIBLE parameter to the target database release, you cannot downgrade to an earlier release with FLASHBACK DATABASE or the database downgrade procedure. The COMPATIBLE value can be increased once you are comfortable with the upgrade.

7. Set the LOG_FILE_NAME_CONVERT parameter to the appropriate location. It is a best practice to set this parameter, regardless of whether the location structures between the two sites are the same. Setting this parameter optimizes log clearing and switchover capabilities:

   ```
   ALTER SYSTEM SET LOG_FILE_NAME_CONVERT= ' ',' ' SCOPE=SPFILE;
   ```

---

[2] See MetaLink Note 300479.1: "10g Rolling Upgrades with Logical Standby"

8. Ensure that flashback logging is enabled on the primary. If it is not enabled, it will require a small outage (database shutdown and startup mount) to enable it.

```
SHUTDOWN IMMEDIATE  <- For Oracle RAC, perform on all instances
STARTUP MOUNT
ALTER DATABASE FLASHBACK ON
ALTER DATABASE OPEN
```

9. Install an upgraded ORACLE_HOME on each node. This can be done using an Oracle home cloning utility and then patching this ORACLE_HOME location accordingly. Establish the new ORACLE_HOME:

```
cp -pr /u01/app/oracle/product/11.1.0.6 /u01/app/oracle/
product/11.1.0.7
```

Use the Oracle-provided cloning utility to update the Oracle Software Inventory with the new ORACLE_HOME location:

```
/u01/app/oracle/product/11.1.0.7/clone/bin/clone.pl
ORACLE_HOME=/u01/app/oracle/product/11.1.0.7 ORACLE_HOME_NAME=11gR1d07 '-
O"CLUSTER_NODES={node1,node2}"' '-O"LOCAL_NODE=node1"'
```

10. As root user, run /u01/app/oracle/product/11.1.0.7/root.sh.

11. Now upgrade the new ORACLE_HOME to 11.1.0.7.

12. Create a GRP on the primary:

```
CREATE RESTORE POINT JUSTB4_UPGRADE1 GUARANTEE FLASHBACK DATABASE
```

13. Prepare to convert the existing physical standby to a logical standby. First, stop managed recovery on the physical standby:

```
ALTER DATABASE RECOVER MANAGED STANDBY DATABASE CANCEL;
```

At this point redo is still being sent to the standby database, it is just not applied.

14. Execute the following on the primary database:

```
EXECUTE DBMS_LOGSTDBY.BUILD;
```

This will build the LogMiner dictionary, which will be sent to the standby by the standard Redo Transport mechanism.

15. Back on the standby, make sure that it is mounted exclusive if in a RAC configuration, and instruct the physical standby database to apply all redo up to but not including the LogMiner dictionary using the 'RECOVER TO LOGICAL STANDBY' qualifier:

```
ALTER SYSTEM SET CLUSTER_DATABASE=FALSE SCOPE=SPFILE;
SHUTDOWN IMMEDIATE
STARTUP MOUNT
ALTER DATABASE RECOVER TO LOGICAL STANDBY KEEP IDENTITY
ALTER DATABASE OPEN;
```

The Oracle Database 11g SQL statement ALTER DATABASE RECOVER TO LOGICAL STANDBY has a new clause, KEEP IDENTITY. This clause ensures that the logical standby database retains its internal database ID (DBID), which is identical to the DBID of the primary database.

At this point, the LogMiner dictionary created on the primary database has transmitted via redo stream and applied to the standby database, and you now have an open logical standby database.

16. Prevent any automatic archive log deletion and enable SQL Apply:

```
EXECUTE DBMS_LOGSTDBY.APPLY_SET('LOG_AUTO_DELETE', 'FALSE');
ALTER DATABASE START LOGICAL STANDBY APPLY IMMEDIATE
```

17. Wait for this query to display "IDLE":

```
SELECT SESSION_ID, STATE FROM V$LOGSTDBY_STATE;
```

To ensure you meet your RPO, it is advisable to have a second physical standby database that will continue to operate using the original software version and receive the current redo stream while the logical standby is being upgraded. However, you can create an archived redo log repository with the same database release (the target release) and COMPATIBLE setting as the primary database so that redo is still received while applying the patch or upgrading the database. See Oracle MetaLink Note 434164.1.[3] Creating a repository ensures that you can meet the RPO if the primary site fails during the upgrade of the logical.

18. Perform pre-upgrade steps on the primary:

```
ALTER SYSTEM SET LOG_ARCHIVE_DEST_STATE_2=DEFER SCOPE=MEMORY
```

19. Perform pre-upgrade steps on the logical standby.

The upgrade will be performed on the logical standby database, so you will need to stop SQL Apply. It is also recommended that you create another GRP on the logical standby. This restore point will be used in case of issues in the upgrade process and a fallback recovery is needed.

```
ALTER DATABASE STOP LOGICAL STANDBY APPLY;
CREATE RESTORE POINT PRE_UPGRADE_3 GUARANTEE FLASHBACK DATABASE;
SHUTDOWN IMMEDIATE
```

20. Perform the upgrade on the logical standby. For upgrades, set the ORACLE_HOME environment variable to the new software location. Note that DBUA should be used for most upgrade scenarios, such as from 10gR2 to 11g upgrades. For an Oracle patchset apply, such as 11.1.0.7, use the Oracle Universal Installer. In our example case, we will need to use OUI for the 11.1.0.7 upgrade.

21. Perform maintenance on unsupported data types.

22. If an archived redo log repository was used, you can use the RMAN CATALOG command to catalog the archived redo log repository logs to avoid resending those logs:

```
RMAN> CATALOG START WITH '+PSTBY/MATRIX_DR0/ARCHIVELOG/';
```

23. Once the upgrade is completed, you can restart the redo transport to the logical standby and also start up SQL Apply. On the primary:

```
SQL> ALTER SYSTEM SET LOG_ARCHIVE_DEST_STATE_2=ENABLE SCOPE=MEMORY;
```

On the logical standby:

```
SQL> STARTUP
SQL> ALTER DATABASE START LOGICAL STANDBY APPLY IMMEDIATE;
```

---

[3] See MetaLink Note 434164.1: "Data Guard Archived Redo Log Repository Example"

**24.** As a protective measure, disable redo transmission on the logical standby so that it does not try to send redo once it becomes the primary:

```
ALTER SYSTEM SET LOG_ARCHIVE_DEST_STATE_2=DEFER SCOPE=MEMORY;
```

**25.** At this point, the primary is running the lower version of the software. To finish up the rolling upgrade process, upgrade/patch the primary. This will require a switchover. A switchover will be performed to move the primary database to the current logical standby, and then go through the same process for current primary:

```
ALTER DATABASE COMMIT TO SWITCHOVER TO LOGICAL STANDBY;
```

Once this command has completed on the primary database, before you proceed with the switchover, query the V$DATABASE view for the switchover_status. If the status indicates TO PRIMARY, then it is safe to proceed. Finish the switchover on the logical standby database:

```
ALTER DATABASE COMMIT TO SWITCHOVER TO PRIMARY;
```

**26.** The former primary database is now currently running as the transient logical standby. The former standby database is now the primary database and is also running the latest upgraded code. However, the new standby cannot receive or apply redo because it is running at a lower database version than the new primary database. Therefore, you must convert your original primary database back into a physical standby database. Shut down and restart the new logical standby and then perform a Flashback Database to the guaranteed restore point created in step 13:

```
SHUTDOWN IMMEDIATE;
STARTUP MOUNT;
FLASHBACK DATABASE TO RESTORE POINT JUSTB4_UPGRADE;
```

**27.** Shut down the new logical standby, and using the new cloned ORACLE_HOME (from step 9), start the standby in mount mode and convert it to a physical standby:

```
SHUTDOWN IMMEDIATE;
STARTUP MOUNT;
ALTER DATABASE CONVERT TO PHYSICAL;
```

As stated earlier, the database upgrade includes two components: updating the binary files and updating the database objects. The binary upgrade was picked up with the leverage of the new ORACLE_HOME. For the upgrade of database objects, once the physical standby has caught up to the new primary, it will automatically be upgraded (by virtue of Redo Apply).

**28.** Note that the CONVERT TO PHYSICAL statement will implicitly dismount the database. Therefore, you will need to restart the physical database again and put it into the MOUNT state. Additionally, managed recovery will need to be started:

```
SHUTDOWN IMMEDIATE;
STARTUP MOUNT;
ALTER DATABASE RECOVER MANAGED STANDBY DATABASE
USING CURRENT LOGFILE DISCONNECT;;
```

**29.** Once you are satisfied with the new Oracle version, it is recommended that you set the COMPATIBLE settings to the rolling upgraded versions.

**30.** Optionally, for customers who want to return back to the original configuration (prior to starting the rolling upgrade), a switchover can be performed.

## Caveats and Restrictions

Some restrictions apply to using the transient logical standby rolling upgrade process:

■  When you perform the initial switchover in the rolling upgrade process, you cannot use the PREPARE TO SWITCHOVER operation because the primary and standby databases are running different Oracle releases.

■  In this transient logical standby configuration, no bystander logical standby databases can exist. A *bystander logical standby database* is a logical standby database that exists in the same Data Guard configuration as the physical standby that will become the transient logical standby. If an existing logical standby database is in this configuration, it is highly recommended that you use this for the rolling upgrade.

Note that for Oracle Database10g, if the primary database in a rolling upgrade configuration is a RAC database, ensure that all but one instance are shut down. If you are running with COMPATIBLE set to lower than 10.2.0.2, disable the threads before initiating a switchover. Do the same to the logical standby database except for the instance where SQL Apply is running. Re-enable the threads and start the instances after the switchover operation has completed successfully. Although the instances are shut down, the role change will be automatically propagated to these instances when they are restarted.

Options for using rolling upgrade when unsupported data types exist are as follows:

■  Suspend or prohibit changes to the unsupported data type objects. Temporarily suspend or prohibit changes to the unsupported tables for the period of time it takes to perform the upgrade procedure.

■  Use DBA_LOGSTDBY_EVENTS with Oracle Data Pump or with the Export/Import utility. If you cannot prevent changes to unsupported tables during the upgrade, any unsupported transactions that occur are recorded in the DBA_LOGSTDBY_EVENTS table on the logical standby database. After the upgrade is completed, use Oracle Data Pump or the Export/Import utility to import the changed tables to the upgraded databases. Review section 12.4 in *Oracle Data Guard Concepts and Administration* for more information.

■  Use Extended Datatype Support (EDS), which enables SQL Apply to replicate changes to tables that contain some data types not natively supported from one database to another. Beginning with Oracle Database 10g Release 10.2.0.4, SQL Apply supports the ability for triggers to fire on the logical standby database, which provides the basis of EDS. For an overview of EDS, see the MAA whitepaper "Extended Datatype Support: SQL Apply and Streams."[4] For details and examples of using EDS to support data types that are not natively supported by SQL Apply, see MetaLink Note 559353.1.[5]

---

[4] See www.oracle.com/technology/deploy/availability/pdf/maa_edtsoverview.pdf.
[5] MetaLink Note 559353.1: "Extended Datatype Support (EDS) for SQL Apply"

# Conclusion

Performing software upgrades is not only a painstaking process, but it also creates large downtime outages. Data Guard can be leveraged to minimize most of this downtime impact. This chapter reviewed how a logical standby database can be leveraged to enable an upgrade of a database or complete stack version. When the standby upgrade is deemed successful, a Data Guard switchover is executed to transition the standby database to the production role running on the new release of the software or stack. While the standby database operates in this production role, the database on the original primary is converted back to a physical standby. This physical standby is then restarted with a newer software stack version and the database is implicitly upgraded to new release via Redo Apply. This method not only provides a low-impact environment to the user community, but this configuration can also be used to validate the new software stack, minimizing unplanned outages.

# CHAPTER
## 12

# Backup and Recovery
# Considerations

ost database administrators will agree that protecting data is one of the most important aspects of their job. As a DBA, you are responsible for the availability of the databases in your environment, and a sound backup and recovery strategy is critical to administering and managing those databases. The more time you spend planning and testing your backup and recovery strategy, the easier it will be to respond in an efficient and timely manner during a recovery situation. Operating system commands such as cp and dd can be used to back up an Oracle database, but they are not database-aware commands. Although many third-party tools are available for database backup and recovery, we will focus on the usage of Oracle's Recovery Manager (RMAN) utility to back up and recover your Oracle databases.

Several backup options are available for databases in a Data Guard environment. This chapter will look at those options as well as factors that can influence your backup strategy decisions. In addition, we will review some of the most common recovery scenarios that you can use as a guide when testing your own strategies.

Improvements in Oracle Database 11*g* have focused on the integration of RMAN and Data Guard, and we will briefly cover some of these features.

Here is a summary of the topics that will be covered in this chapter:

- RMAN Basics
- RMAN Integration with Data Guard
- RMAN Configuration
- Backup Strategies
- Backup Scenarios
- Recovery Strategies
- Recovery Scenarios
- Best Practices

# RMAN Basics

RMAN provides several benefits when compared with user-managed backup and recovery. The following highlights some of those benefits:

- Eliminates the need for complex backup scripts
- Minimizes human error by keeping track of all the backup information
- Performs error checking during backups and recoveries
- Supports high-speed incremental backups
- Supports compression of backup files
- Repairs corrupt data blocks without needing to restore a file from a backup (block media recovery)
- Simulates restores as well as backups
- Simplifies the process of cloning a database
- Integrates with third-party media management tools

We assume that you are familiar with the RMAN utility, so we will not be covering details about how to set up and configure RMAN. However, we will focus on components and functionality that are necessary to back up and recover databases in a Data Guard environment. As you read this chapter, you will find that the examples are based on backups and recoveries to disk. We will highlight some of the nuances specific to using tape where necessary.

Following is a list of some RMAN terminology that will be used throughout this chapter:

- **Target database**   The database against which RMAN commands are run

- **Catalog database**   The database that houses the recovery catalog schema

- **Auxiliary database**   When cloning a database, represents the name of the actual clone database

- **Recovery catalog**   The catalog that contains metadata information about the backups

- **Backup piece**   The file that contains the backup of a control file, archived logs, or a datafile

- **Backupset**   One or more relevant backup pieces

- **Image copy**   The copy of a datafile, control file, or archive log that is similar to copies made of files with the `cp` or `dd` operating system command

- **Channel**   The server session used to perform backups and recoveries; identifies a specific device, disk, or tape to be used for a backup or recovery

# RMAN Integration with Data Guard

Several improvements have been included in Oracle Database11*g* regarding backup and recovery; however, our focus will be on features that improve the integration of RMAN with Data Guard. You can now set persistent RMAN configurations for a primary or physical standby database. This enables you to use backups made on one database for the restore and recovery of another database in your Data Guard configuration. In addition, metadata on the primary and standby databases can be managed from the same recovery catalog. We will discuss this in more detail later in this chapter.

## Block Change Tracking Support

Incremental backup performance has been improved over past releases by backing up only the changed data blocks. You can now enable block change tracking support on a physical standby database to quickly identify the blocks that changed since the last incremental backup. (Block change tracking on a physical standby requires a license for Oracle Active Data Guard.)

```
SQL> alter database enable block change tracking
  2  using file '/media/orclvol3/oradata/matrix_dr0/chgtrack.log';
Database altered.
SQL> Select filename, status, bytes
  2  from v$block_change_tracking;
FILENAME                                              STATUS    BYTES
---------------------------------------------------   --------  ----------
/media/orclvol3/oradata/matrix_dr0/chgtrack.log       ENABLED   11599872
```

Contrary to what many DBAs think, the size of the block change tracking (BCT) file is not related to the amount of updates performed on the database. The size of the BCT file depends on the size of the database, the number of database files and redo threads, and information collected for up to eight backups. Normally, the space required is about 1/30000 the size of the data blocks to be tracked. So for a 1-terabyte database, you might need a BCT file of 34MB. However, to avoid the overhead of allocating space as the database grows, the BCT file starts at 10MB and increases in size by 10MB chunks. In addition, RMAN reserves 320KB of space in the BCT file for each data file, so the BCT file would be 40MB.

## Control File Management

Backups of the control files are interchangeable between a primary database and its physical standby databases. You can restore a standby control file on a primary database and a primary control file on a physical standby database. It is no longer necessary to back up a standby control file on the primary database when creating a standby database using the new 11*g* DUPLICATE FOR STANDBY FROM ACTIVE DATABASE method. Nor do you need to create a backup control file on all your standby sites. RMAN will now automatically synchronize the control file information with the standby databases when using an RMAN catalog. Depending on the role that the database is playing according to the RMAN catalog, the current control file and/or standby control file backup can be used to restore a control file with the RESTORE CONTROLFILE command.

## Resynchronizing the RMAN Catalog

You can now resynchronize the RMAN catalog from a remote database using the RESYNC CATALOG command with the CONNECT IDENTIFIER clause. Prior to doing the resync, you must define the connect identifiers for the standby databases:

```
RMAN> CONFIGURE DB_UNIQUE_NAME MATRIX_DR0 CONNECT IDENTIFIER 'MATRIX_DR0';
```

The RESYNC CATALOG command can be used to resynchronize the catalog with a specific standby's site information. In addition, the ALL clause will synchronize all of the sites:

```
RMAN> RESYNC CATALOG FROM DB_UNIQUE_NAME ALL;
```

# RMAN Configuration in Data Guard

The RMAN catalog contains backup and recovery information in one centralized location. The recovery catalog consists of a set of tables, indexes, and packages that reside in a database somewhere in your network. These tables store the information about RMAN backups that occur for all the target databases. The server where the catalog resides should be separate from the primary and standby sites so that in the event of a disaster at either the standby or primary site, the ability to recover from the latest backups will not be impacted. An RMAN catalog is required so that backups taken on one database server can be restored to another database server. Use of the control file as the repository will not work because the primary database will have no knowledge of backups that occur on the standby database.

RMAN uses the DB_UNIQUE_NAME parameter to distinguish one database site from another. As of Oracle Database 11*g*, it is mandatory that the uniqueness of DB_UNIQUE_NAME be maintained in a Data Guard configuration. Only the primary database must be explicitly registered using the REGISTER DATABASE command. Physical standby databases are registered automatically in the catalog when you use RMAN to connect to them as the TARGET while connected to the recovery catalog. The recovery catalog tracks the files in the Data Guard environment by associating every database file with a DB_UNIQUE_NAME. A backup remains associated with the database that created it unless you use the following command to associate the backup with a different database: use the CHANGE command with the RESET DB_UNIQUE_NAME option to alter the association of files from one database to another within a Data Guard environment. This command is useful when disk backups or archive logs are transferred and you want to use them on the database to which they were transferred. You can also change the association of a file from one database to another database without having to connect directly to either database using the FOR DB_UNIQUE_NAME and RESET DB_UNIQUE_NAME options:

```
RMAN> CHANGEBACKUP TAG='STANDBY_BACKUP_LVL0'
        FOR DB_UNIQUE_NAME MATRIX_DR0 RESET DB_UNIQUE_NAME;
```

Use the CONFIGURE command to set the RMAN configurations. When the CONFIGURE command is used with the FOR DB_UNIQUE_NAME option, it sets the RMAN site-specific configuration for the database with the DB_UNIQUE_NAME you specify. If this is used with the CONFIGURE, SHOW, and LIST commands, it is possible for you to view and modify persistent RMAN configuration parameters without connecting to that database using the TARGET option. If you use the DB_UNIQUE_NAME clause with the ALL option instead of the site_name option, RMAN will connect to all databases registered in the catalog and will update their control files with the new settings.

The following are examples of the use of the FOR DB_UNIQUE_NAME clause:

```
RMAN> show all for db_unique_name matrix_dr0;
starting full resync of recovery catalog
full resync complete
RMAN configuration parameters for database
     with db_unique_name MATRIX_DR0 are:
CONFIGURE RETENTION POLICY TO REDUNDANCY 3;
CONFIGURE BACKUP OPTIMIZATION OFF; # default
CONFIGURE DEFAULT DEVICE TYPE TO DISK;
CONFIGURE CONTROLFILE AUTOBACKUP ON;
CONFIGURE CONTROLFILE AUTOBACKUP FORMAT FOR DEVICE TYPE DISK TO 'cf%F';
CONFIGURE DEVICE TYPE DISK PARALLELISM 1 BACKUP TYPE TO BACKUPSET; # default
CONFIGURE DATAFILE BACKUP COPIES FOR DEVICE TYPE DISK TO 1; # default
CONFIGURE ARCHIVELOG BACKUP COPIES FOR DEVICE TYPE DISK TO 1; # default
CONFIGURE CHANNEL 1 DEVICE TYPE DISK FORMAT   '/media/orclvol3/matrix_
dr0%t_%s_%p';
CONFIGURE MAXSETSIZE TO UNLIMITED; # default
CONFIGURE ENCRYPTION FOR DATABASE OFF; # default
CONFIGURE ENCRYPTION ALGORITHM 'AES128'; # default
CONFIGURE COMPRESSION ALGORITHM 'BZIP2'; # default
CONFIGURE ARCHIVELOG DELETION POLICY TO NONE; # default
CONFIGURE SNAPSHOT CONTROLFILE NAME TO '/u01/app/oracle/product/11.1.0/db_1/
dbs/sncfmatrix_dr0.ora';

RMAN> report schema for db_unique_name matrix;
Report of database schema for database with db_unique_name MATRIX
List of Permanent Datafiles
===============================
```

```
File Size(MB) Tablespace              RB segs Datafile Name
---- -------- -------------------- ------- ------------------------
1    610      SYSTEM                  YES
/media/orclvol1/oradata/matrix/system01.dbf
2    498      SYSAUX                  NO
/media/orclvol1/oradata/matrix/sysaux01.dbf
3    1024     UNDOTBS1                YES
/media/orclvol2/oradata/matrix/undotbs01.dbf
4    1024     USERS                   NO
/media/orclvol1/oradata/matrix/users01.dbf
5    20       ACTOR_D                 NO
/media/orclvol2/oradata/matrix/actor_d_01.dbf
6    20       ACTOR_I                 NO
/media/orclvol2/oradata/matrix/actor_i_01.dbf
List of Temporary Files
=======================
File Size(MB) Tablespace              Maxsize(MB) Tempfile Name
---- -------- -------------------- ----------- --------------------
1    1024     TEMP                    32767
/media/orclvol2/oradata/matrix/temp01.dbf
```

Certain configuration parameters will stay consistent, such as backup retention and default destinations of disk and tape. You will need to connect to both the primary database and the RMAN catalog. Configure the retention policy to keep the necessary backups to perform a database recovery to any point in time within a specific period.

Following are some example RMAN configuration commands along with a description of what they do. In these examples, we are taking our backups from the standby database, and as such we need to maintain archive logs only at the primary until they have been applied (or shipped) to the standby database.

# Example Configuration for a Primary Database

Follow these steps to configure a primary database:

1. Configure the retention policy for the database as *n* days:

   ```
   RMAN> CONFIGURE RETENTION POLICY TO RECOVERY WINDOW OF 7 DAYS;
   ```

2. Specify when archived logs can be deleted:

   ```
   RMAN> CONFIGURE ARCHIVELOG DELETION POLICY TO SHIPPED TO ALL STANDBY;
   ```

   Or use this:

   ```
   RMAN> CONFIGURE ARCHIVELOG DELETION POLICY TO APPLIED ON ALL STANDBY;
   ```

3. Configure the connect string for the primary database and all standby databases. This will enable RMAN to connect remotely and perform resynchronizations. Note that this applies even if the other database instance where the resynchronization occurs is on the local host.

   ```
   RMAN> CONFIGURE DB_UNIQUE_NAME MATRIX CONNECT IDENTIFIER 'MATRIX';
   ```

4. After connect identifiers are configured for all standby databases, you can verify the list of standbys by using the `LIST DB_UNIQUE_NAME OF DATABASE` command.

## Example Configuration for a Backup Standby Database

Follow these steps to configure a physical standby database where backups are taken:

1. Issue the following commands after connecting to the physical standby database and the recovery catalog. Enable automatic backups of the control file and server parameter file:

   ```
   RMAN> CONFIGURE CONTROLFILE AUTOBACKUP ON;
   ```

2. Skip backing up datafiles for which a valid backup already exists with the same checkpoint:

   ```
   RMAN> CONFIGURE BACKUP OPTIMIZATION;
   ```

3. Configure the tape channels to create backups as required by media management software:

   ```
   RMAN> CONFIGURE CHANNEL DEVICE TYPE SBT PARMS '<channel parameters>';
   ```

4. Specify when the archived logs can be deleted with the `CONFIGURE ARCHIVELOG DELETION POLICY` command. Since the logs are backed up at the standby site, you should specify the `NONE` option for the log deletion policy:

   ```
   RMAN> CONFIGURE DELETION POLICY TO NONE;
   ```

   This will enable automatic deletion of archived logs on the standby database (where backups are being taken) that are outside of the retention period or that have already been backed up to tape, if additional space is needed for new backups or archived logs.

## Example Configuration for Other Physical Standby Databases

Follow these steps to configure another physical standby database where backups are not taken.

Issue the following command after connecting to each of the other physical standby databases and the recovery catalog:

```
RMAN> CONFIGURE ARCHIVELOG DELETION POLICY TO APPLIED ON STANDBY;
```

Setting this configuration on each of the other physical standby databases (where backups are not being taken) will enable automatic deletion of archived logs on this standby database that have been applied to all other remote standby destinations. Archived logs are deleted if space in the flash recovery area needs to be reclaimed for new files. Using this policy requires that the database uses a Flash Recovery Area (FRA).

Refer to Note 305565.1 "Persistant Controlfile Configurations for RMAN in Oracle 9*i* and Oracle 10*g*" for additional information.

# Backup Strategies

Several backup strategies should be considered depending on your business's recovery point objective (RPO) and recovery time objective (RTO). (Refer to Chapter 2 for detailed information on defining your business requirements.) These objectives, along with your budget, will drive your decisions in terms of infrastructure as well as strategy. Even with Data Guard configured and in use, RMAN should be included as a part of your overall strategy. When you do have that failure of the primary database and successfully failover to your standby database, you may still have to use a backup to rebuild the old primary database, especially if you are not using Flashback Database. And without Flashback Database, you may have to restore and recover your entire Data Guard setup if you do not discover the user error before the Apply Delay you set has expired. Of course, you could also experience that dreaded multiple failure and lose the primary database and your standby databases and need to restore from backup to get back up and running. Having a well-thought-out backup strategy will help in all of these cases.

The data change frequency and the amount of data included in your environment also factor into how you set up your backup strategy. The following options can be evaluated to determine whether they fit within your acceptable mean time to recover (MTTR).

Consider doing weekly full (level 0) and fast incremental backups when the frequency of data changes is low to medium. During fast incremental backups, only the changed blocks are read and written if you have enabled BCT. Archived logs kept on disk can be used to recover the database to any point in the day.

If your tolerance for an outage is extremely low, you could take a full database image copy or image copies of the most critical tablespaces followed by nightly incremental backups. The image copy can be rolled forward with the most current incremental to produce a new disk full backup on a daily basis. The time to recover is reduced because the image copy is updated with the latest block changes, and fewer redo logs are required to bring the database back to the current state. Archived logs are backed up and retained on disk as needed.

As mentioned earlier, RMAN database backups can be offloaded in a Data Guard environment to the physical standby database. This will help alleviate the impact of the backups on the primary database. You must use an RMAN catalog instead of the control file so that the primary database will be aware of backups taken on the standby, and vice versa. You can perform a backup on a physical standby database and restore it to the primary database, and vice versa. However, keep in mind that backups of a logical standby database are not usable at the primary database and can only be used to restore the logical standby.

Backups of physical standby control files and primary control files are interchangeable. This means that you can offload control file backups in a Data Guard environment. RMAN will update the filenames for database files during restore and recovery at the database.

**NOTE**
*As of Oracle Database 11g you no longer need to make separate control file backups on your primary and standby. However, in 10g, you still have to take a special standby control file backup when using RMAN to back up your physical standby.*

In a Data Guard environment, the recovery catalog considers disk backups accessible only to the database where the backups were taken. On the other hand, a tape backup created on one database is accessible to all of the databases. Commands such as backup, restore, and crosscheck work on any accessible backup. RMAN considers only image copies that are associated with the database as eligible to be recovered. In addition, incremental backups on disk and tape are eligible to roll forward image copies. In a database recovery, however, RMAN considers only the disk backups associated with the database and all files on tape as eligible to be restored.

One last consideration is the backup and deletion of the archive logs. If you back up from the standby, the archive logs will never be removed from the primary unless you set the correct archive log deletion policy, as mentioned earlier. If you do not set the policy, you will have to set up another backup on the primary to clean up the archive logs on the primary site.

# Backup Scenarios

Several backup scenarios are applicable in a Data Guard environment: full backups, incremental backups, backup copies, backups of the flash recovery area (FRA), and archive backups.

## Backup Database Not Backed Up

DBAs can perform database backups using the BACKUP DATABASE NOT BACKED UP. When you back up the database with BACKUP DATABASE NOT BACKED UP keywords, you are instructing RMAN to back up datafile and archive logs that have not been previously backed up.

You can also specify the syntax with the SINCE TIME 'SYSDATE -1'; clause to back up files not backed up since the specified time. The optional syntax, such as NOT BACKED UP 2 TIMES, also comes in handy for the extra-cautious DBA. You can also include the archive log with the PLUS ARCHIVELOG syntax. Putting it all together, you can perform backups on the primary database like so:

```
RMAN> BACKUP NOT BACKED UP SINCE TIME 'SYSDATE -1' DATABASE PLUS ARCHIVELOG;
```

This particular backup strategy is recommended if you are making copies from the flash recovery area to tape. If you perform backups to the flash recovery area and then back up the flash recovery area to tape, you should consider using the BACKUP DATABASE NOT BACKED UP syntax.

## Full Backups on Primary

When it comes to performing full backups on the primary database, we recommend one of the three backup strategies: full level 0 backup, full level 0 compressed backup, and database image copy backup with RMAN. To perform a complete level 0 backup, you would normally issue the command BACKUP AS BACKUPSET INCREMENTAL LEVEL 0 FORMAT ... (DATABASE). The key difference in performing a compressed backup is to incorporate the key reserved word COMPRESSED in the BACKUP DATABASE command.

Here's a comprehensive backup script example that takes advantage of the compressed option while backing up both database files and archive logs. In addition, the control file and spfile are preserved as part of the backup strategy:

```
run
{
allocate channel d1 type disk;
allocate channel d2 type disk;
allocate channel d3 type disk;
allocate channel d4 type disk;
backup as compressed backupset incremental level ###_BACKUP_LEVEL_###
tag='###_ORACLE_SID_###_bkup_###_BACKUP_LEVEL_###z_###_DATE_###'
filesperset 1 format
'/apps/oracle/admin/###_ORACLE_SID_###/bkups/%d.%s.%p.%t.L###_BACKUP_
```

```
LEVEL_###.DB' (database) ;
###_sqlspfile_### "create pfile=''/apps/oracle/admin/###_ORACLE_SID_###/bkups/
init_###_ORACLE_SID_###_###_DATE_###.ora''from spfile";
sql "alter system archive log current";
sql "alter system switch logfile";
sql "alter system switch logfile";
change archivelog all validate;
sql "alter database backup controlfile to trace";
sql "alter database backup controlfile to
''/apps/oracle/admin/###_ORACLE_SID_###/bkups/control01_###_ORACLE_
SID_###_###_DATE_###.ctl.bkup''";

backup as compressed backupset format
'/apps/oracle/admin/###_ORACLE_SID_###/bkups/%d.%s.%p.%t.A' skip
inaccessible (archivelog all not backed up 2 times);
backup tag='###_ORACLE_SID_###_CTL_###_DATE_###' format
'/apps/oracle/admin/###_ORACLE_SID_###/bkups/%d.%s.%p.%t.CTL'
(current controlfile);

delete noprompt archivelog until time 'sysdate -
###_NUMBER_OF_DAYS_TO_RETAIN_###'
backed up 2 times to device type disk;

release channel d1;
release channel d2;
release channel d3;
release channel d4;
}
```

Notice in this example that a pfile is created from the spfile as part of the backup strategy. You can alternatively back up the spfile as well. Pay particular attention to the backup strategy implemented to back up the control file. The control file is backed up three times:

- To trace to the UDUMP directory
- Using RMAN syntax to the backup destination
- Using SQL*Plus syntax to the file system backup destination

Most importantly, take note of the DELETE command for the archive logs. You do not want to back up and delete input on all the archive logs. For databases participating in a Data Guard configuration, RMAN will not delete archive logs on the primary database that have not been shipped to the physical standby database. If you try to delete them, you will encounter the RMAN-08137 error, as shown here:

```
RMAN-08137: WARNING: archive log not deleted as it is still needed
```

In our real-world example, we delete only the archive logs if they've been backed up twice to disk and are older than two days. This archive log purge strategy happens to be one of several practiced in the industry. You can change and adopt a strategy that works best for your organization.

# Backup as Copy

Backing up the database as image copies for performing rolling updates may be of particular interest for DBAs with very large databases (VLDBs) and/or that have extremely short backup windows. Companies in the past abandoned Oracle backup solutions to settle with hardware vendor solutions that provide business continuity volumes (BCVs), such as the technologies provided by EMC and Hitachi. This chapter does not cover the topic of BCVs, but a high-level overview is provided in the appendix of this book.

Oracle database image copies can now provide equivalent technologies once offered only by hardware vendors. Oracle provides a one-stop–shop solution with the concept of performing baseline level 0 backups and updating the database with incremental level 1 backups to keep the backup database in sync with the source database. Basically, you can justify the budget for additional disk space for image copies since you are trading for the cost associated with the BCV hardware and software.

Obviously, disk space requirements can decrease significantly if you are compressing your backupsets. Even if you are not compressing your backupsets, the storage requirement for the backup area may decrease if you have a lot of preallocated free space inside the database, since RMAN does not back up blocks that have never been modified before. In the case of an image copy, the size of the database backup area is directly proportional to the size of the database, plus the number of days of incremental backups and the number of days of archive logs to keep on disk. A simplified equation to determine the amount of space required is shown here:

Backup file system or FRA = Database size
+ number of incremental backups to retain
+ number of days of archive log backups to keep
+ control files to keep on disk

For some databases, the disk space requirements for the backup file system can be 1.25 to 1.5 times the size of the database itself.

To perform image copies of the database, you must leverage the key reserved words BACKUP AS COPY. The following example provides a comprehensive syntax to perform an image copy of the database, similar to how you copy database files using the cp command in UNIX:

```
RMAN> BACKUP AS COPY INCREMENTAL LEVEL 0 TAG='###_TAG_###'
FORMAT '/apps/oracle/admin/DB/bkups/%U' DATABASE;
```

RMAN copies three kinds of files: datafiles, archive log files, and control files. With the %U format, datafiles are copied with the data-D-%d_id-%I_TS-%N_FNO-%f_%u format, archive logs are copied with the arch-D_%d-id-%I_S-%e_T-%h_A-%a_%u format, and control files are copied with the cf-D_%d-id-%I_%u format. The following list provides the explanation of the above-mentioned RMAN format options:

- %c specifies the copy number of the backup piece within a set of multiplexed backup pieces. If you did not multiplex a backup (that is, with the COPIES parameter), this variable is 1 for backupsets and 0 for proxy copies.

- %d specifies the name of the database.

- %e specifies the archived log sequence number.

- %N specifies the tablespace name.

- `%h` specifies the archived redo log thread number.

- `%f` specifies the absolute file number.

- `%I` specifies the database ID (DBID).

- `%u` specifies an eight-character name constituted by compressed representations of the backupset or image copy number and the time the backupset or image copy was created.

The `BACKUP AS COPY` syntax at the database level is new to Oracle Database 10g. This syntax replaces the previous `COPY DATAFILE` and `COPY TABLESPACE` commands. The `BACKUP AS COPY` at the database level will make an image copy of the entire database in the location specified in the `FORMAT` parameter. Instead of the file system destination, you may have an ASM diskgroup destination such as the flash recovery area, `+FLASH`. You will notice that the `TAG` name plays an integral role in applying incremental backups to baseline image copies. We recommend that you define a customized `TAG` to refer symbolically to your backupset or database copy. The `TAG` can be up to 30 characters in length.

## Image Copy Rolled Forward

After you've created an image copy of our database, what's next? The answer is simple. You need to take incremental backups and apply them to your new image copy. Consider, for example, a particular customer in the financial sector that chose to perform full level 0 backup to disk on a monthly/quarterly basis. Your backup schedule looks like this:

- Sunday: Level 1 Merge with Level 0—now it is LEVEL 0

- Monday: Level 1 Merge with Level 0—now it is LEVEL 0

- Tuesday: Level 1 Merge with Level 0—now it is LEVEL 0

- Wednesday: Level 1 Merge with Level 0—now it is LEVEL 0

- Thursday: Level 1 Merge with Level 0—now it is LEVEL 0

- Friday: Level 1 Merge with Level 0—now it is LEVEL 0

- Saturday: Level 1 Merge with Level 0—now it is LEVEL 0

At a specified weekend near the end or beginning of the quarter, full level 0 backups to disk are performed. Daily incremental level 1 backups are performed and applied to the baseline backup. This process is repeated until the next quarter, when level 0 images backups are performed.

Even though quarterly full level 0 database copy backups are performed, conceptually, you do not need to perform another full backup again, and the biggest benefit is that in the event of catastrophic failure to the primary disks, you can switch the database to the image copy and start the database. For multi-node RAC implementation, the target destination of your image copy must be on a clustered file system or Automatic Storage Management (ASM). In the event that you lose your primary database, you can switch to your copy (assuming that it is not a complete outage at the Storage Area Network level or data center level), and start up the database. If your database copy image location is not on a shared storage, you will not be able to bring the database in a cluster mode. You will end up running the database in a single instance mode. This may be acceptable for some companies as defined by the SLA to run in a reduced capacity. Once you fix the database issue or corruption or whatever caused the initial outage, you can perform another baseline level 0 image copy to the clustered file system or ASM and switch the database back to run in the original configuration. In a granular level, if the loss on the primary database is a tablespace or datafile, you can simply copy the affected datafiles from the copy using the RMAN COPY command. In a nutshell, database image copies on the primary database can effectively provide your first level of protection from possible database outages.

Of course, since you are using Data Guard, you would have failed over to your standby and used the on-disk copy to re-create the old primary as a standby database if you did not have Flashback Database enabled or that catastrophic failure occurred at the primary disk level.

As stated earlier, when it comes to performing database copies and applying level 1 incremental backups to the parent backup image, use of the RMAN TAG syntax plays an important role and simplifies the architecture and maintenance. As you can see in the following code example, the RECOVER COPY OF DATABASE syntax uses the TAG to identify the incremental backup to apply to:

```
run
{
[ … ]
recover copy of database with tag '###_BASELINE_TAG_###';
BACKUP INCREMENTAL LEVEL ###_BACKUP_LEVEL_### tag='###_TAG_###'
FOR RECOVER OF COPY WITH TAG '###_BASELINE_TAG_###'
format '/apps/oracle/admin/###_ORACLE_SID_###/bkups/%d.%s.%p.%t.L1.4R.DB'
DATABASE;
[ … ]
}
```

On a nightly basis, incremental level 1 backups are performed with the FOR RECOVER OF COPY WITH TAG syntax. This backs up only the blocks that have changed since the last incremental backup.

**TIP**
*Two kinds of backups can occur: differential incremental backups and cumulative incremental backups. The differential incremental backup backs up changed blocks since the last level 0 or level 1 backup. If a level 1 backup exists, it will back up changes since the last level 1 backup. If a level 1 backup does not exist, it will look for a level 0 backup and back up changed blocks since the level 0 backup. A cumulative incremental backup, on the other hand, backs up changed blocks since the last level 0 backup.*

Each night a level 1 backup from the previous night will be applied before another level 1 backup occurs. Here's a sample output showing how the level 1 changed blocks from the previous night are recovered on top of the parent backup:

```
Starting recover at 17-JAN-09
channel d1: starting incremental datafile backupset restore
channel d1: specifying datafile copies to recover
recovering datafile copy fno=00001
name=/apps/oracle/admin/MATRIX/bkups/data_D-MATRIX_I-3231931562_TS-SYSTEM_
FNO-1_2rk3in4b
```

```
recovering datafile copy fno=00003
name=/apps/oracle/admin/MATRIX/bkups/data_D-MATRIX_I-3231931562_TS-SYSAUX_
FNO-3_2ok3in33
recovering datafile copy fno=00006
name=/apps/oracle/admin/MATRIX/bkups/data_D-MATRIX_I-3231931562_TS-DOCS_TBL_
FNO-6_28k3imhd
recovering datafile copy fno=00007
name=/apps/oracle/admin/MATRIX/bkups/data_D-MATRIX_I-3231931562_TS-DOCS_IDX_
FNO-7_29k3imkc
recovering datafile copy fno=00033
name=/apps/oracle/admin/MATRIX/bkups/data_D-MATRIX_I-3231931562_TS-TRACKING_
IDX_FNO-33_3ck3in7i
recovering datafile copy fno=00034
name=/apps/oracle/admin/MATRIX/bkups/data_D-MATRIX_I-3231931562_TS-EDI_TBL_
FNO-34_2kk3in1i
recovering datafile copy fno=00051
name=/apps/oracle/admin/MATRIX/bkups/data_D-MATRIX_I-3231931562_TS-user_ts_
FNO-51_27k3imac
recovering datafile copy fno=00052
name=/apps/oracle/admin/MATRIX/bkups/data_D-MATRIX_I-3231931562_TS-INDEX_TS_
FNO-52_3nk3in8h
channel d1: reading from backup piece
/apps/oracle/admin/MATRIX/bkups/MATRIX.250.1.676260017.L1.4R.DB
channel d2: starting incremental datafile backupset restore
channel d2: specifying datafile copies to recover
...
...
channel d4: reading from backup piece
/apps/oracle/admin/MATRIX/bkups/MATRIX.248.1.676260016.L1.4R.DB
channel d2: restored backup piece 1
piece handle=/apps/oracle/admin/MATRIX/bkups/MATRIX.247.1.676260016.L1.4R.DB
tag=MATRIX1_1_16JAN09_0200
channel d2: restore complete, elapsed time: 00:00:03
channel d3: restored backup piece 1
piece handle=/apps/oracle/admin/MATRIX/bkups/MATRIX.249.1.676260016.L1.4R.DB
tag=MATRIX1_1_16JAN09_0200
channel d3: restore complete, elapsed time: 00:00:04
channel d4: restored backup piece 1
piece handle=/apps/oracle/admin/MATRIX/bkups/MATRIX.248.1.676260016.L1.4R.DB
tag=MATRIX1_1_16JAN09_0200
channel d4: restore complete, elapsed time: 00:00:04
channel d1: restored backup piece 1
piece handle=/apps/oracle/admin/MATRIX/bkups/MATRIX.250.1.676260017.L1.4R.DB
tag=MATRIX1_1_16JAN09_0200
channel d1: restore complete, elapsed time: 00:00:05
Finished recover at 17-JAN-09
```

On a nightly basis, you should implement a scheduled job to update your image copy of the database. You can perform a new image copy of the database and update your existing image copy of the database by taking advantage of the rman2disk.ksh script provided at the Data Guard

Handbook website (www.dataguardbook.com/). This comprehensive script will perform level 0 backups, compressed backups, and database copies; perform level 1 backups; update level 0 image copies with incremental backups; back up archive logs; back up control files; back up the spfile, and so on. Once you perform a level 0 baseline backup using the rman2disk.ksh script, you can perform nightly updates with the following cron job:

```
0 1 * * *  /apps/oracle/general/sh/rman2disk.ksh -d MATRIX -l 1
   -r merge > /tmp/rman2disk_MATRIX.merge.log 2>&1 &
```

**NOTE**
*The rman2disk.ksh script is fully documented on the Data Guard website and updated on an ongoing basis.*

As a part of backup strategy, you should back up the baseline level 0 backup to tape. In addition, you should plan to back up the level 1 incremental backup to tape.

## Standby Database Creation

You can use a couple of methods to create the standby database using a backup of the primary database. You can use the DUPLICATE command to clone the primary database as a standby database or an image copy that you manage yourself. In both cases, the BACKUP VALIDATE DATABASE command can be used to check the integrity of all data files.

Both the original DUPLICATE FOR STANDBY and the new Oracle Database 11*g* DUPLICATE FOR STANDBY FROM ACTIVE DATABASE methods are described in Chapter 2 with examples.

```
RMAN> DUPLICATE TARGET DATABASE FOR STANDBY DORECOVER;
```

Alternatively, you can use image copies to create a standby database. One of the requirements is that the primary database must be closed cleanly and then mounted. This restriction may make the use of image copies for a standby creation less attractive when compared to the use of a backupset. To use this method, you would shut down the primary database and then restart it in mount mode. You can then create an image copy of all of the datafiles and create a standby control file. After this is done, you can open the primary database and archive the current log. This image copy can then be taken to the remote site and, after fixing the parameters as usual, mounted using the standby control file.

**NOTE**
*We added this example here for your information—but, to be honest, with its downtime requirements, we recommend using one of the DUPLICATE FOR STANDBY methods in RMAN.*

## Backups on a Standby Database

The following example shows all the current configuration settings on our standby database and then the settings for taking a full backup:

```
RMAN> show all;
RMAN configuration parameters for database
     with db_unique_name MATRIX_DR0 are:
CONFIGURE RETENTION POLICY TO REDUNDANCY 3;
```

```
CONFIGURE BACKUP OPTIMIZATION OFF; # default
CONFIGURE DEFAULT DEVICE TYPE TO DISK;
CONFIGURE CONTROLFILE AUTOBACKUP ON;
CONFIGURE CONTROLFILE AUTOBACKUP FORMAT FOR DEVICE TYPE DISK TO 'cf%F';
CONFIGURE DEVICE TYPE DISK PARALLELISM 1 BACKUP TYPE TO BACKUPSET; # default
CONFIGURE DATAFILE BACKUP COPIES FOR DEVICE TYPE DISK TO 1; # default
CONFIGURE ARCHIVELOG BACKUP COPIES FOR DEVICE TYPE DISK TO 1; # default
CONFIGURE CHANNEL 1 DEVICE TYPE DISK FORMAT
'/media/orclvol3/matrix_df%t_%s_%p';
CONFIGURE MAXSETSIZE TO UNLIMITED; # default
CONFIGURE ENCRYPTION FOR DATABASE OFF; # default
CONFIGURE ENCRYPTION ALGORITHM 'AES128'; # default
CONFIGURE COMPRESSION ALGORITHM 'BZIP2'; # default
CONFIGURE ARCHIVELOG DELETION POLICY TO NONE; # default
CONFIGURE SNAPSHOT CONTROLFILE NAME TO '/u01/app/oracle/product/11.1.0/db_1/
dbs/sncfmatrix_DR0.ora';

RMAN> backup incremental level 0 database TAG='standby_lvl0';

Starting backup at 05-JAN-09
allocated channel: ORA_DISK_1
channel ORA_DISK_1: SID=142 device type=DISK
channel ORA_DISK_1: starting incremental level 0 datafile backup set
channel ORA_DISK_1: specifying datafile(s) in backup set
input datafile file number=00004
name=/media/orclvol1/oradata/matrix_dr0/users01.dbf
input datafile file number=00003
name=/media/orclvol2/oradata/matrix_dr0/undotbs01.dbf
channel ORA_DISK_1: starting piece 1 at 05-JAN-09
channel ORA_DISK_1: finished piece 1 at 05-JAN-09
piece handle=/media/orclvol3/matrix_df675356527_14_1 tag=STANDBY_LVL0
comment=NONE
channel ORA_DISK_1: backup set complete, elapsed time: 00:00:01
channel ORA_DISK_1: starting incremental level 0 datafile backup set
channel ORA_DISK_1: specifying datafile(s) in backup set
input datafile file number=00001
name=/media/orclvol1/oradata/matrix_dr0/system01.dbf
input datafile file number=00005
name=/media/orclvol2/oradata/matrix_dr0/actor_d_01.dbf
input datafile file number=00006
name=/media/orclvol2/oradata/matrix_dr0/actor_i_01.dbf
input datafile file number=00002
name=/media/orclvol1/oradata/matrix_dr0/sysaux01.dbf
channel ORA_DISK_1: starting piece 1 at 05-JAN-09
channel ORA_DISK_1: finished piece 1 at 05-JAN-09
piece handle=/media/orclvol3/matrix_df675356588_15_1 tag=STANDBY_LVL0
comment=NONE
channel ORA_DISK_1: backup set complete, elapsed time: 00:01:15
Finished backup at 05-JAN-09
```

```
Starting Control File and SPFILE Autobackup at 05-JAN-09
piece handle=/u01/app/oracle/product/11.1.0/db_1/dbs/cfc-2215364109-20090105-
00 comment=NONE
Finished Control File and SPFILE Autobackup at 05-JAN-09
RMAN>
```

Once the backup is complete, we can display the backups we have made by using the LIST
BACKUPSET SUMMARY command:

```
RMAN> list backupset summary;
List of Backups
===============
Key     TY LV S Device Type Completion Time #Pieces #Copies Compressed Tag
------- -- -- - ----------- --------------- ------- ------- ---------- ------------------
382     B  F  A DISK        04-JAN-09       1       1       NO         TAG20090104T150544
383     B  F  A DISK        04-JAN-09       1       1       NO         TAG20090104T150911
384     B  F  A DISK        04-JAN-09       1       1       NO         TAG20090104T150952
385     B  F  A DISK        04-JAN-09       1       1       NO         TAG20090104T151104
648     B  0  A DISK        05-JAN-09       1       1       NO         STANDBY_LVL0
649     B  0  A DISK        05-JAN-09       1       1       NO         STANDBY_LVL0
663     B  F  A DISK        05-JAN-09       1       1       NO         TAG20090105T150510
```

Then, using the LIST BACKUPSET command, we can see the details of a specific backup:

```
RMAN> list backupset 649;
List of Backup Sets
===================

BS Key  Type LV Size       Device Type Elapsed Time Completion Time
------- ---- -- ---------- ----------- ------------ ---------------
649     Incr 0  810.53M    DISK        00:01:59     05-JAN-09
        BP Key: 652   Status: AVAILABLE  Compressed: NO  Tag: STANDBY_LVL0
        Piece Name: /media/orclvol3/matrix_df675356588_15_1
  List of Datafiles in backup set 649
  File LV Type Ckp SCN    Ckp Time  Name
  ---- -- ---- ---------- --------- ----
  1    0  Incr 708412     05-JAN-09
/media/orclvol1/oradata/matrix_dr0/system01.dbf
  2    0  Incr 708412     05-JAN-09
/media/orclvol1/oradata/matrix_dr0/sysaux01.dbf
  5    0  Incr 708412     05-JAN-09
/media/orclvol2/oradata/matrix_dr0/actor_d_01.dbf
  6    0  Incr 708412     05-JAN-09
/media/orclvol2/oradata/matrix_dr0/actor_i_01.dbf

RMAN>
```

## Archive Backups

Periodically, you will want to (or may have to) take backups of your archive log files so that you have the information necessary to roll forward one of your restored backups from all these level 0 and level 1 backups you have been taking:

```
RMAN> backup archivelog from scn=708389  TAG='STANDBY_ARCHIVE';
Starting backup at 05-JAN-09
using channel ORA_DISK_1
channel ORA_DISK_1: starting archived log backup set
channel ORA_DISK_1: specifying archived log(s) in backup set
input archived log thread=1 sequence=48 RECID=26 STAMP=675356631
channel ORA_DISK_1: starting piece 1 at 05-JAN-09
channel ORA_DISK_1: finished piece 1 at 05-JAN-09
piece handle=/media/orclvol3/matrix_df675357372_17_1 tag=STANDBY_ARCHIVE
comment=NONE
channel ORA_DISK_1: backup set complete, elapsed time: 00:00:01
Finished backup at 05-JAN-09

Starting Control File and SPFILE Autobackup at 05-JAN-09
piece handle=/u01/app/oracle/product/11.1.0/db_1/dbs/cfc-2215364109-20090105-
01 comment=NONE
Finished Control File and SPFILE Autobackup at 05-JAN-09
```

In Oracle11*g*, the archived redo log failover feature will enable RMAN to complete a backup even when some of the logs are missing or corrupt. If you have multiple archivelog destinations configured and at least one archived log exists for a given sequence and thread in either of the destinations, then RMAN will attempt to back it up. If RMAN encounters issues during the backup, it will check the other archivelog destinations for that file.

# General Recovery Strategies

It is important that you understand what your recovery options are under different scenarios. In addition, you need to ensure that your backup strategy will support those recovery options. Subsequently, you should test these scenarios as frequently as possible for different types of failures, such as media failure, block corruption, user error, and disaster recovery. These failure types along with other recovery concepts are discussed in detail in Chapter 3.

## Media Failure

Media failures occur when the database cannot read from or write to a datafile. This could be the result of hardware failures, or it could be a result of the file being accidentally deleted or overwritten.

## Block Corruption

Data block corruptions occur in files as a result of memory corruptions that are written to the files as well as I/O errors on the underlying disks. You can verify data block corruption using the following tools.

In RMAN, you can run the following command to check for physical and logical corruptions in the database as well as archive logs:

```
RMAN> BACKUP VALIDATE DATABASE ARCHIVELOG ALL;
Starting backup at 14-JAN-09
starting full resync of recovery catalog
full resync complete
allocated channel: ORA_DISK_1
channel ORA_DISK_1: SID=127 device type=DISK
channel ORA_DISK_1: starting archived log backup set
channel ORA_DISK_1: specifying archived log(s) in backup set
input archived log thread=1 sequence=19 RECID=2 STAMP=675075647
. . .
input archived log thread=1 sequence=54 RECID=73 STAMP=676072884
channel ORA_DISK_1: backup set complete, elapsed time: 00:00:45
List of Archived Logs
=====================
Thrd Seq     Status Blocks Failing Blocks Examined Name
---- ------- ------ -------------- --------------- ---------------
1    19      OK     0              196894
/media/orclvol3/MATRIX/archivelog/2009_01_02/o1_mf_1_19_4owc0n2t_.arc
. . .
1    54      OK     0              196861
/media/orclvol3/MATRIX/archivelog/2009_01_13/o1_mf_1_54_4ptrvyh5_.arc
channel ORA_DISK_1: starting full datafile backup set
channel ORA_DISK_1: specifying datafile(s) in backup set
input datafile file number=00004
name=/media/orclvol1/oradata/matrix/users01.dbf
input datafile file number=00003
name=/media/orclvol2/oradata/matrix/undotbs01.dbf
channel ORA_DISK_1: backup set complete, elapsed time: 00:01:25
List of Datafiles
=================
File Status Marked Corrupt Empty Blocks Blocks Examined High SCN
---- ------ -------------- ------------ --------------- ----------
3    OK     0              86136        131072          1156673
  File Name: /media/orclvol2/oradata/matrix/undotbs01.dbf
  Block Type Blocks Failing Blocks Processed
  ---------- -------------- ----------------
  Data       0              0
  Index      0              0
  Other      0              44936

File Status Marked Corrupt Empty Blocks Blocks Examined High SCN
---- ------ -------------- ------------ --------------- ----------
4    OK     0              131030       131072          703802
  File Name: /media/orclvol1/oradata/matrix/users01.dbf
  Block Type Blocks Failing Blocks Processed
  ---------- -------------- ----------------
  Data       0              10
```

```
Index       0            3
Other       0           29
```

```
channel ORA_DISK_1: starting full datafile backup set
channel ORA_DISK_1: specifying datafile(s) in backup set
input datafile file number=00001
name=/media/orclvol1/oradata/matrix/system01.dbf
input datafile file number=00005
name=/media/orclvol2/oradata/matrix/actor_d_01.dbf
input datafile file number=00006
name=/media/orclvol2/oradata/matrix/actor_i_01.dbf
input datafile file number=00002
name=/media/orclvol1/oradata/matrix/sysaux01.dbf
channel ORA_DISK_1: backup set complete, elapsed time: 00:00:55
List of Datafiles
=================
File Status Marked Corrupt Empty Blocks Blocks Examined High SCN
---- ------ ------------- ------------ --------------- ----------
1    OK     0             12863        78080           1156673
   File Name: /media/orclvol1/oradata/matrix/system01.dbf
   Block Type Blocks Failing Blocks Processed
   ---------- -------------- ----------------
   Data       0              54058
   Index      0              8928
   Other      0              2231


File Status Marked Corrupt Empty Blocks Blocks Examined High SCN
---- ------ ------------- ------------ --------------- ----------
2    OK     0             18222        64920           1156673
   File Name: /media/orclvol1/oradata/matrix/sysaux01.dbf
   Block Type Blocks Failing Blocks Processed
   ---------- -------------- ----------------
   Data       0              15367
   Index      0              13749
   Other      0              17582


File Status Marked Corrupt Empty Blocks Blocks Examined High SCN
---- ------ ------------- ------------ --------------- ----------
5    OK     0             2544         2560            676361
   File Name: /media/orclvol2/oradata/matrix/actor_d_01.dbf
   Block Type Blocks Failing Blocks Processed
   ---------- -------------- ----------------
   Data       0              5
   Index      0              0
   Other      0              11


File Status Marked Corrupt Empty Blocks Blocks Examined High SCN
---- ------ ------------- ------------ --------------- ----------
6    OK     0             2548         2560            676360
   File Name: /media/orclvol2/oradata/matrix/actor_i_01.dbf
   Block Type Blocks Failing Blocks Processed
   ---------- -------------- ----------------
```

```
Data        0              0
Index       0              1
Other       0              11

channel ORA_DISK_1: starting full datafile backup set
channel ORA_DISK_1: specifying datafile(s) in backup set
including current control file in backup set
including current SPFILE in backup set
channel ORA_DISK_1: backup set complete, elapsed time: 00:00:01
List of Control File and SPFILE
================================
File Type    Status Blocks Failing Blocks Examined
------------ ------ -------------- ---------------
SPFILE       OK     0              2
Control File OK     0              598
Finished backup at 14-JAN-09

RMAN>

Recovery Manager complete.
```

You can also use the DBVERIFY utility to identify corrupted datafiles. The ANALYZE command can also be used to identify corrupted data blocks.

You can refer to the following documents for additional information on handling data corruption errors: Note 428570.1 "Best Practices for Avoiding and Detecting Corruption" and Note 35512.1 "DBVERIFY—Database Verification Utility."

# User Errors

Accidents happen. Tables can be accidentally dropped, jobs can be run in the wrong order, or the wrong jobs can be executed. In any case, the end result will be that the data needs to be backed out. You could do a point-in-time recovery, or you could consider some of the following options instead:

- **Flashback query**    Retrieves data from a previous point in time
- **Flashback table**    Restores table to a previous point in time
- **Flashback drop**    Recovers a dropped table
- **Flashback transaction backout**    Backs out a transaction
- **Flashback Database**    Repairs database-wide logical errors

When configuring the primary and standby databases, it would be to your advantage to configure a flash recovery area for each database. The FRA is a storage location where all of the files needed for a recovery are kept. These files would include the control files, archived redo logs, online redo log copies, flashback logs, and RMAN backups. You should consider placing the FRA on disks separate from those that are used for the database. To configure the flash recovery area in ASM, you will need to set the following parameters. (If you are not using ASM, you would use a directory path as the FRA.)

```
DB_RECOVERY_FILE_DEST = +FLASH
DB_RECOVERY_FILE_DEST_SIZE = 52400M
```

Enable Flashback Database on the primary and standby databases. This will enable you to roll back the database to an earlier point in time without requiring a complete restore. When Flashback Database is enabled, flashback logs are kept in the flash recovery area. These logs can be used to roll back the database without requiring a complete restore. Refer to Chapters 8 and 9 for additional details on the flashback technology as it applies to a Data Guard environment. In addition, you can refer to Note 305648.1 when configuring your flash recovery area.[1]

# Recovery Scenarios

In any recovery situation, the analysis should be done up front to determine the exact cause of the error and the most time-efficient manner to recover the database. This may seem like common sense, but when you're in this situation and management and customers are calling and everyone is in a rush to get the database back online, bad decisions can be made. This section will cover some of the recovery scenarios that you may encounter as well as options to use to recover from these situations.

It is recommended that you practice different recovery scenarios. Not only does this help to validate that you can meet your recovery requirements, but it will help you avoid mistakes that you may have otherwise made when recovering your database. Refer to Oracle® Database Backup and Recovery User's Guide 11*g* Release 1 (11.1) and Oracle® Data Guard Concepts and Administration 11*g* Release 1 (11.1) for additional detailed recovery scenarios.

## Loss of a Datafile on a Primary Database

Two options are available to you when you lose a datafile on the primary database: You can use a backup to recover the datafile or use files on a standby database to recover the datafile as of Oracle Database 11*g*.

### Using a Backup to Recover the Datafile

The following summarizes the steps that you would take if you were using a backup to recover the datafile on the primary:

1. Connect to the primary database as the target:

   ```
   RMAN TARGET / CATALOG rman/<pswd>@RCAT
   ```

2. Alter the datafile offline:

   ```
   RMAN> SQL "ALTER DATABASE DATAFILE 1 OFFLINE";
   ```

3. Restore and recover the datafile:

   ```
   RMAN> RESTORE DATAFILE 1;
   RMAN> RECOVER DATAFILE 1;
   RMAN> SQL "ALTER DATABASE DATAFILE  1 ONLINE";
   ```

---

[1] Note: 305648.1 "What Is a Flash Recovery Area and How to Configure It"

### Using a Standby Database to Recover the Datafile

The following summarizes the steps that you would take if you were using the datafiles from the standby database to recover a lost datafile:

1.  Connect to the standby database as the target database, and connect to the primary database as the auxiliary database:

    ```
    RMAN TARGET sys/<pswd>@MATRIX_DR0 CATALOG rman/<pswd>@RCAT auxiliary /
    ```

2.  Back up the datafile on the standby and transfer to the primary:

    ```
    RMAN> BACKUP AS COPY DATAFILE 1 AUXILIARY FORMAT
       2> '/u04/oradata/MATRIX_DR0/users.dbf';
    ```

3.  Start RMAN and connect to the primary database as target and to the recovery catalog:

    ```
    RMAN TARGET / CATALOG rman/<pswd>@RCAT
    ```

4.  Use the CATALOG DATAFILECOPY command to catalog this datafile copy so that RMAN can use it:

    ```
    RMAN> CATALOG DATAFILECOPY '/u04/oradata/MATRIX_DR0/users.dbf';
    ```

5.  Use the SWITCH DATAFILE command to switch the datafile copy so that this file becomes the current datafile:

    ```
    RUN {
    SET NEWNAME FOR DATAFILE 1 TO '/u04/oradata/MATRIX/users.dbf';
    SWITCH DATAFILE 1;
    }
    ```

# Loss of a Datafile on a Standby Database

Use the following steps to recover a lost datafile on a standby database:

1.  Stop the Redo Apply using the ALTER DATABASE command:

    ```
    SQL> ALTER DATABASE RECOVER MANAGED STANDBY DATABASE CANCEL;
    ```

2.  Start RMAN and connect both to the standby and recovery catalog:

    ```
    RMAN TARGET / CATALOG rcat/<pswd>@RCAT
    ```

3.  Issue the following commands to restore and recover datafiles on the standby database:

    ```
    RMAN> RESTORE DATAFILE 1;
    RMAN> RECOVER DATAFILE 1;
    ```

4.  Restart SQL Apply:

    ```
    SQL> ALTER DATABASE RECOVER MANAGED STANDBY DATABASE
    USING CURRENT LOGFILE DISCONNECT;
    ```

## Loss of Standby Controlfile

You can restore the control file from backups by executing the RESTORE CONTROLFILE command. You can use several ways to do this depending on whether you're using an RMAN catalog or FRA. Here are some of the options:

```
RMAN> RESTORE CONTROLFILE FROM AUTOBACKUP;
RMAN> RESTORE CONTROLFILE FROM '/BACKUP_DIR/PIECE_NAME';
RMAN> RESTORE CONTROLFILE;                 => MOST RECENT BACKUP.
```

You can then start and mount your database. Depending on your configuration you can also refer to Note: 459411.1 "Steps to Re-create a Physical Standby Controlfile" and Note 734862.1 "Step by Step Guide on How to Recreate Standby Control File When Datafiles Are on ASM And Using Oracle Managed Files" for details.

## Loss of Primary Controlfile

You can restore the control file from a backup by executing the RESTORE CONTOLFILE and the RECOVER DATABASE commands. The RECOVER DATABASE command automatically fixes the filenames in the control file to match the files existing at that database and recovers the database to the most recently received log sequence at the database. Lastly, you may also create a new control file using CREATE CONTROLFILE. As a part of your backup process, you may want to include a step to back up your control file to trace. This will come in handy if you ever need to rebuild your control file.

```
RMAN> SQL "ALTER DATABASE BACKUP CONTROLFILE TO TRACE";
```

Or use this:

```
SQL> ALTER DATABASE BACKUP CONTROLFILE TO TRACE;
```

In the alert log, you will see a line similar to the following, which tells you where the control file create script has been written:

```
Backup controlfile written to trace file
/OracleHomes/diag/rdbms/matrix/Matrix/trace/Matrix_ora_ 28431.trc
```

## Loss of an Online Redo Log File

If the online redo log files are multiplexed, then the loss of one member will not impact the database. You can then shut down the database and copy the other members of the group over the missing or damaged member:

1. Shut down the database.

2. Copy the existing multiplexed member over the missing or damaged member.

```
[matrix]$ ls
control01.ctl   redo02a.rdo   sysaux01.dbf   users01.dbf
redo01a.rdo     redo03a.rdo   system01.dbf
[matrix]$ cp redo03a.rdo /media/orclvol2/oradata/matrix/redo03b.rdo
[matrix]$ cd /media/orclvol2/oradata/matrix
```

```
[matrix]$ ls
actor_d_01.dbf   control02.ctl   redo02b.rdo   temp01.dbf
actor_i_01.dbf   control03.ctl   redo01b.rdo    redo03b.rdo   undotbs01.dbf
```

**3.** Start up the database.

If all of the members of an inactive group that has been archived are lost, the group can be dropped and re-created.

If the current group or an inactive group that has not yet been archived is damaged or missing, you must failover to the standby database, or take a loss of data and recover primary to a time just prior to that current or inactive group.

In Oracle Database 11*g*, a tool called Data Recovery Advisor can help you diagnose and fix media failures. It will determine the best recovery options and can perform the recovery.

Once the database has detected the failure or you've run diagnostic checks or executed the VALIDATE commands, the results are stored in the Automatic Diagnostic Repository (ADR). Once ADR records the failures, you can invoke the Data Recovery Advisor. Here's an example of what you would see if the failure has not been placed in ADR:

```
RMAN> list failure;
no failures found that match specification
```

The following is an example of a Data Recovery Advisor report for a missing redo log:

```
RMAN> advise failure;
starting full resync of recovery catalog
full resync complete
List of Database Failures
=========================
Failure ID Priority Status    Time Detected Summary
---------- -------- --------- ------------- -------
702        HIGH     OPEN      05-JAN-09     Redo log file
/media/orclvol2/oradata/matrix/redo03b.rdo is missing
  Impact: Database might be unrecoverable or become unrecoverable
analyzing automatic repair options; this may take some time
allocated channel: ORA_DISK_1
channel ORA_DISK_1: SID=135 device type=DISK
analyzing automatic repair options complete

Mandatory Manual Actions
========================
no manual actions available

Optional Manual Actions
=======================
1. If file /media/orclvol2/oradata/matrix/redo03b.rdo was unintentionally
renamed or moved, restore it

Automated Repair Options
========================
```

```
Option Repair Description
------ ------------------
1      Drop and re-create redo log group member
/media/orclvol2/oradata/matrix/redo03b.rdo
  Strategy: The repair includes complete media recovery with no data loss
  Repair script:
/u01/app/oracle/diag/rdbms/matrix/matrix/hm/reco_2237002612.hm
```

The LIST FAILURE command cannot be used on a physical standby database. If you try, you will see the following error:

```
RMAN> LIST FAILURE;
RMAN-00571: ===========================================================
RMAN-00569: =============== ERROR MESSAGE STACK FOLLOWS ===============
RMAN-00571: ===========================================================
RMAN-03002: failure of list command at 02/15/2009 18:33:58
RMAN-05533: LIST FAILURE is not supported on STANDBY database
```

The Data Recovery Advisor is also available in Grid Control and Database Control in a GUI format. In Grid Control it is under the Availability tab for the primary database in the Perform Recovery action. The Data Recovery Advisor (without any errors showing) is displayed in Figure 12-1.

The RESTORE PREVIEW command can be used to determine which backups will need to be restored and recovered and what checkpoint you must exceed to open the database reset logs. The RECOVER DATABASE command automatically fixes the filenames in the control file to match the files existing at that database and recovers the database to the most recently received log sequence at the database.

Here's the restore DATABASE preview command:

```
RMAN> restore DATABASE preview;
Starting restore at 04-JAN-09
starting full resync of recovery catalog
full resync complete
allocated channel: ORA_DISK_1
channel ORA_DISK_1: SID=125 device type=DISK
List of Backup Sets
===================
BS Key  Type LV Size       Device Type Elapsed Time Completion Time
------- ---- -- ---------- ----------- ------------ ---------------
63      Incr 0  780.04M    DISK        00:01:20     03-JAN-09
        BP Key: 65   Status: AVAILABLE  Compressed: NO  Tag:
TAG20090103T115553
        Piece Name: /media/orclvol3/matrix_df675172553_2_1
  List of Datafiles in backup set 63
```

---

**Perform Recovery**

**Oracle Advised Recovery**

Oracle did not detect any failures.                    ( Advise and Recover )

---

**FIGURE 12-1.** *Data Recovery Advisor*

```
   File LV Type Ckp SCN    Ckp Time   Name
   ---- -- ---- ---------- --------- ----
    1    0  Incr 580819     03-JAN-09
/media/orclvol1/oradata/matrix/system01.dbf
    2    0  Incr 580819     03-JAN-09
/media/orclvol1/oradata/matrix/sysaux01.dbf
    3    0  Incr 580819     03-JAN-09
/media/orclvol2/oradata/matrix/undotbs01.dbf
    4    0  Incr 580819     03-JAN-09
/media/orclvol1/oradata/matrix/users01.dbf

BS Key   Type LV Size       Device Type Elapsed Time Completion Time
------- ---- -- ---------- ----------- ------------ ---------------
228     Incr 1  22.17M     DISK        00:01:25     04-JAN-09
        BP Key: 234   Status: AVAILABLE  Compressed: NO  Tag:
TAG20090104T195543
        Piece Name: /media/orclvol3/matrix_df675287744_8_1
   List of Datafiles in backup set 228
   File LV Type Ckp SCN    Ckp Time   Name
   ---- -- ---- ---------- --------- ----
    3    1  Incr 652440     04-JAN-09
/media/orclvol2/oradata/matrix/undotbs01.dbf
    4    1  Incr 652440     04-JAN-09
/media/orclvol1/oradata/matrix/users01.dbf

BS Key   Type LV Size       Device Type Elapsed Time Completion Time
------- ---- -- ---------- ----------- ------------ ---------------
229     Incr 1  5.73M      DISK        00:00:30     04-JAN-09
        BP Key: 235   Status: AVAILABLE  Compressed: NO  Tag:
TAG20090104T195543
        Piece Name: /media/orclvol3/matrix_df675287836_9_1
   List of Datafiles in backup set 229
   File LV Type Ckp SCN    Ckp Time   Name
   ---- -- ---- ---------- --------- ----
    1    1  Incr 652474     04-JAN-09
/media/orclvol1/oradata/matrix/system01.dbf

BS Key   Type LV Size       Device Type Elapsed Time Completion Time
------- ---- -- ---------- ----------- ------------ ---------------
230     Incr 1  29.46M     DISK        00:00:23     04-JAN-09
        BP Key: 236   Status: AVAILABLE  Compressed: NO  Tag:
TAG20090104T195543
        Piece Name: /media/orclvol3/matrix_df675287868_10_1
   List of Datafiles in backup set 230
   File LV Type Ckp SCN    Ckp Time   Name
   ---- -- ---- ---------- --------- ----
    2    1  Incr 652488     04-JAN-09
/media/orclvol1/oradata/matrix/sysaux01.dbf
using channel ORA_DISK_1
```

```
List of Archived Log Copies for database with db_unique_name MATRIX
=====================================================================

Key     Thrd Seq     S Low Time
------- ---- ------- - ---------
226     1    31      A 04-JAN-09
        Name:
/media/orclvol3/MATRIX/archivelog/2009_01_04/o1_mf_1_31_4p2t9wb5_.arc

Media recovery start SCN is 652440
Recovery must be done beyond SCN 652488 to clear datafile fuzziness
Finished restore at 04-JAN-09
```

Here's the RESTORE ARCHIVELOG ALL PREVIEW command:

```
RMAN> RESTORE ARCHIVELOG ALL PREVIEW
Starting restore at 04-JAN-09
using channel ORA_DISK_1
List of Backups
===============
Key     TY LV S Device Type Completion Time #Pieces #Copies Compressed Tag
------- -- -- - ----------- --------------- ------- ------- ---------- ------------------
63      B  0  A DISK        03-JAN-09       1       1       NO         TAG20090103T115553
228     B  1  A DISK        04-JAN-09       1       1       NO         TAG20090104T195543
229     B  1  A DISK        04-JAN-09       1       1       NO         TAG20090104T195543
230     B  1  A DISK        04-JAN-09       1       1       NO         TAG20090104T195543

List of Archived Log Copies for database with db_unique_name MATRIX
=====================================================================

Key     Thrd Seq     S Low Time
------- ---- ------- - ---------
226     1    31      A 04-JAN-09
        Name:
/media/orclvol3/MATRIX/archivelog/2009_01_04/o1_mf_1_31_4p2t9wb5_.arc

Media recovery start SCN is 652440
Recovery must be done beyond SCN 652488 to clear datafile fuzziness
```

# Incomplete Recovery of the Primary Database

Several options are available when you need to perform an incomplete recovery of the primary database. If flashback is enabled on the primary, you can recover the primary and standby database prior to the error occurring. However, if media recovery is required, a restore and recovery will be needed. On the primary, do the following.

1. Mount the database exclusive:

   ```
   SQL> startup mount exclusive
   ORACLE instance started.
   Total System Global Area 1.0737E+10 bytes
   Fixed Size                  2101912 bytes
   Variable Size            4160753000 bytes
   ```

```
Database Buffers           6492782592 bytes
Redo Buffers                 81780736 bytes
Database mounted.
```

2.  Flash back the database:

    ```
    SQL> flashback database to '<timestamp>;
    Flashback complete.
    ```

3.  Open the database reset logs:

    ```
    SQL> alter database open resetlogs;
    Database altered.
    ```

On the standby database, you will need to issue the same FLASHBACK STANDBY DATABASE statement on the standby database before restarting apply services. Note that you do not execute OPEN RESETLOGS on a physical standby database after the flashback command.

# Recovering from a Dropped Table

The following is an example of recovering from the accidental dropping of a table.

1.  Drop the table:

    ```
    SQL> drop table matrix_user.movie_titles;
    Table dropped.
    ```

2.  Flash back the table:

    ```
    SQL> flashback table matrix_user.movie_titles to before drop;
    Flashback complete.
    ```

# Recover a Missing Datafile from a Backup Taken on the Standby

The following covers the procedures you will need to follow to restore a datafile to the primary database with a backup that was taken on a physical standby.

```
RMAN> list failure;
List of Database Failures
=========================
Failure ID Priority Status     Time Detected Summary
---------- -------- ---------  ------------- -------
402        HIGH     OPEN       12-FEB-09     One or more non-system datafiles
are missing

RMAN> repair failure preview;
List of Database Failures
=========================
```

```
Failure ID Priority Status     Time Detected Summary
---------- -------- --------- ------------- -------
402        HIGH     OPEN       12-FEB-09     One or more non-system datafiles
are missing

analyzing automatic repair options; this may take some time
allocated channel: ORA_DISK_1
channel ORA_DISK_1: SID=125 device type=DISK
analyzing automatic repair options complete

Mandatory Manual Actions
========================
no manual actions available

Optional Manual Actions
========================
1. If file /media/orclvol2/oradata/matrix/location_d_01.dbf was unintentionally
renamed or moved, restore it
2. If file /media/orclvol1/oradata/matrix/location_i_01.dbf was unintentionally
renamed or moved, restore it
Automated Repair Options
========================
Option Repair Description
------ ------------------
1      Restore and recover datafile 7; Restore and recover datafile 8
  Strategy: The repair includes complete media recovery with no data loss
  Repair script:
/u01/app/oracle/diag/rdbms/matrix/matrix/hm/reco_515388588.hm

RMAN>
Strategy: The repair includes complete media recovery with no data loss
Repair script: /u01/app/oracle/diag/rdbms/matrix/matrix/hm/reco_515388588.hm

contents of repair script:
   # restore and recover datafile
   sql 'alter database datafile 7, 8 offline';
   restore datafile 7, 8;
   recover datafile 7, 8;
   sql 'alter database datafile 7, 8 online';
```

1. Offline the missing datafiles:

   ```
   RMAN> sql 'alter database datafile 7, 8 offline';
   sql statement: alter database datafile 7, 8 offline
   ```

2. Associate the standby backup with the primary database:

   ```
   RMAN> change backup tag='ORALINUX2_FULL_021209' from db_unique_name
   matrixdr reset db_unique_name;
   change backup piece db_unique_name
   backup piece handle=/media/orclvol3/matrix_df678591310_24_1 RECID=15
   STAMP=678591326
   ```

```
change backup piece db_unique_name
backup piece handle=/media/orclvol3/matrix_df678591351_25_1 RECID=16
STAMP=678591366
change backup piece db_unique_name
backup piece handle=/media/orclvol3/matrix_df678591452_26_1 RECID=17
STAMP=678591467
Changed 3 objects db_unique_name
```

3. Run a list summary to ensure that the backups are now accessible by the primary database:

```
RMAN> LIST BACKUPSET SUMMARY;
List of Backups
===============
Key     TY LV S Device Type Completion Time #Pieces #Copies Compressed Tag
------- -- -- - ----------- --------------- ------- ------- ---------- ---
1017    B  0  A DISK        11-FEB-09       1       1       NO
ORALINUX1_FULL_021109
1018    B  0  A DISK        11-FEB-09       1       1       NO
ORALINUX1_FULL_021109
1019    B  0  A DISK        11-FEB-09       1       1       NO
ORALINUX1_FULL_021109
1037    B  F  A DISK        11-FEB-09       1       1       NO
TAG20090211T223025
1096    B  0  A DISK        12-FEB-09       1       1       NO
ORALINUX2_FULL_021209
1097    B  0  A DISK        12-FEB-09       1       1       NO
ORALINUX2_FULL_021209
1098    B  0  A DISK        12-FEB-09       1       1       NO
ORALINUX2_FULL_021209
```

4. Restore the datafiles from the standby backup:

```
RMAN> restore datafile 7, 8 from tag='ORALINUX2_FULL_021209';
Starting restore at 12-FEB-09
using channel ORA_DISK_1

channel ORA_DISK_1: starting datafile backup set restore
channel ORA_DISK_1: specifying datafile(s) to restore from backup set
channel ORA_DISK_1: restoring datafile 00007 to
/media/orclvol2/oradata/matrix/location_d_01.dbf
channel ORA_DISK_1: reading from backup piece
/media/orclvol3/matrix_df678591351_25_1
channel ORA_DISK_1: piece handle=/media/orclvol3/matrix_
df678591351_25_1 tag=ORALINUX2_FULL_021209
channel ORA_DISK_1: restored backup piece 1
channel ORA_DISK_1: restore complete, elapsed time: 00:00:03
channel ORA_DISK_1: starting datafile backup set restore
channel ORA_DISK_1: specifying datafile(s) to restore from backup set
channel ORA_DISK_1: restoring datafile 00008 to
/media/orclvol1/oradata/matrix/location_i_01.dbf
channel ORA_DISK_1: reading from backup piece
/media/orclvol3/matrix_df678591452_26_1
```

```
channel ORA_DISK_1: piece handle=/media/orclvol3/matrix_
df678591452_26_1 tag=ORALINUX2_FULL_021209
channel ORA_DISK_1: restored backup piece 1
channel ORA_DISK_1: restore complete, elapsed time: 00:00:03
Finished restore at 12-FEB-09
```

5. Recover the missing datafiles:

```
RMAN> recover datafile 7, 8 from tag='ORALINUX2_FULL_021209';
Starting recover at 12-FEB-09
using channel ORA_DISK_1

starting media recovery
media recovery complete, elapsed time: 00:00:01

Finished recover at 12-FEB-09
```

6. Set the datafiles online:

```
RMAN> sql 'alter database datafile 7, 8 online';
sql statement: alter database datafile 7, 8 online
```

# General Best Practices

Following industry best practices[2] can save you lot of headaches and possible reimplementation of architectural changes. The following shows some general best practices:

- The RMAN catalog should be stored on a separate server from the primary and standby databases. In the case of a disaster, there will be no impact to the recovery of either site.

- Take backups at both the primary and standby databases to reduce recovery time in case of double outages.

- Maintain multiple copies of the backup files as well as archive logs in different locations. Refer to Note 443814.1 "Managing Multiple Archive Log Destinations with RMAN" for details.

- Specify FILESPERSET = 1 when backing up. Have each datafile in a single backupset. When doing a partial restore, RMAN must read through the entire piece to get the datafile/archive log requested. The smaller the backup piece, the quicker the restore can complete.

- Specify MAXOPENFILES = 1 for each channel defined. This will ensure that each RMAN channel reads from only a single file at any one time.

- Define additional channels to increase the number of parallel backup processes running. With FILESPERSET set to 1 and MAXOPENFILES set to 1, you will need to specify additional channels and/or degrees of parallelism that will allow RMAN to keep more data moving into the backupsets.

---

[2] Note: 388422.1 "Top 10 Backup and Recovery Best Practices"

- Turn on logical block checking to detect memory and data corruptions as soon as they occur. There is overhead associated with enabling it depending on the level of checking that you've selected and the workload in your environment.

- Turn on block change tracking when using RMAN backups. RMAN can use the block change tracking file to identify the blocks that have changed for incremental backups, thus avoiding the need to scan every block in the datafile.

- When backing up a database, use the `check logical` parameter. To ensure that you have a good backup, this will check for logical corruption within a block as well as the normal head/tail checksums.

- If you're using tape, ensure that your retention period is in line with your tape retention policy requirements. If you're not using a catalog, ensure that your control file record keep time matches the retention policy.

- Set AUTOBACKUP to ON. This will ensure that you always have an up-to-date control file and spfile available that has been taken at the end of the current backup, not during it.

- Don't use `DELETE ALL INPUT` when backing up archive logs. It will back up from one destination and delete all copies of the archive log in the other destinations, whereas `DELETE INPUT` will back up from one location and then delete only what has been backed up. Use the RMAN command `BACKUP RECOVERY FILES` to copy disk backups in the flash recovery area to tape.

# Conclusion

As a database administrator, you are responsible for the availability of the databases in your environment. In this chapter, we've discussed backup and recovery strategies, techniques, and the integration of RMAN in a Data Guard environment. It is crucial that you spend time planning, testing, and documenting your backup and recovery strategies. Your understanding of backup and recovery concepts and your knowledge of which techniques to use during a specific type of recovery will enable you to respond in a timely and efficient manner during an emergency. You will also want to review Oracle® Data Guard Concepts and Administration 11*g* Release 1 (11.1) manual as well as the Oracle® Database Backup and Recovery User's Guide 11*g* Release 1 (11.1) for more detailed information.

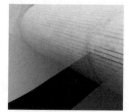

# CHAPTER
## 13

## Troubleshooting
## Data Guard

n the previous chapters, you learned industry best practice techniques to set up and enable Data Guard. Just as with any kind of database administrative tasks, Data Guard often requires "nurturing and feeding." When configuring and maintaining a Data Guard environment, you will inevitably run into issues. In this chapter, we will focus on some of the common issues and resolutions regarding the configuration and maintenance of a Data Guard environment. We'll cover where to look for information to help you pinpoint the issue as well as steps for corrective action to resolve the most common problems.

Several great sources of diagnostic information are available to aid you in determining the root cause of your Data Guard issues. Available at your disposal are the alert log and trace files, database health checks, the Data Guard Broker, Oracle Enterprise Manager, and performance views. The majority of the potential Data Guard errors can be divided into the following categories, which are covered in this chapter:

- Common management issues
- Physical standby issues
- Logical standby issues
- Switchover troubleshooting
- Failover troubleshooting
- Data Guard Broker issues
- Data Guard Snapshot standby issues

Troubleshooting methodologies and techniques evolve and mature over time. Although we try to provide you the most amount of troubleshooting information in this chapter, we cannot cover all the possible errors that a DBA can encounter in a Data Guard environment. We will address the common issues that you may encounter. For future updates and latest troubleshooting tips, please visit the Data Guard Handbook blog site at blog.dataguardbook.com.

# Diagnostic Information

Oracle provides common diagnostic information in database alert logs, observer logs, Data Guard trace files, and the Data Guard Broker log files. In addition to describing how to use the log files, we will include a brief description of some of the performance views that you can use to monitor a Data Guard configuration. We will also provide you with relevant information about where to look to determine the root cause of an issue with your Data Guard configuration.

## Database Alert Logs

The database alert logs provide a great source of information in investigating issues with both the primary and standby databases. You should start diagnosing the problem by investigating the contents of the database alert logs. Most issues can be identified here, but you will frequently need to obtain additional information to resolve them. The Data Guard Broker also writes information to the alert logs as well as its own Disaster Recovery Center (DRC) log files. Prior to Oracle Database 11*g*, the alert log could be found in the background destination directory in the format alert<*dbname*>.log. Starting with Oracle Database 11*g*, the text alert log file resides in the trace subdirectory of the diagnostic destination along with the trace files and the XML version in the alert subdirectory. These are found under the Oracle base directory in the following format: ${ORACLE_BASE}/diag/rdbms/${ORACLE_SID}/${ORACLE_SID}. To determine the exact directories you can query the V$DIAG_INFO view on your primary or standby database as in the following example (slightly edited here to fit the page).

```
SQL> SELECT NAME,VALUE FROM V$DIAG_INFO WHERE VALUE LIKE '%OracleHomes%';

NAME            VALUE
-------------   -----------------------------------------------------------

ADR Base        /scratch/OracleHomes

ADR Home        /scratch/OracleHomes/diag/rdbms/matrix_dr0/Matrix_DR0

Diag Trace      /scratch/OracleHomes/diag/rdbms/matrix_dr0/Matrix_DR0/trace

Diag Alert      /scratch/OracleHomes/diag/rdbms/matrix_dr0/Matrix_DR0/alert

Diag Incident   /scratch/OracleHomes/diag/rdbms/matrix_dr0/Matrix_DR0/incident

Diag Cdump      /scratch/OracleHomes/diag/rdbms/matrix_dr0/Matrix_DR0/cdump

HealthMonitor   /scratch/OracleHomes/diag/rdbms/matrix_dr0/Matrix_DR0/hm
```

Chapter 7 contained a comprehensive alert log monitoring shell script that you can employ to monitor your database by mining the text alert log. Oracle 11*g* also comes with a new utility called adrci that allows you to interactively examine the XML formatted alert log. The nice thing about this utility is that it will find all the logs that currently reside in your Oracle Database 11*g* diagnostics directory structure.

```
[Matrix_DR0] adrci

ADRCI: Release 11.1.0.6.0 - Beta on Sat Apr 25 11:49:38 2009

Copyright (c) 1982, 2007, Oracle.  All rights reserved.

ADR base = "/scratch/OracleHomes"
adrci> SHOW ALERT
Choose the alert log from the following homes to view:
1: diag/clients/user_oracle/host_1716447713_11
2: diag/asm/+asm/+ASM
3: diag/tnslsnr/lcarpent-lnx/listener
4: diag/rdbms/matrix_dr0/Matrix_DR0
5: diag/rdbms/bogus/Matrix_DR0
Q: to quit

Please select option:
```

Selecting one from the list will convert the XML file into a text file and load it directly into an editor so you can examine the alert log. Or you can use a single command to search for a certain type of message. For example, to look for all occurrences of `ORA-12nnn` messages (usually TNS errors) you use the following command.

```
adrci> SHOW ALERT -P "MESSAGE_TEXT LIKE '%ORA-12%'"

Choose the alert log from the following homes to view:

1: diag/clients/user_oracle/host_1716447713_11
2: diag/asm/+asm/+ASM
3: diag/tnslsnr/lcarpent-lnx/listener
4: diag/rdbms/matrix_dr0/Matrix_DR0
5: diag/rdbms/bogus/Matrix_DR0
Q: to quit

Please select option: 4

Output the results to file: /tmp/alert_12564_3086_Matrix_DR0_3.ado
```

Which would then put you into the editor where you would see the results of the query as follows.

```
2009-02-03 23:49:05.418000 -05:00
Errors in file /scratch/OracleHomes/diag/rdbms/matrix_dr0/Matrix_DR0/trace/
Matrix_DR0_lns1_28677.trc:

ORA-12528: TNS:listener: all appropriate instances are blocking new connections

2009-02-03 23:49:13.090000 -05:00
Errors in file /scratch/OracleHomes/diag/rdbms/matrix_dr0/Matrix_DR0/trace/
Matrix_DR0_arc3_19858.trc:

ORA-12528: TNS:listener: all appropriate instances are blocking new connections

2009-02-11 00:08:23.537000 -05:00
Errors in file /scratch/OracleHomes/diag/rdbms/matrix_dr0/Matrix_DR0/trace/
Matrix_DR0_lgwr_2660.trc:

ORA-12514: TNS:listener does not currently know of service requested in connect
descriptor
```

You could then repeat the same query on one of the other log files in the list. Of course if you have a `grep` capability you could do the same thing on the text alert log file. However, there is a lot more to `ardci` than meets the eye. For example, using the `SHOW PROBLEM` command gives you a list from all alert logs on the system that are considered a problem.

```
adrci> SHOW PROBLEM
ADR Home = /scratch/OracleHomes/diag/clients/user_oracle/host_1716447713_11:
*************************************************************************
0 rows fetched
ADR Home = /scratch/OracleHomes/diag/asm/+asm/+ASM:
*************************************************************************
0 rows fetched
ADR Home = /scratch/OracleHomes/diag/tnslsnr/lcarpent-lnx/listener:
*************************************************************************
```

```
0 rows fetched
ADR Home = /scratch/OracleHomes/diag/rdbms/matrix_dr0/Matrix_DR0:
*************************************************************************
PROBLEM_ID PROBLEM_KEY            LAST_INCIDENT LASTINC_TIME
---------- -------------          ------------- -------------------------
5          ORA 600 [1433]         20422 2009-03-25 10:17:23.029677 -04:00
6          ORA 239                19833 2009-03-24 21:31:00.990974 -04:00
4          ORA 600 [600]          19801 2009-03-22 03:35:30.344734 -04:00
3          ORA 494                19378 2009-03-22 00:45:12.459292 -04:00
2          ORA 7445 [ksmdgidx()+24] 16921 2009-03-07 15:05:08.714188 -05:00
5 rows fetched
adrci>
```

Type **HELP** to get a list of all the commands or refer to the Oracle documentation for more information on `ardci`.

## Observer Log Files

If you are using the Fast-Start Failover (FSFO) feature of Data Guard, additional diagnostic information is available in the observer log file. If you use the Data Guard command-line interface (DGMGRL), you can configure the log file to track observer events. In addition, the observer maintains a file with the configuration information, called FSFO.dat by default. As we mentioned in Chapter 8, you can change the name of this file. If you're using Enterprise Manager to configure the observer, the observer datafiles are kept in the ${ORACLE_HOME}/dbs directory and the log files are in the ${ORACLE_HOME}/rdbms/log directory. The datafiles are called afo<*nnnnn*>.dat and the log files are called dgmgrl<*nnnnn*>.log. The <*nnnnn*> is a system-generated number that will change each time the observer is started. You can use the DGMGRL -logfile option to start the observer so that all of the troubleshooting actions can be captured in a file. Here's an example:

```
% DGMGRL -LOGFILE observer.log / "START OBSERVER"
```

All the observer output is then recorded in an observer.log file in the current working directory where you issued the DGMGRL command. In general, the observer.log file often provides useful information for troubleshooting problems with the observer as well as problems with FSFO.

## Data Guard Trace Files

Data Guard trace files can also provide crucial information to diagnosing Data Guard configuration issues and/or identify areas in the Data Guard topology that need attention. Oracle will write an audit trail of the archived redo logs received from the primary database into a trace file when the LOG_ARCHIVE_TRACE initialization parameter is enabled. You can also set this parameter for the standby databases to generate trace output for the remote file services (RFS), archiver process ARCn, and Managed Recovery Process (MRP0) processes. The trace files will be located in the user_dump_ dest directory. The format for the parameter is as follows, where *nn* is the trace level:

```
LOG_ARCHIVE_TRACE=nn
```

To enable, disable, or change the parameter on a standby database, issue the following command; for example, here we set it to 16:

```
SQL> ALTER SYSTEM SET LOG_ARCHIVE_TRACE=16
```

The higher the trace level, the more detailed the information generated. The following examples show some of the trace file formats:

- **Remote file server** *<instance_name>*_rfs_*<number>*.trc

- **Management recovery process** *<instance_name>*_mrp_*<number>*.trc

- **Virtual timekeeper** *<instance_name>*_vktm_*<number>*.trc

# Data Guard Broker Log Files and Tools

The Data Guard Monitor (DMON) process also writes status information to a log file. DMON log files can be useful in diagnosing Data Guard failures and can be found in the background_dump_ dest directory. The name of the DMON log file is drc<DB_UNIQUE_NAME>.log.

With Grid Control (which uses the Broker), you can identify the root cause of errors by executing the VERIFY command to run a series of checks on the Broker configuration, including a health check of each database in the configuration. You can also invoke tracing for more detailed information. This information will be found in the alert log and trace files.

The Data Guard Broker will also automatically check the overall health of the primary and standby databases by checking each component of the Data Guard configuration. It takes the current database state and current parameter settings and matches those with the Broker configuration file. Table 13-1 identifies the fundamental health checks the Data Guard Broker will perform on both the primary and standby databases.

The following database properties can be used to query the database status through DGMGRL:

- **StatusReport** Lists all the issues detected during a database health check

- **LogXptStatus** Lists all the log transport errors detected on all of the instances on the primary database

- **InconsistentProperties** Lists all of the properties with inconsistencies between the Broker configuration and the database settings

- **InconsistentLogXptProps** Lists all of the redo transport inconsistencies between the Broker configuration and the redo transport settings

| Database | Data Guard Broker will check |
|---|---|
| Primary | Database settings are the same as those specified in the Broker configuration. |
| | Redo transport settings match those in the redo transport–related properties of the standby database. |
| | Redo transport services do not have any errors. |
| | Database is in the correct data protection mode. |
| | Data protection level is consistent with configured data protection mode. |
| | Supplemental logging is turned on when a logical standby database exists. |
| Standby | Database settings are consistent with those specified within the Broker configuration. |
| | Primary and standby databases are synchronized or within lag limits (if FSFO is enabled). |

**TABLE 13-1.** *Data Guard Broker Health Checks*

Here's an example of how to query this information via the DGMGRL SHOW DATABASE command:

```
DGMGRL>  SHOW DATABASE 'MATRIX_DR0' 'StatusReport'
```

**NOTE**
*For more detailed information on the health check, see Chapter 5.*

# Dynamic Performance Views

Table 13-2 shows the dynamic performance views and brief descriptions that provide troubleshooting information for common Data Guard issues.

| Name | Description |
|---|---|
| DBA_LOGSTDBY_EVENTS | Contains the last 100 (default) events that occurred on the logical standby |
| DBA_LOGSTDBY_PROGRESS | Checks whether SQL Apply is progressing |
| DBA_LOGSTDBY_LOG | Checks whether archive logs are being delivered to a logical standby |
| DBA_LOGSTDBY_UNSUPPORTED | Identifies SQL Apply unsupported data types |
| V$ARCHIVE_DEST | Describes all the destinations in the Data Guard configuration, including each destination's current settings |
| V$ARCHIVE_DEST_STATUS | Displays runtime and configuration information for the redo transport destinations |
| V$ARCHIVE_GAP | Displays information to help you identify a gap in the archived redo log files on a physical standby |
| V$DATAGUARD_CONFIG | Lists the DB_UNIQUE_NAME parameters defined in the Data Guard configuration in LOG_ARCHIVE_CONFIG |
| V$DATAGUARD_STATUS | Displays and records events that would typically be triggered by any message to the alert log or server process trace files limited to the last 256 messages |
| V$LOG | Displays information from the online redo log files |
| V$LOGFILE | Contains information about the online redo log files and standby redo log files |
| V$LOG_HISTORY | Contains archive log history information from the control file |
| V$ARCHIVED_LOG | Contains more detailed archived log information from the control file. |
| V$LOGSTDBY_PROCESS | Shows whether logical standby process is running; if query returns no rows, it is not running |
| V$MANAGED_STANDBY | Displays current status information for Oracle Database processes related to Data Guard |
| V$STANDBY_LOG | Contains standby log file information |

**TABLE 13-2.**  *Database Performance Views*

# Data Guard Configuration and Management Errors

The majority of DBAs will encounter common errors that could impact their physical and/or logical standby databases as well as those that impact the Data Guard Broker. We will discuss the common errors that plague DBAs and corrective actions to resolve the issues that DBAs may run into when trying to configure and maintain a Data Guard environment. In addition, we'll address issues relating to the failover and switchover processes.

## Common Management Issues

Several situations can cause problems with your Data Guard configuration. We'll discuss the common issues that can occur at a standby environment, starting with errors associated with the password file.

### The Password File

You may encounter a couple of errors associated with the password file. For instance, you may have problems connecting to the standby database and may see the "ORA-01034: ORACLE not available" error message. Check your password for the SYS account on the primary and standby databases to make sure that they are the same.

If you encounter an ORA-16191 error when the primary attempts to connect to the standby, verify that the SYS password is the same on the primary and standby databases. Ensure that the primary and standby databases are using a password file and that the REMOTE_LOGIN_PASSWORD parameter is set to SHARED or EXCLUSIVE. You will need to push a new copy of the password file from the primary and replace the password file on the standby to fix the issue. In a Real Application Clusters (RAC) environment for the primary and standby, verify the timestamps of all of the password files and copy the latest file to all other nodes.

Remember that as of Oracle Database 11*g* you can no longer just create a new password file for a physical standby database. You must always copy the primary database password file to all physical standby databases whenever a privileged user's password is changed.

### SQL Apply Fails with ORA-01031

This error tells you that SQL Apply has failed with insufficient privileges. The problem is that background processes are not running with SYSDBA privileges. They will need to be granted manually on both the primary and standby databases. You will see the following in the alert log on the logical standby:

```
LOGSTDBY stmt: grant sysdba to maxtrix_user
LOGSTDBY status: ORA-01031: insufficient privileges
```

### SYS User and Data Guard

The password of the SYS user is used to authenticate redo transport sessions when a password file is used. In Oracle 11*g* the REDO_TRANSPORT_USER parameter can be used to select a different user for redo transport authentication by setting this parameter to the name of any user who has been granted the SYSOPER privilege.

At the standby site, execute the following commands to grant the appropriate role to the matrix_user:

```
SQL> alter session disable guard;
SQL> grant sysdba to matrix_user;
SQL> alter session enable guard;
```

Once the privilege has been granted, you will need to skip the transaction that caused the error on the standby and start the logical apply again. You can run the following command to determine the transaction in question:

```
SQL> SELECT XIDUSN, XIDSLT, XIDSQN, STATUS, STATUS_CODE
        FROM DBA_LOGSTDBY_EVENTS
        WHERE EVENT_TIME = (SELECT MAX(EVENT_TIME) FROM DBA_LOGSTDBY_EVENTS);
```

Pass the information from this query to the following stored procedure to skip the transaction:

```
SQL> EXECUTE DBMS_LOGSTDBY.SKIP_TRANSACTION (xid,xidslt,xidsqn);
```

However, we strongly recommend that you do *not* just randomly skip transactions. You must fix the problem that caused SQL Apply to stop in the first place (as above) before you can skip the errant transaction.

## Resolving Gaps Manually

A redo gap occurs whenever redo transmission is interrupted. Redo Transport Services will automatically detect the redo gap and resolve it by sending the missing redo to the destination once redo transmission resumes. In some cases, though, gap resolution can't be performed automatically and must be done manually. For example, redo gap resolution must be performed manually on a standby database if the primary database is unavailable or if the missing archive log is no longer on disk at the primary.

To determine whether a redo gap exists on your physical standby, you can run the following query. It gives you the lowest and highest sequence number of the log files received on the standby database. The thread# value will be 1 in the case of a single instance. If you are running a RAC configuration, this number will be different for each node.

```
SQL> SELECT * FROM V$ARCHIVE_GAP;
      THREAD# LOW_SEQUENCE# HIGH_SEQUENCE#
    ----------- ------------- --------------
        2         6233          6233
        3         4531          4531
        4         4938          4939
```

In this example, the query indicates for thread 2 that the standby is missing a log file with the sequence number of 6233. On thread 3, the log file with the sequence number of 4531 is missing, and on thread 4, log files with the sequence numbers between 4938 and 4939 are missing. You can use the low and high sequence numbers to identify the actual log files that are missing. Run the following query on the primary to capture this information:

```
SQL> SELECT name
        FROM v$archived_log
        WHERE thread# = 2
```

```
      AND dest_id = 2
      AND sequence# = 6233;
NAME
--------------------------------------------------
/u06/oradata/MATRIX/recovery_area/arch_2_6233_656445787.arc
```

If gaps exist, the output from this query will indicate which log files are missing. You may need to run this query multiple times because it returns only the gap that is currently preventing Redo Apply from continuing. Generally Data Guard will automatically resolve these gaps. However, if Data Guard does not resolve them you need to investigate why by examining the alert logs of both the primary and standby databases. If necessary, copy these files either from the production site or from backups to the physical standby site and register them with the physical standby database using the following command:

```
SQL>ALTER DATABASE REGISTER LOGFILE '<log file name>';
```

To determine whether other archived redo log files are missing, query the V$ARCHIVED_LOG view on the standby database to obtain the last sequence received and V$LOG to get the last sequence sent based on information in the control file for a specific thread:

```
SQL> SELECT MAX(R.SEQUENCE#) LAST_SEQ_RECD, MAX(L.SEQUENCE#) LAST_SEQ_SENT
     FROM V$ARCHIVED_LOG R, V$LOG L
     WHERE R.DEST_ID=2 and L.ARCHIVED='YES';
LAST_SEQ_RECD  LAST_SEQ_SENT
-------------  -------------
    11071          11073
```

If possible, copy any archived redo log files from the primary database that have sequence numbers higher than the highest sequence number available on the standby database to the standby site and register them. This must be done for each thread. But do not forget to investigate why Data Guard could not resolve this gap in the first place and fix that problem as well, so that it does not happen again!

On a logical standby database, run the following query to determine whether gaps exist. The DBA_LOGSTDBY_LOG view contains information about logs registered for the logical standby database. The NEXT_CHANGE# is the system change number (SCN) of the next archive log and FIRST_CHANGE# is the SCN of the current archive log:

```
SQL> SELECT THREAD#, SEQUENCE#, FILE_NAME
     FROM DBA_LOGSTDBY_LOG L
     WHERE NEXT_CHANGE# NOT IN
         (SELECT FIRST_CHANGE#
          FROM DBA_LOGSTDBY_LOG
          WHERE L.THREAD# = THREAD#)
     ORDER BY THREAD#, SEQUENCE#;
   THREAD# SEQUENCE#  FILE_NAME
---------- ---------- ------------------------------------------------
      1         6
/u06/oradata/MATRIX_DR0/recovery_area/arch_1_6_656445787.arc
      1        10
/u06/oradata/MATRIX_DR0/recovery_area/arch_1_10_656445787.arc
```

This example indicates that a gap exists in the sequence of the archive log files for thread 1. The highest log file is at sequence 10; however, a gap exists between this file and the log file at sequence 6. You will need to copy the missing log files over and register them.

## Use an Incremental RMAN Backup to Roll a Standby Forward

In cases where the standby has fallen behind for a long period of time, you may want to use an incremental backup as a more efficient method for handling large gap scenarios. You should use this method only if the standby has fallen significantly behind the primary or no NOLOGGING operations have been performed on the primary. This solution can be used only on a physical standby database.

1. The first step is to stop Redo Apply on the standby database:

```
SQL> ALTER DATABASE RECOVER MANAGED STANDBY DATABASE CANCEL;
```

2. Next, determine the current SCN for the standby database. You can use the following method if the standby is lagging behind the primary database:

```
SQL> SELECT CURRENT_SCN FROM V$DATABASE;
CURRENT_SCN
----------
885952
```

3. Use the value for the current SCN to take your incremental backup on the primary database:

```
RMAN> run
{
allocate channel d1 type disk;
allocate channel d2 type disk;
backup incremental from scn 885952 database format
'/tmp/dba/bkups/MATRIX_%U';
release channel d1;
release channel d2;
}
```

4. On the primary, obtain a new standby control file and copy it to physical standby:

```
SQL> alter database create standby controlfile as '/tmp/std.ctl'
```

5. Copy the backupset and the standby control file backup to the physical standby server using the `scp` or `sftp` command. Shut down the physical standby, and replace the control file on the physical standby database with /tmp/std.ctl. Issue the `startup mount` command on the physical standby.

6. After you finishing copying the backupset to the standby system, catalog the backup using the target database control file:

```
RMAN> CATALOG START WITH '/tmp/dba/bkups';
List of Files Unknown to the Database
=====================================
```

```
File Name: /tmp/dba/bkups/MATRIX_0ijmc1cn_1_1
File Name: /tmp/dba/bkups/MATRIX_0hjmc1ck_1_1
File Name: /tmp/dba/bkups/MATRIX_0jjmc1es_1_1
Do you really want to catalog the above files (enter YES or NO)? YES
cataloging files...
cataloging done
List of Cataloged Files
=======================
File Name: /tmp/dba/bkups/MATRIX_0ijmc1cn_1_1
File Name: /tmp/dba/bkups/MATRIX_0hjmc1ck_1_1
File Name: /tmp/dba/bkups/MATRIX_0jjmc1es_1_1
```

7. Recover the database from the incremental backup using NOREDO:

```
RMAN> recover database noredo;
```

8. Restart the MRP:

```
SQL> ALTER DATABASE RECOVER MANAGED STANDBY DATABASE
        USING CURRENT LOGFILE DISCONNECT;
```

If your databases uses OMF (or ASM which uses OMF by default) you will need to take care when you recreate the standby control file. For more detail refer to MetaLink Note 734862.1[1].

## Standby Database Is Not Receiving Redo Logs

If the redo data is not being transported to the standby database, query the V$ARCHIVE_DEST view and check for error messages. Here is an example of the query:

```
SQL> SELECT DEST_ID, STATUS, ERROR
      FROM V$ARCHIVE_DEST;
DEST_ID STATUS     ERROR
------- --------- ------------------------------------
    1   ERROR     ORA-16012: Archivelog standby database identifier mismatch
    2   INACTIVE
    3   INACTIVE
```

If the output of the query does not help you, check the following list of possible issues. If any of the following conditions exists, log transport services will fail to transmit redo data to the standby database.

### Listener Issues

- The listener.ora file has not been configured correctly.

- The listener has not been started on the standby.

- The service name for the standby instance is not configured correctly in the tnsnames.ora file on the primary database.

  - If you cannot log in remotely to the standby database using the TNSNAME identifier, then Data Guard cannot log in either. Try the remote login yourself:

    ```
    SQL> CONNECT SYS/PASSWORD@MYTNSNAME AS SYSDBA;
    ```

---

[1] Note 734862.1: Step By Step Guide on How to Recreate Standby Control File When Datafiles Are on ASM and Using Oracle Managed Files

### Archive Destination Issues

- The service name specified by the LOG_ARCHIVE_DEST_*n* parameter for the primary database is incorrect.

- The LOG_ARCHIVE_DEST_STATE_*n* parameter for the standby database is not set to the value ENABLE.

- A disconnect occurred and the number of seconds specified by REOPEN has not yet passed.

- The standby instance is not started.

- The standby control file was created incorrectly.

- The correct backup was not used to build the standby.

## Standby Waiting on Log Files that Exist at the Standby

If the standby is waiting on logs that are in the standby destination area, the logs are most likely not properly registered on the standby. Check the appropriate views (physical is V$ARCHIVED_LOG and logical is DBA_LOGSTDBY_LOG) to see if they are registered. If they are not registered, the file on disk is unusable and you should use the manual procedure if Data Guard cannot resolve the gaps automatically. *Do not try to use the file on disk!* Also verify that the local archival destination on the standby is correct.

## Receive an ORA-16032 on Alter System Archive Log All

One of the LOG_ARCHIVE_DEST_*n* parameters is not configured correctly. Verify the local destinations on the primary.

## Media Recovery Failures

If media recovery fails on the standby, leaving your standby in an unrecoverable state, you will see the following messages:

```
ORA-01578: ORACLE data block corrupted
ORA-26040: Data block was loaded using the NOLOGGING option.
```

In this example the problem is the result of a nologging operation on the primary database. The steps required to recover from this error or any other data file problem are the same. Following is a summary of steps to follow to recover from media failures on your standby databases (the steps would be similar if the failure is on the primary database).

First, take a full backup of the primary database and restore the necessary files to the physical standby database. On the physical standby database, you will need to do the following:

1. Offline the corresponding datafiles.

2. Copy the backup datafiles from the primary database.

3. Replace the corrupted datafiles.

4. Stop the Redo Apply.

5. Online the corresponding datafiles.

6. Restart the Redo Apply.

**Resync Logical Standby Database When Nologging Issue Occurs**   Keep in mind that SQL Apply will skip over nologging operations. Therefore, the datafiles will not be affected by the data block corruption. You will eventually see an "ORA-01403: No Data Found on the standby" error. To resync the table with the primary table, you will need to re-create it with the INSTANTIATE table procedure.

If you see an "ORA-00308: cannot open archived log," cancel SQL Apply and manually retrieve the missing files.

### Renaming Datafiles with the ALTER DATABASE Statement

You cannot rename a datafile on the standby site when the STANDBY_FILE_MANAGEMENT initialization parameter is set to AUTO. In addition, you are not permitted to use any of the following SQL statements:

```
SQL> ALTER DATABASE RENAME
SQL> ALTER DATABASE ADD/DROP LOGFILE
SQL> ALTER DATABASE ADD/DROP STANDBY LOGFILE MEMBER
SQL> ALTER DATABASE CREATE DATAFILE AS
```

If you attempt to use any of these statements on the standby database, the following error is returned if STANDBY_FILE_MANAGEMENT is set to AUTO:

```
ORA-01511: error in renaming log/data files
ORA-01270: RENAME operation is not allowed
```

You can still add and delete standby redo log files:

```
SQL> ALTER DATABASE ADD/DROP STANDBY LOGFILE;
```

# Physical Standby Issues

You will likely encounter several common issues when managing a physical database:

- You cannot mount the physical standby database.
- The standby archive destination is not defined properly.
- The standby site does not receive logs.
- The standby site is not processing the logs (MRP down, and so on).

### Unable to Mount the Physical Standby Database

The physical standby can't be mounted if the control file was created with an operating system– created backup or a backup created using an ALTER DATABASE statement *without* the STANDBY options. The standby control file must be created with the ALTER DATABASE CREATE STANDBY CONTROLFILE statement or the RMAN BACKUP CURRENT CONTROLFILE with the FOR STANDBY option.

### Primary Database Shutdown

If you have configured standby redo log files on your standby database, the size of the current standby redo log file on each standby database must be the same size as the redo log file on the primary database. After a log switch, if no available standby redo log files match the size of the redo log file on the primary database, the primary will shut down if it is in Maximum Protection mode.

The primary database becomes unsynchronized if it is in Maximum Availability mode. You will see the following message in the alert log:

```
No standby log files of size <#> blocks available.
```

To avoid this message, make sure that when you add a redo log group to the primary database, you add a corresponding standby redo log group to the standby database of the same size. At a minimum, you should have at least one standby redo log file group more than the number of online redo log file groups per thread on the primary database.

## ORA-16066

You will encounter this error when the REMOTE_ARCHIVE_ENABLE parameter is set to FALSE. This parameter controls whether the archival of the redo logs to remote destinations is permitted. This parameter has been deprecated, but if you are using it you will have to set REMOTE_ ARCHIVE_ENABLE=TRUE in your parameter file and bounce the primary database.

## ORA-16204: Parameter %s Cannot Be Parsed

The value for the LOG_ARCHIVE_DEST_*n* parameter is incorrect. Some of the common causes are an option that is missing a required value, a misplaced equal sign, or an unrecognized option. You will need to correct the value for the LOG_ARCHIVE_DEST_*n* parameter.

## Remote Archival to Standby Database Fails with an ORA-01031

You will see this error if an archiver process (ARCn) or LogWriter Network Service (LNS) process at the primary database fails with the ORA-01031 and the redo is not getting transferred to the standby. This is a result of a missing password file on the standby database. Copy the password file from the primary to the standby database, and restart the standby database.

```
SQL> SELECT STATUS, ERROR
       FROM V$ARCHIVE_DEST;
STATUS    ERROR
--------- ----------------------------------------------------------
VALID
ERROR     ORA-01031: insufficient privileges
INACTIVE
INACTIVE
INACTIVE
INACTIVE
INACTIVE
```

## Standby Database Cannot Apply Redo

If you encounter issues with applying the logs to the standby database, and you see the ORA-00326 message in your alert log, you'll see the following:

```
ORA-00326: log begins at change <SCN> , need earlier change <SCN>
```

This means that media recovery has found an archive log which was generated after the required archive log. It needs the correct log. When you are using Data Guard Redo Apply, this error cannot occur since the managed recovery process (MRP) will provide media recovery only with the logs in the correct order. If the next log is not in the correct order, the MRP will not pass anything to media recovery. This usually occurs when Data Guard ends up performing gap resolution.

If you were using manual recovery and feeding media recovery archive logs one at a time, it normally means that you provided an archive log generated after the required log. You can remedy the problem by providing the correct file.

In reality, the ORA-00326 error should strike fear in the heart of the Data Guard DBA. When you get this error in your Data Guard configuration, it means that someone did something very bad. Since the MRP will never pass a media recovery log file out of order, it is impossible for a physical standby that has always been maintained by Data Guard to encounter this error.

However, if someone had used manual recovery on a physical standby without paying attention to the log files they were providing, it is possible to have media recovery apply a log that it should not have and get into this situation. This is because Data Guard, in the earlier releases, tried to help out in a failover situation by leaving partial archive logs on disk in case you needed to failover. Of course, if you were using standby redo logs (SRLs), this was never necessary because the SRL file would contain the last bit of redo for the failover. However, if you were not using SRL files or if Data Guard was in the process of resolving a gap and a failure occurred at the primary, then one of these partial archive log files would be left on disk, but never registered in the physical standby control file. Since it is not registered, the MRP would ignore it. If the primary came back online and you did not perform a failover, then that partial archive log would be overwritten by the real archive log and the MRP would continue correctly. If you had to failover, then you could manually register this partial archive log file and the MRP would process it and you could activate the physical standby.

If everyone obeyed the rules, these problems would not occur. However, when a large gap appears, someone will often copy over a bunch of archive log files and run manual recovery on those files until they are caught up, and then restart the MRP. If the person were not careful, media recovery would pick up one of these partial archive log files and apply it since internally it looked like a normal archive log. The problem would become apparent when Data Guard Redo Apply was restarted and the MRP passed the next proper log to media recovery. Since the previous archive log was a partial, the starting SCN of the new log would not follow in order and media recovery could not continue. At this point, all you could do would be completely re-create the physical standby since media recovery would not reapply the archive log that was mistakenly applied (as a partial) since that thread/sequence log file had already been processed.

When you plan to use manual recovery on a physical standby for any reason, you must first examine the standby database control file to determine what archive logs have been registered for each thread. Then you must make sure that you copy all archive logs from the primary that follow the last registered sequence for each thread. You cannot rely on what you see on disk—you must use the control file of the standby.

Because of this problem, Data Guard no longer leaves partial archive log files on disk. If you are using versions of Oracle Database prior to 10.1.0.5, these partial archive logs could still be on disk at your standby database. In this case, be very careful if you decide to use manual recovery.

## Log Shipment Errors—ORA-12570

You may encounter sporadic "ORA-12570: TNS packet reader failure" messages when shipping redo data between the primary and standby when the connection is going through a firewall. If you can't disable the firewall timeout or bypass the firewall, set `sqlnet.expire_time` in the sqlnet.ora file on both servers. This will enable Dead Connection Detection (DCD). For a more detailed explanation, refer to MetaLink Notes 550103.1 and 151972.1[2].

---

[2] Note 550103.1: Log Shipment Intermittently Errors with ORA-12570 and Note 151972.1: Dead Connection Detection (DCD) Explained

# Logical Standby Database Failures

Several issues can occur with a logical standby environment:

- SQL Apply stops.
- SQL Apply hangs.
- SQL Apply cannot keep up with the primary.
- Data is not applied to the logical standby.

## What to Do if SQL Apply Stops

Log apply services cannot apply unsupported Data Manipulation Language (DML) statements, Data Definition Language (DDL) statements, and Oracle-supplied packages to a logical standby database running SQL Apply. The following sections summarize some of the conditions under which SQL Apply will stop.

**Determine What Has Failed**   You can find the last statement that SQL Apply tried to process in the DBA_LOGSTDBY_EVENTS view:

```
SQL> SELECT XIDUSN, XIDSLT, XIDSQN, STATUS, STATUS_CODE
  2 FROM DBA_LOGSTDBY_EVENTS
  3 WHERE EVENT_TIME =
  4 (SELECT MAX(EVENT_TIME)
  5 FROM DBA_LOGSTDBY_EVENTS);
```

The output of the query will reveal the statement and error that caused SQL Apply to fail. If an incorrect SQL statement caused SQL Apply to fail, transaction information as well as the statement and error information can be viewed. The following sections discuss using some of the "skip" procedures in SQL Apply to avoid some of these problems. Just remember that you cannot randomly skip errors or transactions in SQL Apply without first fixing the issue that caused the problem in the first place. Are we repeating ourselves? Yes, because this is extremely important. Never randomly skip transactions at a Logical Standby!

**Database Management Issues**   If a database management issue occurs, such as running out of space in a particular tablespace or adding a datafile on the primary with a file specification that doesn't match that in the logical standby environment, fix the problem and resume SQL Apply using the ALTER DATABASE START LOGICAL STANDBY APPLY IMMEDIATE; statement.

**Incorrect SQL Statements**   Fix the problem by executing the correct SQL statement and using the SQL Apply skip procedure, DBMS_LOGSTDBY.SKIP_TRANSACTION, to ensure that the incorrect statement is ignored the next time SQL Apply is run. Then, restart SQL Apply using the ALTER DATABASE START LOGICAL STANDBY APPLY IMMEDIATE; statement.

Another important tool for handling logical standby database failures is the DBMS_LOGSTDBY.SKIP_ERROR procedure. Depending on the circumstances of the error, you might want to do one of the following:

- Ignore failures for a table or specific DDL.
- Associate a stored procedure with a filter so at runtime a determination can be made about skipping the statement, executing the statement, or executing a replacement statement.

Taking one of these actions prevents SQL Apply from stopping. Later, you can query the DBA_ LOGSTDBY_EVENTS view to find and correct any problems that exist.

**ORA-01403: No Data Found**   You will encounter the ORA-01403 error when DML is executed on the logical standby to tables maintained by SQL Apply. This will generally occur if someone makes these changes with SYSDBA privileges or if the logical standby guard was disabled. The primary and the logical can get out of sync and the error won't show up until the table on the primary standby is updated.

To resolve the issue, you would need to skip and re-instantiate the table. Make sure that you have a database link defined to connect to the primary database. You can use the DBMS_ LOGSTDBY.SKIP and DBMS_LOGSTDBY.INSTANTIATE_TABLE procedures to accomplish this, as demonstrated here:

```
SQL> EXEC DBMS_LOGSTDBY.SKIP('DML','ACTORS','%');
SQL> EXECUTE DBMS_LOGSTDBY.INSTANTIATE_TABLE
  2 ('MATRIX_USER', 'ACTORS', 'MATRIX_DBLINK');
```

**ORA-16211: Unsupported Record Found in the Archived Redo Log**   You will encounter the ORA-16211 error when log apply encounters a record in the archived redo log that could not be interpreted. This error could occur under any number of circumstances; however, a few documented potential causes for this error do exist:

- Nologging on an object on the primary
- Changes made to an Indexed Organized Table (IOT) on the primary
- Direct path inserts on a partition table

To resolve this error, you can re-instantiate the object or drop the object. In either case, you will want to determine the archive log with the error and send it to Oracle support for analysis.

**Handling DDL Issues**   You will often face issues with DDL statements in a standby database. For example, a DBA may add a datafile to the primary and the path is not valid on the logical standby. Remember that the DB_FILE_NAME_CONVERT parameters are not used on a logical standby. Keep in mind that the following statements are skipped automatically on the standby:

- CREATE and ALTER DATABASE commands
- CREATE and DROP DATABASE LINK commands

The following procedures can be used to help resolve issues with DDL:

- **DBMS_LOGSTDBY.SKIP**   Skips a schema or object or a type of statement
- **DBMS_LOGSTDBY.SKIP_ERROR**   Ignores a class of errors and continues the SQL Apply
- **DBMS_LOGSTDBY.SKIP_TRANSACTION**   Skips a failed transaction provided that you issued a compensating transaction

For additional information pertaining to skipping SQL statements on the logical standby database, refer to Chapter 4.

### SQL Apply Hanging

If it appears that SQL Apply is hanging, perform the following steps for investigative procedures:

1. Check `DBA_LOGSTDBY_PROGRESS` to see if any activity is occurring:

   ```
   SQL> SELECT APPLIED_SCN, APPLIED_TIME, READ_SCN,
           READ_TIME, NEWEST_SCN, NEWEST_TIME
        FROM DBA_LOGSTDBY_PROGRESS;
   ```

2. Check the `HIGH_SCN` from the `V$LOGSTDBY` view. The SCN should change as the SQL Apply progresses:

   ```
   SQL> SELECT TYPE, HIGH_SCN, STATUS
           FROM V$LOGSTDBY;
   ```

3. Check `V$LOGSTDBY_STATS` for information on the activity on the standby. You can look at the number of transactions applied or transactions ready and tell whether the transactions are being applied as fast as they are being read.

**NOTE**
*Additional information for monitoring a SQL Apply delay or hanging situation is available in Chapter 7.*

# Switchover Issues

You may encounter several common issues when performing a switchover. For example, if the switchover to standby fails on the primary, then you probably have sessions connected. In this scenario, you can use the `WITH SESSION SHUTDOWN` option. If the switchover fails on the standby, take a look at the alert log to determine what happened. If it is sessions, one thing to look at, if you are running an older version of Oracle, is the setting for the `JOB_QUEUE_PROCESSES` initialization parameter, to confirm that it is set to 0. Otherwise, just use the `WITH SESSIONS SHUTDOWN` qualifier.

### Switchover Fails—Redo Data Was Not Transmitted

It is also possible that the standby never received the final redo from the primary during the first part of the switchover. Query the `THREAD#`, `SEQUENCE#`, `ARCHIVED`, `APPLIED`, and `STATUS` columns in the `V$ARCHIVED_LOG` view of the standby to determine whether the last redo data was transmitted from the primary database and was applied on the standby database. If the last redo data was not transmitted to the standby database, you can copy the archived redo log file containing the final End-of-Redo data from the primary database to the standby database and register it. Restart log apply services and the archived redo log file will then be applied automatically.

### Switchover Fails—ORA-01102 Error

If both the standby database and the primary database reside on the same server and switchover fails with an ORA-01102 error "Cannot mount database in EXCLUSIVE mode," you should verify that you've specified a `DB_UNIQUE_NAME` in the initialization parameter file that is used by the original primary database (standby database). Keep in mind that if the `DB_UNIQUE_NAME` parameter of the standby database is not set, the standby and the primary databases both use the same mount lock and will cause the ORA-01102 error during the startup of the second database. To fix the issue, add the `DB_UNIQUE_NAME` to the initialization parameter file of the standby database and shutdown and restart the standby and primary databases.

## Switchover Fails—Active SQL Sessions

If you receive the following error during switchover, "ORA-01093: Alter Database Close only permitted with no sessions connected," then you need to make sure that you include the `WITH SESSION SHUTDOWN` clause as a part of the `ALTER DATABASE COMMIT TO SWITCHOVER TO PHYSICAL STANDBY` statement. Active SQL sessions will prevent a switchover from being processed. Some of the other processes that can prevent the switchover are

- Job queue scheduler process
- Advance queue time manager
- Oracle Enterprise Manager agent

You can reset the `job_queue_processes` and `aq_tm_processes` to 0 dynamically to fix the issue. If the OEM agent is preventing the switchover, you can stop it with the `EMCTL STOP AGENT` command. Most of these issues have been resolved in Data Guard in later versions of Oracle Database.

## Back Out from an Unsuccessful Switchover

You may end up with two physical standbys if the switchover fails in the middle. In this case, go back to the original primary database that was converted to a physical standby and perform the second part of the switchover—the `ALTER DATABASE COMMIT TO SWITCHOVER TO PRIMARY;`—and make it the primary database. Identify the root cause of the switchover failure by examining the alert log files of both databases and resolve the issues before proceeding. Remember that once you resolve the problem, which was most probably a gap in the redo that existed before you started the switchover, and restart the MRP, it will stop again once it processes the End-of-Redo from the original switchover attempt. All you have to remember is to restart the MRP again before continuing with the second switchover.

If you need to back out from an unsuccessful switchover on a physical standby, you may be able to accomplish this with the following steps:

1. Issue the following command on the original primary database:

   ```
   SQL> ALTER DATABASE COMMIT TO SWITCHOVER TO PRIMARY;
   ```

   If this statement is successful, shut down and restart the database. The database will be running in the primary database role. However, if the statement is not successful, you will need to continue with the next steps.

2. When the switchover was started, a trace file was written in the log directory. This trace file contains the SQL statements needed to re-create the original primary control file. Capture the statements from this file and execute them from SQL*Plus on the new standby database. The new standby database will revert back to the primary role.

3. Shut down the original physical standby database and create a new standby control file on the primary database. Copy the standby control file to the original physical standby site. The following is an example of how to re-create the standby control file:

   ```
   SQL> ALTER DATABASE RECOVER MANAGED STANDBY DATABASE CANCEL;
   SQL> SHUTDOWN IMMEDIATE;
   ```

On the primary database do the following:

```
SQL> ALTER DATABASE CREATE STANDBY controlfile as '<file name>';
```

4. Restart the original physical standby instance. If this procedure is successful and archive gap management is enabled, the Fetch Archive Log (FAL) processes will start and rearchive any missing archived redo log files to the physical standby database. You can now attempt the switchover again after correcting any issues that led to the failure of initial switchover.

### Switchover—Archived Redo Logs Are Not Applied

After a successful switchover, if the archived logs are not applied to the standby database, you will need to verify that your environment and the initialization parameters are set correctly. You can take the following steps to find the problem:

1. Verify that the LOG_ARCHIVE_DEST_*n* parameter is set correctly on the primary:

```
SQL> SELECT DEST_ID, STATUS, DESTINATION
        FROM  V$ARCHIVE_DEST;
```

   If you do not see an entry corresponding to the standby database, you need to set the LOG_ARCHIVE_DEST_*n* and LOG_ARCHIVE_DEST_STATE_*n* parameters.

2. Verify the local archiving LOG_ARCHIVE_DEST_*n*, STANDBY_ARCHIVE_DEST, and LOG_ARCHIVE_FORMAT parameters at the standby database so that the archived redo log files are configured to the correct location.

3. On the standby database, set the DB_FILE_NAME_CONVERT and LOG_FILE_NAME_CONVERT parameters. Set the STANDBY_FILE_MANAGEMENT parameter to AUTO if you want the standby to automatically add new datafiles that are created at the primary site.

4. Verify that the listener.ora file on the standby site has an entry for the listener. In addition, check the tnsnames.ora file at the primary site to ensure that a corresponding service name exists at the primary site.

5. Verify that the listener is up on the standby site. If not, then start it.

# Failover Issues

During a failover process, errors are more likely to occur when a standby database is transitioning to the primary role. To address the issue, analyze the errors to find the root cause of the issue and correct it.

If you have a gap in the redo, then a normal failover will not succeed. In this case, you have two choices: resolve the problem of the missing redo or use the ACTIVATE STANDBY command and failover, losing the missing redo.

Another example of this occurs when the primary database is still running. This is usually indicated by the presence of Remote File Server (RFS) processes on the standby database. If the primary database is still running but can no longer function as a primary database, shut it down and retry the failover. In Oracle Database 10g Release 2, you could use the FORCE qualifier to the ALTER DATABASE RECOVER MANAGED STANDBY DATABASE FINISH command and Data Guard would terminate the errant RFS processes automatically. As of Oracle Database 11g terminating the RFS processes is the default.

# Data Guard Broker Issues

The following sections cover common configuration errors, problems with failover and switchover processing, and common FSFO observer problems.

### ORA-16627 on the Standby Database

You may receive an "ORA-16627: Operation disallowed since no standby databases would remain to support protection mode" for several reasons. Table 13-3 summarizes the causes and resolutions to this error.

| Causes | Action |
|---|---|
| Attempt to change a configuration's overall protection mode and no online, enabled standby databases support the proposed protection mode | Confirm that at least one standby database satisfies the new protection mode. |
| Attempt to enable a configuration and no online, enabled standby databases support the overall protection mode | Confirm that at least one standby database has a LogXptMode configuration property setting that supports the current overall protection mode when enabling a configuration. |
| A switchover attempt that would violate the configuration's overall protection mode | Confirm that at least one other standby database has a LogXptMode configuration property setting that supports the overall protection mode. In addition, ensure that the LogXptMode configuration property established for the primary database supports the overall protection mode. After the switchover, the old primary database will become the standby database and its LogXptMode configuration property setting must support the overall protection mode. |
| An attempt to disable or remove a database that, if successful, would result in no available standby databases that could support the configuration's overall protection mode | Confirm that at least one other standby database has a LogXptMode configuration property setting that supports the overall protection mode. |
| Trying to set a configuration or database offline that would result in violating the configuration's overall protection mode | Confirm that at least one other standby database has a LogXptMode configuration property setting that supports the overall protection mode. You may have to downgrade the protection mode setting to maximum performance if attempting to offline the configuration. |
| The Broker returns this error during a health check | Confirm that at least one standby database has a LogXptMode configuration property setting that supports the current overall protection mode. |

**TABLE 13-3.** *Root Cause and Resolutions for ORA-16627*

The `LogXptMode` parameter is dynamic and can be viewed or updated via Enterprise Manager or DGMGRL. This parameter enables you to set the redo transport service on the standby database. The database must be configured with standby redo logs. The following are the valid options for this parameter:

- ASYNC
- SYNC

Here's an example of how to change this parameter:

```
DGMGRL> EDIT DATABASE 'MATRIX_DR0' SET PROPERTY 'LogXptMode'='SYNC';
```

### Redo Is Not Being Sent to Standby Databases

In a Data Guard Broker configuration, you determine that the redo are not being sent to the standby databases. To identify the root cause of the problem you can check the following:

- Verify that the state of the primary database is in the `TRANSPORT-ON` state using the `SHOW DATABASE` command.
- Verify that the standby database is available.
- Verify that the listener is up.
- Verify that the value of the `LogShipping` configurable database property of the standby database is `ON`.
- Check the status of the redo transport services on the primary database using the `LogXptStatus` database property. Check for error messages associated with redo transport services. This can provide additional information to help you find the issue.

### Redo Received by the Standby but Not Applied

Redo might not be applied to the standby database for several reasons. You can investigate the cause of the failure by doing the following:

- Determining whether or not the log apply services might be stopped
- Checking to see if a failed transaction has occurred, if this is a logical standby database
- Verifying the state of the standby database is `APPLY-ON`
- Verifying the state of the primary database is `TRANSPORT-ON`
- Checking to see if log files are building up because the value of the `DelayMins` property is set too large

If you cannot see any errors, compare the transport rate to the apply rate on the Performance page in Enterprise Manager to see if the apply rate is lower than the transport rate.

### Physical Standby Switchover Failures

You can perform the following steps to recover from a failed switchover on a physical standby that's being managed by Data Guard Broker:

1. Investigate the error messages returned by the Broker to find the source of the problem on the standby database. Examine the alert log file information and the contents of the

Broker log file for the standby database. If FSFO is enabled, disable it. You can use DGMGRL to enable and disable this configuration:

```
DGMGRL> ENABLE CONFIGURATION
DGMGRL> SHOW CONFIGURATION
Configuration
Name: MATRIX
Enabled: NO
Protection Mode: MaxAvailability
Fast-Start Failover: DISABLED
Databases:
MATRIX - Primary database
MATRIX_DR0 - Physical standby database
```

2. Convert the standby back to a primary database.

3. Finish the recovery.

4. Re-enable the configuration.

5. Perform the switchover operation again.

## Logical Standby Switchover Failures

Perform the following steps to recover from a failed switchover on a logical standby that's being managed by Data Guard Broker:

1. Analyze and correct the detected failure. (If FSFO is enabled, disable it.)

2. Remove the configuration.

3. Convert back to the primary database.

4. Re-create the configuration.

5. Re-enable the configuration.

6. Perform the switchover operation again.

## Transition the Primary Database to the Standby Role

If you have problems transitioning the primary database to the standby role, you can try the following to fix the issue:

1. Disable the configuration using DGMGRL.

2. Investigate the error message returned by the Broker to find the source of the problem on the primary database and correct it. You can review the alert log and the Broker log file to determine the root cause of the issue.

3. Re-enable the configuration to restore the databases to their original roles and states.

4. Perform the switchover again.

## Transition the Standby Database to the Primary Role

If you encounter a problem when transitioning the target standby database to the primary role, use these general guidelines to restore to the pre-switchover state. If FSFO is enabled, the Broker does not allow switchover to any standby database except to the target standby database. In addition, switchover to the target standby database is allowed only when the value of the FS_FAILOVER_ STATUS column in the V$DATABASE on the standby database is set to READY or SUSPENDED.

## ORA-16596: Object Not Part of the Data Guard Broker Configuration

You will see this error in a couple of scenarios. The following shows those conditions:

- The Broker fails to locate a Broker configuration for the database that is running.
- The database instance in which you made a request to the Broker is not a part of the Broker configuration.
- The Broker configuration file for one of its databases was accidentally removed or is outdated.

Verify that a database does exist in the Broker configuration that has a name that matches the DB_UNIQUE_NAME of the database that returned the error. If the configuration does exist, remove the database from the Broker configuration and delete the configuration file for the standby database.

Try to enable the configuration. Once the configuration is enabled, create a new database profile from the previously deleted standby database. You can use Enterprise Manager or the DGMGRL.

### Problems with Starting Multiple Observers

When enabling the observer for FSFO, you need to be aware of a few things during the enabling and maintaining the configuration.

Only one observer can be observing the Broker configuration at any given time. If you attempt to start additional observers, one of the following errors is returned:

```
ORA-16647: could not start more than one observer
DGM-16954: Unable to open and lock the Observer configuration file
```

Use the DGMGRL SHOW CONFIGURATION VERBOSE command to determine the location of the observer that is currently associated with the Broker configuration. If it is not correct, you can issue the STOP OBSERVER command and restart the observer on another system. In addition, if you try to start the observer for another Broker configuration in the same home directory as an existing observer you can encounter this error. Use the FILE qualifiers noted in Chapter 8.

### Observer Has Stopped

If the observer server is no longer available, you can move it to a new host. As with the preceding situation, to move the observer, you must terminate the link between the observer and the Broker configuration:

```
DGMGRL> STOP OBSERVER;
```

Issue the DGMGRL SHOW CONFIGURATION VERBOSE and SHOW DATABASE commands to verify that the configuration is no longer being observed:

```
DGMGRL> SHOW CONFIGURATION VERBOSE;
```

Note that you do not need to issue the DGMGRL SHOW commands to verify that the observer has actually stopped. Successful completion of the DGMGRL STOP OBSERVER command will allow a new observer to become associated with the configuration. You can issue the START OBSERVER command to initiate a new observer on a different host:

```
DGMGRL> START OBSERVER;
```

## Errors Converting to a Snapshot Standby

You must be in MOUNT state and the MRP must be stopped to convert a database to a snapshot standby. You will receive the following error messages when invoking the ALTER DATABASE CONVERT TO SNAPSHOT STANDBY command if this is not the case:

```
ORA-38784: Cannot create restore point .......
ORA-01153: an incompatible media recovery is active
```

The same applies when converting back to a physical standby. The database must be in MOUNT mode or you will receive the following error when issuing the ALTER DATABASE CONVERT TO PHYSICAL STANDBY Command:

```
ORA-01126:  database must be mounted in this instance and not open in any
instance.
```

For additional information on converting to a Snapshot Standby, please review Chapter 9.

# Helpful Hints and Tips

As always, when using Data Guard to protect your primary database, you'll benefit by following a few recommendations. Some of the items in the following sections are reiterations of issues discussed earlier in the book but bear repeating here.

## Avoid Refreshing the Standby Control File

If at all possible, avoid refreshing the standby control file. This will remove all archived log information from the standby and replace it with the information from the primary database. You can set STANDBY_FILE_MANAGEMENT to AUTO and any operating system file additions or deletions on the primary database are replicated on your physical standby. You would refresh the standby control file when STANDBY_FILE_MANAGEMENT is set to MANUAL under the following circumstances:

- Rename or delete a datafile
- Add or drop a tablespace
- Add or drop online redo logs
- Alter control file

## Avoid Using the NOLOGGING Clause

As mentioned in earlier chapters, nologging operations at the primary database will render your standby databases unrecoverable and in need of attention before you need to use the standby. At worst, the following operations can completely destroy the standby and you'll have to re-create it from scratch. Remember that no logging operations can occur at all levels in the database if you do not use `ALTER DATABASE FORCE LOGGING` on the primary database. The hierarchy of no logging operations are

- Database
- Tablespace
- Objects
- SQL*Loader

As a last resort, if you choose to use the no logging option for performance considerations, please review Chapter 7 on monitoring your production database for no logging activities. You want to proactively monitor and assess your situation before switching or failing over to your disaster recovery site.

# OMF—Copying Control File

The datafile names will be different in the primary and physical standby if you are using Automatic Storage Management (ASM), because ASM enforces Oracle Managed Files (OMF). When you copy over the standby control file, you lose all the information in the control file about your datafiles, archive logs, and so on. The following steps show you how to handle this scenario:

1. On the primary database, create the standby control file:

   ```
   rman target /
   RMAN> BACKUP CURRENT CONTROLFILE FOR STANDBY FORMAT '/tmp/standby.ctl.
   bkup';
   ```

   Or do this:

   ```
   SQL> ALTER DATABASE CREATE STANDBY CONTROLFILE AS '/tmp/standby.ctl';
   ```

2. Copy the control file to the standby site.

3. On the standby database, shut down all the instances.

4. Restore the standby control file:

   ```
   rman target /
   RESTORE STANDBY CONTROLFILE FROM '/tmp/standby.ctl.bkup';
   ALTER DATABASE MOUNT;
   EXIT
   ```

5. Catalog all the disk groups for your datafiles:

   ```
   rman target /
   CATALOG START WITH '+DG_DBA_DF501/MATRIX_DR0/';
   CATALOG START WITH '+DG_DBA_DD501/MATRIX_DR0/';
   SWITCH DATABASE TO COPY;
   EXIT
   ```

6. Re-enable flashback:

```
sqlplus / as sysdba
ALTER DATABASE FLASHBACK OFF;
ALTER DATABASE FLASHBACK ON;
```

7. Re-create standby control files:

```
ALTER DATABASE RECOVER MANAGED STANDBY DATABASE
USING CURRENT LOGFILE DISCONNECT;
```

For a more detailed explanation of these steps, refer to MetaLink Note 734862.1.

# Conclusion

This chapter offers you a great starting point for diagnosing many issues that you may encounter in a Data Guard environment. We have covered where to find diagnostic information, what tools are available to aid in resolving issues, and resolutions to some of the most common errors. You will find that many of these errors can be avoided by spending the majority of your time planning and configuring your environment, and of course, by reading this book, which you have just about completed.

Again, make sure that you visit our blog site at blog.dataguardbook.com to review the latest and greatest tips and tricks to troubleshooting a Data Guard environment. We will help you maintain a healthy Data Guard ecosystem.

# CHAPTER
## 14

# Deployment Architectures

ne of the most important things this book has sought to accomplish is to show how Data Guard is more than just a solution for disaster recovery. Data Guard also addresses requirements for high availability by offering a unique combination of high performance, functionality, and simplicity. Data Guard can boost primary database performance and response time by offloading read-only queries, reporting, and backups to a standby database. Data Guard can increase availability by enabling rapid failover to a standby database in the event that mundane events such as data corruption, critical component failure, or human error bring down the primary database—events that occur much more frequently than natural disasters.

Data Guard rolling database upgrades increase availability by minimizing planned downtime when installing new patch sets or new Oracle releases, executing a technology refresh, moving data centers, and performing other types of planned maintenance described in this book. Data Guard standby databases can also improve the quality and efficiency of quality assurance testing, increasing availability by eliminating disruption due to unforeseen consequences of introducing change to the production environment.

Yes, Data Guard is a disaster recovery solution for the Oracle Database, but it offers so much more value to the daily operation of any mission-critical database that no DBA should ever "leave home without it", even if their company is never hit by a power outage, fire, flood, hurricane, earthquake, or other event of similar magnitude.

Data Guard's rich feature set and flexibility creates opportunities for many different deployment architectures. The preceding chapters have covered technical details for implementing and managing Data Guard configurations. This chapter explores deployment architectures which address requirements which extend beyond traditional disaster recovery. The architectures discussed are derived from the collective experiences of the authors of this book with Data Guard users worldwide and are representative of those deployed by the following users:

- A manufacturing company
- A utility company
- A retail brokerage firm
- A government agency
- A pharmaceutical company
- A web retailer
- An insurance firm

### Myth Buster: Data Guard Is a DR Solution

This chapter is chock-full of Data Guard solution architectures, but not one of them has disaster recovery as its primary objective. Data Guard is used to achieve objectives for high availability, data protection, and high performance, and for enabling the confidence to introduce change to a production system. Disaster protection comes along as a by-product of simply choosing a remote location for your standby database.

# Manufacturing Company: HA Configuration

Assume you work for a small manufacturing company that has limited DBA resources—you are the only DBA and you also wear other hats. Scalability for the mission-critical database you manage is not a concern. A single node, while at times used more heavily than you would like to see, has proven sufficient to meet service-level expectations. Your priority is on high availability (HA) and data protection. The company previously implemented cold failover cluster solutions to protect against server failure. This configuration is perceived as "single-node simple" because applications run on only one server at a time. The server running the application (in this case an Oracle instance) is the active node. The second server in the cluster is a passive node and will host an Oracle instance only if the first server fails. The active and passive nodes each have access to the storage hosting the Oracle database files, and their status is monitored by cluster software that restarts the Oracle instance on the passive node if the active node fails.

Contrast the cold failover cluster to a Data Guard configuration where primary and standby databases are located on a local area network (LAN) in the same facility. This meets the criteria of being a single-node simple configuration in that production always runs on one Oracle instance at a time. A Data Guard standby database, however, is a much more powerful HA solution than a passive node in a cold cluster configuration. While a standby database provides the same HA protection against server failure, the other attributes of a standby database provide better data protection, higher availability for additional hardware failures, better system utilization, better performance, and more scalability than a cold failover cluster. A Data Guard HA configuration provides this manufacturing company the following advantages:

- Data Guard Redo Apply (physical standby) provides optimal protection against data corruptions and industry-unique protection from lost writes caused by hardware or operating system failures that can corrupt your database.

- Zero data loss recovery point objective from any component failure, including network attached storage (NAS)/Storage Area Network (SAN) failure, network failure, and/or complete database failure—eliminating single points of failure that are not addressed by cluster environments. Note that best practices for a Data Guard configuration with a local standby database always requires that the standby database be hosted on separate storage from the primary database, either locally attached or on a separate NAS or SAN.

- Zero data loss recovery point objective for any event that destroys a computer room while the rest of the manufacturing plant is viable. The primary and standby databases are deployed in two different computer rooms located at either end of the plant.

- A worst-case recovery time objective of less than 60 seconds, utilizing Oracle-integrated automatic failure detection, database failover, and application failover.

- Fast point-in-time recovery from user error and logical corruptions using Oracle Flashback Database without the management overhead and increased storage costs required to maintain multiple rolling snapshots. Note that unlike a full database snapshot, Flashback Database requires disk space only to hold flashback logs (data changes) used to rewind the database back to your desired point in time.

- Rolling database upgrades to minimize planned downtime when upgrading to new patchsets and major database releases.

> ### Myth Buster: Cold-Failover Clusters Are an HA Solution
> Addressing server failure alone does not an HA solution make. HA solutions are designed to eliminate single points of failure (SPOFs). The single database management system to which all nodes in a cluster share access becomes an SPOF, whether those nodes are active-active as with Oracle Real Application Clusters (RAC) or active-passive as with cold failover clusters. Hardware and software failures can cause the database management system to become corrupt and/or fail. A comprehensive HA solution eliminates SPOF by intelligently maintaining a synchronized replica of the database management system on separate servers and storage that is isolated from events that can impact the availability of the primary database, protecting against a wider range of failures. This makes Data Guard a necessary component of any comprehensive HA architecture designed for the Oracle Database.

- Greater scalability and maximum return on investment (ROI) by offloading read-only queries, reports, and fast incremental backups from the production database to the standby databases while in standby role. Queries and reports on the standby are able to return up-to-date results. Using the standby database for read-only workload does not impact recovery point objectives (RPOs) or recovery time objectives (RTOs).

The manufacturing company chose to implement a simple Data Guard HA configuration illustrated in Figure 14-1. The company selected Data Guard not for protection against site failure, because in this case the database is of no value if the plant is destroyed. Data Guard was selected for the express purpose of providing HA and data protection for failure events that occur within the site.

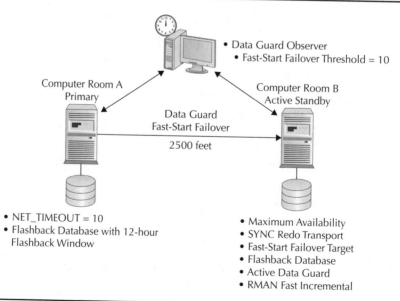

**FIGURE 14-1.** *Manufacturing company HA configuration*

## Optimal Corruption Protection

`DB_ULTRA_SAFE = DATA_AND_INDEX` is new for Oracle Database 11g and sets the following parameters:

- `DB_BLOCK_CHECKSUM=FULL`  Block checking prevents memory and data corruptions.
- `DB_BLOCK_CHECKING=FULL`  Redo and data block checksum detects corruptions on the primary and protects the standby.
- `DB_LOST_WRITE_PROTECT=TYPICAL`  Losts write protection enables a physical standby database to detect lost write corruptions on the primary or standby.

The HA configuration consists of primary and standby databases using Data Guard Maximum Availability protection mode (zero data loss) and synchronous redo transport services (SYNC). Primary and standby databases are located in different computer rooms at opposite ends of the plant so that the destruction of a computer room will not impact operations as long as the rest of the plant remains viable. Data Guard Broker is used to manage the configuration and Data Guard Fast-Start Failover[1] is used to automate database failover. The following are highlights of the significant elements for this configuration:

- Because primary and standby are on the same LAN with reliable quality of service from a network perspective, the `FastStartFailoverThreshold` property has been reduced from the default of 30 seconds to just 10 seconds to accelerate failover time without increasing the risk of "false failovers" caused by transient network issues.

- Likewise, the value of `NET_TIMEOUT` has been reduced from the default of 30 seconds to 10 seconds without increasing the risk of transient network issues impacting data protection.

- Client failover best practices described in Chapter 10 are followed to automatically break application clients connected to the failed primary out of TCP timeout, and all connections are all automatically directed to the new primary database.

- For maximum corruption protection in Oracle Database 11g, they set `DB_ULTRA_SAFE = DATA_AND_INDEX` on primary and standby databases. Note that one of the checks enabled with this setting is `DB_BLOCK_CHECKING=FULL`. While this will have little impact on primary performance, it can have significant impact redo apply performance on a physical standby. If testing proves that the standby overhead is too great, then change the standby settings to `DB_BLOCK_CHECKSUM=FULL` and `DB_LOST_WRITE_PROTECT=TYPICAL` in lieu of using `DB_ULTRA_SAFE`.

- Flashback Database is configured with a 12-hour retention period on both primary and standby databases to enable fast point-in-time recovery from user error or logical corruptions, as well as automatic database reinstatement should a Data Guard automatic failover occur.

---

[1] MAA Best Practices for Data Guard Fast-Start Failover; see www.oracle.com/technology/deploy/availability/pdf/ MAA_WP_10gR2_FastStartFailoverBestPractices.pdf

- Oracle patchset releases and major versions are upgraded in rolling fashion using the Data Guard rolling upgrade process.[2] They use the existing physical standby database for the upgrade during off-peak hours by transitioning read-only users back to the primary database for the duration of the upgrade. The concern is that this impacts RTO/RPO if a failure event occurs while the upgrade is being executed. To eliminate this concern, a second standby database is provisioned on a temporary basis to execute the rolling upgrade.

- The standby database uses the Active Data Guard Option[3] so that it is open read-only while it continues to be synchronized with the primary database. This provides more headroom for primary database processing, mitigating past concerns in which CPU utilization ran uncomfortably high.

- The standby database is also used to offload backups from production using an RMAN-based online backup strategy of one full backup, then subsequent fast incremental backups that are merged with the previous full backup on-disk to roll forward a complete image backup of the production database.

This Data Guard HA configuration allows the manufacturing company the simplicity of a cold-failover cluster plus the ability to improve performance and scalability by using all servers and storage at all times. Data Guard's integrated automatic failover more closely monitors the status of the primary database than an external cluster manager and increases availability by eliminating the need to restart Oracle before the failover node can become active. Unlike clustered solutions that share access to a common database, the independent synchronized replica maintained by Data Guard eliminates the database and the storage on which it resides from being a single point of failure. Should the SAN fail or if other issues cause the database to become unavailable, production automatically transitions to the standby database without downtime or data loss. Continuous Oracle validation before data is applied to the standby database isolates the replica from physical corruptions that impact the primary database due to hardware or software errors. Data Guard enables the Oracle Database to be in continuous recovery mode on the standby server, making it a validated "hot" synchronized copy ready to assume primary processing at any time.

# Utility Company: Zero Data Loss HA/DR

A utility company is also seeking a simple HA architecture, but it wants to "have its cake and eat it too" when it comes to disaster recovery. Management quickly realizes they can achieve both HA and DR by simply moving their standby database to a remote location. While the distance between primary and standby is limited by the influence of network latency in synchronous configurations, the inherent efficiency of Data Guard Redo Transport enables a greater degree of geographic separation and thus better data protection than third-party storage-centric alternatives.

For an optimal combination of protection and performance, the utility company will separate their primary and standby databases at a distance where testing shows the performance impact of

---

[2]MAA Best Practices for Rolling Database Upgrades; see www.oracle.com/technology/deploy/availability/pdf/MAA_WP_10gR2_RollingUpgradeBestPractices.pdf

[3]MAA Best Practices for Active Data Guard; see www.oracle.com/technology/deploy/availability/pdf/maa_wp_11gr1_activedataguard.pdf

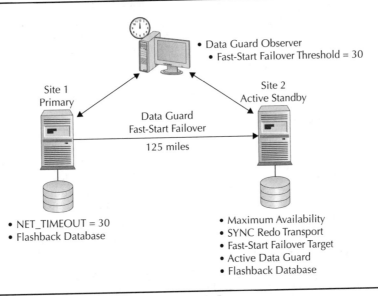

**FIGURE 14-2.** *Utility company: zero data loss HA/DR*

SYNC redo transport can still be tolerated by their applications and service level agreements. Performance testing shows that despite the combination of variables that impact synchronous performance—network latency, congestion, message size, commit concurrency, and so on—the company can successfully use an existing data center located 125 miles from their primary site.[4] Figure 14-2 illustrates the classic HA/DR Data Guard configuration chosen by the utility company to address their requirements.

High-level details of this HA/DR configuration are identical to the previous HA deployment: Maximum Availability protection mode (zero data loss) and synchronous redo transport services (SYNC) with Data Guard Broker to manage the configuration and Data Guard Fast-Start Failover (FSFO) to automate database failover. The same provisions made in the preceding example are

### Myth Buster: I Can't Use SYNC—It Will Hang My Primary Database

You know this is a myth because you have read this book and understood the difference between Maximum Protection and Maximum Availability modes. In Maximum Availability, the primary database will never stall for any longer than NET_TIMEOUT seconds if the primary is not able to communicate with the standby database, a value over which you have complete control.

---

[4]MAA Best Practices for Data Guard Redo Transport and Network Configuration; see www.oracle.com/technology/deploy/availability/pdf/MAA_WP_10gR2_DataGuardNetworkBestPractices.pdf

made in this case for automating client failover, using Flashback Database, preventing corruptions, and performing rolling database upgrades. Active Data Guard is also used to offload read-only queries, reporting, and backups from the primary database.

The minor differences between the HA/DR configuration and the preceding HA configuration all stem from the fact that the disaster recovery site is deployed on a wide area network (WAN), specifically as follows:

- `FastStartFailoverThreshold` property is increased to 30 seconds to reduce the risk of false failovers caused by transient network issues.

- The same WAN quality of service concerns, combined with the zero data loss objective, lead to raising the value of `NET_TIMEOUT` to 30 seconds. The potential to stall primary database processing for 30 seconds is accepted in return for the increased likelihood of preserving zero data loss protection throughout transient disruptions of service. A `NET_TIMEOUT` value of 15 seconds would be used if a greater emphasis was placed on performance than on data protection.

- The Data Guard observer process that monitors the FSFO configuration and initiates failover is located at the disaster recovery site on a system separate from the system hosting the standby database. Ideally, the observer can be hosted at a third site, and will thus not be impacted by failures at either primary or standby sites. Under no circumstances would the observer be located at the site that predominantly functions as the primary data center location.

This HA/DR configuration illustrates how Data Guard has evolved far beyond traditional DR solutions. The utility company has simply moved their standby to a remote site, with few differences between this configuration and the HA architecture deployed by the manufacturing company in the preceding example.

# Retail Brokerage Firm: HA/DR with Zero Data Loss and Extended Geographic Separation

A retail brokerage firm seeks zero data loss HA/DR along with an additional level of protection from events that impact a wider geographic area extending more than 500 miles from their production data center. In addition to HA/DR, they require active use of standby systems, storage, and software while in standby role for maximum ROI. Their requirements are the following:

- A zero data loss RPO for outages caused by any event within a 75-mile radius of the primary data center, and an associated complete RTO of less than 60 seconds from time a failure occurs to the time that applications can reconnect to the new production database.

- A maximum data loss exposure not to exceed a 10-second RPO for outages caused by any event within a 500-mile radius of the primary data center, with an associated RTO of 30 minutes following detection of the failure.

- Optimal protection against data corruptions and lost writes.

- Fast point-in-time recovery from user error and logical corruptions.

- Rolling database upgrades to minimize planned downtime.

- Active use of all systems by offloading read-only queries, reports, and fast incremental online backups from the production database to standby databases while they are in standby role. Queries and reports must return up-to-date results. Using the standby database for such workloads must not impact RPO or RTO.

- The ability to use a standby database for preproduction testing of hot patches and other changes without compromising RPO objectives.

These requirements are addressed with an architecture that uses as building blocks the zero data loss HA/DR configuration deployed by the utility company in the preceding example, and a second remote standby database that uses Data Guard Maximum Performance mode and ASYNC redo transport services, illustrated in Figure 14-3.

The HA/DR building block differs from that used by the utility company in that it is located just 75 miles from the production database, and they have shaved 10 seconds off the value of the `FastStartFailoverThreshold` property to afford more time for application clients to failover to the new production database within the required 60-second RTO. Active Data Guard is used to address the requirement for offloading read-only queries, reports, and online backups from the primary database.

The next building block in this architecture is a second remote standby database deployed more than 500 miles from the primary site and configured for Maximum Performance mode and ASYNC redo transport. Earlier in this book we discussed the fact that a primary database can have up to nine directly attached standby databases. A remote standby database using ASYNC redo transport addresses the second tier RPO/RTO objective to survive events that impact up to

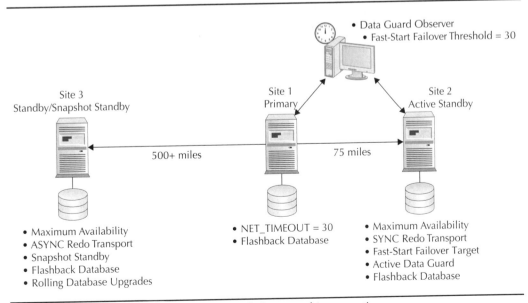

**FIGURE 14-3.** *Retail brokerage firm: extended geographic separation*

a 500-mile radius from the production database, without subjecting the primary database to overhead caused by high–round trip time (RTT) network latency at such distances. During normal operation, the ASYNC standby can be converted to a Data Guard Snapshot standby and used for preproduction testing without impacting RPO or RTO objectives. Redo data continues to be received by the Snapshot standby the entire time it is open read-write for testing to maintain the RPO. The RTO objective for the second standby has enough leeway to accommodate the conversion and resynchronization of the snapshot back to its original role as a standby database if a failover is required.

In the event of a failure occurring within a 75-mile radius, an automatic failover is executed to the SYNC standby with zero data loss, and the second remote standby automatically recognizes the new primary database. Should a failure destroy both the primary production site and the FSFO target, a manual failover is executed to transition the ASYNC standby to the primary role.

# Government Agency: Protection from Multi-site Threats

This government agency is very concerned about continuous operations even when confronted with a multi-site threat. On the surface, this requirement sounds as though it could be achieved by the preceding configuration deployed by the retail brokerage firm—but different requirements and additional operating philosophies motivate this user to deploy a slightly different architecture.

Data protection is critical—but near-zero data loss, measured in single-digit seconds, is sufficient to meet the RPO requirement because safeguards at the application level mitigate this small exposure to data loss. The combination of data protection, performance, and availability are critical to maintaining confidence in these systems. A multi-site architecture was designed to meet the following requirements:

- A three-site architecture that can survive intentional acts of violence that may occur against two different locations at the same time.

- More than 500 miles of separation between each site so that two of the three sites will survive large-scale geographic disasters, making it possible to provide continuous data protection even after a failover has occurred.

### General MAA Best Practices

While the representative architectures presented in this chapter have Data Guard as their focus, they all assume that related HA best practices are followed, including the use of `DB_ULTRASAFE` for optimal corruption protection, a flash recovery area for automated management of recovery-related files, Flashback Database for fast point-in-time recovery, and more.[5]

---

[5] Oracle Database High Availability Best Practices, 11g Release 1 (11.1), B28282-01, Section 2.6, Configuring Oracle Database 11g with Data Guard; see http://otn.oracle.com/goto/maa

- Multiple mission-critical Oracle Databases are to be hosted by this disaster recovery configuration. The user has high expectations for the operating efficiency and state of production readiness at each site. For this reason, the organization wants to disperse the production instances across all three sites. Each site will host standby databases for the production instances hosted at the other sites. In this manner, each location is a production site at all times, eliminating any chance of complacency due to the perception of being a standby site. This also limits the impact of a single site outage to just a third of the agency's total production instances, while spreading the burden of recovering from that loss across the two remaining sites.

- The three-site architecture and the requirements stated require that each primary database be able to synchronize two standby databases—each one located at each of the other sites.

- This agency is incredibly conservative by nature due to the implications that failure to perform their mission will have for the community it serves. This conservatism leads agency officials to prefer manual failover in lieu of automatic failover, so that they have complete control of all role transitions.

- Data protection must be continuous at failover time—the remaining standby database must automatically recognize the new primary database and continue to protect the latest transactions.

- Officials prefer the simplicity and high performance of physical versus logical replication to maintain standby replicas, assuming a physical replica can meet their additional requirements as stated.

- All standby databases must be able to provide read-only access to data for adhoc queries and reports. Latency between the standby and primary databases must be minimal, not to exceed 10 seconds at peak and this activity must not impact the RTO or RPO.

- When not being used for adhoc queries and reports, standby databases must be able to support test activities that require independent read-write access to verify planned system and software changes before they are placed into production, while continuing to provide disaster protection. It is understood that using a standby database for test activity can impact the RTO, but it must not impact the RPO.

- The user had evaluated storage-based replication solutions for disaster protection. These solutions were eliminated from consideration due the inability to have Oracle mounted and able to access the database while a remote-mirroring session is active. The agency also requires a solution that is data-aware and able to perform Oracle validation before data is applied to any standby database for optimal protection against corruption caused by hardware, OS, and firmware failures. All these things are not possible with storage solutions.

- The solution must include an integrated capability for very fast point-in-time recovery—also referred to as Continuous Data Protection (CDP). This feature is required given the distributed nature of some transactions executing against the various databases. The disaster recovery solution must support distributed transactions as well as provide a mechanism for coordinated distributed point-in-time recovery.

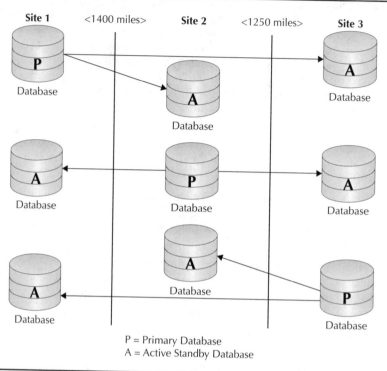

**FIGURE 14-4.**   *Government agency: protection against multi-site threats*

The architecture selected is depicted in Figure 14-4. It is a multi-site architecture in which each standby database is configured using Data Guard Maximum Performance and ASYNC redo transport services. It uses Flashback Database in combination with manual procedures to execute change-based recovery to re-establish global consistency for distributed transactions.[6] It uses

## Automatic Recognition of Role Transitions

In a multiple-standby configuration having any combination of physical and logical standbys, failover/switchover to any physical standby will result in all other standbys seamlessly recognizing and accepting redo data from the new primary database. The only caveat is that for this process to be automatic, the applied SCN on other standby databases cannot be in the future of the SCN at which the standby became primary. If that is the case, then manual intervention using Flashback Database will be required. For this reason and to achieve minimum data loss, it is always recommended to failover to the standby database that is most closely synchronized with the primary at the time it failed.

---

[6]Oracle Database High Availability Best Practices, 11g Release 1 (11.1), B28282-01, Recovering Databases in a Distributed Environment, Section 4.2.9; see http://otn.oracle.com/goto/maa

Active Data Guard to provide read-only access to an up-to-date physical standby and Data Guard Snapshot standby to enable a physical standby to be dual purposed for DR and quality assurance testing. (See Chapter 9 for more details on Active Data Guard and Snapshot standby.) The long distance between sites provides enough geographic separation to prevent any single event from taking down more than one data center at a time. The three-site architecture also enables two sites to survive a disaster, leaving an operational standby database to provide continuous protection for each primary database after a failover has occurred. This user has achieved their operational objective of making each site a production site in its own right. Data Guard Redo Apply, with its simplicity, high performance, high reliability, and rich functionality, has enabled the user to deploy an architecture where all sites are active and all systems are utilized.

# Pharmaceutical Company: Centralized HA/DR and Data Distribution

A pharmaceutical company has a mission-critical database that supports applications used to comply with federal regulatory requirements. The company is required to maintain a secure, synchronized replica of the production database at a remote location for zero data loss in the event of primary site failure. The company must also replicate various subsets of data from the production database to research and manufacturing facilities located worldwide. While the primary database and remote replica used for data protection use the same hardware architecture and operating system, the research facilities host their Oracle databases on an assortment of hardware architectures and operating systems. Ideally, the pharmaceutical company can offload the primary database of the overhead of replicating data subsets to many different sites. This also would make it easier to insure the security of the source data by limiting direct access to the primary database. The replication targets at the remote research facilities can be up to 5 minutes behind the primary database.

The pharmaceutical company selected an architecture described in Figure 14-5. They have configured Data Guard Maximum Availability (SYNC) to maintain a zero data loss physical standby database located 150 miles from the primary data center. The physical standby database is always the failover/switchover target. A second standby database using SQL Apply is deployed on separate storage at the same remote location. The logical standby is configured using Data Guard Maximum Performance (ASYNC) and serves as the source database from which Oracle Streams replicates different subsets of data to each of the remote research facilities. All Streams capture processing required to replicate subsets to remote targets is performed on the logical

### Myth Buster: You Can't Run Streams on a Logical Standby Database

This *used* to be true for Oracle Database releases prior to 11.1.0.7 and (coming soon we hear) 10.2.0.5. You can now run Streams on a logical standby database, which makes a logical standby very useful for creating a stage database to offload Streams upstream capture processing from a primary database. An additional advantage is that logical standby integrates seamlessly into a configuration that uses physical standby databases for HA/DR. The logical standby will automatically recognize when a failover or switchover to the physical standby has occurred and continue to receive data from the new primary database.

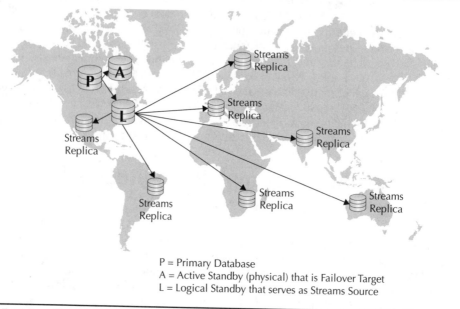

P = Primary Database
A = Active Standby (physical) that is Failover Target
L = Logical Standby that serves as Streams Source

**FIGURE 14-5.** *Pharmaceutical company: centralized HA/DR and data distribution*

standby database. During role transitions when the physical standby becomes the primary, the logical standby will automatically recognize the new primary database and continue to replicate data to the remote sites. Note that should the logical standby fail, the company will need to recover the database using a previous backup of the logical and allow Data Guard to resynchronize the logical standby with the primary to resume Streams replication.

# Web Retailer: HA/DR with Reader-farm Scale Out

A popular retail web site has an extensive inventory of products for sale that is constantly being updated. Consumers frequently access the site to browse the company's online catalog. Query volume, while high during normal periods, can peak at 10-times normal volume during holiday and promotional periods. This user is already using Data Guard to protect their mission-critical databases,

### Myth Buster: There Are Only Three Ways to Scale Read Performance

Buying a bigger box, deploying Oracle RAC, or using SQL-based replication technology to maintain a reporting/query replica have been the traditional approaches to scaling real-time read performance. A new alternative is to use Active Data Guard to implement a reader-farm comprising multiple, low-cost, single-node physical standby databases. An Active Data Guard reader farm can be cheaper than a big box, simpler to manage than a cluster, offering better performance, reliability, and less complexity and effort than SQL-based replication.

with primary and standby sites located 90 miles apart. The company prefers to run simple HA/DR configurations with a single node primary and a single node Data Guard physical standby database. The company also wants to build a reader farm by creating read-only replicas of their primary database to scale performance for catalog browsing during holiday periods without increasing the complexity of their current environment. Updates must be propagated to all read-only replicas within 5 seconds of the original update on the primary database.

The company's chosen architecture is described in Figure 14-6. One standby database is located at their DR site configured for Maximum Availability (SYNC). Between two and eight additional Active Data Guard standby databases are deployed to support online web access from outside the firewall. For security reasons, web access to the DR copy is not allowed.

As seasonal query volume expands or contracts, the company simply deploys/decommissions standby database instances as appropriate. At failover or switchover time, all active standby databases automatically recognize the new primary database and continue to provide read-only access. Similar to how it has implemented HA/DR by having the primary database and failover target located at separate sites, the company has also dispersed their Active Data Guard standby databases across both data centers. In this fashion, the failure of an entire site does not impact data protection or availability for either online customer access or internal operations.

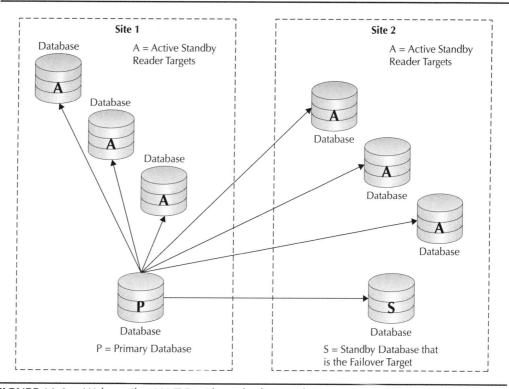

**FIGURE 14-6.** *Web retailer: HA/DR with reader-farm scale out*

# Insurance Company: Maximum Availability Architecture

An insurance company determined that a mission-critical claims application was no longer meeting its business needs. Antiquated application design made it very difficult to respond quickly to new business opportunities, and the mainframe platform on which it was running was inflexible and costly to maintain.

The mainframe model used by the legacy application partitioned claims processing and data by geographic region—each region had its own regional operations center served by its own mainframe, database, and instance of the claims application. While this configuration isolated failures to individual regions, it also resulted in many operational challenges and costly investment in idle capacity, all stemming from the fact that there was no single consolidated database to serve claims processing. Operational reporting on the mainframe was also severely constrained by the lack of a consolidated database for all regions and by concern for the impact that it would have on OLTP processing. This was ironic because operational reporting is most critical during troubled times when claims processing is at its peak, yet this would be the very moment when claims processing could least afford to be impaired by overhead from operational reporting.

The company decided to implement a complete redesign of their application and system architecture. The goal was to achieve better than mainframe performance, scalability, and availability with a more flexible application design and lower cost system architecture that could quickly evolve to meet the changing needs of their business. Key criteria for their new architecture included the following:

- **High scalability**   More than 12,000 concurrent users access the system during peak work hours and sudden increases in workload occur with little warning. A hurricane on the Gulf Coast, wildfires on the West Coast, or ice storms in New England can cause dramatic increases in the volume of claims applications—the expectation is that response time will be the same during these critical times as it is on a holiday morning when all is calm.

- **High availability**   Server failure must not impact all 12,000 users at the same time. The new application design assumes a single consolidated database. The systems architecture must find a way to support this while providing the necessary level of high availability.

- **Operational reporting**   Claims processing and operational reporting must each be able to scale independently, without impacting the performance of the other. Operational reporting must have access to a data that can be no more than 10 seconds behind the OLTP system.

- **Reducing planned downtime windows**   The mainframe environment offers little in the way of reducing planned downtime. Operating system upgrades, hardware maintenance, database upgrades, and new patchsets all require extended periods of downtime that the business is seeking to eliminate or minimize to the greatest degree possible.

- **RPO**   There is a very small tolerance for data loss—an RPO of less than 10 seconds—regardless of the nature or scope of failure, be it from data corruption caused by component failure or a catastrophic event that destroys the production database and impacts an area within a 350-mile radius of the primary site.

■ **RTO**   Server failure can never impact more than 25 percent of the user population at one time and must have an accompanying RTO of less than 1 second for the affected users. RTO for database failover following site failure is less than 60 seconds once administrators are able to respond to the failure event and make the decision to execute a failover operation.

The insurance company selected the combination of Oracle RAC and Data Guard as the foundation for its next generation architecture, as depicted in Figure 14-7. A four-node Oracle RAC primary database has a corresponding four-node Oracle RAC physical standby database, with primary and standby data centers separated by 350 miles. Oracle RAC meets both the scalability requirements of a consolidated database and the HA requirements for server failure. The primary database serves all claims processing from a single database. All nodes process claims applications. Additional nodes can be quickly provisioned should additional capacity be required.

Active Data Guard is deployed at the standby database to address requirements for operational reporting while having zero impact on OLTP performance of the primary database. Standby database capacity is provisioned to match the primary database so that service levels for OLTP processing are not impacted if a failover or switchover occurs. Active Data Guard uses two of the standby cluster nodes for Redo Apply and operational reporting during steady state processing while in standby role. If more capacity is required for operational reporting, additional nodes can be added to the standby database to meet that requirement with zero impact to the availability of the reporting system or to primary database processing. The remaining standby nodes are used to host other databases used for test and development to use all available systems to the fullest. These nodes are quickly reallocated to production processing if a failover is required. Similarly, since OLTP and operational reporting will both run on the same database after a failover, a degraded level of operational reporting is acceptable during a failover scenario—OLTP processing takes priority.

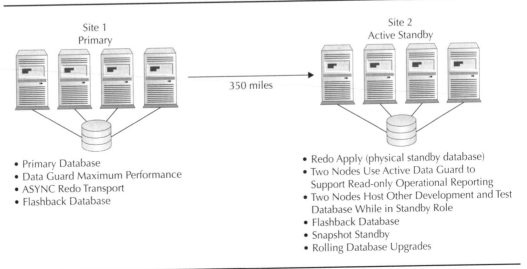

FIGURE 14-7.   *Insurance company: maximum availability architecture*

The standby database is also used as a Snapshot standby for full-blown QA testing. Such testing is reserved for periods of low activity when the primary cluster has enough idle capacity to handle both OLTP and operational reporting.

Data Guard Maximum Performance (ASYNC) is used to achieve RPO and RTO requirements with near zero performance impact on the primary database. Data Guard FSFO has not been used to automate database failover (ASYNC support included in Oracle Database 11*g* onwards) due to the user's preference for manual control. Testing confirmed that manual failover would meet RTO objectives.

Oracle RAC rolling upgrades are used to eliminate planned downtime for hardware and operating system maintenance and installation of one-off patches for the Oracle Database. Such maintenance is performed in a rolling fashion, one node at a time, without impacting the availability of the primary or standby Oracle RAC clusters. Data Guard rolling upgrades are used to minimize downtime for installation of Oracle patchsets and major database releases that cannot be upgraded using the RAC rolling upgrade functionality. A second standby instance is created to use Data Guard SQL Apply on a temporary basis when a database rolling upgrade is performed.

In addition to Oracle RAC and Data Guard, they make extensive use of ASM, Oracle Recovery Manager, flash recovery area, Flashback Database, and Oracle Enterprise Manager using the best practices described in this book and documented in Oracle Database High Availability Best Practices.[7]

# Conclusion

This chapter covered seven different deployment architectures. The first six used Data Guard to address requirements for high availability, data protection, and scalability using configurations that are single-node simple to deploy and manage resources. Data Guard's rich feature set and ability to use all computing resources create new opportunities to solve complex problems using a lower cost architecture that has fewer moving parts and thus is simpler to implement and manage.

The last example, however, acknowledges that single-node simple won't solve your problem if you must scale beyond what a single server can support, or if you desire a level of high availability in which server failure is completely transparent. The good news is that you can take all of the same elements of data protection and availability that Data Guard enables for single-node architectures and address additional requirements for scalability and HA by simply adding Oracle RAC to your Data Guard configuration.

To illustrate this point, let's assume that you work for the retail brokerage firm discussed earlier in this chapter and have implemented the architecture depicted in Figure 14-3. Things run fine for a year, and then the business customer you support informs you that a new initiative is being rolled out that will increase your OLTP workload to double the volume that your current system is sized to handle. You need a fast, low-cost, low-risk solution to accommodate this extra workload and meet the needs of your customer.

You decide to add a second node to one of your standby databases and create an Oracle RAC cluster. You test the new cluster using read-only queries while it is in standby role. Then you test the new cluster in primary role by using Snapshot standby and Real Application Testing. Once you

---

[7] Oracle Database High Availability Best Practices, 11*g* Release 1 (11.1), B28282-01; see http://otn.oracle.com/goto/maa

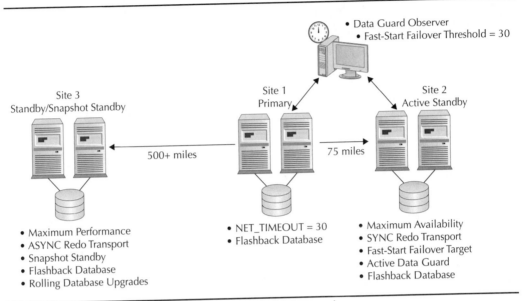

**FIGURE 14-8.** *Retail brokerage firm after Oracle RAC upgrade*

are 100-percent confident that the new cluster is optimally configured and stable, you convert the Snapshot standby back to a synchronized standby database, and at a convenient time you take a 5-minute planned maintenance window to switchover production to the new cluster. You then upgrade the original primary database and the second standby database in your configuration to Oracle RAC clusters. The result of this work is depicted in Figure 14-8.

Adding Oracle RAC has doubled the volume of workload that you can support while completely preserving your previous hardware investment and the bulk of your previous management practices. Rather than expensive forklift upgrades, the integration of Data Guard and Oracle RAC has enabled you to efficiently and safely scale beyond single-node capacity. You have also set yourself up for near-unlimited future growth. If other initiatives come along with even more workload, you can simply add more Oracle RAC nodes to your existing clusters online—with zero downtime. You can use Snapshot standby and Real Application Testing so that you always have confidence in any new changes that you introduce.

The breadth of Oracle's high availability technologies provides users with the flexibility to choose the right tools for the job at hand, without incurring additional costs or complexity for capabilities that you do not need today. At the same time, you can proceed with complete confidence that you can evolve the architecture you begin with to easily address whatever the future may bring.

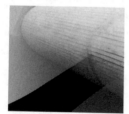

# APPENDIX

# Data Guard vs. Array-based Remote Mirroring Solutions

ou've made it through the book! Congratulations! But we're not quite done with you yet. Throughout your voyage, you have been learning about all the features and every nuance of Data Guard. You have been following along as we peeked into every dark corner and examined every knob, tool, and option available to you. We sincerely hope that it has been worthwhile for you and that your Data Guard knowledge has been considerably expanded. If there is any doubt still in your mind about using Data Guard, we hope to expel it completely by comparing Data Guard against the other most popular disaster recovery solution, *remote mirroring*.

# The Basics

Array-based remote mirroring is available from several mainstream storage vendors, including EMC, Hitachi, and Network Appliance. While the technology employed by each vendor differs somewhat, in principle the method by which they replicate data to the remote site is very similar. Because of this similarity, we'll discuss the differences between remote mirroring solutions and Data Guard in terms of topology, performance, and solution reliability when applied to disaster recovery (DR).

Very rarely, if ever, is the execution of real-world DR plans the result of planned events. Disasters of any type that would take out a primary production database simply don't give us advance notice that they are going to occur. To the contrary, they occur with no warning, and allow us no time to test or make ready our DR site to accept the transition of our production workload. It's assumed that regardless of whether we are using Data Guard or an array-based remote mirroring solution, we will have run DR exercises to test the readiness and thoroughness of our DR planning at some time prior to the disaster occurring.

Many companies create task forces dedicated to business continuity in the event of disasters, and those divisions of the IT group often perform DR exercises on a quarterly or semi-annual basis. The processes involved in bringing up the DR infrastructure are thoroughly documented so that in the event of a catastrophe, the failover of the application and database can occur without errors—and, of course, with minimum or no data loss.

With a mirroring strategy, even though we may have tested our DR readiness earlier through exercising controlled tests, when we completed those tests, the DR site had to be rebuilt from scratch.

In other words, the DR site in place at the time of the actual disaster has never been tested. In the simplest of terms, it will start and work, or it won't.

Oracle Data Guard gives us the same flexibility of the array-based replication (and more) in validating our DR readiness, without requiring the complete rebuild of the DR site. In Oracle Database 10g Data Guard, we can open the standby database in read-only, or even read-write mode executing Data Manipulation Language (DML) during our testing, and then return the DR site to its previous state with absolutely no need to reinstantiate the DR site. We saw the operation of this capability in Chapter 9 in the section on opening an Oracle Database 10g Release 2 Data Guard standby in read-only and read-write mode. Also in Chapter 9, we demonstrated the significant increase in flexibility for opening a DR standby database with Oracle Database 11g Data Guard in both read-only and read-write mode with the introduction of snapshot standby databases and Active Data Guard. In both Oracle Database 10g and 11g Data Guard, we are able to return the opened DR standby database to its role as a managed DR standby.

The flexibility and effectiveness of Data Guard in managing your DR standby databases provides the ultimate return on investment (ROI) since expenditures for additional space utilization do not have to be incurred.

Data Guard does not minimize the value of array-based remote mirroring when it comes to storage not directly tied to the Oracle database data files themselves, such as file system data and files. Often, the combination of Data Guard and storage array-based replication proves to be the best combination, especially with application data not in the database. Of course, this does not include the Oracle home, since with Data Guard you have separately installed homes on the primary and standby systems.

# Topology

The backbone of topology for Oracle Data Guard and array-based remote mirroring solutions is a network and its associated components, the database servers, underlying storage supporting the databases, and the databases themselves. It is a given that for a DR site to be an effective mirror of the production site, ready to take over the production role at any time, it must be continuously updated as changes occur on the production site. This is where the two technologies diverge from one another and take very distinct and different approaches to keeping the DR site in sync with the production site.

Array-based remote mirroring solutions by definition enable synchronization of the databases via transmission of changed data as observed at the storage level from the primary database to the standby database. Synchronization at the storage level requires the transmission of the database redo that initiated the synchronization, in addition to every write to data files, other members of the online redo log groups, archived log files, temporary data files, undo data files, and control files. In addition, if flashback recovery is enabled, all writes to the flashback logs, and multiplexed online redo and archive logs if they exist, need to be synchronized. All of this synchronization activity must occur across the network and its associated components that are connecting the primary and remote DR sites to each other. Contrast the requirements of array-based mirroring with that of Oracle Data Guard, where only the writes to the online redo logs of the primary database must be transmitted to the standby database.

When array-based remote mirroring solutions are implemented across WANs over long distances, their underlying topology itself can become a limiting factor to its practicality as a DR solution. When run synchronously for maximum data protection, a distance of around 60 miles can be achieved using specialized network devices. Distances beyond this require additional hardware in the form of repeaters and converters from third-party vendors. From a practical standpoint, going beyond the distance of normal LAN coverage will most likely introduce latencies that produce significant performance degradation to primary databases.

# Performance

In primary and standby DR sites of close proximity, network latencies may not be high, and hence any performance impact on the primary production database may be negligible. On the other hand, true standby DR sites are rarely in close proximity to the primary production database. Generally, true standby DR sites target zero data loss as a tenant of their design. It is important to note that both array-based remote mirroring and Data Guard provide for zero data loss. The mechanisms by which they achieve this are quite different, as noted earlier.

Zero data loss dictates that a commit on the primary production database must be written to disk on the remote standby database before the next transaction can proceed. As you know, when transactions commit, their redo must be written out to the online redo log and that redo must be transmitted to the remote standby database before the transactions actually commit. Both mirroring and Data Guard have to obey this rule but what is happening underneath is slightly different. With mirroring, the I/O to the online redo log is not acknowledged back to the log writer process (LGWR) until the same blocks are sent over the network to the DR site, an additional I/O performed on the DR disks, and the acknowledgment sent back. With Data Guard, the online redo log file I/O is performed once, and then the LogWriter Network Service (LNS) process takes the redo from memory, sends it over the network where it is written to the standby redo log, and sends the acknowledgment to the LGWR process—still, two-disk I/Os and a network roundtrip for both operations. This is why we tell users that it makes no sense to mirror the database and use Data Guard at the same time, because you just end up with a minimum of three disk I/Os and two network roundtrips.

But you should also consider that with mirroring, while the online redo log file (ORL) processing from above is going on, any change to the database as a result of a write on the primary database requires a corresponding change on the remote standby database. The bottom line is many, many more writes are required with array-based remote mirroring than are required with Data Guard. In addition, significantly more network roundtrips are required to maintain the remote standby database in sync with the primary database when using array-based remote mirroring.

One study using an OLTP workload that generated 3 MB/sec of redo with a synchronous zero data loss configuration, and varying degrees of network latency, compared an off-the-shelf remote mirroring solution with Data Guard. The remote mirroring solution introduced more than six times the performance overhead of Data Guard at 10ms round trip times (RTT). As distances between the primary database and the remote standby database increase, it is reasonable to assume the latencies or RTT will also increase. This fact, coupled with the dramatically larger amount of data that must be sent, received, and acknowledged in a zero data loss environment, reduces the practicality of implementing array-based remote mirroring as a viable solution for DR. The converse of this demonstrates the practicality of implementing Oracle Data Guard over large geographic distances, improving the separation of a primary and standby DR database.

# Reliability

As mentioned in the opening of this appendix, you don't know if the mirrored database is actually going to open until you have to activate it, which is usually during one of those "unplanned disasters." The biggest reason why this is so frightening is because you really don't know what is going on during the mirroring other than the changes are going over to the DR site. Should a corrupt block occur on the primary database, an array-based remote mirroring solution will likely replicate the corrupt block, as it would a clean block. You won't find this out until you activate the mirror during a failover and discover that the database will not start up. Oracle Data Guard, on the other hand, validates all redo blocks before transmitting and applying them to the remote standby database, eliminating the chance that corruptions will be propagated to the remote standby database.

# Final Thoughts

Oracle Data Guard has been built for one purpose: the reliable, successful propagation of data from an Oracle primary database to one or more Oracle remote standby databases. Data Guard provides the following significant advantages over array-based remote mirroring:

- No additional disk space nor special hardware is required.
- The network requirements are substantially less with Data Guard.
- Protection can be maintained across far greater geographic distances.

Both array-based replication and Data Guard provide compression algorithms to compress the packets/blocks before the changed data is transmitted over the WAN, but many more implementation options are available with Oracle Data Guard out of the box. With Data Guard, you have real-time validation and application of redo. You can open the remote standby databases in read-only or read-write mode (depending on the type of standby), and for the Oracle Database 11g physical standbys, you also can have real-time apply of redo while the database is open in read-only mode. Data Guard allows you to open a physical standby in read-write mode, complete thorough testing of DR plans, application upgrades, or break-fix, and then return the database to its standby mode fully utilizing your DR site. Snapshot standby databases, Real Application Testing (RAT), and active standby databases offer a complete and comprehensive suite of availability configurations for nearly any purpose.

Array-based remote mirroring can enable some of the same functionality by mounting the remote file systems and then opening the remote standby database. The most significant difference, though, is that once you have opened the remote standby database, it can no longer be maintained in sync with the primary database, eliminating it from service as a DR site. Once the remote standby database has been opened, you can return it to service as a DR site by shutting down the instance, dismounting the file systems or ASM disks, and resynchronizing them from the preserved image (Snapshot Image or business continuity volumes [BCV]). You can also snap off a copy of the mirror database, activate it, and use it for testing. But not only does this require double the disk space on the DR site and you are testing on stale data, it provides no guarantee that the actual mirrored database is going to work when you need it.

Both array-based remote mirroring and Oracle Data Guard serve in many locations as the primary DR vehicle that companies rely on in the event of a disaster. Before choosing your environment, you should carefully consider all facets of your requirements and understand how you can leverage your remote standby database to maximize the ROI of the significant outlay that will be made to deploy a true disaster recovery site.

Think about this: If the head of IT comes to you and asks, "Are we ready for any kind of failure?", which of these answers would you prefer to give:

- "We know that the mirroring is working and the information is getting over there."
- "Sure, we're running our reporting over on the Active Data Guard standby database as we speak, and we test with switchover every other Saturday."

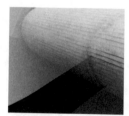

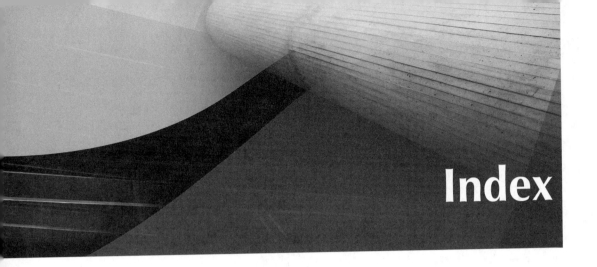

# Index

## A

ABORT command, 316
ACID properties, 108–109
ACTIVATE STANDBY DATABASE
    command, 57, 463
Active Data Guard, 371–375
    basic configuration, 372–373
    configuring, 374–375
    overview, 13, 371–372
    reader farms, 373–374
    Real-Time Query, 373, 375
    reporting, 26
    vs. read-only physical standby, 351
active rate, 271–272
Active Session History (ASH), 146
active SQL sessions, 462
active standby databases, 26–29
ADD DATABASE command, 195, 200
ADDRESS_LIST, 380–382, 389
ADR (Automatic Diagnostic Repository), 433–434
adrci utility, 445–447
Advanced Compression option, 9, 59–60, 83, 99
AFFIRM attribute, 81, 83
AFFIRM processing, 57
AFFIRM standby database, 39
alert log files
    historical information, 264–265
    mining, 259–264
    overview, 444–447
    redo generation rate, 43
    searching, 229
    viewing, 228–229

alerts, severity categories, 263
aliases, 380
ALL setting, 134
ALL_LOGFILES value, 82
ALL_ROLES value, 82
ALTER command, 193
ALTER DATABASE statement, 456
ALTER SYSTEM commands, 199, 206
ALTER SYSTEM SET command, 204
ALTERNATE attribute, 84
Alternate property, 210
AlternateLocation property, 210
analysis, Database Replay, 366–367
ANALYZE command, 429
ANALYZER process, 147, 154
applications
    JDBC, 389, 391–392
    OCI, 385, 386, 391, 392
    Real Application Clusters. See RAC
    Real Application Testing, 28,
        364–365, 398
    Transparent Application Failover, 382–384
APPLIER processes, 147
apply engine, 163–164
apply lag, 159, 227, 231–233, 252, 272
apply method, 36, 61–62
apply rate, 271–272
apply services, 11–17. See also Redo Apply;
  SQL Apply
    considerations, 19–20
    described, 4, 114
ApplyInstanceTimeout property, 202–203
ApplyParallel property, 207–208

ARCH (archive) processes
    compression, 83
    dedicated, 80
    deprecated for redo transport, 11, 56,
       198, 304, 312
    described, 115
    gap resolution and, 10, 58
    number of, 83–84
    REMOTE_ARCHIVE_ENABLE
       parameter, 79–80
ARCH transport, 11, 18, 56
architecture, 1–29
archive destination issues, 455
archive log files, 264–271
    archivelog mode, 282–284
    backing up, 426
    deleting, 417, 418
    destinations, 269–271
    partial, 57, 304, 458
    splitting, 102
archive processes. *See* ARCH
archived redo logs, 108, 463
ARCHIVE_LAG_TARGET parameter, 37, 266
archivelog mode, 282–284
array-based remote mirroring systems, 491–495
ASH (Active Session History), 146
ASH reports, 146, 157, 159
ASM (Automatic Storage Management)
    migrating to, 396
    standby data file location, 69–71
    storing configuration files, 180–181
ASM disk groups, 57, 180, 269–271, 420
ASM instance, 69–70
ASM standby files, 69–70
ASMCMD utility, 180–181
ASSM (Automatic Segment Space
    Management), 396
ASYNC attribute, 81
ASYNC (asynchronous) redo transport
    architecture, 8
    compression, 9
    enhancements, 7
    LNS send size and, 45
    Maximum Performance mode, 36–37
    optimizing, 8, 59–61
    overview, 7–9
    vs. SYNC transport, 38
asynchronous redo transport. *See* ASYNC
asynchronous standby destinations, 61
asynchronous transmission, 20
atomic, 108

atomicity, 108
attributes, deprecated, 84–85
AUTOBACKUP to ON parameter, 441
Automatic Diagnostic Repository (ADR),
    433–434
automatic failover, 22–24, 335–347, 377–394
automatic gap resolution, 9–11
automatic log switch, 37
Automatic Segment Space Management
    (ASSM), 396
automatic site/client failover, 377–394
Automatic Workload Repository. *See* AWR
auxiliary database, 411
availability
    high. *See* high availability
    maximum, 38–39
    monitoring, 252–255
    threats to, 2
AWR (Automatic Workload Repository), 43
AWR reports, 43–44, 146, 369, 397, 398

# B

backouts
    flashback, 429
    from unsuccessful switchovers, 462–463
BACKUP AS COPY command, 419–420
backup files
    physical standby database, 68–71
    RMAN Oracle Database 10g, 94–97
backup pieces, 411
BACKUP RECOVERY FILES command, 441
backups, RMAN, 409–426
    archive log deletion and, 417
    archive log files, 426
    canceling, 314
    control files, 412, 418
    creating standby database,
       88–89, 91, 423
    cumulative, 421
    differential, 421
    fast incremental, 27
    full, 417–418
    as image copies, 419–420
    image copies rolled forward, 420–423
    incremental, 411–412, 416, 421
    incremental RMAN, 453–454
    missing data files, 437–440
    multiple copies, 440
    offload, 27

primary database, 417–418
scenarios, 417–426
standby control file, 416
on standby database, 423–425
strategies, 415–417
backupsets, 411, 425
bandwidth
compression and, 60
considerations, 43–44
described, 43
determining requirements for, 43–44
I/O, 119
latency and, 43–46
network, 43–46
tuning, 43–46
bandwidth-delay product. See BDP
base table trigger, 136, 137, 139
BCT (block change tracking), 411–412, 441
BCT files, 412
BCVs (business continuity volumes), 419
BDP (bandwidth-delay product), 49–50
BDP calculator, 50
bits, vs. bytes, 50
block change tracking (BCT), 411–412, 441
block checking, 125
blog.dataguardbook.com, 470
broker. See Data Guard broker
Broker log, 181, 323
Broker log files, 181, 323, 444, 448, 466
brokerage firm configuration, 478–480
BrokerResource Manager (RSM), 173–175
buffer cache locks, 111
buffered redo records, 3
BUILD command, 102–103
business continuity volumes (BCVs), 419
bystander logical standby database, 407
bytes, vs. bits, 50

# C

cache, 111, 119. See also LCR cache; memory
Calibrate_IO utility, 119
"Cannot Open Archived Log" error, 456
catalog database, 411
catalogs, RMAN, 412
CHANGE command, 413
change vectors, 3, 108
channels, 411
check logical parameter, 441
checkpoint recovery phase, 117

checkpoints, 108, 149–150
clients
configuring, 387–392, 389
failover, 378, 387–394
client-side load balancing, 380–381
cloning database, 400, 423
Clusterware utility, 390, 400
cold failover clusters, 35, 473, 474
collections, 135
commands. See also specific commands
SQL, 102, 103, 173, 201, 301
switchover, 20, 303, 316–319, 348
commit records, 3
COMMIT statements, 4–5
COMMIT TO SWITCHOVER TO PRIMARY
command, 348
committing transactions, 111
CommunicationTimeout property, 175, 202
compatibility issues, 307, 320
COMPATIBLE parameter, 399, 403
COMPATIBLE setting, 405
compression
Advanced Compression, 9, 59–60, 83, 99
advantages of, 60
archive processes, 83
ASYNC redo transport, 9
asynchronous standby destinations, 61
considerations, 60–61
CPU resources and, 60
Data Guard Broker and, 61
enabling, 60–61
gap resolution, 61
purpose of, 60–61
redo, 45, 59–61, 282
COMPRESSION attribute, 83
configuration
Active Data Guard, 374–375
ASYNC redo transport, 59–61
clients, 387–392
Data Guard Broker. See Data Guard Broker
databases, 388, 390, 391, 392–394
displaying, 73
options for, 35–62
protection modes. See protection modes
redo transport mode, 42
RMAN, 412–415
SRL files, 56–58, 75–77
TAF, 382–384
tuning network, 42–56
verifying with Grid Control, 224–226
zero data loss and, 33–34, 39

configuration errors, 450–456
configuration files
    Data Guard Broker, 174, 176–178
    storing, 180–181
configuration-level properties, 201–202
CONFIGURE command, 413
CONNECT command, 178, 190, 193–195
connect identifiers, 72, 222, 223
connect strings, 183–186, 188, 413–414
connect time failover, 380–381
CONNECT_DESCRIPTOR, 381
connection load balancing, 380–381
consistency, 108
control files
    backing up, 412, 418
    losing, 432
    managing, 412
    primary, 412, 432
    recovering, 432
    restoring, 412
    standby, 412, 432
    troubleshooting, 469–470
CONVERT TO PHYSICAL statement, 406
COORDINATOR process, 147, 154, 167
COPY DATAFILE command, 420
COPY TABLESPACE command, 420
corruption, 3, 13
corruption protection, 13–14, 475
CPU resources, 60
CREATE CONFIGURATION command, 181,
    193–194, 195
CURRENT_SCN value, 273–275

**D**

data blocks
    block change tracking support,
      411–412, 441
    checking, 125
    corrupted, 426–429
    logical block checking, 441
    soft-corrupt, 112
Data Center migration, 396
Data Definition Language. See DDL
Data Guard
    accessing features, 220–221
    architecture, 1–29
    categories, 35–62
    components, 114–124
    goals of, 11–12

    health checks, 224–225
    implementing. See implementation
    managing. See management
    monitoring. See monitoring
    overview, 2–5
    planned migration, 396–398
    planning for, 32–63
    protection modes. See protection modes
    rolling upgrades, 15, 396, 398–407
    troubleshooting. See troubleshooting
    vs. remote-mirroring, 3, 491–495
Data Guard Apply, 11, 12, 114, 118–119
Data Guard Broker, 171–217. See also
    DGMGRL
    basics, 179–193
    Broker log, 181, 323
    bypassing, 92
    changing configuration properties, 200–210
    changing database state, 200, 211–212
    changing protection mode with, 212–213
    compression and, 61
    configuration files, 174, 176–178
    configuring, 66–67, 72, 73, 88, 221–224
    configuring Oracle Net Services, 187
    connect strings, 183–185
    connecting to, 190–196
    considerations, 26, 63, 71, 72, 173
    creating/enabling configurations, 193–200
    database connections, 72
    described, 25
    health checks, 448–449
    illustrated, 64
    log files/tools, 444, 448–449, 466
    managing Data Guard with, 193–213
    monitoring Data Guard with, 214–216
    Oracle Net Services, 183–187
    overview, 25, 172–178
    parameters, 179–183
    performing failover with, 334
    performing switchover with, 323
    process flow, 174–176
    process model, 173–174
    Real Application Clusters, 176, 187–190
    reliability of, 172
    removing from production
      database, 216–217
    removing standby database, 250–251
    troubleshooting, 464–468
    using, 92
Data Guard Broker CLI, 178
Data Guard Handbook website, 422–423

Data Guard home page, 73–75, 220, 248, 251
Data Guard (DG) Menu utility, 276–297
Data Guard Monitor. *See* DMON
Data Guard Net Server, 174
Data Guard Setup, 63, 66–77
Data Guard Switchover, 395–408
Data Guard wizard, 63, 68, 77, 178
data loss
    acceptable loss, 33–34
    failover and, 303–308
    network considerations, 34
    overview, 33–34
    time loss, 33
    transaction loss, 33
    zero. *See* zero data loss
Data Recovery Advisor, 433–434
data types, unsupported, 130, 135, 407
database administrator. *See* DBA
database alert logs, 444–447
database checkpoint, 108
Database Control, 221, 366–368
database ID (DBID), 404
database image copies, 419–420
database level enforcement, 113
database management. *See* management
database metrics, 226–228
database monitoring. *See* monitoring
Database Replay, 364, 365–370, 398
database status, 448
Database Unique Name, 71
Database Upgrade Assistant (DBUA), 400–401
database writer process (DBWn), 4, 5
database-level properties, 202–209
`database_role` attribute, 142, 143
databases
    active standby, 26–29
    alternate destinations, 84
    cloning, 400, 423
    configuring, 388, 390, 391, 392–394
    connect string, 183–186, 188, 413–414
    Flashback. *See* Flashback Database
    logical standby. *See* logical standby
        databases
    names, 78–79
    physical standby. *See* physical standby
        databases
    primary. *See* primary databases
    remote mirroring systems, 3, 13, 491–495
    rolling upgrades, 15, 396, 398–407, 476
    snapshot standby, 27, 250, 353–364, 468
    "split brain" condition, 24

    standby. *See* standby databases
    states, 200, 211–212
    switching primary/standby. *See* switchover
    target, 411
    unique names, 41, 79, 81–82, 412, 461
    VLDB, 419
datafile checkpoint, 108
datafiles
    losing on primary database, 430–431
    losing on standby database, 431
    missing, 437–440
    recovering, 430–431, 437–440
    renaming, 456
    standby, 69–71
dataguardbook.com, 276
datasets
    available at logical standby, 128
    creating at logical standby, 141–145
    local, 141–145
    replicated from primary database,
        129–134
DBA (database administrator)
    monitoring and, 164, 258, 269
    protecting data, 410
    SYSDBA role, 72, 277
DBA_LOGSTDBY_EVENTS view, 164, 168,
    289–290, 407, 449
DBA_LOGSTDBY_LOG view, 449
DBA_LOGSTDBY_PARAMETERS view, 292
DBA_LOGSTDBY_PROCESS view, 292–294
DBA_LOGSTDBY_PROGRESS view, 449
DBA_LOGSTDBY_STATS view, 291–292
DBA_LOGSTDBY_UNSUPPORTED view, 449
DB_BLOCK_CHECKING parameter, 125, 475
DB_BLOCK_CHECKSUM parameter, 475
DB_CACHE_SIZE parameter, 119
DB_CREATE_FILE_DEST parameter, 80
DB_CREATE_ONLINE_LOG_DEST
    parameter, 75
DB_FILE_NAME_CONVERT attribute, 86
DBID (database ID), 404
DB_LOST_WRITE_PROTECT parameter, 475
DB_LOST_WRITE_PROTECTION
    parameter, 125
DBMS_JOBS, 142
`dbms_logstdby.apply_set` parameter, 148
DBMS_LOGSTDBY.SKIP procedure, 130–131
`dbms_logstdby.skip_transaction`
    procedure, 167
DBMS_SCHEDULER, 142–145, 387
DBMS_SERVICE PL/SQL package, 390

DB_NAME parameter, 78–79
DB_ROLE_CHANGE system event, 386–387, 388, 390, 393
DBUA (Database Upgrade Assistant), 400–401
DB_ULTRA_SAFE parameter, 125, 126
DB_UNIQUE_NAME attribute, 41, 79, 81–82
DB_UNIQUE_NAME parameter, 41, 78–79, 195, 412, 461
DBVERIFY utility, 112, 429
DBWn (database writer process), 4, 5
DBWR processes, 111, 119
DDL (Data Definition Language), 87–88
DDL issues, 460
DDL statements, 131, 135, 164
DDL transactions
    skipping, 167–168, 295–296
    SQL Apply, 153–157
deadlocks, 165–167
DELAY attribute, 84, 118, 383
DelayMins property, 207
DELETE ALL INPUT, 441
delete command, 418
dependent transactions, 304
deployment architectures, 471–489
    data distribution, 483–484
    extended geographic separation, 478–480
    government agency configuration, 480–483
    high availability configurations, 473–480
    high availability/disaster recovery, 476–485
    insurance company configuration, 486–488
    manufacturing configuration, 473–476
    maximum availability, 486–488
    multi-site threat protection, 480–483
    overview, 472
    pharmaceutical company configuration, 483–484
    retail brokerage firm configuration, 478–480
    utility company configuration, 476–478
    web retailer configuration, 484–485
    zero data loss configurations, 476–480
DESCRIPTION_LIST, 380–381
DG (Data Guard) Menu utility, 276–297
DG_BROKER_CONFIG parameters, 176–177, 179
__DG_BROKER_SERVICE_NAMES parameter, 183–184
DG_BROKER_START parameter, 173, 181–183
dg.conf file, 276

DGConnectIdentifier property, 184, 185, 188
DGConnectionIdentifier property, 210
DGMGRL (Data Guard command-line interface), 25, 66, 178, 447
DGMGRL CLI. See also Data Guard Broker
    accessing, 178, 186
    components, 193
    configuring Broker, 193–210
    configuring Data Guard, 181–183
    connecting to Broker, 190–196
    considerations, 173, 178, 186, 193, 205
    disabling configuration, 466
    help, 178
    observer operations, 447, 467–468
    performing failover, 334
    performing manual restate, 341–342
    performing switchover, 323
    querying database, 448, 449
    stopping processes, 362
    using with Broker, 178
    vs. Grid Control, 178
diagnostic information, 444–449
diagnostic scripts, 296
directories, 94, 180–181, 356
disaster recovery. See DR
Disaster Recovery Center (DRC) log files, 444–447
DML statements, 131
DML transactions, 151–153
DML triggers, 136, 137
DMON log files, 448
DMON process, 173, 175, 177
DMON (Data Guard Monitor) process, 173, 448
DNS caching, 388
DNS name mapping, 388
DNS servers, 388
DR (disaster recovery), 26, 300, 302, 472, 476–485
DR solutions, 26, 300, 302, 472
DRC log, 183, 194, 216
DRC (Disaster Recovery Center) log files, 444–447
DRC processes, 174
dropped tables
    flashback, 429
    recovering from, 437
DUPLICATE command, 423
DUPLICATE FOR STANDBY command, 423
durability, 109
dynamic performance views, 449

# E

_EAGER_SIZE parameter, 150
EDIT command, 200–210
EDIT CONFIGURATION command,
    202, 212–213
EDIT DATABASE command, 209,
    211, 216
EDIT INSTANCE command, 209–210
EDS (Extended Datatype Support),
    135, 407
ENABLE DATABASE command, 199
End Of Redo (EOR) marker, 301, 303, 348
Enterprise Manager (OEM), 25–26, 64, 124.
    *See also* Grid Control
EOR (End Of Redo) marker, 301, 303, 348
error messages
        "Cannot Open Archived Log," 456
        "No Data Found," 456, 460
        "Object Not Part of Data Guard Broker
            Configuration," 467
        "Operation Disallowed," 464–465
        "ORACLE not available," 450
        "Parameter %s Cannot Be
            Parsed," 457
        "TNS Packet Reader Failure," 458
        "Unsupported Record," 460
errors. *See also* troubleshooting
        configuration, 450–456
        converting to snapshot standby, 468
        log shipment, 458
        management, 450–456
        ORA. *See* ORA error codes
        password file, 450
        SQL Apply, 450–451
        TNS, 175
        user, 429–430
        V$DATAGUARD_STATUS,
            284–285
        VERIFY command, 448
escape character, 131
events
        checking for, 289–290
        DB_ROLE_CHANGE system, 386–388,
            390, 393
        FAN, 385, 386, 389, 392
        ONS, 392–393
exclusive locks, 111
Export/Import utility, 407
Extended Datatype Support (EDS), 135, 407

# F

failback, 300, 397
failover, 302–309. *See also* switchover
        automatic, 22–24, 335–347, 377–394
        client, 378, 387–394
        client notification, 378
        complete, 378–379, 387–394
        connect time, 380–381
        with Data Guard Broker, 324
        data loss and, 303–308
        DB_ROLE_CHANGE system event,
            386–387
        efficient reconnection, 378
        Fast-Start Failover, 335–347, 447
        Flashback Database and, 243
        flashback technologies and, 309–310
        gap resolution and, 308, 331
        inevitabiity of, 53, 310–311
        issues, 463
        logical standby database, 303, 328–329
        manual, 22–24, 240–243
        Maximum Availability mode, 325, 339
        Maximum Performance mode, 303, 306,
            308, 328, 340
        Maximum Protection mode, 42, 303, 307,
            325, 328, 339
        multiple standbys and, 348
        outbound connect timeout, 381–382
        overview, 21–24, 302
        partial, 379, 388–389
        performing, 324–347
        performing with Grid Control,
            240–243, 334
        physical standby, 303, 326–328
        primary databases and, 22
        redo gaps and, 326, 328
        reinstating primary, 329–333
        service relocation, 378
        site, 378–379
        "split brain" condition, 24
        TCP timeouts, 381–382, 384, 386,
            390–391
        thread merging and, 304, 307–308
        timeouts, 381–382
        Transparent Application Failover, 382–384
        triggers, 387, 390, 393–394
        vs. switchover, 309
failover process, 303
FAL (Fetch Archive Log), 87, 266

FAL client, 87
FAL requests, 308
FAL_CLIENT parameter, 87
FAL_SERVER parameter, 87
FAN (Fast Application Notification), 384–386
FAN events, 385, 386, 389, 392
FAN messaging, 385, 390, 392
FAN OCI (Oracle Call Interface), 385–386
FAN Oracle Notification Service (ONS), 385
Fast Application Notification. See FAN
Fast Connection Failover (FCF), 385
Fast-Start Failover (FSFO) feature, 243,
    335–347, 447
FCF (Fast Connection Failover), 385
FDDI (fiber distributed data interface), 44
Fetch Archive Log. See FAL
fiber distributed data interface (FDDI), 44
files
    ASM standby, 69–70
    backup. See backup files
    BCT, 412
    configuration. See configuration files
    listener, 48, 52, 53, 65, 89, 185
    log. See log files
    OMF, 226, 469–470
    ORL. See ORL files
    password, 89, 104, 278–279, 450
    pfile, 61, 104, 216, 418
    spfile, 61, 95, 179, 216, 418
    SRL. See SRL files
    standby, 284
    TNSNAME, 183, 184, 192
    trace, 447–448
FILESPERSET parameter, 440
FINISH APPLY qualifier, 328
FINISH command, 326, 327, 330
fire_once_only property, 136, 137, 140
flash recovery area, 71, 85, 230–231, 255
Flash Recovery Area (FRA), 429
Flashback Database, 309–311
    considerations, 309, 311
    database rollbacks, 429–430
    described, 230, 309
    enabling, 230–231
    failovers and, 243
    logging capabilities, 230–231
    uses for, 310
flashback drop, 309, 429
flashback logging, 404
flashback query, 309, 429
flashback SCN, 331, 332

flashback table, 429
flashback technologies, 309–311
flashback transaction backout, 429
FLASHBACK_SCN number, 332
FLASHBACK_TRANSACTION_QUERY
    view, 168
FOR DB_UNIQUE_NAME clause, 413–414
force logging, 63, 113–114, 279, 281
FORCE LOGGING clause, 279, 281
FORCE qualifier, 327
FRA (Flash Recovery Area), 429
FROM ACTIVE DATABASE method, 67
FSFO (Fast-Start Failover) feature, 243,
    335–347, 447
FSFO.dat file, 447

**G**

gap resolution
    automatic, 9–11
    compression, 61
    considerations, 39
    failover and, 308, 331
    network and, 58
    ORLs and, 8
    proactive, 87
    reactive, 87
gaps
    archive log, 266–268
    redo. See redo gaps
global checkpoint, 108
government agency configuration, 480–483
Grid Control, 219–256
    accessing Data Guard features, 220–221
    adding standby redo logs, 224–226
    canceling apply, 76–77
    changing protection modes with,
        234–236
    configuring Data Guard Broker, 221–224
    configuring FSFO, 243, 345–347
    creating logical standby databases,
        244–250
    creating standby databases, 67–73,
        221–222
    editing standby database properties,
        236–238
    enabling FlashBack Database, 230–231
    High Availability Console, 252–255
    metrics, 226–228
    modifying standby databases, 222–224

overview, 220
performing failover, 240–243, 334
performing switchover, 238–240,
    323–324
power user method, 78–98
Real-Time Query, 375
reviewing Data Guard performance,
    231–234
specifying backup files, 68–71
specifying standby SID, 68–69
starting Observer from, 342–343
using, 65–77
using with Broker, 178
verifying configuration, 224–226
viewing alert log files, 228–229
vs. Database Control, 221
vs. DGMGRL, 178
Grid Control Jobs page, 74
Grid Control snapshot convert, 363
group commits, 4
GRP (guaranteed restore point), 27–28, 310,
    315, 354, 400
guaranteed restore point (GRP), 27–28, 310,
    315, 354, 400
GUARD setting, 134

**H**

HA. *See* high availability
health checks, 224–225, 324, 448–449
HELP command, 178, 447
HEXTORAW function, 168
high availability (HA), 35, 252–255
high availability (HA) configurations, 473–480
High Availability Console, 252–255
high availability/disaster recovery (HA/DR),
    476–485
high-speed networks, 43

**I**

image copies
    backups as copies, 419–420
    described, 411
    rolled forward, 420–423
implementation, 31–106
    configuration options, 35–62
    creating logical standby database, 98–105
    creating physical standby database, 63–98

determining requirements, 33–35
planning for, 32–63
RAC and, 105–106
InconsistentLogXptProps property, 448
InconsistentProperties property, 448
incremental backups, 27, 453–454
INDEX REBUILD statements, 155
InitialConnectIdentifier property,
    184, 185, 188
instance recovery, 109
instance-level properties, 209–210
instances
    Maximum Availability mode, 38–39
    Maximum Performance mode, 37
    Maximum Protection mode, 40–41
insurance company configuration, 486–488
INSVs (internode servers), 176
internode servers (INSVs), 176
I/O bandwidth, 119
IP addresses, 379, 387, 388
isolation, 109

**J**

Java Database Connectivity. *See* JDBC
Java Virtual Machine (JVM), 385
JDBC (Java Database Connectivity), 380, 385
JDBC applications, 389, 391–392
JDBC clients, 380, 382, 385
JDBC driver, 386
jobs, canceling, 314
JVM (Java Virtual Machine), 385

**K**

KEEP IDENTITY clause, 15, 404
kernel slaves (KSV), 119–120
kilobits, 50
KSV (kernel slaves), 119–120

**L**

lag
    apply, 272
    SQL Apply, 296–297
    transport, 272
LANs (local area networks), 44
large objects (LOBs), 135

latency
  ASYNC model and, 44
  availability and, 38
  bandwidth calculations and, 43–46
  BDP and, 49–50
  third-party replication products, 153
LatestLog property, 216
LCR cache, 159–163
  considerations, 165
  increasing size of, 157, 161–162
  overview, 147–149
  paging and, 295
LCR paging, 295
LGWR (log writer) process
  asynchronous redo transport, 7–8
  described, 3, 115
  flushing redo buffers, 111
  redo transport and, 5
  SRL file I/O and, 56
  writing to ORL, 4
LIST BACKUPSET SUMMARY command, 425
LIST DB_UNIQUE_NAME OF DATABASE
  command, 415
LIST FAILURE command, 434
listener, 185–187
listener files, 48, 52, 53, 65, 89, 185
LISTENER.ORA file, 47–48, 51–52, 186, 454, 463
LNS (Log Network Server), 5–10
LNS (LogWriter Network Service), 115
LNS process
  improving read speed, 59
  reconnection, 81
  timeouts, 81
LNS send size, 45
load balancing
  client-side, 380–381
  connection, 380–381
  server-side, 380
LOBs (large objects), 135
local area networks (LANs), 44
local checkpoint, 108
LOCATION attribute, 84–85
log buffers
  hit ratio, 8
  increasing size of, 59
  resizing, 59
  tuning, 59
log files
  alert. See alert log files
  archive. See archive log files
  archivelog mode, 282–284

  bad, 233, 234
  Broker, 181, 323, 444, 448, 466
  DMON, 448
  DRC, 444–447
  FAL, 87, 266
  gaps in, 9–11
  MV logs, 141
  nologging issue, 456, 468–469
  observer, 447
  ORL. See ORL files
  SRL. See SRL files
  standby database waiting on, 455
  standby redo, 37
  switching, 37, 56
  target standby alert log, 315, 317–318
  values for, 82
Log Network Server (LNS), 5–10
log read recovery phase, 117
log shipment errors, 458
log switches
  archive, 264
  automatic, 37
  forcing, 37, 266
  redos and, 56
  SYNC standby database and, 38–39
log writer. See LGWR
LOG_ARCHIVE_CONFIG parameter, 41, 79
LOG_ARCHIVE_DEST parameter, 403
  attributes, 80–86
  considerations, 399
  Data Guard Broker, 197–198, 205–207
  deprecated attributes, 84–86
  enabling compression, 61
  Maximum Availability mode, 42
  Maximum Performance mode, 42
  Maximum Protection mode, 42
  overview, 36, 80, 205–207
  upgrades, 403
LOG_ARCHIVE_DEST_STATE attribute, 86
LOG_ARCHIVE_MAX_PROCESSES
  parameter, 79–80
LOG_ARCHIVE_TRACE parameter, 45
log-based replication, 130, 134, 135, 144–145
LOG_BUFFER parameter, 59
LOG_FILE_NAME_CONVERT
  parameter, 87, 403
log-force at commit, 111
logging
  at database level, 113
  flashback, 404
  supplemental, 101, 103

at table level, 114
at tablespace level, 113
logging table trigger, 136, 137, 140
logging tables, 136–141
logical block checking, 441
logical standby databases, 127–170. *See also*
   SQL Apply
      alert log file entries, 264
      bystander, 407
      considerations, 128–129
      creating, 98–105
      creating local dataset at, 141–145
      creating via physical standby database,
         101–105
      creating with Grid Control, 244–250
      customizing, 141–145
      dataset replicated from primary, 129–134
      datasets available at, 128
      DG Menu utility, 285–297
      diagnostic scripts, 297
      failover, 303, 328–329
      materialized views, 141–142
      monitoring, 285–297
      nologging issue, 456
      operational aspects, 145–170
      overview, 128–129
      parameters, 292
      prerequisites, 98–101
      processes, 292–293
      properties, 208–209
      protecting replicated tables on, 134–141
      reinstating primary after failover, 331–333
      resyncing, 456
      role transitions, 129
      rolling upgrade, 399–407
      scheduler jobs, 142–144
      skipping DDL transactions, 295–296
      skipping table entries, 245–250
      status codes, 293–294
      steady state issues, 34, 42–44, 128
      streams and, 483
      Streams capture, 144–145
      stuck appliers, 294–295
      support for, 98–101
      switching to, 320–323
      switchover, 301–302, 320–323
      switchover failures, 466
      transient, 15, 402–407
      troubleshooting, 459–461
      uses for, 128
      using physical database for, 98–101
Logical Standby Process (LSP), 15–17, 115
logical standby properties, 208–209
LogMiner dictionary, 102–105, 154, 404
logminer memory spill, 149
LogMiner utility, 167–169
LogShipping property, 204, 205
LOGSTDBY status, 264
LogWriter Network Service (LNS), 115
LogXptMode parameter, 465
LogXptStatus property, 448
lost writes, 125–126
LSP (Logical Standby Process), 15–17, 115

## M

MAA (Maximum Availability Architecture),
   29, 480
MAA team, 58
managed recovery, 113
MANAGED RECOVERY command, 319
Managed Recovery Process. *See* MRP
management
      with Broker, 193–213
      errors, 450–456, 459
      memory, 147–149
      overview, 24–26
      troubleshooting, 450–456, 459
MANDATORY attribute, caution about, 85
manufacturing configuration, 473–476
materialized views (MVs), 141–142
MAX_CONNECTIONS attribute, 83–84
MAX_FAILURE attribute, caution about, 85–86
Maximum Availability Architecture. *See* MAA
Maximum Availability mode
      failover and, 325, 339
      LOG_ARCHIVE_DEST parameter, 42
      overview, 18–19, 38–39
      vs. Maximum Protection mode, 40
Maximum Performance mode
      failover and, 303, 306, 308, 328, 340
      LOG_ARCHIVE_DEST parameter, 42
      mixing standby databases, 39
      overview, 18, 36–37
Maximum Protection mode
      failovers and, 42, 303, 307,
         325, 328, 339
      FSFO and, 339
      LOG_ARCHIVE_DEST parameter, 42
      overview, 19, 39–41
      vs. Maximum Availability mode, 40

MAXOPENFILES parameter, 440
MAX_SGA setting, 148, 150, 157, 158, 295
mean time to recover (MTTR), 416
media failures, 426
media recovery, 13, 110, 119–120
Media Recovery Coordinator (MRP0), 12
media recovery failures, 455–456
megabits, 50
megabytes, 50
memory. *See also* cache
    media recovery and, 119
    mining engine and, 148, 162
    SQL Apply, 147–149
    System Global Area, 3, 109, 146, 148, 150
    TCP tuning and, 49
memory spill, 149
merged redos, 304, 305
METHOD attribute, 383
metrics, 226–228
migration, planned, 396–398
mining engine
    checkpoints and, 149–150
    DDL statements and, 154
    memory and, 148, 162
    processes in, 146
    transaction chunking and, 150
    tuning, 159–162
mirroring, remote, 3, 13, 491–495
monitoring, 257–297
    active rate, 271–272
    alert log files, 259–264
    apply lag, 272
    apply rate, 271–272
    archive log files, 264–271
    archive log mode, 282–284
    current environment, 277–297
    with Data Guard Broker, 214–216
    DG Menu utility, 276–297
    events, 289–290
    LCR paging, 295
    logical standby databases, 285–297
    MRP status, 275–276
    nologging activities, 279–282
    overview, 258–259
    password file, 278–279
    redo transport delays, 268–269
    SQL Apply lag, 296–297
    standby databases, 272–276
    standby file management, 284
    stats, 291–292
    stuck appliers, 294–295

    transport lag, 272
    V$DATAGUARD_STATUS errors, 284–285
MOUNT state, 189, 190
MRP (Managed Recovery Process)
    applying redo, 73, 74
    described, 115
    errors, 457–458
    reporting status of, 275–276
    restarting, 47, 77
    shutting down, 72, 73
    stopping, 46, 76–77, 319
MRP0 (Media Recovery Coordinator), 12
MTTR (mean time to recover), 416
multiplexing, 57, 75–77, 90
MV logs, 141
MVs (materialized views), 141–142

## N

names, unique. *See* unique name
nested tables, 135
NET_TIMEOUT attribute
    Data Guard Broker, 198, 206
    high availability and, 475, 477, 478
    overview, 81
    protection modes, 18–19, 38
network bandwidth. *See* bandwidth
networks
    data loss and, 34
    gap resolution, 58
    high-speed, 43
    LANs, 44
    latency. *See* latency
    throughput, 44
    tuning, 42–58
    WANs, 44
"No Data Found" error, 456, 460
NOAFFIRM attribute, 83
NOLOGGING activities, 279–282
NOLOGGING clause, 279–282, 468–469
nologging issue, 456, 468–469
nologging operations, 111–114
NOREGISTER attribute, caution about, 86
NSV processes, 174

## O

OBJECT data type, 99, 135
"Object Not Part of Data Guard Broker Configuration" error, 467

Observer, 335–347, 447
observer log files, 447
observer servers, 467–468
OCI (Oracle Call Interface), 385–386
OCI applications, 385, 386, 391, 392
OEM (Enterprise Manager), 25–26, 64, 124.
    *See also* Grid Control
offload backups, 27
offload read-only queries, 13, 26
OLTP (online transaction processing), 44
OLTP database, 144
OLTP nodes, 44
OMF (Oracle Managed Files), 226, 469–470
online redo log files. *See* ORL files
online transaction processing. *See* OLTP
ONLINE_LOGFILE value, 82
ONS (Oracle Notification Service), 385
ONS daemons, 385, 392
ONS events, 392–393
ONS publisher, 392–393
OPEN RESETLOGS command, 309, 310, 437
OPEN state, 302
operating systems, migrating to different
    platform, 396
"Operation Disallowed" error, 464–465
optimization. *See also* performance
        ASYNC redo transport, 8, 59–61
        log clearing, 403
        queries, 176
        switchover, 403
optimizer statistics, 365
ORA error codes, 259–263
ORA-00257 error, 269–271
ORA-00308 error, 456
ORA-00326 error, 57, 457–458
ORA-600 3020 error, 126
ORA-00600 error, 259
ORA-752 error, 126
ORA-01031 error, 457
ORA-01034 error, 450
ORA-01102 error, 461
ORA-01403 error, 456, 460
ORA-3133 error, 386
ORA-4031 error, 164–165
ORA-04042 error, 169–170
ORA-12514 error, 186
ORA-12570 error, 458
ORA-16032 error, 455
ORA-16066 error, 457
ORA-16191 error, 450
ORA-16204 error, 457

ORA-16211 error, 460
ORA-16596 error, 467
ORA-16627 error, 213, 464–465
ORA-16642 error, 193–194
ORA-17503 error, 183
ORA-26786 error, 167
ORA-26787 error, 167
ORA-38500 error, 118
Oracle Advanced Compression
    option, 9, 59–60, 83, 99
Oracle Call Interface. *See* OCI
Oracle Clusterware, 400
Oracle Data Pump, 133, 407
Oracle Database 10*g* Release
        parallel recovery, 119
        read-write standby, 353–357
        RMAN, 94–98
Oracle Database 11*g* Release. *See also* databases
        data protection changes, 124–125
        MAX_CONNECTIONS attribute caution, 84
        parallel recovery, 119
        RMAN, 88–94
Oracle Enterprise Manager. *See* OEM
Oracle Managed Files (OMF), 226, 269–470
Oracle Net aliases, 380
Oracle Net Services, 5, 6, 53, 54, 183–187
"ORACLE not available" error, 450
Oracle Notification Service. *See* ONS
Oracle Real Application Clusters. *See* RAC
Oracle recovery. *See* recovery
Oracle Recovery Manager. *See* RMAN
ORACLE_HOME location, 400–401, 404, 405
ORL (online redo log) files
        described, 3, 108
        gap resolution and, 8
        LGWR writing to, 4
        MANDATORY attribute and, 85
        not receiving, 454–455
        recovering, 432–436
        size, 56, 116
        SRL files and, 37, 116
        transmitting, 8
O/S. *See* operating systems
outbound connect timeout, 381–382

# P

parallel media recovery (PMR), 119–120
PARALLEL option, 118
parallel query (PQ) slaves, 117, 119–120

"Parameter %s Cannot Be Parsed" error, 457
parameters, 78–88. *See also specific parameters*
    considerations, 41
    primary role, 80–86
    protection modes, 41
    role-independent, 78–80
    standby role, 86–88
password files, 89, 104, 278–279, 450
passwords
    physical standby database, 68–69
    problems with, 450
    SYS, 277
peak state, 34
performance. *See also* optimization
    I/O best practices, 57–58
    maximum, 36–37
    Redo Apply, 13
    remote mirroring, 493–494
    reviewing with Grid Control, 231–234
    SQL Apply, 157–164
    standby apply, 17
pfile, 61, 104, 216, 418
PGA (Program Global Area), 111
pharmaceutical company configuration,
    483–484
physical standby
    switchover, 301–302, 315–320
physical standby databases. *See also* Redo Apply
    backup files, 68
    checking capability, 125–126
    choosing interface, 63–64
    components of, 114–124
    corruption detection, 124–126
    creating, 63–98
    creating logical standby database via,
        101–105
    data file location, 69–71
    data protection, 124–126
    failover, 303, 326–328
    Grid Control and, 65–77
    location, 69
    manual recovery on, 457–458
    naming, 71–72
    opening after switchover, 302
    password, 68–69
    power user method, 78–98
    prerequisites, 64–65
    primary redo and, 28
    read-only mode, 350–353
    read-write mode, 352–353
    reinstating primary after failover, 329–331

snapshot, 353–364
specifying SID for, 68–69
switching to, 301–302, 315–320
switchover failures, 465–466
system ID, 68–69
transfer method, 69
troubleshooting, 456–458
username, 68–69
physical standby method. *See* Redo Apply
pipeline, 159, 163
PL/SQL (Procedural Language/Structured Query
    Language), 122, 130, 277, 284, 398
PL/SQL procedures, 130, 135, 162
PMR (parallel media recovery), 119–120
PQ (parallel query) slaves, 117, 119–120
PR0x processes, 115, 120
`PreferredApplyInstance` property,
    187–188, 203
`PREPARE TO SWITCHOVER` operation, 407
PREPARER processes, 146, 160–161, 292–295
`preserve_commit_order` parameter, 148,
    151–152, 158, 166
primary control files, 412, 432
primary databases
    backups, 417–418
    control file loss, 432
    described, 2
    failover and, 22
    incomplete recovery of, 436–437
    Maximum Availability mode, 38–39
    Maximum Performance mode, 36–37
    Maximum Protection mode, 40–41
    read-write clone, 353–357
    recovering datafiles on, 430–431
    Redo Transport, 14
    registered, 412–413
    reinstating after logical standby failover,
        331–333
    reinstating after physical standby failover,
        329–331
    remote archival failure, 457
    shutdown (unwanted), 456–458
    switching with standby. *See* switchover
    transitioning standby to, 466–467
    transitioning to standby role, 466
primary redo, 28
`PRIMARY_ROLE` value, 82
proactive gap resolution, 87
problems. *See* troubleshooting
Procedural Language/Structured Query
    Language. *See* PL/SQL

proc_name argument, 131
production databases. *See* primary databases
Program Global Area (PGA), 111
properties. *See also specific properties*
    ACID, 108–109
    configuration-level, 201–202
    database-level, 202–209
    instance-level, 209–210
    logical standby, 208–209
    reverse, 204–205
    SQL, 207–208
protection modes. *See also specific*
  *protection modes*
    changing with Broker, 212–213
    changing with Grid Control, 234–236
    choosing, 36–42
    considerations, 20, 41–42
    described, 18, 36
    displaying, 75
    FSFO and, 339
    NET_TIMEOUT attribute, 18–19, 38
    overview, 18–19
    parameters, 41
    RPO and, 62–63
    RTO and, 62–63
    setting, 41–42
psfiles, 418

## Q

QA environment, 353–364
queries
    flashback, 309, 429
    offload read-only, 13, 26
    optimized, 176
    parallel query slaves, 117, 119–120
    Real-Time Query, 212, 236, 373, 375
    SQL, 275
query SCNs, 13
queue lengths, 54–56

## R

RAC (Real Application Clusters)
    Data Guard Apply and, 12
    Data Guard Broker and, 176, 187–190
    Data Guard implementation and, 32,
      105–106
    Maximum Performance mode, 37

    migrating to, 396
    primary database, 77
    redo generation rate, 43–44
RAC instances, 176
RAID controllers, 58
RAT (Real Application Testing), 28, 364–365,
  371, 398
reactive gap resolution, 87
read performance, 484
reader farms, 373–374
READER process, 146, 147–148, 292
reader-farm scale out, 484–485
read-only mode, 350–353
read-write clone, 353–357
read-write mode, 352–353
read-write standby database, 353–357
Real Application Clusters. *See* RAC
Real Application Testing (RAT), 28, 364–365,
  371, 398
Real Time Apply (RTA), 115, 117–119, 207, 353
Real-Time Query, 212, 236, 373, 375
receive buffer, 49, 51–53, 59
receive queue limits, 55
RECOVER DATABASE command, 432, 434
RECOVER TO LOGICAL command, 104
recoveries, RMAN. *See also* recovery; RMAN
    block corruption, 426–429
    control file loss on primary database, 432
    control file loss on standby database, 432
    datafile loss on primary database, 430–431
    datafile loss on standby database, 431
    datafiles, 430–431, 437–440
    dropped tables, 437
    incomplete recovery of primary database,
      436–437
    loss of online redo log files, 432–436
    media failures, 426
    online redo log file, 432–436
    scenarios, 430–440
    strategies, 426–430
    user errors, 429–430
recovery. *See also* redo processing
    ACID properties, 108–109
    checkpoint phase, 117
    concepts/components, 108
    Flashback Database, 429–430
    instance, 109
    log read phase, 117
    managed, 113
    media, 110, 119–120
    monitoring, 120–124

nologging operations, 111–114
overview, 109–110
parallel media, 119–120
redo apply phase, 117
RMAN. *See* recoveries, RMAN
thread merging, 110
types of failures, 109
recovery catalog, 412
recovery database, 411
Recovery Manager. *See* RMAN
recovery phases, 117
recovery point objective. *See* RPO
recovery rate, 118–119
recovery SCN, 331
recovery time objective. *See* RTO
redo allocation latch, 111
Redo Apply, 12–15. *See also* physical standby
  databases
    advantages, 14–15, 17
    considerations, 20
    corruption detection, 13–14
    errors, 457–458
    media recovery, 13
    overview, 12–15
    performance, 13
    process flow, 117
    recovery phase, 117
    rolling database upgrades, 15
    standby databases, 14
    switchover and, 313
    vs. SQL Apply, 11–17
redo change vectors, 108
redo compression, 45, 59–61, 282
redo copy latch, 111
redo data, 3
redo entries. *See* redo records
redo feature
    asynchronous redo transport, 7–9
    described, 2
    merged, 304, 305
    not applied to standby databases, 465
    overview, 2–5
    reducing amount of, 59
    synchronous redo transport, 5–7
redo gaps. *See also* gaps
    failovers and, 326, 328
    resolving manually, 451–452
redo generation rate
    availability and, 252
    considerations, 232–233
    determining, 43–44

redo log buffers, 3, 4, 8, 111
redo log files. *See also* ORL files
redo processing, 107–126, 111–114. *See also*
  recovery
redo records, 3, 108
redo transport
    ARCH, 11, 56, 198, 304, 312
    architecture, 5, 6
    compression, 9, 59–61
    delays in, 268–269
    primary database, 14
    SYNC. *See* SYNC redo transport
redo transport mode, 42–58
Redo Transport Services, 5–11
    described, 4, 5, 114
    optimizing, 59–61
REDO_TRANSPORT_COMPRESS_ ALL
    parameter, 9, 61
redo-write size, 4, 45
refreshing technology stack, 396
REINSTATE DATABASE command, 341
remote archival failure, 457
Remote File Server. *See* RFS
remote mirroring systems, 3, 13, 491–495
REMOTE_ARCHIVE_ENABLE parameter, 79
REMOVE CONFIGURATION command, 217
REMOVE INSTANCE command, 209–210
REOPEN attribute, 81
replica database. *See* standby databases
replicated tables, 134–141
replication
    log-based, 130, 134, 135, 144–145
    skipping, 130–134
    third-party solutions, 151, 153
    trigger-based, 137–141
    unsupported tables, 135–141
reporting
    Active Data Guard, 26
    Database Replay, 365–366
RESET DB_UNIQUE_NAME option, 413
Resource Manager (RSM), 173–175
resources, 470
restarts
    breaking deadlocks with, 165–167
    SQL Apply, 164–167
RESTORE CONTROLFILE command,
  412, 432
restore DATABASE preview command,
  434–436
restore point, 27–28, 310, 315, 354, 400
RESTORE PREVIEW command, 434

restores. *See* recoveries
RESYNC CATALOG command, 412
resynchronization, 414
retail brokerage firm configuration, 478–480
retention period, 441
RETRIES attribute, 383
reverse properties, 204–205
RFS (Remote File Server), 5, 6–7
RFS process, 5–10, 12, 56, 57, 117–118
RMAN (Recovery Manager)
    advantages, 410
    backups. *See* backups, RMAN
    basics, 410–411
    best practices, 440–441
    block change tracking support,
        411–412, 441
    configuration, 412–415
    control file management, 412
    creating physical standby database, 78–98
    format options, 419–420
    incremental backups, 453–454
    integration with Data Guard, 411–412
    Oracle Database 10*g*, 94–98
    Oracle Database 11*g*, 88–94
    recoveries. *See* recoveries, RMAN
    terminology, 411
RMAN catalog, 401, 412–416, 440
rman2disk.ksh script, 423
RMAN-08137 error, 418
Role Management Services, 19–24, 114
role transitions
    automatic recognition of, 482
    basics, 300–309
    considerations, 62
    described, 129, 300
    failover, 302–309
    SQL Apply and, 129
    switchover, 300–302, 309
rolling database upgrades, 15, 396,
    398–407, 476
round trip time (RTT), 7, 44–46
RPO (recovery point objective)
    considerations, 33, 34
    data loss, 33–34
    overview, 32, 33–34
    relating to protection modes, 62–63
    requirements, 33–35
    vs. RTO, 34
RSM (BrokerResource Manager), 173–175
RSM processes, 174
RTA (Real Time Apply), 115, 117–119, 207, 353

RTO (recovery time objective)
    choosing apply method, 61–62
    considerations, 34, 35
    high availability, 35
    low, 35
    overview, 32, 34–35
    real-time apply and, 119
    relating to protection modes, 62–63
    requirements, 34–35
    vs. RPO, 34
    zero downtown, 35
RTT (round trip time), 7, 44–46

# S

SANs (Storage Area Networks), 13
scaling recovery rate, 118–119
scheduler jobs, 142–144
schemas
    not maintained, 129–130
    Statspack, 121–122
SCNs (system change numbers)
    assigned, 3
    comparing, 14
    described, 108
    flashback, 331, 332
    lost writes, 126
    query, 13
    recovery, 331
    reinstating primary database, 329–330
SCN_TO_TIMESTAMP function, 273–275
SDU buffer, 45
SDUs (session data units), 46–48
SecureFile large objects (LOBs), 135
send buffer, 49, 51–53, 59
servers
    Data Guard Net Server, 174
    DNS, 388
    internode, 176
    Log Network Server, 5–10
    observer, 467–468
    Remote File Server, 5–10, 115
server-side load balancing, 380
server-side TAF, 384, 391
SERVICE attribute, 36, 80
service level agreement (SLA), 32
SERVICE_NAME parameter, 390
session data units (SDUs), 46–48
SGA (System Global Area), 3, 109, 146,
    148, 150

SHOW command, 214
SHOW CONFIGURATION command, 190–191, 194–195, 199
SHOW DATABASE command, 214, 449
SHOW DATABASE VERBOSE command, 196–197, 208, 215
SHOW PROBLEM command, 446–447
SHUTDOWN ABORT command, 316, 337, 343
SID (system ID), 68–69
site failover, 378–379
skip rules, 129–133, 248, 249
SKIP_FAILED_TRANSACTION clause, 167–168
skipping
    DDL transactions, 295–296
    failed transactions, 167–168
    replication, 130–134
    table entries, 245–250
    transactions, 167–168, 296
SKIP_TRANSACTION procedure, 167, 168, 296
SLA (service level agreement), 32
snapshot standby database, 27, 250, 353–364, 468
socket size, 49–55
soft-corrupt data blocks, 112
spfile, 61, 95, 179, 216, 418
"split brain" condition, 24
SQL Apply, 15–17. *See also* logical standby databases
    advantages, 16–17
    apply engine, 147
    basics, 145–157
    bottlenecks, 157, 159–164
    checkpoints, 149–150
    considerations, 15, 17, 20
    DDL transactions, 153–157
    DML transactions, 151–153
    errors, 450–451
    hanging, 461
    memory management, 147–149
    mining engine, 146
    overview, 15–16
    parameter values, 158
    performance, 157–164
    problems with, 459–461
    process architecture, 146–147
    redos in, 333
    restarts in, 164–167
    rolling upgrades, 398, 399–402, 407
    row dependency, 153

    setting parameters, 148
    stopped, 167–169
    switchover and, 313–314
    transaction "chunking," 150–151
    troubleshooting, 164–170
    tuning, 157–164
    vs. Redo Apply, 11–17
SQL Apply lag, 296–297
SQL commands, 102, 103, 173, 201, 301
SQL Performance Analyzer, 364, 370–371
SQL queries, 275
SQL statements, 459–460
SQL syntax properties, 207–208
SQL*Plus
    Broker properties and, 205
    considerations, 63, 64, 72
    described, 24
    DG Menu, 276, 277
    stopping MRP, 76–77
    switchovers and, 25, 300, 311
SRL (standby redo log) files
    adding, 224–226
    considerations, 7, 37, 56–58
    correcting, 75–77
    described, 5, 56
    input/output, 56–58
    listing, 76
    Maximum Availability mode, 38
    Maximum Performance mode, 37
    multiplexing, 57, 75–77, 90
    number of, 37
    ORL files and, 37
    size, 116
    uses for, 115–116
    vs. ORL files, 116
standby apply performance, 17
standby control file, 412, 416, 432, 468
standby data files, 69–71
standby databases
    active, 26–29
    alternate destinations, 84
    applying redos to, 11–17
    backups on, 423–425
    control file loss, 432
    creating with Grid Control, 67–73, 221–222
    creating with primary backup, 423
    cross-platform considerations, 77
    described, 2
    determining current time on, 273–275
    editing properties, 236–238

logical. *See* logical standby databases
Maximum Availability mode, 38–39
Maximum Performance mode, 36–37
Maximum Protection mode, 39–41
missing data files, 437–440
mixing, 39
modifying with Grid Control, 222–224
monitoring, 272–276
multiple, 348
not receiving redo logs, 454–455
physical. *See* physical standby databases
read-write, 353–357
recovering datafiles on, 431
Redo Apply, 14
redo not applied to, 465
redo not sent to, 465
registered, 412–413
removing from Broker control, 250–251
reopening, 81
rolling forward, 453–454
snapshot, 27, 250, 353–364, 468
switching with primary. *See* switchover
transitioning primary to, 466
transitioning to primary role, 466–467
unable to apply redo, 457–458
waiting on log files, 455
standby file management, 284
standby locations, 69
standby redo log. *See* SRL
STANDBY setting, 134
StandbyArchiveLocation property, 210
STANDBY_FILE_MANAGEMENT parameter, 87–88
STANDBY_LOGFILE value, 82
STANDBY_ROLE value, 82
START parameter, 173, 181–183
STARTUP MOUNT command, 189, 191
static listener, 88–89
stats, checking for, 291–292
Statspack snapshots, 122–124
Statspack utility, 121–124
StatusReport property, 448
steady state, 34, 42–44, 128
stmt argument, 131
Storage Area Networks (SANs), 13
streams, 483
Streams capture, 144–145
switchback, 300, 397
switchover, 300–302. *See also* failover
with Data Guard Broker, 323
described, 238

health checks, 324
logical standby, 301–302, 320–323
multiple standbys and, 348
opening physical database after, 302
overview, 20–21, 300
performing with Grid Control, 238–240, 323–324
physical standby, 301–302, 315–320
preparing for, 311–314
preprocessing steps, 314–315
procedure for, 311–324
vs. failover, 309
switchover commands, 20, 303, 316–319, 348
switchover issues, 461–463
switchover process, 301–302
symbolic links, 262
SYNC attribute, 80
SYNC (synchronous) redo transport
architecture, 5–6
considerations, 477
latency and, 8
Maximum Availability mode, 38
overview, 5–7
vs. ASYNC transport, 38
SYNC standby database, 38–39
synchronous redo transport. *See* SYNC
synchronous transmission, 19
SYS password, 277
SYS user, 450
SYSDBA role, 277
SYSDBA username, 72
.syspasswd file, 277
system change numbers. *See* SCNs
System Global Area (SGA), 3, 109, 146, 148, 150
system hangs, 477
system ID (SID), 68–69

**T**

table level level enforcement, 114
tables
flashback, 429
logging, 136–141
nested, 135
not replicated, 130
protecting on logical standby, 134–141
replicating subset of, 130
replicating unsupported, 135–141
skipped/skip rules, 130–134

tablespace level enforcement, 113
TAF (Transparent Application Failover), 188, 382–384, 391
TAF attributes, 383–384
TAG name, 420, 421
target database, 411
Target Name, 72
target standby alert log, 315, 317–318
TCP (Transmission Control Protocol)
    buffer space, 48–49
    queue lengths and, 54–56
    queue losses, 54
    timeouts, 381–382, 384, 386, 390–391
    tuning, 48–54
TCP connections, 48–49
TCP network layer, 48–54
TCP socket buffer size, 48–54, 58
TCP/IP (Transmission Control Protocol/Internet Protocol), 44
technology stack, 396
TEOR (Terminal EOR), 326
Terminal EOR (TEOR), 326
test environment, 353–364
testing
    active standby databases, 27–29
    Database Replay, 366–370
    network tuning, 58
thread checkpoint, 108
thread merging, 110, 304, 305, 307–308
threads, closed, 307
thresholds, 226
THROUGH ALL SWITCHOVER qualifier, 319–320, 348
throughput, 44, 58, 119
time, 273–275, 287
time loss, 33
timeouts, 381–382, 384, 386, 390–391
TNS (Transparent Networking Substrate), 46–48, 183–185
TNS descriptors, 53
TNS errors, 174–175
TNS level, 46
"TNS Packet Reader Failure" error, 458
TNSNAME definition, 36
TNSNAME entries, 184–186, 189, 192
TNSNAME files, 183, 184, 192
TNSNAME identifier, 72
TNSNAMES descriptor, 80
TNSNAMES.ORA file, 47, 48, 72, 189, 277, 463
TopWaitEvents property, 216
trace files, 447–448

transaction loss, 33. See also data loss
transactions
    "chunking," 150–151
    committing, 111
    DDL. See DDL transactions
    dependent, 304
    DML, 151–153
    failed, 167–168
    life cycle, 116–117
    life of, 111
    skipping, 167–168, 296
transfer methods, 69
transient logical standby database, 15, 402–407
transitions, role. See role transitions
transmission, 19–20
Transmission Control Protocol. See TCP
transmit queue limits, 54–55
Transparent Application Failover. See TAF
Transparent Networking Substrate. See TNS
transport lag, 8, 36, 159, 231–233, 272
trigger-based replication, 137–141
triggers
    base table, 136, 137, 139
    database role changes, 393–394
    database startup, 390
    DML, 136, 137
    failover, 387, 390, 393–394
    logging table, 136, 137, 140
    SQL Apply, 135
troubleshooting, 443–470. See also errors
    archive destination issues, 455
    blog.dataguardbook.com, 470
    control file, 469–470
    data block corruption, 426–429
    Data Guard Broker issues, 464–468
    Data Guard Broker log files/tools, 448–449
    database alert logs, 444–447
    database management issues, 450–456, 459
    DDL issues, 460
    diagnostic information, 444–449
    dynamic performance views, 449
    failover issues, 463
    health checks, 448–449
    HELP command, 447
    hints/tips, 468–469
    logical standby database, 459–461
    media recovery failures, 455–456
    nologging issue, 456, 468–469
    not receiving redo logs, 454–455
    observer log files, 447

OMF, 469–470
overview, 444
password file problems, 450
physical standby databases, 456–458
primary database shutdown, 456–458
redo gaps, 451–452
renaming datafiles with, 456
rolling standby forward, 453–454
SHOW PROBLEM command, 446–447
snapshot standby, 468
"split brain" condition, 24
SQL Apply, 164–170, 459–461
standby waiting on log files, 455
switchover issues, 461–463
trace files, 447–448
TRUNCATE operation, 155–156
tuning
    apply engine, 163–164
    bandwidth, 43–46
    log buffers, 59
    mining engine, 159–162
    networks, 42–56, 58
    recovery rate, 118–119
    SQL Apply, 157–164
    TCP, 48–54
TYPE attribute, 383

## U

unique name, 78–79
    FOR DB_UNIQUE_NAME, 413–414
    DB_UNIQUE_NAME (attribute), 41, 79,
        81–82
    DB_UNIQUE_NAME (parameter),
        41, 78–79, 195, 412, 461
    LIST DB_UNIQUE_NAME OF
        DATABASE, 415
    RESET DB_UNIQUE_NAME, 413
UNRECOVERABLE option, 112
"Unsupported Record" error, 460
upgrades
    DBUA, 400–401
    rolling, 15, 396, 398–407, 476
    TNS name and, 185
user errors, 429–430. See also errors
username
    considerations, 191
    physical standby database, 68–69
    SYSDBA, 72
utility company configuration, 476–478

## V

validation, 3
VALID_FOR attribute, 82–83, 206
V$ARCHIVE_DEST view, 282–284, 449
V$ARCHIVE_DEST_STATUS view, 282–284,
    312, 449
V$ARCHIVED_LOG view, 268, 449
V$ARCHIVE_GAP view, 449
VARRAY data type, 99, 135
V$DATABASE_BLOCK_CORRUPTION view,
    124–125
V$DATAGUARD_CONFIG view, 449
V$DATAGUARD_STATS view, 120–121, 272
V$DATAGUARD_STATUS view, 284–285, 449
V$DIAG_INFO view, 445
VERIFY command, 448
very large databases (VLDBs), 419
views. See also specific views
    Data Guard, 120–121
    dynamic performance, 449
    materialized, 141–142
    for monitoring recovery progress,
        120–121
VIP (virtual IP) address, 106, 189, 379, 387, 388
virtual IP (VIP) address, 106, 189, 379, 387, 388
Virtual Private Database (VPD) policies, 130
VLDBs (very large databases), 419
V$LOG view, 449
V$LOGFILE view, 449
V$LOG_HISTORY view, 264, 449
V$LOGSTDBY_PROCESS view, 147,
    292–294, 449
V$LOGSTDBY_PROGRESS view, 287, 313,
    449, 461
V$LOGSTDBY_STATS view, 291
V$MANAGED_STANDBY view, 120,
    275–276, 449
VPD (Virtual Private Database) policies, 130
V$PWFILE_USERS view, 279
V$RECOVERY_PROGRESS view, 121,
    271–272
V$STANDBY_APPLY_SNAPSHOT view, 121
V$STANDBY_LOG view, 449

## W

WANs (wide area networks), 44
web retailer configuration, 484–485
web site, dataguardbook.com, 276

wide area networks (WANs), 44
workload capture, 365, 367
workload processing, 365
workload replay, 365
write-ahead logging protocol, 111
write-behind logging protocol, 111

# X

XML, 135, 445
XML files, 445
XPT service, 183, 185

# Z

zero data loss
    Maximum Availability mode, 38–39
    Maximum Protection mode, 39–41
    mixed databases and, 33
    production downtime and, 39
    production throughput and, 33
zero data loss configurations, 39, 476–480
zero data loss method, 5
zero downtime, 35